T0215775

Communications
in Computer and Information Science   924

Commenced Publication in 2007
Founding and Former Series Editors:
Phoebe Chen, Alfredo Cuzzocrea, Xiaoyong Du, Orhun Kara, Ting Liu,
Dominik Ślęzak, and Xiaokang Yang

More information about this series at http://www.springer.com/series/7899

Kang Li · Minrui Fei
Dajun Du · Zhile Yang
Dongsheng Yang (Eds.)

Intelligent Computing and Internet of Things

First International Conference on Intelligent Manufacturing
and Internet of Things and 5th International Conference on Computing
for Sustainable Energy and Environment, IMIOT and ICSEE 2018
Chongqing, China, September 21–23, 2018
Proceedings, Part II

 Springer

Editors
Kang Li
The University of Leeds
Leeds
UK

Minrui Fei
Shanghai University
Shanghai
China

Dajun Du
Shanghai University
Shanghai
China

Zhile Yang
Shenzhen Institute of Advanced Technology
Chinese Academy of Sciences
Shenzhen
China

Dongsheng Yang
Northeastern University
Shenyang
China

ISSN 1865-0929   ISSN 1865-0937   (electronic)
Communications in Computer and Information Science
ISBN 978-981-13-2383-6   ISBN 978-981-13-2384-3   (eBook)
https://doi.org/10.1007/978-981-13-2384-3

Library of Congress Control Number: 2018953021

This Springer imprint is published by the registered company Springer Nature Singapore Pte Ltd.
The registered company address is: 152 Beach Road, #21-01/04 Gateway East, Singapore 189721, Singapore

Preface

This book constitutes the proceedings of the 2018 International Conference on Intelligent Manufacturing and Internet of Things (IMIOT 2018) and International Conference on Intelligent Computing for Sustainable Energy and Environment (ICSEE 2018), which were held during September 21–23, in Chongqing, China. These two international conference series aim to bring together international researchers and practitioners in the fields of advanced methods for intelligent manufacturing and Internet of Things as well as advanced theory and methodologies of intelligent computing and their engineering applications in sustainable energy and environment. The new conference series IMIOT is jointly organized with the well-established ICSEE conference series, under the auspices of the newly formed UK-China University Consortium in Engineering Education and Research, with an initial focus on intelligent manufacturing and sustainable energy.

At IMIOT 2018 and ICSEE 2018, technical exchanges within the research community took the form of keynote speeches, panel discussions, as well as oral and poster presentations. In particular, two workshops series, namely the Workshop on Smart Energy Systems and Electric Vehicles and the Workshop on Communication and Control for Distributed Networked Systems, were held again in parallel with IMIOT 2018 and ICSEE 2018, focusing on the two recent hot topics of the integration of electric vehicles with the smart grid, and distributed networked systems for the Internet of Things.

The IMIOT 2018 and ICSEE 2018 conferences received 386 submissions from over 50 different universities, research institutions, and companies from both China and UK. All papers went through a rigorous peer review procedure and each paper received at least three review reports. Based on the review reports, the Program Committee finally selected 135 high-quality papers for presentation at the IMIOT 2018 and ICSEE 2018. These papers cover 22 topics and are included in three volumes of the CCIS series, published by Springer. This volume of CCIS includes 52 papers covering 9 relevant topics.

Located at the upstream Yangtze basin, Chongqing constitutes the most important metropolitan area in the southwest of China. It has a glorious history and culture and serves as a major manufacturing center and transportation hub. Chongqing is also well-known for its spicy food and hotpot, attracting tourists and gourmets from around the world. In addition to academic exchanges, participants were treated to a series of social events, including receptions and networking sessions, which served to build new connections, foster friendships, and forge collaborations. The organizers of IMIOT 2018 and ICSEE 2018 would like to acknowledge the enormous contribution of the Advisory Committee, who provided guidance and advice, the Program Committee and the numerous referees for their efforts in reviewing and soliciting the papers, and the Publication Committee for their editorial work. We would also like to thank the editorial team from Springer for their support and guidance. Particular thanks are of course due to all the authors, as without their high-quality submissions and presentations the conferences would not have been successful.

Finally, we would like to express our gratitude to our sponsors and organizers, listed on the following pages.

September 2018

Fusheng Pan
Shilong Wang
Mark Price
Ming Kim Lim
Kang Li
Yuanxin Luo
Yan Jin

Organization

Honorary Chairs

Fusheng Pan	Chongqing Science and Technology Society/Chongqing University, China
Shilong Wang	Chongqing University, China
Mark Price	Queen's University Belfast, UK

General Chairs

Ming Kim Lim	Chongqing University, China
Kang Li	Queen's University Belfast, UK

Advisory Committee Members

Erwei Bai	University of Iowa Informatics Initiative, USA
Zhiqian Bo	China Xuji Group Corporation, China
Tianyou Chai	Northeastern University, China
Phil Coates	Bradford University, UK
Jaafar Elmirghani	University of Leeds, UK
Qinglong Han	Swinburne University of Technology, Australia
Deshuang Huang	Tongji University, China
Biao Huang	University of Alberta, Canada
Guangbin Huang	Nanyang University of Technology, Singapore
Minrui Fei	Shanghai University, China
Sam Ge	National University of Singapore, Singapore
Shaoyuan Li	Shanghai Jiaotong University, China
Andy Long	University of Nottingham, China
Dong Yue	Nanjing University of Posts and Communication, China
Peter Taylor	University of Leeds, UK
Chengshan Wang	Tianjin University, China
Jihong Wang	University of Warwick, UK
Xiaohua Xia	Petoria University, South Africa
Yulong Ding	University of Birmingham, UK
Yugeng Xi	Shanghai Jiaotong University, China
Sarah Supergeon	University College London, UK
Derong Liu	University of Illinois, USA
Joe Qin	The Chinese University of Hong Kong, Hong Kong, China
Savvas Tassou	Brunel University London, UK
Qinghua Wu	South China University of Technology, China
Yusheng Xue	China State Grid Electric Power Research Institute, China
Jiansheng Dai	King's College London, UK

I-Ming Chen	Nangyang Technological University, Singapore
Guilin Yang	Institute of Advanced Manufacturing Technology, Ningbo, China
Zhuming Bi	Indiana University Purdue University Fort Wayne, USA
Zhenyuan Jia	Dalian University of Technology, China
Tian Huang	Tianjin University, China
James Gao	University of Greenwich, UK
Weidong Li	Coventry University, UK
Stan Scott	Queen's University Belfast, UK
Dan Sun	Queen's University Belfast, UK

International Program Committee

Chairs

| Yuanxin Luo | Chongqing University, China |
| Yan Jin | Queen's University Belfast, UK |

Local Chairs

Xuda Qin	Tianjin University, China
Fuji Wang	Dalian University of Technology, China
Yingguang Li	Nanjing University of Aeronautics and Astronautics, China
Adam Clare	University of Nottingham, UK
Weidong Chen	Shanghai Jiaotong University, China
Rui Xiao	Southeast University, China
Furong Li	Bath University, UK
Min-Sen Chiu	National University of Singapore, Singapore
Petros Aristidou	University of Leeds, UK
Jinliang Ding	Northeastern University, China
Bing Liu	University of Birmingham, UK
Shan Gao	Southeast University, China
Mingcong Deng	Tokyo University of Agriculture and Technology, Japan
Zhengtao Ding	The University of Manchester, UK
Shiji Song	Tsinghua University, China
Donglian Qi	Zhejiang University, China
Wanquan Liu	Curtin University, Australia
Patrick Luk	Cranfield University, UK
Guido Maione	Technical University of Bari, Italy
Chen Peng	Shanghai University, China
Tong Sun	City University London, UK
Yuchu Tian	Queensland University of Technology, Australia
Xiaojun Zeng	The University of Manchester, UK
Huaguang Zhang	Northeastern University, China
Shumei Cui	Harbin Institute of Technology, China
Hongjie Jia	Tianjin University, China
Youmin Zhang	Concordia University, USA

Xiaoping Zhang	University of Birmingham, UK
Peng Shi	University of Adelaide, Australia
Kay Chen Tan	National University of Singapore, Singapore
Yaochu Jin	University of Surrey, UK
Yuchun Xu	Aston University, UK
Yanling Tian	University of Warwick, UK

Organization Committee

Chairs

Congbo Li	Chongqing University, China
Minyou Chen	Chongqing University, China
Adrian Murphy	Queen's University Belfast, UK
Sean McLoone	Queen's University Belfast, UK

Special Session Chairs

Qian Tang	Chongqing University, China
Xin Dai	Chongqing University, China
Johannes Schiffer	University of Leeds, UK
Wenlong Ming	Cardiff University, UK

Publication Chairs

Zhile Yang	Chinese Academy of Sciences, China
Jianhua Zhang	North China Electric Power University, China
Hongjian Sun	Durham University, UK
Trevor Robinson	Queen's University Belfast, UK

Publicity Chairs

Qingxuan Gao	Chongqing University, China
Junjie Chen	Southeast University, China
Brian Falzon	Queen's University Belfast, UK
Ben Chong	University of Leeds, UK

Secretary-General

Yan Ran	Chongqing University, China
Dajun Du	Shanghai University, China
Rao Fu	Queen's University Belfast, UK
Yanxia Wang	Queen's University Belfast, UK

Registration Chairs

| Guijian Xiao | Chongqing University, China |
| Shaojun Gan | Queen's University Belfast, UK |

Program Committee Members

Stefan Andreasson	Queen's University Belfast, UK
Andy Adamatzky	University of the West of England, UK
Petros Aristidou	University of Leeds, UK
Vijay S. Asirvadam	Universiti Teknologi Petronas, Malaysia
Hasan Baig	University of Exeter, UK
Lucy Baker	University of Sussex, UK
John Barry	Queen's University Belfast, UK
Xiongzhu Bu	Nanjing University of Science and Technology, China
Jun Cao	University of Cambridge, UK
Yi Cao	Cranfield University, UK
Xiaoming Chang	Taiyuan University of Technology, China
Jing Chen	Anhui University of Science and Technology, China
Ling Chen	Shanghai University, China
Qigong Chen	Anhui Polytechnic University, China
Rongbao Chen	HeFei University of Technology, China
Weidong Chen	Shanghai Jiaotong University, China
Wenhua Chen	Loughborough University, UK
Long Cheng	Chinese Academy of Science, China
Min-Sen Chiu	National University of Singapore, Singapore
Adam Clare	University of Nottingham, UK
Matthew Cotton	University of York, UK
Xin Dai	Chongqing University, China
Xuewu Dai	Northeastern University, China
Li Deng	Shanghai University, China
Mingcong Deng	Tokyo University of Agriculture and Technology, Japan
Shuai Deng	Tianjin University, China
Song Deng	Nanjing University of Posts and Telecommunications, China
Weihua Deng	Shanghai University of Electric Power, China
Jinliang Ding	Northeastern University, China
Yate Ding	University of Nottingham, UK
Yulong Ding	University of Birmingham, UK
Zhengtao Ding	University of Manchester, UK
Zhigang Ding	Shanghai Academy of Science and Technology, China
Dajun Du	Shanghai University, China
Xiangyang Du	Shanghai University of Engineering Science, China
Geraint Ellis	Queen's University Belfast, UK
Fang Fang	North China Electric Power University, China
Minrui Fei	Shanghai University, China
Dongqing Feng	Zhengzhou University, China
Zhiguo Feng	Guizhou University, China
Aoife Foley	Queen's University Belfast, UK
Jingqi Fu	Shanghai University, China
Shaojun Gan	Queen's University Belfast, China
Shan Gao	Southeast University, China

Xiaozhi Gao	Lappeenranta University of Technology, Finland
Dongbin Gu	University of Essex, UK
Juping Gu	Nantong University, China
Zhou Gu	Nanjing Forestry University, China
Lingzhong Guo	Sheffield University, UK
Yuanjun Guo	Chinese Academy of Sciences, China
Bo Han	Xi'an Jiaotong University, China
Xuezheng Han	Zaozhuang University, China
Xia Hong	University of Reading, UK
Guolian Huo	North China Electric Power University, China
Weiyan Hou	Zhengzhou University, China
Liangjian Hu	Donghua University, China
Qingxi Hu	Shanghai University, China
Sideng Hu	Zhejiang University, China
Xiaosong Hu	Chongqing University, China
Chongzhi Huang	North China Electric Power University, China
Sunan Huang	National University of Singapore, Singapore
Wenjun Huang	Zhejiang University, China
Tan Teng Hwang	University College Sedaya International University, Malaysia
Tianyao Ji	South China University of Technology, China
Yan Jin	Queen's University Belfast, UK
Dongyao Jia	University of Leeds, UK
Jongjie Jia	Tianjin University, China
Lin Jiang	University of Liverpool, UK
Ming Jiang	Anhui Polytechnic University, China
Youngwook Kuo	Queen's University Belfast, UK
Chuanfeng Li	Luoyang Institute of Science and Technology, China
Chuanjiang Li	Harbin Institute of Technology, China
Chuanjiang Li	Shanghai Normal University, China
Dewei Li	Shanghai Jiao Tong University, China
Donghai Li	Tsinghua University, China
Guofeng Li	Dalian University of Technology, China
Guozheng Li	China Academy of Chinese Medical Science, China
Jingzhao Li	Anhui University of Science and Technology, China
Ning Li	Shanghai Jiao Tong University, China
Tongtao Li	Henan University of Technology, China
Weixing Li	Harbin Institute of Technology, China
Xiaoli Li	Beijing University of Technology, China
Xin Li	Shanghai University, China
Xinghua Li	Tianjin University, China
Yunze Li	Beihang University, China
Zhengping Li	Anhui University, China
Jun Liang	Cardiff University, UK
Zhihao Lin	East China University of Science and Technology, China
Paolo Lino	University of Bari, Italy
Bin Liu	University of Birmingham, UK

Chao Liu	Centre national de la recherche scientifique, France
Fei Liu	Jiangnan University, China
Guoqiang Liu	Chinese Academy of Sciences, China
Mandan Liu	East China University of Science and Technology, China
Shirong Liu	Hangzhou Dianzi University, China
Shujun Liu	Sichuan University, China
Tingzhang Liu	Shanghai University, China
Wanquan Liu	Curtin University, Australia
Xianzhong Liu	East China Normal University, China
Yang Liu	Harbin Institute of Technology, China
Yunhuai Liu	The Third Research Institute of Ministry of Public Security, China
Patrick Luk	Cranfield University, UK
Jianfei Luo	Chinese Academy of Sciences, China
Yuanxin Luo	Chongqing University, China
Guangfu Ma	Harbin Institute of Technology, China
Hongjun Ma	Northeastern University, China
Guido Maione	Technical University of Bari, Italy
Marion McAfee	Institute of Technology Sligo, Ireland
Sean McLoone	Queen's University Belfast, UK
Gary Menary	Queen's University Belfast, UK
Gillian Menzies	Heriot-Watt University, UK
Wenlong Ming	Cardiff University, UK
Wasif Naeem	Queen's University Belfast, UK
Qun Niu	Shanghai University, China
Yuguang Niu	North China Electric Power University, China
Bao Kha Nyugen	Queen's University Belfast, UK
Ying Pan	Shanghai University of Engineering Science, China
Chen Peng	Shanghai University, China
Anh Phan	Newcastle University, UK
Meysam Qadrdan	Imperial College London, UK
Donglian Qi	Zhejiang University, China
Hua Qian	Shanghai University of Engineering Science, China
Feng Qiao	Shenyang Jianzhu University, China
Xuda Qin	Tianjin University, China
Yanbin Qu	Harbin Institute of Technology at Weihai, China
Slawomir Raszewski	King's College London, UK
Wei Ren	Shaanxi Normal University, China
Pedro Rivotti	Imperial College London, UK
Johannes Schiffer	University of Leeds, UK
Chenxi Shao	University of Science and Technology of China, China
Yuntao Shi	North China University of Technology, China
Beatrice Smyth	Queen's University Belfast, UK
Shiji Song	Tsinghua University, China
Yang Song	Shanghai University, China
Hongye Su	Zhejiang University, China

Guangming Sun	Beijing University of Technology, China
Tong Sun	City University of London, UK
Xin Sun	Shanghai University, China
Zhiqiang Sun	East China University of Science and Technology, China
Wenhu Tang	South China University of Technology, China
Xiaoqing Tang	The University of Manchester, UK
Fei Teng	Imperial College London, UK
Yuchu Tian	Queensland University of Technology, Australia
Xiaowei Tu	Shanghai University, China
Gang Wang	Northeastern University, China
Jianzhong Wang	Hangzhou Dianzi University, China
Jingcheng Wang	Shanghai Jiaotong University, China
Jihong Wang	University of Warwick, UK
Ling Wang	Shanghai University, China
Liangyong Wang	Northeastern University, China
Mingshun Wang	Northeastern University, China
Shuangxin Wang	Beijing Jiaotong University, China
Songyan Wang	Harbin Institute of Technology, China
Yaonan Wang	Hunan University, China
Kaixia Wei	NanJing XiaoZhuang University, China
Lisheng Wei	Anhui Polytechnic University, China
Mingshan Wei	Beijing Institute of Technology, China
Guihua Wen	South China University of Technology, China
Yiwu Weng	Shanghai Jiaotong University, China
Jianzhong Wu	Cardiff University, UK
Lingyun Wu	Chinese Academy of Sciences, China
Zhongcheng Wu	Chinese Academy of Sciences, China
Hui Xie	Tianjin University, China
Wei Xu	Zaozhuang University, China
Xiandong Xu	Cardiff University, UK
Juan Yan	University of Manchester, UK
Huaicheng Yan	East China University of Science and Technology, China
Aolei Yang	Shanghai University, China
Dongsheng Yang	Northeastern University, China
Shuanghua Yang	Loughborough University, UK
Wankou Yang	Southeast University, China
Wenqiang Yang	Henan Normal University, China
Zhile Yang	Chinese Academy of Sciences, China
Zhixin Yang	University of Macau, Macau, China
Dan Ye	Northeastern University, China
Keyou You	Tsinghua University, China
Dingli Yu	Liverpool John Moores University, UK
Hongnian Yu	Bournemouth University, UK
Kunjie Yu	Zhengzhou University, China
Xin Yu	Ningbo Institute of Technology, Zhejiang University, China
Jin Yuan	Shandong Agricultural University, China

Jingqi Yuan	Shanghai Jiao Tong University, China
Hong Yue	University of Strathclyde, UK
Dong Yue	Nanjing University of Posts and Communications, China
Xiaojun Zeng	The University of Manchester, UK
Dengfeng Zhang	University of Shanghai for Science and Technology, China
Huifeng Zhang	Nanjing University of Posts and Communications, China
Hongguang Zhang	Beijing University of Technology, China
Jian Zhang	State Nuclear Power Automation System Engineering Company, China
Jingjing Zhang	Cardiff University, UK
Lidong Zhang	Northeast Electric Power University, China
Long Zhang	The University of Manchester, UK
Qianfan Zhang	Harbin Institute of Technology, China
Xiaolei Zhang	Queen's University Belfast, UK
Xiaoping Zhang	University of Birmingham, UK
Youmin Zhang	Concordia University, USA
Yunong Zhang	Sun Yat-sen University, China
Dongya Zhao	China University of Petroleum, China
Guangbo Zhao	Harbin Institute of Technology, China
Jun Zhao	Tianjin University, China
Wanqing Zhao	Cardiff University, UK
Xingang Zhao	Shenyang Institute of Automation Chinese Academy of Sciences, China
Min Zheng	Shanghai University, China
Bowen Zhou	Northeastern University, China
Huiyu Zhou	Queen's University Belfast, UK
Wenju Zhou	Ludong University, China
Yimin Zhou	Chinese Academy of Sciences, China
Yu Zhou	Shanghai Tang Electronics Co., Ltd., China
Yunpu Zhu	Nanjing University of Science and Technology, China
Yi Zong	Technical University of Denmark, Demark
Kaizhong Zuo	Anhui Normal University, China

Sponsors

Chongqing Association for Science and Technology, China
Shanghai University, China

Organizers

Chongqing University, China
Queen's University Belfast, UK

Co-organizers

Southeast University, Beijing Institute of Technology, Dalian University of Technology, Harbin Institute of Technology, Northwestern Polytechnical University, South China University of Technology, Tianjin University, Tongji University, Shanghai University, University of Birmingham, Cardiff University, University College London, University of Nottingham, University of Warwick, University of Leeds.

Contents – Part II

Fault Diagnosis and Maintenance

Intelligent Computing in Robotics

Intelligent Control and Automation

IoT Systems

Neural Networks and Deep Learning

Precision Measurement and Instrumentation

Image Processing

Advanced Evolutionary Computing Theory and Algorithms

Improved Shuffled Frog Leaping Algorithm for Multi-objection Flexible Job-Shop Scheduling Problem

Mingli Gou, Qingxuan Gao[✉], and Su Yang

College of Mechanical Engineering, Chongqing University, Chongqing 400044, China
grace_qx@126.com

Abstract. This paper proposes an improved shuffled frog leaping algorithm (SFLA-PSO) to solve multi-objective flexible job-shop problem. Pareto optimization strategy is used to balance three objectives including minimum the maximum completion time, maximum workload of all machines and the total processing time of all job. In the new algorithm, the particle swarm flight strategy is innovatively embedded into the local update operator of the SFLA-PSO. A dynamic crowding density sorting method is used to update external elite archive which holds the non-dominated population. To further improve the quality of the solution and the diversity of the population, a new local optimization strategy is developed associated with a neighborhood search strategy for achieving a high development ability of the new algorithm. The test results of benchmark instances illustrate the effectiveness of the new algorithm.

Keywords: Flexible job-shop scheduling · Multi-objective optimization
Pareto optimum solution · Shuffled frog leaping algorithm
Particle swarm algorithm

1 Introduction

The multi-objective flexible shop scheduling problems (MOFJSP) evolved from flexible shop scheduling problems (FJSP) which has been proven to be NP-hard problem [1]. It can comprehensively consider multiple targets and better meet modern production requirements, but it is more complicated combinatorial optimization problem than FJSP because of its increased machine selection, extended search scope as well as multiple choices of optimization objectives. Therefore, this issue has attracted more and more attention from academia and industry.

Two optimization approaches are ususlly developed for multi-objective flexible job shop scheduling problem. The first method is weighted sum approach, namely, the multi-objective optimization problems is transformed into a single objective optimization problem by assigning different weights to each objective, and then solved by some meta-heuristic approaches. Neverthless, this method only obtains a single solution, thus it is difficult to find Pareto-optimal solutions for decision maker's choice. The second approach is called Pareto-based multi-objective evolutionary algorithms which is

© Springer Nature Singapore Pte Ltd. 2018
K. Li et al. (Eds.): ICSEE 2018/IMIOT 2018, CCIS 924, pp. 3–14, 2018.
https://doi.org/10.1007/978-981-13-2384-3_1

developed to reduce the influence of decision-maker's preference. Instead of finding a single optimal solution, this method generates Pareto non-inferior solutions with sufficient number and uniform distribution that satisfy multiple objectives. The most typical algorithms is called NSGA- II proposed by Deb et al. [2], which is the improved version of NSGA that is highly dependent on the parameters of the fitness sharing. Another modified version of the NSGA-II is called non-dominated ranking genetic algorithm (NRGA) [3] using Rolette-wheel strategy instead of tournament selection strategy. In solving MOFJSP, Shao et al. [4] proposed a hybrid discrete particle swarm optimization (DPSO) and simulated annealing (SA) to identify an approximation of the Pareto front for FJSP. Zhong et al. [5] proposed a niching and particle swarm optimization algorithms for multi-objective flexible job-shop scheduling problem. a new meta-heuristic is designed based on ICA and VNS to minimize total tardiness and makespan under the constraint by Lei et al. [6]

Since Shuffled frog leaping algorithm (SFLA) [7] put forward, SFLA has made great progress in its applications [8, 9] because of its advantages of fewer parameters, fast computation and global optimization ability. In solving job shop scheduling. Xu et al. [10] proposed the shuffled frog leaping algorithm (SFLA) to solve the hybrid flow-shop problem with multiprocessor tasks. A novel SFLA, where the search process within each memeplex is done on its non-dominated member, is proposed based on a three-string coding method to solve two conflicting goals by Xiuping Guo et al. [11] To our knowledge, the research of the shuffled frog leaping algorithm hybriding other algorithms to find Pareto solutions for multi-objective job shop scheduling problem seem relatively less.

In this paper, we proposed an improved shuffled frog leaping algorithm to solve multi-objective job scheduling problem. Most importantly, the particle swarm flight strategy was embedded into the local location update operator of the shuffled frog leaping algorithm to increase global exploration capability, a new local optimization strategy for external elite archive is developed associated with a neighborhood search strategy for achieving a high development ability of the new algorithm. The objectives in this paper are to minimize makespan, the workload of the critical machine and the total workload of machines simultaneously.

This paper is organized as followed. We define the multi-objective flexible job shop scheduling problem in Sect. 2, Sect. 3 presents the framework of the SFLA-PSO algorithm, SFLA-PSO algorithm is explained in Sect. 4 including the meme evolution, the external elite document's maintenance and so on. In Sect. 5, SFLA-PSO is compared with other heuristic algorithm for classic instance. Section 6 gives the conclusion of the paper.

2   Multi-objective Flexible Job Shop Scheduling Problem

The MOFJSP can be described as a set of n jobs J_i where $i = 1, 2, \ldots n$ which have to be processed on a set of m machines M_k where $k = 1, 2, \ldots m$. Each job contains a predetermined sequence of fixed operations, each operation can be processed on one or more different machines and the processing time varies with the machine. The goal of the MOFJSP is to select the right machine for each operation and determine the optimum processing order of each operation on the machine, so as to optimize the manufacturing system as much as possible. The following assumptions and constraints are considered.

(1) All jobs and machines are available at time zero and each machine can only execute one operation at a given time.
(2) There are no sequential requirements for the operations between the different jobs, the operation of the same job must be finished in the previous operation before starting the next process 3.
(3) Each operation cannot be interrupted during processing
(4) Once a job is completed on a machine, it is transported to the next machine immediately and the transportation time is negligible.
(5) Breakdowns are not considered for the machines.

The notation used in this paper are as following,

(1) Let $J = \{J_i\}$, $1 \leq i \leq$ n, indexed I, be a set of n jobs to be scheduled.
(2) Let $M = \{M_j\}$, $1 \leq j \leq$ m, indexed j, be a set of m machines.
(3) Let $O_{i,j}$ be the jth operation of J_i, n_i donates the total number of operation of job J_i.
(4) let $P_{i,j,k}$ be the processing time of $O_{i,j}$ on the machine M_k, $T_{i,j}$ be the completion time of the operation $O_{i,j}$.
(5) Decision variables $X_{i,j,k} = 1$ if machine Mk is selected for operation $O_{i,j}$, otherwise $X_{i,j,k} = 0$.

In this paper, three objectives are simultaneously considered, which are given as follows.

$$\text{Min}\, T_{\text{max}} = \max_{1 \leq i \leq n}\{T_{i,j}\} \tag{1}$$

$$\text{Min}\, W_{\text{max}} = \max_{1 \leq k \leq m}\{W_k\} = \max_{1 \leq k \leq m} \sum_{i=1}^{n} \sum_{j=1}^{m} P_{i,j,k} X_{i,j,k} \tag{2}$$

$$\text{Min}\, L_{\text{max}} = \sum_{i=1}^{n} \sum_{j=1}^{n_i} \sum_{k=1}^{m} P_{i,j,k} X_{i,j,k} \tag{3}$$

Where T_{max} is the maximum completion time of all jobs; W_{max} is the maximum workload of all machines; L_{max} is the total processing time of all jobs.

3 Framework of SFLA-PSO Algorithm

In this paper, we propose an improved SFLA (SFLA-PSO) as showed in Fig. 1, which is divided into three phases including initializing phase, evolution phase and update external elite document phase.

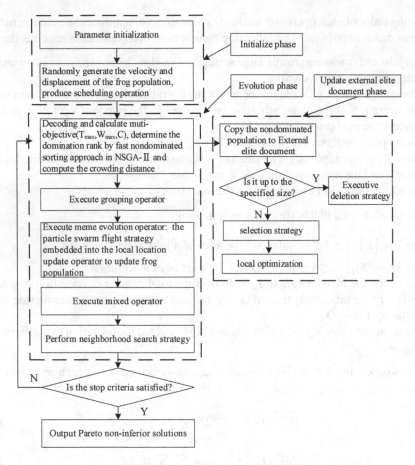

Fig. 1. The framework of SFLA-PSO

4   The Hybrid Algorithm SFLA-PSO

4.1   The Meme Evolution Operator

The SFLA is a novel meta-heuristic algorithm, which makes use of the cultural environment information named as "meme" among the population to perform its evolution. The searching process is performed using the instruction of memes generated by the cooperation and competition among the population. In addition, the redistribution of the sub-population makes searching process less possible to be trapped in local minima. The traditional meme evolution operator are shown below.

$$\Delta X = r \, and \, () * (X_b - X_w) \tag{4}$$

$$newX_w = X_w + \Delta X \left(\Delta X_{max} \geq \Delta X \geq -\Delta X_{min} \right) \tag{5}$$

$$\Delta X = r \operatorname{and}() * \left(X_g - X_w\right) \tag{6}$$

$$newX_w = X_w + \Delta X \left(\Delta X_{max} \geq \Delta X \geq \Delta X_{min}\right) \tag{7}$$

Where, in Eq. (4) ΔX denotes the moving step of frog individual, rand() represents the random number uniformly distributed between 0 and 1, X_b and X_w represents the best and worst frog in each meme group respectively, Eq. (5) denotes the update of the location of the worst frog individuals in the meme group, if the frog could produce a better position after the above update, then replace the original position with a new position, otherwise replace X_g with X_b, and update with (6) (7) formula above. A new solution is randomly generated instead of the worst frog if the above method still fails to produce better frog individuals.

In this paper, the fly strategy of particles in PSO is embedded into the local update operator of SFLA to guide the evolution of frog individuals in the meme group, the local position update operator is adjusted as follows,

$$V_{id}^{k+1} = wV_{id}^k + c_1 r_1 \left(P_{id}^k - X_{id}^k\right) + c_2 r_2 \left(P_{gd}^k - X_{gd}^k\right) \tag{8}$$

$$X_{id}^{k+1} = X_{id}^k + V_{id}^{k+1} \tag{9}$$

$$V_{id}^{k+1} = wV_{id}^k + c_3 r_3 \left(P_{gd}^k - X_{id}^k\right) \tag{10}$$

$$X_{id}^{k+1} = X_{id}^k + V_{id}^{k+1} \tag{11}$$

Where, in Eqs. (8), (9), (10) and (11) the parameters such as c_1, c_2, c_3, r_1, r_2, r_3 and w are the same meaning as those in the standard PSO algorithm. But the difference is that X_{id}^k represents the worse frog individual in the meme group, P_{id}^k and P_{gd}^k denotes the optimal position of the meme group and all frog individuals respectively. According to Eqs. (8) and (9),the frog individual' speed and displacement is updated, The objective function (Objv') of the updated individual is calculated and compared with objective function (Objv) of frog individual before update in Pareto dominance relation,

(a) if Objv'> Objv, then the speed and displacement of the individual is replaced with the updated frog individual's.
(b) if Objv > Objv', then update the speed and displacement according to Eqs. (10) and (11), a new individual is randomly generated instead of the original individual if the frog is still dominated by the original individual.
(c) if Objv'~ Objv, then accept the speed and displacement of the updated individual at a probability of 50%.

The Pareto relation can be described as followed, for multi-objective optimization problem, $\min[f_i(x), i = 1, 2, \cdots, n]$, if $f_i(X^a) \leq f_i(X^b)$ and a strict inequality exists at least, then X^b is dominated by X^a, symbolized as $X^a > X^b$, if the two vectors do not dominate each other, it can be symbolized as $X^a \sim X^b$.

4.2 External Elite Document's Maintenance

In order to solve the multi-objective optimization problem, the key is to find enough uniformly distributed Pareto sets which are close to the real Pareto front. This paper uses elitist strategy to store the non-dominated individuals generated during the evolution of each generation and delete the dominant individuals that may exist in the elite document, The algorithm steps are as follows.

(1) Copy the non-dominated individual generated by the individual flight to the elite document, and delete the duplicated individuals and dominating ones in the document.

(2) If the number of individuals in the document exceeds the specified scale N, the individuals of the same rank are descending order by the crowding-distance, and then the first N individuals are retained. The method of computing crowding-distance is the fast non-dominated sorting approach proposed by Deb et al. [8] in NSGA II, however, the crowding-distance of the Pareto solution is calculated only once in each iteration, thereby resulting in poor diversity and evenness of Pareto solution. Therefore, in this paper each individual is removed and the crowding-distance of the remaining individuals is recalculated until the specified size is satisfied in the process of maintaining elite documents. Otherwise, the elite document is not reduced. The proposed method avoids the increase of the number of non-dominated individuals in the process of external document iteration, and removes the redundant crowding individuals to ensure the uniformity of Pareto solution distribution.

4.3 A Local Optimization Strategy for External Elite Documents

The outside elite documents stored non-dominated individuals in the iteration which overcome the defects of NSGA II algorithm without using external elite population to preserve the historical non-dominated individuals which caused some better solutions to be lost, falling into premature convergence. However, the external elite document is only used to store the non- dominated individuals searched in the iteration, and these individuals do not react to the evolutionary population, resulting in reducing the convergence speed of the algorithm and decreasing the diversity of Pareto solutions. Therefore, this paper proposes the local optimization strategy including selection strategy and local optimization to optimize the external Pareto solution set. The selection strategy decides how to choose the important search area to avoid blind search and the local optimization is to optimize the important search regions. The selection strategy is as follows.

(1) Strategy 1, In order to avoid the repeated search for a region, a non-dominated individuals on the current stored in the external elite document is designated the largest number of local search, once more than the search times, the search area is discarded.

(2) Strategy 2, A sphere radius (R) is specified in advance, aiming at guiding the search toward promising regions. For non-dominated individuals that do not reach the search upper limit (L), the number of non-dominated individuals within the radius

of the hyper-sphere is counted as the center, the smaller amount means the less non-dominated individuals around it, indicating the new non-dominated individuals are discovered with the high probability. If the minimum number exceeds one, the average euclidean distance is calculated within the radius of the hyper-sphere, The larger distance means the more sparse distribution of solutions, resulting in more likely to find new non-dominated solutions. The local optimization algorithm for external elite documents is given in Fig. 2.

Procedure 1 Local optimization algorithm for external elite documents

Input, Non-dominated individuals S_0, the upper search limit (L), the hyper-sphere radius (R), the maximum number of iterations N, the number of current search of the individual (i) N_i

Output, a new non-dominated archive after local search

// start selection strategy

1. $S_0' = \{a \in S_0 \mid N_a < L\}$.

2. Calculate $\beta(a) = \{\theta \in S_0 \mid \|f(\theta) - f(a)\| \leq R \,\forall a \in S_0'\}$

   $\gamma = \{\theta \mid \min|\beta(\theta)|, \forall \theta \in S_0\}$

3. If $|r|<1$ then   choose randomly a non-dominated individual to local search.

   else if $|r|==1$ choose a unique non-dominated individual to local search.

   else then

$$d(a) = \frac{\sum_{\theta \in \beta(a)} \|f(\theta) - f(a)\|}{|\beta(a)|} \quad a \in \gamma \text{ // Calculate the average euclidean distance}$$

$$\dot{\gamma} = \{a \in \gamma \mid \max d(a)\}$$

choose non-dominated individual (a) to local research.

// start local search

4. While $N_a<N$ do

   For each a' $\in\delta$(a) do   //Neighborhood exploration

   If a$\prec$a' then   a=a', N_a=0

   Else if a$\sim$a' then   update (a',S), N_a=0   // add to the non-dominated set

   $N_a=N_a+1$

   If $N_a>L$ then   break

Fig. 2. Local optimization algorithm for external elite documents

4.4 Selection of Global Optimal Solution

In the SFLA-PSO algorithm, the worst individual in the meme group uses the fly strategy of the particle in PSO to track its historical optimum position and global optimum position to update its speed and displacement. For a single objective optimization problem, the global optimal solution can be obtained by directly comparing the fitness values of individual populations, but for multi-objective optimization, the Pareto solution sets obtained in each evolution process are mutually exclusive, and there is no global optimal solution in the traditional angle of view. In order to ensure the diversity of the Pareto solutions and the uniformity, we can select non-dominated individuals randomly from the descending order based on crowding-distance after the first 20% as a global optimal solution to guide the meme within the group of the worst individual updates.

4.5 The Encoding and Decoding of Frog Populations

In order to deal with the chromosome encoding in MOFJSP, we should not only choose the machine to process, but also arrange the order of the operations on the machine. Therefore, the double coding based on operation and machine is adopted in this paper. The position vectors of individual frogs can be represented as vectors of a dimension (total operation number $L = \sum_{i=1}^{n} n_j$), each L dimension vector is represented by $X_p[L]$, $X_m[L]$ respectively. Take 3×4 FJSP as an example, $O_1 = \{O_{11}, O_{12}, O_{13}\}$, $O_2 = \{O_{21}, O_{22}, O_{23}\}$, $O_3 = \{O_{31}, O_{32}, O_{33}\}$, The chromosome encoding and decoding corresponding to a feasible solution is shown in Table 1.

Table 1. Examples of chromosome coding and decoding

encoding	$X_m[L]$	3	4	2	4	3	3	2	2	1
	$X_p[L]$	1	3	2	2	1	3	3	1	2

decoding	$X_p[L]$	O_{11}	O_{31}	O_{21}	O_{22}	O_{12}	O_{32}	O_{33}	O_{13}	O_{23}
	$X_m[L]$	M_3	M_4	M_2	M_4	M_3	M_3	M_2	M_2	M_1

Where O_{ij} represents the j-th operation of the i-th job, when decoding, the procedure firstly reads the operation coding successively and then randomly select a machine in a given optional machine table of operation. The operations processed on each machine after decoding are $\{M_1: O_{23}\}$, $\{M_2: O_{21}, O_{33}, O_{13}\}$, $\{M_3: O_{11}, O_{12}, O_{32}\}$, $\{M_4: O_{31}, O_{22}\}$.

4.6 The Adjustment of Frog Population's Displacement

The velocity vector of the worst individual in the meme group is updated according to the Eqs. (8) and (10), and the position vector is updated according to the Eqs. (9) and (11). Since FJSP belongs to integer encoding, there may be a decimal fraction after updating, so it is necessary to adjust the infeasible solution. The feasible operation is obtained according to the reordered new displacement in ascending order. The adjustment results are shown in the following Table 2. At the same time, the process also has machine constraint, hence there is a need to reselect the machine after the adjustment

Table 2. Example of the adjusted displacement of the frog individual

The displacement $X_p[L]$	1	3	2	2	1	3	3	1	2
The updated displacement $X'_p[L]$	1.3	2.4	0.8	1.5	1.8	2.1	5	4.8	2.9
The ordered displacement $X'_p[L]$	0.8	1.3	1.5	1.8	2.1	2.4	2.9	4.8	5
The adjusted displacement $X_p[L]$	2	1	2	1	3	3	2	1	3

operation, according to the procedure to find the process of optional machine set in the optional machine table, and then randomly select a processing machine.

4.7 Neighborhood Search Strategy

SFLA-PSO has the advantages of few parameters, global searching ability and fast convergence speed, but it is easy to fall into local optimum. In order to improve the local search ability and increase the diversity and dispersion of Pareto front, the neighborhood search strategy adopted in this paper is as follows.

(1) Exchange operations based on operation genes

The two positions which is selected randomly from the operation genes $X_P[L]$ are interchanged, the rest remains the same and $X'_P[L]$ is obtained. As shown in Table 3(a), the operation of gene position 3 and 6 interchange and the machine genes are adjusted accordingly. The objection function of the individual after the interchange is calculated. If the individual after the neighborhood search dominates the original individual, the original individual is replaced.

Table 3. The operation base on operation

(a) Exchange operations based on operation

$X_p[L]$	2	1	2	1	3	3	2	1	3
$X_p[L]$	2	1	3	3	1	2	2	1	1

(b) Reverse operation based on operation

$X_p[L]$	2	1	2	1	3	3	2	1	3
$X_p[L]$	2	1	3	3	1	2	2	1	1

(2) Reverse operation based on operation genes

Reverse the operation between two positions which is selected randomly from the operation genes $X_P[L]$, the rest remains the same, $X'_P[L]$ is obtained. As shown in Table 3(b), the operation gene between position 3 and 6 reverse and the machine genes are adjusted accordingly. The objection function of the individual after reversing is calculated.If the individual after the neighborhood search dominates the original individual, the original individual is replaced.

(3) Mutation based on machine genes

Select a position randomly at $X_m[L]$ and find the operation corresponding to the position, choose a machine randomly that is different from the original machine at optional machine set. The objective function is calculated. If the mutated individual dominates the original one, the original individual is replaced.

5 Computational Results

To evaluate the performance of the proposed SFLA-PSO algorithm, we conducted a number of computational experiments. The AL + CGA algorithm [12], PSO + SA algorithm [13], PSO + TS algorithm [14] and SCAO algorithm [15] are used to compare with the proposed SFLA-PSO algorithm.

In this paper, the SFLA-PSO algorithm was implemented in MATLAB environment on an Intel Core i5-4200M 2.5 GHz PC. The Five Kacem instances are selected to test, each instance can be characterized by the followed parameters, number of jobs (n), number of machines (m), and each operation O_{ij} of job i.

5.1 Problem 8 × 8

This is an instance of 8 × 8 with 27 operations. The comparison of the SFLA-PSO algorithm with others is showed in Table 4, in which S_i denote i th solution. The comparison result shows that the proposed hybrid algorithm in this paper obtains more Pareto solutions than other algorithm. Moreover, the optimal solution for the maximum load of all machines is not under the premise of sacrificing the other two goals.

Table 4. Comparison of results on problem 8 × 8

	AL + CGA		PSO + SA		PSO + TS		SCAO		SFLA-PSO		
	S1	S2	S1	S2	S1	S2	S1	S2	S1	S2	S3
T_{max}	15	16	16	16	15	14	15	14	16	16	16
L_{max}	79	79	75	73	75	77	76	77	73	75	77
W_{max}	–	–	12	13	12	12	12	12	13	12	11

5.2 Problem 10 × 10

This is an instance of 10 × 10 with 30 operations taken from Kacem et al. [12]. The comparison of the SFLA-PSO algorithm with others is showed in Table 5, in which S_i denote i th solution. The comparison result shows that the proposed SFLA-PSO algorithm obtains more and better Pareto solutions than other algorithms.

Table 5. Comparison of results on problem 10 × 10

	AL + CGA		PSO + SA		PSO + TS		SCAO		SFLA-PSO		
	S1	S2	S1	S2	S1	S2	S1	S2	S1	S2	S3
T_{max}	7	–	7	–	7	8	7	8	8	7	8
L_{max}	45	–	44	–	42	42	42	42	41	42	42
W_{max}	5	–	6	–	6	5	6	5	7	6	5

5.3 Problem 15 × 10

This is an instance of 15 × 10 with 56 operations taken from Du et al. (2008). The comparison of the SFLA-PSO algorithm with others is showed in Table 6, in which Si denote i th solution. The comparison result shows that the proposed SFLA-PSO algorithm is not bad.

Table 6. Comparison of results on problem 15 × 10

	AL + CGA		PSO + SA		PSO + TS		SCAO		SFLA-PSO		
	S1	S2	S1	S2	S1	S2	S1	S2	S1	S2	S3
T_{max}	23	24	12	–	11	11	11	11	11	11	–
L_{max}	95	94	93	–	91	93	91	93	91	93	–
W_{max}	11	11	11	–	11	10	11	10	11	10	–

6 Conclusions

This paper studies a multi-objective flexible job shop scheduling problem with the goal of minimum the maximum completion time, maximum workload of all machines and the total processing time of all job, and establishes a multi-objective optimization model. Since it is NP-hard, an improved shuffled frog leaping algorithm were proposed to heuristically solve them. The key contribution of this paper is that The particle swarm flight strategy is embedded in the SFLA, and the dynamic crowding density sorting method is used to update the non-dominant population external elite files, to improve the performance of algorithm. Moreover,A new local optimization strategy is adopted to achieve the high development ability of the new algorithm. The comparison results with other typical algorithms demonstrated the effectiveness of the proposed algorithm.

The improved shuffled frog leaping algorithm proposed in this paper improves the search performance of the shuffled frog leaping algorithm and extends the applicability of the algorithm. How to improve the SFLA algorithm in solving more complex problems and improve the convergence precision of the algorithm, simulated annealing algorithm, the chaotic theory and immune algorithm with strong local search ability is an important research direction in the future of the authors.

References

1. Garey, M.R., Johnson, D.S., Sethi, R.: The complexity of flowshop and jobshop scheduling. Math. Oper. Res. **1**(2), 117–129 (1976)
2. Deb, K.: A fast and elitist multiobjective genetic algorithm. NSGA-II. IEEE Trans. Evol. Comput. **6**(2), 182–197 (2002)
3. Jadaan, O.A., Rajamani, L., Rao, C.R.: Non-dominated ranked genetic algorithm for solving multi-objective optimization problems, NRGA. J. Theor. Appl. Inf. Technol. **1**, 60–67 (2008)
4. Shao, X.Y., Liu, W.Q., Liu, Q.: Hybrid discrete particle swarm optimization for multi-objective flexible job-shop scheduling problem. Int. J. Adv. Manuf. Technol. **67**(9–12), 2885–2901 (2013)

5. Zhong, Y., Yang, H., Mo, R., Sun, H.: Optimization method of flexible job-shop scheduling problem based on niching and particle swarm optimization algorithms. Comput. Integr. Manuf. Syst. **12**(21), 3231–3238 (2015)
6. Lei, D., Li, M., Wang, L.: A two-phase meta-heuristic for multiobjective flexible job shop scheduling problem with total energy consumption threshold. IEEE Trans. Cybern. **PP**(99), 1–13 (2018)
7. Eusuff, M., Lansey, K.: Optimization of water distribution network design using the shuffled frog leaping algorithm. J. Water Resour. Plann. Manage. **129**(2003), 210–225 (2003)
8. Luo, X.H., Yang, Y., Li, X.: Modified shuffled frog-leaping algorithm to solve traveling salesman problem. J. Commun. **30**(7), 130–135 (2009)
9. Ren, W.L., Zhao, C.W.: A localization algorithm based on SFLA and PSO for wireless sensor network. Inf. Technol. J. **12**(3), 502–505 (2012)
10. Xu, Y., Wang, L., Liu, M., Wang, S.Y.: An effective shuffled frog-leaping algorithm for hybrid flow-shop scheduling with multiprocessor tasks. Int. J. Adv. Manuf. Technol. **68**(5–8), 1529–1537 (2013)
11. Lei, D., Zheng, Y., Guo, X.: A shuffled frog-leaping algorithm for flexible job shop scheduling with the consideration of energy consumption. Int. J. Prod. Res. **55**(11), 3126–3140 (2017)
12. Kacem, I., Hammadi, S., Borne, P.: Approach by localization and multiobjective evolutionary optimization for flexible job-shop scheduling problems. IEEE Trans. Syst. Man Cybern. Part C Appl. Rev. **32**(1), 1–13 (2002)
13. Xia, W.J., Wu, Z.M.: An effective hybrid optimization approach for multi-objective flexible job-shop scheduling problems. Comput. Ind. Eng. **48**(2005), 409–425 (2005)
14. Zhang, G.H., Shao, X.Y., Li, P.G., Gao, L.: An effective hybrid particle swarm optimization algorithm for multi-objective flexible job-shop scheduling problem. Comput. Ind. Eng. **56**(2009), 1309–1318 (2009)
15. Xing, L.N., Chen, Y.W., Yang, K.W.: Multi-objective flexible job shop schedule, design and evaluation by simulation modeling. Appl. Soft Comput. **9**(2009), 362–376 (2009)

Hysteretic Model of a Rotary Magnetorheological Damper in Helical Flow Mode

Jianqiang Yu[1,2], Xiaomin Dong[1(✉)], Shuaishuai Sun[2], and Weihua Li[2]

[1] State Key Laboratory of Mechanical Transmission, Chongqing University, Chongqing 400044, China
xmdong@cqu.edu.cn
[2] School of Mechanical, Materials and Mechatronic Engineering, University of Wollongong, Wollongong, NSW 2522, Australia

Abstract. To capture the accurate hysteretic characteristics of a rotary magnetorheological (MR) damper in reciprocating motion, a new model with reversibility is proposed and analyzed. The rotary MR damper in helical flow mode is designed and tested on MTS under different current to obtain the hysteretic characteristics. To portray hysteresis effectively and accurately, the proposed model composed of a shape function and hysteresis factor is introduced. To obtain the reversibility, the model is separated to the hysteretic part and current-dependent part based on normalization method. The two parts follow the multiplication rule. To improve computational efficiency, Constriction Factor Particle Swarm Optimization (CFPSO) algorithm is used to identify the model's parameters. Feasibility and effectiveness of the identified model are validated through comparison with two typical dynamic models.

Keywords: Rotary magnetorheological damper · Helical flow mode
Model · Hysteresis factor

1 Introduction

To suppress the vibration in transmission devices and suspensions, semi-active magnetorheological (MR) systems have been investigated in recent years. MR dampers in the semi-active systems can provide tunable damping with rapid response and lower energy consumption. To ensure the MR systems to be feasible and efficient, the accurate dynamic model should be constructed to capture the MR dampers' nonlinear hysteresis. So far, different modeling methods and dynamic models are proposed and applied in semi-active control procedures [1]. MR dampers in different working modes exhibit various hysteretic characteristics. The damping in valve mode is magnetic field- and rate-dependent while the shear mode is mainly influenced by magnetic field. The hysteresis of MR damper in squeeze mode is rate-independent and gap width-dependent [2]. Therefore, the dynamic model should be established based on the unique characteristics of MR damper.

© Springer Nature Singapore Pte Ltd. 2018
K. Li et al. (Eds.): ICSEE 2018/IMIOT 2018, CCIS 924, pp. 15–24, 2018.
https://doi.org/10.1007/978-981-13-2384-3_2

The hysteretic characteristics of dampers working at valve mode can be predicted by bi-viscous models [3], viscoelastic models [4], Bouc-wen models [5], Dahl models [6], hyperbolic tangent models [7], sigmoid function models [8], polynomial model [9], hysteretic-division model [10], and so on [11]. The parametric models contain the Bouc-wen model [12, 13], Dahl model [14] and LuGre friction model [15] have been used to describe damping characteristics of dampers in shear mode. Different from the models of valve mode damper, the effects of stiffness are not considered in most of shear mode models [16]. Improved Bouc-wen model can also be used to describe the characteristics of dampers in squeeze mode [2].

As a new working mode, helical flow mode has been proposed and analyzed in our prior work [17]. It is different from the conventional valve mode, shear mode and their mixed mode. The dampers working at helical flow mode have high damping density and can avoid sedimentation. Nowadays, vehicle or seat suspensions utilized rotary magnetorheological dampers (RMRDs) have been studied because of the rotary damper's unique advantages [18, 19]. The rotary dampers don't need accumulator to provide volume and temperature compensation. Besides, the rotary dampers are beneficial to integrate self-power and self-sensing systems. RMRD in helical flow mode is also suitable for application in vehicle or seat suspensions. Considering high torque density, the damping system with helical flow mode damper can save the force amplifier such as gear box and rack and pinion. For its application and control, the dynamic model should be established based on its hysteretic characteristics.

In this study, a novel dynamic model with inverse ability is proposed to capture the characteristics of rotary MR damper in helical flow mode. Construction of this study is as follows. The hysteretic characteristics are tested and analyzed in Sect. 2. Section 3 shows the details of the dynamic model. Parameters identification is conducted in Sect. 3.2. Conclusions are made in Sect. 4.

2 Hysteretic Characteristics of RMRD in Helical Flow Mode

The configuration of RMRD in helical flow mode is shown in Fig. 1. It mainly consists of outer cylinder, inner cylinder, piston, coil and rod. The inner cylinder rotates with the rod while piston and outer cylinder keep still. Spiral groove in the rod is filled with fluid. MR fluid flows in duct 1 and duct 2. The details of helical flow mode can be seen in Ref. [17].

Total torque derived from three ducts can be calculated by Eqs. (1)–(4).

$$T_{max} = T_1 + T_2 + T_3 \tag{1}$$

$$T_1 = \int_0^l \frac{\Delta P}{l} x h dx \cos \theta (r_d - 0.5 r_h) \tag{2}$$

$$T_2 = 2\pi r_2^3 L \eta \frac{w}{d} + 2\pi r_2^2 l_a \tau_2 \tag{3}$$

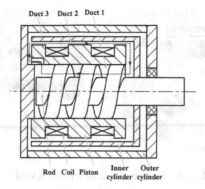

Fig. 1. Configuration of RMRD in helical flow mode

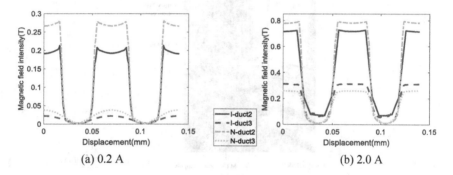

(a) 0.2 A   (b) 2.0 A

Fig. 2. Magnetic field intensity distribution in the duct 2 and duct 3

$$T_3 = 2\pi r_3^3 L\eta \frac{w}{d} + 2\pi r_3^2 l_a \tau_3 \tag{4}$$

here, T_1, T_2 and T_3 are torque in duct 1, duct 2 and duct 3, respectively. T_1 is derived from the effects of helical flow mode. T_2 and T_3 are both calculated based on working principle of shear mode. In our prior work [17], a rotary damper is designed and tested. In this study, the thickness of duct 2 and duct 3 is changed from 1.5 mm and 2 mm to 1 mm and 1 mm, respectively. Figure 2 shows the comparison of the magnetic field intensity between the initial damper and novel one. The novel one shows higher magnetic field intensity than the initial one both under 0.2 A and 2.0 A. The higher magnetic field intensity is beneficial to improve coulomb damping force.

The components and assembly of the novel damper can be seen in Fig. 3. The volume of MR fluid in RMRD is $385 \times 10^{-6} m^3$ which is also smaller than the initial damper. Test apparatus of the RMRD is shown in Fig. 4. Rack-and-pinion is applied to convert the linear motion to rotational motion. Characteristics of torque-angle and torque-velocity loops are displayed in Figs. 5, 6 and 7. The torque can be improved by

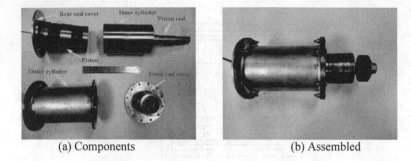

(a) Components   (b) Assembled

Fig. 3. Picture of manufactured RMRD

Fig. 4. Test apparatus of the RMRD

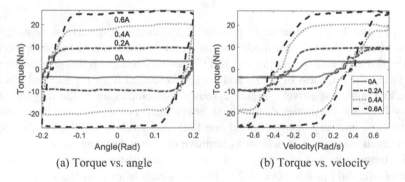

(a) Torque vs. angle   (b) Torque vs. velocity

Fig. 5. Torque characteristics at amplitude of 6 mm and frequency of 0.6 Hz

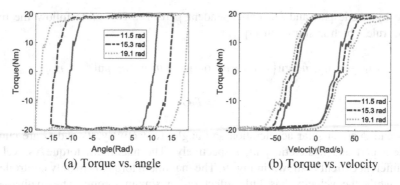

Fig. 6. Torque characteristics at frequency of 0.8 Hz and current of 0.4 A

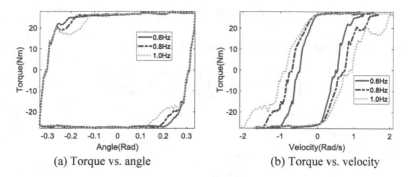

Fig. 7. Torque characteristics at amplitude of 10 mm and current of 0.6 A

increasing current obviously. The curve mutation appears in torque-angle loops especially in Fig. 7 due to the cooperation problem of the rack-and-pinion at larger damping force.

3 Modeling and Parameters Identification

3.1 Modeling Method

To capture the characteristics of torque-angle and torque-velocity curves, a model based on a shape function shown in Eq. (5) and hysteresis factor is proposed. The parameter sensitivity analysis of shape function is conducted and displayed in Fig. 8.

$$z = \frac{1 - e^{\beta w}}{1 + e^{\beta w}} \tag{5}$$

Even though these type curves are enough to capture torque-angle or force-displacement, the nonlinear hysteretic characteristics cannot be captured accurately. To describe the hysteresis, hysteresis factor in Eq. (6) is introduced to replace the velocity term in Eq. (5). To realize the reversibility of model, normalization method is used to separate hysteretic part and current-dependent part. The two parts follow the multiplication rule which is shown in Eq. (7).

$$w \rightarrow n_1 w + n_2 \text{sgn}\left(\ddot{\phi}\right) + n_3 \ddot{\phi} \text{ or } w \rightarrow n_1 w + n_2 \text{sgn}(\phi) + n_3 \phi \tag{6}$$

$$T_d = T_I G \tag{7}$$

here, $\ddot{\phi}$ and ϕ are angular acceleration and angle, respectively. T_I and G are current-dependent part and hysteretic part, respectively. The maximum torque vs. velocity under different current is shown in Fig. 9. The maximum torque is mainly controlled by current while the velocity has little effect on maximum torque. The mathematical expression of current-dependent part is shown in Eq. (8).

$$T_1 = c_1 e^{c_2 I^2 + c_3 I} + c_4 \tag{8}$$

here, I is current. c_1, c_2, c_3 and c_4 are model's parameters.

$$T_1 = \left(c_1 e^{c_2 I^2 + c_3 I} + c_4\right) \frac{1 - e^{n_1 w + n_2 \text{sgn}(\phi) + n_3 \phi}}{1 + e^{n_1 w + n_2 \text{sgn}(\phi) + n_3 \phi}} \tag{9}$$

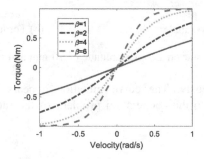

Fig. 8. Parameters analysis of the shape function

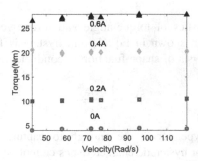

Fig. 9. Maximum force vs. velocity under different current

The inverse model is

$$I = \frac{-c_3 - \sqrt{c_3^2 + 4c_2\kappa}}{2c_2}$$

(10)

Here, $\kappa = \ln[(T_d/G - c_4)/c_1]$ and $G = \frac{1 - e^{a_1 w + a_2 \operatorname{sgn}(\phi) + a_3 \phi}}{1 + e^{a_1 w + a_2 \operatorname{sgn}(\phi) + a_3 \phi}}$.

3.2 Parameter Identification

To identify the dynamic model parameters efficiently, Constriction Factor Particle Swarm Optimization (CFPSO) algorithm is introduced. Constriction factor in CFPSO is used to ensure convergence of conventional PSO algorithm. The update mode is dependent on Eq. (11).

$$v_{id}^{k+1} = \chi\left(v_{id}^k + c_1 rand_1^k\left(pbest_{id}^k - x_{id}^k\right) + c_2 rand_2^k\left(pbest_d^k - x_{id}^k\right)\right)$$

(11)

in which, $\chi = 2/\left|2 - \sigma - (\sigma^2 - 4\sigma)^{0.5}\right|$ is constriction factor. $\sigma = C_1 + C_2$ and $\sigma > 4$. The values of parameters are selected based on prior knowledge: $C_1 = C_2 = 2.05$ and convergence tolerance is $1.0e^{-20}$. Objective function is as follows.

$$J = \sum_{k=1}^{N}\left[\hat{T}_t - T_s\right]^2$$

(12)

here, N is the number of data. $\hat{T}_t$ and T_s are the model torque and test data, respectively. The optimization results can be seen in Table 1.

Table 1. Values of parameters in the novel dynamic model

Parameters	c_1	c_2	c_3	c_4	n_1	n_2	n_3
Values	−1.5938	−8.1292	9.4075	−2.0948	0.0995	0.8785	0.1447

Experimental and theoretical results are compared in Fig. 10. The hysteresis characteristics can be captured by the model in the visual. To further evaluate the accuracy of the novel model, the arctangent model and hyperbolic tangent model are identified and compared. Their equations are shown in Eqs. (13) and (14). The mean deviation, root-mean-square error (RMSE) and coefficient of determinations R^2 [20] are set as evaluation coefficients. Values of the arctangent model, the hyperbolic tangent model and the novel model about mean deviation are 1.6638, 1.6744 and 1.3808, respectively. The values about RMSE are 96.7687, 96.5282 and 86.1562, respectively. The lower values of mean absolute error and RMSE show that the novel model has more accuracy than the other two models. Besides, the values about R^2 are 0.9658, 0.9660 and 0.9729, respectively. The higher determination coefficient verifies the trustable ability of the novel model. The differences between experimental results and theoretical results are also calculated and shown in Fig. 11. It is noted that the novel model owing better accuracy.

$$T_d = \frac{a_1}{1 + a_2 e^{a_3 I}} \dot{\phi} + \frac{2}{\pi} \frac{a_4}{1 + e^{a_5(a_6 + I)}} \text{a} \tan[a_7(\dot{\phi} + \frac{a_8 \text{sgn}(\dot{\phi})}{1 + a_9 e^{a_{10} I}})] \tag{13}$$

$$T_d = (a_1 I + a_2)\dot{\phi} + (a_3 I + a_4)\phi + (a_5 I^2 + a_6 I + a_7) \tanh[a_8 \dot{\phi} + a_9 \text{sgn}(\dot{\phi})] \tag{14}$$

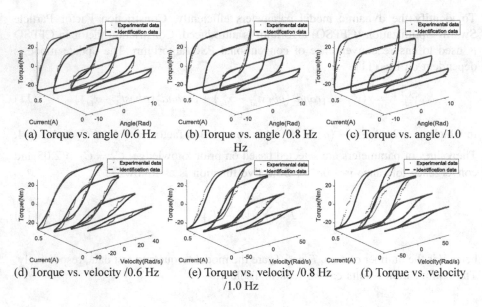

(a) Torque vs. angle /0.6 Hz   (b) Torque vs. angle /0.8 Hz   (c) Torque vs. angle /1.0 Hz

(d) Torque vs. velocity /0.6 Hz   (e) Torque vs. velocity /0.8 Hz   (f) Torque vs. velocity /1.0 Hz

Fig. 10. Comparison of theoretical and experimental results

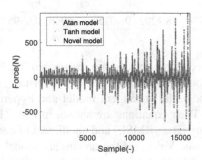

Fig. 11. Comparison of the accuracy of models

4 Conclusion

To capture the hysteretic characteristics of the RMRD in helical flow mode, a novel model is proposed and analyzed based on the experimental results. The hysteretic characteristics are captured by a shape function and hysteresis factor. The current-dependent part and the hysteretic part are separated to ensure the reversibility. The model are identified by CFPSO algorithm and compared with two typical models. The mean absolute error, RMSE and coefficient of determinations are introduced to evaluate accuracy of the models. Results show that the novel model can describe the nonlinear hysteretic characteristics with feasibility.

Acknowledgments. We would like to thank the authors of the references for their enlightenment. This research is also supported financially by the National Natural Science Foundation of People's Republic of China (Project No. 51675063), the Program for New Century Excellent Talents in University (No. NCET-13-0630) and the State Scholarship Fund of China Scholarship Council (No. 201706050094). These supports are gratefully acknowledged.

References

1. Wang, D.H., Liao, W.H.: Magnetorheological fluid dampers: a review of parametric modelling. Smart Mater. Struct. **20**, 1–34 (2011)
2. Chen, P., Bai, X.-X., Qian, L.-J., Choi, S.-B.: A new hysteresis model based on force–displacement characteristics of magnetorheological fluid actuators subjected to squeeze mode operation. Smart Mater. Struct. **26**, 1–10 (2017)
3. Wereley, N.M., Panng, L., Kamath, G.M.: Idealized hysteresis modeling of electrorheological and magnetorheological dampers. J. Intell. Mater. Syst. Struct. **9**, 642–649 (1998)
4. Li, W.H., Yao, G.Z., Chen, G., Yeo, S.H., Yap, F.F.: Testing and steady state modeling of a linear MR damper under sinusoidal loading. Smart Mater. Struct. **9**, 95–102 (2000)
5. Ismail, M., Ikhouane, F., Rodellar, J.: The hysteresis Bouc-Wen model, a survey. Arch. Comput. Methods Eng. **16**, 161–188 (2009)
6. Dahl, P.R.: Solid friction damping of mechanical vibrations. AIAA J. **14**, 1675–1682 (1976)
7. Şahin, İ., Engin, T., Çeşmeci, Ş.: Comparison of some existing parametric models for magnetorheological fluid dampers. Smart Mater. Struct. **19**, 1–11 (2010)
8. Ma, X.Q., Wang, E.R., Rakheja, S., Su, C.Y.: Modeling hysteretic characteristics of MR-fluid damper and model validation. In: Proceedings of the IEEE Conference on Decision and Control, vol. 2, pp. 1675–1680 (2002)
9. Choi, S.-B., Lee, S.-K., Park, Y.-P.: A hysteresis model for the field-dependent damping force of a magnetorheological damper. J. Sound Vib. **2**, 375–383 (2001)
10. Yu, J., Dong, X., Zhang, Z.: A novel model of magnetorheological damper with hysteresis division. Smart Mater. Struct. **26**, 1–15 (2017)
11. Chen, P., Bai, X.-X., Qian, L.-J., Choi, S.B.: An approach for hysteresis modeling based on shape function and memory mechanism. IEEE/ASME Trans. Mech. **23**, 1270–1278 (2018)
12. Pawlus, W., Karimi, H.R.: A comparative study of phenomenological models of MR brake based on neural networks approach. Int. J. Wavelets Multiresolut. Inf. Process. **11**, 1–30 (2013)
13. Miah, M.S., Chatzi, E.N., Dertimanis, V.K., Weber, F.: Nonlinear modeling of a rotational MR damper via an enhanced Bouc-Wen model. Smart Mater. Struct. **24**, 1–14 (2015)

14. Tse, T., Chang, C.: Shear-mode rotary magnetorheological damper for small-scale structural control experiments. J. struct. Eng. ASCE **130**, 904–911 (2004)
15. Boston, C., Weber, F., Guzzella, L.: Modeling of a disc-type magnetorheological damper. Smart Mater. Struct. **19**, 1–12 (2010)
16. Imaduddin, F., Mazlan, S.A., Zamzuri, H.: A design and modelling review of rotary magnetorheological damper. Mater. Des. **51**, 575–591 (2013)
17. Yu, J., Dong, X., Wang, W.: Prototype and test of a novel rotary magnetorheological damper based on helical flow. Smart Mater. Struct. **25**, 1–15 (2016)
18. Sun, S.S., Ning, D.H., Yang, J., Du, H., Zhang, S.W., Li, W.H.: A seat suspension with a rotary magnetorheological damper for heavy duty vehicles. Smart Mater. Struct. **25**, 1–10 (2016)
19. Yu, J., Dong, X., Zhang, Z., Chen, P.: A novel scissor-type magnetorheological seat suspension system with self-sustainability. J. Intell. Mater. Syst. Struct. **29**, 1–12 (2018)
20. Dong, X., Yu, J., Wang, W., Zhang, Z.: Robust design of magneto-rheological (MR) shock absorber considering temperature effects. Int. J. Adv. Manuf. Tech. **90**, 1735–1747 (2017)

Dynamic Production Scheduling Modeling and Multi-objective Optimization for Automobile Mixed-Model Production

Zhenyu Shen, Qian Tang, Tao Huang$^{(\boxtimes)}$, Tianyu Xiong,
Henry Y. K. Hu, and Yi Li

State Key Laboratory of Mechanical Transmissions,
Chongqing University, Chongqing 400044, China
thuang@cqu.edu.cn

Abstract. Due to inventory redundancy problem caused by automakers mixed-model production mode, a practical scheduling modeling and multi-objective optimization strategy is presented to increase production and inventory efficiency in this paper. Numerous factors including the general assembly shop, the painting shop, and linear buffer between two workshops have been considered, and a novel dynamic production scheduling model is proposed to achieve three optimization goals: (i) equalize parts consumption rate in the general assembly shop so changes in parts inventory can be predicted; (ii) reduce color switching frequency in the painting shop's production queue; (iii) reduce waiting time in car body's buffer zone. Based on this model, an embedded heuristic algorithm with NSGA-2 (No-domination Sorting Genetic Algorithms-II) is employed to solve multi-objective optimization problem. Simulations are finally conducted, when compared with a traditional algorithm, the results are obviously better than traditional algorithm, which validate effectiveness of the proposed model and optimization algorithm.

Keywords: Shop scheduling · Inventory control · Multi-objective optimization
Genetic algorithm

1 Introduction

Due to end customers' diversified demands, more companies have adopted production by order strategy, resulting in multiple types of products are collinearly produced on mixed-model production lines. In consequence, wide variety of parts need to be assembled which results in higher inventory cost. When formulating a production plan, the amount of parts inventory needs to be known, so production sequence can be reasonably arranged. Since production flow sequence determines parts usage sequence,

Foundation items: This work was supported in part by the Key Technology Research and System Integration of Discrete Intelligent Manufacturing Workshop, China (No. cstc2016zdcy-ztzx60001), the Fundamental Research Funds for the Central Universities of China under Grant 2018CDXYJX0019, and the National Nature Science Foundation of China under Grant 51805053 as well as Grant 51575069.

K. Li et al. (Eds.): ICSEE 2018/IMIOT 2018, CCIS 924, pp. 25–33, 2018.
https://doi.org/10.1007/978-981-13-2384-3_3

optimizing production queue can help to balanced parts consumption ratio. The purpose of equalization is to reduce fluctuations in consumption rate. This not only increases the robustness of production line, it is also possible to predict the consumption rate of parts, which is the key to keeping inventory at a low level. Through the strategy of milk run [1], stocks will eventually reach a dynamic balance, and it will ultimately achieve the goal to reduce inventory costs.

Prior to the use of intelligent algorithms, most of production scheduling was done manually. Shop scheduling problem is a typical NP-hard problem with exponential explosion characteristics [2], and it is difficult to find the optimal solution relies on manual scheduling. However, the emergence of intelligent algorithms solves this problem. The results filtered by tens of millions of iterations are often much better than the results of manual scheduling [3].

Therefore, this article introduces a dynamic scheduling model that covers the general assembly shop, the painting shop, and painted body storage (PBS) which is a buffer zone connects the two shops. Parts inventory in the general assembly shop will dynamically change as time goes. The optimization goal of the general assembly shop is to equalize the consumption rate of various parts as much as possible while ensuring each car can be assembled on time; the painting shop is to reduce the number of color switching in production queue and lower spraying cost; and PBS is to rearrange the production queues coming out of the painting shop, and to reduce waiting time of vehicles in the buffer zone, under the premise of meeting the general assembly shop's requirements. The NSGA-2 has been selected to achieve these multiple optimization goals. This algorithm has a reliable performance in solving multi-objective optimization problems and is widely used [4].

2   Mathematical Model

Many car companies are currently running on order production mode. An order information represents a specific model of car. In the workshop, an order i corresponds to a list of parts M_i, so the optimization of production queue is essentially the optimization of $\{M_i\}$. Pre-definition is mandatory for each model of car. Considering extensibility of the mathematical model, 42 different models are predefined, shown in Table 1.

Table 1. Configuration table.

Model	Number of configurations	Number of colors
A	5	4
B	4	3
C	3	2
D	2	2

Meanwhile, a collection of parts lists required for 42 models $\{M : M_{i,j} \in M, i \in N_1, j \in N_2\}$ is defined, and all parts are assigned to 10 stations. Dissimilar parts have been divided into 4 categories, totaling 52, as shown in Table 2.

Table 2. Parts list.

Station	Number of parts	Type	Station	Number of parts	Type
1	10	T1	6	4	T3
2	3	T2	7	3	T2
3	1	T4	8	4	T3
4	4	T3	9	3	T2
5	10	T1	10	10	T1

Among them, T1 are customized parts that can be used only for the specified model of the specified configuration, such as seats and engines. T2 are common parts in different car models that can be used only for the specified configuration, like in various electronic auxiliary systems. T3 are common parts in different configurations that can be used only for specified models, like interior trimming panels and wheels. T4 are common parts for all vehicles, like different fasteners.

For the general assembly shop, the parts consumption speed needs to be more balanced. The theoretical consumption rate of each part is

$$EV_j = \bar{V}_J = \frac{N_1}{\sum_{i=1}^{N_1} M_{i,j}} \tag{1}$$

Deviation between actual consumption rate and theoretical consumption rate is the optimization goal of the general assembly shop.

$$\min f_1 = \frac{\sum_{j=1}^{N_2} (V_j - \bar{V}_J)^2}{N_1} \tag{2}$$

For the painting shop, reducing the frequency of color switching can reduce coating costs. The number of color switching can be expressed as

$$S_i = \begin{cases} 0, & i = 1 \\ 0, & color(i) = color(i-1) \\ 1, & color(i) \neq color(i-1) \end{cases} \tag{3}$$

Therefore, the optimization goal of the painting shop is

$$\min f_2 = \sum_{i=1}^{N_1} S_i \tag{4}$$

There are many kinds of buffers for connecting the general assembly shop and the painting shop, linear, circular, backward and so on [5]. In general, waiting buffer time of car body is always proportional to the optimization effect of buffer. Therefore, linear buffer has been selected for our model.

For PBS, the less time car bodies are waiting in PBS, the more efficient PBS will be. The waiting time can be expressed as

$$W_i = \begin{cases} i(i'), & i' = 1 \\ i(i'), & i(i'-1) < i(i') \\ i(i'-1), & i(i'-1) \geq i(i') \end{cases} \tag{5}$$

So, the optimization goal of PBS is

$$\min f_3 = T_{t2} \sum_{i'=1}^{N_1} (W_i - i) \tag{6}$$

3 NSGA-2 and Heuristic Buffer Algorithm

Three optimization objectives have strong correlations and involve many variables. Changes in any workshops' production queue will affect another workshop queue and buffer. Therefore, a multi-objective optimization algorithm is necessary. The typical multi-objective evolutionary algorithms are NSGA-2, PESA-2 and SPEA-2. Each of these three algorithms has its advantages and disadvantages. The advantage of NSGA-2 is that it has high operational efficiency and good distribution of solution sets in low-dimensional problems; its disadvantage is that the diversity of solution sets is not ideal in high-dimensional problems. The advantage of PESA-2 is that the convergence of its solution is very good; but the disadvantage is that the selection operation can only select one individual at a time, the time consumption is very large, and the class diversity is not good. The advantage of SPEA-2 is that it can obtain a well-distributed solution set, but its clustering process takes a long time to maintain diversity, and the operating efficiency is not high.

In order to balance the running time with the quality of reconciliation, NSGA-2 was eventually selected. Besides, we have designed a heuristic algorithm that can directly calculate the downstream shop queue within constraints of the linear buffer, based on the queue of upstream shop and the optimization goal of downstream shop which are embed it in the NSGA-2.

The heuristic algorithms are divided into inbound rules and outbound rules. The inbound rules are as follows:

1. If the last car in a lane has the same color of the waiting car, enter the lane.
2. Enter a lane with least car.

   Its outbound rules are as follows:

1. In the waiting outbound car, select the same color as the last outbound car.
2. Unless the number of waiting cars in PBS is greater than M, otherwise there is no car outbound.
3. When the number of waiting cars in PBS is greater than M, select the lane with the highest number of cars, and outbound.

It should be pointed out that the general assembly shop is set to be the upstream workshop and the painting shop as the downstream workshop. The reason is that the optimization of the painting shop is simpler than the general assembly shop. A simple heuristic algorithm can be selected if it achieves a good optimization effect. By adjusting the parameter M, we can balance with waiting time and optimization effect. When M is larger, there will be reduce color switching in the painting shop production queue, but longer waiting time in PBS.

For the actual buffer, its inbound and outbound order are opposite to our algorithm. When the algorithm is used in the real buffer, actual outbound rule will be different to the outbound rule that we have designed, but inbound rule stays the same. The actual outbound has only one rule: outbound is order specified from the general assembly shop.

This heuristic algorithm needs to be embedded in NSGA-2, and through iterative filtering, the scheduling plan which meets our optimization goals can be identified. Algorithm flow chart is shown in Fig. 1.

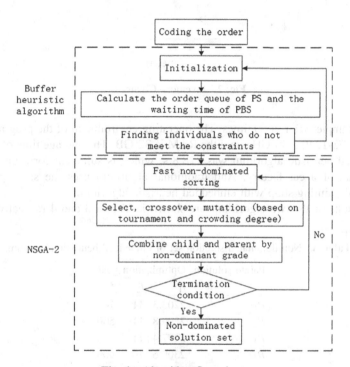

Fig. 1. Algorithm flow chart.

4 Simulation Examples

The simulated data is based on the production plan of 1,000 cars in a car factory within one day. In addition, a traditional algorithm is designed to compare with the above algorithm. This traditional algorithm is actually applied to the factory, rely on PLC control and will determine the inbound and outbound sequence of body in PBS according to a fixed priority. Both that embedded heuristic algorithm based on NSGA-2 and traditional algorithms are programmed by Matlab.

Due to computational complexity, the production plan has been divided into 10 equal proportions smaller plans, so only one portion (100 cars) production queue needs to be calculated. Then connect them end to end in a cyclic manner to get the total production queue, so this total production queue is "equalized". Inventory changes of parts should conform to the rule in Fig. 2.

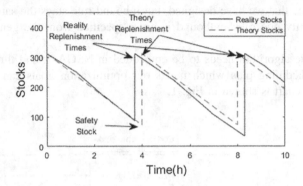

Fig. 2. Inventory Changes.

Two example was run 50 times. The operating environment of the program is Intel Xeon CPU E3-1240 3.50 GHz, and the RAM is 32 GB. The average time of operation of embedded heuristic algorithm was 278.8 s, which is sufficient for a one-day production plan of a car factory. And traditional algorithm uses the same production sequence of painting shop with embedded heuristic algorithm.

The results of the two algorithms are shown in Tables 3 and 4 respectively.

Table 3. Non-dominated solution set of embedded heuristic algorithm.

Pareto solution	Optimization goal		
	f_1	f_2	f_3
P_1	2203.3	11	700
P_2	2209.8	11	500
P_3	2297.4	11	450
P_4	2309.6	10	900
Average	2582.7	12.8	810

Taking P_3 as an example, cars are numbered from 1 to 42 according to their models, configurations and colors. Starting from the time when first car arrives at station 10 in the general assembly shop, record the time $t = T_0$. Then parts inventory status and production line status at $t = T_1 = T_0 + 10 * T_{t1}$, $t = T_2 = T_1 + 10 * T_{t1}$ are respectively as shown in Figs. 3 and 4.

The solution obtained by the traditional algorithm have lower waiting time, but the consumption rate of parts is very uneven. The consumption rate of parts will directly

Table 4. Corresponding solution set of traditional algorithm.

Solution	Optimization goal		
	f_1	f_2	f_3
P'_1	7354.8	11	450
P'_2	8785.4	11	450
P'_3	7927.5	11	450
P'_4	7651.7	10	450
Average	7885.1	12.8	450

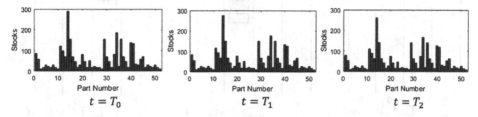

Fig. 3. The status of inventory at different times.

affect the inventory of the assembly shop, but the waiting time will not be. In order to study what negative impact the waiting time would have on the production line, some inspection work was done.

When observing the results of the calculation, an unrealistic situation was discovered. The results show that when waiting time is bigger, a kind of defect is more likely to appear. This defect will result vacancies at the production queue of the general assembly shop. The reason for this defect is that there are fewer bodies available in the PBS when the queue is first started. If there is no body that meets the outbound rules, there will be a vacancy in the assembly shop queue.

To avoid this situation, the production speed of the painting shop needs to be greater than the general assembly shop, and the M value increases over time for a short period of time when the queue is just starting to run. When the available car body in the PBS is sufficient, the M value no longer increases.

Actually, as long as the car body can meet the constraints of continuous outbound, they are all equivalent regardless of the waiting time. If the embedded heuristic algorithm can ensure continuous outbound car body in PBS. The traditional algorithms do not have obvious advantages in Optimization goal 3. Instead, there is a clear disadvantage in optimizing goal 1. It can be considered that the embedded heuristic algorithm has a comparative advantage over the traditional algorithms.

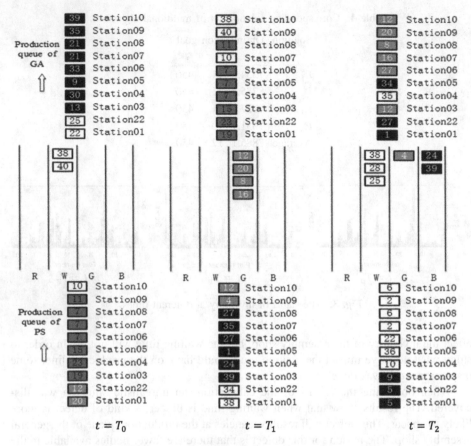

Fig. 4. The status of the production line at different times.

5   Conclusion

In this paper, a dynamic scheduling model is proposed for automobile mixed-model production. By scheduling the sequence reasonably, this model can balance the consumption rate of parts in the general assembly shop, reduce the number of color switching in the painting shop, and improve reordering efficiency of the linear buffer. When compared with a traditional algorithm, the result is obviously better than the traditional algorithm. In addition, this is beneficial to achieve a more accurate inventory control and sequence tracking by monitoring status of parts inventory and production queues. It can be known for any order, it is where and how to complete, and even which batch of parts are being used at the time. The value calculated by this model can be serve as an important reference for the automakers who want to reduce their production cost.

References

1. Sadjadi, S.J., Jafari, M., Amini, T.: A new mathematical modeling and a genetic algorithm search for milk run problem. Int. J. Adv. Manuf. Technol. **44**(1–2), 194–200 (2009)
2. Jalilvand-Nejad, A., Fattahi, P.: A mathematical model and genetic algorithm to cyclic flexible job shop scheduling problem. J. Intell. Manuf. **26**(6), 1085–1098 (2015)
3. Soleimani, H., Kannan, G.: A hybrid particle swarm optimization and genetic algorithm for closed-loop supply chain network design in large-scale networks. Appl. Math. Model. **39**(14), 3990–4012 (2015)
4. Deb, K.: A fast elitist non-dominated sorting genetic algorithm for multi-objective optimization: NSGA-2. Lect. Notes Comput. Sci. **1917**, 849–858 (2000)
5. Chen, GY: Research on buffer design and resequence in automobile production line. Huazhong University of Science and Technology (2007)

Tandem Workshop Scheduling Based on Sectional Coding and Varying Length Crossover Genetic Algorithm

Hao Sun and Xiaojun Zheng[⊠]

School of Mechanical Engineering, Dalian Jiaotong University, Dalian, China
zhengxj@djtu.edu.cn

Abstract. For the tandem workshop scheduling problem, the objective of optimization is to obtain minimum total distribution time. To achieve that goal, we propose an optimization model, considering the rated load of automated guided vehicles (AGV) and the different regional transportation speeds. This model has three features. First, the sectional coding rules are adopted because materials need to be transported in batches between machines. Second, the crossover operation with varying length is used because the superior characteristics of the previous generation population could be better passed down to the offspring, thus accelerating the convergence rate of the population. Finally, the mutation operation combining insertion and reverse can maintains the diversity of the population and improve the local search ability of the algorithm. The tandem workshop scheduling problem can apply our algorithm, and the effectiveness of the improvement is demonstrated.

Keywords: Tandem workshop scheduling · Genetic algorithm
Sectional coding

1 Introduction

In the Flexible Workshop Scheduling Problem (FJSP), the material transportation system is one of the important design aspects. Research shows that the cost of material transportation links takes up 30–95% of the total production cost [1]. As a tool for material transportation and distribution, AGV can improve the automation, flexibility, efficiency and safety of the modern flexible workshops. It is mainly to design the route of transportation by considering the constraints (Such as speed, the number of AGV, deadweight and so on) in order to achieve the goal of the shortest path or time.

With the increasing amount of material transportation in the flexible workshops, the demand for AGVs from the system has also increased, which greatly increases the complexity of the scheduling tasks, and it is easy to cause traffic jam, collision and other problems. Bozer and Srinivasan [2] proposed the concept of a tandem workshop scheduling system, effectively avoiding the conflicts and collisions. Zhang [3] proposed a tandem workshop hybrid scheduling model based on cloud computing environment, the model could efficiently realized the load balance. Zhou et al. [4] putted the tabu search into the genetic algorithm to solve single-field tandem workshop scheduling

© Springer Nature Singapore Pte Ltd. 2018
K. Li et al. (Eds.): ICSEE 2018/IMIOT 2018, CCIS 924, pp. 34–43, 2018.
https://doi.org/10.1007/978-981-13-2384-3_4

optimization problem. Bai et al. [5] proposed a tandem workshop control model, which reduced the complexity of AGVs scheduling and improved the efficiency of the system. Tang et al. [6] solved the problem of task scheduling and coordination control in tandem AGV systems by neuro-endocrine coordination mechanisms. Hou et al. [7] developed a collaborative optimization method to solve the problem of machine allocation and loop layout for tandem AGV systems. Reza et al. [8] putted forward a method based on tabu search and genetic algorithm to avoid infeasible solutions from crossover operation.

The paper will be organized as follows: in Sect. 2, a tandem workshop scheduling system model was defined. And we established the mathematical model in Sect. 3. Next, we explained the proposed sectional coding and the varying length crossover genetic algorithm (VGA) as detailed in Sect. 4. In the Sect. 5, we compared the result of the proposed algorithm with the fixed length crossover genetic algorithm (FGA) to verity the effectiveness of the algorithm. At last, we made a conclusion.

2 Problem Description

In a tandem workshop scheduling system, the distribution of the machines are given, the AGVs move in a bi-directional path, and only one AGV is worked in different areas to avoid collisions. In different areas, the location of a machine is designated as a transfer station, which is used to handle transportation tasks between different areas, and all transfer stations constitute a transfer center. AGV has different operating speeds in different areas, which can save transportation time, increase production efficiency, and save costs. The tandem workshop scheduling model is shown in Fig. 1.

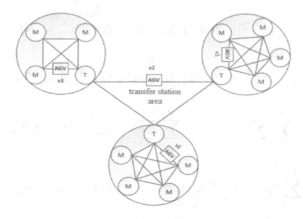

Fig. 1. The tandem workshop scheduling model

The optimization for tandem AGV workshop aims to provide the excellent scheme of path planning, so that the material distribution time of tandem workshop scheduling system is reduced effectively.

3 Mathematical Model

In a tandem workshop scheduling system, the machine layout is given, There is a material transfer station (A machine can be regarded as a transfer station) in different areas, and only one AGV is available for scheduling, without considering the loading and unloading time of the material. The speed of AGVs for material transport between machines is v_1, the speed of AGVs for material transport between different transfer stations is v_2. A kind of material can be transported between different machines at a time.

The maximum load capacity of AGV is Q, The number of AGV is $i \in \{1, 2, \dots, R\}$, The number of different areas (Which include machine areas and transfer centers) is $r_j, s_j \in \{1, 2, \dots, M_j\}$, M_j is the total number of machines in area j.

A preferable AGV path scheduling optimization scheme is obtained, and the shortest time for the entire tandem workshop scheduling system is calculated. We establish the following mathematical model:

Objective function:

$$Min \sum_{i=1}^{R} \sum_{j=1}^{N} \sum_{r_j=1}^{M_j} \sum_{s_j=1}^{M_j} \delta_{ijr_js_j} T_{ijr_js_j}. \tag{1}$$

Constraints:

$$\sum_{j=1}^{N} \sum_{r_j=1}^{M_j} \sum_{s_j=1}^{M_j} \delta_{ijr_js_j} q_{jr_js_j} \le Q \quad \forall i \in \{1, 2, \dots, R\}. \tag{2}$$

$$t_{ijr_js_j} = \frac{d_{ijr_js_j}}{v_1} \quad \forall i \in \{1, 2, \dots, R\} \quad \forall j \in \{1, 2, \dots, N\}. \tag{3}$$

$$t'_{ijr_js_j} = \frac{d'_{ijr_js_j}}{v_2} \quad \forall j \in \{1, 2, \dots, N\} \quad \forall i \in \{1, 2, \dots, R\}. \tag{4}$$

$$T_{ijr_js_j} = \sum_{r_j,s_j=1}^{M_j} \sum_{j=1}^{N} \delta_{ijr_js_j} t_{ijr_js_j} + \sum_{r_j,s_j=1}^{M_j} \sum_{j=1}^{N} \delta_{ijr_js_j} t'_{ijr_js_j} \quad \forall i \in \{1, 2, \dots, R\}. \tag{5}$$

$$\sum_{s_j=1}^{M_j} \delta_{ij1s_j} = 1 \quad \forall i \in \{1, 2, \dots, R\} \quad \forall j \in \{1, 2, \dots, N\}. \tag{6}$$

$$\sum_{r_j=1}^{M_j} \delta_{ijr_j1} = 1 \quad \forall i \in \{1, 2, \dots, R\} \quad \forall j \in \{1, 2, \dots, N\}. \tag{7}$$

$$\sum_{r_j=1}^{M_j} \delta_{ijr_jh} - \sum_{s_j=1}^{M_j} \delta_{ijhs_j} = 0 \quad \forall h \in \{1, 2, \ldots, M\} \quad \forall i \in \{1, 2, \ldots, R\}$$

$$\forall j \in \{1, 2, \ldots, N\}. \tag{8}$$

Where:

Formula (1) shows the total time for AGV to perform all transportation tasks in tandem workshop.

Formula (2) indicates that the load of a AGV cannot exceed the load-carrying quota.

Formula (3) indicates that in the machine area, the operating time of AGV transport materials between two machines.

Formula (4) indicates that in the transfer center, the operating time of AGV transport materials between two machines.

Formula (5) represents the total time of different areas to accomplish tasks.

Formula (6)–(8) means that different AGV will return to the starting position after completing all the transportation tasks from the transfer station.

Notes:

$T_{ijr_js_j}$: In the area j, the time for the i-th AGV to complete the transportation tasks from the machine r_j to the machine s_j.

$q_{jr_js_j}$: In the machine area j, transport the weight of the material from machine r_j to machine s_j.

$d'_{ijr_js_j}$: In the transfer center j, the distance of the i-th AGV from the machine r_j to the machine s_j.

$d_{ijr_js_j}$: In the transfer center j, the distance of the i-th AGV from the machine r_j to the machine $sssss_j$.

$$\delta_{ijr_js_j} \begin{cases} = 1 \text{ If the i-th AGV is arranged for material transportation from} \\ \quad \text{machine } r_j \text{ to machine } s_j. \\ = 0 \text{ Other} \end{cases}$$

4 Sectional Coding and Varying Length Crossover Genetic Algorithm

In this paper, a tandem workshop AGV scheduling model is established based on the minimum material transportation time as the objective function. Compared with the traditional genetic algorithm, the coding method of chromosomes is redesigned, which could generate chromosomes to meet the needs of the optimization problem. The objective function is used as the fitness function of the algorithm. With improved crossover and mutation operation, the certain cross rate and mutation rate are set, so that the superior individuals of the previous generation are not lost, and this can ensure the variety.

4.1 Coding Design

There are many encoding strategies for genetic algorithms. A sectional coding based on the order of transportation tasks is used in this paper. One AGV is only responsible for transport tasks in the current area, so the chromosome should be segmented according to the number of AGV in the system. Each segment represents the sequence of an AGV transportation path. Each gene represents the transportation tasks required between two machines. Since the load-carrying quota of different AGVs cannot exceed the load capacity, there will be the same serial number of the transportation path. Figure 2 shows an example of chromosome coding design, which indicates that the entire scheduling system consists of two areas, in which the numbers represent the transportation path from start to finish. The same number represents the same path, and the times indicate the number of transportation along the path.

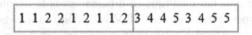

Fig. 2. An example of chromosome coding design

4.2 Selection Operation

For the selection operation, tournament selection method is adopted. Selecting a certain size of individuals from the population (Which is known as the scale of the tournament, the value is two), comparing different individuals, and retaining individuals with higher fitness values to the next generation, and this operation is repeated until the scale of next generation reaches the preset value.

4.3 Crossover Operation

For genetic algorithms, chromosomes are cross-processed to generate new individuals. Due to real-valued sectional coding is adopted, it is unsatisfactory to employ the cross-rules of traditional genetic algorithm for addressing this complex optimization problem, and it is easy to produce infeasible solutions. In literature [9], the use of the crossover operation fixed cross-block size may make the population converge slowly and prone to local optimum. However, the crossover operation of the varying length crossover can not only make the excellent characteristics of the two parent retained, but also accelerate the convergence rate of the population. The crossover operation improved is as follows:

Step 1:   In different gene coding segments of the chromosome, two random numbers (Between 0 and L, where L represents the length of the coding segment) are generated, respectively, as the cross-block size of the two individuals of the parent.

Step 2:   In the parental chromosome Parent1, a crossing place A1 is randomly generated, then the length of the cross-block is added to generate the second crossing place A2. Therefore, the genes between the two crossing places are the cross-block A12.

Step 3:   In the chromosome Parent2, the operation of step 2 is repeated to form a cross-block B12.

Step 4:   The value of each gene bit of the cross-block A12 is placed into the offspring2 in turn, and the value of each gene bit of the cross-block B12 is placed into offspring1 in turn.

Step 5:   Finding the extra genes in Parent1 and Parent2 relative to B12 and A12 respectively, and putting them into the offspring1 and offspring2.

The following Figs. 3, 4 and 5 show the specific operation of the crossover operation:

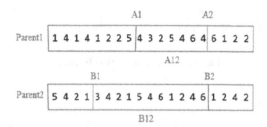

Fig. 3. Selecting the crossing place and the cross-block

4.4 Mutation Operation

The mutation operation applying the insertion (The gene of one place is inserted into another place) and reverse sequence (Reversing sequence of genes between different places) were considered for the VGA. This method can improve the search ability of the whole algorithm, avoid premature phenomena, and maintain the diversity of the whole population. The specific mutation operation for different gene encoding segment is as follows:

Step 1:   Selecting a gene at a certain position (Where P1 is located) in the Parent, randomly.

Step 2:   A place P2 (P1 and P2 are not equal) is randomly selected in the Parent, and the gene selected in the previous step is inserted into the place of P2, and the rest of the genes are moved forward.

Step 3:   Then, two places randomly selected in the Parent are P3 and P4. If P3 is equal to P4, then P4 is the value of the L-2 gene place (L is the length of this chromosome segment).

Step 4:   Reversing the sequence of genes between P3 and P4, and replacing the original gene block. Thus, a new chromosome offspring Offspring is formed.

As shown in Figs. 6 and 7, the specific operation for the mutation operation.

A12
3 2 5 4 6 4
B12
3 4 2 1 5 4 6 1 2 4 6
Parent1
1 4 1 4 1 2 2 5 4 3 2 5 4 6 4 6 1 2 2
Parent2
5 4 2 1 3 4 2 1 5 4 6 1 2 4 6 1 2 4 2

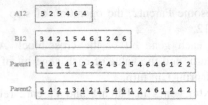

Fig. 4. Finding the extra genes

Offspring1
3 4 2 1 5 4 6 1 2 4 6 1 4 1 4 2 2 5 2
Offspring2
3 2 5 4 6 4 5 4 2 1 4 2 1 4 6 1 2 1 2

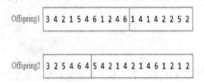

Fig. 5. Generating new offspring

Parent
1 4 1 4 1 2 2 5 4 3 2 5 4 6 4 6 1 2 2
P1
P2
Offspring
1 4 1 4 2 2 5 4 3 2 5 1 4 6 4 6 1 2 2

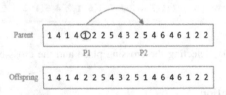

Fig. 6. Insertion mutation operation

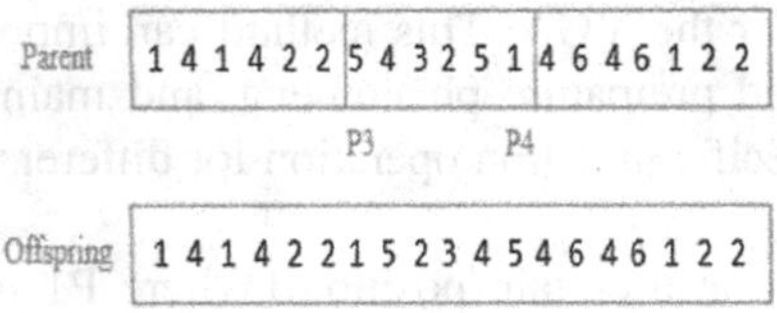

Parent
1 4 1 4 2 2 5 4 3 2 5 1 4 6 4 6 1 2 2
P3
P4
Offspring
1 4 1 4 2 2 1 5 2 3 4 5 4 6 4 6 1 2 2

Fig. 7. Reversing sequence mutation operation

5 Experimental Verification

In order to analyze the advantages of VGA, a tandem workshop material transportation is taken as an example. The workshop consists of five areas (Which include four machine areas and one transfer center) and 24 machines, and different areas contain the machine serial number as shown in Table 1, the space position of different machines is given (As shown in Table 2 below). There are 5 AGVs in the workshop for transportation work. The AGV speed is 40 m/min in the four machine areas and the AGV speed in the transfer center area is 60 m/min. The material loading and unloading time in the workshop is negligible. The maximum load of different AGVs is 100 kg. The materials required to be transported between the machines in the workshop are shown in Table 3 below.

Table 1. Machine serial number in different areas

Area	Machine	Area	Machine
Machine area 1	1, 2, 3, 4, 5, 6	Machine area 4	19, 20, 21, 22, 23, 24
Machine area 2	7, 8, 9, 10, 11, 12	Transfer center 5	4, 11, 13, 20
Machine area 3	13, 14, 15, 16, 17, 18		

The problem is solved by applying our algorithm. The detailed parameters are as follows: The population size is N = 100, the crossover rate is 0.6, and the maximum iteration number of the algorithm is 10000 times. The algorithm of DE, the fixed length crossover genetic algorithm and the genetic algorithm of this paper were performed 50 times respectively. The data results are shown in Table 4 below:

The VGA proposed in this paper adopts the sectional coding rules, which can avoid illegal solutions in the crossover and mutation operation. The crossover operation with varying length crossover enables the population to have more potential, retain the fine quality of the individual and improve the computing capability of the algorithm. At the same time, the mutation operation combining insertion mutation and reverse sequence mutation can maintains the diversity of the population and increases the local search ability of the algorithm to avoid premature phenomena.

Figure 8 shows the average fitness value curve of different algorithms when reaching the termination condition. Since the VGA that we proposed employs thc mutation operation combining two mutation methods, the DE algorithm with different mutation rates is used for comparison. For the DE, the optimal value decreases as the mutation rate increases. In the case of high mutation rate, the optimal value of DE is obviously larger than that of FGA and VGA. According to the experimental results, sectional coding and varying length crossover genetic algorithm have faster convergence rate and better value of the objective function than the traditional algorithm.

Table 2. The space position of the machine

Machine	Coordinate	Machine	Coordinate	Machine	Coordinate
1	(2500, 21000)	9	(19100, 17431)	17	(13650, 3000)
2	(5000, 20000)	10	(20375, 11654)	18	(12000, 4000)
3	(5600, 14500)	11	(9958, 10580)	19	(3600, 5300)
4	(5300, 9800)	12	(10079, 16650)	20	(5600, 5300)
5	(4780, 10000)	13	(10150, 7250)	21	(5600, 4000)
6	(3100, 15000)	14	(15600, 7250)	22	(5600, 3000)
7	(11340, 23450)	15	(19800, 5600)	23	(4300, 3000)
8	(16434, 22341)	16	(19800, 3100)	24	(3600, 3500)

Table 3. Material transport table

Route	Weight	Route	Weight	Route	Weight	Route	Weight
1–2	300	11–7	550	16–13	224	24–21	300
1–3	450	9–11	280	17–14	245	19–20	180
3–5	50	12–9	70	18–15	77	19–22	95
4–6	980	7–10	360	18–16	114	4–20	460
2–5	510	9–7	240	20–24	350	4–11	160
1–4	320	13–15	810	20–23	650	11–13	190
4–3	780	13–16	970	21–19	80	13–20	310
11–8	760	13–18	260	22–24	110	20–4	490
8–10	200	14–15	315	23–20	450	13–11	100

Table 4. Experimental results

Algorithm	The optimal value	Average value	Mutation rate	
			Insertion mutation	Reverse mutation
FGA	37875	38132	0.9	0.7
VGA	37579	37796	0.9	0.7
DE	38631	39505	0.9	

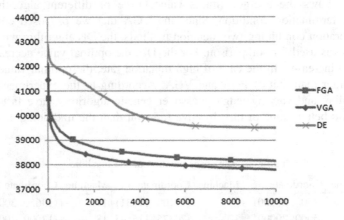

Fig. 8. The comparison of average fitness value

6 Conclusion

An optimization model is proposed to optimize the tandem AGV workshop with the goal of minimizing the total distribution time. Only one AGV is responsible for material transportation in different areas, the coding rules, crossover and mutation operation of traditional genetic algorithms are improved, and the proposed algorithm is validated by the example of tandem workshop scheduling problem. Experimental results show that the average fitness curve of the proposed algorithm falls faster, its convergence speed is faster, and a more excellent objective value can be obtained, compared with the fixed length crossover genetic algorithm and DE.

To sum up, the genetic algorithm proposed in this paper is suitable for the selection of work schemes for the tandem workshop scheduling problem, which can effectively improves the production efficiency and improves the economic efficiency of the enterprises.

Acknowledgements. This work was supported by the Guidance Program for Natural Science Foundation of Liaoning (No. 20170540138).

References

1. Pen C.T., Du Z.J.: Design of AGV based on AT89S52 MCU. Wireless Internet Technology 13 (2017)
2. Bozer, Y.A., Srinivasan, M.M.: Tandem configuration for automated guided vehicle systems and the analysis of single vehicle loops. IIE Trans. **23**, 72–82 (1991)
3. Zhang, H.: Design and implementation of a hybrid scheduling model for tandem workshop resources in cloud computing environment. CIT **5**, 8–11 (2017)
4. Zhou, Q., Liu, J., Wei, F.L.: Single-field tandem workshop scheduling optimization based on genetic taboo search algorithm. I J. Chang. Univ. Sci. Technol. (Nat. Sci.) **4**, 32–38 (2014)
5. Bai, S.F., Tang, D.B., Gu, W.B., Zheng, K.: Research of multiple AGV systems based on tandem workshop control module. CNEU **3**, 8–12 (2012)
6. Tang, D.B., Lu, X.C., Zheng, K.: Research on tandem AGV scheduling based on neuro-endocrine coordination mechanism. Mach. Build. Autom. **4**, 112–115 (2015)
7. Hou, L.Y., Liu, Z.C., Shi, Y.J., Zheng, X.J.: Optimizing machine allocation and loop layout in tandem AGV workshop by the collaborative optimization method. Neural Comput. Appl. **4**, 959–974 (2016)
8. Rezapour, S., Zanjirani-Farahani, R., Miandoabchi, E.: A Machine-to-loop assignment and layout design methodology for tandem AGV systems with single-load vehicles. Int. J. Prod. Res. **49**, 3605–3633 (2011)
9. Chen, Z.T.: Research and application on job shop scheduling problem based on improved genetic algorithm, p. 32. Dalian University of Technology, Dalian

Robust Bi-level Routing Problem for the Last Mile Delivery Under Demand and Travel Time Uncertainty

Xingjun Huang[1], Yun Lin[1]([✉]), Yulin Zhu[1], Lu Li[1], Hao Qu[1], and Jie Li[2]

[1] College of Mechanical Engineering, Chongqing University, Chongqing, China
linyun313@163.com
[2] School of Automotive Engineering, Chongqing University, Chongqing, China

Abstract. Designing the last mile delivery system in a lean way has become an important part of serving customers efficiently and economically. However, in practice, the uncertainty in customer demand and travel times often means vehicles capacity may be exceeded along the planed route and vehicles miss theses time windows, increasing the cost, reducing efficiency and decreasing the customer satisfaction. Previous studies have lacked an uncertainty-based view, and few studies have discussed how to develop an uncertain model. To address this issue, the bi-level routing problem for the last mile delivery is formulated as a robust vehicle routing problem with uncertain customer demand and travel times. In addition, a modified simulated annealing algorithm is proposed and tested in computational experiments. The results show that the proposed model has good performance for uncertainty processing.

Keywords: Last mile delivery · Uncertainty
Modified simulated annealing algorithm · Robust optimization

1 Introduction

The bi-level multisized terminal location-routing problem (*BL-MSTLRP*) for the last mile delivery, as a classical combinatorial optimization problem, first is introduced by Zhou [8] under the e-commence environment, that aims to find the optimal set of terminals and the optimal set of routes for a fleet of vehicle delivering products or service to a given set of customers groups. It is worthy that the

Supported by the National Social Science Fund of China (Grant No. 18BJY066), Fundamental Research Funds for the Central Universities (Grant No. 106112016CDJXZ338825), Chongqing key industrial generic key technological innovation projects (Grant No. cstc2015zdcy-ztzx60009), Chongqing Science and Technology Research Program (Grant No. cstc2015yykfC60002).

© Springer Nature Singapore Pte Ltd. 2018
K. Li et al. (Eds.): ICSEE 2018/IMIOT 2018, CCIS 924, pp. 44–54, 2018.
https://doi.org/10.1007/978-981-13-2384-3_5

BL-MSTRP, as the classical optimization for last mile delivery, assumes that all the input data, such as customer demands and travels time, are both deterministic and are known in advance. However, the solutions derived by deterministic model are often infeasible when applied to the real-world situation, particularly in the era of on-time delivery [7]. To tackle problem, this paper proposes robust bi-level routing problem (*RBLRP*) for the last mile delivery under demand and travel time uncertainty, an extended version of the *BL-MSTRP* for the last mile delivery. Note that robust optimization is advantageous due to its computational tractability and its ability to deal with the practical applications, in which only partial information or a small amount of historical data about the uncertain parameters is available [1–4]. In this study, the uncertainty sets of customer demand and uncertainty sets of travel times of bi-level were derived with partial information about the distributions of the uncertain parameters and a modified SA algorithm was proposed to tackle this issue.

The reminder of this paper is organized as follows. Section 2 describes the considered *RBLRP* and the process of uncertainty transformation. In addition, the corresponding robust mathematical model is also presented. In Sect. 3, a modified SA algorithm is designed for the *RBLRP*. Section 4 presents a computational experiment using the modified versions of Zhou 's instances [8]. Finally, conclusions are drawn and presented in Sect. 5.

2 Problem Description and Model Formulation

2.1 Problem Description

The RBLRP is defined on a complete undirected digraph $G = (N, A)$, where the set of vertex is represented by $N = \{N_0 \cup N_C \cup N_D\}$ and the set of the arcs is represented by $A = \{A_C \cup A_D\}$. Vertex N_0 represents the *DC* where several identical vehicles k with capacity Q are located. The set of customer groups is denoted as $N_C = \{1, 2, ..., n_c\}$, where the distance between the two customer groups is defined as the A_C. Similarly, the set of terminals is denotes as N_D, where the distance between the two terminals is defined as the A_D. For the first level, vehicles start at the DC and deliver parcels to a set of terminals and the vertex set of the level 1 is denoted by $N_1 = \{N_0 \cup N_D\}$; for the second level, vehicles deliver parcels from the DC but directly to customer groups, serving individual customers and the vertex set of the level 2 is denoted by $N_2 = \{N_0 \cup N_C\}$. In addition, a subset of N is denoted by $N_l = \{N_C \cup N_D\}$. Customers in each group can freely choose between *HD* and CP services. Vehicles serve customers with *HD* demand directly, and those with *CP* demand pick up parcels themselves at the closest terminals. An example of the *RBLRP* is illustrated to describe such situation in Fig. 1, which consists of one *DC*, four terminals and four customer groups. Note that customer demand and travel times will fluctuate within a certain range, and the uncertain customer demand and travel times is modeled as symmetric and bounded random variables.

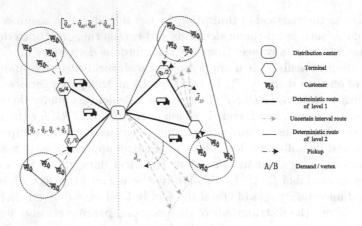

Fig. 1. The problem description of *RBLRP* with uncertainty for last mile delivery with *HD* and *CP* service programming.

2.2 Uncertain Transformation of Customer Demand

The customer demand uncertainty set $U_{q_i}^k$ and the travel distance uncertainty set U_d^k is defined as follows based on the robust optimization approach [4].

$$u_{q_i} = \times_{k \in K} U_{q_i}^k, q_i = \{q_{iC} \cup q_{iH}\} \tag{1}$$

with

$$U_{q_i}^k = \left\{ \tilde{q}_i \in R^{|N_i^k|} \mid \tilde{q}_i = \bar{q}_i + \alpha_i \hat{q}_i , \sum_{i \in N_i^k} |\alpha_i| \le \Gamma_{q_i}^k, \right. \tag{2}$$

$$\left. |\alpha_i| \le 1, \Gamma_{q_i}^k = \left\lceil \theta_{q_i} \left| N_C^k \right| \right\rceil, \forall i \in N_C \right\}$$

Equation (1) reflects the overall demand uncertainty set u_{q_i} of customer groups $i \in N_C$ is the Cartesian product of the demand uncertainty set for each vehicle, which consists of CP demand and *HD* demand. Equation (2) denotes the uncertain demand of customer groups with *HD* demand; $\bar{q}_i$ represents the nominal value of uncertain demand; and $\hat{q}_i$ denotes the maximum deviation from the nominal value for each vertex $i \in N_C$. α_i is the auxiliary variable, and $\Gamma_{q_i}^k$ is the uncertainty budget that controls the level of uncertain demand of customer groups. Since the uncertainty experienced by each vehicle is related to the number of customers in each customer group visited, $\Gamma_{q_i}^k$ change by at most $\left\lceil \theta_{q_i} \left| N_C^k \right| \right\rceil$, where $\left\lceil \theta_{q_i} \left| N_C^k \right| \right\rceil$ represents the smallest integer that is larger than or equal to $\theta_{q_i} \left| N_C^k \right|$. And θ_{q_i} is the demand uncertainty budget coefficient of customer groups, and takes value in the interval $[0, 1]$. If $\theta_{q_i} = 0$, $\Gamma_{q_i}^k = 0$ and $\tilde{q}_i = \bar{q}_i$ – the influence of the demand uncertainty of customer groups can be ignored completely. If $\theta_{q_i} = 1$, $\Gamma_{q_i}^k = \left| N_C^k \right|$ – each customer demand $\tilde{q}_i$ of customer groups can take any value in the interval $[\bar{q}_i - \hat{q}_i, \bar{q}_i + \hat{q}_i]$.

In addition, we defined the actual HD demand in customer group $i \in N_C$ and the actual CP demand in vertex $i \in N_l$, namely q_{iH} and q_{iC}. Each is defined as nominal customer demand polytope, as discussed by Zhou et al. [8].

$$p_{ijCH} = f(d_{ij}), i \in N_C, j \in N_D \tag{3}$$

$$\tilde{q}_{iC} = \tilde{q}_i - \tilde{q}_{iH}, \forall i \in N_C \tag{4}$$

$$w_{k1} + w_{k2} \le 1, \forall k \in K \tag{5}$$

Equation (3) reflects that probability of customers in groups $i \in N_C$ with initial CP demand tending to choose HD service when terminal j is selected to serve it. In Eq. (4), $\tilde{q}_{iH}$ denotes the overall uncertain HD demand in customer group $i \in N_C$; p_{iH} and p_{iC} are the initial percentages of the two types of services, respectively, where $p_{iH} + p_{iC} = 1$ and z_{ij} is a binary variable that 1 if customer group i choose the terminal j to serve itself; 0, otherwise. Equation (5) show the overall CP demand in customer group $i \in N_C$. Equation (6) guarantee that each vehicle can only be allocated neither level 1 or level 2.

2.3   Uncertain Transformation of Travel Distance

For the distance within the customer groups, because of the spatial aggregation feature of customers locations for the last mile delivery, the overall delivery demand of a customer group keeps constant while individual demand constantly changes, which is difficult to calculate the tour travel distance for all customers. Here, the approximate continuous model for customer group (modified from Zhou et al. [8]) was introduced to model the nominal travel distance $\bar{L}(n)$ of the tour in customer group with n customers, which is given by

$$\bar{L}(n) = k_1 \sqrt{S \lceil n/\eta \rceil} \tag{6}$$

$$n = n_C p_I p_S \cdot \frac{q_{iH}}{q_{iC}} \cdot p_E \tag{7}$$

where S is the customer group distribution area. η denotes the agglomeration degree which represents the customer group's customer density or degree of aggregation; k_1 is a constant, generally $k_1 = 0.57$. n is the number of the customers with HD demand in certain customer group; n_C is the number of customer in a customer group; p_I is the probability of the internet users; p_S is the probability of online shopping of customer group; q_{iH}/q_{iC} is the probability that the customer group selects HD service; p_E is the probability that the customer group buys online every day. Based on the construction process of uncertainty set of robust optimization, the travel time uncertainty set $u_{L(n)}$ of the tour in customer group is denoted.

$$u_{L(n)} = \times_{k \in K} U^k_{L(n)} \tag{8}$$

with

$$U_{L(n)}^k = \left\{ \tilde{L}(n) \in R^{|N_C^k|} \middle| \tilde{L}(n) = \bar{L}(n) + \lambda_i \hat{L}(n) , \sum_{i \in N_C^k} |\lambda_i| \leq \Gamma_{L(n)}^k , \right.$$
$$\left. |\lambda_i| \leq 1, \Gamma_{L(n)}^k = \lceil \theta_{L(n)} |N_C^k| \rceil , \forall i \in N_C^k \right\} \tag{9}$$

Equation (9) shows the overall distance uncertainty set $u_{L(n)}$ of the tour in customer groups is the Cartesian product of the travel time uncertainty set $U_{d_A}^k$ of the tour in a customer group for each vehicle. N_C^k denotes the set of customer groups on the route of the vehicle. Similarly, the parameters in the Eq. (10) has the resemble meanings to those in Eq. (2). N_C^k represents the nominal value of uncertain demand $\tilde{L}(n)$ and $\hat{L}(n)$ denotes the maximum deviation from the nominal value for each customer group $\forall i \in N_C^k$. λ_i is the auxiliary variable, and $\Gamma_{L(n)}^k$ is the uncertainty budget that controls the level of uncertain travel distance of the tour in the customer groups and $\Gamma_{L(n)}^k$ is defined as equaling $\lceil \theta_{L(n)} |N_C^k| \rceil$, where $\lceil \theta_{L(n)} |N_C^k| \rceil$ represents the smallest integer that is larger than or equal to $\theta_{L(n)} |N_C^k|$. And $\theta_{L(n)}$ is the travel time uncertainty budget coefficient of the tour in a customer group, and takes value of between 0 and 1. For the distance between terminals in level 1 and between customer groups in level 2, without loss of generality, the travel time uncertainty set u_{d_A} between terminals and customer groups is given by

$$u_{d_A} = \times_{k \in K} U_{d_A}^k, A = \{A_C \cup A_D\} \tag{10}$$

with

$$U_{d_A}^k = \left\{ \tilde{d} \in R^{|A^k|} \middle| \tilde{d}_{ij} = \bar{d}_{ij} + \beta_{ij} \hat{d}_{ij} , \sum_{(i,j) \in A^k} |\beta_{ij}| \leq \Gamma_{d_A}^k , \right.$$
$$\left. |\beta_{ij}| \leq 1, \Gamma_{d_A}^k = \lceil \theta_{d_A} |A^k| \rceil , \forall (i,j) \in A^k \right\} \tag{11}$$

Equation (11) shows the overall distance uncertainty set u_{d_A} is the Cartesian product of the travel time uncertainty set $U_{d_A}^k$ for each vehicle. Similarly, in Eq. (12), A^k denotes the set of arcs on the route of the vehicle k, which consists of the set between customer groups and the set between terminals. $\bar{d}_{ij}$ represents the nominal value of uncertain distance $\tilde{d}_{ij}$ and $\tilde{d}_{ij}$ denotes the maximum deviation from the nominal value for each arc $\forall (i,j) \in A^k$. β_{ij} is the auxiliary variable, and $\Gamma_{d_A}^k$ is the uncertainty budget that controls the level of uncertain travel time of customer groups and terminals and $\Gamma_{d_A}^k$ is defined as equaling $\lceil \theta_{d_A} |A^k| \rceil$ – where $\lceil \theta_{d_A} |A^k| \rceil$ represents the smallest integer that is larger than or equal to $\theta_{d_A} |A^k|$. And θ_{d_A} is the distance uncertainty budget coefficient, and takes value of between 0 and 1.

2.4 Mathematical Formulation

The considered $RBLRP$ given the route-dependent uncertainty sets is presented, starting with the objective function:

$$(RBLRP) \quad \min \ Z = \sum_{i \in N_1} \sum_{j \in N_1} \sum_{k \in K} \tilde{t}_{ij} x_{ijk} w_{k1} + \sum_{i \in N_2} \sum_{j \in N_2} \sum_{k \in K} \tilde{t}_{ij} x_{ijk} w_{k2}$$
$$+ \sum_{i \in N_c} \sum_{j \in N_2} \sum_{k \in K} \tilde{t}_i (n) x_{ijk} w_{k2}$$

$$(12)$$

Objective (13) minimizes the total travel time, including vehicle travel time between vertexes in level 1, vehicle travel time between customer groups, travel time and service time in customer groups of level 2.

$$\sum_{j \in N_1} x_{ijk} \leq 1, \forall i \in N_D, k \in K \tag{13}$$

$$\sum_{j \in N_1} x_{0jk} = 1, \forall k \in K \tag{14}$$

$$\sum_{i \in N_1} x_{i0k} = 1, \forall k \in K \tag{15}$$

$$\sum_{j \in N_1} x_{jik} - \sum_{j \in N_1} x_{ijk} = 0, \quad \forall i \in N_D, k \in K \tag{16}$$

$$U_{0uk} = \sum_{i \in N_1} \sum_{j \in N_D} \tilde{q}_{jC} x_{ijk}, \quad \forall u \in N_D, k \in K \tag{17}$$

$$\sum_{j \in N_1} U_{jik} - \sum_{j \in N_1} U_{ijk} = \tilde{q}_{iC}, \quad \forall i \in N_D, k \in K \tag{18}$$

$$U_{ijk} \leq Q, \quad \forall i, j \in N_1, k \in K \tag{19}$$

$$\sum_{i \in N_1} \sum_{j \in N_1} \tilde{d}_{ij} x_{ijk}/s_1 + \sum_{i \in N_1} \sum_{j \in N_D} t_{jC} x_{ijk} \leq T_k, \forall k \in K \tag{20}$$

$$\sum_{i \in N_1} U_{i0k} = 0, \forall k \in K, k \in K \tag{21}$$

Constraints (13)–(22) are used for limiting the vehicle routing of level 1. Constraints (14) guarantee that each terminal is served at most once. Constraints (15)–(17) are the flow conservation constraints, which ensure that vehicle starts from DC and ends at DC. Constraints (18) ensure calculate the load of vehicles. Constraints (19) are the flow constraints for demand. Constraints (20) make sure that remaining demand of a vehicle should not exceed its capacity. Constraints (21) stipulate that vehicle's maximum working hours should not be exceeded. Constraints (22) ensure that the remaining demand of a vehicle is zero after serving the final vertex. Note that constraints (20)–(22) are both related to both level 1 and level 2.

$$\sum_{j \in N_C} x_{ijk} = 1, \forall i \in N_2, k \in K \tag{22}$$

$$\sum_{m \in N_D} z_{im} = 1, \forall i \in N_C \tag{23}$$

$$\sum_{j \in N_2} x_{0jk} = 1, \forall k \in K \tag{24}$$

$$\sum_{i \in N_2} x_{i0k} = 1, \forall k \in K \tag{25}$$

$$\sum_{j \in N_2} x_{jik} - \sum_{j \in N_2} x_{ijk} = 0, \ \forall i \in N_C, k \in K \tag{26}$$

$$U_{0uk} = \sum_{i \in N_2} \sum_{j \in N_C} \tilde{q}_{jH} x_{ijk}, \ \forall u \in N_C, k \in K \tag{27}$$

$$\sum_{j \in N_2} U_{jik} - \sum_{j \in N_2} U_{ijk} = \tilde{q}_{iH}, \ \forall i \in N_C, k \in K \tag{28}$$

$$U_{ijk} \leq Q, \ \forall i, j \in N_2, k \in K \tag{29}$$

$$\sum_{i \in N_2} \sum_{j \in N_2} \tilde{d}_{ij} x_{ijk} \Big/ s_1 + \sum_{i \in N_C} x_{ijk} \left(k_1 \sqrt{S \lceil n_i / \eta_i \rceil} \Big/ s_2 + \sum_{i \in N_C} \tilde{q}_{iH} t_H \right) \leq T_k, \forall k \in K \tag{30}$$

$$\sum_{i \in N_C} \tilde{q}_{iC} z_{im} \leq b_m y_m, \ \forall k \in K, m \in N_D \tag{31}$$

Constraints (23)–(32) are used for limiting the level 2. Constraints (23) guarantee that each customer group is served exactly once by a level 2. Constraints (24) ensure that each customer group is assigned to a terminal exactly once. Constraints (25)–(31) have a similar meaning with constraints (15)–(21). Constraints (32) make sure that the terminal's capacity cannot be exceeded by customers assigned.

3   The Modified SA Algorithm for the RBLRP

3.1   Solution Representation and Encoding

In this work, permutation representation is used and the splitting procedure [5, 6] is integrated into the encoding strategy. As far as the chromosome of level 1 and level 2, the DCs, denoted as 0 between the head and tail of the chromosome, are generated at random, aiming to split the giant tour into some small routes without violating the vehicle capability and working time constraints.

3.2   The Neighborhood Search Structure

For the SA heuristic, we employ a random neighborhood structure that features three types of moves [4], including intra-route swap, intra-route relocate and intra-route 2-opt. The local optimum solution of R^{search} is generated from the solution of $R^{initial}$ based on the neighborhood search operators and a graphic illustration of the three neighborhood operators appears in Fig. 2.

Intra-route Swap. Intra-route swap is executed by randomly selecting the ith and jth positions located in the same chromosome and therefore exchanging the genes in the two positions.

Intra-route Relocate. We implement the move by randomly selecting the jth position, remove it from the chromosome and reinsert it into the middle of the jth and j-1th positions of the same chromosome.

Intra-route 2-opt. This neighborhood operator is executed by randomly selecting the ith and jth positions located in the same chromosome and reverse the order of (i, j).

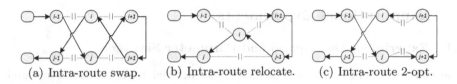

(a) Intra-route swap.   (b) Intra-route relocate.   (c) Intra-route 2-opt.

Fig. 2. Three neighborhood operators.

3.3   The Modified SA Method

As is shown in the Algorithm 1, the modified SA procedure is depicted. For the parameters setting, initialize the terminate temperature T_{min} and initial temperature T that is calculated, $T = 100 * n$, where n is the number of the vertexes. For the acceptance decision, the Metropolis criterion is used in the local search step. Generate a neighborhood solution R^{search} from $R^{current}$ and calculate its fitness function. The solution generated form the local search R^{search} is compared to the current solution $R^{current}$. If the fitness function difference of R^{search} and $R^{current}$, namely $\triangle$, is greater than 0, the R^{search} replaces the current solution $R^{current}$. Otherwise, R^{search} is accepted with the probability of acceptance $\exp(-\triangle/T)$ when $\exp(-\triangle/T)$ is greater than 0–1 random number. Implement the iterations until i = iter. If the temperature is greater than T_{min}, the current temperature is updated by $T = T * r$, where r is the temperature update factor.

Algorithm 1. The procedure of modified SA

1: Define neighborhood research structure N_J^{search}, $J = 1, \cdots, J_{max}$;
2: Set the solution of giant tour as the initial solution $R^{initial}$ and improve $R^{initial}$ by local search;

3: Set current solution $R^{current} \leftarrow R^{initial}$;
4: **repeat**
5:   **repeat**
6:     {Local search}
7:     Generate a local optimal solution $R^{search} \in N_J^{search}(R^{current})$;
8:     {Acceptance decision} STATE $\Delta = F(R^{search}) - F(R^{current})$;
9:     **if** $\Delta < 0$ **then**
10:        $R^{current} \leftarrow R^{search}$;
11:     **else**
12:        **if** $\exp(-\Delta/T) > $ rand **then**
13:           $R^{current} \leftarrow R^{search}$;
14:        **end if**
15:     **end if**
16:     i $\leftarrow$ i + 1
17:   **until** i $\leq$ iter
18:   $T = T * r$ $(r < 1)$;
19: **until** $T < T_{min}$

---

4   Computational Experiments

4.1   Experiment Description and Parameter Setting

The computational experiment instance was derived from the latest research instance of Zhou [8] designed for the *BL-MSTLRP* with deterministic customer demands and travel times. To simplify the calculation, the datasets of terminal size information and vehicle type information were ignored. The speed of vehicles is 30 km/h between nodes and 20 km/h in customer groups with working time about 8 h. In addition, the customer demand transfer coefficient is subject to distribution as follows.

$$P_{ijCH} = f(d_{ij}) = \begin{cases} 0, & 0 \leq d_{ij} \leq 500 \\ 0.3, & 500 < d_{ij} \leq 800 \\ 0.7, & 800 < d_{ij} \leq 1000 \\ 1, & d_{ij} > 1000 \end{cases} \tag{32}$$

For the robust purpose, the nominal value $\bar{q}_i$ ($i \in N_C$) and $\bar{t}_{ij}$ ($(i, j) \in A$) was assumed to equal to the corresponding customer demand and travel time in case set data from the *Zhou*, respectively. Moreover, we assumed that the maximal demand deviation $\hat{q}_i$ was $0.2\bar{q}_i$, and the maximal travel time deviation $\hat{t}_{ij}$ was $0.2\bar{t}_{ij}$ and $\theta_{q_i} = \theta_{L(n)} = \theta_{d_A}$ was 0.6. For the SA, The terminal temperature $T_{min} = 0.001$, maximal evolutional generation $I_{iter} = 100$ and temperature update factor $r = 0.99$. Finally, the computational experiments were implemented using *MATLAB R2014a*, and the experiments on a computer with an AMD *A8-7650K* Radeon R7 CPU at 3.30 GHz and 8 GB RAM under Windows X64 system.

4.2 Computational Results

The result of comparison with two strategies is shown in the Table 1. Compared with the deterministic solution, the robust strategy will result in a lower vehicle travel time, which is reduced by 1.63%. This is mainly because the disturbance of the uncertainty factor makes the distance from the customer to the terminal increase, and customers also prefer CP services. This can be seen from the average load rate of vehicles transferred from (54.78%, 89.66%) to (55.41%, 84.61%). To examine the impact of customer demand and travel time uncertainty, two sets of experiments were added, *Rob-T* and *Rob-D*. One interesting finding is that travel time uncertainty has a stronger influence on deterministic solution strategy than the demand uncertainty, for example, 1.60% vs 0.15%. This is mainly because the uncertainty of demand does not affect the choice of customer service, while the uncertainty of the path directly leads to the shift of customer service selection. Finally, The result of robust optimization is shown in the Fig. 3.

Table 1. Comparison of two solutions strategies on the considered instances

Type	NO.	N.V.	OBJ	Reduce	Avg.loadrate	Level-1		Level-2			
						$Sobj_{11}$	$Sobj_{12}$	$Sobj_{21}$	$Sobj_{22}$	$Sobj_{23}$	$Sobj_{24}$
Det	2\4	6	28.1019	-	54.78%\89.66%	4.7693	0.5270	4.5405	5.9162	6.1567	6.1921
Rob	2\4	6	27.6440	1.63%	55.41%\84.61%	1.2462	4.0485	7.2201	5.6179	4.3403	5.1710
Rob-T	2\4	6	27.6512	1.60%	57.72%\88.14%	0.8779	4.4156	5.1710	6.5562	5.6711	4.9595
Rob-D	2\4	6	28.0595	0.15%	52.59%\86.07%	4.7624	0.5355	5.7462	5.8996	6.5549	4.5609

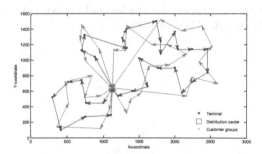

Fig. 3. The best solution of robust optimization of the instance.

5 Conclusion

The last mile delivery problem has gained widespread attention in recent years, but the previous studies lack enough analysis of the uncertain phenomenon. This paper focus on the research on the uncertainty optimization of the last mile. We found that robust optimization performed outstandingly on uncertainties and also had good performance in dealing with large-scale network uncertainties.

Future research should consider more uncertainty and establish a last-mile optimization model that is closer to reality. In addition, future research should also pay more attention to empirical research and enrich relevant research results.

References

1. Ben-Tal, A., Ghaoui, L., Nemirovski, A.: Robust Optimization (2009)
2. Bertsimas, D., Sim, M.: The price of robustness. Oper. Res. 52(1), 35–53 (2004). https://doi.org/10.1287/opre.1030.0065
3. Han, J., Lee, C., Park, S.: A robust scenario approach for the vehicle routing problem with uncertain travel times. Transp. Sci. 48(3), 373–390 (2014). https://doi.org/10.1287/trsc.2013.0476
4. Hu, C., Lu, J., Liu, X., Zhang, G.: Robust vehicle routing problem with hard time windows under demand and travel time uncertainty. Comput. Oper. Res. 94, 139–153 (2018). https://doi.org/10.1016/j.cor.2018.02.006
5. Kloimüllner, C., Papazek, P., Hu, B., Raidl, G.R.: A cluster-first route-second approach for balancing bicycle sharing systems. In: Moreno-Díaz, R., Pichler, F., Quesada-Arencibia, A. (eds.) EUROCAST 2015. LNCS, vol. 9520, pp. 439–446. Springer, Cham (2015). https://doi.org/10.1007/978-3-319-27340-2_55
6. López-Santana, E., Rodríguez-Vásquez, W., Méndez-Giraldo, G.: A hybrid expert system, clustering and ant colony optimization approach for scheduling and routing problem in courier services. Int. J. Ind. Eng. Comput. 9(3), 369–396 (2018). https://doi.org/10.5267/j.ijiec.2017.8.001
7. Taş, D., Dellaert, N., Van Woensel, T., De Kok, T.: Vehicle routing problem with stochastic travel times including soft time windows and service costs. Comput. Oper. Res. 40(1), 214–224 (2013). https://doi.org/10.1016/j.cor.2012.06.008
8. Zhou, L., Lin, Y., Wang, X., Zhou, F.: Model and algorithm for bilevel multisized terminal location-routing problem for the last mile delivery. Int. Trans. Oper. Res. (2017). https://doi.org/10.1111/itor.12399

A Comprehensive Fault Diagnosis System and Quality Evaluation Model for Electromechanical Products by Using Rough Set Theory

Jihong Pang[1,3](✉), Ruiting Wang[1], and Yan Ran[2]

[1] College of Mechanical and Electronic Engineering, Wenzhou University,
Wenzhou 325035, China
pangjihong@163.com
[2] College of Mechanical Engineering, Chongqing University, Chongqing
400030, China
[3] College of Mechanical Engineering, Zhejiang University, Hangzhou 310027,
China

Abstract. Electromechanical product is an important part of mechanical and electrical control system, and its quality plays a key role in the normal operation process. In this paper, a comprehensive fault diagnosis system and quality evaluation model for electromechanical products is analyzed. Firstly, the feature extraction of different faults is carried out, and the fault features of electromechanical products are simplified by using the approximation set information system properties of rough set theory. Secondly, the subjective weight index model is determined based on the rough information system properties of rough set theory. Then, the evaluation weight of each index of quality evaluation model for electromechanical products is obtained by the importance measurement of information system properties. Finally, this paper illustrates that the results of fault diagnosis and quality evaluation of ball valves as well as the availability of scientific.

Keywords: Fault diagnosis system · Quality evaluation model
Electromechanical products · Rough set

1 Introduction

Reliability and quality performance for electromechanical products will directly affect the stability of the operational stability. Thus, every company should make the most of its sources and regulating the cost from time to time to product quality [1]. It is introduced that during the manufacturing process of electromechanical products, the fault diagnosis system and quality evaluation of their key procedures must be

J. Pang—This work was supported by the National Natural Science Foundation of China (No. 71671130, No. 71301120, No. 51705048).

K. Li et al. (Eds.): ICSEE 2018/IMIOT 2018, CCIS 924, pp. 55–64, 2018.
https://doi.org/10.1007/978-981-13-2384-3_6

strengthened to ensure the qualification and stability to materials and workmanship [2]. The fault diagnosis system is a key part of product quality evaluation, and product working performance is affected by the processing quality in through their manufacturing process [3]. Moreover, the quality evaluation goals can be translated into a set of preference or utility functions that represent the value of alternative sets of consequences by decision theorists [4]. Through introducing the reliability specifications and quality test methods specified for electromechanical products, the basic fault diagnosis and quality control requirements can be understood by the application [5]. This paper presents a fault diagnosis system for alarm processing and fault diagnosis in product manufacturing process.

On the other hand, a comprehensive fault diagnosis system and quality evaluation model for electromechanical products is the basis of scientific decision-making. Fault diagnosis system is an important part for quality evaluation model, a comprehensive evaluation with rough set theory can improve the electromechanical products quality [6]. Furthermore, combination with rough sets and decision-making theory has enormous development potentials in the field of fault diagnosis system and quality evaluation for electromechanical products [7]. To ensure the accuracy and stability of quality evaluation, this comprehensive fault diagnosis system sets up fault recognition mechanism before acting [8]. Domestic and foreign scholars have done a lot of research work on comprehensive quality evaluation methods. In the next, under the framework of rough set theory, this study presents a multi-stage innovation quality evaluation model with the theory of rough set analysis. A quality evaluation model for identification, diagnosis, estimation and forecast of fault diagnosis system using the data fusion technique and the rough set theory was established [9]. This paper describes how to apply rough set theory in quality evaluation model validity of fault diagnosis systems. Objective weighting evaluation method based on actual data source to make quantitative evaluation of indicators, the weight is determined according to the correlation or variation coefficient of each index.

Considering the above aspects, a new method for quality evaluation and its application in ball valve fault diagnosis with rough set theory is proposed in this study. This study will be arranged as follows. The implement process comprehensive fault diagnosis system and quality evaluation model for electromechanical products by using rough set theory in the following section. In the case study, a testing attribute evaluation is set up, the attributes of t quality evaluation model are calculated, and the experimental data are analyzed to verify or identify the model's key attributes for a high fault diagnosis system. In the last section, some conclusions on the approved diagnosis system and evaluation model are given.

2 Implement Processes by Using Rough Set Theory

Rough set theory is an effective tool to deal with vagueness and uncertainty. It provides effective means for people to understand things correctly and make scientific decisions. The rough set theory was proposed by Poland scientist in 1982, and after the continuous development of scientific researchers on rough set theory [10]. Rough set theory is a new mathematical tool with strong knowledge obtaining ability after probability theory, fuzzy sets, mathematical theory of evidence [11]. At present, rough set theory has been applied to various fields, such as machine learning, fault diagnosis, control algorithm acquisition, process control and knowledge acquisition in relational database, and has achieved great success [12].

In brief, the rough set theory and method is quite an efficient means to deal with complex system, which is applied to a lot of fields. An algorithm of attribute reduction based on attribute importance of rough set was used to fault diagnosis system [13]. An extraction method of decision rules for fault diagnosis by using rough set theory is presented to extract simple and effective diagnostic rales for quality evaluation in this paper. The implement process of fault diagnosis system and quality evaluation model for electromechanical products by using rough set theory is shown in Fig. 1.

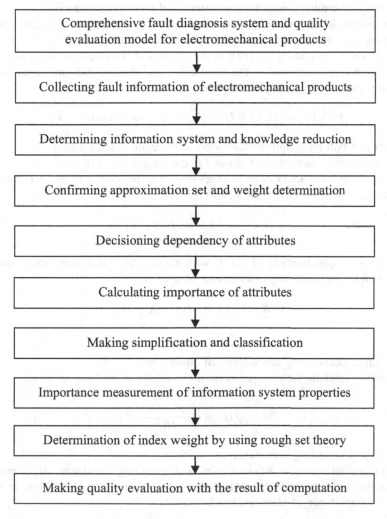

Fig. 1. Implement process of quality evaluation by using rough set theory

2.1   Information System and Knowledge Reduction

Knowledge reduction is the core of rough set theory. In this paper, the association and their relation between information system and knowledge reduction were described. A new object of value reduction is proposed to get the rules with maximal support measurement. Rough set theory has two important objectives of classification and reduction [14].

Let $S = (U, A, V, f)$ is an information system, where U represents a nonempty finite set of objects, $U = \{x_1, x_2, \ldots, x_n\}$ is called a domain. A represents a nonempty finite set of attributes, $A = \{a_1, a_2, \ldots, a_m\}$, $a_j\ (j \leq m)$ is called an attribute. Va is the range of the attribute a, $f\colon U \times A \to V$ is an information function for each attribute of object given a value of information, namely $a \in A, x \in U, f(x, a) \in Va$.

Step one: Determining information system and knowledge reduction
A rough set model to mine default rules was used to solve the decision question with incomplete information. Rough set theory is a new mathematical tool to deal with fuzzy and uncertain knowledge [15]. In the process of classification, individuals with little difference are attributed to the same class, and their relationship is an indistinguishable relationship, which is shown as:

$$IND(P) = \{(x, y) \in U \times U : f(x, a) = f(y, a), a \in P\} \tag{1}$$

Step two: Confirming approximation set and weight determination
The next approximation of set X about I is the largest set of objects, which must be based on the existing knowledge belongs to X, and remember to make $POS(X)$, the specific calculation formula is as follows (2):

$$I_*(X) = \{x \in u : I(x) \subseteq X\} \tag{2}$$

The upper approximation of set X with respect to I is x-intersecting *non-null* equivalent $I(X)$, the following formula can be used as:

$$I^*(X) = \{x \in u : I(x) \cap X \neq \phi\} \tag{3}$$

Step three: Decisioning dependency of attributes
The decision attribute set D depends on the conditional attribute set C.

$$\gamma_c(D) = \frac{|POS_c(D)|}{|U|} \tag{4}$$

Step four: Calculating importance of attributes
Different attributes play a different role in determining the degree of dependency between the decision attributes. Add attribute a to the conditional attribute set R, and define the importance of classification $U/IND(P)$:

$$sgf(a, R, P) = \gamma_R(P) - \gamma_{R-\{a\}}(P) \tag{5}$$

Step five: Making simplification and classification

In a decision-making system, there are often some dependencies and classifications between the conditional attributes. Simplification can be understood as the easiest way to represent the decision attribute of the decision system to the set of condition attributes without losing the information Dependencies and classification.

A given decision system $S = \{U, A = C \cup D, V, f\}$. The simplification of the conditional attribute C is a nonempty subset C'' of C,

(1) $IND(C', \{d\}) = IND(C, \{d\})$.
(2) This explains that $IND(C'', \{d\}) = IND(C, \{d\})$.

It satisfies that all the reduced sets of C is denoted $RED\ (C)$, and the intersection of all reduced sets of C is called a kernel, denoted $CORE\ (C)$, $CORE\ (C) = \cap RED\ (C)$.

Therefore, any simplification B of C can be used instead of C without losing any information in the information table, resulting in a simplified message.

2.2 Importance Measurement of Information System Properties

Based on the information system of rough set theory, we can suppose that $U/IND(P) = \{X_1, X_2, \ldots, X_n\}$. And P is defined as:

$$I(P) = \sum_{i=1}^{n} \frac{|X_i|}{|U|} \Big| 1 - \frac{|X_i|}{|U|} = 1 - \frac{1}{|U|^2} \sum_{i=1}^{n} |X_i^2| \tag{6}$$

Where X represents the cardinal number of the set X, X_i/U represents the relative cardinality of the equivalent class X_i in U.

And the importance of attribute A_a is defined as:

$$SGF_{A-\{a\}}(a) = I(A) - I(A - \{a\}) \tag{7}$$

The above definition shows the importance of attribute a in A is a change in the amount of information caused by A removed after $\{a\}$ size measurement.

2.3 Determination of Index Weight by Using Rough Set Theory

Due to the shortcomings of the single evaluation method, the subjective weight is organically combined by the rough set theory in this paper.

And the attribute of $a_i \in A$ is representative of $SGFA - \{a_i\} - (a_i)$, $a_i \in A$ are defined as weight:

$$\omega(a_i) = SGF_{A-\{a_i\}}(a_i) \backslash \sum_{i=1}^{m} SGF_{A-\{a_i\}}(a_i) \tag{8}$$

3 A Case Study

A method of fault diagnosis of ball valve by using rough set theory is proposed in the case study. A ball valve is widely used in the pneumatic and hydraulic control system, which controls the circulation of the medium in the pipe through opening and closing of the ball valve. The existing problems of manufacturing process of ball valve were analyzed, including unstable machining quality, imperfect technics, incongruous process design and low assembly quality. The comprehensive evaluation method consists of objective weighting method and subjective weighting method. Rough set theory was introduced to solve this problem, and further the quality evaluation model for fault diagnosis ability was proposed.

In this paper, the comprehensive evaluation method is used to evaluate the index of the quality of the ball valve. With the use of rough set theory, the operational quality of ball valve was improved and optimized. In the process of work, if the valve leakage or failure cannot start normally, it will cause the system fail to achieve the prescribed workflow and affect the environmental pollution. Typical application of the ball valve of quality improving and enhancement of processing capacity were introduced in this case study. Rough set theory is applied to evaluate the quality of ball valve. The index that affects the quality of ball valve is determined through comprehensive index weight values, and the key part is controlled during the production process of ball valve quality. To realize the complementary advantages of uncertainty, the final comprehensive evaluation result is more reasonable.

To determine the reliability correction factor, it is necessary to comprehensively consider the composition structure, manufacture and assembly, and use of the product. However, the above indicators are too general and difficult to quantify in practice. Therefore, it is necessary to divide the above several large segments into easily quantified indicators, establish a more comprehensive index system to evaluate the degree of difference.

In view of the quality characteristics and consulting related manuals and large number of failure data, the ball valve can be obtained the factors which affecting the quality of life cycle. Then, the comprehensive evaluation hierarchy model of numerical control machine tool subsystem quality correction factor is established, which is shown in Fig. 2.

The layered model consists of three layers, the top layer is the target layer, the middle layer is the criterion layer and the bottom layer of the index layer. Rule layer contains leakage of packing, leakage of main seal, side snapping or bite motion, abnormal pneumatic actuator. And each factor contains number of factors for the specific comparative indicators, which is used to build the hierarchical model of index layer. Then, the simplification of rough set theory to the index system is described below. Firstly, the indexes of two level in Fig. 2 are set as the attributes of the information system, that is, $A = \{X_1, X_2, \ldots, X_{11}\}$. Ball valve can be evaluated as a collection of objects in the system, for the convenience of processing, there are eight ball valves, namely $U = \{I, II, \ldots, VIII\}$.

In the evaluation process, the corresponding evaluation results of each secondary index are measured in four grades, which is shown in Table 1.

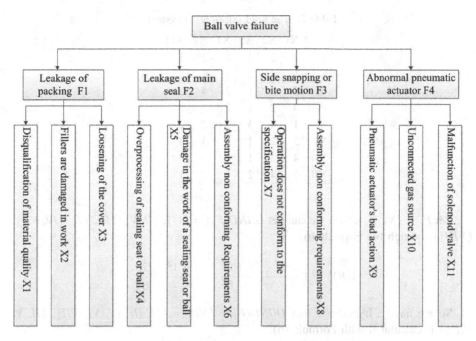

Fig. 2. Quality evaluation index system of ball valve

Table 1. Information system of ball valve

	X_1	X_2	X_3	X_4	X_5	X_6	X_7	X_8	X_9	X_{10}	X_{11}
I	3	2	2	1	2	3	1	2	2	1	1
II	1	4	2	3	2	1	3	2	2	2	2
III	2	2	4	3	1	2	2	4	4	1	2
IV	4	2	3	2	1	4	2	3	3	3	3
V	1	4	2	3	3	1	3	2	2	2	2
VI	2	2	3	2	1	2	2	3	3	3	3
VII	4	2	4	2	1	4	1	4	3	3	3
VIII	3	4	2	1	2	3	1	2	2	1	1

In the next, the information system $S = (U, A, V, f)$ of rough set is simplified, and a simple set is $R_1 = \{X_1, X_2, X_5, X_7, X_9, X_{11}\}$. And the Table 1 corresponding to the information system S can be further reduced to Table 2.

From Table 2, comprehensive assessment standards are namely "excellent", "good", "general" and "poor", and can be respective by $4, 3, 2, 1$, which are used to build an information system S of rough set. And the corresponding level one and two levels index sets are $\{F_1, F_2, F_3, F_4\} = \{\{X_1, X_2\}, \{X_5\}, \{X_7\}, \{X_9, X_{11}\}\}$.

Then, the computing process of secondary classes is simplified with the framework among $U = \{I, II, III, IV, V, VI, VII, VIII\}$ and $A = \{X1, X2, X5, X7, X9, X11\}$.

Table 2. The brief information system

	X1	X2	X5	X7	X9	X11
I	3	2	2	1	2	1
II	1	4	2	3	2	2
III	2	2	1	2	4	2
IV	4	2	1	2	3	3
V	1	4	3	3	2	2
VI	2	2	1	2	3	3
VII	4	2	1	1	3	3
VIII	3	4	2	1	2	1

Let $F_1 = \{X_1, X_2\}$, then we can get $U/IND(F_1) = \{\{I\}, \{II, V\}, \{III, VI\}, \{IV, VII\}, \{VIII\}\}$ through the Formula (6):

$$I(F1) = 1 - \frac{1^2 + 2^2 + 2^2 + 2^2 + 1^2}{8^2} = \frac{50}{64}.$$

So we have a hypothesis that $U/IND(F_1 - \{X_1\}) = \{\{I, III, IV, VI, VII\}, \{II, V, VIII\}\}$ is calculated with Formula (6):

$$I(F1 - \{X1\}) = 1 - \frac{5^2 + 3^2}{8^2} = \frac{30}{64}.$$

Next, the calculating results can be get through the Formula (7):

$$SGF_{F1-\{X1\}}(X1) = I(F1) - I(F1 - \{X1\}) = \frac{50 - 30}{64} = \frac{20}{64}.$$

So similarly, the results can be obtained:

$$SGF_{F1-\{X2\}}(X2) = I(F1) - I(F1 - \{X2\}) = \frac{50 - 48}{64} = \frac{2}{64}.$$

Then, the weight can be counted through the Formula (8):

$$\omega(X1) = SGF_{F1-\{X1\}}(X1) \backslash \sum_{i=1}^{2} SGF_{F1-\{Xi\}}(Xi) = \frac{20}{20 + 2} \approx 0.9091.$$

In much the same way, the other weights can be obtained as:

$$\omega(X5) = 1.0000, \; \omega(X5) = 1.0000.$$

$$\omega(X9) = 0.3333, \; \omega(X11) = 0.6667.$$

$$\omega(F1) = 0.4000, \ \omega(F2) = 0.2000.$$

$$\omega(F3) = 0.2000, \ \omega(F4) = 0.2000.$$

After that, depending on the results, we can meet with the comprehensive fault diagnosis system and quality evaluation model of ball valve to discuss further action. Data collection module is the base of the condition monitoring and quality evaluation model in the manufacturing process. Next, we point out the merits and main problems of the ball valve quality evaluation model. Development of the multiparameter condition monitoring and quality evaluation model for ball valve. The experimental results demonstrate that the proposed fault diagnosis system and quality evaluation model is correct and effective.

4 Conclusions

This paper studies the decision rules acquisition methodology by using rough set theory for fault diagnosis and quality evaluation. The application of comprehensive quality evaluation model of ball valve in a manufacturing firm was discussed. This study offers one new approach for automatic diagnosis rules knowledge in intelligent quality evaluation. Rough set theory not only can enrich intelligent decision theory, but also effectively provides the reference to the research of relative areas. Moreover, a fault diagnosis system and quality evaluation model for electromechanical products is developed based on the information fusion technology and rough set theory. Examples show that the evaluation is feasible effective and provides a new way for the evaluation of the quality of the ball valve. The method of fault diagnosis and quality evaluation model can be also prospected for other electromechanical products by using rough set theory.

Acknowledgments. This work was supported by the National Natural Science Foundation, China (No. 71671130, No. 71301120, No. 51705048), the postdoctoral program of Zhejiang University & Zhejiang Linuo Fluid Control Technology Company of China (No. 174102), the key project of teaching reform of Wenzhou University (No. 15jg07), engineering practice education center of Wenzhou University & Zhejiang Linuo Fluid Control Technology Company of China.

References

1. Bassi, F., Clerici, R., Aquario, D.: Evaluating quality of the didactics at university: the opportunities offered by latent class modeling. TQM J. **30**(2), 168–180 (2018)
2. Huang, H.B., Li, R.X., Yang, M.L., Lim, T.C., Ding, W.P.: Evaluation of vehicle interior sound quality using a continuous restricted Boltzmann machine-based DBN. Mech. Syst. Sig. Process. **84**, 245–267 (2017)
3. Oliveira, J.C.M., Pontes, K.V., Sartori, I., Embirucu, M.: Fault detection and diagnosis in dynamic systems using weightless neural networks. Expert Syst. Appl. **84**, 200–219 (2017)

4. Vidal Legaz, B., Maia De Souza, D., Teixeira, R.F.M., Anton, A., Putman, B., Sala, S.: Soil quality, properties, and functions in life cycle assessment: an evaluation of models. J. Clean. Prod. **140**, 502–515 (2017)
5. Ma, C., et al.: Sound quality evaluation of the interior noise of pure electric vehicle based on neural network model. IEEE Trans. Ind. Electron. **64**(12), 9442–9450 (2017)
6. Gao, Z., Chin, C.S., Chiew, J.H.K., Jia, J., Zhang, C.: Design and implementation of a smart lithium-ion battery system with real-Time fault diagnosis capability for electric vehicles. Energies **10**(10), 1503 (2017)
7. Zhao, R., Li, C., Tian, X.: A novel industrial multimedia: rough set based fault diagnosis system used in CNC grinding machine. Multimed. Tools Appl. **76**(19), 19913–19926 (2017)
8. Moayyedian, M., Abhary, K., Marian, R.: Optimization of injection molding process based on fuzzy quality evaluation and Taguchi experimental design. CIRP J. Manuf. Sci. Technol. **21**, 150–160 (2018)
9. Nazari, R., Seron, M.M., De Dona, J.A.: Actuator fault tolerant control of systems with polytopic uncertainties using set-based diagnosis and virtual-actuator-based reconfiguration. Automatica **75**, 182–190 (2017)
10. Chiaselotti, G., Ciucci, D., Gentile, T., Infusino, F.: Rough set theory and digraphs. Fundam. Inform. **153**(4), 291–325 (2017)
11. Gardiner, E.J., Gillet, V.J.: Perspectives on knowledge discovery algorithms recently introduced in chemoinformatics: rough set theory, association rule mining, emerging patterns, and formal concept analysis. J. Chem. Inf. Model. **55**(9), 1781–1803 (2015)
12. Hu, D., Yu, X., Wang, J.: Statistical inference in rough set theory based on Kolmogorov-Smirnov goodness-of-fit test. IEEE Trans. Fuzzy Syst. **25**(4), 799–812 (2017)
13. Huang, C.-C., Tseng, T.-L., Tang, C.-Y.: Feature extraction using rough set theory in service sector application from incremental perspective. Comput. Ind. Eng. **91**, 30–41 (2016)
14. Khan, M.A.: A probabilistic approach to rough set theory with modal logic perspective. Inf. Sci. **406–407**, 170–184 (2017)
15. Yao, Y., Zhang, X.: Class-specific attribute reducts in rough set theory. Inf. Sci. **418–419**, 601–618 (2017)

The Research of Improved Wolf Pack Algorithm Based on Differential Evolution

Yingxiang Wang[✉], Minyou Chen, Tingli Cheng,
and Muhammad Arshad Shehzad Hassan

State Key Laboratory of Power Transmission Equipment and System Security
and New Technology, School of Electrical Engineering, Chongqing University,
Chongqing 400044, China
jxgzwyx@126.com

Abstract. Aiming at the problems of traditional wolf pack algorithm (WPA): easy to fall into local optimal, large computational resource cost and low robustness, an improved wolf pack algorithm based on differential evolution (DIWPA) is proposed. By introducing the search factor for search wolves, maximum number of raid wolves, adaptive siege step size and differential evolution strategy, the proposed algorithm can not only reduce the computational cost but also improve the global search ability. The DIWPA is used to conduct optimization test on 12 benchmark functions and compare to 3 typical optimization algorithms. The test results show that DIWPA has great robustness and global search ability, especially has excellent performance in multi-peak, high-dimension, indivisible functions.

Keywords: Wolf pack algorithm · Local optimal · Differential evolution
Robustness · Global search ability

1 Introduction

1.1 A Subsection Sample

Swarm intelligence algorithms such as Particle Swarm Optimization (PSO) [1–3], Fish Swarm Optimization (FSA) [4, 5], Ant Colony Optimization (ACO) [6], Differential Evolution Algorithm (DE) [7], are widely used to solve optimization problems and have their own merits in solving different problems. The wolf pack search (WPS) was proposed by Yang et al. [8] in 2007. The Wu et al. [9] proposed a new Wolf Pack algorithm (WPA) on the basis of analyzing the behavior of hunting and prey among wolves in 2013. The WPA simulates the characteristics of wolves and groups to collaboratively hunt. In addition, the abstract behavior of walking, summoning, raids, siege, "winner is king" head wolf generation mechanism and the "strong survival" group update their mechanism to solve the optimization problems. Although the algorithm has a short time of introduction due to its good performance in multi-peak, high-dimension functions. In addition, it has been widely used in three-dimensional underwater track planning [10], hydropower reservoir optimization scheduling [11] and other human production activities. However, there are inevitably some shortcomings:

© Springer Nature Singapore Pte Ltd. 2018
K. Li et al. (Eds.): ICSEE 2018/IMIOT 2018, CCIS 924, pp. 65–76, 2018.
https://doi.org/10.1007/978-981-13-2384-3_7

easy to fall into local optimal solution, large computational resource cost and low robustness. Authors in [12] proposed an improved wolf pack algorithm, which proposed the wolf updating rules and introduced the phase factor according to the basic idea of the traditional wolf pack algorithm. At the same time, it optimized the types of step lengths of the traditional wolves and designed a new wolves. The location update formula is validated by the test function simulation. Literature [13] proposed a cultural wolf pack algorithm combined with cultural algorithm. This algorithm can effectively solve the blindness problem of artificial wolf search. Through testing and analyzing three complex functions, the validity of the culture wolf pack algorithm is verified. In Literature [14], the idea of solving the current local optimum in the PSO algorithm was introduced into the walking and summoning behavior of the wolf pack algorithm, and the suboptimal solution obtained by the chaos method is optimized. The improved algorithm greatly improves the accuracy of the search and avoids falling into local optimal. The effectiveness of the algorithm is verified by simulation.

Aiming at the deficiencies of WPA, this paper proposes an improved wolf pack algorithm based on differential evolution (DIWPA). Based on the intelligent behavior improvement of WPA, DIWPA introduces crossover, mutation and selection in differential evolution, which greatly improves the optimization performance and robustness of the algorithm.

This paper introduces the basic principle of DIWPA firstly. Then, DIWPA is used to conduct optimization test on 12 benchmark functions and compare to 3 typical optimization algorithms. The test results show that DIWPA has good performance for all kinds of test function optimization, and can avoid premature algorithm.

2 Basic Principle of the DIWPA

The DIWPA inherits all the behavior of the WPA and improves it. The main improvements are as follows:

① Due to the lack of guidance in wandering in WPA, the algorithm is unable to fully search the solution space and easily fall into a local optimum. The DIWPA introduces the search factor to the search wolves to make the algorithm traverse the entire space.

② In the face of high-dimensional function optimization, it may inevitably consume a lot of computing resources and may be difficult to jump out of the optimization process and reduce the robustness in WPA. The DIWPA introduces the maximum number of raid wolves to improve computational efficiency and algorithm robustness.

③ All the artificial wolves will siege at the same determined step size in siege behavior in WPA, so the adaptive siege step length is introduced in the siege behavior and the differential evolution strategies is introduced to improve the global search capabilities in DIWPA.

In summary, the DIWPA consists of seven kinds of behaviours such as walking, summoning, raid, siege, mutation, crossover, and selection, as well as two kinds of mechanisms, such as the generation of the wolf with the winner as the king and the group renewal with the survival of the strong.

The following minimum optimization problem as an example to introduce the main process of the DIWPA algorithm in detail:

(1) Initialization

Using the formula (1) to initialize the wolves, producing n artificial wolfs:

$$X_i^t = X_i^L + rand \times \left(X_i^U - X_i^L\right), i = 1, 2, \cdots, n \tag{1}$$

where X_i^t represents the ith artificial wolf in the tth generation; X^L and X^U are the lower and upper bounds of the variable $X = (x_1, x_2, \cdots, x_D)$ respectively; D is the variable dimension.

(2) The head wolf produces rules

In the initialized population, the fitness value of each artificial wolf is calculated by Eq. (2). The artificial wolf with minimal fitness value will be elected to be the head wolf in the iterative process and the fitness value of head wolf is Q_{lead}. During the process, the artificial wolf with the optimal fitness value after each evolution need to compare with the head wolf in the previous generation. If the current fitness value of the artificial wolf is better, the artificial wolf will replaces the head wolf and to be a new head wolf. For the minimum problem, Q_i is considered better than Q_{lead} when $Q_i < Q_{lead}$.

$$Q = f(X) \tag{2}$$

where $f(X)$ is the objective function of the minimum optimization problem.

(3) Walk behaviour

In addition to the head wolf, the S_{num} wolves with the best fitness value are selected as the search wolves in the current prey group to search for prey in space. S_{num} takes an integer between $[n/(\alpha+1), n/\alpha]$, where α is the scale factor of search wolf. The search wolves heads in the h directions respectively and records the fitness value of each position. And then they return to the original position, and proceeds to the pth (p = 1, 2, ..., h) direction. The location of wolf i in the dth (d = 1, 2, ..., D) dimensional space is shown in Eq. (3):

$$x_{id}^P = x_{id} + \gamma \times step_a^d \tag{3}$$

where $step_a$ is the walking distance of the search wolf, γ is the search factor of search wolf, and is a random number within $[-1, 1]$.

At that time, the fitness value of the position where the search wolf is located is Q_{ip}. The direction in which the fitness value is the smallest and smaller than the current position fitness value Q_{io} is selected to be further advanced, and the search wolf information X_i is updated. Comparing the artificial wolf with the minimal fitness value Q_{min} with the head wolf Q_{lead} after the end of one-time walking behaviour. If $Q_{min} < Q_{lead}$, the wolf with the minimal fitness value becomes the new head wolf and initiate the summoning; otherwise, repeat the walking behaviour until a certain wolf i with the fitness value $Q_i < Q_{lead}$, or the number of walks T_1 reaches the maximum number of walks T_{1max}. It should be pointed out that each search wolf has different fitness values so the search directions h of each search wolf is different, it will be taken within $[h_{min}, h_{max}]$.

(4) Raid behaviour

The head wolf initiates the summoning action by howling, calling the raid wolves to approach the head wolf quickly. The position of the raid wolf i in the dth (d=1, 2, ..., D) dimensional space at the $(k + 1)$th evolution is shown in Eq. (4):

$$x_{id}^{k+1} = x_{id}^k + step_b^d \times (g_d^k - x_{id}^k)/\left|g_d^k - x_{id}^k\right| \tag{4}$$

where $step_b$ is the step size of the raid wolf, and g_d^k is the position of the head wolf of the kth generation in the dth (d = 1, 2, ..., D) dimensional space.

In the process of wolves rushing, the wolf with the minimal fitness value Q_{min} is compared with the head wolf Q_{lead} after each raid. If $Q_{min} < Q_{lead}$, the wolf with the minimal fitness value becomes a new head wolf, the raid behaviour ends; otherwise, the raid continues until the fitness value of a certain wolf i is smaller than the head wolf fitness value or the raid reaches the maximum raid T_{2max}.

(5) Siege behaviour

The raid wolves will unite all the search wolves and move to the position where the head wolf is after the raid behaviour. For all the wolves of kth generation, assuming that the position of the head wolf in the dth (d = 1, 2, ..., D) dimensional space is G_d^k, the siege behaviour of wolves is shown in Eq. (5):

$$x_{id} = x_{id}^k + \lambda \times step_i^d \times (G_d^k - x_{id}^k)/\left|G_d^k - x_{id}^k\right| \tag{5}$$

where λ is a random number distributed uniformly between $[-1, 1]$; $step_i$ is the adaptive siege step size of wolf i. Taking the difference between the fitness difference in the search space upper and lower bound and the search space and the optimal value as the reference value, a positive correlation relationship between the adaptive siege step length and the difference between the fitness value of wolf i and the fitness value of head wolf is established. Adaptive siege step size $step_i$ is shown in Eq. (6):

$$step_i = (Q_i - Q_{lead}) \times \frac{X^U - X^L}{maxQ_0 - minQ_0}$$ (6)

where $maxQ_0$ and $minQ_0$ are the worst fitness value and optimal fitness value of the artificial wolf produced by the algorithm initialization.

If the fitness value of the position of the artificial wolf after the siege is smaller than the fitness value of the original position, the position information of the artificial wolf will be updated; otherwise, the position of the artificial wolf is not changed.

In particular: the $step_a$ and $step_b$ have the relationship is shown in Eq. (7):

$$step_a = step_b/2 = |X^U - X^L|/S$$ (7)

where S is the step size factor, it is the physical quantity that describes the artificial wolf to search for fine degree in the space to be searched for.

(6) Variation behaviour

After the siege behaviour, two different artificial wolf (kth generation) X_1^k, X_2^k are randomly selected in the group, and the vector difference is assigned to the weight and then the third randomly selected artificial wolf X_3^k is added. Artificial wolf variation vector v_i^{k+1} for any artificial wolf target vector X_i^k has expressed in Eq. (8):

$$v_i^{k+1} = X_3^k + F * (X_1^k - X_2^k)$$ (8)

where F is a scaling factor, it's a value between [0, 2], indicating the degree of scaling of the vector difference. The larger of F, the greater influence of the difference vector on v_i^{k+1}, which is beneficial to keeping the diversity of wolves; on the contrary, F can promote the local refined search.

(7) Crossover behaviour

After the variation behaviour, the artificial wolf variation vector v_i^{k+1} and the artificial wolf target vector X_i^k are mixed according to the Eq. (9) to generate the artificial wolf test vector u_i^{k+1} :

$$u_{ij}^{k+1} = \begin{cases} v_{ij}^{k+1} & rand(j) \leq CRorj = randn(i) \\ x_{ij}^k & rand(j) > CRorj \neq randn(i) \end{cases}$$ (9)

where j represents the jth variable of the artificial wolf, $randn(i) \in [1, 2, \cdots, D]$ is the identification of the randomly selected dimension variable; CR is the crossover probability factor, generally in the value between [0, 1]. The larger the CR is, the more favourable of the algorithm performs local search and also to speed up the convergence rate; the smaller the CR is, the more conducive to maintaining the diversity of wolves and global search.

(8) Choice behaviour

After the crossover behaviour, the artificial wolf test vector u_i^{k+1} and the artificial wolf target vector X_i^k are obtained. If the fitness value of the test vector is smaller than the target vector, u_i^{k+1} is replaced by X_i^k to become the $(k + 1)$th generation and the artificial wolf position is updated. Otherwise, use X_i^k directly as the $(k + 1)$th generation and update. It is shown in Eq. (10):

$$X_i^{k+1} = \begin{cases} u_i^{k+1} & Q(u_i^{k+1}) < Q(X_i^k) \\ X_i^k & Q(u_i^{k+1}) \geq Q(X_i^k) \end{cases} \tag{10}$$

For the artificial wolf vector X_i^{k+1}, the artificial wolf with the minimal fitness value Q_{min} should be found and compared with the head wolf fitness Q_{lead}. If $Q_{min} < Q_{lead}$, the artificial wolf with the minimal fitness value is selected as the head wolf.

(9) Wolves update mechanism

The prey hunted by the wolves is not evenly distributed to every wolf and will be distributed according to the principle of "weak meat and strong food". This may lead to the weak wolves to be starved to death. This principle will be simulated by removing R wolves with worst fitness and produced R artificial wolves according to formula (1). R is a random integer between $[n/(2 \times \beta), n/\beta]$ and β is the updates scale factor of wolves.

Through the above actions, the wolves constantly update and evolve until the algorithm reaches the maximum number of iterations G_{max} or when the optimal value obtained by the algorithm reaches the preset precision.

3 Simulation Test and Analysis of DIWPA

3.1 Introduction of Benchmark Functions

In order to test the performance and validity of DIWPA, this paper selects 12 benchmark functions shown as Table 1 to test it. In Table 1, "U" represents unimodal function; "M" represents multimodal function, it is usually used to detect the abilities of global optimization and avoid precocity [15] of the algorithm; "S" represents a separable function, "N" represents an inseparable function. The inseparable function will be more complex than the separable function, and the performance requirement of the algorithm is higher in the optimization process. In the definition field column of Table 1, the set part is the range of the variable value, and the index is the dimension D of the function. The higher the test function dimension D, the greater the computational complexity of the algorithm and the higher the performance requirement of the algorithm.

Table 1. 12 benchmark functions

Function name	Function expressions	Feature	Domain	Global optimum
Sphere	$f_1 = \sum\limits_{i=1}^{D} x_i^2$	US	$[-10, 10]^2$	0
Matyas	$f_2 = 0.26(x_1^2 + x_2^2) - 0.48x_1x_2$	UN	$[-10, 10]^2$	0
Booth	$f_3 = (x_1 + 2x_2 - 7)^2 + (2x_1 + x_2 - 5)^2$	MS	$[-10, 10]^2$	0
Eggcrate	$f_4 = x_1^2 + x_2^2 + 25(sin^2x_1 + sin^2x_2)$	MN	$[-\pi, \pi]^2$	0
Trid6	$f_5 = \sum\limits_{i=1}^{D} (x_i - 1)^2 - \sum\limits_{i=2}^{D} x_ix_{i-1}$	UN	$[-36, 36]^6$	-50
Sumsquares	$f_6 = \sum\limits_{i=1}^{D} ix_i^2$	US	$[-10, 10]^{10}$	0
Rastrigin	$f_7 = \sum\limits_{i=1}^{D} [x_i^2 - 10cos(2\pi x_i) + 10]$	MS	$[-10, 10]^{60}$	0
Griewank	$f_8 = \frac{1}{4000}\sum\limits_{i=1}^{D} x_i^2 - \prod\limits_{i=1}^{D} cos(\frac{x_i}{\sqrt{i}}) + 1$	MN	$[-600, 600]^{100}$	0
Quadric	$f_9 = \sum\limits_{i=1}^{D} (\sum\limits_{k=1}^{i} x_k)^2$	MS	$[-30, 30]^{100}$	0
Rosenbrock	$f_{10} = \sum\limits_{i=1}^{D-1} \left[100(x_{i+1} - x_i^2)^2 + (x_i - 1)^2\right]$	MN	$[-30, 30]^{100}$	0
Ackley-1	$f_{11} = -20exp\left(-0.2\sqrt{\frac{1}{D}\sum\limits_{i=1}^{D} x_i^2}\right) - exp\left(\frac{1}{D}\sum\limits_{i=1}^{D} cos(2\pi x_i)\right) + 20 + e$	MN	$[-32, 32]^{100}$	0
Ackley-2	$f_{11} = -20exp\left(-0.2\sqrt{\frac{1}{D}\sum\limits_{i=1}^{D} x_i^2}\right) - exp\left(\frac{1}{D}\sum\limits_{i=1}^{D} cos(2\pi x_i)\right) + 20 + e$	MN	$[-32, 32]^{200}$	0

3.2 Algorithm Verification and Analysis

In order to test the performance of DIWPA, this paper uses DIWPA, WPA, PSO, and DE algorithms to perform 100 optimization tests on the 12 functions listed and records the optimal value, the worst value, the average value, the standard deviation, the calculation success rate and average consuming time to compared and analysed. Experimental environment are as follows: Intel(R) Core(TM) i5-4590 CPU @3.30 GHz, 16 GB of memory, Win7 Professional 64-bit operating system, Matlab R2013b.

The calculation success rate is defined as the percentage of successful calculations in the total number of calculations [9]. For each result Q obtained by the optimization calculation, when Q satisfies formula (11), it means the search is successful:

$$\begin{cases} \left|\frac{Q-Q_{best}}{Q_{best}}\right| < 1E-03 & Q_{best} \neq 0 \\ |Q - Q_{best}| < 1E-03 & Q_{best} = 0 \end{cases} \tag{11}$$

where Q_{best} is the theoretical global optimal value of the function.

The maximum number of iterations for the optimization calculation are set to 2000, and the population size of the DIWPA, WPA, PSO, and DE algorithms are 50, where: the parameters of the WPA algorithm are selected according to the literature [9], the parameters of the PSO algorithm are selected according to the literature [1], and the parameters of the DE algorithm are selected according to the literature [7], as shown in Table 2.

Table 2. Parameters of each algorithm

Algorithm	Parameters
PSO	Inertia weight $\omega = 0.7298$, learning factor $c_1 = c_2 = 2$, individual velocity range $[-0.5, 0.5]$
DE	Scale factor $F = 0.6$, crossover probability factor $CR = 0.9$
WPA	Scale factor of search wolf $\alpha = 4$, maximum number of walks $T_{max} = 20$, distance determination factor $\omega = 500$, step size factor $S = 1000$, update scale factor $\beta = 6$
DIWPA	Scale factor of search wolf $\alpha = 4$, maximum number of walks $T_{1max} = 10$, maximum number of raids $T_{2max} = 10$, step size factor $S = 1500$, update scale factor $\beta = 3$, scale factor $F = 0.6$, crossover probability factor $CR = 0.9$

The standard deviation, average value, optimal value, calculation success rate, worst value, and average consuming time of the four algorithms on the 12 functions are shown in Table 3. The average convergence curves of the functions are shown in Fig. 1.

Table 3. Optimization results of each algorithm

Function	Algorithm	Optimal value	Worst value	Average value	Standard deviation	Calculation success rate	Average consuming time(s)
Sphere	PSO	3.92E−87	4.64E−81	1.69E−81	2.09E−81	100%	1.74
	DE	0	0	0	0	100%	4.98
	WPA	0	2.44E−187	1.22E−188	0	100%	16.8
	DIWPA	0	0	0	0	100%	8.4
Matyas	PSO	1.35E−71	2.85E−65	7.63E−66	1.08E−65	100%	4.89
	DE	0	0	0	0	100%	9.09
	WPA	0	0	0	0	100%	34.95
	DIWPA	0	0	0	0	100%	16.64
Booth	PSO	0	0	0	0	100%	4.03
	DE	0	0	0	0	100%	6.93
	WPA	3.77E−07	1.26E−04	4.22E−05	5.23E−05	100%	27.40
	DIWPA	0	0	0	0	100%	13.04
Eggcrate	PSO	8.03E−88	2.17E−75	1.09E−76	4.73E−76	100%	2.62
	DE	0	0	0	0	100%	6.01
	WPA	1.27E−171	1.25E−164	2.65E−165	0	100%	21.58
	DIWPA	0	0	0	0	100%	11.35
Trid6	PSO	−4.49E+01	−4.93E+01	−4.75E+01	1.31E+00	0	2.47
	DE	−5.00E+01	−5.00E+01	−5.00E+01	0	100%	5.88
	WPA	−5.00E+01	−5.00E+01	−5.00E+01	0	100%	20.88
	DIWPA	−5.00E+01	−5.00E+01	−5.00E+01	0	100%	9.08
Sumsquares	PSO	3.22E−17	1.33E−15	5.48E−16	5.91E−16	100%	2.40
	DE	1.08E−70	5.29E−67	4.64E−68	1.17E−67	100%	7.08
	WPA	1.54E−56	8.99E−55	4.26E−55	3.81E−55	100%	23.7
	DIWPA	0	0	0	0	100%	11.86
Rastrigin	PSO	7.63E+01	1.56E+02	1.13E+02	2.16E+01	0	3.07
	DE	2.28E+02	4.98E+02	3.83E+02	7.03E+01	0	16.9
	WPA	4.41E−09	3.37E−06	3.75E−07	7.48E−07	100%	49.93
	DIWPA	0	2.41E−12	1.58E−13	5.20E−13	100%	22.69
Griewank	PSO	4.72E+00	2.03E+00	3.55E+00	8.68E−01	0	6.16
	DE	1.99E+01	1.97E+01	1.98E+01	3.28E−04	0	18.90
	WPA	3.11E−12	3.88E−01	1.49E−01	9.73E−02	94%	62.65
	DIWPA	2.44E−15	6.68E−12	1.59E−12	1.95E−12	100%	32.98
Quadric	PSO	3.16E−28	4.65E−23	4.45E−24	1.10E−23	100%	15.67
	DE	2.08E−10	4.29E−02	4.01E−03	9.25E−03	50%	32.79
	WPA	5.93E−10	8.64E−07	2.33E−07	3.06E−07	100%	121.15
	DIWPA	4.15E−12	8.48E−08	1.11E−08	1.89E−08	100%	57.70
Rosenbrock	PSO	1.46E+02	4.43E+02	2.78E+02	7.86E+01	0	3.45
	DE	3.83E+02	2.81E+03	8.06E+02	5.62E+02	0	26.90
	WPA	2.59E−11	5.26E−02	3.83E−02	8.48E−03	90%	75.88
	DIWPA	3.23E−13	2.82E−10	2.39E−11	6.20E−11	100%	39.93
Ackley-1	PSO	5.92E−01	4.30E+00	2.43E+00	9.00E−01	0	4.28
	DE	1.99E+01	2.01E+01	2.00E+01	5.95E−03	0	25.29
	WPA	7.30E−13	6.36E−02	5.73E−02	1.76E−02	87%	73.93
	DIWPA	8.88E−16	8.88E−16	8.88E−16	0	100%	36.97
Ackley-2	PSO	2.26E+00	4.91E+00	3.04E+00	6.29E−01	0	6.19
	DE	1.96E+01	1.99E+01	1.98E+01	8.26E−04	0	46.14
	WPA	1.52E−11	7.17E−01	2.39E−01	4.68E−01	75%	136.06
	DIWPA	8.88E−16	8.88E−16	8.88E−16	0	100%	68.11

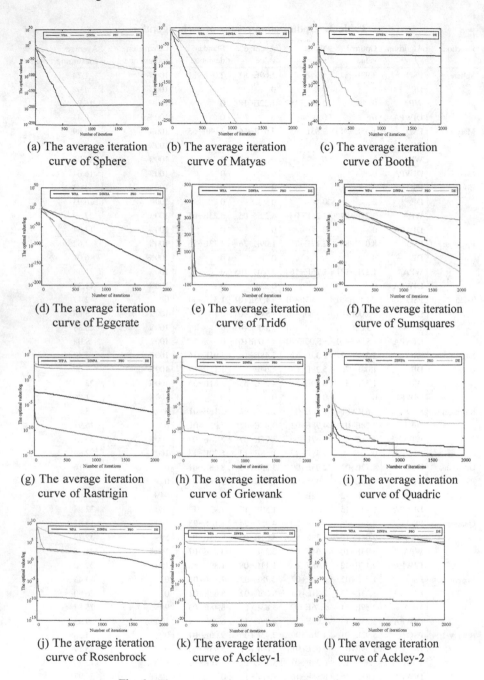

(a) The average iteration
curve of Sphere

(b) The average iteration
curve of Matyas

(c) The average iteration
curve of Booth

(d) The average iteration
curve of Eggcrate

(e) The average iteration
curve of Trid6

(f) The average iteration
curve of Sumsquares

(g) The average iteration
curve of Rastrigin

(h) The average iteration
curve of Griewank

(i) The average iteration
curve of Quadric

(j) The average iteration
curve of Rosenbrock

(k) The average iteration
curve of Ackley-1

(l) The average iteration
curve of Ackley-2

Fig. 1. The average iteration curve of each function

From Table 3 and Fig. 1, we can get the results as follows:

① For the single-peak, low-division and separable function of Sphere, the four algorithms are all successfully searched. Among them, DIWPA and DE have the best search capability, and the search capability of WPA is worse than DIWPA.

② For the single-peak, low-dimension and indefinable function of Matyas, the four algorithms are all successfully searched. Among them, DIWPA, WPA and DE have the same search capability and excellent performance.

③ For the multi-peak, low-dimension and separable function of Booth, the four algorithms are all successfully searched, among which DIWPA, PSO, and DE have the same search capability, and WPA has worse ability to search than the other three algorithms.

④ For the multi-peak, low-dimension and indefinable function of Eggcrate, the four algorithms are all successfully searched, among which DIWPA and DE have better search capability, and WPA has worse ability than DIWPA.

⑤ For the single-peak and indefinable function of Trid6, DIWPA, WPA, and DE are successfully searched and have good performance. The PSO is trapped in a local optimal and lead to fail.

⑥ For the single-peak and separable function of Sumsquares, the four algorithms are all successfully searched, among which the DIWPA has the best search capability and the WPA is worse than it.

⑦ For the multi-peak and separable function of Rastrigin, The PSO and DE fall into a local optimal lead to fail. DIWPA and WPA are successful and the DIWPA has better performance.

⑧ For the high-dimensional, multi-modal and indefinable functions of Griewank and Rosenbrock, the PSO and DE were failed. The DIWPA optimization was all successful and has good performance. The WPA may fallen into a local optimal and made the optimization ability unstable at some time.

⑨ For the high-dimensional, multi-peak and separable function of Quadric, the PSO, WPA and DIWPA are all successfully searched, among which the PSO has the best search capability. The DIWPA and WPA have the same optimization capability, but the DE suffers from local optimal values lead to the optimization ability unstable.

⑩ For high-dimensional, multi-modal and indefinable function of Ackley, the PSO and DE completely fail. The DIWPA has been successfully optimized. WPA has fallen into a local optimal situation, which results in a decrease in the search capability at some time. With the increase of the dimensionality of Ackley function, The probability of falling into a local optimum is further increased, and its ability to find optimization will be further reduced.

In summary, the DIWPA has a good ability for computing various types of uni-/multi-peak, low-dimensional/high-dimensional, and separable/inseparable functions. Compared with WPA, the DIWPA has better performance in multi-peak, high-dimension, indivisible functions. The robustness and accuracy of the solution are strengthened, and takes less time of the DIWPA.

4   Conclusion

In order to improve the optimization performance of traditional wolf pack algorithm, this paper proposes an improved wolf pack algorithm based on differential evolution (DIWPA). The main improvements are as follows: (1) The DIWPA introduces the search factor of search wolf in the walking behaviour, which makes the algorithm optimization can traverse the entire space; (2) The DIWPA introduces the maximum number of raid wolves to improves computational efficiency and algorithm robustness; (3) the adaptive siege step size and the differential evolution strategies is introduced to improve the global search capabilities in DIWPA. The DIWPA is used to conduct optimization test on 12 benchmark functions and compare to 3 typical optimization algorithms. The test results show that DIWPA has great robustness and global search ability, especially has excellent performance in multi-peak, high-dimension, indivisible functions.

References

1. Kennedy, J., Eberhart, R.: Particle swarm optimization. In: 1995 Proceedings of IEEE International Conference on Neural Networks, vol. 4, pp. 1942–1948. IEEE (2002)
2. Tehsin, S., Rehman, S., Saeed, M.O.B., et al.: Self-organizing hierarchical particle swarm optimization of correlation filters for object recognition. IEEE Access **PP**(99), 1 (2017)
3. Wei, L.X., Li, X., Fan, R., et al.: A hybrid multi-objective particle swarm optimization algorithm based on R2 indicator. IEEE Access **PP**(99), 1 (2018)
4. Singhal, P.K., Naresh, R., Sharma, V.: Binary fish swarm algorithm for profit-based unit commitment problem in competitive electricity market with ramp rate constraints. Gener. Transm. Distrib. IET **9**(13), 1697–1707 (2015)
5. Li, X.L., Shao, Z.J., Qian, J.X.: An optimizing method based on autonomous animate: fish swarm algorithm. Syst. Eng.-Theory Pract. **22**, 32–38 (2002)
6. Li, Y., Zhang, C., Yang, Q., et al.: Improved ant colony algorithm for adaptive frequency-tracking control in WPT system. IET Microwaves Antennas Propag. **12**, 23–28 (2017)
7. Wu, L.H.: Differential Evolution Algorithm and Its Application. Hunan University (2007)
8. Yang, C., Tu, X., Chen, J.: Algorithm of marriage in honey bees optimization based on the wolf pack search. In: International Conference on Intelligent Pervasive Computing, pp. 462–467. IEEE Computer Society (2007)
9. Wu, H.S., Zhang, F.G., Wu, L.H.: A new swarm intelligence algorithm—wolf pack algorithm. Syst. Eng. Electron. **35**(11), 2430–2438 (2013)
10. Zhang, L., Zhang, L., Liu, S., et al.: Three-dimensional underwater path planning based on modified wolf pack algorithm. IEEE Access **5**(99), 22783–22795 (2017)
11. Wang, J.Q., Jia, Y.Y., Xiao, Q.Y.: Wolf pack algorithm in the optimal operation of hydropower station reservoirs. Adv. Sci. Technol. Water Resour. **35**(3), 1–4 (2015)
12. Hui, X.B., Guo, Q., Wu, P.P., et al.: An improved wolf pack algorithm. Control Decis. **32**(7), 1163–1172 (2017)
13. Qian, R.X.: A wolf algorithm based on cultural mechanism. Inf. Technol. **2015**(12), 98–102 (2015)
14. Cao, S., Jiancheng, A.: Otsu image segmentation method for improved wolf group optimization algorithm. Microelectron. Comput. **34**(10), 16–21 (2017)
15. Solano-Aragón, C., Castillo, O.: Optimization of benchmark mathematical functions using the firefly algorithm with dynamic parameters. In: Castillo, O., Melin, P. (eds.) Fuzzy Logic Augmentation of Nature-Inspired Optimization Metaheuristics. SCI, vol. 574, pp. 81–89. Springer, Cham (2015). https://doi.org/10.1007/978-3-319-10960-2_5

Multi-objective Optimization Genetic Algorithm for Multimodal Transportation

Xiong Guiwu[1,2(✉)] and Xiaomin Dong[2]

[1] School of International Business, Sichuan International Studies University, Chongqing 400031, China
gwxiong@126.com
[2] College of Mechanical Engineering, Chongqing University, Chongqing 400044, China

Abstract. The multimodal transportation is an effective manner in reducing the transportation time and cost. However, the programming of multimodal transportation is very complex and belongs to NP difficulty problems. Therefore, an optimal model based on the graph structure was firstly formulated for the multimodal transportation with two optimal objectives including the transportation time and the transportation cost. An optimized algorithm with two layers was then proposed after characterizing the formulated model. The upper level was applied to find the global optimal Pareto fronts and the transportation path, whereas the lower level was to find the optimal path and the transportation manner. At last, a numerical simulation was performed to validate the model and the proposed algorithm. The results show that the proposed algorithm can find a series of Pareto front solutions, which indicates that the formulated model and proposed algorithm are effective and feasible.

Keywords: Fourth party logistics · Time window · Multi-agent
Hybrid Taguchi genetic algorithm

1 Introduction

As the economic globalization continues to intensify, resources, products, and markets are scattered all over the world. Market demands are changing rapidly and competition is becoming increasingly fierce. How to make all members in the logistics business closer to each other in the supply chain? The information in the process of business processing is highly integrated to achieve collaborative operation of the supply chain, shorten the relative length of the supply chain, make the logistics business on the supply chain smoother, yield higher, and respond faster. Meeting the needs of customers has become an urgent issue in management science and engineering. The multimodal operation is an important task of logistics and transportation organization and has become an effective measure for the fourth party logistics company to improve its competitiveness and thus reduce logistics costs. Compared to a single mode of transport, multimodal transport can increase efficiency, enhance safety and flexibility, and at the same time meet the requirements of the cargo carrier. However, compared to a single mode of transport, due to multi-participation, multiple objectives need to be taken into account. This makes multimodal transportation planning much more complicated and difficult.

© Springer Nature Singapore Pte Ltd. 2018
K. Li et al. (Eds.): ICSEE 2018/IMIOT 2018, CCIS 924, pp. 77–86, 2018.
https://doi.org/10.1007/978-981-13-2384-3_8

Therefore, it is very important to develop a multi-objective optimization algorithm for multimodal transportation planning.

At present, scholars have studied the modeling and algorithm problems of multimodal transport planning from different perspectives. However, most of works belong to single-objective optimization problems. There are few studies on multi-objective optimization problems that consider cost and transit time. For example, Angelica Lozano et al. [1] studied the shortest feasible path problem under multimodal transportation and solved it by using the sequential algorithm. Boussedjra and Moudni [2] adopted a bi-directional research strategy to establish an intermodal transport network model and presented the shortest path algorithm between source and destination. Some scholars consider multi-objective optimization when passengers use multiple transport modes. Brands et al. [3] studied the multi-objective optimization problem of multimodal passenger transportation in urban passengers considering uncertain demand. The results show that the demand is uncertain. The Pareto frontier solution of multi-objective optimization has a great influence on them. They [4] also applied this algorithm to solve multimodal network design problems. Zhang et al. [5] applied the uncertain optimization method to study the shortest path of passenger multimodal transport. They considered the difference in transit time and transportation cost caused by the uncertainties of different transport modes. The goal of the double-objective optimization problem was verified by numerical methods. Osuji et al. [6] studied the multi-objective transportation problem based on fuzzy optimization. Zhang et al. [7] proposed a generalized shortest path algorithm for solving optimal transportation routes based on the multimodal transport model established by Reddy. Wei et al. [8] considered the time-varying conditions of cost, transit time, and risk in the transportation process, and established the short-circuit model of time-varying multimodal transportation through the deformation of the transportation network and solved it. Zhang et al. [9] established an optimal distribution model for multimodal transport networks, and quantitatively analyzed the rational organization mode of multimodal transport to minimize total costs. Wang et al. [10] proposed an optimization model for transportation modes based on the analysis of the transport characteristics of various transportation modes and presented a solution algorithm. Wei et al. [11] established the shortest time path-transportation cost model for multimodal transportation, and proposed the iterative algorithm to solve the shortest path. Yang et al. [12] studied the multimodal transport model with time windows, proposed a bi-level optimization model, and used ant colony algorithm to achieve path optimization. These studies have established and solved the multimodal transport model for a single logistics transport task under certain conditions, which belongs to the single-objective optimization problem.

From the above analysis, it can be seen that there are still few researches on the multi-objective optimization of logistics multimodal transport planning problems. The research on modeling methods and algorithms still needs to be in-depth. Therefore, based on the previous research [13], this paper intends to investigate multi-objective modeling and solving algorithms for multimodal transport planning. In the previous research, considering the integration of multimodal transport and multi-agent logistics operations with time windows, a multimodal transportation optimization model based on graph structure was established and a two-layer search algorithm was designed to solve it. For further in-depth research, this paper proposes to build a multi-objective optimization model based on a multimodal transport network that considers transportation time and transportation cost in Sect. 2. In Sect. 3, a two-layer multi-objective hybrid Taguchi algorithm is proposed. The numerical examples verify the established models and algorithms in Sect. 4. Section 5 will conclude it.

2 Modeling of Multimodal Transportation

In order to facilitate modeling and analysis, the virtual network is defined as follows. Let $G = (V, E, M)$ be the network graph under consideration. It is the abstraction of logistics nodes and traffic connections in the geographical map under consideration. V is a set of the nodes in the actual logistics transportation network correspond. E is a set of edges, corresponding to all possible transportation paths. M is a collection of transportation modes. To facilitate problem solving, the following assumptions are made.

Hypothesis 1 the same shipment cannot be transported separately;

Hypothesis 2 there are multiple modes of transport between two adjacent transfer stations to choose from, but only one mode of transport can be selected;

Symbol description:

x_{ijm} commodity is shipped at (i, j) with mode m;
c_{ijm} unit shipment price of commodity at (i, j) with mode m;
d_{ijk} shipment length at (i, j) with mode m;
v_m unit shipment velocity for mode m;
tt_{ikl} the unit transfer time from mode k to l at node i;
tc_{ikl} the unit transfer cost from mode k to l at node i;
ω_i^{kl} changing sign from mode k to l at node i;
q_{ijm} Commodity volume at (i, j);
D_i Schedule time at node i, $D_i = 0$ for no schedule time;

$G = (V, E, M)$ is a multimodal transport network with time windows, which includes reducing total transportation time and transportation costs. The decision variables are x_{ijm} and ω_i^{kl}. The multi-objective optimization model with the goal of transportation cost and transportation time is as follows:

$$Z_1 = \min\left\{ \sum_{ij} \sum_m c_{ijm} q_{ijm} d_{ijm} x_{ijm} + \sum_{ij} \sum_i \sum_{kl} q_{ijm} \omega_i^{kl} tc_{ikl} \right\}$$

$$Z_2 = \min\left\{ \sum_{ij} \sum_m d_{ijm}/v_m + \sum_{ij} \sum_i \sum_{kl} \max(D_i, q_{ijm} tt_{ikl}) \right\} \qquad (1)$$

S.T.

$$\sum_j q_{ijm} - \sum_i q_{jim} = \begin{cases} Q & if\ i = O \\ -Q & if\ i = D \quad \forall\ i \in V,\ m \in M \\ 0 & otherwise \end{cases} \qquad (2)$$

$$\max(D_i, q_{ijm} tt_{ikl}) + d_{ijm}/v_m - A_j = 0 \ \forall \ i, j \in V, \ (i, j) \in E, \ m \in M \tag{3}$$

$$l_i \le A_i \le u_i, \ \forall \ i \in V \tag{4}$$

$$\sum_m x_{ijm} \le 1 \ \forall \ (i, j) \in E, \ m \in M, \tag{5}$$

$$\omega_i^{kl} = \begin{cases} 1 & k \ne l \\ 0 & k = l \end{cases}, \tag{6}$$

$$x_{ijm} \in \{0, \ 1\} \ \forall \ (i, j) \in E, \ m \in M. \tag{7}$$

The first optimization objective function in Eq. (1) is to reduce the total transportation cost, and the second optimization goal is to reduce the total transportation time. Equation (2) is the traffic balance condition in the network flow. Formula (3) ensures the tolerance of time requirements. Equation (4) represents that the node should meet the predetermined time window constraints. Formula (5) indicates that there is at most one transport mode for each link. The values of variables (6) and (7) are limited.

3 Multi-objective Genetic Algorithm Based on Time Window

In order to make the multimodal transportation model closer to the real scene, we studied the customized time window, the transportation distances of different transportation modes, different transportation speeds, the conversion costs and conversion time of different nodes, which is different from the previous issue of multimodal transportation routes. There are multiple edges between some nodes. Moreover, once the mode of transportation has changed at certain nodes, additional conversion costs and time are still included. The problem has become very complicated, and the key is to find it difficult to find a best multimodal transport network. Therefore, a two-layer multi-objective hybrid Taguchi algorithm is proposed to find the optimal transport path.

The dual-layer multi-target hybrid Taguchi algorithm consists of two layers. The upper layer aims to find the overall global optimal Pareto frontier and transportation mode, while the lower layer searches for the local optimal Pareto frontier of the fixed path and transport mode. The lower level optimization method determines the upper feasible solution space. The multimodal transport path problem model can be reduced to the following two-level multi-objective optimization problem.

$$\min_{(x_{ijm}, \omega_i^{kl})} Z = \{Z_1, Z_2\}$$

S.T.

$$\omega_i^{kl} \in \arg \min_{\omega_i^{kl}} \{Z_1, Z_2\}, \tag{8}$$

$$\sum_j q_{ijm} - \sum_i q_{jim} = \begin{cases} Q & if\ i = O \\ -Q & if\ i = D \\ 0 & otherwise \end{cases} \forall\ i \in V,\ m \in M, \qquad (9)$$

$$\max(D_i, q_{ijm}tt_{ikl}) + d_{ijm}/v_{ijm} - A_j = 0,\ \forall\ i, j \in V,\ (i, j) \in E,\ m \in M, \qquad (10)$$

$$l_i \le A_i \le u_i,\ \forall\ i \in V, \qquad (11)$$

$$\omega_i^{kl} = \begin{cases} 1 & k \ne l \\ 0 & k = l \end{cases}, \qquad (12)$$

$$\sum_m x_{ijm} \le 1\ \forall\ (i, j) \in E,\ m \in M, \qquad (13)$$

$$x_{ijm} \in \{0, 1\}\ \forall\ (i, j) \in E, m \in M. \qquad (14)$$

3.1 Solution Algorithm for the Upper Level

The task of this layer is to find the global Pareto frontier and provide effective and feasible transport paths for the lower levels. As far as multimodal transport path optimization is concerned, if network agents have only one mode of transport to choose from, the shortest path algorithm should be the optimal solution. Taking into account the existence of various modes of transport, it is very difficult to directly apply the k shortest path algorithm. To this end, multimodal transport networks are transformed, standardized, and weighted.

Algorithm 1. Initial feasible path population generation
Step 1: Read the data of the multimodal network.
Step 2: Calculate the normalized weighting matrix according to the weights
Step 3: Calculate k shortest paths using the K-shortest path algorithm
Algorithm 2. Check and replace operation
Step 1: If the path is feasible, stop it;
Step 2: Generate a random weight factor. Calculate normalization matrix and apply K shortest path algorithm to calculate k shortest paths;
Step 3: Select a feasible path from the K feasible paths to replace the infeasible path.

3.2 Optimization Algorithm for the Lower Transportation Mode

Since the position of the Pareto front before the optimization is not known, it is hoped that the chromosomes of the initial population can be evenly dispersed throughout the feasible solution space, and there is a potential advantage of using the Taguchi experimental method to generate these chromosomes.

Algorithm 3. Generation of the initial population of transport modes
Step 1: Read the path provided by the upper layer

Step 2: All the edges in the path have the same transport method available? If applicable, apply to select chromosomes and go to step 4. If not, go to step 3

Step 3: Divide the path into several sections based on the same available transport method. Sides with the same available transport methods are connected together. Each section chooses its own orthogonal table.

Step 4: Calculate the shipping cost and time for each chromosome.

Step 5: Sort the chromosomes according to the fast non-dominated sorting method.

Step 6: Select the chromosome based on chromosome rankings.

The Taguchi experiment method also incorporates crossovers in order to inherit good genes from the father. This article uses a two-level orthogonal array with l factors, where l is the length of the feasible path. Two levels correspond to the parents of two chromosomes.

Algorithm 4. Crossing based on taguchi experimental method

Step 1: Randomly select the parents of the two paired pools;

Step 2: Select the orthogonal table according to the length of the chromosome;

Step 3: Use orthogonal experiments to generate progeny;

Step 4: Sort children according to the fast non-dominated sorting method;

Step 5: Select two chromosomes based on the chromosomes.

3.3 Two-Level Multi-target Taguchi Genetic Algorithm

Based on the above analysis, the two-level multi-object Taguchi genetic algorithm can be summarized as follows.

Algorithm 5. Bi-level multi-target Taguchi genetic algorithm

Step 1: Read the array and graphics structure. Read the initial value of all parameters.

Step 2: parameter settings: For the upper level, including population size, crossover rate and mutation rate. For the lower layer, population size, crossover rate, mutation rate

Step 3: Apply algorithm 1 to generate the initial population of feasible paths

Step 4: Upper Population Evolution

If (stopping conditions are not met) proceed

Start

Step 4.1: Apply Algorithm 3 to generate the initial population of transport methods for each feasible path

Step 4.2: Lower population evolution

If (stopping conditions are not met) proceed

Start

Step 4.3: Select: Select chromosomes to cross, crossover probability. Continue to choose until the number of selected chromosomes is half of it.

Step 4.4: Crossover: Crossing selected chromosomes using algorithm 4

Step 4.5: Variation: The probability of variation in each chromosome

Step 4.6: Sort all chromosomes using fast non-dominated sorting

Step 4.7: Keep the next generation of the previous chromosome

End
Step 5: Select: Intersect each chromosome with crossover probability. Continue to choose until the selected number of chromosomes reach to half of it
Step 6: Cross: Crosses the selected chromosome. If the crossed path is feasible, then go to Step 8
Step 7: Execute Algorithm 2
Step 8: Variation: The probability that each chromosome will mutate. If the crossover path is feasible, then go to Step 10.
Step 9: Execute Algorithm 2
Step 10: Use the fast non-dominated sorting method to sort all chromosomes
Step 11: Preserve the next chromosome of the next generation
End

4   Numerical Simulation

In order to verify the models and algorithms constructed, based on the logistics network in Eastern China, it is assumed that there are a batch of containers that need to be transported. The transport can be carried out in 35 city nodes. The transportation methods include roads, railways and waterways, but not all cities have three links. An example was constructed with 35 nodes and 136 edges. Figure 1 shows the map of logistics and transportation in eastern China. Many major cities along the Yangtze River rely on waterways, railroads and trucks for transportation. There is a simple and effective model in the multimodal network environment. The model can provide some good trade-off solutions. These nodes next to the Yangtze River can be connected to each other by barges, such as to nodes 1, 3, 9, ..., 93. The following parameters $G_1 = 220$, $p_{c1} = 0.1$, $p_{m1} = 0.1$, $G_2 = 50$, $p_{c2} = 0.2$ and $p_{m2} = 0.2$ are used in the simulation. The stop condition is simply to reach the highest iteration of the predetermined upper and lower levels. The two predetermined maximum iterations are 20 generations.

Fig. 1. Logistics transportation network in China eastern region

There are three common modes of transportation, namely roads, railways and waterways. The total transportation costs include transportation costs and transportation costs.

The mode of transportation determines the cost of transportation. Transit costs include labor costs and equipment costs during transportation. The transfer container is a standard container, 8 feet high, 8 feet wide and 20 to 55 feet long. Containers can be transported by trucks, railroads and barges. In general, containers can hold 15 tons. Because there is no universal standard to describe the shipping rate, transshipment rate, transportation speed and transit time. This article uses the relevant data provided by [14] as the basis for calculation, as shown in Tables 1, 2 and 3. The transport rates and speeds given in Table 1 are shown in Tables 2 and 3, respectively.

Table 1. Transportation rates and speed

Transportation rates (USD dollars/container)	High way	Rail way	Water
Cost (USD dollars)	0.90	0.3510	0.1234
Speed (miles/hour)	42	37	6.7

Table 2. Transfer rate (cost for each container)

	High way	Rail way	Water
High way	0	58	100
Rail way	58	0	100
Water	100	100	0

Table 3. Transfer time (time for each container)

	High way	Rail way	Water
High way	0	0.1	0.17
Rail way	0.1	0	0.17
Water	0.17	0.17	0

Consider one task is 1000 containers from node 1 (Shenzhen) to node 93 (Dandong). The goods are more focused on the quality of transportation. Assuming that the transportation continues until it reaches the destination, simulations are performed. The results are shown in Fig. 2. The Pareto solution and other non-dominated optimal solutions are given in the figure. These solutions become alternatives to the carrier's decision. The carrier needs to select according to the shipper's requirements (Table 4).

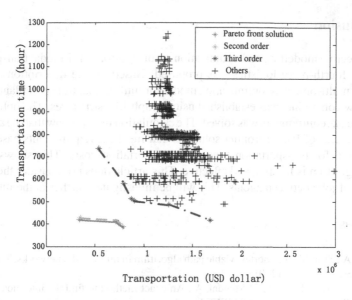

Fig. 2. No-dominated solution plan

Table 4. Transportation path and manner from Shenzhen to Dandong

Plan	Transportation path and manner	Cost (USD Dollars)	Time (hours)
1	1-9-10-15-31-32-33-47-45-44-43-51-56-62-69 -74-75-80-89-85-84-93 Water-Water-Water-Water-Water-Rail-Rail-Rail-Rail-Rail-Rail-Rail-Rail-Rail-Rail-Rail-Rail-Rail-Rail-Rail-Rail	7.9405 e + 005	388.35
2	1-10-15-31-46-47-48-50-57-56-62-69-74-75-8 0-89-85-84-93 Water-Water-Water-Water-Water-Rail-Rail-Rail-Rail-Rail-Rail-Rail-Rail-Rail-Rail-Rail-Rail	7.156 e + 005	412.97
3	1-10-15-31-32-46-45-44-50-57-56-62-69-74-7 5-80-89-85-84-93 Water-Water-Water-Water-Water-Rail-Rail-Rail-Rail-Rail-Rail-Rail-Rail-Rail-Rail-Rail-Rail-Rail	7.4644 e + 005	403.81
4	1-9-10-15-31-46-58-93 Water-Water-Water-Water-Water-Water-Water	3.4699 e + 005	419.68
5	1-9-10-15-31-46-45-44-50-51-56-62-69-74-75 -80-89-85-84-93 Water-Water-Water-Water-Water-Rail-Rail-Rail-Rail-Rail-Rail-Rail-Rail-Rail-Rail-Rail-Rail-Rail	7.5566 e + 005	404.52

5 Conclusion

A multi-objective modelling and optimization algorithm for multi-modal transport optimization of fourth-party logistics was proposed. Based on the description of model problems, a multi-objective optimization model for multimodal transport planning with time window constraints was established using graph-like structures. The optimization of different task requirements was solved. The calculation results show that the algorithm can solve a series of Pareto frontier solutions that meet the requirements based on the user's demand for transportation time and transportation costs. This shows that the proposed algorithm is feasible and effective. This article does not consider the issue of the transfer of jobs between agents. This will be investigated further in the future.

References

1. Lozano, A., Storchi, G.: Shortest viable path algorithm in multimodal networks. Transp. Res. Part A **35**(3), 225–241 (2001)
2. Boussedjra, M., Bloch, C., EI Moudni, A.: An exact method to find the intermodal shortest path. In: Proceedings of the 2004 IEEE International Conference on Networking, Sensing & Control, Taiwan, China (2004)
3. Brands, T., Wismans, L.J.J., Berkum, E.C.V.: Multi-objective optimization of multimodal passenger transportation networks: Coping with demand uncertainty. In: Papadrakakis, M., Karlaftis, M.G., Lagaros, N.D. (eds.) An International Conference on Engineering and Applied Sciences Optimization, Kos Island, Greece, 4–6 June 2014, pp. 547–561 (2014)
4. Brands, T., Berkum, E.C.V.: Performance of a genetic algorithm for solving the multi-objective, multimodal transportation network design problem. Int. J. Transp. **2**(1), 1–20 (2014)
5. Zhang, Y., et al.: A bi-objective model for uncertain multi-modal shortest path problems. J. Uncertainty Anal. Appl. **3**(8), 1–17 (2015)
6. Osuji, G.A., Okoli Cecilia, N., Opara, J.: Solution of multi-objective transportation problem via fuzzy programming algorithm. Sci. J. Appl. Math. Stat. **2**(4), 71–77 (2014)
7. Yunhe, Z., Dong, L.B.L., Hongyan, G.: Research on a generalized shortest path method of optimizing intermodal transportation problems. J. China Railway Soc. **28**(4), 22–26 (2006)
8. Wei, H., Li, J., Liu, N.Z.: An algorithm for shortest path with multimodal in time - varying network. Chin. J. Manag. Sci. **14**(4), 56 (2006)
9. Jianyong, Z., Yaohuang, G.: A multimodal transportation network assignment model. J. China Railway Soc. **24**(4), 114–116 (2002)
10. Tao, W., Gang, W.: A combined optimization model for transportation modes of multimodal transport. Eng. Sci. **7**(10), 46–50 (2005)
11. Zhong, W., Jinsheng, S., Ailing, H., et al.: Research on model of the shortest time path and transport cost in multimodal transportation. Eng. Sci. **8**(8), 61–64 (2006)
12. Wendong, Y., Wenfang, W.: Analyzing and modeling of multimodal transportation with time window. J. Nanjing Unv. Aeronaut. Astronaut. **41**(1), 111–115 (2009)
13. Guiwu, X., Yong, W.: Optimization algorithm of multimodal transportation with time window and job integration of multiagent. J. Syst. Eng. **26**(3), 379–387 (2011)
14. Manuel, D., Rossetti, H.N.: WebShipCost - Intermodal Transportation Linkage Cost Assessment Via the WWW. The Mack-Blackwell Transportation Center (2005)

Big Data Analytics

The Research of 3D Power Grid Based on Big Data

Bing He$^{(\boxtimes)}$, Jin-xing Hu, and Ge Yang

Shenzhen Institutes of Advanced Technology, CAS, Shenzhen, China
bing.he@siat.ac.cn

Abstract. The visual graphics can reflect the hiding relationships between different data by color, location, and the topological structure. This paper proposes a 3D power grid framework by integrating big data and 3D visualization technologies to achieve flexible, multidimensional, dynamic, and panoramic display of power data. The proposed framework consists of data acquisition, data analysis and mining and 3D visualization module. We detailed the 3D method from modeling, management and visualization techniques, and analyzed the modeling elements from geospatial data, electric graphic data, electric attribute data and data mining result dataset. Finally, we give two scenarios of 3D power system. Most of tools used in this paper are open source software. This can ensure the system stability, flexible and easy to use for the management of large distributed data resources and avoid duplication system development.

Keywords: Geospatial database · Time series data · CityGML
Power GIS

1 Introduction

As the power system becomes more and more complex and complicated, the control of the safe and stable operation of power grid becomes very complicated. In order to improve the operation level of power grid, the power system imposes higher requirements on high-performance computing and visualization technologies. But, due to the heterogeneous nature of power systems, it's difficult to achieve interoperation between various power databases. This results in the phenomenon of information islands [1]. However, a new trend in IT service is managing, analyzing and visualizing the multi-source power big data by high-performance computer clusters to construct smart power grid [2–5]. Big data has 4 V characteristics, focusing on the fusion, analysis and mining of multi-source and multi-type data. It has high data throughput speed, distributed computing, and multi-source data association mining analysis capabilities. Therefore, the characteristics of big data technology fit the needs of massive power data analysis and calculation.

Currently, 2D visualization technology has been widely used in the power industry. The power data is displayed by two-dimensional lines, charts, scatter plots and images [6, 7], or by geographic information system (GIS) [8–10]. However, big data technology and GIS technology have been decentralized in the power sector. Also, 2D GIS is based on two-dimensional abstract graphical symbols, which have limited ability to

© Springer Nature Singapore Pte Ltd. 2018
K. Li et al. (Eds.): ICSEE 2018/IMIOT 2018, CCIS 924, pp. 89–98, 2018.
https://doi.org/10.1007/978-981-13-2384-3_9

present information to users. And it's difficult to accurately deal with many 3D problems in 2D GIS. Therefore, if the high-performance computing capability of big data technology can be effectively combined with geographical 3D visualization technology, the real-time power grid operation and control will become clear, intuitive and effective. Therefore, this paper represents a power grid framework based on big data and 3D technologies to achieve flexible, dynamic visualization of power data.

2   3D Power Data Visualization Framework

This section introduces a framework based on big data technologies and 3D techniques to manage and visualize large amounts of power data. This framework consists of data acquisition and conversion modules, big data platform, power data analysis and mining modules, and 3D visualization modules.

(1) *Data acquisition and conversion modules:* in the proposed framework, power data is mainly extracted from the internal system [11], for example, wide area measurement system, energy management system, device detection and monitoring system, etc. External data is collected from socio-economic, urban population, geographic information system. The two kinds of data are imported into big data platform by three ways. Traditional relational data is converted by Apache Sqoop [12]. Streaming data or timing data is processed by Apache Storm [13]. Unstructured data could be imported by Apache Flume [14]. Specifically, the data which will be managed and processed in big data platform includes power topology elements, 3D models, related attribute data (such as electric equipment information) and geospatial data (e.g. streets, buildings, roads, water, etc.)

(2) *Big data platform:* We use Apache Hadoop [15] to build big data platform. The underlying storage form is HDFS which will be analyzed directly. In order to facilitate the scheduling and management of cluster resources, we adopt YARN [16] as the manager. Above data management module is data processing services, including off-line processing, machine learning, memory computing. Offline processed data can be stored by HBASE [17]. HIVE [18] generates SQL query statement and submits to other analysis and processing modules. Offline processing is mainly used to meet non-real-time requirements. But for time-critical computing, we use memory computing, such as Impala [19] or Spark [20].

(3) *Data analysis and mining modules*: Multi-source heterogeneous data often implies valuable relationship. For this purpose, machine learning library (such as Spark R and Spark Mllib) is employed. Except for providing simple data query and general analysis capabilities, this framework includes the 3D modeling method for domain application, For example, the data mining results of equipment state evaluation, risk assessment, load capacity assessment and fault prediction. The modeling results will be submit to visualization client (such as web browser, desktop 3D viewer) (Fig. 1).

(4) *3D visualization of analysis modules*: 3D visualization module is the core of this framework. It consists of two parts. One part is power data spatialization module, the other is the power data visualization module. Spatialization module access to

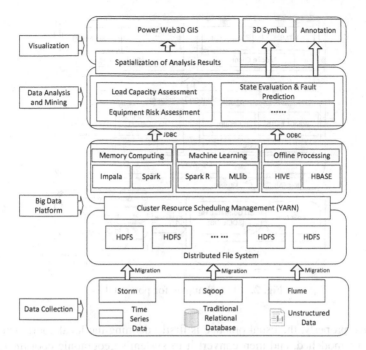

Fig. 1. 3D power data visualization framework

power big data platform through JDBC, ODBC or Hive. The spatialized objects include data mining and analysis results and static attribute data. Then, the spatialized results are transferred into three-dimensional symbols (such as points, lines, and surfaces) and annotations. Finally, three-dimensional client utilizes digital terrain models, remote sensing images, power equipment, 3D symbols and annotations to construct a panoramic virtual scene.

3 3D Techniques

Comparing with the 2D power GIS, 3D modelling process is complex and requires a combination of different software to construct power and geospatial objects. This section will detail the visualization techniques for 3D power system (Fig. 2).

3.1 Modeling Techniques

- SketchUp [21] is an open source software for 3D modelling. It has been used in a wide range of applications such as architectural and civil design. Power tower and electric equipment can be easily modelled in SketchUp. However, due to lack of geographical projection information, 3D models created by SketchUp can't be directly import into 3D power system. In order to ensure that the model can be

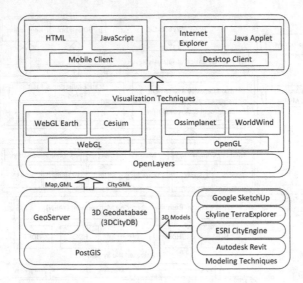

Fig. 2. 3D techniques for power GIS

displayed properly, the usual practice is firstly defining the local coordinates of the area to be modelled, and then convert it to system's geographic coordinate.

- Skyline TerraExplorer Pro [22], ESRI CityEngine [23] are two commercial 3D GIS desktop viewer and creator. They provide a wide range of powerful terrain analysis tools to improve decision making. They can manage and visualize geospatial features, imageries, elevation raster, urban models and dynamic objects. These data could be published and utilized by web or desktop client. Secondary development power 3D system could have rich functionality based on this two software, and the development process is easier.

- 3D GIS has been used to the acquisition, management, analysis in macroscopic geographical environment, and show buildings generalization appearance and location. It's unable to obtain further constructional details (such as indoor pattern, various pipelines and facilities configuration and materials, etc.). The inner components of 3D objects haven't explicit spatial relationship. This results in today's power 3D GIS staying in viewing three-dimensional appearance. For the city power 3D map based on big data technologies, the detailed power information is very helpful for power management staff to know the panorama operation status of power network. Autodesk Revit [24] software is a such tool to build Building Information Modelling (BIM). In order to achieve three-dimensional multi-scale power map visualization, it needs BIM models integrated into 3D GIS.

3.2   3D Geospatial Database

With the growth of 3D power models, it's need effective storage and management tools. Meanwhile, in order to support data access into big data platform, the 3D model management method should be migrated to web environment, and ultimately realizing

3D models sharing. Currently model data management often adopts relational database such as SQL Server, Oracle, and associates model files with database to achieve read and display. For the model retrieval, each model will be classified, labelled and added property, and then establish text index database to achieve quick search. This method is inefficient. It requires an efficient way for large data management in big data platform.

The 3D City Database (3DCityDB) is a free Open Source package consisting of a database schema and a set of software tools to import, manage, analyse, and visualize virtual 3D city models according to the CityGML standard. 3D power models can be transformed to CityGML. The geometry, topology, semantics between the different classes of the power objects are kept in the CityGML file. Then, 3DCityDB import tool could be used to save the CityGML file into relational database, and tile the large, complex 3D power objects to easily visualize in virtual globes like Google Earth or Cesium WebGlobe.

3.3   Web3D Visualization

Common 3D power system is tightly coupled to the 3D commercial software. It's difficult for sharing modules between different power systems and departments. For the cross-platform demand, there are two techniques to achieve 3D visualization in web browser. One is based on WebGL, the other is based on OpenGL. Each produces corresponding visualization software or library.

Cesium [26] and WebGL Earth [27] are two types of JavaScript library for creating 3D globes and 2D maps in a web browser without a plugin. They provide a mechanism to inserting interactive maps into webpages. They use WebGL for hardware-accelerated graphics. The power 3D objects in the format of CityGML are viewable. The geospatial data sources of 3D power GIS can be other web map services as well as image tiles services. Power management staff can rotate and zoom in or out on the globe, or even tilt the viewing angle.

World Wind [28] and ossimPlanet [29] are based on object-oriented programming language. They are open source. World Wind is a Java library and uses satellite imagery and elevation data to allow users to experience earth terrain in visually rich 3D. ossimPlanet is a C++ library. It supports native file access to a wide variety of geospatial data sets - including raster, vector, and view elevation data sets and OGC Web Mapping Services over the web (Fig. 3).

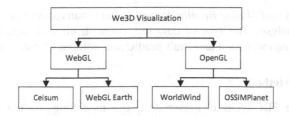

Fig. 3. 3D visualization in web browser

4 Power 3D GIS Modeling

4.1 Modeling Elements

In the general power system, geographic and power data are visualized by 2D geometries, colors and symbols, and the power assessment results are pie charts, bar charts, graphs. Power management staff can't grasp the spatial distribution of analysis results. In this paper, power 3D data will be divided into four categories: geospatial data, electric graphic data, electric attribute data and power analysis and data mining result dataset.

(1) *Geospatial data*: geospatial data is mainly used to build a three-dimensional virtual scene, including DEM, remote sensing images and other geographic features, such as buildings, roads, bridges, and related information. There data will be modelled by 3D software and saved into 3D database. Based on LOD technology and spatial indexing technology, the display efficiency can be improved (Fig. 4).

Fig. 4. 3D visualization of geographic data

(2) *Electric graphic data*: this type of data includes geographic wiring diagram for power facilities such as (overhead lines, cable lines), equipment (substations, switching stations, towers, substations, transformers, switches, etc.). The other three types of data could be associated with electric graphic data to build a 3D panoramic visualization environment (Fig. 5).

(3) *Electric attribute data:* include monitoring data, power sales data, social statistics, and etc.

(4) *Data Analysis and Mining Results*: Power system management process involves a lot of data analysis. This type of data sets comes from load capacity assessment, equipment state evaluation and fault prediction, equipment risk assessment, etc.

4.2 Modeling Method

According to the 3DCityDB characteristics, the modelling method includes static symbols and dynamical spatialization. When static symbolization, different types of visualization objects will be separately established the appropriate static symbol library, and stored into 3D model database. The visualization process of these types of objects

Fig. 5. 3D modeling of power devices

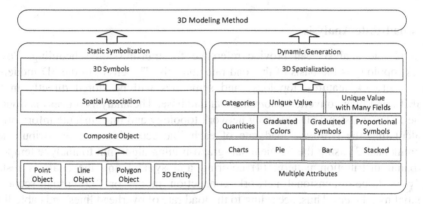

Fig. 6. 3D modeling method for power system

will be displayed by setting colors, geometries and symbol size by analysed data value. Dynamic spatialization is used to visualize the data analysis and mining results. The obtained graphics data sets will be directly graded and classified for visualization. The spatialization method includes inverse distance weighted method, ordinary kriging, cubic splines, and etc. The visualization method includes categories (unique value, unique value with many Fields), quantities (graduated colors, graduated symbols, proportional symbols), charts (pie, bar, stacked), and multiple attributes (Fig. 6).

5 Scenarios

This section will describe the using of 3D power visualization framework in the following two scenarios:

5.1 Operation State Monitoring of Power Grid

The sensors deployed in the power network can real-time access the status of related equipment. The acquired data is based on the form of flow and time series. This paper uses Storm to process it. According to the purpose of the application, the visualization method is divided into three types: abnormal state detecting, real-time operation state visualization, post hoc analysis. During the abnormal status detecting process, the abnormal value combine with the devices coordinate will be transmit to visualization client and symbolized by abnormal types to achieve equipment malfunction status alerts. Real-time status could be visualized by time interval and associated with the observed value of the related equipment and power lines. The status value need to the space-time transformation to convert the indicator data or time data into three-dimensional space, and the format index axis is the Z-axis three-dimensional graphics, and can also be used hierarchical, categorical displayed. The post hoc analysis is focused on the need for large amounts of data analysis requirements. According to the specified interval, the analysis results will be symbolized, colored and loaded into 3D scene.

5.2 Load Rate Analysis

Line load rate analysis can provide reference for transmission scheduling. Power network topology is the basis of the load rate analysis. Therefore, in the 3D modeling process, network features, topology, and semantics will be stored directly in the CityGML, and then converted into relational database. The analysis process is divided into the following steps: (1) obtaining network topology and line attribute information; (2) calculating the real-time load rate of each line according to line attribute and measurements; (3) using the frequent sub-graph mining algorithm to analyze temporal and spatial distribution pattern; (4) coloring and symbolizing the analysis results directly in three-dimensional network connection model or 3D virtual scene as geospatial map layers. Thus, according to the load rate of overhead lines and cable lines and taking the value as the Z-axis coordinate, the results can be dynamical visualized by line types, width, colors, or the combinations form. As well, the continuous-time mining results can constitute a three-dimensional time-series map animation, and shown the change of load rate, as well as spatial distribution at different time periods (Fig. 7).

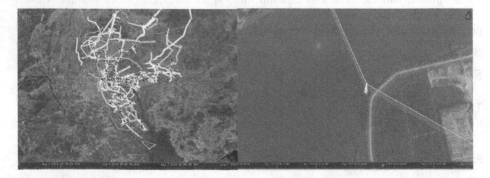

Fig. 7. Dynamic visualization of load status

6 Conclusions

Considering the drawback of common 2D power system, this paper proposes a 3D power visualization framework based on big data technologies and 3D modeling techniques to achieve flexible display of large multidimensional power data in dynamic panoramic scene. The proposed framework consists of data acquisition and conversion, big data platform, power data analysis and mining, and 3D spatialization of analysis results. Then, we detailed the visualization techniques and modeling elements in 3D power system from geospatial data, electric graphic data, electric attribute data and power analysis and data mining result dataset. Finally, we give two use case of power system. Most of the mentioned tools and software are open source and integrated together to ensure high performance and presentation capabilities of the 3D framework while avoiding unnecessary duplication of development work. This research can guide researchers and power company for the development of 3D big data power system.

Acknowledgment. The work described in this paper is supported by the National High Technology Research and Development Program of China (863 Program) (2015AA050201), and the Chinese National Natural Science Foundation (41701167) and (6433012). We gratefully acknowledge the valuable cooperation and help of Guangzhou Power Supply Co. Ltd.

References

1. Liu, Q.: Data fusion and application of power equipment based on big data on Panorama. Informatization Constr. (9), 63–65 (2015)
2. Zhou, J.Z., Hu, R.Q.Y., Qian, Y.: Scalable distributed communication architectures to support advanced metering infrastructure in smart grid. IEEE Trans. Parallel Distrib. Syst. **23**(9), 1632–1642 (2012)
3. Fang, X., Yang, D.J., Xue, G.L.: Evolving smart grid information management cloudward: a cloud optimization perspective. IEEE Trans. Smart Grid **4**(1), 111–119 (2013)
4. Vu, H., Liu, J.K., Huang, X.: A secure cloud computing based framework for big data information management of smart grid. IEEE Trans. Cloud Comput. **3**(2), 233–244 (2014)
5. Maheshwari, K., Birman, K., Wozniak, J., Zandt, D.V.: Evaluating cloud computing techniques for smart power grid design using parallel scripting. In: Proceedings of 2013 13th IEEE/ACM International Symposium on Cluster, Cloud and Grid Computing (CCGrid), Persistent Link, pp. 319–326 (2013)
6. Ravikumar, G., Pradeep, Y., Khaparde, S.A.: Graphics model for power systems using layouts and relative coordinates in CIM framework. IEEE Trans. Power Syst. **28**(4), 3906–3915 (2013)
7. W.Zhangjin,H.Xingwen,D.Ying,Z.Rui,Z.Qingguo, "A CGI + AJAX + SVG based monitoring method for distributed and embedded system," in Proc. 2008 IEEE 1st Int. Conf. UBI-Media Computing,2008,pp. 144–148
8. Tang, K., Zhong, Y.J., Wu, H.F., He, P.Y., Xu, L.J., Qi, W.Q.: Design and implementation of GIS basic data quality management tools for power network. Electr. Power Inf. Commun. Technol. **14**(2), 98–101 (2016)
9. Bai, Y.Q., Nie, J., Chen, Y., Li, Z., Chen, T.: Construction of GIS platform for Chongqing grid. J. Geomatics **37**(5), 73–75 (2012)

10. Wei, W., Liu, B.H., Dai, J.Z., Xia, H., Li, Z.: Design and implementation of GIS-based Wuhan Grid management systems. China Electr. Power **37**(1), 161–163 (2009)
11. Zhang, D.X., Miao, X., Liu, L.P., Zhang, X., Liu, K.Y.: Research on development strategy for smart grid big data. Proc. CSEE **35**(1), 2–12 (2015)
12. Apache Sqoop. http://sqoop.apache.org/
13. Apache Storm. http://storm.apache.org/
14. Apache Flume. http://flume.apache.org/
15. Apache Hadoop. http://hadoop.apache.org/
16. YARN. http://hadoop.apache.org/docs/current/hadoop-yarn/hadoop-yarn-site/YARN.html
17. HBASE. http://hbase.apache.org/
18. HIVE. http://hive.apache.org/
19. Impala. http://impala.io/
20. Spark. http://spark.apache.org/
21. SketchUp. http://www.sketchup.com/
22. Skyline TerraExplorer Pro. http://www.skylinefrance.com/en/home
23. ESRI CityEngine. http://www.esri.com/software/cityengine/
24. Autodesk Revit. http://www.autodesk.com/products/revit-family/ overview
25. 3D City Database. http://www.3dcitydb.org/3dcitydb/3dcitydbhomepage/
26. Cesium. https://cesiumjs.org/
27. WebGL Earth. http://www.webglearth.com/
28. World Wind. https://goworldwind.org/
29. ossimPlanet. https://trac.osgeo.org/ossim/

Identifying Service Gaps from Public Patient Opinions Through Text Mining

Min Tang[1], Yiping Liu[1(✉)], Zhiguo Li[1], and Ying Liu[2]

[1] School of Management, Chongqing Technology and Business University,
Chongqing 400067, China
tangmin@ctbu.edu.cn, 466952855@qq.com
[2] School of Engineering, Cardiff University, Cardiff, CF24 3AA, UK

Abstract. Nowadays, healthcare systems have become increasingly patient-centered and the unstructured, open-ended and patient-driven feedback has drawn a significant attention from medical and healthcare organizations. Based on this, we are motivated to harness various machine learning algorithms to process such a large amount of unstructured comments posted on public patient opinion sites. We first used sentiment analysis to automatically predict the concerns of patients from the training set which was already labelled. Then, with the help of the clustering, we extracted the hot topics related to a specific domain to reflect the service issues that patients concern most. Through experimental studies, the performance of different algorithms and the influence of different parameter were compared. Finally, refering to the survey and previous studies, the results were analyzed to obtain the conclusions.

Keywords: Text mining · Sentiment analysis · Clustering analysis
Public health service

1 Introduction

At the present stage, it is widely accepted that collecting, responding and processing the comments from customers is extremely important to the organizations. The feedback from customers has been a crucial source to evaluate the quality of service and products. With the development of the technology, reporting their experience and public opinions on the Internet has become a popular way for patients and customers [1]. In the area of the service industry, large organizations have performed a huge number of studies to discover the reasonable approaches to process the comments from consumers. Sentiment analysis and text mining based on the natural language processing and machine learning algorithms play a critical role in these studies [2]. Obviously, it could be meaningful if sentiment analysis can be conducted in the field of healthcare. Through this, the information of sentiment and emotion can be captured from the textual data of patients' experience. Academic research in this area has largely focused on establishing the models with higher accuracy for 'automatically predicting the sentiment embedded within the text'. Additionally, based on the research of the National Health Service (NHS) (2013) in England, the sentiment analysis witnessed it could become the novel

© Springer Nature Singapore Pte Ltd. 2018
K. Li et al. (Eds.): ICSEE 2018/IMIOT 2018, CCIS 924, pp. 99–108, 2018.
https://doi.org/10.1007/978-981-13-2384-3_10

resource for patients when they were making choice of hospitals. Based on this, the test for patients' satisficing to the service of hospitals will be conducted by analysis a vast amount of textual data on the Patient Opinion website in this project. Three questions will be focused on, which are whether this hospital could be proposed by the specific patient, whether the attitude of the staff is appropriate and whether the waiting time is reasonable.

1.1 Feedback Collection

In recent years, the study of recipient experience has drawn a significant interest. And the researchers continue in the field of extraction and analysis. As introduced by the study performed by Sun and Li (2011), it is important for organizations to collect and analyze the recommendations of customers, since it allows companies to adopt the service to customers' expectations in a developing manner. Based on the research of McAfee and Brynjolfsson (2012), there is five percent growth of productivity and six percent growth of profitability in the companies can process the comments. The technological advances expand the source for hospitals to collect the customer comments. Then the sentiment analysis, which is helpful to assess people's feelings for the services and products, is convenient to be carried out. In addition to these, comparing with the traditional methods, which often have the low response rate [3], the quantity of the materials from the Internet and social media is extremely wide. Above all, the usage of the Internet can obtain the achievement of the wide source, timeliness and convenience.

1.2 Text Analysis

Textual comments have attracted considerable attention for the past few years. Literature highlights that marketing department had used manual and machine learning methods to process the information. The deeper understanding of the comments can be gained if the analysis is performed with the manual manners. However, the review for the huge quantity of text might be inconsistent without 'procedural models' [4].

In terms of the medical service, online health communities and the patient-authored text they contained, accompanied by the potential value, have attracted more and more attention. Graebner et al. (2012) suggested that the major direction of consumer comments analysis with text mining has basically focused on establishing more accurate models for forecasting the sentiment embedded within the textual recommendations. Previous studies showed that the linguistic text mining approaches had better performance than that of manual methods in the categorization of the comments because they performed better in the precision of prediction. In the field of medicine, enterprises like Google Flu [5] and HealthMap [6] have already demonstrated that the PAT (patient-authored text) is a dependable source for illness tracking and medical research. Additionally, websites such as CureTogether and PatientLikeMe have put great effort into the research for effect exerted by the patient opinions on the healthcare service.

A large number of works focused on the sentiment analysis, which was also regarded as opinion mining. It involved the study of the analysis of person's opinion, sentiments to the product, services etc., and the factors influence them. Machine learning means the model is trained on the structure of the data. In terms of sentiment analysis, the literature displays several key aspects of it. The bag-of-words approach can be used to process the text with unigrams, bigrams and trigrams in the analysis. With consideration of potential emotional comments, the sentiment could be determined in several ways by the algorithm. As can be seen in the research of the feedback of the healthcare experience on Twitter in the US, monitoring social media can obtain the meaningful, unsolicited and real-time data, while the traditional survey system cannot capture it. One of the most important reasons is social media can provide the opinions from patients that cannot be obtained from other routes with the cautious observation [7].

Besides those manners of classification, automatic topic detection based on document clustering is an alternative approach for extracting health-related hot topics in online communities [8]. Patterson (2011) illustrated that document clustering is a valid manner to clearly differentiate the groups of clinical narratives. Recently, many studies applied clustering manners to this user-generated medical text to discover the topics that interest patients who post their experience online. The study of Denecke focused on blogs related to healthcare and separated the topics of these blogs into two groups: informative and affective [9]. Brody (2010) processed the texts based on Latent Dirichlet Allocation (LDA) topic models to explore the salient directions of online evaluations of healthcare systems. Therefore, it is valuable to perform the clustering approaches in text mining.

In summary, the main mission of the service industry, such as the healthcare systems, is offering the satisfactory service to meet the requirements of the recipients. Additionally, since people rely increasingly upon the internet and social networks, the amount of the text present online continues to rise sharply, which provides organizations with a source to exploit business intelligence. Moreover, collecting and analyzing consumer comments witness their importance have a continuous increase. Hence improving the service quality based on the advice from the Internet and social media has drawn significant attention because of its vast potential value, outstanding convenience and high efficiency. Previous literature highlights several research limitations, such as the manual preprocess, size of the dataset and the variety of specialities, which also point out the directions of further research.

2 Methodology

The data analysis techniques were conducted to the textual comments from Patient Opinion about the service experience of cancer patients. The objective was to test whether the prediction for patients' views on several topics could be obtained automatically based on their feedback. The machine learning classification approach was chosen and trained from the labelled data, which was regarded as the training group. And the comments can be classified into various categories based on the given examples, with the help of the open-source data mining software—Weka, which had been widely adopted in the previous researches of text mining in many domains. To scale the reliability of the experiments, the results of this research were compared with the quantitative rating provided by the Patient Opinion. There were two domains of the service of healthcare predicted, which were waiting for time and attitude of the staff. In terms of clustering, after converting the textual data into the valid format of Weka, the expectation maximization (EM) clustering was conducted.

2.1 Source of Data and Pre-processing

In this study, Patient Opinion website was used as the data source. Next, the representative comment fields should be determined. Based on the statistical widgets of Patient Opinion, cancer was one of the most common diseases of the comments. There were the tools can analyse the 5 most concerned words mentioned in the feedback for 'What could be improved' in the last week. 'Waiting time' and 'communication', which had the most occurrence, were chosen as the measurements - 'whether the waiting time is reasonable' and 'whether the communication between patients and staffs is unblocked'. Thus, this paper chose cancer patients as research subjects and collects the comments related to waiting time and communication.

In the area of sentiment analysis, we conducted data processing techniques on all the online free-text comments posted by cancer patients about the treatment attitude and waiting time on a Patient Opinion website. The Patient Opinion was asked for helping to collect the textual data as the training set for the research, which included the works like removing the meaningless labels, lowercasing the text and tuning each sentence into a separate line. The texts were split into two parts, which establishes two contents - 'neg' and 'pos'. The comments with positive sentiment labels were stored in 'pos' content. In contrast, the 'neg' content was composed of the negative evaluation. Each comment was an individual file. For clustering analysis, Offline Explorer, one of the web crawler tools, was used to receive all the web pages from the comment platform. Additionally, to obtain the better topic clustering results, some sentences unrelated to the topics were dislodged.

2.2 Sentiment Analysis and Text Classification

Sentiment analysis, which is also named opinion mining, is to process people's opinions and extract the sentiments towards the products and services [10]. Machine learning is about learning from the structure of predefined data and discover the principles and functions can process the unlabelled information [11]. There are two main types of machine learning algorithms, which is supervised and unsupervised respectively. Sentiment analysis or text classification should be involved by supervised fields, which means that the training data should have already had the class labels by the start of the operation. The fundamental process of supervised machine learning method for sentiment analysis was shown in Fig. 1, the labelled data should be provided as the training set and the algorithm can learn and output the trained model. The reliability of the model should be tested with the unlabelled data.

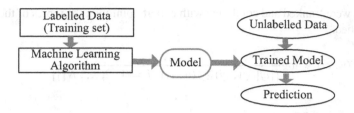

Fig. 1. The fundamental process of supervised machine learning method for sentiment analysis

A large number of different technical methods could be conducted in classification in machine learning. In this paper, 3 popular supervised machine learning algorithms were selected to perform the sentiment analysis, which was 'Naïve Bayes Multinomial' (NBM), Decision Trees and Support Vector Machines.

2.3 Clustering Analysis

Recently, text clustering has been extensively adopted to discover the most concerned topics related to medical service. Since there were a significant amount of medical-related words occur in those comments, UMLS Metathesaurus, which had often been used in previous studies, was adopted to extract medical concepts. As listed in Table 1, the most frequent health-related and service-related concepts were extracted. And all the features' domains used in this research are also shown in Table 1. However, to input the received features to the topic clustering, the results should be quantified as feature vectors, which are characterized by 'high dimensionality, redundancy and high correlation among individual attributes, which is unfavourable for clustering' [12]. Principle component analysis (PCA), which had been proved by many experiments as the effective method to reduce features, was adopted to solve this problem.

Table 1. All the features' domains used in this research

Category	Types of key phrases	Category	Types of key phrases
Keywords	n-gram	Semantic terms	
1-gram		Service domain	Service terms
2-gram		Semantic terms	
Medical domain	Medical terms		

In this paper, one of the typical probability-based clustering-Expectation Maximization (EM) clustering was selected. To enhance the performance of distinguishing the different clusters and identifying the topics from the clusters, many keywords were selected to differentiate the topics. These key phrases were n-gram words and included the medical concepts and terms in service evaluation from UMLS lexicon. Several approaches to extract these keywords had been used, in this paper, they were selected from the function below, where f is the frequency of w in the cluster ci, and the bottom of the formula is 'the total number of clusters with a term w frequency greater than or equal to the term w frequency of the cluster being evaluated'. Once the key phrases have high scores were 'ranked and combined with expert opinions', the topics of the clusters were identified.

$$f(w, ci) * log\frac{N}{|\{cj|f(w, cj) \geq f(w, ci), j = 1, 2, \ldots, N|\}|}$$ (1)

2.4 Performance Measurement

A large number of different technical methods could be conducted in classification in machine learning. In this paper, 3 popular supervised machine learning algorithms were selected to perform the sentiment analysis, which was 'Naïve Bayes Multinomial' (NBM), Decision Trees and Support Vector Machines. The principle of Decision Trees is classifying the data into different classes by 'recursively separating the feature space into two parts and assigning different classes based upon which region in the divided space the sentence is' [13]. The Support Vector Machines method obtains the classes with the help of the support vectors, which represents the boundary of different groups. These vectors are continuously maximized until it is large enough to differentiate the difference [14]. In addition to this, the comparison was also applied to detect which gave the quickest and most accurate outcomes. In feature extraction, the feature matrix was established by separating the sentences and texts into words. Within the matrix, the sentences and texts were the indexes in a row and the column consisted of all of the words occurred in the documents. The measurement of the value was calculated based on the frequency count of each word in each comment, the size of the comment and the occurrence of every word in the whole document. After the matrix had been built up, the feature matrix can be operated by each model to output the results and the performance could also be evaluated. The measurements are accuracy (the percentage of correct outputs from the whole database), F-measure ('the harmonic mean of precision and recall' [11]), Recall index and cost time. Finally, the J48 Decision Trees was selected to process the test set.

3 Results and Discussion

3.1 Sentiment Analysis

To reduce the processing time of classification, the number of words in the learning process was limited to no more than 10,000 based on the frequency of each word. After the experiment, the prediction performance of every method was compared with that of others. The results outputted by Naïve Bayes Multinomial, J48 Decision Trees and Support Vector Machine of 3 domains of healthcare service (overall evaluation to the service, whether the communication is good and whether the waiting time is reasonable) were shown as follow (Tables 2 and 3).

Table 2. The results of the overall evaluation, waiting time, communication and the overall evaluation without 'Stop Word List'

	Overall rating			Waiting time			Communication			Overall rating without 'Stop Word List'		
	NBM	J48	SVM	NBM	J48	SVM	NBM	J48	SVM	NBM	J48	SVM
Accuracy	86.60%	76.30%	78.60%	80.20%	80.30%	81.60%	83.60%	81.60%	80.70%	85.90%	72.60%	72.90%
F-measure	0.87	0.81	0.82	0.83	0.85	0.82	0.85	0.8	0.81	0.85	0.81	0.8
Recall	0.87	0.81	0.82	0.83	0.85	0.82	0.85	0.8	0.81	0.85	0.81	0.8
Time (s)	0.08	226	316	0.03	36	61	0.03	92	106	0.09	252	332

Table 3. The performance of three algorithms in overall evaluation without 'Tokenizer'

NBM	Accuracy	F-measure	Recall	Time	No. of extraction
2-gram	73.60%	0.74	0.74	0.06	2676
3-gram	71.20%	0.71	0.71	0.05	1360
N(1-3)-gram	83.20%	0.84	0.84	0.04	7960
WordTokenizer	83.60%	0.85	0.85	0.03	863
Alphabetic	80.90%	0.85	0.85	0.03	792
J48	Accuracy	F-measure	Recall	Time	No. of extraction
2-gram	72.90%	0.73	0.73	151	2676
3-gram	72.10%	0.71	0.71	140	1360
N(1-3)-gram	82.80%	0.8	0.8	106	7960
WordTokenizer	83.50%	0.8	0.8	92	863
Alphabetic	80.30%	0.8	0.8	87	792

Based on the results, the NBM algorithm observed that it had the best performance in the overall assessment. Then, obviously, the accuracy of 3 approaches changed in the experiment for 'waiting time' and 'communication'. On the one hand, the J48 Decision Trees and Support Vector Machine performed better, which increased roughly 3%. The comparison also suggests that the NBM could perform better with the large database. Conversely, the J48 DT and SVM algorithms could outperform the NBM if the size of the dataset is not large enough. In terms of the influence of 'StopWordList', it displayed that the list had a helpful effect on the work of the algorithms. All 3 methods became more accurate with using the Weka's list of stop words. Moreover, the F-measure and Recall index also increased slightly with the time taken to complete the process becoming less. For the final prediction of the test set (Table 4), there was 77% comments showed the service satisfied the patients, which was fundamentally in a similar range with the quantitative survey and the statistical analysis of Patient Opinion.

Table 4. The results of the trained model

Overall rating	Positive	Negative
Overall	770	230
Waiting time	926	74
Communication	756	244

The results indicate that the output of the sentiment analysis of the comments can be efficient and have reasonable accuracy [15]. And it can accomplish the effective extraction and identification of the critical issues of the review. It can also prove that there are dramatic meaningful information in the unstructured feedback of patients and it could significantly benefit the organizations if processed appropriately. With the help of the sentiment analysis, in both overall view and certain domains, an aggregate evaluation of objectives can be provided.

3.2 Clustering Analysis

In the area of clustering analysis, after pre-processing and features extraction, the EM clustering was conducted by Weka. After operating the EM cluster, the results were organized based on their ranks and semantic relation to the medical care and service evaluation. The final results were displayed as follow (Table 5).

Table 5. Clustering analysis results

Label	Key phrases
Staff	Good, bad, brilliant, excellent, professional, amazing, impressed, shortage
Communication	Respect, lack of efficient, nice, ignore, wait, staff manner
Care	Good, patient, professional, empathy, dignity, compassion, brilliant
Nurse	Nice, excellent, lack, patient, amazing, ignored, professional
End of life	Well treated, respect, appreciate
waiting time (negative)	Hour, still, emergency, appointment
Communication (negative)	Lack of, ignore, rude, waiting

In the 'staff' group, basically, the patients' views to doctors and staffs were satisfactory. There was one word deserved to be mentioned - 'professional', which was mentioned more times in writers' praises than other words. It suggested that the patients may pay more attention to attitudes and skills in the professional field instead of characters and personalities. On the negative side, patients and reporters often criticized the topic of 'shortage', which showed that the shortage of staffs was still the critical problem in the healthcare system. Comparing the topics around 'staff', the second group labelled 'communication' was comprised of features much more specific. 'Respect' and 'efficient' are two domains with which the criticisms were most concerned. There were also 4 words displayed the drawbacks of the communication, which was 'poor', 'ignored', 'lack of' and 'no', and showed the ignorance, might partly as a result of overworked status, of the staffs and nurses is the most serious problem. In terms of 'care' label, it involved the key features of the care service itself and the results observed the similar situation. The praises from patients were almost full of the texts about care and 'patience', 'empathy', 'dignity' and 'compassion' are the aspects with the most concern of recipients. The number of comments about nurses was considerably more than that about other workers in the healthcare systems, which made the nurse become the essential part of the hospitals. Among all of these words, 'patience' played the most important role in service provided by nurses. There was the other special label is 'end of life', which represented the status of cancer patients in their last time. These comments were often written by their relatives and families. The praise also occupied most of the texts and the most important word in this field was 'respect', which suggested, to the patients in their final time, respect was crucial to them.

To discover the drawbacks of the healthcare service, the comments with negative sentiment in the fields of 'waiting time' and 'communication' were selected as our objectives. Obviously, it can be observed that patients with emergency and appointments were more likely to complain about the waiting time. Since the words involve 'hour' were much more the phrases have 'minute'. Therefore, the further study of the limit needs to be performed here. In the area of 'communication', which the ignorance and rude manners of staffs mentioned most times in the comments.

Above all, professional skills of staff, nurses' patience and the manners of communication have drawn the most attention from patients. The shortage of staff, overworked schedules and ignorance for an effective communication are the problems that need to be improved immediately.

4 Conclusion

This work demonstrates that it is possible for organizations to predict the evaluation embedded with the huge amount of comments through sentiment analysis and explore the hot medical related topics through clustering analysis. By conduct these approaches based on text mining, several valuable conclusions can be drawn from the obtained results. Most of the reporters from Patient Opinion have a basically satisfactory experience but the comments mention the 'waiting time' observe that the negative feedback occupies the larger part than the positive group, which is mostly because of the appointment and emergency. Then, in the field of communication, more than 70% of the comments tagged with positive sentiment and efficiency and manners of staff play the crucial roles in communication between patients and hospitals. The criticism for the communication mainly focuses on the ignorance of the help workers. In addition, for nurses, patients and their families, they pay more attention to their patience while doctors and staffs are praised mainly because of their professional skills. Finally, respect plays the most important role in the healthcare for cancer patients in their last days.

References

1. Greaves, F., Millett, C.: Consistently increasing numbers of online ratings of healthcare in England. J. Med. Internet Res. **14**(3), e94 (2012)
2. Tumasjan, A.: Predicting elections with Twitter: what 140 characters reveal about political sentiment. In: Fourth International AAAI Conference on Weblogs and Social Media, Washington DC, pp. 178–185 (2010)
3. Zimlichman, E., Levin-Scherz, J.: The coming golden age of disruptive innovation in health care. J. Gen. Intern. Med. **28**, 865–867 (2013)

4. Ziegler, C., Skubacz, M., Viermetz, M.: Mining and exploring unstructured customer feedback data using language models and treemap visualizations. In: IEEE/WIC/ACM International Conference on Web Intelligence and Intelligent Agent Technology, pp. 932–937. IEEE, Sydney (2008)
5. Ginsberg, J.: Detecting influenza epidemics using search engine query data. Nature **457**, 1012–1014 (2008)
6. Freifeld, C.C.: HealthMap: global infectious disease monitoring through automated classification and visualization of internet media reports. J. Med. Res. **15**, 150–157 (2008)
7. Greaves, F., et al.: Use of sentiment analysis for capture patient experience from free-text comments posted online. J. Med. Internet Res. **15**(11), e239 (2014)
8. Lin, Y., et al.: A document clustering and ranking system for exploring MEDLINE citations. J. Am. Med. Inform. Assoc. **14**, 651–661 (2007)
9. Denecke, K., Nejdl, W.: How valuable is medical social media data? Content analysis of the medical web. Inf. Sci. **179**, 1870–1880 (2009)
10. Pang, B., Lee, L.: Opinion mining and sentiment analysis found. Trends Inf. Retr. **2**(1–2), 1–138 (2008)
11. Ivanciue, O.: Weka machine learning for predicting the phospholipidosis including potential. Curr. Top. Med. Chem. **8**(18), 1691–1709 (2008)
12. Witten, I.H., Frank, E.: Data Mining: Practical Machine Learning Tools and Techniques. Morgan Kaufmann Publishers, San Francisco (2005)
13. Frank, E., et al.: Data mining in bioinformatics using Weka. Bioinformatics **20**(15), 2479–2481 (2004)
14. Li, J., et al.: Discovery of significant rules for classifying cancer diagnosis data. Bioinformatics **19**(Suppl. 2), 1193–2103 (2003)
15. Alemi, F., et al.: Feasibility of real-time satisfaction surveys through automated analysis of patients' unstructured comments and sentiments. Qual. Manag. Health Care **21**(1), 9–19 (2012)
16. Abegaz, T., Dillon, E., Gilbert, J.E.: Exploring affective reaction during user interaction with colors and shapes. Proc. Manuf. **3**(Suppl. C), 5253–5260 (2015)
17. Dong, A., Lovallo, D., Mounarath, R.: The effect of abductive reasoning on concept selection decisions. Des. Stud. **37**(Suppl. C), 37–58 (2015)
18. Evans, P.: From deconstruction to big data: how technology is reshaping the corporation. MIT Technol. Rev. (2015). Stanford, California
19. Hsu, F.-C., Lin, Y.-H., Chen, C.-N.: Applying cluster analysis for consumer's affective responses toward product forms. J. Interdiscip. Math. **18**(6), 657–666 (2015)
20. Chen, R., Xu, W.: The determinants of online customer ratings: a combined domain ontology and topic text analytics approach. Electron. Commer. Res. **17**(1), 31–50 (2017)
21. Holy, V., Sokol, O., Cerny, M.: Clustering retail products based on customer behaviour. Appl. Soft Comput. **60**(Suppl. C), 752–762 (2017)

How to Verify Users via Web Behavior Features: Based on the Human Behavioral Theory

Jiajia Li, Qian Yi[⊠], Shuping Yi, Shuping Xiong, and Su Yang

College of Mechanical Engineering, Chongqing University, Chongqing 400044, China
Yiqian@cqu.edu.cn

Abstract. Nowadays, the Internet has penetrated into people's daily life in many ways, and people usually use the form of web account to carry out web activities. However, the problem of user account being illegally occupied by others has become increasingly prominent, and the security of user account is not guaranteed. On the other side, the network's advantage of recording data easily provides a valuable opportunity to comprehensively record a tremendous amount of human behaviors. Based upon the status and problems, we present an approach to distinguish genuine account owners from intruders. This study constructs a series of web behavior features based on web usage logs, and uses machine learning to identify users based on Bayesian theorem and structural risk minimization criterion. Experiments show that web behavior analysis is a feasible way for user verification.

Keywords: Human behavior · Human web behavior · User verification Machine learning

1 Introduction

With the rapid development of Internet technology, people are becoming more and more inseparable from the Internet. According to the 39th report of CNNIC (China Internet Information Center) "By the end of 2016, the number of netizens in China has reached 731 million, and the total number of new netizens has increased 42 million 990 thousand over the whole year" [1]. The development of mobile Internet has brought great convenience to people's life. It also provides support platform for information sharing, which further reduces transaction costs and facilitates communication. In general, it improves the efficiency of the overall resource utilization. But at the same time, there are also various security problems of network. So far, the common risk we faced is that the user's account number is embezzled. Under the condition of account password leakage, there are some shortcomings in traditional protection methods, which makes user verification become one of the key issues in account security. In order to solve these problems, we decide to use the real time updated web log and adopt the web behavior features which based on the behavior analysis to carry on the continuous security monitoring to the user.

K. Li et al. (Eds.): ICSEE 2018/IMIOT 2018, CCIS 924, pp. 109–120, 2018.
https://doi.org/10.1007/978-981-13-2384-3_11

The field of human web behavior, elucidation of human behavior in the web environment is quickly gaining eminent position [2]. Guo et al. establish a dynamics model of human interest attenuation based on the data of blog releasing. The results show that blog arrival time interval distribution is a mixed distribution with exponential and power-law feature. It demonstrates the variety of human web behavior dynamics [3]. Neelima et al. dig the frequency of users accessing each page, and find users' sessions to analyze users' time spent on a specific page [4]. Zhong et al. calculate the features for every page based on analysis of association rules, then build up a personalized user browsing behavior model [5]. Via click stream analysis, Leung et al. contrast the different behavioral patterns of consumers which during weekdays and weekends [6]. Cui et al. conducts a pioneering research in how to use model or method to represent human behaviors. They mention that forecasting and predicting are major goals in modeling human behaviors, but it also faces various challenges [7]. In most of existing research, some of which discuss web behavior from the time dimension, and others focus on the analysis of the connection between users and browsing pages. But unlike those studies, this paper maps the behavior theory of the real world into the virtual world, so as to explore the user web behavior from different dimensions.

On Classification and Prediction, Lin et al. use three integrated feature sets (EEG + Modeling, EEG + Task, and EEG + Task + Condition) training a linear discriminant analysis classifier, then integrating human behavior modeling and data mining to predict human errors [8]. By leveraging observable information of the user's Twitter feedback, Pennacchiotti and Popescu use Gradient Boosted Decision Trees-GBDT to build user classification model. Finally, automatically infer the values of user attributes, such as political orientation or ethnicity [9]. According to the characteristics of user interaction with the mouse, Feher et al. introduce a method to verifies users [10]. Pao et al. propose a user verification approach based on user trajectories. Such as on-line game traces, mouse traces, handwritten characters, and traces of the movements of animals in their natural environments [11]. These studies not considered user behavior related to physiological and psychological needs comprehensively, therefore, the current methods do not fully reflect the individual differences of users, nor can they guarantee enough effectiveness. Based on the web behavior which is refined by web log analysis, we propose a general user verification approach, which does not require any extra sensing equipment.

Based on the characteristics of individual differences in human web behavior, this paper is no longer just a study of the relationship between users and web pages but make use of Web logs to construct a series of behavior features which are related to user habits, and then, it draws support from two kinds of machine learning methods to verify users identity.

2 Feature Construction

2.1 Human Web Behavior

Human behavior is a meaningful reaction, which is in order to adapt the external environment. Generally speaking, most of these daily activities are some customary patterns of action, besides, people's attitude will change their behavior accordingly when they are in a state of discomfort [12]. In this study, web behavior refers to the action that takes place on human-computer interface when people surf the Internet. Compared with the traditional entity scene, the existence of the web log to make it possible for accurately and comprehensively collection of human behaviors in the absence of other additional equipment. The internal drive of web behavior includes psychological and physiological demands together with the way of thinking, which same as the offline behavior. Moreover, it combined with the constraints on actual conditions can decide the possibility and trend of behavior. In the same way, web behavior also shows five major characteristics as bellows: Adaptability; combined with the work and rest time, user always choose the most convenient time to surf on Internet, besides, the size of browser window is also depend on their vision and operating environment. Relevance; in fact, most of the time user care more about what they are interested in, and the occurrence of web behavior is related to it, meanwhile, it also affects the persistence and frequency of behavior. Diversity; user can perform web browsing, mouse clicking, input text and other multiple forms of action on the human-computer interaction interface. Dynamic and Controllability; If the external environment or user's motivation changes, user can decide whether to change the current action and how to change it.

2.2 Definitions

Based on the above theory, we analyze the web logs of AML (Advanced Manufacturing Technology) to get 13 features of user behavior. The definitions and descriptions of these web behavior features used in this study are given below.

(1) Week: It indicates that the behavior is happened in which day of the week. It transforms by the 'timestamp' which is recorded on web log. First, read the data of 'timestamp' from web log, such as 2017-05-25T19:47:19.123Z. Next, the information of year, month and date was selected. Finally, convert it to 'week'. For example: '2017-05-25T19:47:19.123Z' is transformed into 'Thur'.

(2) Time: It indicates that the behavior is happened in which time of the day. It transforms by the 'timestamp' which is recorded on web logs. First of all, we divide the 24 h of a day into 6 parts, and the partition rule is shown in Table 1. After that, we extract the information in the 'timestamp' which represents hours, and transform it into the Time's value in the end.

Table 1. The partition rule of a day

No.	Time	Hours
1	Before dawn	00:00–06:00
2	Morning	06:00–11:00
3	Noon	11:00–13:00
4	Afternoon	13:00–16:00
5	Evening	16:00–18:00
6	Night	18:00–24:00

For example: '2017-05-25T19:47:19.123Z' is transformed into 'Night'.

(3) W/H: The ratio of width of height of user browser window, and it can reflect the interface shape of human-computer interaction. The size of the browser window is variable, and which is determined by the user's usage habits. We set 5 ranges of this value according to the shape that has appeared, as showed in Fig. 1. The width and height of the browser window are directly recorded by web logs. After calculating their ratios, the results are classified into 5 ranges.

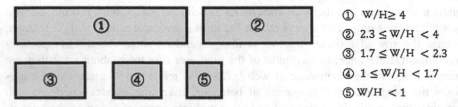

① W/H≥ 4
② 2.3 ≤ W/H < 4
③ 1.7 ≤ W/H < 2.3
④ 1 ≤ W/H < 1.7
⑤ W/H < 1

Fig. 1. The shape of the browser window

(4) P-Web: The ratio of web browsing height to the total height of the web page. It should be noted that the height of user's mouse sliding on a Web page is called web browsing height. Generally, users will browse more content when the page is more consistent with his interests. The height of web browsing and the total height of web page are directly given by web logs.

(5) Event: The type of operation event that user does on web pages. There are 8 types involved in this study, as illustrated in Table 2.

Table 2. The event types of web page

Event	Explain
View	Users browse web pages
Click	Click behavior of the mouse
Behave	Stay for a time on web pages
Fomel	The act of filling out a form
Formsub	The act of submitting a form
Download_paper	Downloading operations
Trail	Mouse movement
Error	Do the wrong operation

(6) Language: The language used by the user for typing. In our study, this feature's value is mostly English or Chinese, which reflects users' habitual language and is related to their living environment.

The features involved in this paper also include:

(7) NumS: It's the number of views of the current session.
(8) UP: The web page where the user is located.
(9) URL: The destination page of a jump in a web site.
(10) Tp: The staying time of a web page.
(11) LTp: The loading time of a web page.
(12) Click-X: The X axis position of the mouse click.
(13) Click-Y: The Y axis position of the mouse click.

The above web behavior features directly or indirectly reflect the characteristics of web behavior. Figure 2 describes the correspondence between the 13 features and the 5 characteristics.

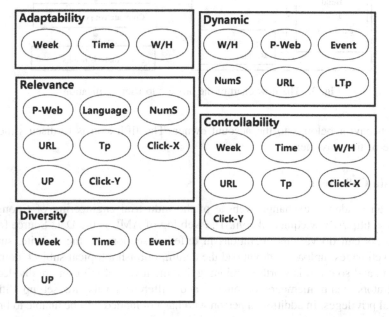

Fig. 2. The correspondence between features and characteristics

3 Methodologies

In this section, we describe the process of user verification and explain the two machine learning methods that we use: Naïve Bayes and Support Vector Machine (SVM). The flow chart of the process is shown in Fig. 3. The process is implemented in five steps. The first step is to obtain the data from the data source, then select the high frequency operation users as the research objects. The second step is to deal with the data according to the principle of feature construction in the Sect. 2. The third step is to further process the data so that it meets the input requirements of machine learning. The fourth step is to use the classifier called Naïve Bayes and SVM to determine whether

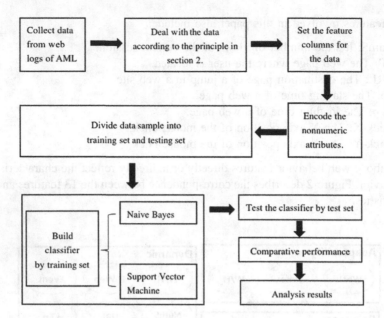

Fig. 3. The flow chart of the process to user verification

the web behavior belongs to the account owner. The fifth step is to discuss the performance of the classifiers.

3.1 Data Collection

AML is an academic exchange website of the industrial engineering of Chongqing University: http://www.cquieaml.com. The web log of AML is the Data Source for our study. Users can do various operations in different sections of the website, such as browse web pages, upload or download the datum, publish a topical subject, comment interaction and so on. It is worth mentioning that the levels of the user are divided into administrators, team members or others, and different levels are set up different functional privileges. In addition, a person who has not landed will be unable to browse the website.

3.2 Classification Model

The essence of user verification is to determine whether users are themselves through web behavior features. It is a problem of binary classification, and the mathematical definitions of the classification problem is as follows:

$$C : C = \{y_1, y_2, \ldots, y_n, \ldots\}$$

The set C represents the set of all categories, y_n represents the category n.

$$I : I = \{x_1, x_2, \ldots, x_m, \ldots\}$$

The elements in set I are waiting to be classified, x_m represents the element m.

There is a mapping rule: $y = f(x_i)$

It makes any $x(x_i \in I)$ has one and only one y ($y_j \in f(x_i)$) corresponded to it. Among them, f is called classifier, and the task of classification algorithm is to construct classifier f.

A. Naïve Bayes

Classification ideology of Naïve Bayes is to solve the probability of occurrence of category $y_j(j = 1, 2\ldots, n, \ldots)$ when element x_i appears. After that, the probable maximum category y will be selected as the category of element x_i. The classification process of Naïve Bayes is divided into three phases, and the specific content arrangements are as follows:

(1) Preparation; above all, the feature attributes are determined and partitioned according to the practical matter, next a part of the elements is selected and classified though known data, in the last step, we take it as a training set. In this phase, the input is all the data to be classified, and the output includes both the feature attributes and the training set. The quality of the features and training samples plays a decisive role in the design of classifier, therefore, this is a crucial phase.
(2) Classifier Design; in this phase, a classifier will be generated after input feature attributes and training dataset. The main work of this phase is not only to calculate the probability of each category in the training set, but also to solve the conditional probability, that is to calculate the probability of occurrence of all categories when the feature $i(i = 1, 2, \ldots, n)$ occurs. Ultimately, the results are recorded to design a classifier.
(3) Application; the test data is used to verify the classification models which build in phase (2).

Naïve Bayes classification is a typical generative learning method which has the advantages of simple logic and easy implementation. Bayes faster than other complex methods in learning and classification, indeed, it has excellent performance in text classification and spam filtering.

B. Support Vector Machine

Support vector machine (SVM) is a binary model by Computing support vector which has strong generalization capability. By the way, it is widely applied into fields such as face recognition and speech recognition. This algorithm maximizes the interval between different types of samples in the feature space by learning a linearity classification facet, and then transforms it into a convex two order programming problem. That means maximizing the interval of two classes of sampling points under constraint conditions. Similar to Naïve Bayes, the classification process of SVM has been three phases: Preparation, Classifier Design and Application. In the second phases, the main task is to find a hyperplane of optimal decision for classification.

3.3 Evaluation Metrics

In this study, we use accuracy and confusion matrix to compare the performance of two classifiers.

A. Accuracy

In general, we utilize accuracy to judge the performance of the classifier. The definition of accuracy is that the ratio of the correct classification numbers to the total samples in a given dataset.

B. Confusion Matrix

Confusion matrixes are usually used to compare the true class and predicted class. In a general way, the class we will focus on is defined as the positive case (+1), and the other classes are negative cases (−1). There are 4 situations about classifiers prediction on the test set, as shown in Table 3.

Table 3. Prediction performance of classifier

	−1(true class)	+1(true class)
−1(predicted class)	True negative(TN)	False negative(FN)
+1(predicted class)	False positive(FP)	True positive(TP)

The interpretations of each symbol are as follows:

TN – The numbers that the model predicts negative sample to negative sample.
FN – The numbers that the model predicts positive sample to negative sample.
FP – The numbers that the model predicts negative sample to positive sample.
TP – The numbers that the model predicts positive sample to positive sample.

The precision, recall and F1-score are common metrics for binary classification.

(1) Precision (P):

$$P = TP/(TP + FP)$$

Precision can measure the correct rate of the model in predicting positive samples.

(2) Recall (R):

$$R = TP/(TP + FN)$$

Recall can measure the reliability of the model in predicting positive samples

(3) F_1-score (F_1):

$$2/F_1 = 1/P + 1/R$$

$$F_1 = 2TP/(2TP + FP + FN)$$

F_1 is a harmonic mean which comprehensive reflects the precision and recall.

4 Experimental Result

Firstly, we collected the web usage log of AML which in the period of May 2017 to March 2018. Secondly, according to the user's operation frequency, the top ten user's data set has been retained. And then, the data are preprocessed by the principle of feature construction in part 2 of this paper. Thirdly, since most of the machine learning methods can only accept the input of quantitative features, we use the encoding method which called One-Hot to convert the non-numeric features into numerical. After that, in order to gain as much effective information as possible from the data set, we use cross

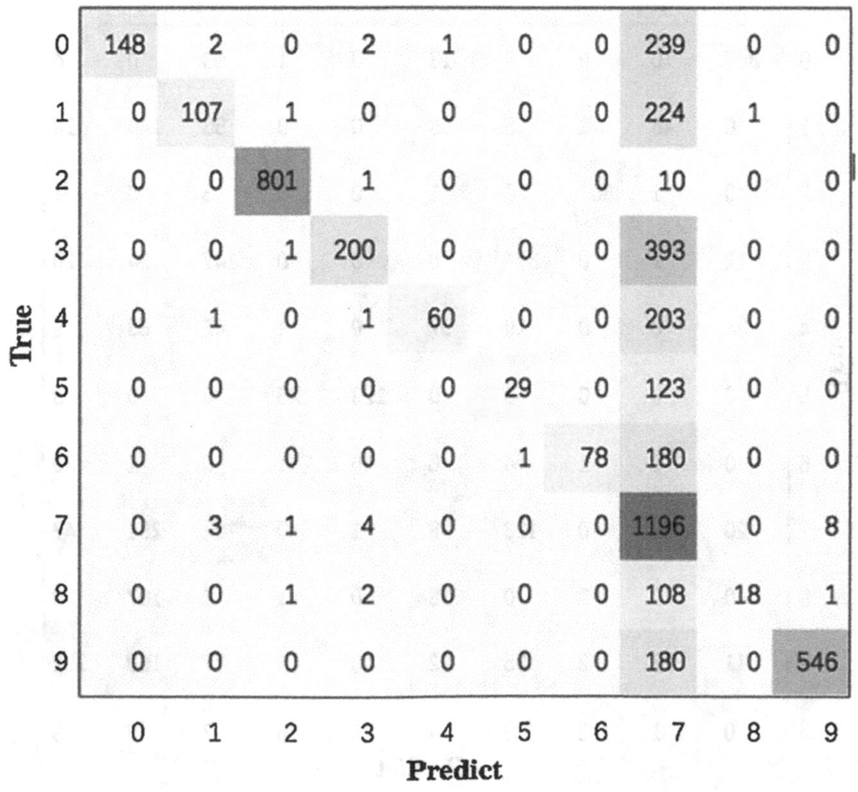

True	0	1	2	3	4	5	6	7	8	9
0	148	2	0	2	1	0	0	239	0	0
1	0	107	1	0	0	0	0	224	1	0
2	0	0	801	1	0	0	0	10	0	0
3	0	0	1	200	0	0	0	393	0	0
4	0	1	0	1	60	0	0	203	0	0
5	0	0	0	0	0	29	0	123	0	0
6	0	0	0	0	0	1	78	180	0	0
7	0	3	1	4	0	0	0	1196	0	8
8	0	0	1	2	0	0	0	108	18	1
9	0	0	0	0	0	0	0	180	0	546

Predict

Fig. 4. Prediction results of SVM

validation to partition the training set and test set, and the proportion of the two is 7:3. At the same time, this can also help us evaluate the predictive performance of the model. After the data preparation is completed, we use Naïve Bayes and SVM algorithms to implement user identity recognition based on web behavior. This process is implemented in Python Programming.

Figure 4 below shows the prediction results of SVM for the test set, and the prediction accuracy is 65%. According to the predicted results by SVM, there are 812 and 1212 web behaviors that belong to user 2 and user 7, of which has 801 and 1196 are correctly classified to their owns, and only a few are misjudged as other users. But for other users, the prediction is not satisfactory. Among them, 203 web behaviors belong to user 4 are wrongly awarded to users 7. Moreover, only 18 of the 130 web behaviors that belong to user 8 are correctly classified. On the whole, many behaviors that are not user 7 are wrongly classified to him.

The accuracy of Naïve Bayes is 64%, as shown in Fig. 5. The prediction result for user 2 is the most ideal, and 800 of web behavior records which belongs to him are correctly identified. But from the point of view of the user 1, the prediction results are not good. There are 333 web behavior records in the test set which belongs to the user 1. Among it has 146 records are classified to user 8, and there is also having 59 and 53

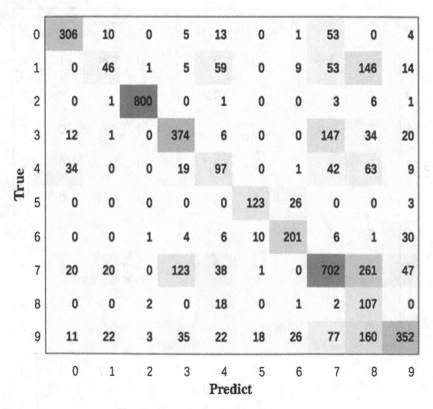

Fig. 5. Prediction results of Naïve Bayes

Table 4. Model performance

	SVM			Naïve Bayes		
	Precision	Recall	F1-score	Precision	Recall	F1-score
0	1	0.38	0.55	0.8	0.78	0.79
1	0.95	0.32	0.48	0.46	0.14	0.21
2	1	0.99	0.99	0.99	0.99	0.99
3	0.95	0.34	0.5	0.66	0.63	0.65
4	0.98	0.23	0.37	0.37	0.37	0.37
5	0.97	0.19	0.32	0.81	0.81	0.81
6	1	0.3	0.46	0.76	0.78	0.77
7	0.42	0.99	0.59	0.65	0.58	0.61
8	0.95	0.14	0.24	0.14	0.82	0.24
9	0.98	0.75	0.85	0.73	0.48	0.58
Avg	0.84	0.65	0.64	0.7	0.64	0.65

records are misjudged to user 4 and user 7. It is disappointing that only has 46 records are correctly identified.

Table 4 shows the overall performance of SVM and Naïve Bayes. The value of prediction, recall and F_1-score of each user is presented in this report, and the last row express the model performance with regard to the whole test set. From this one report we can see that SVM is better than Naïve Bayes in precision and recall, but for F_1-score, Bayes is slightly higher than SVM.

As the result of analysis, SVM has higher accuracy but less reliable for positive samples. But for Bayes, it is more balanced for the distribution of accuracy and reliability.

5 Conclusions

We present 13 web behavior features which associated with the physiological, psychological and living environment of users to verify their identity. It is proved that this is a feasible task under the support of machine learning method, although the results vary with the choice of the model. It is a valuable study to verify user identity with the help of web behavior features, which is because the user's equipment information and network environment are very easy to fake, but the behavior of someone is hard to copy owing to his uniqueness, so that we could guarantee the security of accounts by the user web behaviors, without using other additional devices.

The future direction of work includes the following points: (1) We will try diverse classification and prediction methods to improve the accuracy and reliability of user identification. (2) On the basis of the existing research, we will further explore more features of human web behavior. (3) The importance and contribution of every web behavior feature under different approaches will be discussed in the next step, and the web user is presented in a comprehensive way from the perspective of human behavioral science.

Acknowledgment. This work was supported by Fundamental Research Funds for the Central Universities NO. 106112016CDJXY110003, 2016.1-2017.12 and the National Natural Science Foundation of China under Grant No. 71671020.

References

1. CNNIC: The thirty-ninth statistical report on the development of Internet in China (2017). http://www.cnnic.net.cn/hlwfzyj/hlwxzbg/hlwtjbg/201701/t20170122_66437.htm
2. Géczy, P., Izumi, N., Akaho, S., et al.: Human behavior on web: what is known. In: International Proceedings of Economics Development & Research (2011)
3. Guo, J.L., Fan, C., Guo, Z.H.: Weblog patterns and human dynamics with decreasing interest. Eur. Phys. J. B **81**(3), 341–344 (2011)
4. Neelima, G., Rodda, S.: Predicting user behavior through sessions using the web log mining. In: International Conference on Advances in Human Machine Interaction, pp. 1–5. IEEE (2016)
5. Zhong, J., Yan, C., Yu, W., et al.: A kind of identity authentication method based on browsing behaviors. In: Seventh International Symposium on Computational Intelligence and Design, pp. 279–284. IEEE Computer Society (2014)
6. Leung, R., Law, R., Masiero, L., et al.: Behavior of online visitors to hotel ICON: a weekday-weekend analysis. e-Rev. Tour. Res. **7** (2016)
7. Cui, P., Liu, H., Aggarwal, C., et al.: Uncovering and predicting human behaviors. IEEE Intell. Syst. **31**(2), 77–88 (2016)
8. Lin, C.J., Wu, C., Chaovalitwongse, W.A.: Integrating human behavior modeling and data mining techniques to predict human errors in numerical typing. IEEE Trans. Hum.-Mach. Syst. **45**(1), 39–50 (2017)
9. Pennacchiotti, M., Popescu, A.M.: A machine learning approach to Twitter user classification. In: International Conference on Weblogs and Social Media, Barcelona, Catalonia, Spain. DBLP, July 2011
10. Feher, C.: User identity verification via mouse dynamics. Inf. Sci. **201**(19), 19–36 (2012)
11. Pao, H.K., Fadlil, J., Lin, H.Y., et al.: Trajectory analysis for user verification and recognition. Knowl.-Based Syst. **34**(5), 81–90 (2012)
12. Von Mises, L., Greaves, B.B.: Human Action: The Treatise on Economics. Liberty Fund, Carmel (2007)

Authentication Using Users' Mouse Behavior in Uncontrolled Surroundings

Fan Mo, Shiquan Xiong[✉], Shuping Yi, Qian Yi, and Anchuan Zhang

Department of Industrial Engineering, Chongqing University,
Chongqing, People's Republic of China
Xiongshquan@163.com

Abstract. Trusted interaction mechanism is very crucial to ensure the online security, but almost all studies of authentication using behavioral biometrics are based on controlled experiment. In order to generalize the authentication, data were continuously gathered from websites. The experimental system, which was designed as websites, can be regarded as an uncontrolled experiment. Eight users used the websites for more than three months. No specific tasks were asked to be finished, so the users could use the websites as their will. The system gathered users' mouse data automatically, and based on that, mouse behavior models were built. Only left click and movement sequence of mouse events are considered, but error rates are lower than 3.36% in terms of left click and 4.21% in terms of the movement sequence. The results of a case study show that the authentication accuracy using users' mouse behavior in uncontrolled surroundings is quite high. This research has verified a rapid and general approach to authentic user behavior on the network environment.

Keywords: Trusted interaction mechanism · Authentication
Uncontrolled surroundings · Network environment · Mouse behavior

1 Introduction

Human's behavior is continuous in both real world or online. Before using the Internet, they already develop behavioral patterns on many things from using a pen to pressing a button. After they get online, their behaviors continue with offline behavioral patterns, develop into online patterns, and become stable gradually. Based on that, analysis of their online behavior is meaningful and feasible, since each people's behavior online probably could only match with himself/herself. Studies on trusted interaction mechanism are extremely important nowadays, because of the rapid development of the Internet and security needs of persons and institutions online.

Authentication using behavioral biometrics is a very important issue waiting to be tackled nowadays. People use access control mechanisms, like username, password, token, fingerprints, or signature, to protect against another person's unauthorized access. This means that a user needs to give his/her identity's proof when logging in a web. Another drawback of user verification methods is that they require dedicated hardware devices such as fingerprint sensors are expensive and are not always available. Although

© Springer Nature Singapore Pte Ltd. 2018
K. Li et al. (Eds.): ICSEE 2018/IMIOT 2018, CCIS 924, pp. 121–132, 2018.
https://doi.org/10.1007/978-981-13-2384-3_12

fingerprint verification is becoming widespread in laptops, it is still not popular enough and it cannot be used in web applications.

Authentication in the web environment is also a critical issue because of the development of the Internet. Existing authentication usually focuses on a specific device, such as using the identical computer by one participant, which is not suitable for network environment. Today's people tend to use diverse devices, and the authentication of their behavioral biometrics should be more tolerant and should be established based on complex surroundings, may be based on front-end web development.

There are numerous studies focus on behavioral authentication in experimental surroundings, but a real situation of invading usually is in complex conditions and uncontrolled environments. These previous research explored controlled authentication from different aspects, including keyboard, mouse, etc. Using experiments to analysis users' behaviors is able to get a higher performance in terms of prediction results, since the sample size is similar even identical, and the equipment that participants used is the same. In uncontrolled surroundings, users are allowed to use different devices (tablets, smartphones, personal computers, etc.). Also, the data sizes of different users are not similar. It means that the authentication need to be adopted in real conditions. This can develop prior studies on behavioral authentication, and make them more practical.

Therefore, in this research, authentication using behavioral biometrics based on front-end web development which collects data from the uncontrolled experimental environment is explored.

2   Literature Review

Behavioral biometrics is the process of measuring behavioral tendencies of a user that results from both physiological and psychological differences from person to person. It does not require special designated hardware since they use common devices such as the keyboard and mouse [1]. The common behavioral biometric authentication methods include keystroke dynamics [2, 3], mouse dynamics [4–6], and Graphical User Interface (GUI) usage analysis [7]. A major benefit to usage-based biometrics is that authentication can occur actively throughout the session of a user as opposed to once during initial login [8, 9]. After the initial login has occurred, this can prevent session of a user from being hijacked. This is extraordinarily important for online authentication such as shopping on the internet.

Gaines, Lisowski, Press, and Shapiro [10] introduced the idea of using behavioral biometrics as a supplement to traditional authentication. Keystroke timing data was initially used to supplement password entry [11, 12] this evolved into being able to analyze long structured text as a basis for authentication [13–15], and finally long free text samples [3, 16]. Research on mouse dynamics that are based biometric authentication [17] that is started in 2003 when Everitt and McOwan [18] showed a promising result of static authentication, but most recently Shen, Cai, Guan, Du, and Maxion [19] showed mouse dynamics' potential for static authentication as an alternate access control solution. Ahmed and Traore [4, 20] integrated mouse dynamics and keyboard into a single architecture that could act as an intrusion detection system. Twenty-two subjects were asked to install a monitoring system and ran the software for nine weeks. These fusion methods were able to achieve high accuracy [21]. However, the time for collecting data was too long, and their methods cannot be used on websites.

Overall, authentication for websites generally needs more varied than that on a traditional computer. Studies that used behavioral biometrics designed experiment to collect data from users who used the same computer, and their variable control is strict. This means that the generalization of these authentications models is not so easily into the daily usage of web development. First, one person may have several devices to access the websites. The mouse or computer used by a person may be different. Second, on the condition of the Internet, invaders are highly possible to use different computers and measures to remote control users' data. To deal with this problem, this research considers the complex environment of using computers and tries to build models to verify mouse behavior of individuals.

3 Uncontrolled Experimental System Design

3.1 Participants

There were more than twenty participants in this experiment. The participants were recruited from the Department of Industry Engineering, Chongqing University. They were asked to use online websites to search information, to read texts and pictures, and to download files if they want. There were no specific tasks they are asked to finish, and there is no target amount of tasks, so the participants can choose to use the web a lot, only use it a little, or even not use it. In that conditions, only data from eight participants (two are females and six are males) were chosen to be analyzed in next analysis because of their data were from the period more than 3 months. The average age of participants was 31.25 (SD = 12.848). Six of them were postgraduate students, and two were professors. All the participants had more than 10 years' experience of using internet and mouse. Participants used mouse normally because there is no target in this experiment. The data were collected when they used websites to browse webs, so it was a normal mouse surfing.

3.2 Procedure

A behavioral biometric system fusing user data from mouse, which is based on front-end web development, is presented in this research. There are mainly four steps (the last three steps are as shown Fig. 1.

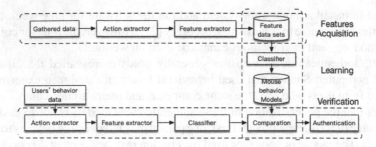

Fig. 1. The process of features acquisition, modeling, and verification.

First, users log into the websites, and use it of his/her own free will; meanwhile, the system records users mouse data. An example JavaScript code can be seen as follows. The second phase is features acquisition. The gathered data are processed by R, and the specific actions (e.g. click, or move) are extracted. Then, features of the action are calculated. These features are saved as feature data sets. The third phase is modeling and the fourth phase is verification. More details about the last three parts are described in Sect. 4.

3.3   Equipment and Programming

A data collection system was developed. Javascript and Java EE in front-end web are used to develop the system which is official websites of the research group (http://www.cquieaml.com/) as shown in Fig. 2. The websites include several parts, such as academic research, business exchanges and cooperation, blog article, about us, and the management system. Javascript codes recorded users mouse data, like click and move, and then transformed the data into back-end server and saved them. The data that are used in following analyses can be downloaded in the management system.

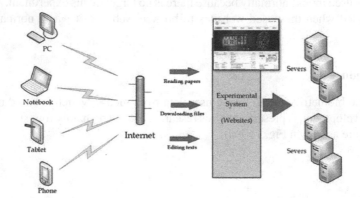

Fig. 2. The system framework of the uncontrolled experimental system.

Two personal computers (Dell Inspiron 3268-R1308) are used for controlling the management system. Participants access the online websites using their own computers, including MacBook Air (2015 early), Lenovo (ThinkPad X1 CAR), Acer (4750G), and Acer (TMP238-M-P6J9). The sampling rate of the mouse data is not consistent, from 10 Hz to 200 Hz. By resampling, the rate is fixed at 100 Hz, so the interval time between two data records (e.g. two movement segments) is 0.01 s.

Eight users' behavior of this system is recorded for more than 3 months, from April 2017 to July 2017. All of them are members of the research group and have their own accounts on the websites. Although the users know the websites can record their behavior, they do not pay attention to it since they generally do some basic work, such as downloading papers or posting a message on the forum, and the recording of their behavior does influence their feelings, so it can be regarded as uncontrolled surroundings.

4   Data Processing

4.1   Features Acquisition

Data on mouse behavior are cleaned, classified, and featured through R programming. User characteristics that relate to the way that a particular user interacts with the websites are collected by the system. This is done by monitoring mouse movements. Features are calculated on these actions. After data collection, the raw data is processed to create features for active authentication testing and identification. The calculated features are selected from prior works. These features are used in many related studies associated with authentication, since they have relatively high reliable.

The original data only involved five values, including type of the mouse event, x-coordinate of the mouse pointer (x), y-coordinate of the mouse pointer (y), time of the mouse event (t), and users ID. R codes are developed to classify the type of mouse event and extract the features. The main mouse events in webs are left-click (LC) and the movement sequence (MS). Unlike the mouse behaviors when interacting with files systems or games, right-click (LC) is not commonly used on websites. The right click motion on pages is to open the webpage 'tab', which helps users to have advanced functions with the websites. These functions are usually not used when surfing the web, so the right click is not going to be analyzing in follow analysis.

Therefore, the research focused on the two behavior and extracted features of them. Features used in this research are from existing studies. The data format changes as shown in Fig. 3.

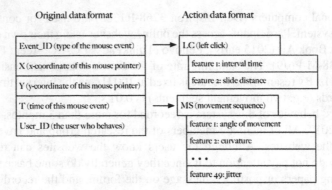

Fig. 3. Changed data format.

The basic events of mouse behavior include pressing the mouse button (including left button and right button), lifting the mouse button (also including left button and right button), and the movement of the mouse which is recognized by a photoelectric detector.

$$\begin{cases} Event_{PR} = \left(PR_i, x_i, y_i, t_i, ID_{user}\right) \\ Event_{LL} = \left(LL_i, x_i, y_i, t_i, ID_{user}\right) \\ Event_{LR} = \left(LR_i, x_i, y_i, t_i, ID_{user}\right) \\ Event_M = \left(M_i, x_i, y_i, t_i, ID_{user}\right) \\ Event_{MS} = \left(MS_i, x_{1:n}, y_{1:n}, t_{1:n}, ID_{user}\right) \end{cases} \tag{1}$$

Left click usually is composed of three sequential basic events: pressing the mouse button (PL), small movement (M), and lifting the mouse button (LL). Users may not keep still when pressing the button, which is the reason why there is a small movement. Features of left click involved interval time between pressing and lifting the mouse button and the slide distance between them.

$$Event_{LC} = \left\{ \left(LC_i, [(PL_i, x_i, y_i, t_i), (MS_i, x_{1:n}, y_{1:n}, t_{1:n}), (LL_i, x_i, y_i, t_i)], ID_{user} \right\} \tag{2}$$

Interval time in LC equals that t_i of LL_i minus t_i of PL_i, and that is, interval time in $LC = t_{LL_i} - t_{PL_i}$. Similarly, slide distance in LC is:

$$\sqrt{\left(x_{LL_i} - x_{PL_i}\right)^2 + \left(y_{LL_i} - y_{PL_i}\right)^2} \tag{3}$$

Features of movement sequence involved 49 aspects in this research. Nine features are shown in Table 1.

Table 1. Nine features used to evaluate a motion curve.

Variables	Definition	Details
Angle of movement	The angle of the path tangent with the x-axis	$\theta_i = \arctan(\delta y_1/\delta x_1) + \sum_{j=1}^{i} \delta\theta_j$ $\delta\theta_j = \delta\arctan(\delta y_1/\delta x_1)$ is the minimal angle change given in $[-\pi, \pi]$ between the j and $j+1$ points
Curvature	The relative angle change to the traveled distance	$c = \delta\theta/\delta s$
Curvature change rate	The rate of the curvature change	$\Delta c = \delta c/\delta s$
Horizontal velocity	Velocity with respect to the x-axis	$v_x = \delta x/\delta t$
Vertical velocity	Velocity with respect to the y-axis	$v_y = \delta y/\delta t$
Velocity	The first displacement moment	$v = \sqrt{v_x^2 + v_y^2}$
Acceleration	The second displacement moment	$\dot{v} = \delta v/\delta t$
Jerk	The third displacement moment	$\ddot{v} = \delta\dot{v}/\delta t$
Angular velocity	To the angle change rate	$w = \delta\theta_t/\delta t$

Each movement has values of all above features, so the minimum, maximum, range, mean, and standard deviation of them are used to reflect the features of the movement sequence. In this part, 45 features are used to measure the movement sequences.

There are also four features that are able to use to reflect the movement, including duration of movement t_n, traveled distance S_n, jitter S'/S_n, straight distance $S' = \sqrt{(x_1 - x_n)^2 + (y_1 - y_n)^2}$. Therefore, there are 49 features in total.

4.2 Learning

R codes are used to build the machine learning methods. Classifiers are constructed for both left-click (LC) and movement sequence (MS). Specifically, the two actions instance forms a row whose columns contain the features that are associated with the action, and its label is given by the ID of the user who performed the action, so it is the supervised learning. Support Vector Machine, Random Forest, and K-Mean Clustering are tested, and then the method of random forest is used to establish models, because of its relatively high accuracy and lesser time consumption. This research not aims to get the best results of machine learning methods; it just shows a good learning results can be gained in uncontrolled surroundings. The mouse data is organized using the techniques of classification and regression trees. An algorithm in the random forest runs, and then randomly selects the predictor and repeats the process. Hundreds of regression trees are generated. The random selection of the predictive factor is averaged as a result of the classification.

The data from feature data sets are split into two parts: training sets (60%) and testing sets (40%), using random sampling methods. This method picks sample randomly and put it into a set. Each training sample is used to construct a decision tree. 'randomForest' library of R is used. The number of trees to grow is 500. The importance of predictors is set as needed to be assessed, and the proximity measure among the rows is set as needed to be calculated. Other parameter settings in the randomForest function is default. The models are firstly built on the data of training sets by classifier; features of users' mouse behavior are categorized by the random forest. The results of classification are the mouse behavior models of the user, so the results can reflect this specific user. After training, testing sets are used to test the accuracy of prediction. Prediction results are visualized though confusion matrix. The model costs about 20 s to get training models and costs around 1 min to get prediction results. 'corrplot' library of R is used to visualize the prediction result.

4.3 Verification

In the end, authentication is conducted based on the two behavior sub-models of LC and MS. The authors comprise an inducer used to build verification model for the user by training on past behavior, often given by samples. During verification, the induced model is used to classify new samples that are acquired from the user. There are two main kinds of models which are models of click and models of movement. Invaders' mouse behavior is recorded by using the account of members in the group, the reliability of his/her click behavior and movement behavior are calculated respectively.

To give the final reliability of users' mouse behavior, the two reliabilities are mixing. To reasonably and simply mix the two authentication results from the models, below equation is used.

$$\alpha \geq A \& \beta \geq B \tag{4}$$

Where α is the reliability of models of left click, and β is the reliability of models of the movement sequence. A is the toleration of reliability of left click, and B is the toleration of reliability of movement sequence. When both reliabilities from the two models reach the threshold, the individual's behavior can be considered as credible.

5 Results and Discussions

5.1 Models Without Sample Balance

Data of mouse behavior are gathered from March 29th, 2017 to August 25th, 2017, and there are more than 1.6 million records of mouse events from eight people. Users' click behavior and movement behavior are modeling using Random Forest based on the training data sets, respectively. There are 500 trees for both of the two models. After that, testing data sets are used to verify the accuracy of the models. As shown in Fig. 4, the accuracy is not very high. In terms of the event of left click, the only accuracy of three participants' behavior is up to 50%, including MF (72%), YS (55%), and ZHJ (79%). The results are not good even worse than random guessing. Several predictions are very bad. For instance, YJ's left clicks are all classified into XHQ (55%) and ZAC (45%). None of LJJ left clicks are grouped to other. With regards to the event of movement sequence, there are five participants who have accuracy up to 50%, including LJJ (66%), MF (64%), XSQ (64%), ZAC (52%), and ZSJ (51%). These results are better than the results of left click but still very poor. The reasons for it is the unbalanced sample size of different participants, because the data are collected from uncontrolled experimental surroundings.

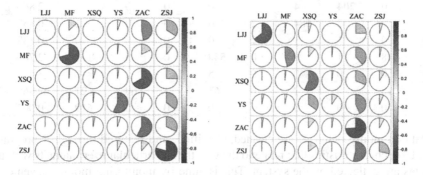

Fig. 4. Left figure: Pie figure of classifying events of LC. Pie figure of classifying events of MS.

5.2 Models with Sample Balance

In order to improve the prediction accuracy, the sample size is balanced by multiplying the size of a small sample group, and random sampling the large sample group. Then, the models are rebuilt using these new data sets. As shown in Tables 2 and 3, the accuracy significantly increases. The last column is the error rates of grouping. As to the left click, the error rates of MF, SHY, and XSQ are 0%, which means that all the predictions are absolutely right. The error rates of LJJ are the highest, up to 15.58%. The overall error rate is 3.36%.

Table 2. The accuracy of left click using testing sets.

	LJJ	MF	SHY	XSQ	YS	YSP	ZAC	ZSJ	Error rates
LJJ	195	0	0	0	34	2	0	0	15.58%
MF	0	216	0	0	0	0	0	0	0.00%
SHY	0	0	550	0	0	0	0	0	0.00%
XSQ	0	0	0	498	0	0	0	0	0.00%
YS	1	0	0	0	638	0	1	0	0.31%
YSP	0	0	0	0	12	168	0	0	6.67%
ZAC	2	0	0	0	26	2	320	0	8.57%
ZSJ	1	3	0	0	2	0	9	149	9.15%

As to the accuracy of the movement sequence, the overall error rate is 4.21%, which is also low. All the predictions of participants' movement sequence behavior are relatively high, except for the predictions of ZAC. The error rate of predicting ZAC's movement sequence is 62.96%. It should be noticed that ZAC is the most active participants in the data collection system, so the data of ZAC is maximum; nevertheless, in the results of the accuracy of movement sequence, the sample size of ZAC is the minimum. That is why the result is not reasonable.

Table 3. The accuracy of movement sequence using testing sets.

	LJJ	MF	SHY	XSQ	YS	YSP	ZAC	ZSJ	Error rates
LJJ	**569**	0	0	0	9	0	1	1	1.90%
MF	0	**204**	4	2	0	0	0	0	2.86%
SHY	0	2	**584**	2	0	0	0	1	0.85%
XSQ	0	1	1	**602**	0	0	0	0	0.33%
YS	8	1	0	0	**540**	0	5	1	2.70%
YSP	0	0	0	0	5	**167**	1	0	3.47%
ZAC	15	0	2	0	63	1	**60**	21	62.96%
ZSJ	0	0	0	0	0	0	0	**619**	0.00%

Data on mouse behavior are cleaned, classified, and featured through R programming. User characteristics that relate to the way that a particular user interacts with the websites are collected by the system. This is done by monitoring mouse movements. Features are calculated on these actions. After data collection, the raw data is processed to create features for active authentication testing and identification. The original data only involved five values, including the type of the mouse event, x-coordinate of the mouse pointer (x), y-coordinate of the mouse pointer (y), time of the mouse event (t), and users ID. R codes are developed to classify the type of mouse event and extract the features. The main mouse events in webs are left click (LC) and the movement sequence (MS), so the researchers focused on the two behavior and extracted features of them. Features used in this research are from existing studies. The data format changes as shown in Fig. 3. Interviews of one participant showed that he used both mouse and the MacBook touchpad. As we can see, behavior of the two interaction ways must be very different, but results indicated that all mouse behavior from one person can be learned, and the classifiers can be strong. That is, although participants used several different devices to log in the system, it seems that the models could handle this problem. Therefore, in some extent, this finding may be extended to other studies, so researchers do not need to control the experiment strictly, which can reduce the cost and also make models fit with real conditions better.

5.3   A Case of Unauthorized Behavior from an Invader

However, the results are high enough, so a test of unauthorized behavior from an invader is conducted. There is an invader whose code is ZSJ. ZSJ used MF's account to login to the websites and tried to simulate MF's mouse behavior. After about ten minutes' use, 35 left click events and 42 movement events are recorded. No matter left click events and movement events, none of ZSJ's mouse behavior is recognized as MF's, and the accuracy of authentication is 100%.

Prediction results in Sect. 5.2 are hard to reach a really high accuracy (i.e. 100%), but when the system knows the behavior from the identical account, the accuracy of authentication could be much higher. This situation conforms to the real environment that an invader knows others' account by stealing or password breaker. The uncontrolled mouse behavior models provide the second protection to prevent invader's unauthorized behavior. However, the system needs to collect enough data in seconds in order to extract them into mouse action, so it may cost several minutes to ensure the accuracy of recognition.

6 Conclusion

This research uses data from websites which can be considered as an uncontrolled experiment. Data are continuously gathered from websites, which means the data are unbalanced and quite conform to the real situation. The data for the uncontrolled experiment is further used to build mouse behavior models through the machine learning method (i.e., random forest). Only left click and movement sequence of mouse events are considered, but error rates are still very high. In terms of left click, error rates lower than 3.36%, and in terms of movement sequence, the error rates lower than 4.21%. In the end, a case study of unauthorized behavior from an invader is conducted. The results institute that the authentication using users' mouse behavior is quite high. This research provides a rapid and general approach to authentic user behavior on the network, which is meaningful for the development of authentication using behavioral biometrics in the uncontrolled environment.

Further work should focus on conducting this experiment on larger sample size. Real Environment usually involves a large group of users on websites, and the identification of potential invaders need to base on all these users' behavior. Besides, mass data might lead to more processing time, so how to improve the classifiers is vital. In addition to that, the influence of users' psychological characteristics, as well as their age and experience of using smart devices, on their mouse behavior may deserve further research. This could explore more about how online behavior related to the specific users who take the behavior.

Acknowledgment. This work was supported by Fundamental Research Funds for the Central Universities NO. 106112016CDJXY110003, 2016.1-2017.12 and the National Natural Science Foundation of China under Grant No. 71671020.

References

1. Multi factor user authentication on multiple devices (2017). https://patents.google.com/patent/US20180097806A1/en. Accessed 26 Apr 2018
2. Joyce, R., Gupta, G.: Identity authentication based on keystroke latencies. Commun. ACM **33**(2), 168–176 (1990)
3. Monrose, F., Rubin, A.D.: Keystroke dynamics as a biometric for authentication. Future Gener. Comput Syst. **16**(4), 351–359 (2000)
4. Ahmed, A.A.E., Traore, I.: A new biometric technology based on mouse dynamics. IEEE Trans. Dependable Secur. Comput. **4**(3), 165–179 (2007)
5. Muthumari, G., Shenbagaraj, R., Pepsi, M.B.B.: Mouse gesture based authentication using machine learning algorithm. In: 2014 IEEE International Conference on Advanced Communications, Control and Computing Technologies, pp. 492–496 (2014)

6. Zheng, N., Paloski, A., Wang, H.: An efficient user verification system via mouse movements. In: Proceedings of the 18th ACM Conference on Computer and Communications Security, CCS 2011, pp. 139–150. ACM, New York (2011). http://doi.acm.org/10.1145/2046707.2046725. Accessed 25 Aug 2017

7. Gamboa, H., Fred, A.: A behavioral biometric system based on human-computer interaction, pp. 381–392 (2004). http://adsabs.harvard.edu/abs/2004SPIE.5404..381G. Accessed 25 Aug 2017

8. Mondal, S., Bours, P.: Combining keystroke and mouse dynamics for continuous user authentication and identification. In: 2016 IEEE International Conference on Identity, Security and Behavior Analysis, ISBA, pp. 1–8 (2016)

9. Park, J., Han, S.H., Kim, H.K., Moon, H., Park, J.: Developing and verifying a questionnaire for evaluating user value of a mobile device. Hum. Factors Ergon. Manuf. Serv. Ind. 25(6), 724–739 (2015)

10. Gaines, R.S., Lisowski, W., Press, S.J., Shapiro, N.: Authentication by keystroke timing: some preliminary results. Report No. RAND-R-2526-NSF. Rand Corp Santa Monica CA, May 1980. http://www.dtic.mil/docs/citations/ADA484022. Accessed 25 Aug 2017

11. Brown, M., Rogers, S.J.: User identification via keystroke characteristics of typed names using neural networks. Int. J. Man-Mach. Stud. 39(6), 999–1014 (1993)

12. Haider, S., Abbas, A., Zaidi, A.K.: A multi-technique approach for user identification through keystroke dynamics. In: 2000 IEEE International Conference on Systems, Man, and Cybernetics, vol. 2, pp. 1336–1341 (2000)

13. Han, S.J., Kim, S.-U.: Placement of a touchpad and click-buttons to relieve arm fatigue and discomfort in a laptop PC. Hum. Factors Ergon. Manuf. Serv. Ind. 27(3), 131–137 (2017)

14. Monrose, F., Rubin, A.: Authentication via keystroke dynamics. In: Proceedings of the 4th ACM Conference on Computer and Communications Security, CCS 1997, pp. 48–56. ACM, New York (1997). http://doi.acm.org/10.1145/266420.266434. Accessed 25 Aug 2017

15. Pusara, M.: An examination of user behavior for user re-authentication (2007). https://search.proquest.com/openview/1bd296a5f59df64c30768646f674eeab/1?pq-origsite=gscholar&cbl=18750&diss=y. Accessed 25 Aug 2017

16. Bergadano, F., Gunetti, D., Picardi, C.: User authentication through keystroke dynamics. ACM Trans. Inf. Syst. Secur. 5(4), 367–397 (2002)

17. Pusara, M., Brodley, C.E.: User re-authentication via mouse movements. In: Proceedings of the 2004 ACM Workshop on Visualization and Data Mining for Computer Security, VizSEC/DMSEC 2004, pp. 1–8. ACM, New York (2004). http://doi.acm.org/10.1145/1029208.1029210. Accessed 26 Apr 2018

18. Everitt, R.A.J., McOwan, P.W.: Java-based internet biometric authentication system. IEEE Trans. Pattern Anal. Mach. Intell. 25(9), 1166–1172 (2003)

19. Shen, C., Cai, Z., Guan, X., Du, Y., Maxion, R.A.: User authentication through mouse dynamics. IEEE Trans. Inf. Foren. Secur. 8(1), 16–30 (2013)

20. Ahmed, A.A.E., Traore, I.: Anomaly intrusion detection based on biometrics. In: Proceedings from the Sixth Annual IEEE SMC Information Assurance Workshop, pp. 452–453 (2005)

21. Bailey, K.O., Okolica, J.S., Peterson, G.L.: User identification and authentication using multi-modal behavioral biometrics. Comput. Secur. 43, 77–89 (2014)

Construction of Network User Behavior Spectrum in Big Data Environment

Mengyao Xu, Fangfei Yan, Biao Wang, Shuping Yi[(✉)], Qian Yi,
and Shiquan Xiong

College of Mechanical Engineering, Chongqing University, Chongqing 400044,
China
ysp@cqu.edu.cn

Abstract. Studying the behavior patterns of network users is important for understanding the individual needs and identifying the identity of users. In this paper, the behavior patterns of network users are built by constructing the behavior spectrum of network users. Network users' behavior spectrum is constructed by dividing the behaviors of users into perceptual state and physiological state. The perceptual state is divided into other features according to the actual situation. The data of the enterprise is used to establish a method of user behavior spectrum based on perceptual state. The physiological state is represented by the features of mouse behavior. The data of self-built website is used to explore a method of user behavior spectrum based on the physiological state. Finally, an example is used to establish a user's behavior spectrum based on two methods.

Keywords: Network user behavior spectrum · Perceptual state
Physiological state · Big data

1 Introduction

With the development of Internet technology, people's lives have become more convenient. At the same time, information security issues have also received more and more attention. Identification of user identities can be achieved by studying the behavior patterns of network users, thus a new method can be offered for the establishment of information security protection mechanism. At present, many scholars have explored how to reflect the behavior patterns of network users. Frhan [1] developed a visualization model named as Social Pattern Clustering WebClickviz (SPCWebClickviz) to visualize the social networking data based on user activities and then clusters them into specified groups. Qiang and Ji-min [2] analyzed Web logs to build user behavior patterns. Zhu et al. [3] proposed a method for defining user roles based on behavior patterns and clusters the behavior of telecommunication network users during socialization. Katerina and Nicolaos [4] investigated the potential correlation between mouse behavioral patterns or keystroke dynamics and a set of End-User Development (EUD) behavioral attributes. These studies are currently only from a single point of view to establish the user behavior patterns, either only use the front-end data (mouse or keyboard related data), or only use the back-end data (log data),

© Springer Nature Singapore Pte Ltd. 2018
K. Li et al. (Eds.): ICSEE 2018/IMIOT 2018, CCIS 924, pp. 133–143, 2018.
https://doi.org/10.1007/978-981-13-2384-3_13

research is too one-sided, therefore, the user's behavior patterns should be described in a more comprehensive and three-dimensional manner by establishing a network user behavior spectrum.

The concept of behavior spectrum was first used by Makkink's in 1936 in the study of European pied Avocet. The behavior spectrum is widely seen in animal behavior. Nishida et al. [5] used behavior spectrum to list and describe all behavior patterns recorded by chimpanzees in the Mahale Mountains National Park, Hall and Heleski [6] demonstrated that the horse's behavior spectrum plays an important role in assessing training methods; Ivanov and Krupina [7] studied Contagion behavior cause changes in the behavior spectrum in Rats. There are few literatures that human behavior is studied by using behavioral spectrum, only one paper can be found so far. The behavior spectrum was defined by Qin et al. [8] as an effective user network access behavior monitoring and measurement method. However, the data that reflect the physiological behavior is not collected, that is, the data collected in the article does not fully represent the behavior of the user.

All the behaviors of the network user are recorded by using the behavior spectrum of the network user in this paper, and then the behavior pattern of the network user are constructed. Perceived behavioral features and physiological behavioral features can be used to construct a network user's behavioral spectrum. Perception [9] is the organization, identification, and interpretation of sensory information in order to represent and understand the presented information, or the environment. In this paper, perception refers to the direct reaction of an objective thing through the sensory brain in the human brain. After the brain perceives the object, user will be guided to make an action. For example, when the operating system's own language is unfamiliar to the user, the language will immediately be transformed into his familiar language. Therefore, the user's perceived behavior is defined that the influence of the external environment, personality traits, and the habits formed during the growth process on the user's network behavior. Physiology [10] is the scientific study of normal mechanisms, and their interactions, which works within a living system. In this paper, physiology refers to the life activities of living organisms and the functions of various organs. Therefore, the user's physiology is different and the user's behavior is also different. For example: The elderly move the mouse generally slower than young people. Therefore, the user's actions using the input tools (mouse, keyboard), including movement direction and movement speed, movement trajectory, movement time, tapping rate, tapping time are defined as the user's physiological behavior.

The remainder of this paper is organized as follows. The data collection is described in Sect. 2. The method for constructing a network user behavior spectrum is described in Sect. 3 and an example is given in Sect. 4. Finally, the concluding remarks are addressed in Sect. 5.

2   Data Collection

Data collection is an essential step before data analysis. In this paper, the data is analyzed from the third person point of view to get the user's behavior features and a one-to-one mapping with the actual behavior is achieved, so different types of data are needed to collect. At present, data is obtained through the self-built website and the enterprise management system, and data from the system's background log and using embedding code technology is collected.

The enterprise management system data is obtained from the background log of the cooperative enterprise. The operations of all employees in the system are recorded, these employees belong to different departments and have different responsibilities, but each user has a clear operation task. As shown in Fig. 1, the collected features are divided into four basic categories (time attributes, operational attributes, individual basic attributes and company related attributes) and used to analyze user behaviors. As shown in Fig. 2, the self-built website data is obtained from the background log and embedding code technology of the academic exchange website established by the laboratory.

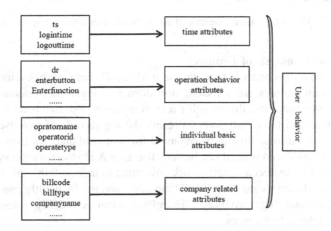

Fig. 1. Enterprise data

3 Method of Constructing Network User Behavior Spectrum

From the Sect. 2, the user behavior features are divided into perceptual state and physiological state. The network user behavior spectrum is constructed by analyzing the network behavior of the perceptual state and physiological state. Next, the enterprise data is used to establish a network behavior analysis method based on the perception state and the mouse data of a self-built website is used to establish a network behavior analysis method based on physiological state.

3.1 Network Behavior Analysis Method Based on the Perception State

As mentioned above, a company's ten-year log records are collected by us. In this part, one-month log records are used, including 6738 log records.

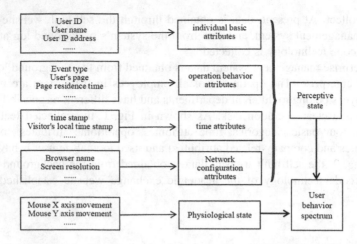

Fig. 2. The composition diagram of the network user behavior spectrum

3.1.1   Statistical Analysis of Features

Since the purpose of this paper is to study the individual's network behavior spectrum, five more relevant features are selected: operatorname, logintime, operatorid, enterfuction and enterbutton. First, this month's record is filtered into two parts according to the operatorname, and these two parts represent the log records of two users (user A and user B). Some information can be obtained for statistical analysis from two users.

From Fig. 3a and b and time, it can be seen that user A always uses the system from 9:30 am to 6:00 pm, and occasionally works overtime to around 9:00 pm. In addition, the frequently used buttons are "save" and "modify", and the frequently used functions are "making lists" and "sales invoices". Therefore, it can be roughly judged that user A's position is related to finances.

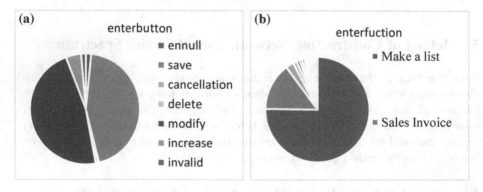

Fig. 3. (a) "enterbutton" for user A. (b) "enterfuction" for user A

3.1.2 Users Behavior Spectrum Based on Perceptual State

The correlation between the various features is tried to be found by us, and a user's behavior spectrum based on perceptual state is expressed as follows:

operatename $= A \sim$ logintime $=$ pm $\sim$ operateid $= 192.168.11.43 \sim$ enterfuction $=$ order management $\sim$ enterbutton $=$ save

In this expression, the processing of the logintime is expressed as 8:00–12:00 as am, 12:01–18:00 as pm, 18:01–00:00 as night, and 00:01–7:59 as representing for early morning. The correlation strength is expressed by calculating the degree of confidence, the confidence calculation formula: confidence(R) = NR/Noperatename = A, NR indicates the number of records that satisfy the behavior spectrum, and Noperatename = A indicates the number of records for user A. The behavior spectrum result for user A is as follows (Table 1).

Table 1. Behavior spectrum result for user A

Confidence	N_R	Examples	Instructions
64.18%	1557	A ~ pm ~ 192.168.2.55	User A often logs in to the system using ID = 192.168.2.55 in the afternoon
48.27%	1171	A ~ pm ~ 192.168.2.55 ~ make a list	User A often logs in to the system with ID = 192.168.2.55 in the afternoon. The often used enterfuction is "make a list"
22.67%	550	A ~ pm ~ 192.168.2.55 ~ make a list ~ modify	User A often logs in to the system with ID = 192.168.2.55 in the afternoon. The often used enterfuction is "make a list", the often used enterbutton is "modify"

3.2 Network Behavior Analysis Method Based on the Physiological State

Physiological behavior refers to the moving, clicking and tapping of input tools (mouse, keyboard) used by the user in the human-computer interaction environment, including the input tool's moving direction, moving distance, moving speed, click rate, tap rate, etc. The mouse movement is used as an example to explain the analysis method of physiological behavior in this section.

3.2.1 The Features Value of Mouse Moving

Five eigenvalues are calculated to represent the physiological and temporal behavior characteristics in time and space. The eigenvalues are described as follows: ① $Sx(k) = x(k + 1) - x(k)$, $k = 1, 2,..., n$, The moving distance on the X axis during the Kth mouse moving; ② $Sy(k) = y(k + 1) - y(k)$, $k = 1, 2, .., n$, The moving distance on the Y axis during the Kth mouse moving; ③ $T(k) = t(k + 1) - t(k)$, $k = 1, 2.., n$, The time required for the Kth mouse moving; ④ $Vx(k) = Sx(k)/T(k)$, $k = 1, 2.., n$, The moving rate per unit time on the X-axis during the Kth mouse moving; ⑤ Vx(k) = Sy(k)/T(k), k = 1, 2.., n, The moving rate per unit time on the X-axis during the Kth mouse moving.

From the eigenvalues, not only the user's range of moving distance and moving rate can be gotten, but also the standard deviation of the sample eigenvalues can be calculated, from which you can see the difference in user behavior.

3.2.2   Mouse Moving Analysis

200 data are randomly selected from 2 users (33rd and 40th) during the period of 2017.7.17–2018.1.3 from both spatial and temporal dimensions as samples, and the first two eigenvalues are selected on the spatial dimension, the second eigenvalues are selected on the temporal dimension.

(1) Analyze the user's mouse moving from the spatial dimension

The moving distance refers to the displacement distance of the mouse in a specific direction each time the mouse is moved. Everyone has different habits of operating the mouse, and the length of the mouse's moving distance is also different.

From Fig. 4a and b, it can be seen that there is a significant difference in the moving distance of the mouse in different directions between the NO. 33 and the NO. 40. The horizontal moving distance range [−1040, 1040] of NO. 40 is wider than [−18, 16] of NO. 33, the moving distance standard deviation 202.5287 is greater than 5.4268 of NO. 33, and the vertical moving distance range [−245, 236] is wider than [12,100] of No. 33, the standard deviation of the moving distance 55.2566 is greater than 8.1125 of No. 33.

(2) Analyze user mouse moving from the temporal dimension

The mouse's moving rate refers to the speed of the mouse's moving in a specific direction within a unit time. Each person's physical function is different, so each person's moving rate is also different.

From Fig. 5a and b, it can be seen that there is a significant difference in the moving rate of the mouse in different directions between the NO. 33 and the NO. 40. The horizontal moving rate range [−0.0622, 7.5] of the NO. 40 is narrower than [−3, 10] of the NO. 33, the moving distance standard deviation 1.4975 is greater than the 0.9027 of the NO. 33, and the vertical moving rate range [−4.64, 2.5] of the NO. 40 is wider than [−1.125, 1.5] of the NO. 33, the moving distance standard deviation 1.1518 is greater than 0.4136 of NO. 33.

4   Case Study

Based on the analysis method of the Sect. 3 for network user's perceptual state behavior and physiological state behavior, an example is used to illustrate the user's network behavior spectrum building process. 150 data from No. 46 are used for experimental analysis.

In terms of perceptual behavior, according to the four attributes, five features are selected: user name, date, IP, head and browser; In terms of physiological behavior,

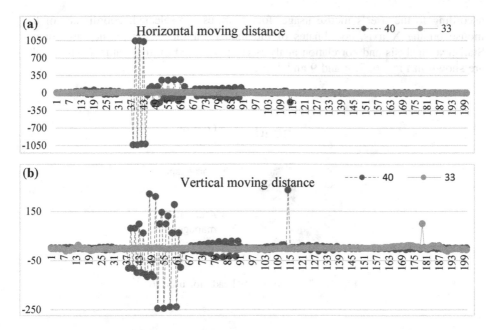

Fig. 4. (a) The moving distance of the mouse in the horizontal direction of the number 33 and 40. (b) The moving distance of the mouse in the vertical direction of the number 33 and 40

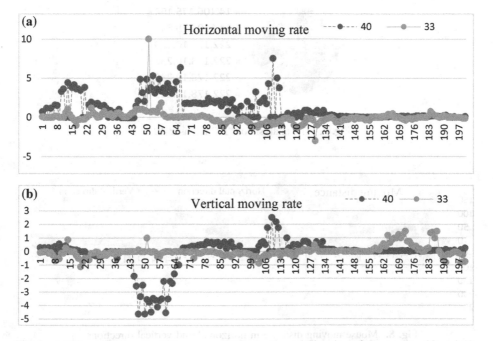

Fig. 5. (a) The moving rate of the mouse in the horizontal direction of the number 33 and 40. (b) The moving rate of the mouse in the vertical direction of the number 33 and 40

according to the user's mouse usage, four features are selected: coordinates of the mouse on the X axis, coordinates of the mouse on the Y axis, time, user name. Statistical analysis and correlation analysis are performed on the features. The results are shown in Figs. 6, 7, 8 and 9 and Table 2.

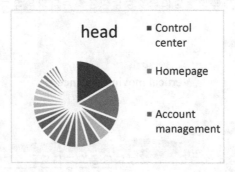

Fig. 6. The analysis of "head" for user 46

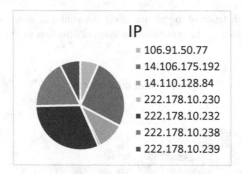

Fig. 7. The analysis of "IP" for user 46

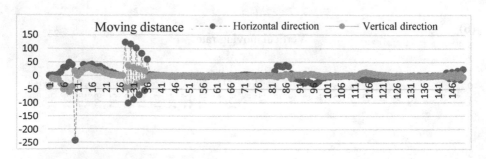

Fig. 8. Mouse moving distance in horizontal and vertical directions

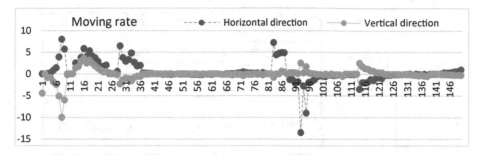

Fig. 9. Mouse moving rate in the horizontal and vertical directions

Table 2. Behavior spectrum result for user 46

Confidence	N_R	Examples	Instructions
82.00%	123	C ~ pm ~ Chrome	User C often uses chrome to log in to the website in the afternoon
31.30%	47	C ~ pm ~ Chrome ~ 222.178.10.232	User C often uses chrome to log in to the website in the afternoon. The often used IP is "222.178.10.232"
16.67%	25	C ~ pm ~ Chrome ~ 222.178.10.232 ~ control center	User C often uses chrome to log in to the website in the afternoon. The often used IP is "222.178.10.232". The often used head is "control center"

The user behavior spectrum of No. 46 is shown in the Fig. 10.

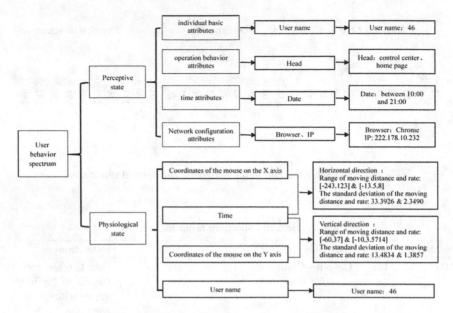

Fig. 10. The user behavior spectrum of No. 46

5 Conclusions

In this article, a method of representing user behavior patterns based on the user behavior spectrum is proposed by us. Firstly, the related definitions of perceptual behavior and physiological behavior are given. Then, the feature values of the user's perceptual behavior and physiological behavior are used for statistical analysis and correlation analysis. Thus, analytical methods based on perceptual behavior and physiological behavior are established. Finally, these analysis methods are used to establish one user's behavior spectrum, and the results showed that the combination of two behaviors to construct the user's behavior pattern is more comprehensive and three-dimensional than analyzing only a single behavior. The purpose of describing the behavior can be achieved by establishing the behavioral spectrum. Only after the description of the behavior, problems such as the behavior's development, mechanism, function and evolution can be proposed. Moreover, the establishment of user behavior spectrum is significant for the identification of user identities.

In the future, there is still a lot of work that needs to be done by us. The analysis of the combination of perception and physiological behavior needs to be more thorough, the mining of behavioral data needs to be deeper, and the construction of the user's behavioral spectrum needs to be more complete. In addition, only the data from self-built websites is used by us to establish a behavioral spectrum. However, self-constructed websites are short-lived and have less data. In the future, more data from cooperative companies will be collected and the establishment of user behavior spectrum for employees in the company will be completed. Also, corporate data will be used to study the evolution of user behavior.

Acknowledgment. This work was supported by Fundamental Research Funds for the Central Universities NO. 106112016CDJXY110003, 2016.1-2017.12 and the National Natural Science Foundation of China under Grant No. 71671020.

References

1. Frhan, A.J.: Visualization and analysis of user behaviour patterns for multimedia content view in social networks. In: 5th ISEEE International Symposium on Electrical and Electronics Engineering, pp. 1–7. IEEE Press, Galati, Romania (2017)
2. Qiang, W., Ji-min, L., Wan-hai, Y., et al.: User identification in the preprocessing of web log mining. Comput. Sci. **29**(4), 64–66 (2002)
3. Zhu, T., Wang, B., Wu, B., et al.: Role defining using behavior-based clustering in telecommunication network. Expert Syst. Appl. **38**(4), 3902–3908 (2011)
4. Katerina, T., Nicolaos, P.: Mouse behavioral patterns and keystroke dynamics in end-user development: what can they tell us about users' behavioral attributes? Comput. Hum. Behav. **83**, 288–305 (2018)
5. Nishida, T., Kano, T., Goodall, J., et al.: Ethogram and ethnography of Mahale chimpanzees. Anthropol. Sci. **107**(2), 141–168 (1999)
6. Hall, C., Heleski, C.: The Role of the ethogram in equitation science. Appl. Anim. Behav. Sci. (2017)
7. Ivanov, D.G., Krupina, N.A.: Changes in the ethogram in rats due to contagion behavior. Neurosci. Behav. Physiol. **47**(8), 987–993 (2017)
8. Qin, T., et al.: Behavior spectrum: an effective method for user's web access behavior monitoring and measurement. In: IEEE Global Communications Conference, pp. 961–966 (2013)
9. Schacter, D.L.: Psychology. Worth Publishers, New York (2011)
10. Prosser, C.L.: Comparative Animal Physiology, Environmental and Metabolic Animal Physiology, 4th edn, pp. 1–12. Wiley-Liss, Hoboken (1991). ISBN 0-471-85767-X

Relation Analysis of Heating Surface's Steam Temperature Difference and Fouling Degree Based on the Combination of Thermodynamic Mechanism and Production Data Mining

Jiahui Wang[1(✉)], Hong Qian[1,2], and Cheng Jiang[1]

[1] School of Automation Engineering,
Shanghai University of Electric Power, Shanghai, China
`5976982ll@qq.com, qianhong.sh@163.com,`
`jcfxf_219@163.com`
[2] Shanghai Power Plant Automation Technology Key Laboratory,
Shanghai, China

Abstract. This paper aims to monitor heating surface fouling degree of boiler without fume temperature data recorded. Based on the thermodynamics, this paper analyzes the heat balance mechanism of the heat transfer characteristics of the convection heating surface of the boiler and the endothermic characteristics of the steam and obtains the relationship between the heat transfer coefficient and the temperature difference and it is proved that the temperature difference between the heating surface and heat transfer coefficient has a strong correlation through the gray correlation analysis method. This paper analyzes the actual production data by correlation analysis and regression analysis: the amount of heat released from the combustion of the boiler is certain when the load is stable, and based on the model for the temperature difference of the working fluid to represent the degree of dust accumulation is established. This paper validates the result that the model is able to reflect the degree of dust deposition on the convective heating surface well by simulation and field data verification methods.

Keywords: Steam temperature difference · Fouling degree · Data mining
Characteristics of heating surface · Ebsilon simulation

1 Introduction

It is a common phenomenon that ash particles produced during solid fuel combustion adhere to surfaces of heat transfer tubes inside boilers. How to estimate fouling degree is one of the most urgent puzzles for electric engineers in industry. As for now, the soot blowing of large coal-fired power station boilers generally employs a fixed quantitative method to purge each heated surface every certain time [1]. This blind and centralized soot-blowing method is likely to result in insufficient soot-blowing or excessive soot-blowing, which will not only damage boiler tube but also affect the stability of the operation, and reduce the generator unit's operating efficiency [2]. Therefore, it is very

© Springer Nature Singapore Pte Ltd. 2018
K. Li et al. (Eds.): ICSEE 2018/IMIOT 2018, CCIS 924, pp. 144–154, 2018.
https://doi.org/10.1007/978-981-13-2384-3_14

necessary to transform the "timed and quantitative" soot-blowing method into "on-demand distribution" soot-blowing methods so as to improve the safety and economy of boiler operation.

Researchers at home and abroad have optimized the boiler soot-blowing system through various methods [3–5]: Prof. Wei of North China Electric Power University proposed the concept of clean factor [3], the ratio of real heat absorption and maximum transferable heat of ideal heat exchanger [4], that is, the ratio of heat transfer effectiveness to characterize the degree of dust accumulation; the method of exporting temperature of flue gas as a whole reflects the total degree of ash pollution in the furnace and its effect. And as for specific heated surface, there is no way to know its fouling degree.

This paper takes a 300 MW coal-fired power plant boiler (DC furnace) as the research object, and analyzes the gray correlation between the temperature difference between the inlet and outlet working surface of the convective heating surface and the cleaning factor calculated based on the thermodynamic mechanism based on the excavation of a large amount of actual production data. The characteristics prove that the temperature difference on the side of the heating surface can reflect the degree of dust accumulation. This method can characterize the degree of dust accumulation based on limited measurement points of heated temperature without calculating the endothermic enthalpy value. This method is proved to be reliable through field test.

2 Modeling of the Relationship Between Ash Fouling and Temperature Difference of the Working Fluid

The characteristics of convective heat transfer and endothermic absorption of the working fluid are analyzed. The model of the cleaning factor that characterizes the ash content of the heated area was determined and the idea of using the temperature difference at the inlet and outlet of the heated surface to characterize the degree of dust accumulation was proposed.

2.1 Analysis of Heat Transfer Characteristics of Convective Heating Surface

For the type Π boiler studied in this paper, heating surfaces mainly absorb the heat in the flue gas by convection. The basic formula for convection heat transfer is [6]

$$Q_1 = KH\Delta t/B_j. \tag{1}$$

In the formula, H is heat surface area, m^2; Δt is heat transfer temperature and pressure, $°C$; B_j Calculated fuel consumption, kg/s; K is heat transfer coefficient, $kW/(m^2 \cdot °C)$.

For the heated surface of the fouling external surface of the pipe, the heat transfer coefficient K, which does not take into account the thermal resistance and scaling of the metal pipe, is calculated as

$$K = \frac{1}{1/\alpha_1 + \varepsilon + 1/\alpha_2} \tag{2}$$

In the above formula, α_1 and α_2 are the exothermic coefficient of the flue gas against the wall and the wall of the working medium, $kW/(m^2 \cdot {}^\circ C)$; ε is the coefficient of ash pollution, $(m^2 \cdot {}^\circ C)/kW$. As the degree of dust accumulation on the heated surface increases, the fouling coefficient ε will gradually increase, and the value of heat transfer coefficient K will gradually decrease.

2.2   Analysis of Endothermic Characteristics of Convective Heating Surface

For superheaters, reheaters, and economizers, the convective heat absorption of the working fluid Q_2 is generally calculated as follow:

$$Q_2 = D(h_2 - h_1)/B_j. \tag{3}$$

In the formula, B_j is calculated fuel volume, kg/s; D is steam flow, kg/s; h_1, h_2 is enthalpy of heated inlet and outlet surface respectively, kj/kg.

Calculation of the enthalpy of the working fluid can refer to the "Water and Steam Thermodynamic Properties Chart" [7] written by Yan Jialu. Through the look-up table, the steam enthalpy corresponding to temperature and pressure can be obtained.

To obtain the relationship between difference in enthalpy and that in temperature, this paper sets the enthalpy value at 265 °C as calculated base, and calculates the difference between enthalpy at different temperature every 25 °C and that at 265 °C in 3 different pressure conditions, as the diagram below shows in the left. In the same way, the diagram in the right is drawn, and its base is the enthalpy value at 350 °C, and temperature difference is every 15 °C in 7 different pressure conditions Fig. 1.

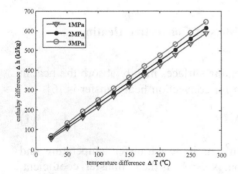

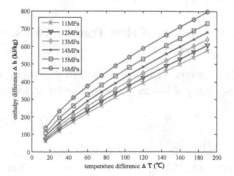

Fig. 1. Characteristic of enthalpy difference caused by temperature difference.

Fig. 2. Characteristic of enthalpy difference caused by temperature difference.

From the above two figures, it can be found that the enthalpy difference is approximately linear with a certain pressure and temperature difference Fig. 2.

$$\Delta h = \alpha \Delta T. \tag{4}$$

Thus, the convective heat absorption can also be expressed by the following formula

$$Q_2 = D\alpha \Delta T / B_j \tag{5}$$

2.3   The Relationship Between Dust Accumulation and Temperature Difference

Qualitative Analysis of Relevance. For a specific convective heating surface, the heat Q1 transferred by the convection and the heat Q2 absorbed by the working fluid should be in balance [7]. The conclusion can be made from (1) and (5),

$$\frac{KH\Delta t}{B_j} = \frac{D\alpha \Delta T}{B_j}. \tag{6}$$

So, the formula of heat transfer coefficient K can be inferred,

$$K = \frac{D\alpha \Delta T}{H\Delta t}. \tag{7}$$

From the formula (7), the heat transfer temperature and pressure can be calculated through the inlet and outlet temperature parameters on the steam side and the flue gas side, however, it will inevitably be limited in practical applications. Based on the above formula, it can be implied that there is a certain correlation between heat transfer coefficient K and the temperature difference ΔT.

Correlation is defined as the measure of the size of systems' association with time or different objects [8]. In the process of system development, if the trend of heat transfer coefficient K is consistent with that of temperature difference ΔT of the working fluid, it means the degree of synchronization changes is relatively high, vice versa.

Quantitative Analysis of Relevance. The degree of correlation is essentially the degree of difference between the geometric shapes of the curves. The correlation coefficient for the reference sequence K and the comparison sequence ΔT at each time can be calculated by the following formula:

$$\xi = \frac{\Delta_{min} + \rho\Delta_{max}}{\Delta(t) + \rho\Delta_{max}}. \tag{8}$$

Among them, the resolution coefficient ρ is generally between 0 and 1; $\Delta(t)$ is the absolute difference between each point on the K curve and the ΔT curve, Δ_{min} is minimum of the absolute difference at all time, and Δ_{max} is the maximum one.

The correlation r is a number that represents the correlation degree which is calculated by merging the correlation coefficients at each time (i.e., each point in the curve) into one value. And take this value as the index to evaluate the relationship between ΔT and K. The formula is as follows:

$$r = \frac{1}{N} \sum_{t=1}^{N} \xi(t). \qquad (9)$$

In this paper, the heat transfer coefficient K model is established using the low-temperature reheater with a wide range of working surface heat and temperature measurement points in the research object, and the correlation between heat transfer coefficient and the temperature difference at the working side is analyzed by the gray correlation analysis method to verify that the temperature difference in the working side reflects the degree of dust accumulation.

3   Analysis of the Correlation Between the Temperature Difference and the Degree of Fouling Degree on the Side of the Convective Heating Surface

Take the above 300 MW coal-fired power plant boiler (DC furnace) as an example. In the load range of [160 MW, 300 MW], the load stability section was selected to analyze the soot blowing system.

3.1   Change in Fouling Degree in Heated Area

The form of fouling in heated area is a dynamic and balanced process. Heat transfer coefficient is determined based on the flow rate of the low-temperature reheater, the temperature difference between the inlet and outlet sides of the cryogenic heat exchanger and the flue gas side when a stable operating condition is selected. According to the soot-blowing records, the load curve of the day and the Heat transfer coefficient (Pu) curve of the low-temperature reheater were plotted, as shown in Figs. 3 and 4:

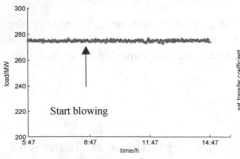

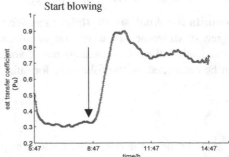

Fig. 3. Real-time load data of coal-fired boiler.

Fig. 4. Heat transfer coefficient (Pu) of Low-temperature reheater curve.

From Fig. 4, it can be seen that the per-unit value of heat transfer coefficient (K) of the heating surface in the low-temperature reheater increases from 0.3 to 0.9 after the start of soot blowing. As the time go by, the degree of dust accumulation in the low reheating area gradually increases, and the K value gradually decreases.

3.2 Correlation Between Heat Transfer Coefficient and Temperature Difference on Heating Surface Side

Similarly the curve of the temperature difference between the inlet and outlet of the cryogenic reheater on day A is drawn, as shown in Fig. 5. It can be seen that the curves of Figs. 4 and 5 are very similar. Using the gray correlation analysis method, the relationship coefficients of 541 moments in this time period are calculated, as shown in Fig. 6.

The average value of the 541 relationship coefficients, known as correlation degree r, is obtained. The correlation between the temperature difference at the inlet and outlet side of the low-temperature reheater and the heat transfer coefficient is 0.61, which is a strong correlation.

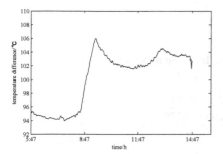

Fig. 5. Temperature difference curve diagram for the inlet and outlet of the low-temperature reheater.

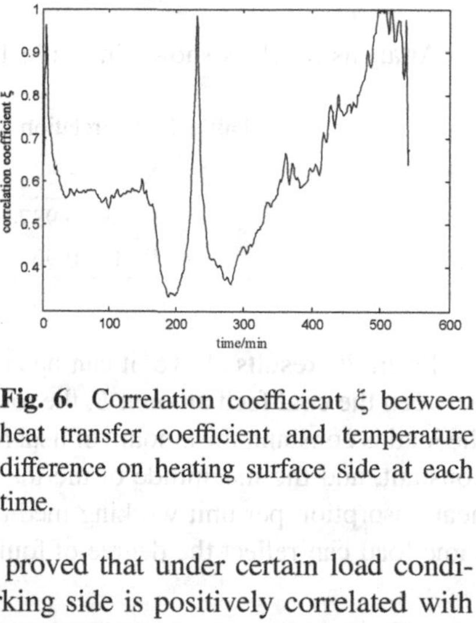

Fig. 6. Correlation coefficient ξ between heat transfer coefficient and temperature difference on heating surface side at each time.

Through the analysis of the field data, it is proved that under certain load conditions, the temperature difference ΔT on the working side is positively correlated with the heat transfer coefficient K, so the temperature difference on the working side can reflect the degree of dust accumulation on the heated surface.

4 Fouling Degree Model in Convection Heating Surface Side Through Temperature Difference

4.1 Fundamentals of Fouling Degree Model

This study does not consider influence of the types of coal, and the heat released from fuel combustion is mainly determined by the amount of coal. According to the actual data, the data of 1440 moments in a certain day were taken, and the load P was used as the independent variable, and the coal supply B and the wind volume W were used as the dependent variables to perform the linear regression analysis.

The relationship between the amount of actual coal B on one day and the amount of coal fitted by the load $\hat{B}$ is shown in Fig. 7. And the relationship between the amount of actual wind W and the amount of wind fitted by the load is shown in Fig. 8.

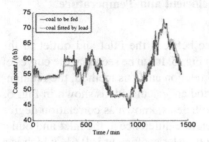

Fig. 7. Linear fitting of coal quantity to load.   **Fig. 8.** Linear fitting of wind W to load

Analysis result is shown in Table 1.

Table 1. Correlation analysis and linear fitting results

X	Y	r	R^2	a	b
P	W	0.987	0.975	0.295	29.618
P	B	0.962	0.914	0.205	9.320

From the results above, it can be concluded that there is a good linear relationship between the coal feed amount B, the total air flow rate W, and the load P. That is, when the load is constant, the amount of heat released from the combustion of the boiler is also constant, and the magnitude of the load is corresponding. Therefore, the difference in heat absorption per unit working medium on the convective heating surface under the same load can reflect the degree of fouling degree on the convective heating surface.

4.2   Fouling Degree Model Establishment

The difference in heat absorption per unit working medium at the convective heating surface under the same load can reflect the degree of dust accumulation on the convective heating surface. The coefficient that defines the degree of fouling of the convective heating surface is β, and the calculation formula for β is:

$$\beta = \begin{cases} 1 & \Delta T \leq T_L. \\ \frac{\Delta T - T_L}{T_H - T_L} & T_L \leq \Delta T \leq T_H. \\ 0 & T_H \leq \Delta T. \end{cases} \tag{10}$$

In the above formula, ΔT is the actual value of the temperature difference between the inlet and the inlet of the convective heating surface whose unit is °C. From formula

(10), it can be inferred that the fouling degree coefficient β is between 0 and 1, and β approaching 0 means that the heated area is severely covered by ash; while β approaching 1 means that the heated surface tends to be clean.

According to the boiler's 696,960 samples in 484 days of operation, 287 samples with stable load in the range of [160 MW, 300 MW] are analyzed. Since for different heat receiving surfaces under different loads, the working medium heat absorption interval values differs as well, and the temperature difference between the import and export of the lower limit value of the TL, the upper limit value TH and the load relationship is shown in Table 2:

Table 2. Upper and lower limit of inlet and outlet heater surface temperature.

Heating surface	Lower limit TL	Upper limit TH
Screen superheater	$-0.0136 \times P+86.1$	$-0.155 \times P+149.7$
High temperature superheater	$-0.017 \times P+37.66$	$-0.066 \times P+58.09$
Low temperature superheater	$-0.08 \times P+55.26$	$-0.23 \times P+115.34$
High temperature reheater	$0.028 \times P+74$	$-0.13 \times P+139.5$
Low temperature reheater	$-0.09 \times P+169.73$	$-0.3 \times P+207.33$

That is, the temperature difference of the working surface of the heating surface indicates the degree of dust accumulation, which needs to be analysed and determined in conjunction with the load at that time. The larger the load, the greater the temperature difference of the working fluid will be correspondingly larger, and the difference in the dust level represented by the temperature difference of the working fluid under different loads is different.

5 Verification of Fouling Degree Model

5.1 Software Simulation

EBSILON Professional is used to calculate the physical quantities such as heat, work, thermal cycle efficiency, and thermal state parameters in the thermal process. Of course, the actual process should be revised on the basis of the ideal process.

There are many component models in the EBSILON component library, which can be used to build the power station based on the complexity of the power station system or the accuracy of the research problem. Therefore, two models are established, which are low-temperature reheater heat transfer model and high-temperature superheater heat exchange model respectively shown in Figs. 9 and 10.

In order to verify that the temperature difference of the working surface of the heating surface represents the degree of dust accumulation, the real-time data of five groups of low retest points under the same conditions of the load are input into the two models to determine the heat transfer coefficient. Though lack of data on the high-temperature superheater flue gas side in the field data, it is still possible to obtain heat transfer coefficient by simulation based on the boundary condition of the data on the

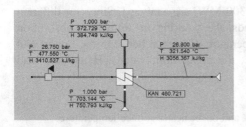

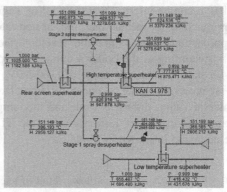

Fig. 9. Low-temperature reheater heat excha- **Fig. 10.** High-temperature superheater heat
nge model.   exchange model.

flue gas side, the working side of the low temperature superheater, and the flue gas side
of the rear screen superheater. The results are shown respectively in Table 3 and
Table 4.

According to the output results in Tables 3 and 4, it can be concluded that whether
on the surface of the low temperature reheater or on that of high temperature

Table 3. Simulation results of low-temperature reheater model.

Part of the input			Part of the output
Steam inlet/outlet temperature(°C)		Temperature difference(°C)	Coefficient of heat transfer(kW/K)
305.74	467.674	161.934	485.873
306.48	465.27	158.79	461.458
321.54	477.55	156.01	460.721
307.15	460.260	153.11	434.006
317.14	469.915	152.775	399.982

Table 4. Simulation results of high temperature superheater model.

Part of the input			Part of the output
Steam inlet/outlet temperature(°C)		Temperature difference (°C)	Coefficient of heat transfer(kW/K)
489.537	524.536	34.999	34.978
485.648	521.820	36.172	50.830
486.938	524.873	37.935	80.673
485.889	524.463	38.574	95.746
485.833	525.893	40.06	119.800

superheater, when the temperature difference between the inlet and outlet working fluids decreases, the heat transfer coefficient will also decrease.

5.2 Verification of Field Data

According to the soot-blowing records, the load is relatively stable from 11:05 to 21:05 on a certain day, and the soot-blowing time is 17:05. The soot blowing area is the heated surface of the high-temperature superheater (taking the heated surface as an example). The temperature difference curve of the outlet steam and the high-temperature superheater, β curve of the high-temperature superheater is shown in Figs. 11 and 12, respectively.

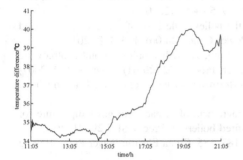

Fig. 11. Temperature difference curve of working fluid in high temperature superheater

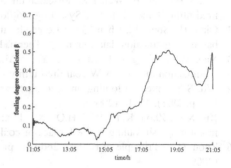

Fig. 12. Fouling degree coefficient β curve of high-temperature superheater.

From the above figure, it can be seen that the temperature difference of the working surface of the high-temperature superheater heating surface after soot blowing rises from 35 °C to 40 °C, and the fouling degree coefficient β increases from 0.1 to 0.5. As time went by, the high reheating area gradually accumulated ash, and the temperature difference and coefficient of dust accumulation gradually decreased.

6 Conclusion

The temperature difference varies between the inlet and outlet side on different heating surfaces under different load. However, it is not difficult to find the relationship between the temperature difference limit of each heating surface and the load through the production data. And to some extent, the real-time temperature difference data can effectively reflect the degree of fouling degree. The results show that:

(1) The degree of correlation between the temperature difference on the heating surface side of the working surface and the heat transfer coefficient is strong.
(2) The temperature difference on the heating surface of the heating surface can effectively reflect the degree of dust accumulation.

(3) In the case of a smokeless temperature measurement point of the boiler, it can provide guidance to the working personnel and help achieve on-demand blowing.

This study only focused on stable conditions, the unit parameters themselves have a certain degree of volatility, and further processing was done using data filtering methods. Under varying conditions, the parameters of the unit have a wide range of changes and needs to be further explored in the future.

References

1. Shi, Y.H., Yun, F., Wei, T.Z.: Research on ash fouling monitoring of heating surface in coal fired utility boiler. J. Power Syst. Eng. **26**(06), 49–50 + 53 (2010)
2. Qian, H., Song, L., Chen, Q.Q.: Research on the believe rule base of soot blowing demand based on production data mining. J. Therm. Power Gener. **46**(06), 113–118 (2017)
3. Yan, W.P., Liang, X.J., Zhou, J., Ye, X.M., Zheng, Z.: Ash monitoring and sootblowing optimization of a 300 MW coal-fired utility boiler. Proc. CSEE **20**(01), 58–61 + 129 (2007)
4. Wu, S.Y.: Effect of fouling on heat transfer performance of heat exchanger. J. Petro-Chem. Equip. **29**(1), 10–12 (2000)
5. Xu, X.H., Zhou, K.Y., Wei, H.Q., Xu, J.Q.: Increment of furnace exit gas temperature for monitoring ash fouling in the furnace of coal-fired boilers. J. Proc. CSEE **29**, 21–26 (2011)
6. Zhou, Q.T.: Principle of Boilers, 2nd edn, pp. 183–185. China Electric Power Press, Beijing (2009)
7. Yan, J., Yu, X., Wang, Y.: Water and Steam Thermodynamic Properties Chart, 3rd edn, pp. 13–53. Higher Education Press, Beijing (2015)
8. Sun, C.Z., Song, Y.T.: Theory discussion about grey interconnect degree model. J. Global Geol. **19**(03), 248–252 + 270 (2000)

Variable Selection Methods in Dredger Production Model

Yinfeng Zhang, Zhen Su, and Jingqi Fu[✉]

Department of Automation, College of Mechatronics Engineering and
Automation, Shanghai University, No.149, Yanchang Rd., Shanghai 200072,
China
jqfu@staff.shu.edu.cn

Abstract. The production of earthwork is an important index to evaluate the performance of dredgers. Because the parameters affecting production are numerous and not independent of each other, it is easy to overfit the production model and have low accuracy. In view of this problem, based on the measured data of a Trailing Suction Hopper Dredger (TSHD), three variable selection methods are applied to select the parameters that can affect the yield most and the inputs of the final production model are determined. The results show that the deleted and retained parameters conform to the actual working conditions. Finally, the advantages and disadvantages of these three methods and their applicability under different working conditions of dredgers are analyzed.

Keywords: Hopper dredging · Yield model · Variable selection

1 Introduction

Dredgers are designed and manufactured for underwater earth and rock works. They can be used to excavate canals, widen waterways, remove siltation from reservoirs, dig trenches, collect ore and so on. The TSHD is more popular than other kinds of dredgers because of its ability to complete the work of digging, loading, transporting, discharging (blowing) independently and change the site itself. Nowadays, the dredging equipment and auxiliary equipment of TSHDs are becoming gradually perfect. However, the operation and management level of TSHDs is generally not high, which affects the dredging efficiency of TSHDs directly.

The optimization of the dredging parameters of TSHD is to obtain the relevant construction parameters, so that the dredger can be in good operation condition and achieve the purpose of high efficiency, high quality and low consumption when dredging under the guidance of these parameters. However, giving proposed construction parameters are not simple, the main difficulties are as follows: 1. It is unrealistic to establish an accurate input-output mechanism model for a complex nonlinear multivariable time-varying system such as dredging operation system from a basic principle. 2. The characteristics of the actual dredging equipment are greatly influenced by the construction environment and operation conditions. 3. The dredging process must ensure the safety of the slurry transport system and unreasonable parameter

© Springer Nature Singapore Pte Ltd. 2018
K. Li et al. (Eds.): ICSEE 2018/IMIOT 2018, CCIS 924, pp. 155–165, 2018.
https://doi.org/10.1007/978-981-13-2384-3_15

adjustment will cause abnormal situations such as blockage, rupture and forced shutdown.

Holland IHC company is one of the most important dredger manufacturing and research units in the world. They also studied the optimization of dredging operations and put forward new concepts such as "Efficient Dredging" and "Accurate Dredging" [1]. But the results of their dredging optimization are not detailed, testing results and key technologies not transparent, usually only a concept. In China, the research reports on the optimization of dredging work are rare and floating on the surface, so it is difficult to study their essence and specific performance.

Modeling and optimization of dredging operations often use model predictive control [2], and the relationship between production and influencing factors must be understood before modeling. In this paper, we focus on maximizing the production of dredging. According to the experience of actual operator and some simulation experiments, the factors that affect the yield can be summarized as follows: speed to ground, vacuum degree of dredge pump, depth and pressure of drag head, soil characteristics [3, 4], pump speed, high pressure flushing system, overflow using [5] and so on. Accordingly, there are many parameters related to production. If taking all the parameters as the inputs of TDS model, it is easy to have problems such as over fitting, low precision and long modeling time. The purpose of variable selection is to select a certain feature set from production-related parameters as inputs to establish an effective TDS model, which can improve the accuracy while removing redundant information, reducing the complexity, improving the generalization performance and simplifying the model. Three methods are applied to realize the screening of production-related parameters, namely, least absolute shrinkage and selection operator (LASSO), mean impact value (MIV) and genetic algorithm (GA).

2 Method Description

Taking the magnitude and dimensional difference of measured data of dredgers into account, the data is first normalized in the early stage of variable screening. This paper uses deviation normalization to process data and the formula is as follows:

$$x_k = \frac{x_k - x_{\min}}{x_{\max} - x_{\min}} \tag{1}$$

where $x_{\min}$ is the minimum number of data series and $x_{\max}$ is the largest number.

2.1 Variable Screening by LASSO

Define the dredging output with tones of dry soil (TDS):

$$\text{TDS}(t) = \frac{\frac{m_t(t)}{v_t(t)} - \rho_w}{\rho_q - \rho_w} v_t(t)\rho_q = \frac{m_t(t) - \rho_w v_t(t)}{\rho_q - \rho_w}\rho_q \tag{2}$$

where ρ_w (1.024 ton/m^3) and ρ_q (2.65 ton/m^3) denote the density of water and quartz; m_t and v_t are loading quality and capacity.

When establishing the yield model, it is assumed to be a linear model. The production-related parameters are recorded as $x_1, x_2, \ldots \ldots x_p$ as independent variables, and the TDS is calculated according to the real data and Eq. (2) and recorded as y as the dependent variable. Supposing that n groups measurement data of TSHD have been standardized as follows: $y_1, x_{11}, x_{12}, \ldots x_{1p}$; $y_2, x_{21}, x_{22}, \ldots x_{2p} \ldots \ldots y_n, x_{n1}, x_{n2}, \ldots x_{np}$.

Create a linear model of production and production-related parameters:

$$y = \beta_1 x_1 + \beta_2 x_2 + \ldots \ldots \beta_p x_p + \varepsilon \tag{3}$$

$$\text{where } y = \begin{pmatrix} y_1 \\ \vdots \\ y_n \end{pmatrix} \quad x = \begin{pmatrix} x_{11} & \cdots & x_{1p} \\ \vdots & \ddots & \vdots \\ x_{x1} & \cdots & x_{np} \end{pmatrix} = (x_1 \quad \cdots \quad x_p) \quad \beta = \begin{pmatrix} \beta_1 \\ \vdots \\ \beta_p \end{pmatrix} \quad \varepsilon = \begin{pmatrix} \varepsilon_1 \\ \vdots \\ \varepsilon_n \end{pmatrix}$$

$$\tag{4}$$

The above production model can be written as:

$$y = x\beta + \varepsilon \tag{5}$$

It is easy to obtain coefficients β according to the thought of ordinary least square (OLS). The basic idea of LASSO [6] is to impose $\ell 1$ punishment on basis of OLS, that is, to limit the length of parameters and the expression is as follows:

$$\hat{\beta} = \underset{\beta \in R^P}{\arg \min} \{(y - x\beta)^T (y - x\beta)\} \quad s.t. \sum_{i=1}^{P} |\beta_i| \leq t \tag{6}$$

Where $t \geq 0$ and it is a regulating parameter that controls the degree of compression. When t is smaller, it means stronger compression and more coefficients will become 0. The above expression can be written as the following equivalent form:

$$\hat{\beta} = \underset{\beta \in R^P}{\arg \min} \{(y - x\beta)^T (y - x\beta)\} + \lambda \sum_{i=1}^{P} |\beta_i| \tag{7}$$

Where λ is a penalty parameter and $\lambda \geq 0$.

Solving LASSO is essentially a solution of a quadratic programming problem with linear inequality constraints. In addition to modern optimization theory and methods based on constraints, least angle regression (LAR) is also commonly used in LASSO. The solution flow of LAR [7] is presented in Algorithm. 1.

Algorithm 1. Least angle regression

1. Standardize the independent variables to have mean zero and unit norm. Start with the residual $r = y - \overline{y}$, $\beta_1, \beta_2, \ldots\ldots\beta_p = 0$.

2. Find the independent variable x_j most correlated with r.

3. Move β_j from 0 towards its least-squares coefficient $\langle x_j, r \rangle$, until some other competitor x_k has as much correlation with the current residual as does x_j.

4. Move β_j and β_k in the direction defined by their joint least squares coefficient of the current residual on $\langle x_j, x_k \rangle$, until some other competitor x_l has as much correlation with the current residual.

5. Continue in this way until all p predictors have been entered. After min ($n-1, p$)steps, algorithm stops.

2.2   Variable Screening by MIV

The idea of MIV is to fluctuate the measured value of the production-related parameters to affect the TDS output, and then sort the parameters according to the magnitude of the output change. It is based on the TDS model and improved BP network [8] with GA is used for TDS modeling.

Using GA to improve BP neural network is divided into 3 stages: determining the structure of BP network, GA optimizing the weight and threshold of BP network and predicting BP network. The structure of BP network is determined firstly according to the number of input and output parameters, and then determine the length of GA individual. Individual coding is implemented by real number, so each individual is a real string, which is composed of 4 parts: the connection weight of the input layer and the hidden layer, the threshold of the hidden layer, the connection weight of the hidden layer and the output layer, and the threshold of the output layer.

GA optimization refers to optimizing the weights and thresholds of BP network. Each individual in population contains all the weights and thresholds of a network. GA evaluates the pros and cons of the individual through fitness function and then finds the individual who has the optimal fitness value by selection, crossover and mutation operation. The sum of absolute errors between real TDS and predicted TDS is used as individual fitness function.

The prediction of BP neural network is the assignment of the initial weights and thresholds of BP network by the optimal individuals obtained by GA, and then the BP network is trained to predict TDS.

MIV is considered as one of the best indexes in neural network to evaluate the degree of input affecting output. The symbol of MIV value represents the relative direction (positive and negative correlation) and absolute value represents the relative degree. The specific calculation process [9] is shown in Algorithm. 2.

Algorithm 2. Selecting variables with MIV
1. Use training sample P to train improved BP network.
2. Training sample P is added 10% to get new training sample P1 and reduced 10% to get P2. $P1 = P \times (1+10\%)$ $P2 = P \times (1-10\%)$
3. Test the network with P1 and P2 to get new outputs A1 and A2. $A1 = sim(P1)$ $A2 = sim(P2)$
4. The impact value(IV) due to the change of training sample P is the difference between A1 and A2. $IV = A1 - A2$
5. Calculate the mean impact value. $MIV = \dfrac{IV}{N}$
6. Sort the independent variables according to the absolute value of the MIV.

2.3 Variable Screening by GA

In the field of variable selection, GA could be utilized to search for latent variables spontaneously [10]. When using GA to solve the problem of variable selection in TSHD, two designs are mainly considered: one is how to use production-related parameters for chromosome coding, and the other is how to design the fitness function.

In this paper, the encoding length is designed to be 18 (corresponding to the number of parameters in Table 1). A population of binary strings (i.e. chromosomes) is created randomly from all the variables. Each position (i.e. gene) of the binary string corresponds to one specific variable, which is coded as "1" if the variable is selected and "0" if not [11].

The fitness function in this paper is used to evaluate the effectiveness of a certain set of production-related parameters in the establishment of TDS model. Therefore, the reciprocal of the squared sum of the errors of the actual TDS and the network predicted TDS can be chosen as fitness function and the expression is as follows:

$$f(X) = \frac{1}{SE} = \frac{1}{sse(\hat{T} - T)} = \frac{1}{\sum\limits_{i=1}^{n} (\hat{t}_i - t_i)^2} \tag{8}$$

In the formula, $\hat{T} = \{\hat{t}_1, \hat{t}_2, \ldots \hat{t}_n\}$ is the TDS of test set; $T = \{t_1, t_2, \ldots t_n\}$ is the real TDS of test set; n is the number of samples for the test set.

To avoid the influence of randomness of the initial weights and thresholds of BP network on the fitness function calculation, the weights and thresholds of BP neural network are optimized by GA for each individual in calculating the fitness function value, that is, the improved BP network using GA mentioned above.

Table 1. Primary selection of production-related parameters.

Variable number	Variable name	Variable type
1	Depth of portside drag	Control parameter
2	Angle of portside drag	Control parameter
3	Differential pressure of portside drag	Measurement parameter
4	Pressure of portside wave compensator	Control parameter
5	Motor speed of portside jet water pump	Control parameter
6	Vacuum degree of portside dredge pump	Measurement parameter
7	Speed of portside dredge pump	Control parameter
8	Position of portside diversion window	Control parameter
9	Depth of starboard drag	Control parameter
10	Angle of starboard drag	Control parameter
11	Differential pressure of starboard drag	Measurement parameter
12	Pressure of starboard wave compensator	Control parameter
13	Motor speed of starboard jet water pump	Control parameter
14	Vacuum degree of starboard dredge pump	Measurement parameter
15	Speed of starboard dredge pump	Control parameter
16	Position of starboard diversion window	Control parameter
17	Speed of dredger	Control parameter
18	Current depth of overflow weir	Control parameter

The total design flow of variable selection with GA is shown in Algorithm. 3.

Algorithm 3. Selecting variables with GA

1. Encode individuals and generate initial populations.
   Encoding rules: If a bit value of the chromosome is "1", it means that the corresponding input variable of the bit participates in the final TDS modeling; conversely, "0" means not participating in modeling.
2. Use population to train improved BP network.
3. Calculate fitness function value.
4. If the termination condition is satisfied, the optimization result is output; otherwise, the selection, crossover, and mutation operations are performed to obtain a new population and jump to step 2.
5. Decode the optimal individual and obtain the selected parameters.

---

3 Experimental Result

3.1 Sources of Data

Modern TSHDs are equipped with advanced equipment, such as DGPS high-precision positioning systems, draft gauge indicators, drag arm position indicators, concentration meters, flowrate indicators and output calculating devices. So various parameters in the process of dredging can be measured.

The experimental data in this paper are taken from the measured dredging data of a TSHD in Xiamen. According to the actual operator's experience and some simulation results, the primary selection of production-related parameters is listed in Table 1.

3.2   The Result of Variable Selection

LAR and modern optimization theory are introduced to solve LASSO, and the results are shown in Figs. 1 and 2. The horizontal axis of the graph represents the penalty terms and the vertical axis represents the coefficients of production-related parameters. The paths of the different color lines represent coefficients solution and we can see that the coefficients solution paths of LAR and LASSO are highly similar. From right to left, with the increase of penalty, the coefficients of parameters gradually decrease to 0. Selecting appropriate penalty item and deleting the production-related parameters with coefficients of 0 can achieve the purpose of variable selection.

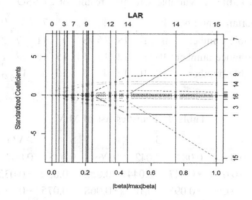

Fig. 1. LAR coefficient solution path.

More generally, it is possible to sort the importance of production-related parameters according to the LASSO coefficients by selecting the appropriate penalty and the result is shown in Table 2.

The MIV algorithm is trained for 5 times to obtain average value (AVG) and the specific training results are shown in Table 3. The average MIV value of motor speed of jet water pump and diversion window position are 0, indicating that their changes do not affect the TDS.

According to the absolute value of MIV, the importance ranking of production-related parameters is arranged, and the result is shown in Table 4.

Figure 3 is the evolution curve of population fitness function, which is optimal in the 75th generation.

The results of variable selection with GA cannot sort the variables according to the degree of importance. Compared with the two methods above, the deleted variables are angles of portside and starboard drags, pressures of portside and starboard wave compensators positions of portside and starboard diversion windows and motor speed of starboard jet water pump.

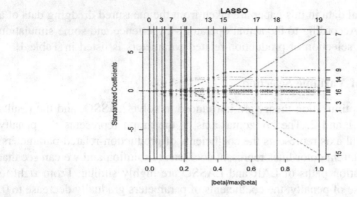

Fig. 2. LASSO coefficient solution path.

Table 2. Variable screening results of LASSO.

Importance number	1	2	3	4	5	6	7	8	9
Variable number	6	14	18	15	3	9	11	17	2
Importance number	10	11	12	13	14	15	16	17	18
Variable number	1	10	12	4	7	16	5	13	8

Table 3. Statistics list of MIV.

	1	2	3	4	5	AVG
1	0.066	0.082	0.042	0.069	0.075	0.067
2	−0.016	−0.047	−0.044	−0.022	−0.034	−0.033
3	−0.056	−0.095	−0.103	−0.068	−0.075	−0.080
4	0.024	0.006	0.007	0.003	0.014	0.011
5	0	0	0	0	0	0
6	−0.104	−0.059	−0.063	−0.159	−0.105	−0.098
7	0.022	0.198	0.061	0.099	0.069	0.090
8	0	0	0	0	0	0
9	0.095	0.094	0.016	0.066	0.080	0.070
10	−0.060	−0.035	−0.035	−0.052	−0.159	−0.068
11	−0.029	−0.038	−0.074	−0.063	−0.063	−0.053
12	0.004	0.022	0.032	0.002	0.026	0.017
13	0	0	0	0	0	0
14	−0.107	−0.092	−0.104	−0.077	−0.092	−0.094
15	0.132	0.364	0.138	0.046	0.342	0.204
16	0	0	0	0	0	0
17	−0.077	−0.039	−0.015	−0.047	−0.067	−0.049
18	0.231	0.238	0.198	0.217	0.261	0.229

Table 4. Variable screening results of MIV.

Importance number	1	2	3	4	5	6	7	8	9
Variable number	18	15	6	14	7	3	9	10	1
Importance number	10	11	12	13	14	15	16	17	18
Variable number	11	17	2	12	4	5	8	13	16

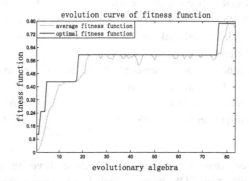

Fig. 3. Evolution curve of fitness function.

According to the 3 methods above and the order of importance, pressures of portside and starboard wave compensators positions of portside and starboard diversion windows and motor speed of starboard jet water pump deleted in GA are ranked in the end of the other two methods and the motor speed of portside jet water pump in LASSO and MIV also ranks behind, so delete these 6 variables. In addition, angles of portside and starboard drags deleted in GA are ranked in the middle of the other two methods, so these two are preserved temporarily.

Stated thus, the final selected variables can be shown in Table 5.

In combination with the actual situation, the variables removed are all related to soil properties. The wave compensator is used to compensate the ship's pressure on the river bed due to the rise and fall of waves. Usually, when the dredging soil is hard, the pressure of the wave compensator should be reduced and if soil is loose and easy to dig, the pressure should be increased. The high pressure flushing system can change the soil moisture content, making the dredging soil loose and easy to dig. For water diversion window, when the dense soil is excavated, the opening of the water diversion window should be enlarged to increase the inflow and should be reduced if soil is loose. Therefore, these three items should not be deleted.

However, according to the measured data, it is found that the pressure of the wave compensator at the stage of dredging is kept near a certain value and the speed of the high pressure flushing motor is 0. Besides, the measured value of the position of diversion window remains unchanged. This indicates that the high pressure flushing system and the opening of the water diversion windows has not been activated or changed. It is preliminarily concluded that the sediment characteristics and the wind and wave currents have not changed significantly. Therefore, their changes have no effect on yield, so that the importance of ranking is behind and especially in the MIV

Table 5. The optimal production-related parameters.

Variable number	Variable name	Variable type
1	Depth of portside drag	Control parameter
2	Angle of portside drag	Control parameter
3	Differential pressure of portside drag	Measurement parameter
6	Vacuum degree of portside dredge pump	Measurement parameter
7	Speed of portside dredge pump	Control parameter
9	Depth of starboard drag	Control parameter
10	Angle of starboard drag	Control parameter
11	Differential pressure of starboard drag	Measurement parameter
14	Vacuum degree of starboard dredge pump	Measurement parameter
15	Speed of starboard dredge pump	Control parameter
17	Speed of dredger	Control parameter
18	Current depth of overflow weir	Control parameter

screening method, their mean value being 0. But these three items must not be considered as having no effect on TDS, because their functions are obvious in the sea area where sediment characteristics and wind waves change significantly. Especially in the maritime space where soil is dense and influence of wave flow is great, it is necessary to open the high-pressure flushing system to break the soil and increase the pressure of the wave compensator and the opening of the water diversion window.

Accordingly, it can be concluded that the results of these three variable selection methods above conform to actual measurement data. However, the results cannot be used as input for all TDS models, because the soil characteristics and construction environments encountered in each working condition are different.

4 Conclusion

The screening results of three methods above are not entirely consistent, but the variables that should be kept are roughly the same. The main difference is reflected in the ranking of importance, which is caused by the algorithm principle of LASSO and MIV. LASSO pays attention to the linear fitting degree of production-related parameters to TDS, while MIV method takes the sensitivity of parameters as the importance.

LASSO has a greater impact on the penalty item. When the penalty parameter λ is larger, more coefficients tend to be 0 and less production-parameters are persisted. In addition, it assumes that the TDS model is a linear model. Although it is not in line with the actual situation, it has obvious advantages in solving the collinearity problem.

MIV takes the sensitivity of production-related parameters as importance, leading to some important but constant parameters missing. But for the specific working environment, if the soil or environmental factors in dredging process have not changed significantly, these important control variables can remain unchanged.

GA is the best way to establish effective TDS model, but it only works for specific conditions, and has no universality like MIV. What's more, MIV and GA are based on the BP network model, and there are inherent defects in the BP network, such as the randomness of initial weight and threshold value, local minimization, slow convergence speed, different choice of network structure and sample dependence. Although the BP network is optimized by GA, it cannot make up for all the defects of the BP network, at the same time, the application of GA algorithm increasing the running time of the program.

Concluding, these three methods above have their own advantages and disadvantages, and GA is the best in terms of modeling effect. They also have one thing in common: the final input variables are not universal, but they are in line with the actual situation of the specific dredging operation. Therefore, for the different sea areas, these three methods above should be reused to determine the best input parameters.

Acknowledgments. This work was financially supported by the Science and Technology Commission of Shanghai Municipality of China under Grant (No. 17511107002).

References

1. Increased accuracy in data for Dutch dredging operations. World Pumps, **2017**(26), 28–29 (2017)
2. Braaksma, J., Babuska, R., Klaassens, J.B., et al.: Model predictive control for optimization the overall dredging performance of a trailing suction hopper dredger. In: Proceedings of the 18th World Dredging Congress (2007)
3. Stano, P.M., Tilton, A.K., Babuska, R.: Estimation of the soil-dependent time-varying parameters of the hopper sedimentation model: The FPF versus the BPF. Control Eng. Pract. **24**, 67–78 (2014)
4. Chen, X., Miedema, S.A., van Rhee, C.: Numerical modeling of excavation process in dredging engineering. Procedia Eng. **102**, 804–814 (2015)
5. Lendek, Z., Babuska, R., Braaksma, J., de Keizer, C.: Decentralized estimation of overflow losses in a hopper dredger. Control Eng. Pract. **16**, 382–406 (2008)
6. Tibshirani, R.: Regression shrinkage and selection via the LASSO: a retrospective. R. Statist. Soc. B **73**(3), 273–282 (2011)
7. Zhang, L., Li, K.: Forward and backward least angle regression for nonlinear system. Automatic **53**, 94–102 (2015)
8. Moradi, M.H., Abedini, M.: A combination of genetic algorithm and particle swarm optimization for optimal DG location and sizing in distribution systems. Int. J. Electr. Power Energy Syst. **1**, 66–74 (2011)
9. Zhang, Z.: An estimation of coal density distributions by weight based on image analysis and MIV-SVM. In: 2015 IEEE Advanced Information Technology Electronic and Automation Control Conference (2015)
10. Chen, D., Hu, B., Shao, X., Su, Q.: Variable selection by modified IPW (iterative predictor weighting)-PLS (partial least squares) in continuous wavelet regression models. Analyst **129** (7), 664–669 (2004)
11. Duan, F., Xiao, F., Jiang, J.J., Ma, L.: Automatic variable selection method and a comparison for quantitative analysis in laser-induced breakdown spectroscopy. Spectrochim. Acta, Part B **143**, 12–17 (2018)

Fault Diagnosis and Maintenance

A New Data Analytics Framework Emphasising Pre-processing in Learning AI Models for Complex Manufacturing Systems

Caoimhe M. Carbery[1,2(✉)], Roger Woods[1], and Adele H. Marshall[2]

[1] Electronic Computer Engineering, Queen's University Belfast, Belfast, UK
{ccarbery02,r.woods}@qub.ac.uk
[2] Mathematical Sciences Research Centre, Queen's University Belfast, Belfast, UK
a.h.marshall@qub.ac.uk

Abstract. Recent emphasis has been placed on improving the processes in manufacturing by employing early detection or fault prediction within production lines. Whilst companies are increasingly including sensors to record observations and measurements, this brings challenges in interpretation as standard approaches for artificial intelligence (AI) do not highlight the presence of unknown relationships. To address this, we propose a new data analytics framework for predicting faults in a large-scale manufacturing system and validate it using a publicly available Bosch manufacturing dataset with a focus on pre-processing of the data.

1 Introduction

Manufacturing is highly competitive and companies have made considerable investments to improve their production analysis capabilities by adding sensors to record information as products undergo manufacture [1]. The abundance of data from multiple sources and in different formats that is monitored continuously, creates challenge for analysis. Moreover, the data may not have been recorded properly, resulting in missing data which has the potential of severely impacting subsequent modeling systems and biasing results. *Missingness* can be due to faults in a machine or sensor, occurrence of noise during processing, power shortages, or some other issues [2]. In addition, imbalanced classes can occur as a result of under-represented classes, such as in binary classification where there can be a majority and minority class. Research has highlighted the problems in assessing classifiers as errors result in inaccuracy as the system is biased towards the majority class. The work here focuses on binary classification where we want to determine whether a product will be grouped into the minority (failure) class dependent on the input parameters.

© Springer Nature Singapore Pte Ltd. 2018
K. Li et al. (Eds.): ICSEE 2018/IMIOT 2018, CCIS 924, pp. 169–179, 2018.
https://doi.org/10.1007/978-981-13-2384-3_16

Review of Relevant Literature: The data in modern manufacturing challenges can suffer from high dimensionality, complexity, non-linearity and inconsistencies [1–4]. To address these challenges, machine learning and data analytics methods have been employed [2–5], which concentrate on predictive maintenance and rare event prediction [6].

Lee et al. [1] presented a cyber-physical system with a case study as an approach to monitor the behaviour of machines using sensor data for Industry 4.0; they also highlighted the need for further work to improve generalisability of the system. Susto et al. [3] presented a new multiple classifier model for predictive maintenance along with a simulation study and benchmark dataset; the data needed to be pre-processed in order to allow for a suitable classifier such as k-NN and support vector machines (SVM), to be trained. In [5], different ML methods were compared for a semiconductor manufacturing dataset and highlighted the benefits of reducing the data through feature selection. Work in [7] emphasised the benefits of AI and ML for manufacturing, but there has been little investigation into the statistical basis of data preprocessing to improve model performance and learning procedures. Kotsiantis et al. [8] has shown the major impact that inefficient data can have on machine learning models.

Motivation and Overview: with increasing complexity in manufacturing processes, machine learning algorithms are being used to ensure earlier detection of defects, improve production performance and prediction of future performance [5]. A framework is presented that collates, pre-processes and generates training data for manufacturing and allows behaviour to be identified that can influence the production outcome. We present an approach that allows AI systems to be built for behavioural analysis and information extraction to be performed which will help engineers to improve machine performance and aid future decision making

This paper is organised as follows; Sect. 2 outlines the framework for analysing manufacturing systems which can be applied to large, inconsistent, imbalanced datasets. Section 3 presents the Bosch case study used to test the framework and create results. Section 4 presents the results of our algorithm and covers conclusions.

2   Manufacturing Data Framework

In this research, we focus on the crucial stages of pre-processing, selecting suitable algorithms and interpretation of the results to generate a suitable method for providing feedback to manufacturing engineers. Our framework shown in Fig. 1, involves four key stages to produce an appropriate learning model [9].

Raw, real-world data which is unstructured and inconsistent in nature, often involves large dimensions, class imbalance issues and missing instances. Therefore its collation is often challenging and involves combining data from different sources e.g. from sensors of varying machines etc. and processing it appropriately.

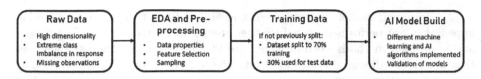

Fig. 1. Visualisation of proposed data analysis design flow for manufacturing data

2.1 Exploratory Data Analysis and Pre-processing

Exploratory data analysis (EDA) and pre-processing are crucial stages in preparing data for AI algorithms [8]. Manufacturing data can contain a large amount of redundant information which if blindly fed into a learning model, can result in a biased or unreliable outcome. Pre-processing can have a critical impact on model performance, therefore effort has been spent on standard approaches e.g. filtering and normalising to ensure that the training dataset is of an appropriate format whilst ensuring that no bias has been introduced.

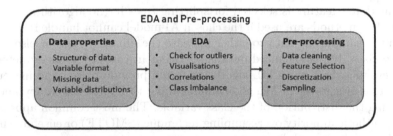

Fig. 2. Detail of the EDA and pre-processing steps required in the framework

Data cleaning removes redundant and unsuitable variables by investigating feature variance and removing those which have near to zero variance as these would not provide useful information to the model build and would only complicate the learning process. Incomplete data is unavoidable but we must try to have reasoning behind our choice for handling *missingness* whilst trying to not influence our model. We can choose from a number of methods which aim to handle missing data [10]. The most common are:

1. Remove any instance with at least one unknown variable value;
2. Mean substitution;
3. Treat missing values as a unique value;
4. K-nearest neighbour imputation method.

For our analysis, there is too much missingness to merely discard these instances, so the chosen approach, as demonstrated by other researchers [6], is to rescale the data and assign the missing instance an unique value, or if the data is of a discrete/categorical format, assign the missing instances an independent group.

To improve model performance and reliability, two feature selection approaches are performed to reduce the number of variables, namely wrapper and embedded methods both of which produce results to indicate the features that are most influential and important. The features retained must encode as much information about the system as possible in order for the final classifier model to perform well. As it is clear that a reduced feature count will improve both performance and accuracy, we want to ensure that we do not remove any features that could be influential to the model outcome [8].

Wrapper methods use a classifier model and conduct an extensive search in the space of subsets of features to determine optimal performance to produce a ranking of features. Often they are superior to filtering approaches, yet they require a larger amount of computation as they involve investigating a large search space. Embedded methods, however, can be seen as a balance between the two approaches as they use internal information of the model. Thus, we have implemented an embedded method to identify the key features for our learning model namely an extreme gradient boosting tree (XGBoost) and thus can determine the most influential and important features for building a suitable classifier [11]. XGBoost generates importance measures based on the number of occasions that a feature is selected for splitting trees in the algorithm.

Sampling methods are used if the chosen AI model cannot handle imbalanced data and re-sample the data to either increase the minority class or else reduce majority class [10]. Imbalanced data is prevalent in cases of anomaly detection or rare events, where some ML algorithms could provide biased and inaccurate results. This is a result of ML algorithms aiming to improve accuracy and not considering the distribution of the class variable. The most common approaches are the synthetic minority over-sampling technique (SMOTE) or ensemble methods which combine weak learners to create stronger learning models.

2.2   Learning Model

Extreme gradient boosting classification trees have the ability to not only uncover important data features, but to construct a robust classification model. It is a popular choice among classification models due to its simple implementation [11]. XGBoost involves the construction of an ensemble of multiple *weaker* trees i.e. small trees. In order to utilise XGBoost models, the data must be in a numeric format. In the first instance of feature selection (see Sect. 2.1), now we can run the learning algorithm on these important variables with multiple iterations to generate a powerful classification model.

2.3   Model Validation

The suitability of an intelligent classification model can be evaluated using standard statistical metrics such as accuracy, sensitivity, specificity, precision and F-measure [12]. We utilised our model and testing dataset to produce values to asses the suitability of our chosen classifier and assess its performance. We calculated the number of correctly classified positive samples (true positives), number of correctly recognised as not in the class (true negative), count of samples that were incorrectly assigned a class (false positive) and those who were not recognised as being in the correct class (false negatives), each denoted by tp, tn, fp, fn respectively [12]. These are used to construct confusion matrices which provide values that are used for calculating the common performance measures to evaluate classification models, for this paper, binary classification (Table 1).

Table 1. General format of confusion matrix.

		True Value		
		Positive	Negative	Total
Predictive	Positive	tp	fp	$tp + fn$
	Negative	fn	tn	$fn + tn$
	Total	$tp + fn$	$fp + tn$	N

The measures are highlighted as follows:

- Accuracy: indicating overall effectiveness of a classifier, calculated using the formulae $\frac{tp+tn}{N}$ but is biased when class imbalance is not addressed;
- Sensitivity and specificity analysis provide values to evaluate the effectiveness of the classifier to identify positive and negative labels respectively, and are given by $Sensitivity = \frac{tp}{tp+fn}$ and $Specificity = \frac{tn}{fp+tn}$;
- Precision is a measure of a class agreement of the data labels with the classifiers output labels, calculated by $\frac{tp}{tp+fp}$;
- F-measure is calculated by $2 \frac{precision.sensitivity}{precision+sensitivity}$ and is more robust to imbalanced data [12].

3   Bosch Manufacturing Case Study

Bosch provided a large anonymised dataset representing one of their production lines with an aim of utilising methods to try to predict the outcome of products and is available on Kaggle [13]. This dataset is one of the largest publicly available manufacturing datasets (14.3 Gb), containing approximately 1.2 million observations and over 4,000 features. The only information provided is the manufacturing line and station associated with each feature which is contained within the variable names e.g. $L1\_S24\_F1695$ indicates that Feature 1695 was observed at Station 24 on Line 1.

The datasets were split into three categories; date, categorical and numeric. Within each of these groups, Bosch have provided the data separated for training and testing thus avoiding in this case, the third stage in Fig. 1. The training sets contain the variable *Response* where a value of 1 indicates a product has failed quality control, and 0 otherwise. No response variable is included in the test dataset as this is the value that our model aims to predict. The quality of the products is extremely high as only 0.58% of products fail at the final testing stage, thus introducing a major class imbalance issue with the data. Figure 3 depicts an example of the flow of a product across the factory floor, highlighting the numerous stations associated with different lines in the build.

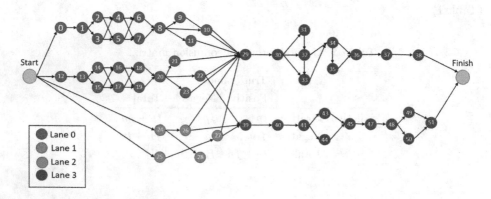

Fig. 3. Example flow of Bosch factory floor depicting stations as circular nodes.

Table 2. Overview of data used for the analysis of Bosch manufacturing.

Data characteristics	Total
Variables	986
Rows	1183747
Lines	4
Stations	51
Percentage missing	78.5
Percentage fail	0.58

3.1 Exploratory Analysis

In the first instance, we perform EDA to identify key properties of the Bosch dataset to identify correlation, redundant variables, underlying structure and issues within the data.

Data Properties: The Bosch manufacturing dataset consists of over 2.4M jobs, each of which have an associated ID and 4364 variables. These variables/features represent either numeric, categorical or date measurements. We performed analysis to determine the proportion of missing observations per feature and also a count of missing observations per ID. Initial investigation into the categorical features indicate an issue of extreme sparsity (around 99% missing) and thus is not included in this paper as done in [6]. Our analysis has focused on the numeric data as preliminaries found it to be most influential, therefore categorical and date variables were not within the scope of this study. Table 2 provides a summary of the dataset used for the research in this paper.

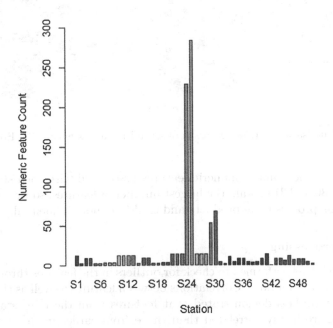

Fig. 4. Bar plot showing the number of features associated with the individual stations of the Bosch production line.

Alongside the properties of the dataset content, a number of other characteristics should be noted prior to any analysis. The chosen processing stages and algorithms must be able to account for each of these challenges if we are to appropriately model the data without introducing bias.

- As the data is anonymised, no expert knowledge can be employed to indicate the higher importance features and learning is fully data-driven.
- Missing observations represents up a large proportion of the data and could be where a product may not pass through a particular station.
- No information is related to each ID, so we could postulate that the manufacturing process involves a number of different products where they may not undergo the same processing steps.
- As the data set is large, any learning procedure must have the capabilities of processing the data of this scale.
- High class imbalance is present within the response variable as only 0.58% of products fail at the final testing stage.

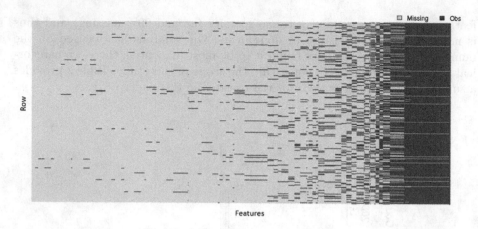

Fig. 5. Visualisation of missing versus observed instances within the Bosch data

Figure 4 shows the count of numeric features associated with each station. Stations 24, 25, 30 and 31 contain the largest number of features, so we assume that these stations process more products and could be more influential.

3.2 Pre-processing

Initial analysis was performed to check for outliers in the features through visualisations of the distributions. Correlations between features as well as the response were calculated. This demonstrated that features from the later stages of the build were more highly correlated than those from earlier in the process. The class imbalance is high, therefore if this is not handled appropriately, any model built with this data will result in a biased approach predicting that the product to be in the majority class i.e. pass. Before implementing sampling methods to handle class imbalance, a number of stages of preprocessing are necessary.

Data Cleaning: Duplicated rows were removed as they provided no further information. Variances for each feature were calculated allowing removal of redundant features with zero variance. Our feature count reduced to 158. Whilst this reduces the dimensionality of a dataset, the relation of the features with the response variable can also be investigated. Figure 5 shows missing data observations in the dataset where the lighter shaded portion represents missing data. It is clear that the later stages are where more information is recorded and would appear in the final model. This needs to be accounted for and our approach was to create an independent category for when an instance was unobserved, by performing discretization on the 158 features to include another factor representing *unobserved* instances.

Feature Selection: Feature selection allows selection of key influential variables which influence the outcome whilst improving the predictive accuracy and improving interpretability. Here we used the top 50 features indicated from the algorithm and their associated observations to train a new XGBoost classifier model. Table 3 shows an example of the 'Gain' values produced by XGBoost.

Sampling: To account for the extreme class imbalance, one must consider sampling methods to rebalance the class variable, but investigation into the XGBoost algorithm demonstrated its robustness to imbalanced data and was not performed for this initial analysis. However, sampling methods must be considered for our general data analysis framework when implementing alternative learning algorithms (Fig. 6).

Table 3. Example of six variables from XGBoost which show the accuracy of model gained by retaining these features.

Feature	Gain
L1_S24_F1723	0.5328070
L1_S24_F1846	0.2248599
L1_S24_F1632	0.1162531
L1_S24_F1695	0.0611954
L3_S34_F3876	0.0403588
L2_S26_F3036	0.0132253

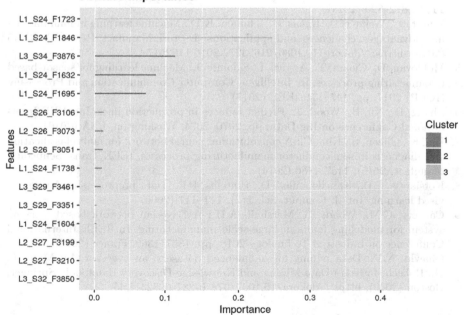

Fig. 6. Output from XGBoost showing the top 15 features of importance

4   Conclusion

In this paper, a new framework has been presented which combines useful analytics tools into a different format from those previously implemented. Using a widely available dataset from Bosch, an appropriate training dataset containing 50 features was produced, allowing an extreme gradient boosting tree to be used as a classification prediction model. Using the framework (Fig. 2), data preprocessing and exploratory analysis was used to create a reduced data size highlighting the most influential features. This allowed us to perform an R implementation of an extreme gradient boosting (XGBoost) model [11] and employ R's inbuilt performance metrics to demonstrate a high accuracy and F-measure. The research highlights the necessity to pre-process and we are currently working with a commercial partner to apply the research to their system to produce an automated system for performing the analysis on manufacturing data.

References

1. Lee, J., Kao, H., Yang, S.: Service innovation and smart analytics for industry 4.0 and big data environment. Proc. CIRP **16**, 3–8 (2014)
2. He, Q.P., Wang, J.: Statistical process monitoring as a big data analytics tool for smart manufacturing. J. Proc. Control **67**, 35–43 (2017). https://doi.org/10.1016/j.jprocont.2017.06.012
3. Susto, G., Schirru, A., Pampuri, S., McLoone, S., Beghi, A.: Machine learning for predictive maintenance: a multiple classifier approach. IEEE Trans. Industr. Inf. **11**(3), 812–820 (2015)
4. Wuest, T., Weimer, D., Irgens, C., Thoben, K.D.: Machine learning in manufacturing: advantages, challenges, and applications. J. Prod. Manufact. Res. **4**(1), 23–45 (2016). https://doi.org/10.1080/21693277.2016.1192517
5. Moldovan, D., Cioara, T., Anghel, I., Salomie, I.: Machine learning for sensor-based manufacturing processes. In: Intelligent Computer Communication and Processing (ICPP) 2017, pp. 147–154. IEEE (2017)
6. Zhang, D., Xu, B., Wood, J.: Predict failures in production lines. In: IEEE International Conference on Big Data, pp. 2070–2074. Washington, USA (2016)
7. Lee, K., Cheon, S., Kim, C.: A convolutional neural network for fault classification and diagnosis in semiconductor manufacturing processes. IEEE Trans. Semicond. Manufact. **25**(5), 1167–1180 (2014)
8. Kotsiantis, S.B., Kanellopoulos, D., Pintelas, P.E.: Data preprocessing for supervised learning. Int. J. Comput. Sci. **1**(2), 111–117 (2006)
9. Carbery, C.M., Woods, R. Marshall, A.H.: A Bayesian network based learning system for modelling faults in large-scale manufacturing. In: IEEE International Conference on Industrial Technology 2018, pp. 1357–1362. France (2018)
10. Chawla, N.V.: Data mining for imbalanced datasets: an overview. In: Maimon, O., Rokach, L. (eds.) Data Mining and Knowledge Discovery Handbook. Springer, Boston (2009). https://doi.org/10.1007/978-0-387-09823-4_45

11. Chen, T., Guestrin, C.: Xgboost: a scalable tree boosting system. In: 22nd International Proceedings on knowledge discovery and data mining, pp. 785–794. ACM (2016)
12. Sokolova, M., Lapalme, G.: A systematic analysis of performance measures for classification tasks. Inf. Proc. Manag. **45**(4), 427–437 (2009)
13. Kaggle.com: Bosch production line performance (2016). https://www.kaggle.com/c/bosch-production-line-performance. Accessed Nov 2017

Performance Assessment of Multivariate Control System Based on Data-Driven Covariance Historical Benchmark

Hong Qian[1,2], Gaofeng Jiang[1(✉)], and Yuan Yuan[1]

[1] Shanghai University of Electric Power, Changyang Road 2588, 200090 Shanghai, China
{qianhong.sh, godfery_Jiang, yuanyuan_shdl}@163.com
[2] Shanghai Power Station Automation Technology Key Laboratory, Shangda Road 99, 200072 Shanghai, China

Abstract. In order to better meet the on-site monitoring requirements and ensure the control system is running well, the performance assessment for multivariate control system (MIMO) is an increasing concern. According to the generalized eigenvalue analysis, multiple performance indexes based on the eigenvalues was proposed, and big data of process output was used to obtain a history data set and establish a historical benchmark, which can not only monitor the adjustment ability of single closed-loop, but also get the change of the overall control performance. A user-definable indicator is put forward to select the historical data set, then, based on the statistical analysis theory, the benchmark is improved and multiple performance levels are divided. Finally, the performance evaluation method is presented for MIMO. An example for monitoring the performance of the coordination control system (CCS) is illustrated to show the use and effectiveness and objectivity of the proposed method.

Keywords: Performance assessment · Data-driven
Multivariate control system · Historical benchmark · Statistical analysis theory
Performance levels

1 Introduction

Modern industrial process controllers can meet design requirements in the early running, but without regular maintenance, the controller performance will decline with time and eventually lead to a huge gap [1]. At present, for MIMO systems on site, such as CCS, the control performance can only be judged by manual analysis, which is difficult to adapt to the requirements of power production automation. It is also necessary to realize the timely detection of performance degradation, provide guidance for the optimization. Therefore, it is an urgent need to implement automatic and effective online performance assessment and monitoring of a MIMO.

Research on control performance was first proposed by Harris [2], which shows the construction of performance benchmark is the key to evaluation index. Depending on the benchmark, performance evaluation methods can be divided into two types [3]. One is a method based on mathematical modeling. The performance benchmark of this

© Springer Nature Singapore Pte Ltd. 2018
K. Li et al. (Eds.): ICSEE 2018/IMIOT 2018, CCIS 924, pp. 180–190, 2018.
https://doi.org/10.1007/978-981-13-2384-3_17

method is mostly from some of the best controllers designed for theoretical goals. Such methods as IMC [4], MVC [5, 6] and LQG [7] are relatively mature, but the monitoring effect depends on the accuracy of the process model. The other is data-driven evaluation methods, such as based on multivariate covariance and principal component analysis statistics [8]. These methods have strong versatility and do not rely on process models. Yu and Qin propose a statistical method for the MIMO process based on historical data [9, 10], in industrial applications, the availability of benchmarks has been validated [11]. However, a practical problem is that the selection of benchmark data for this method requires a certain amount of expert knowledge [12]. Based on data-driven technology, this paper presents a performance evaluation method based on historical benchmarks for MIMO. According to the actual operation of the system, only I/O operation data is needed and it is performed under the closed-loop conditions. It does not require in-depth understanding of the system and does not hinder the normal operation of the industrial process. In order to overcome the limitations of historical benchmarks relying on expert experience, a user-definable indicator was proposed to select historical data sets and perform distribution fitting to obtain a range of index values divided by performance levels.

This paper is organized as follows. In Sect. 2, the performance method based on data-driven is proposed. In Sect. 3, an experiment is illustrated to show the rationality of this method. Finally, the conclusions are given in Sect. 4.

2   Proposed Method

2.1   The Framework of the Proposed Method

In this section, a flowchart of the proposed method is given in Fig. 1. Data mining technology is used to analyze a large number of process data off-line, obtain the benchmark value corresponding to the historical data sets, calculate the current value J_{act} of the system operation online, and compare with the benchmark J_{hist} to obtain the performance indexes, and further multiple performance levels are divided. Finally, a comprehensive analysis of the performance of MIMO is performed.

2.2   Performance Indexes Based on Historical Benchmark for MIMO

The most common approach to loop monitoring is to compare the performance of the monitored loop with that of a benchmark [13], based on historical benchmark, the performance index can be expressed as

$$\gamma(k) = \frac{J_{hist}}{J_{act}}. \tag{1}$$

For a MIMO process, let the benchmark period be I and the monitored period II, to assess the overall control performance during period II, a covariance index similar to that proposed by Mcnabb and Qin [14] as follows:

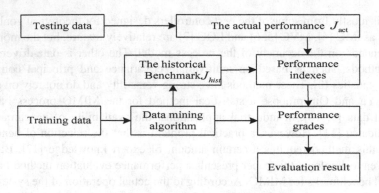

Fig. 1. Flowchart of the proposed method

$$I_v = \frac{|\text{cov}(y_\text{I})|}{|\text{cov}(y_\text{II})|}. \tag{2}$$

The covariance matrix used to characterize performance can be transformed into generalized eigenvalues [9, 15], which is a quantitative indicator. Since MIMO system with q controlled variates has

$$\text{cov}(y_\text{I})P = \text{cov}(y_\text{II})P\Lambda. \tag{3}$$

Where $\Lambda = \text{diag}(\lambda_1, \lambda_2, \cdots, \lambda_q)$ and $P=[p_1, p_2, \cdots, p_q]$.
By Eqs. (2) and (3), then we have

$$|\text{cov}(y_\text{I})||P| = |\text{cov}(y_\text{II})||P||\Lambda|. \tag{4}$$

Noticing that P is non-singular [9], we further deduced the overall performance index of the control system:

$$I_v = \frac{|\text{cov}(y_\text{I})|}{|\text{cov}(y_\text{II})|} = |\Lambda| = \prod_{i=1}^{q} \lambda_i. \tag{5}$$

Besides, the generalized eigenvalue analysis can be also simplified as follow:

$$\{\text{cov}^{-1}(y_\text{II}) \cdot \text{cov}(y_\text{I})\}p = \lambda p. \tag{6}$$

According to the mathematical definition of the eigenvalue, it has:

$$\text{cov}(y_\text{I})P_\text{I} = \Lambda_\text{I}P_\text{I}. \tag{7}$$

$$\text{cov}(y_\text{II})P_\text{II} = \Lambda_\text{II}P_\text{II}. \tag{8}$$

Where $\Lambda_I = \mathrm{diag}(\lambda_{I,1}, \lambda_{I,2}, \cdots, \lambda_{I,q})$ and $\Lambda_{II} = \mathrm{diag}(\lambda_{II,1}, \lambda_{II,2}, \cdots, \lambda_{II,q}), \lambda_{I,i}$ are eigenvalues during period I corresponding to a controlled variate, and $\lambda_{II,i}$ are eigenvalues during period II.

Comparing Eqs. (4), (7) and (8) can yield:

$$\Lambda = \Lambda_I \Lambda_{II}^{-1} = \begin{bmatrix} \frac{\lambda_{I,1}}{\lambda_{II,1}} & & & \\ & \frac{\lambda_{I,2}}{\lambda_{II,2}} & & \\ & & \ddots & \\ & & & \frac{\lambda_{I,q}}{\lambda_{II,q}} \end{bmatrix}. \tag{9}$$

So we get the single closed-loop performance index:

$$I_i = \lambda_i = \frac{\lambda_{I,i}}{\lambda_{II,i}}. \tag{10}$$

2.3   Historical Data Set Selection Rules and Performance Classification

Combining with practical applications, the historical data set to be selected is a series of continuous process data, and at the same time, the indicator does not show a large jump. Therefore, we have proposed an indicator that can be customized according to different needs. It is used to select a historical data set and defines it as follow:

$$\alpha(\Gamma) = \omega_0 \prod_{i=1}^{q} \lambda_{\Gamma,i} + \sum_{i=1}^{q} \omega_i \lambda_{\Gamma,i}. \tag{11}$$

Where Γ is a certain operating phase, $\lambda_{\Gamma,i}$ are the eigenvalues correspondingly. The weight coefficient ω_0 represents the importance of overall control performance, $\omega_0, \omega_1, \cdots \omega_q$ represents the importance of each closed-loop control performance.

In this paper, a large amount of historical process data is used to traverse all historical stages according to Eq. (11) for off-line calculations to obtain index values $\alpha(\Gamma)$ for any stage and regard it as a random variate, denoted as X. Through mathematical statistics analysis, we can the probability distribution of X and further fit the distribution to $f(x)$, take multiple data sets corresponding to multiple stages corresponding to the peak value as historical data sets, in that way, the average value of the eigenvalue values in the multiple stages corresponding to the historical data sets serves as the evaluation benchmark, i.e. $\lambda_{*,1}, \lambda_{*,2}, \cdots, \lambda_{*,q}$.

After fitting, in most cases, X is possible to obey the lognormal distribution, thus $Y = \ln(X) \sim N(\mu, \sigma^2)$, the probability density function expression of X is

$$f(x, \mu, \sigma) = \begin{cases} \frac{1}{\sqrt{2\pi}\sigma x} \exp\left[-\frac{1}{2\sigma^2}(\ln x - \mu)^2\right] & x > 0 \\ 0 & x \le 0 \end{cases}. \tag{12}$$

When $y = \ln(x) = \mu$, which is $x = e^\mu$, $f_{\max}(x, \mu, \sigma)$ exists. As there are M stages in the history data set, the benchmark is

$$\lambda_{*,i} = \frac{1}{M} \sum_{k=1}^{M} \lambda_{*k,i}. \tag{13}$$

When $y = \ln(x) = \mu + p\sigma$, which is $x = e^{\mu + p\sigma}$, corresponding to N data sets, there are

$$\lambda_{\mu + p\sigma, i} = \frac{1}{N} \sum_{k=1}^{N} \lambda_{pk,i}. \tag{14}$$

Then the improved single closed-loop control performance indexes are

$$I_i = \lambda_i = \frac{\lambda_{*,i}}{\lambda_{II,i}}. \tag{15}$$

The improved overall control performance index can be expressed by

$$I_v = \prod_{i=1}^{q} \lambda_i = \prod_{i=1}^{q} \frac{\lambda_{*,i}}{\lambda_{II,i}}. \tag{16}$$

In practical work, Y obeys the normal distribution and has 3σ criteria, so the lognormal distribution X has

$$
\begin{aligned}
P(e^{\mu-\sigma} \leq x \leq e^{\mu+\sigma}) &= 68.27\% \\
P(e^{\mu-2\sigma} \leq x \leq e^{\mu+2\sigma}) &= 95.45\% \\
P(e^{\mu-3\sigma} \leq x \leq e^{\mu+3\sigma}) &= 99.73\%.
\end{aligned} \tag{17}
$$

Therefore, the range of indexes can be divided into 5 intervals in the direction of $(0, \infty)$, corresponding to 5 grades, respectively poor, fair, good, nice and great, as shown in Table 1. In the end the rating criteria is summarized as follows

Table 1. Performance grades

Item	Great	Nice	Good	Fair	Poor
I_i	$(1, \infty)$	$(\frac{\lambda_{*,i}}{\lambda_{\mu+\sigma,i}}, 1]$	$(\frac{\lambda_{*,i}}{\lambda_{\mu+2\sigma,i}}, \frac{\lambda_{*,i}}{\lambda_{\mu+\sigma,i}}]$	$(\frac{\lambda_{*,i}}{\lambda_{\mu+3\sigma,i}}, \frac{\lambda_{*,i}}{\lambda_{\mu+2\sigma,i}}]$	$(0, \frac{\lambda_{*,i}}{\lambda_{\mu+3\sigma,i}}]$
I_v	$(1, \infty)$	$(\frac{\prod_{i=1}^{q}\lambda_{*,i}}{\prod_{i=1}^{q}\lambda_{\mu+\sigma,i}}, 1]$	$(\frac{\prod_{i=1}^{q}\lambda_{*,i}}{\prod_{i=1}^{q}\lambda_{\mu+2\sigma,i}}, \frac{\prod_{i=1}^{q}\lambda_{*,i}}{\prod_{i=1}^{q}\lambda_{\mu+\sigma,i}}]$	$(\frac{\prod_{i=1}^{q}\lambda_{*,i}}{\prod_{i=1}^{q}\lambda_{\mu+3\sigma,i}}, \frac{\prod_{i=1}^{q}\lambda_{*,i}}{\prod_{i=1}^{q}\lambda_{\mu+2\sigma,i}}]$	$(0, \frac{\prod_{i=1}^{q}\lambda_{*,i}}{\prod_{i=1}^{q}\lambda_{\mu+3\sigma,i}}]$

The performance of MIMO is a comprehensive consideration of single closed-loop indexes and the overall index. Therefore, If I_i and I_v are all great, the controller of MIMO system works well, on the contrary, when they all are poor, the adjustment effect is difficult to meet the control requirements.

3   Experiment and Discussion

The process output data from a 600 MW coal-fired heating unit of a thermal power plant under normal operation is used as the data source of the experiment. The dataset contains the set-point and output values of the two controlled variates (output power and main steam pressure). Then, an example for monitoring the performance of CCS is illustrated in this section.

3.1   Performance Indexes for Coordinated Control System

Generally, coordinated control system of the thermal power unit is a tow input tow output control object. From Eqs. (15) and (16), the control performance indexes are

$$I_N = \lambda_N = \frac{\lambda_{*,N}}{\lambda_{\mathrm{II},N}}. \tag{18}$$

$$I_P = \lambda_P = \frac{\lambda_{*,P}}{\lambda_{\mathrm{II},P}}. \tag{19}$$

$$I_v = \lambda_N \lambda_P = \frac{\lambda_{*,N}\lambda_{*,P}}{\lambda_{\mathrm{II},N}\lambda_{\mathrm{II},P}}. \tag{20}$$

Where I_N and I_P is the single closed-loop performance index of power and main steam pressure, respectively, I_v represents the overall performance of the system.

3.2   Experimental Procedure

Due to the large data, only 6 h were shown below. The output power (MW) was in Fig. 2. The main steam pressure (MPa) was in Fig. 3.

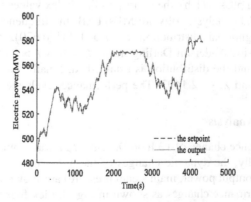

Fig. 2. The set-point and output of electric power

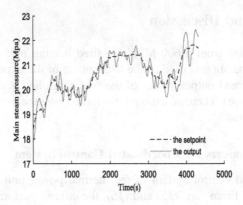

Fig. 3. The set-point and output of main steam pressure

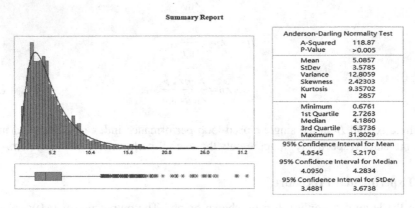

Fig. 4. Statistical summary report of α

By using Eq. (11) ($\omega_0 = 1.5, \omega_1 = 2$ and $\omega_2 = 2$) to perform offline calculations on multiple historical phases (1 h), the corresponding index values for 2 857 phases are obtained. Through data analysis software MINITAB, the frequency of α was counted and fitted to a lognormal distribution $\alpha \sim f(x, 1.431, 0.620)$, showed in Fig. 4. Hypothesis test by using Anderson-Darling shows $P = 0.107 > 0.05$ in Fig. 5, it meets the null hypothesis and the distribution is established. Finally, we can get the benchmark $\lambda_{*,1} = 0.0511$ and $\lambda_{*,2} = 2.1403$. The performance levels are shown in Table 2.

3.3 Results and Analysis

The control performance change of 12 h on December 22 was monitored using the field operation data. Finally, the dynamic changes of the performance indexes for a single controlled quantity (output power, main steam pressure) are shown in Figs. 6 and 7, the overall system performance changes as shown in Fig. 8. Pick four times t1, t2, t3, and t4 during performance monitoring, as shown in Fig. 9, we can get the corresponding index value, showed in Table 3.

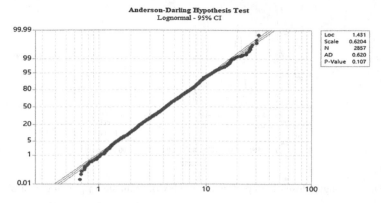

Fig. 5. Anderson-darling hypothesis test

Table 2. Classification of the coordinated control performance

Item	Great	Nice	Good	Fair	Poor
I_N	$(1, \infty)$	$(0.592, 1]$	$(0.406, 0.592]$	$(0.229, 0.406]$	$(0, 0.229]$
I_P	$(1, \infty)$	$(0.568, 1]$	$(0.307, 0.568]$	$(0.164, 0.307]$	$(0, 0.164]$
I_v	$(1, \infty)$	$(0.339, 1]$	$(0.157, 0.339]$	$(0.054, 0.157]$	$(0, 0.054]$

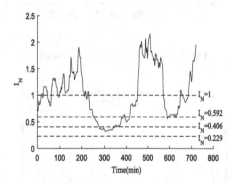

Fig. 6. Single closed-loop performance index of electric power control

The simulation results show that the electric power control performance is great for more than 360 min, and is still nice for a long time, and the performance is good and fair in a short time within 200 min to 400 min. The main steam pressure control performance is great or nice most of the time, nice state time is longer, and performance is good and general in a short time. The overall control performance is great or nice most of time and it is good or fair in a very short time.

At time t1, I_N, I_P and I_v are all greater than 1, control quality of the system better than the benchmark, and is in the great state; At t2, the control performance is general, which needs to be improved. There is a severe attenuation trend in t1 to t2, which

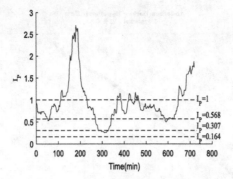

Fig. 7. Single closed-loop performance index of main steam pressure control

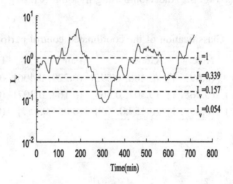

Fig. 8. Overall performance index

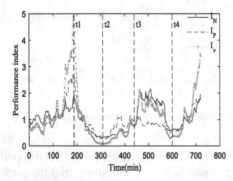

Fig. 9. The dynamic change curve of performance indexes

should be taken seriously. Adjustment quality of the system is nice at t3; it is good at t4. The situation does not occur, that is, the power, main steam pressure, and overall control performance are all in poor, which means that the system is out of control.

Table 3. Performance index values at t1–t4

Item	I_N	I_P	I_v
t1	1.904	2.593	4.937
T2	0.325	0.265	0.086
T3	0.790	0.927	0.732
T4	0.616	0.560	0.345

4 Conclusion

This paper proposes evaluation indexes for MIMO based on data-driven technology combined with the actual operation of the control system. It can not only obtain the control performance of a single closed-loop, but also get the overall performance of MIMO. And a rule for selecting historical sets is also proposed, by which an improved historical benchmark is obtained, and uses distribution fitting to divide the control performance into five levels. The performance evaluation of a 600 MW unit coordinated control system is simulated, and the objectivity and rationality of the method are verified. For the characteristics and control quality requirements, this method can be applied to a large number of multivariate control systems in the field. It can realize online automatic evaluation to monitor the change of control quality, quickly respond to severe performance degradation, and provide guidance for the optimization of control system.

References

1. Desborough, L., Miller, R.: Increasing customer value of industrial control performance monitoring-honeywell's experience.In: AIChE Symposium Series, pp. 169–189 (2002)
2. Harris, T.J.: Assessment of control loop performance. Can. J. Chem. Eng. **67**(5), 856–861 (1989)
3. Xin, Q., Yang, C., et al.: A review of control loop monitoring and diagnosis: prospects of controller maintenance in big data era. Chin. J. Chem. Eng. **24**(8), 952–962 (2016)
4. Zhang, G.M., Li, N., Li, S.Y.: A data driven performance monitoring method for predictive controller. J. Shanghai Jiao Tong Univ. **45**(8), 1113–1118 (2011)
5. Zhang, Q., Li, S.Y.: Performance monitoring and diagnosis of multivariate model predictive control using statistical analysis. Chin. J. Chem. Eng. **14**(2), 207–215 (2006)
6. Wang, X., Huang, B., Chen, T.: Multirate minimum variance control design and control performance assessment: a data-driven subspace approach. IEEE Trans. Control Syst. Technol. **15**(1), 65–74 (2006)
7. Bernstein, D.S., Haddad, W.M.: LQG control with an H∞ performance bound: a Riccati equation approach. In: American Control Conference, pp. 796–802. IEEE (2009)
8. Alghazzawi, A., Lennox, B.: Model predictive control monitoring using multivariate statistics. J. Process Control **19**(2), 314–327 (2009)
9. Yu, J., Qin, S.J.: Statistical MIMO controller performance monitoring, Part I: data-driven covariance benchmark. J. Process Control **18**(3–4), 277–296 (2008)
10. Yu, J., Qin, S.J.: Statistical MIMO controller performance monitoring, part II: Performance diagnosis. J. Process Control **18**(3–4), 297–316 (2008)

11. Li, Q., Whiteley, J.R., Rhinehart, R.R.: A relative performance monitor for process controllers. Int. J. Adapt. Control Sig. Process. **17**(7–9), 685–708 (2010)
12. Wang, L., Li, N.: Performance monitoring of the data-driven subspace predictive control systems based on historical objective function benchmark. Acta Autom. Sin. **39**(5), 542–547 (2013)
13. Desborough, L., Harris, T.: Performance assessment measures for univariate feedback control. Can. J. Chem. Eng. **70**(6), 1186–1197 (1992)
14. Mcnabb, C.A., Qin, S.J.: Projection based MIMO control performance monitoring: I—covariance monitoring in state space. J. Process Control **13**(8), 739–757 (2003)
15. Yuan, Q., Lennox, B., Mcewan, M.: Analysis of multivariate control performance assessment techniques. J. Process Control **19**(5), 751–760 (2009)

Quantitative Safety Assessment Method of Industrial Control System Based on Reduction Factor

Haoxiang Zhu[1]([✉]), Jingqi Fu[1], Weihua Bao[2], and Zhengming Gao[2]

[1] Department of Automation, College of Mechatronics Engineering and Automation, Shanghai University, No.149, Yanchang Rd, 200072 Shanghai, China
18817679228@163.com, jqfu@staff.shu.edu.cn
[2] Shanghai Automation Instrumentation Co Ltd, Shanghai, China

Abstract. Information security assessment is important to the smooth and stable operation of industrial control system (ICS), and provides valuable advices for security policy and measurement. On the basis of analyzing the safety risk assessment standards of industrial control system, this paper puts forward a method of risk assessment for industrial control system based on fuzzy analytic hierarchy process, and creatively introduces fuzzy consistent matrix and entropy method to overcome the lack of fuzziness in the evaluation result of traditional analytic hierarchy process. This method can effectively assess the importance of system assets, the severity of vulnerability and the threats it faces. Through the above steps, the risk of the system is comprehensively evaluated.

Keywords: Industrial control system · Risk assessment · Entropy method
Vulnerability

1 Introduction

With the arrival of intelligent manufacturing and the deep integration of industrialization and information technology [1], in view of the increasing security threat and attack of industrial control system, the network security risk assessment is becoming more and more concerned as a method to recognize the risk of industrial control system [2] in advance. It has become a new hot spot in the research of industrial control network security [3].

Most of the industrial enterprises in our country have not established the information security management system of industrial control system, the safety management system is not perfect, and the establishment of the safety management system [4] is lack of basis and guidance. With the continuous development of the Internet, the proportion of information security risk is becoming more and more serious. Therefore, it is necessary to develop the relevant standards for safety management, put forward the specific process of safety management [5], and put forward the safety requirements of the industrial control system from many aspects such as information security and

© Springer Nature Singapore Pte Ltd. 2018
K. Li et al. (Eds.): ICSEE 2018/IMIOT 2018, CCIS 924, pp. 191–201, 2018.
https://doi.org/10.1007/978-981-13-2384-3_18

functional safety, and guide the industrial enterprises to establish the suitable conditions according to their own actual conditions [6].

In the field of industrial control security, most of them are the combination of analytic hierarchy process and normalization. In this paper, the fuzzy matrix method and entropy method are adopted to reduce the consistency test [7]. The reduction factor can also improve the accuracy of the final evaluation. It is a feasible method.

2 Factors Analysis of Industrial Control Security Assessment

2.1 Asset Identification

First, an object asset library is needed to create, which can not be limited to the hardware and software of the system. The assets of a complete control system should include information, data, hardware, software, communication facilities, personnel, and manufactured products. Generally speaking, the assets of industrial control network can be divided into physical assets, logical assets and personnel assets.

Destroying the availability, integrity and confidentiality of information assets is the main way to affect the system, and most of the system losses also arise. In the process of assigning assets, the value of assets can be expressed qualitatively or quantitatively, and some systems can describe the value of assets in the process of risk analysis by quantitative analysis.

The final assignment is assigned to a level, and asset classification shows a comprehensive description of the importance of different levels. The higher the level is, the more important the assets are, the evaluators can determine the scope of the important assets [8] according to the results of the assets, then the next risk assessment is carried out through the important assets.

2.2 Vulnerability Identification

The vulnerability of industrial control system can be divided into technical vulnerability and management vulnerability according to different attributes. For a long time, industrial control systems have been considered as isolated and isolated systems, and information security is not the first issue to be considered. This makes the industrial control system have many vulnerabilities in the technology of [9] platform and network. In the industrial field, the awareness of information security and protection is weak, and a large part of the industrial control system lacks effective safety management. It is mainly manifested in the imperfect safety management system, the unclear operation process of the safety equipment, the lack of effective supervision, inspection of the security risks faced by the system, the lack of training for the personnel, the backward emergency plan and so on.The degree of vulnerability of the identification is classified to the degree of membership, and then classify the severity of vulnerability according to the difficulty of vulnerability being exploited.

2.3   Threat Recognition

Industrial control system threats mainly come from external environment and human factors. The external environment threats are mainly manifested in the physical environment effects such as hardware and software failures, network attacks and serious natural disasters, such as earthquakes and fires, and human factors are mainly manifested in poor management, operation error, unauthorized access and operation.

The two indicators for assigning threats are the frequency of threats and the impact on assets. The frequency of the earthquake threat is very low, but it is very destructive to the system, and the frequency of network sniffing is very high, but most of the effects on the system can be ignored.

After the identification of assets, vulnerabilities, threats and existing security measures, according to certain rules, an appropriate method is adopted to assign the identified risk factors. The risk values of the organization are related to the importance of the assets, the severity of the vulnerability and the intensity of the threat.

3   Safety Quantitative Analysis

3.1   Level Analysis Method

A hierarchical structure model is established. On the basis of in-depth analysis of practical problems, various factors are decomposed from top to bottom into several levels according to different attributes. The factors of the same layer are influenced by the factors belonging to the upper layer or on the upper factors, and at the same time, the factors of the next layer or the role of the lower factors are dominated. The top level is the target layer, usually has only 1 factors, the lowest level is usually the plan or the object layer, and there is one or several levels in the middle, it is usually the criterion or the index layer. When there are too many criteria (for example, more than 9), the sub criterion level should be further decomposed.

The weight vector is calculated and the consistency check is carried out. For each pair of paired comparison matrices, consistency index is used, random consistency index and consistency ratio to test the consistency of the maximum characteristic root and corresponding eigenvector. If the test is succeed, the feature vector (normalized) is the weight vector; if it is not succeed, the paired comparison matrix needs to be reconstructed.

Calculate the combined weight vector and check the consistency. The lowest combination weight vector is calculated to tend to the target., and do the combination consistency check according to the formula. If the test is succeed, the decision can be made according to the result expressed by the combination weight vector. Otherwise, the model or the pair comparison matrix with large consistency ratio need to be reconsidered.

The analytic hierarchy process is used to decompose the industrial control system into several levels, construct the information security risk hierarchy structure model, and establish multiple evaluation items. The factors of safety evaluation are divided into target level, criterion level and index level. The work of pre-risk assessment includes asset identification, vulnerability identification and threat identification. It's necessary to transform the complex multi factor problem into the contrast problem. By comparing the factors, the fuzzy complementary [10] judgement matrix constructed by the expert is converted into a fuzzy consistent judgment matrix [11].

3.2 Level Analysis Method

The judgement matrix of the analytic hierarchy process needs many times when the consistency is poor. The fuzzy complementary judgement matrix constructed is converted by the expert to the fuzzy consistent judgment matrix. It overcomes the defect that the subjectivity of the judgement matrix is too strong in the analytic hierarchy process, and the difference between consistency [12] and matrix consistency, the difficulty and lack of consistency check.

Judgment matrix:

$$R(r_{ij})_{n*n} = \begin{bmatrix} 1 & \frac{\omega_2}{\omega_1} & \cdots & \frac{\omega_n}{\omega_1} \\ \frac{\omega_1}{\omega_2} & 1 & \cdots & \vdots \\ \vdots & & \ddots & \\ \frac{\omega_1}{\omega_n} & & \cdots & 1 \end{bmatrix}$$

The comparison of the two factors is divided into 6 grades: the same, important, relatively important, obviously important, and absolutely important. It's natural to use digital 0.1–0.9 to quantify, as shown in Table 1.

Table 1. Numerical meaning table

r_{ij}	Meaning
0.5	The two factors are equally important
0.6	Compared with the two elements, the former is slightly more important
0.7	Compared with the two elements, the former is obviously important
0.8	Compared with the two elements, the former is strongly important
0.9	Compared with the two elements, the former is extremely important
0.1–0.4	Contrary to the above

In order to determine the relative membership degree of a single evaluation index, the fuzzy evaluation matrix is used to eliminate the dimensional effect of each evaluation index to make modeling universal.

$$R = (r_{ij})_{n*n} \tag{1}$$

The fuzzy complementary judgement matrix is calculated by line and recorded as:

$$r_i = \sum_{k}^{n} r_{ik} \tag{2}$$

The mathematical transformation is applied to the fact:

$$f_{ij} = \frac{r_i - r_j}{2n} + 0.5 \tag{3}$$

The records are as follows:

$$R_M = (f_{ij})_{n*n} \tag{4}$$

The consistency condition of the judgement matrix is not completely satisfied, and it is objective or even impossible to eliminate in practice.

Use the test index:

$$CI = \frac{\lambda_{\max} - n}{n - 1} \tag{5}$$

When less than 0.1, the judgement matrix conforms to the consistency standard [13], and the result of hierarchical single ranking is acceptable. Otherwise, CI will be revised until it meets the consistency standard. $\lambda_{\max}$ is the maximum eigenvalue of a fuzzy judgment matrix.

3.3   Element Normalization

When the value of a certain index of each evaluation object [14] is different, the entropy value is smaller, which indicates that the effective information provided by the index is larger and its weight should be larger. On the contrary, if the difference of a certain index value is small and the entropy value is larger, the amount of information provided by the index is smaller and the weight of the index should be smaller. When the values of each target are the same, the entropy is maximum, which means that the index has no useful information, and can be removed from the evaluation index system.

Since the measurement units of each index are not unified, it is necessary to standardize them before they are used to calculate the comprehensive indexes [16], which means that the absolute value of the index is converted to the relative value.

$$f_{ij} = |f_{ij}| \tag{6}$$

In order to determine the fuzzy membership matrix of the relative membership degree of a single evaluation index, the dimensional effect of each evaluation index is eliminated, so that the modeling is universal.

$$R_M = (f_{ij})_{n*n} \tag{7}$$

The matrix R_M is used as the original matrix, and linear normalization of it can be got, so as to solve the homogenization problem of different quality indicators. Moreover, because the meaning of the positive and negative index values is different (The higher the positive index is, the lower the negative index value is.). Therefore, different algorithms is used to standardize the data for high and low index. The specific methods are as follows:

For positive indicators:

$$\mu_{ij} = \frac{f_{ij} - \min_{j}(f_{ij})}{\max_{j}(f_{ij}) - \min_{j}(f_{ij})} \tag{8}$$

For negative indicators:

$$\mu_{ij} = \frac{\max_{j}(f_{ij}) - f_{ij}}{\max_{j}(f_{ij}) - \min_{j}(f_{ij})} \tag{9}$$

The entropy of the i index is:

$$h_i = -k \sum_{j=1}^{n} \theta_{ij} \ln \theta_{ij} \tag{10}$$

$$\theta_{ij} = \frac{\mu_{ij}}{\sum_{j=1}^{n} \theta_{ij}} \tag{11}$$

k is defined as a super parameter and can be adjusted according to the actual situation. After calculating the entropy of the i, the entropy weight of the i can be obtained through the following formula:

$$\omega_i = \frac{1 - h_i}{m - \sum_{i=1}^{m} h_i} (\sum_{1}^{m} \omega_i = 1) \tag{12}$$

$$W_i = (\omega_1, \omega_2 \ldots \ldots \omega_n) \tag{13}$$

The result of the evaluation:

$$B_i = W_i \times R_{Ai} \tag{14}$$

3.4 Anti Model Gelatinization Method

According to the negative rule idea, the weight of each part in the industrial control system is obtained by using the reduction factor inverse model gelatinization method, and the risk of the whole system is quantified through it.

The result of fuzzy comprehensive evaluation is a fuzzy vector which belongs to the risk comment set {high, high, general, low, low}. Then, based on the barycenter method, the reduction factor is used to improve the fuzzification method. The factor is derived from the negative rules and μ_i is called the reduction factor. μ_i is the reduction of the normal weight.

Reduction factors make up a reduction vector μ^-.

Using the reduction factor μ_i to change the normal weight in the anti-gelatinization process:

$$B_1^* = \frac{\sum\limits_{j=1}^{n} v_i \omega_i}{\sum\limits_{j=1}^{n} \omega_i} \tag{15}$$

$$B_2^* = \frac{\sum\limits_{j=1}^{n} v_i (\omega_i)^\alpha}{\sum\limits_{j=1}^{n} (\omega_i)^\alpha} \tag{16}$$

α is a compromise parameter that is distributed in the interval $[1, +\infty]$.

v_i takes the intermediate values of the grade of membership degree vector of the evaluation grade.

$$\tau_i = a_i^T \cdot \rho_i \tag{17}$$

a_i is the unit amount of each element, ρ_i is the reduction, If it's not zero, v_i was cut. To ensure that the weight after reduction is not negative, $\tau_i \subset (0, 1)$.

The evaluation score of the upper layer is obtained by the formula 17. Parameter B_i is the weight of the various factors of the I, S_i is the evaluation score for the I factor. In this way, the total score of the system can be finally obtained.

4 Case Analysis

The network risk assessment is carried on to a specific power system. First, the evaluation object is analyzed, and the evaluation target is established by the analysis. Aiming at the total risk target of the system, it is refined into multiple sub targets, and establish a hierarchical structure model of industrial control system with multi-objective, multi-level and multi criteria layer by improved analytic hierarchy process. The level structure model is divided into four layers: the target layer is the security risk of the enterprise control system; the first level index divides the factors affecting the security risk of the control system into three aspects: assets, vulnerabilities and threats; the second index is the identification of the three risk factors and subdivides according to the attributes of each category of risk factors. In order to refine the mapping relationship between target level and target level, the second level index is further refined into families, forming the underlying factor layer. Finally, the hierarchical structure model is determined.

Specifically, the relative importance of each factor index is divided according to the quantitative scaling method of fuzzy matrix priority relation, and the fuzzy judgment matrix is constructed.

Referring to the assignment structure, the numerical results is given in the form of matrix, and get the corresponding fuzzy judgement matrix$R_{P1}, R_{P2}, R_{P3}, R_{P4}$ and R_{P5}.

$$R_{P1} = \begin{bmatrix} 0.5 & 0.7 & 0.8 & 0.9 \\ 0.3 & 0.5 & 0.6 & 0.8 \\ 0.2 & 0.4 & 0.5 & 0.6 \\ 0.1 & 0.2 & 0.4 & 0.5 \end{bmatrix}, R_{P2} = \begin{bmatrix} 0.5 & 0.3 \\ 0.7 & 0.5 \end{bmatrix}, R_{P3} = \begin{bmatrix} 0.5 & 0.5 & 0.2 & 0.3 \\ 0.5 & 0.5 & 0.3 & 0.4 \\ 0.8 & 0.7 & 0.5 & 0.6 \\ 0.7 & 0.6 & 0.4 & 0.5 \end{bmatrix}$$

$$R_{P4} = \begin{bmatrix} 0.5 & 0.2 & 0.3 & 0.4 & 0.6 \\ 0.8 & 0.5 & 0.4 & 0.4 & 0.7 \\ 0.7 & 0.6 & 0.5 & 0.5 & 0.8 \\ 0.6 & 0.6 & 0.5 & 0.5 & 0.6 \\ 0.4 & 0.3 & 0.2 & 0.4 & 0.5 \end{bmatrix}$$

$$R_{P5} = \begin{bmatrix} 0.5 & 0.4 & 0.7 & 0.6 & 0.6 & 0.5 & 0.8 & 0.4 & 0.2 & 0.8 & 0.9 \\ 0.6 & 0.5 & 0.7 & 0.8 & 0.7 & 0.6 & 0.9 & 0.3 & 0.2 & 0.5 & 0.6 \\ 0.3 & 0.3 & 0.5 & 0.4 & 0.3 & 0.4 & 0.6 & 0.2 & 0.3 & 0.7 & 0.8 \\ 0.4 & 0.2 & 0.3 & 0.5 & 0.4 & 0.4 & 0.7 & 0.5 & 0.5 & 0.6 & 0.7 \\ 0.4 & 0.3 & 0.7 & 0.6 & 0.5 & 0.6 & 0.8 & 0.5 & 0.5 & 0.7 & 0.8 \\ 0.5 & 0.4 & 0.6 & 0.6 & 0.4 & 0.5 & 0.7 & 0.5 & 0.5 & 0.6 & 0.8 \\ 0.2 & 0.1 & 0.4 & 0.3 & 0.2 & 0.3 & 0.5 & 0.6 & 0.7 & 0.5 & 0.5 \\ 0.6 & 0.7 & 0.8 & 0.5 & 0.5 & 0.5 & 0.5 & 0.5 & 0.7 & 0.8 & 0.8 \\ 0.8 & 0.8 & 0.7 & 0.5 & 0.5 & 0.5 & 0.3 & 0.3 & 0.5 & 0.2 & 0.1 \\ 0.1 & 0.5 & 0.3 & 0.4 & 0.3 & 0.4 & 0.5 & 0.2 & 0.8 & 0.5 & 0.5 \\ 0.2 & 0.4 & 0.2 & 0.3 & 0.2 & 0.2 & 0.5 & 0.2 & 0.9 & 0.5 & 0.5 \end{bmatrix}$$

According to formula 8 and 9, each matrix is normalized and transform the fuzzy complementary judgement matrix R_{Pi} into fuzzy consistent matrix $R_{MPi}.i = 1, 2...5$. According to formula 10, the entropy weight ω_i of the i index is calculated. Finally, the weight of each factor b_i is calculated based on formula 11. The overall framework is shown in Fig. 1.

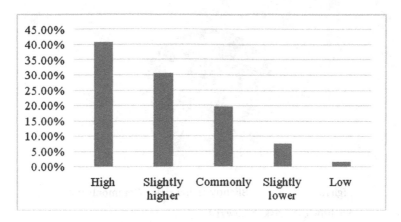

Fig. 1. Distribution of asset importance

It can be known that the weights of each index are as follows:

$$\omega_{P1} = (\,0.405 \quad 0.313 \quad 0.275 \quad 0.007\,)$$

$$\omega_{P2} = (\,0.375 \quad 0.625\,)$$

$$\omega_{P3} = (\,0.224 \quad 0.315 \quad 0.337 \quad 0.124\,)$$

$$\omega_{P4} = (\,0.012 \quad 0.121 \quad 0.221 \quad 0.485 \quad 0.161\,)$$

$$\omega_{P5} = (\,0.135 \quad 0.151 \quad 0.081 \quad 0.094 \quad 0.117 \quad 0.108 \quad 0.071 \quad 0.111 \quad 0.103 \quad 0.013 \quad 0.017\,)$$

Finally, according to the comprehensive evaluation method: $B = \omega \times R$, the final distribution of the importance of assets can be got. As shown in Fig. 2. Effective safety measures adopted by industrial control systems can reduce the possibility of vulnerability to threats. Effective security measures can reduce the possibility of risk occurrence and reduce the damage caused by security events, while invalid security measures may further create vulnerabilities and provide an intrusion approach to threats. It is found that although the deployed security performance is good, there are still some fragile points without any security measures. This is the main approach to the external threat of intrusion. For example, some commonly used industrial protocols use plaintext transmission, and the common control equipment lacks the encryption authentication mechanism and network when communicating with the host computer. The opening of the port is not standard and so on.

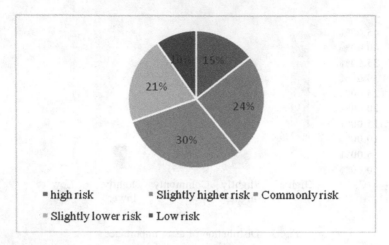

Fig. 2. Risk distribution diagram

5 Conclusion

In this paper, an improved fuzzy analytic hierarchy process is applied to assess the risk of information security in specific power systems. The results of the inverse model gelatinization are improved by entropy method and improved reduction factor, effectively assessing the importance of the system assets, the severity of the vulnerability and the threats faced, and evaluating the system risk synthetically, thus verifying the effectiveness and practicability of the proposed method. At the same time, it provides a good theoretical basis for the risk management of the industrial control system, and further enriches the theory of risk assessment of industrial control system. It has high theoretical value and practical value for the establishment of the strengthening scheme of industrial control system and the improvement of the risk management system.

In the comprehensive fuzzy evaluation of the relative importance of each element and the factors of the evaluation layer, it is one of the key points of the future research to design a better evaluation standard to deal with the evaluation data better and reduce the subjective uncertainty.

Acknowledgments. This work was financially supported by the Science and Technology Commission of Shanghai Municipality of China under Grant (No. 17511107002).

References

1. Peng, y, Jiang, C., Xie, F.: Progress in information security of industrial control systems. J. Tsinghua Univ. (Nat. Sci. Ed.) **52**(10), 1396–1408 (2012)
2. Peng, J., Liu, L.: Information security analysis of industrial control systems. Autom. Instrum. **33**(12), 36–39 (2012)
3. Chin, Z.: Safety and management of industrial network control system. Meas. Control Technol. **32**(2), 87–92 (2013)

4. Xiong, Q., Peng, Y., Dai, Z.: Preliminary study on information security risk assessment of industrial control system. Chin. Inf. Secur. **27**(3), 57–59 (2012)
5. Zhu, X.: Information security risk assessment risk analysis method. Inf. Secur. Technol. **28** (8), 87–89 (2010)
6. Jia, C., Feng, D.: Safety assessment of industrial control system based on fuzzy analytic hierarchy process. J. Zhejiang Univ. **50**(4), 759–765 (2016)
7. Qin, C., Chen, X., Yang, Y.: Research and application of three level assessment on the safety of tailing bank based on FAHP IE algorithm. Control Proj. **21**(6) 995–1000 (2014)
8. Lu, H., Chen, D., Peng, Y.: Quantitative research on information security risk assessment of industrial control system. Autom. Instrum. **35**(10), 21–25 (2014)
9. Yuan, Y.: Research on risk management of construction projects based on fuzzy analytic hierarchy process (FAHP). Chongqing University, Chongqing (2013)
10. Ma, L., Zhang, L., Yang, Y., et al.: Research on the security risk assessment of information systems based on fuzzy neural network. J. Chin. Secur. Sci. **22**(005), 164–169 (2012)
11. Li, J., Yin, X., Hutu, et al.: Research on network security assessment based on extension theory. Comput. Eng. Appl. **48**(21), 79–82 (2012)
12. Krutz, R.L.: Securing SCADA Systems. Wiley, Hoboken (2005)
13. Fan Hong, Feng Dengguo, Wu Yafei. Methods and applications of information security risk assessment. Tsinghua University press, Beijing 2006 49–50
14. Kefeng, F., Ruikang, Z., Lin, L.: Research on information security standard system of industrial control system. Top. Netw. Secur. Stand. **6** (4), 17–21 (2016)
15. Xiaofeng, Z., Xiuzhen, C.: Grey level information security evaluation model. Ind. Control Syst. **1**(6), 15–20 (2014)
16. Nicholson, A., Webber, S., Dyer, S., et al.: SCADA security in the light of cyber-warfare. Comput. Secur. **31**(4), 418–436 (2012)

Intelligent Computing in Robotics

The Electric Field Analysis and Test Experiments of Split Type Insulator Detection Robot

Pengxiang Yin[1,2,3(✉)], Xiao Hong[1,2,3], Lei Zheng[1,2,3], Biwu Yan[1,2,3], and Hao Luo[1,2,3]

[1] NARI Group Corporation Ltd., Nanjing 211106, China
hustypx@qq.com
[2] Wuhan NARI Limited Liability Company, State Grid Electric Power Research Institute, Wuhan 430074, China
[3] Hubei Key Laboratory of Power Grid Lightning Risk Prevention, Wuhan 430074, China

Abstract. The insulator strings of Extra High Voltage (EHV) and Ultra High Voltage (UHV) transmission lines are longer. It is more convenient and effective to detect insulators with robot. Currently, insulator detection robots mainly work by climbing along the insulator string, the structure is bulky and complex, and needs further improvement. Therefore, this paper proposes a split insulator detection robot which is suitable for the detection of suspended insulator string. The electric field distribution around the insulator robot is simulated and analyzed. The test experiment of 220 kV insulator string is carried out. The results indicate that the maximum electric field strength around the split type robot is 1753 kV/m. Partial discharge will not be generated. The measured potential value of the insulator detection robot is less than the original voltage distribution value of the insulator. The actual voltage distribution of insulators can be obtained by compensation and correction, then the detection of low and zero insulators is carried out.

Keywords: Split type robot · Insulator detection · Electric field analysis
Test experiments

1 Introduction

Transmission line insulators work in outdoor environment. Due to severe weather or industrial pollution, they may suffer from erosion of dust, natural hydrochloric acid, haze, acid rain, industrial waste gas and other pollutants [1, 2]. As time goes by, the insulation performance decreases. To ensure the safe operation of transmission line insulators, preventive inspection should be carried out regularly. In addition, insulators should be detected before live working such as replacing insulators and electric power fittings on transmission towers [3, 4]. The disc porcelain insulator string need to be tested for low/zero state, the detection methods can be classified as contact type and non-contact type [5, 6]. At present, the non-contact type detection is mainly carried out by using infrared or ultraviolet detection. The detected temperature difference of the

© Springer Nature Singapore Pte Ltd. 2018
K. Li et al. (Eds.): ICSEE 2018/IMIOT 2018, CCIS 924, pp. 205–214, 2018.
https://doi.org/10.1007/978-981-13-2384-3_19

insulator is small through infrared detection method, while the ultraviolet detection performance is easily affected by the environment of the insulators [7, 8]. Both methods have their own limitations, the data analysis methods need further studied in order to improve the detection accuracy [9]. The data of contact detection is more reliable. Traditional detection methods mainly rely on spark fork method or voltage distribution method by manual work to distinguish the condition of insulators, which are very inconvenient for long string insulators detection because the operating lever is usually too long [10, 11]. With the rapid development of EHV and UHV transmission lines, the insulator strings are too long to use manual detection methods [12, 13]. Insulator detection by robot is convenient and effective for long insulator strings, and also reduces the manpower investment in insulator detection work, reducing the operation and maintenance costs of transmission lines [14, 15].

At present, insulator detection robot moves up and down along the suspension insulator string mainly by climbing. Electric field distribution of each part of the insulator detection robot is simulated and analyzed by researchers. Simulation results show that the robot has a certain influence on electric field distribution of the insulator string, but does not affect its insulation performance [16, 17]. The electric field strength of the robot can be reduced through structural improvement and optimization, it can avoid interference to the detection system and the malfunction of robot by corona discharge and suspended potential discharge [3, 18]. However, due to the combination of power and detection module on robot body, resulting in large volume, heavy weight and complex structure of the robot body.

This paper designs a kind of split insulator detection robot for the suspension string of the disc porcelain insulator in the straight-line tower, which has simple structure, light weight and small volume. By simulating the electric field of the robot body and the insulator string when the robot moves along insulator string, researchers study the influence of the robot on insulator string and the largest field strength of each structure of robot body. The test of 220 kV transmission line insulator string voltage detection by designed insulator robot is carried out, the results of voltage distribution measurement are analyzed.

2 Operating Principle of Split Type Insulator Detection Robot

The structure of split insulators low/zero live detection robot is showed in Fig. 1. It contains two parts: power module and detection module. The power module and the detection module are connected by a thin insulation rope, which can be dissembled and installed flexibly. The detection module transmits instructions to the power module through WIFI communication network, which controls the detection module to move up and down and stop, then insulator detection according to the predetermined procedures is accomplished.

The power module includes cable drive motor, cable rack, guide pulley and fixed plate. The driving motor is consisted of control chip, WIFI communication module, motor driver, rotate speed sensor, grinding motor, power management unit and the battery. The structure of the cable rack and guide pulley are simple and small in size, it

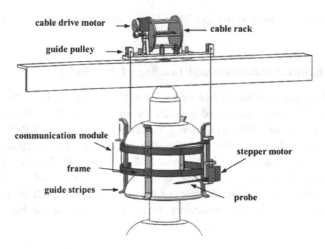

Fig. 1. Structure of the split type insulator detection robot.

is easy to carry onto the tower. The connecting plate can be fixed on the cross arm stably due to the structure of the cross arm, the connecting part is metal, so as to ensure that the power module and the tower body are equipotential.

The detection module includes distance sensor, frame, stepper motor, probe, guide stripes and WIFI communication module. All modules are installed on the frame and are dismountable. The guide stripes can effectively prevent the insulators detection robot from being stuck by the insulator's shed while moving along the insulator string. The detection module identifies the steel cap, shed and steel foot of the insulator through the pre-supposed algorithm by using the range sensor. When the range sensor recognizes the steel cap, the communication module sends the stop instruction to the cable drive motor. When the detection module stops at the detection position, stepper motor controls the two probes to touch the adjacent two insulators' steel caps and measure the voltage of the insulators. Then the voltage data can be transmitted to the hand-held terminal through the communication module, and draw the distribution voltage curve on the terminal which is used to judge low/zero value insulators.

3   Electric Field Analysis of Insulator Detection Robot

Because the power module of the insulator detection robot is installed on the cross arm of the tower and is equipotential with respect to the arm, the influence of the electric field on power module is negligible. But the detection module may change the distribution of the surrounding electric field while moving, and the module body may also produce partial discharge due to the high local field strength, which needs simulation on the electric field for further analysis. Take the disc type porcelain insulator string on the 220 kV single-loop cathead tower as simulation object, the electric field distribution of the robot's body, insulators and gold fittings when the insulator detection robot moves at different positions along the 220 kV disc type porcelain insulator string are analyzed.

3.1   Establishment, Subdivision and Loading of 3D Model

The 3D model includes the tower-line system model and the insulator robot model, as shown in Fig. 2. The tower model adopts 220 kV straight line cathead tower, it height 42 m, and tower size according to drawing. Insulator string type is XP-70. The height of single insulator is 146 mm, the disc diameter is 255 mm, the creepage distance is 280 mm, and one insulator string is composed of 15 insulators. Bundled conductor is considered (vertically arranged). The length of the conductor model is 20 meters, the split spacing is 400 mm, and the diameter of the sub conductor is 21.66 mm. In order to subdivision the model, it is necessary to build a wrapped air bag outside the conductor.

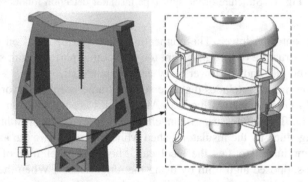

Fig. 2. The 3D model of the tower-line system and the insulator robot.

For the insulator robot, detection part including probe, stepper motor, connecting plate, rack, guide stripes, communication module are built in the model. The probe is divided into front metal and insulated connecting rod, the length of the front section is 120 mm, the length of the connecting rod is 130 mm, the inner radius of the rack is 140 mm, the thickness is 5 mm, the height is 20 mm, the guide stripes is 200 mm long and 20 mm wide, and the radius of the circular arc is 20 mm; The size of the communication module is $30 \times 40 \times 100$ (mm), and the step motor size is $30 \times 40 \times 45$ (mm). For the convenience of model subdivision, the model of the detection part is simplified and the components with less influence on the electric field simulation results are removed.

Then the whole model is subdivided, air bags are added respectively above the insulator string and the tower in order to control their density. The insulator string and the robot get encryption subdivision. The subdivision diagram of the insulator robot is shown in Fig. 3 for example. At last, potential is loaded and the maximum field intensity is studied. The maximum voltage $U_m = \frac{220 \times \sqrt{2}}{\sqrt{3}} = 179.629$ kV is loaded in the phase of the insulator robot, the rest phases are loaded with $-0.5U_m$ according to phase sequence. The insulator is located at the high voltage end, the high potential U_m is loaded on the steel foot and wire connected to it, and 0 potentials are loaded on the low voltage end which is connected with metal fittings, the iron cap, the pole tower, the ground and the outsourced air boundary. The steel foot and iron cap with unknown potential in the calculation model are suspended potential conductors. Coupled free degree method is applied, which means the connected steel feet and steel cap are coupled at equal potential. The probe of the insulator robot also needs to be coupled when measuring the equipotential of the steel cap connected with measuring device.

Fig. 3. Mesh of insulator detection robot.

3.2   Simulation Results and Analysis

Finite element method is used to simulate the static field and to number the insulators starts from the high voltage end. Taking the third insulator for example, the influence of insulator on the surface strength of insulator strings and the distribution characteristics of the electric field of the insulators robot are analyzed. The field strength comparison of the surface of insulator strings of the third insulation with and without robot is shown in Fig. 4. It indicates that although the insulator robot has a certain influence on the local field strength of the third and the fourth insulators, the overall change is little, and the maximum field intensity change of the surface of the insulator is only about 1%, which means that the effect of insulator robot on surface field strength of insulators is small.

When measuring the third insulator, the electric field strength on the rack and guide stripes of the insulator, as shown in Fig. 5, is about 240 kV/m, which is much less than the halo field strength of the air. The field strength at the probe and connecting rod is shown in Fig. 6, with a maximum value of about 1372 kV/m, which is less than that of the air. By comparing and analyzing the maximum field strength of the probe, the field strength of the insulator robot is larger at both ends of the insulator string, and the probe field intensity is the largest near the high end, while the insulator robot's probe field strength is smaller in the middle of the insulator. This is the same with the voltage distribution characteristics of insulators, because the insulators at both ends bear a higher voltage and the insulators in the middle bear a lower voltage, so the voltage

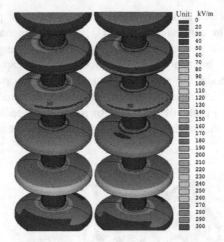

a) Without robot   b) Robot measuring No. 3 insulator

Fig. 4. The influence of detection robot on the electric field intensity of insulator surface.

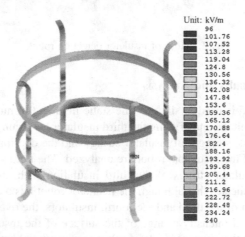

Fig. 5. The electric field distribution of the rack.

difference between two probes is different. The larger the voltage difference is, the greater the field strength is. And this also verifies the effectiveness of the calculation.

The electric field simulation shows that the insulator robot has a certain influence on the distribution of the electric field of the insulators, but it has little influence on the maximum field strength of them, so this influence can be ignored. The maximum field strength of the insulator is about 1753 kV/m. At the probe and the insulated connecting rod, the radius of the probe wire is 0.3 cm. The halo field strength is about 37.6 kV/cm calculated with the Peek formula, and the field strength of the probe surface is 17.53 kV/cm, which is a large margin. So the corona discharge will not occur.

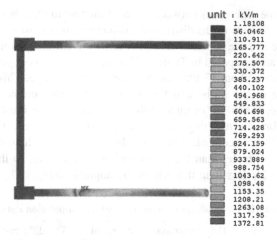

Fig. 6. The electric field distribution of probe and connecting rod.

Fig. 7. Field layout of the test.

4 Test and Analysis of 220 KV Insulator String

The 220 kV insulator string was used for testing in the laboratory. The insulator string has 13 insulators, the field layout is shown in Fig. 7. By using the iron tower to simulate the tower cross arm, the iron frame is grounded through copper wire, the lowest fittings are connected to a high-voltage generator, and the AC voltage effective value is 127 kV. The insulator detection robot is set to measure twice of each insulator when working.

As there are some differences between the environment in the laboratory and for the actual tower, the difference of the distribution voltage in the industry standard between the measured value and the standard value is quite different. The simulation data with the measured data are compared in Table 1. Firstly, the sum of voltage of 13 insulators is 110.03 kV, which is about 17 kV less than the applied voltage. This result is caused by the capacitance of the probe and the impact of the measurement circuit on the distribution voltage. When the insulator robot is measuring the insulator, it is equivalent to a parallel branch, resulting in the reduction of the equivalent impedance, and the distribution voltage is reduced. When the robot moves along the insulator string, the measured values are smaller than that of the original insulators, so the recorded total voltage is about 17 kV less than the sum of the applied voltages.

Table 1. Comparison of measurement and simulation data.

No.	The simulation data without robot/kV	The simulation data with robot/kV	Measured value/kV	The difference of measured value and simulation data with robot/kV
1	29.71	26.26	24.75	1.51
2	20.27	17.16	15.68	1.48
3	15.03	12.85	11.70	1.15
4	11.47	10.01	9.24	0.77
5	9.02	7.87	7.78	0.09
6	7.32	6.39	6.73	−0.34
7	6.09	5.52	5.96	−0.44
8	5.28	4.87	5.42	−0.55
9	4.73	4.26	4.72	−0.46
10	4.45	4.02	4.46	−0.44
11	4.38	3.94	4.33	−0.39
12	4.53	4.11	4.49	−0.38
13	4.71	4.31	4.77	−0.46
SUM	126.99	111.47	110.03	1.44

The robot and the insulator string forms a equivalent parallel circuit structurally. The configuration of this equivalent parallel circuit is constantly varying during measurement, and the measured value from the detection robot has a complex nonlinear relationship with the original voltage distribution.

The whole model of insulator robot detection is established and verified by simulation. Firstly, the three-dimensional model according to the test field layout is set up, distribution parameters are simulated according to the finite element method in Sect. 2, and the equivalent branch of the insulator robot is added to the road model. The insulators at high potential are added to the equivalent branch of the robot to calculate the voltage values at both ends respectively, and the insulators without the robot branch are calculated. Results of voltage distribution is shown in Table 1. When the robot is close to one certain insulator, the voltage distribution of the simulation is different from the original insulator voltage distribution, the maximum single voltage difference appears on the first insulator, the difference is 3.45 kV, which is about 13.14%. The overall difference of the whole series voltage is about 15.5 kV. When the robot is close to insulators, the maximum difference between the simulated data and the measured data is about 1.51 kV, and the difference is about 6.1%.

Because the insulator model is idealized, the material parameters are different from data of the actual insulators, and the measurement error is considered at the same time, the above error values can meet engineering requirements. It shows that the insulator detection robot can effectively measure the insulator distribution voltage. However, due to the difference between the total value of measurement and the actual voltage value, it is not convenient for the staff to analyze. The voltage compensation method can be studied so that the measurement results reflect the original voltage distribution of the insulators as accurate as possible.

5 Conclusion

This paper designed a split type insulator detection robot which is applicable for suspension insulator string detection, and carried out electric field analysis and test study of insulator robot detection. Conclusions are as follows:

(1) The insulator robot has some influence on the local electric field distribution of insulators, but it has little influence on the maximum field strength of insulators which can be neglected. The maximum field strength of the insulator robot itself is less than halo field strength of the air. The same research method can be used to detect the low and zero insulators of the suspension porcelain insulator strings of 500 kV and 1000 kV transmission lines by further improving the insulation of the insulators.

(2) The insulator robot can accurately and effectively measure the distribution voltage of insulators. However, because of the influence of the probe and measuring circuit, the measurement value is different from the actual voltage distribution of the insulator. The measured results should be compensated.

(3) The insulator robot can detect the distribution voltage effectively under the simulated environment with low and zero voltage value insulators. The distinguishing and analysis of low and zero insulators can be carried out with the help of the measured voltage distribution curve.

Acknowledgement. Fund Project: Technology project of State Power Grid Co., Ltd. (No. 524625170046)

References

1. Zhibin, Q., Jiangjun, R., Daochun, H., et al.: Study on aging modes and test of transmission line porcelain suspension insulators. High Volt. Eng. **42**(4), 1259–1267 (2016)
2. Xian, Z., Richeng, L., Ming, Z., et al.: Online detection device of low or zero value insulators in UHVDC Transmission line. Electr. Power **49**(6), 90–94 (2016)

3. Juan, J., Guanbin, W., Shiyou, M., et al.: The electric field analysis and optimal design on a robot for insulator detection. Insul. Surge Arresters **2**, 180–185 (2017)
4. Yuntu, J., Jun, H., Jian, D., et al.: The identification and diagnosis of self-blast defects of glass insulators based on multi-feature fusion. Elect. Power **50**(5), 52–58 (2017)
5. Feng, W., Hongcai, L., Xiang, P., et al.: Optimization research on condition-based maintenance of overhead transmission line with online detection without power cut. Elect. Power **49**(10), 84–89 (2016)
6. Haipeng, S., Weiguo, L., Zhanzhan, Q.: Study on the on-line detection device of hand-held insulator. Insul. Surge Arresters **1**, 22–26 (2012)
7. Jiangang, Y., Ye, Z., Tangbing, L.I., et al.: Analysis of high-voltage ceramic insulators infrared detection blind areas. High Volt. Eng. **43**(9), 2903–2910 (2017)
8. Jing, C., Nan, Z., Zhong, M., et al.: Ultraviolet detection technology of 750 kV resistant to porcelain insulator based on artificial pollution test. Elect. Power **49**(9), 23–29 (2016)
9. Peng, L.: Study on Heating and Discharge Characteristics of Zero Value Insulators Based on Infrared and Ultraviolet Imaging. North China Electric Power University, Beijing (2016)
10. Yong, F., Zongren, P., Peng, L., et al.: Voltage-sharing characteristics of porcelain insulators for UHV AC transmission lines. High Volt. Eng. **36**(1), 270–274 (2010)
11. Xiaowei, L., Linong, W., Junhua, W., et al.: Research on automatic detection technology for faulty porcelain insulators on AC transmission lines. Electr. Meas. Instrum. **53**(11), 110–115 (2016)
12. Liang, Z., Yong, L., Zhigang, R., et al.: Analysis on the influence factor of insulators detection by robots and electric field method. Insul. Surge Arresters **2**, 148–155 (2017)
13. Zhengzi, C., Weiguo, L., Wenbin, C.: Design and implementation of insulator resistance measurement robot based on WiFi wireless remote control. Elect. Power **48**(12), 23–26 (2015)
14. Rui, G., Bing, T., Lei, Z., et al.: Study on cap and pin porcelain insulator detecting technology suitable for robots on transmission line. Insul. Surge Arresters **2**, 141–147 (2017)
15. Yao, C., Dehua, Z., Jie, N.: The impact of zero and low resistance insulator on potential and electric field distribution of long insulator strings in the 500 kV transmission line. Insul. Surge Arresters **3**, 29–34 (2015)
16. Ming, Z., Richeng, L., Jie, X., et al.: Feasibility research and develop of working detecting robot for low/zero insulator. High Volt. Appar. **52**(6), 160–166 (2016)
17. Linhua, Z., Yandong, C.: The research and design of overhead transmission line insulator detecting robot. Electron. Des. Eng. **23**(16), 164–166 (2015)
18. Tao, C., Daqing, S., Deli, Z., et al.: Research on the application of disc type porcelain insulators detection robot in overhead transmission lines. Insul. Surge Arresters **2**, 11–16 (2013)

Study on Early Fire Behavior Detection Method for Cable Tunnel Detection Robot

Biwu Yan[1,2,3(✉)], Guangzhen Ren[1,2,3], Xiaowei Huang[1,2,3],
Junfeng Chi[1,2,3], Lei Zheng[1,2,3], Hao Luo[1,2,3], and Pengxiang Yin[1,2,3]

[1] NARI Group Corporation Ltd., Nanjing 211106, China
nanruixm@qq.com
[2] Wuhan NARI Limited Liability Company, State Grid Electric Power Research Institute, Wuhan 430074, China
[3] Hubei Key Laboratory of Power Grid Lightning Risk Prevention, Wuhan 430074, China

Abstract. With the increase of cable tunnels and improvement of inspection requirements, different types of inspection robots have been designed and applied to the inspection and fire protection of cable tunnels. Due to the complex environment of the cable tunnel, it is difficult for existing robots to conduct fire detection and diagnosis effectively. Therefore, a fire detection method of cable tunnel robot based on support vector machine (SVM) is proposed. According to the actual tunnel size, a simulation model is established to calculate the smoke concentration and temperature variation of tunnels under different fire power. Considering the dynamic detection of robot, the characteristics of the measured data are analyzed. The SVM model is trained by using the sample characteristic data, and then the test data is used for testing. The accuracy of the test is up to 95%.

Keywords: Split type robot · Insulator detection · Electric field analysis
Test experiments

1 Introduction

With the rapid development of cities, more and more cable tunnels have replaced overhead lines. The power cables work under high voltage and high temperature environment for a long time. Breakdown and short circuit may occur with insulation aging. Further, the cable tunnel fire may be produced. In order to ensure the safe and stable operation of power cables, monitoring and maintenance should be carried out. Due to the narrow space and complex environment, it is very inconvenient to operate and maintain the cable tunnel manually. Especially when a tunnel fire accident occurs, it is not easy to find the hidden danger of the fire. Once lighting a fire, the fire will develop rapidly along the cable line. Combustion produces a large amount of smoke, toxic and harmful substances and high temperatures. These pose a threat to the personal safety of the staff in the tunnel. The cable tunnel has a long distance, narrow passageways and few outlets. Rescuers are hard to get close to the source of fire. Therefore, the cable tunnel inspection robot emerges as the times require [1–3].

© Springer Nature Singapore Pte Ltd. 2018
K. Li et al. (Eds.): ICSEE 2018/IMIOT 2018, CCIS 924, pp. 215–224, 2018.
https://doi.org/10.1007/978-981-13-2384-3_20

Intelligent robots are used for inspection work, which can effectively reduce staff burden. Furthermore, there are fixed-point detection systems in general tunnels, but they have monitoring blind area. As a mobile monitoring system, the tunnel robot can effectively compensate for the shortcomings of the fixed-point detection system. The cable tunnel robot can be divided into walking and track type [4, 5]. The walking robot is mainly a caterpillar type. The cable tunnels may have accumulated water, debris, large slopes and complex pipelines, which are not conducive to walking. The orbital robot walking on the track at the top of the tunnel is not affected by the above factors. In 2009, the Shanghai Jiao Tong University developed a lightweight, small crawler patrol robot [6]. The upper part arranged infrared cameras, gas sensors and signal transceivers to collect and transmit the physical environment and gas environment in the tunnel. In 2012, the Hangzhou power company produced a wheeled robot [7]. It carries the gas sensor and the smoke sensor, can effectively perceive the potential danger in the tunnel, and provide the data base for the fire prevention. The fire extinguishing device can take effective measures to extinguish the fire according to the feedback signal of the actual sensing device. However, because the robot carries too many equipment, its weight and size exceed the standard. In 2014, the Xiamen Electric Power Exploration Institute studied and produced a fixed track cable tunnel inspection system [8]. The mobile mechanism marched along the predetermined track. Two infrared camera devices were arranged to collect the images in the tunnel and an ultrasonic sensing device to measure the obstacles. The whole mobile mechanism also carries several gas sensors to detect the gas environment. However, the above research focuses on the robot's motion and data acquisition function. There are few studies on the tunnel fire behavior judging by the collected data. If the fire source is detected in time, the fire can be extinguishing as soon as possible.

In this article, the simulation model is established according to the actual size of the cable tunnel. The tunnel fire is simulated under different fire power sources, and the data of flue gas concentration and temperature in the tunnel are obtained. Consider the dynamic sampling data of robots, the characteristic parameters are analyzed and extracted. A fire detection method of cable tunnel robot based on SVM is proposed. The effectiveness of the above method is verified by simulation data.

2   Modeling and Simulation of Fire in Cable Tunnel

In order to study the early fire behavior detection method, the development law of the tunnel fire needs to be obtained. The cable tunnel robot can measure temperature, characteristic gas, particle concentration, etc. Unlike the fixed-point monitoring device, the tunneling robot detects relevant data in the process of moving. It is necessary to obtain data on temperature and smoke concentration measured by robots. However, the fire tests are destructive and non-recoverable, and full-scale tests are expensive. A more efficient method is as follows: first, the fire development rules are obtained by numerical simulation, and then the simulation data are verified by typical tests. This section will introduce the model building and simulation results.

2.1 Modeling and Parameter Setting

According to the structure and size of an electric single cabin of integrated corridor in Hangzhou, the 1:1 numerical model of cable tunnel is established. The length, width and height of the cable tunnel are 200 × 2.3 × 2.3 m. There is one column on each side of the tunnel, with three rows in each column. The height of the lowest cable to the ground is 0.5 m, and the two rows are separated by 0.4 m. The robot is located on the top of the middle of the tunnel. Its measuring device is 0.8 m from the top, so the probe is set at the same height. 220 kV cables are arranged according to the actual layout. The cable diameter is about 0.11 m. Because of the setting requirement of the calculation software, the rectangle with equal cross section area is used for simulation. Electric power cable is generally copper core XLPE cable. The material is allocated according to the mass ratio of copper and plastic to 6:4. The ignition source is selected in the test simulation, and the fire source size is installed on the cable with a size of 0.1 × 0.1 m. The overall model is shown in Fig. 1. In order to calculate accurately, the mesh is more detailed near the fire source.

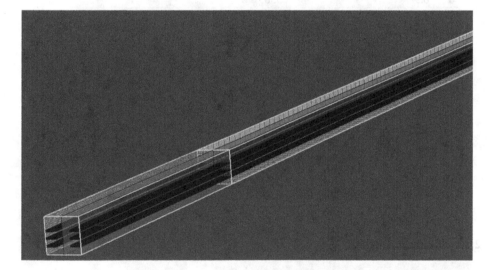

Fig. 1. Fire simulation model of cable tunnel

According to the actual situation, there is ventilation equipment in the cable tunnel under normal working conditions. In the early stage of the fire, the ventilation equipment may be still working. Wind speed has a certain effect on the spread of the fire. When the fire develops to a certain stage, trigger the linkage and close the fire door. It is considered that the wind speed of the port is zero. It can delay the spread of fire and reduce oxygen content. The two cases above are simulated respectively. According to results of previous studies, the heat release rate of the cable material is obtained. Combined with the shape and size of the cable in this article, the maximum heat release rate of different numbers of cables is calculated. The fire power corresponding to different fire sizes is set to 1467 kW/m^2, 2200 kW/m^2 and 3385 kW/m^2, respectively. The fire source is set as the T2 fire growth model. The source of the fire rises to maximum power after 200 s, and then the power remains unchanged. In order to simulate the situation of fire in different layers of cable, The fire source height is set to 0.5 m, 0.9 m, 1.3 m, respectively. Considering the wind speed, the power and the height of the fire source, different working conditions are set up as shown in Table 1.

Table 1. Setting of simulation conditions

No.	Height of the fire source (m)	Heat release power (kW/m^2)	Wind speed (m/s)
1	0.5	1467	1
2	0.5	2200	1
3	0.5	3385	1
4	0.9	1467	1
5	0.9	2200	1
6	0.9	3385	1
7	1.3	1467	1
8	1.3	2200	1
9	1.3	3385	1
10	0.5	1467	0
11	0.5	2200	0
12	0.5	3385	0
13	0.9	1467	0
14	0.9	2200	0
15	0.9	3385	0
16	1.3	1467	0
17	1.3	2200	0
18	1.3	3385	0

2.2   Simulation Result

(1) Analysis of flame spread

In the simulation of different conditions, comparing the conditions 2, 5 and 8 with conditions 10, 11 and 12, it can be found that the spread rate of fire will grow with the increase in the size of the fire source power in the same of fire source setting height and wind speed. For example, in conditions 2, 5 and 8, the fire spread quickly in the vertical direction while it is 77th seconds, 59th seconds, and 46th seconds respectively. Comparing conditions 7, 8, and 9, the spread speed of fire is also related to the space height of the fire. When the cables set at the bottom cable holder is on fire, the flame will rise with the flowing of hot air, and quickly ignites the overhead cable. If the tunnel is well ventilated, it will also accelerate the lateral spread of fire. When the cables in the top is on fire firstly, during the initial stage of the fire, the flame rises up against the ceiling, quickly forming a ceiling jet and moving horizontally along the ceiling. After

200 s, the cables in the top are all ignited. Typical fire spread situation is shown in Fig. 2.

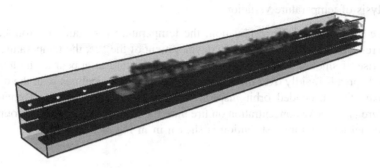

Fig. 2. Typical flame spread schematic

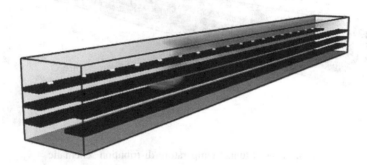

Fig. 3. Smoke diffusion in the early stage of fire

(2) Analysis of fire smoke diffusion

It is very important for early warning of fire detection to study the diffusion of smoke in cable tunnels. As shown in Fig. 3, during the smoldering stage of the cable, although the cable only ignited small flames, the smoke had spread rapidly in the tunnel. In the fire simulation of cable tunnels, it can be observed that under other conditions unchanged, only changing the size of the fire source power, such as conditions 2, 5 and 8, the smoke used 50.8 s, 40.2 s and 31.4 s respectively through the cable tunnel with 20 m, that is, the smoke spread rate grows with the increase of the fire source power.

Consider the effect of ventilation in the cable tunnel on the spread of smoke. When the tunnel is ventilated, lateral wind will make the smoke downstream of fire source pass through the tunnel model first. With growing of the fire, the smoke in the upper reaches of the fire source will gradually increase. As in conditions 8 and 17, it takes 58.6 s and 40.6 s respectively for the smoke to pass through tunnel model with 20 m.

When the tunnel is not ventilated, the smoke spreads more evenly in the tunnel, and the ventilation of the tunnel will intensify the burning of the cable and make the smoke accumulate faster in the tunnel.

(3) Analysis of temperature variation

At the beginning of the combustion, the temperature distribution throughout the tunnel is relatively uniform. During the development of the fire, the temperature grows with the rise of smoke, which causes the high temperature to appear at the top of the tunnel and spreads rapidly over the tunnel. The temperature declines with the distance. This makes the suspended orbit inspection robot better able to detect changes in temperature and smoke concentration on fire than the robot walking on the ground. The typical tunnel temperature distribution is shown in in Fig. 4.

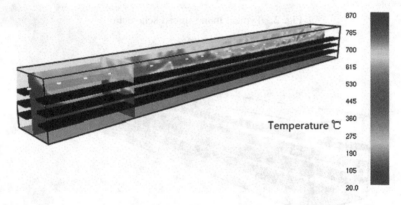

Fig. 4. Typical tunnel temperature distribution schematic

3   Simulation Data Analysis and Fire Behavior Detection Method

Take the following working conditions as an example: height of the fire source 0.9 m, heat release power 3385 kW/m^2 and wind speed 1 m/s. The variation of smoke concentration and temperature in cable tunnel fires is analyzed. The probe is arranged at the height of the robot sensor. The smoke concentration and temperature measured by the probe arranged in proper order from the fire source point are shown in Figs. 5 and 6. It can be seen from Fig. 5 that the temperature of the detection point above the fire source point rises slowly due to the effect of ventilation. The temperature at the second detection points in the downwind direction increased rapidly and the temperature value is higher. For the turbulence produced by combustion has a great influence on the temperature change. The temperature variation of several detection points near the fire source point is obviously different from that of other detection points. The trend of temperature of the detection point beyond the fire source 5 m is similar changing with time. The difference in the rate of rise is small. But there are some differences in the starting time of temperature rise at different locations. Therefore, when sampling sequence is selected for analysis, the point with a certain distance from the fire source is more regular. It can be seen from Fig. 6 that the smog concentration curve is rather chaotic compared with the temperature. This is mainly due to the fact that the generation and diffusion of particles are very irregular under the action of flame turbulence. Especially when the flame is burning fiercely, it is more difficult to make use of smoke concentration. The smoke concentration changes more smoothly at a certain distance from the fire source and when the concentration is low. Therefore, when selecting smoke concentration data, a lower trigger value can be set. When the smoke concentration exceeds the trigger value, a certain length of data is recorded and analyzed.

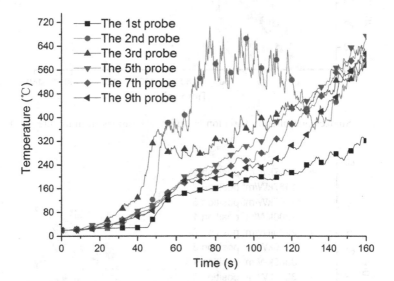

Fig. 5. Temperature variation at different locations from the fire point

When the fire behavior is detected, the tunnel robot moves towards the fire source. The data collected during the movement are different from those obtained directly by simulation. It is necessary to analyze and process data with the speed of mobile robot. In order to conduct fire source detection, it is necessary to determine the starting position of the analysis data. Due to the random time and location of the fire, the robot may begin to judge in different locations. For the temperature varies greatly with the outside world, it is more reasonable to use smoke concentration as trigger criterion. It is assumed that the analysis data begin to record when the smoke concentration exceeds 10%. Take the following working conditions as an example: height of the fire source 0.9 m and wind speed 1 m/s. The heat release power is 1467 kW/m^2, 2200 kW/m^2 and 3385 kW/m^2, respectively. The smoke concentration and temperature detection value under different heat release power and initial measurement position are shown in Figs. 7 and 8. It shows that the sampling data sequence of smoke concentration and temperature under different fire source power has certain rules. But it is difficult to distinguish only through the curve.

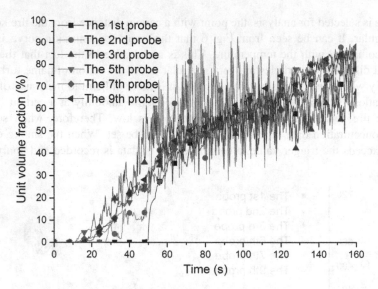

Fig. 6. Smoke concentration variation at different locations from the fire point

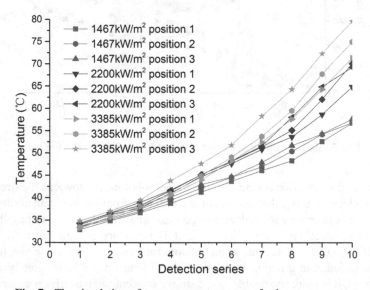

Fig. 7. The simulation of temperature sequence of robot measurement

From the above analysis, it can be seen that fire detection is more accurate based on robot detection data at the early stage of fire. In this paper, a fire detection method based on SVM is proposed. When the smoke concentration exceeds the threshold, 10 temperature values of robot sampling and 10 smoke concentrations are selected to form a characteristic vector. It is input to SVM for classification and judgement. SVM

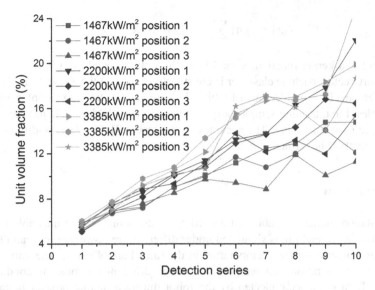

Fig. 8. The simulation of Smoke concentration sequence of robot measurement

classifier constructs a hyper-plane as the edge of classification decision by using support vectors in training set. The training set is given as Formula 1.

$$D = \left\{ (x_i, y_i) \middle\| x_i \in R^P, y_i \in \{-1, 1\}, i = 1, \cdots, n \right\} \tag{1}$$

Where: x_i is a P dimension characteristic vector, y_i is various classifications, n is the total number of characteristic vector.

Support vector machines can maximize the difference between parallel hyper-planes of two categories. Two hyper-planes can be expressed by Formula 2.

$$\begin{cases} H_1/x_i, w + b = 1 \\ H_2/x_i, w + b = -1 \end{cases} \tag{2}$$

Where: w is a normal vector of hyper-plane, b is a bias vector.

The optimization problem can be expressed by formula 3. The constraint condition is formula 4.

$$Min \frac{1}{2} \| W \|^2 + P \sum_{i=1}^{n} \varepsilon_i \tag{3}$$

$$y_i(w \bullet \phi(x_i) + b) \geq 1 - \varepsilon_i, i = 1, 2, \cdots, n \tag{4}$$

The classification of support vector machines can be expressed by formula 5.

$$f(x) = \text{sgn}\left(\sum_{i=1}^{l} a_i^* y_i K(X, X_i) + b^*\right) \tag{5}$$

Where: K a kernel function, a^* and b^* is the optimal coefficient.

Support vector machine classifier is constructed based on the above formula. In this paper, there are 180 sample data, of which 120 are used as training samples and 60 as test samples. First, training samples are used to train the SVM model, and then the test samples are used for testing. The accuracy of the test is 91.7%. The validity of the fire detection method is verified.

4 Conclusion

The simulation model is established according to the actual size of the cable tunnel in this article. The tunnel fire is simulated under different fire power sources, and the data of flue gas concentration and temperature in the tunnel are obtained. The variation law of smoke concentration and temperature under different combustion conditions is analyzed. Data sequence collected by the robot during a mobile process is analyzed. The sampling data sequence of smoke concentration and temperature under different fire source power has certain rules. The characteristic values are selected through simulation data, and the fire detection model based on support vector machine is trained. The accuracy of the test is 91.7%. The validity of the fire detection method is verified.

Acknowledgments. This study was funded by the State Grid Corporation Headquarters Science and Technology Project (524625160014).

References

1. Hui, Z., Ruiming, Q.: Mechanism design of a new kind of inspection robot for cable tunnel and track optimization simulation. Mach. Des. Manuf. Eng. **47**(3), 61–65 (2018)
2. Ingason, H., Li, Y.Z.: Model scale tunnel fire tests with longitudinal ventilation. Fire Saf. J. **45**(8), 371–384 (2010)
3. Rie, D.H., Hwang, M.W., Kim, S.J., et al.: A study of optimal vent mode for the smoke control of subway station fire. Tunn. Undergr. Space Technol. **21**(3), 300–301 (2006)
4. Victores, J.G., Martinez, S., Jardon, A., et al.: Robot-aided tunnel inspection and maintenance system by vision and proximity sensor integration. Autom. Constr. **20**(5), 629–636 (2011)
5. Li, Y.Z., Lei, B., Ingason, H.: The maximum temperature of buoyancy-driven smoke flow beneath the ceiling in tunnel fires. Fire Saf. J. **46**(4), 204–210 (2011)
6. Fu, Z., Chen, Z., Zheng, C., et al.: A cable-tunnel inspecting robot for dangerous environment. Int. J. Adv. Robot. Syst. **5**(3), 243–248 (2008)
7. Wei, H., Zhen, R.G., Ge, J., et al.: Research of patrol robot for electrical cable corridor. Autom. Instrum. **12**, 13–16 (2013)
8. Ling, F., Huaxia, Y., Dong, F.W.: Research on the moving structure of split cable tunnel inspection robot. Process Autom. Instrum. **38**(6), 46–50 (2017)

Speech Endpoint Detection Based on Improvement Feature and S-Transform

Lu Xunbo[✉], Zhu Chunli[✉], and Li Xin[✉]

School of Mechatronic Engineering and Automation, Shanghai University,
Shanghai 200072, China
{xunbolu, zhuspringwinner}@163.com,
su_xinli@aliyun.com

Abstract. In the low SNR and non-stationary noise environment, traditional feature detection methods will lead to a sharp drop in detection performance. This paper proposes an improved speech endpoint detection algorithm based on S-transform (ST). ST has the advantages of both Short Fast Fourier Transform (SFFT) and Wavelet Transform (WT). It can extract more robust MFCC features. In this paper, the ST is combined with spectral subtraction to transform the speech into the time-frequency joint domain in order to obtain a purer speech. Then the dynamic threshold updating mechanism is used to detect the noisy speech with two-parameter double threshold method. Through Matlab simulation, the improved algorithm presented in this paper is compared with two other algorithms. The experimental results reveal that this algorithm has a higher accuracy in endpoint detection. Moreover, it has a great advantage both in detection rate and error rate.

Keywords: Endpoint detection · S-transform · Spectral subtraction
MFCC · Uniform sub-band variance

1 Introduction

Speech enhancement technology plays an important role in speech processing such as speech coding, recognition and endpoint detection. The speech signal is a typical non-stationary signal, but the existing methods usually divide the signal into multiple frames and process each frame. This kind of method causes the loss of information in the signal, especially the key information between two frames. Therefore, it is necessary to make some improvements to the traditional feature extraction methods. The conventional Fourier transform cannot effectively analyze unsteady signals because it is only a global transformation of a signal, and for speech signal processing, the frequency domain characteristics at each moment are also very important. Therefore, it is necessary to combine the time domain and frequency domain when processing speech signals. The s-transform proposed by Stockwell [1] has the advantages of SFFT and WT. The s-transform can not only preserve the phase information of the signal but also provide the changeable time-frequency accuracy. It is a linear transformation and suitable for processing non-stationary signals. Compared with SFFT, WT and other

© Springer Nature Singapore Pte Ltd. 2018
K. Li et al. (Eds.): ICSEE 2018/IMIOT 2018, CCIS 924, pp. 225–235, 2018.
https://doi.org/10.1007/978-981-13-2384-3_21

methods, ST is more intuitive in time-frequency performance, and decomposes more meticulously in the high-frequency part, which means it can extract more features.

Meanwhile, for the problem of unsatisfactory single-feature speech endpoint detection and waveform distortion under low SNR environment, feature parameter improvement techniques and multi-feature parameter fusion techniques become the focus of endpoint detection. Huang and Yang [2] used MFCC as a parameter for judging speech and noise, which creates a new idea [3]. References [4, 5] introduce wavelet transform (DWT) into the extraction of MFCC parameters. Literature [6] combines MFCC cepstrum distance with logarithmic energy for endpoint detection; literature [7] points out that the dual threshold setting of MFCC cepstrum parameters is not suitable and proposes a feature parameter of the cosine of the MFCC; WANG Haibin [8] proposes a novel method called MFCC based on s-transform (SMFCC) for speech feature extraction. These studies have achieved certain improvements in the endpoint detection under low SNR conditions, but still need to be improved in the accuracy and stability of the detection. Therefore, this paper uses ST combined with spectral subtraction to transform the speech into the time-frequency joint domain in order to obtain a purer speech, then the dynamic threshold updating mechanism is used to detect the noisy speech with two-parameter double threshold method.

2   Concept of S-Transform (ST)

S-transform is an effective time-frequency representation method, which combines the advantages of SFFT and WT, and is suitable for the analysis of nonlinear and non-stationary signals (such as speech signals).

For a given signal $x(t)$, its S-transform is defined as:

$$S(t,f) = \int_{-\infty}^{+\infty} x(\tau)g(t-\tau,f)e^{-j2\pi f\tau}d\tau. \tag{1}$$

τ and t are time variables, f is a frequency variable and $g(t-\tau,f)$ is a Gaussian function as follows:

$$g(t-\tau,f) = \frac{|f|}{\sqrt{2\pi}}e^{\frac{-(t-\tau)^2f^2}{2}}. \tag{2}$$

The S-transform is reversible and its inverse transform is:

$$x(t) = \int_{-\infty}^{+\infty}\int_{-\infty}^{+\infty}\{S(t,f)dt\}e^{j2\pi ft}df. \tag{3}$$

From Eq. (1), we can see that ST can be regarded as a phase correction of a continuous wavelet transform(CWT), it changes the corresponding scale parameters, translation parameters of the wavelet transform, thus making up for the disadvantage of phase information lacking in CWT. From Eq. (2), we can see that the window function is characterized by both time and frequency characteristics, and the variance of the window function is equal to the inverse of the frequency. Based on these characteristics, satisfactory results obtained if a signal is transformed into the time-frequency domain by ST and then processed by the method of spectral subtraction.

3 SMFCC Cepstral Distance Feature Extraction

3.1 MFCC Principle

The Mel Frequency Cepstrum Coefficient (MFCC) analysis is based on the auditory mechanism of the human ear, describes the distribution of speech signals in energy, and can well simulate the human auditory system's perception ability [8], which has good recognition and robustness. It is one of the most important and effective feature parameters in the current speech signal processing. MFCC is a cepstrum parameter extracted in the frequency range of the Mel scale, where the Mel scale describes the nonlinear characteristics of the human ear frequency, and the relationship between the Mel frequency and the linear frequency can be approximated by Eq. (4), where the frequency is f, the unit is Hz.

$$f_{mel} = 2595. \log\left(1 + \frac{f}{700}\right). \tag{4}$$

3.2 SMFCC Feature Extraction Steps

SMFCC feature extraction steps are as follows:

(1) Preprocessing: Including pre-emphasis, frame division, and windowing functions. The purpose of pre-emphasis is to compensate for the loss of high-frequency components, enhance the high-frequency components. The usual pre-emphasis filter is:

$$H(z) = 1 - az^{-1}. \tag{5}$$

(2) S-transform
    Transform the speech into the time-frequency joint domain.
(3) Through the Mel filter bank
    Transform the signal into the Mel spectrum.
(4) Take logarithms for energy
    The log energy output for each filter bank is:

$$E(m) = \ln\left(\sum_{k=0}^{N-1} |X_a(k)|^2 H_m(k)\right), 0 \leq m \leq M. \tag{6}$$

where M means the number of trigonometric filters.

(5) Calculate discrete cosine transform (DCT) to get SMFCC cepstrum parameters:

$$smfcc(n) = \sum_{m=0}^{N-1} E(m)\cos\left(\frac{\pi n(m-0.5)}{M}\right). \tag{7}$$

(6) Extract dynamic difference parameters.

The standard cepstrum parameter MFCC only reflects the static characteristics of the speech parameters, and the dynamic characteristics of the speech can be described by the static characteristics of the differential spectrum. Combining dynamic and static features can effectively improve the system's recognition ability.

3.3 SMFCC Cepstrum Distance

Assuming the speech signal is $x_s(n)$, the SMFCC of each frame of the speech signal is $smfcc_{speech}(i, n)$, the leading speechless segment is used as the background noise frame, the average value of several previous frames SMFCC is taken as the estimated value of the background noise of SMFCC. Since it is irrelevant to i after the value is averaged, we denoted it as $smfcc_{noise}(n)$, so the SMFCC cepstrum distance is:

$$d_{smfcc}(i) = \sqrt{\sum_{n=1}^{p}\left(smfcc_{speech}(i, n) - smfcc_{noise}(n)\right)^2}. \tag{8}$$

In Eq. (8), p refers to the order used in the SMFCC cepstrum analysis.

4 SMFCC Cepstrum Distance Feature Extraction Based on Spectral Subtraction

4.1 Discrete S-Transform Based on Spectral Subtraction

Spectral subtraction is one of the most commonly used methods for speech noise reduction. Assumed that the speech signal $x(n)$ can be expressed as:

$$y(n) = x(n) + d(n). \tag{9}$$

Which $x(n)$ is a pure speech signal, $d(n)$ is a noise signal, and the s-transform is performed on both sides of Eq. (9):

$$Y_s(m, n) = X_s(m, n) + D_s(m, n). \tag{10}$$

where m denotes the m-th sample point in the ST, and n denotes the n-th frame.

$Y_s(m, n)$ can be obtained by direct discrete s-transform. However, the noise energy spectrum $D_s(m, n)$ cannot be obtained accurately and has to be obtained approximately by the way of estimation. The normal estimation method in [9, 10] is to take the statistical average $E\left[|D_s(m, n)|^2\right]$ in the absence of speech as $|D_s(m, n)|^2$.

It is known that the length of the noise segment is IS, and the corresponding frame number is NIS. The average energy value of the noise segment can be obtained as:

$$E\left[|D_s(m,n)|^2\right] = \frac{1}{NIS}\sum_{i=1}^{NIS}|X_s(m,n)|^2. \tag{11}$$

By obtaining the power spectrum of the silent speech segment and subtracting the power spectrum of the original speech, then the power spectrum of the relatively pure speech signal is processed by square root, and after the inverse S-transform (IST), a relatively pure speech signal $\widetilde{x}_i(k)$ can be obtained:

$$\widetilde{x}_i(k) = \sum\left(\frac{1}{N}\sum_{m=0}^{N-1}\widetilde{X}_s(m,n)\right)e^{\frac{i2\pi nk}{N}}, 0\leq k\leq N-1. \tag{12}$$

4.2 Spectral Subtractive Feature Extraction of SMFCC

Before extracting the SMFCC cepstrum feature, spectral subtraction is performed on the noisy-added speech signal to remove most of the noise and suppress the distortion of the speech waveform. The principle is illustrated in Fig. 1.

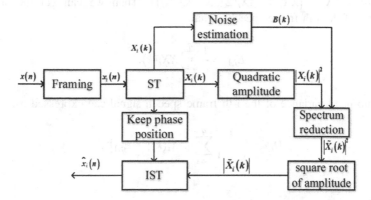

Fig. 1. Principle diagram for spectral subtractive feature extraction of SMFCC.

5 Bandwidth Variance Feature Extraction of Uniform Subbands

The characteristics of noise and speech in the frequency domain are quite different. In general, the voice energy of a voiced segment has a large change with the frequency band, and there is a larger peak at the resonance peak, but the energy value in the noise segment is relatively low, and more evenly distributed within the frequency band. According to this characteristic of the speech signal, the band variance becomes the most commonly used characteristic parameter. The uniform subband separation frequency band variance is proposed as the speech characteristic parameters of the signal based on this characteristic [11].

5.1   Uniform Subband Separation Band Variance

In order to eliminate the effect of noise on the amplitude of each spectral line, a method based on uniform subband separated band variance algorithm is proposed. Assuming the length of each frame is N, there are $(N/2 + 1)$ spectral lines in positive frequency after FFT, we can obtain amplitude spectrum $X_i = \{X_i(1), X_i(2), \ldots, X_i(N/2 + 1)\}$ after DFT, then split it into q subbands, the number of lines contained in each subband is:

$$p = fix[(N/2 + 1)/q] (fix[] \text{ means to get the integer part}). \tag{13}$$

p is so called uniform subband, which means each subband is equal bandwidth. The amplitude of the m-th subband in the i-th frame is:

$$XX_i(m) = \sum_{k=1+(m-1)p}^{1+(m-1)p+(p-1)} |X_i(k)|. \tag{14}$$

Assuming $XX_i = \{XX_i(1), XX_i(2), \ldots, XX_i(q)\}$, Then we can get the sub-band mean value of the i-th frame speech signal:

$$E_{i,1} = \frac{1}{q} \sum_{k=1}^{q} XX_i(k). \tag{15}$$

The sub-band variance of the i-th frame speech signal can expressed as:

$$D_{i,1} = \frac{1}{q-1} \sum_{k=1}^{q} [|XX_i(k)| - E_{i,1}]^2. \tag{16}$$

6   Dynamic Threshold Update and Endpoint Detection

The most commonly method used in endpoint detection is a dual threshold method. By extracting typical characteristic parameters of the speech, an proper threshold is selected to determine the start and end points of speech and to detect speech frames and non-speech frames [12]. This paper selects the improved spectral subtractive SMFCC cepstral distance and uniform subband variance as features, adopts a dynamic threshold estimation mechanism and uses the two-parameter double threshold method to perform endpoint detection. The procedure of the spectral subtraction algorithm based on ST is given as follows:

Step 1.   Preprocessing the speech signal,adding a Hanning window, the frame length is set to 200ms, and the frame shift is 80ms.

Step 2.   Using the spectral subtraction method based on ST to obtain a spectrally-reduced speech sequence $\tilde{x}_i(n)$,calculate $smfcc_{speech}(i,n)$ and $smfcc_{noise}(n)$ according to (7),then calculate $d_{smfcc}(i)$ according to (8).

Step 3.   Using DFT to the processed speech signal, dividing the subbands. We divides it into 25 subbands in this paper, each subband contains 4 spectral lines, then calculate the uniform subband variance of each frame $D_{i,1}$.

Step 4.   Median filtering to $d_{smfcc}(i)$ and $D_{i,1}$ in order to remove some wild points to abtain $d_m(i)$ and $D_m(i)$.

Step 5.   Dynamic threshold update.Setting thresholds firstly:
$$\begin{cases} T_1 = a * d_{mth} + p\delta_1 \\ T_2 = b * d_{mth} + p\delta_1 \end{cases} \begin{cases} T_3 = c * D_{mth} + p\delta_2 \\ T_4 = d * D_{mth} + p\delta_2 \end{cases}$$
Difine the update formula as:
$$\begin{cases} T_1 = T_1 \times \alpha + d_m(i)(1-\alpha) \\ T_2 = T_2 \times \alpha + d_m(i)(1-\alpha) \end{cases} \begin{cases} T_3 = T_3 \times \beta + D_m(i)(1-\beta) \\ T_4 = T_4 \times \beta + D_m(i)(1-\beta) \end{cases}$$

Step 6.   Using the two-parameter double threshold method for endpoint detection:
First-level judgment(based on d_m): Select a higher threshold T_2 to make a rough decision. Above the threshold is the speech segment, otherwise keep setting T_1 and T_2. Then determine a lower threshold T_1, search from the intersection to both sides and find out the two intersections of d_m and T_1, which is the start and end of the speech segment.
Second-level judgment(based on D_m): Select a higher threshold T_4, extend the search from the start and endpoint, which obtained from the first-level judgment, to both sides. Above the threshold is the speech segment, otherwise keep setting T_3 and T_4. Then determine a lower threshold T_3, continue to expand the search from the start and endpoint to both sides, find out the two intersections of D_m and T_3, then we will obtain the start and end point of the speech segment.

The detection algorithm flow is shown in Fig. 2.

7   Experiment Results

The speech database used in the experiments here is 126 pure voices in the TIMIT voice database. The noise signals used in the simulation includes 5 kinds of noise (white, pink, volvo, babble and factory noises) of NOISEX-92 Datebase. The pure speech signals and various noise signals are mixed at 3 different SNR(10 dB, 5 dB, and 0 dB). In order to verify the correctness and robustness of this method, we compared the proposed algorithm with the algorithms mentioned in literature [4] and literature [13]. All three algorithms perform well when SNR is 10 dB, the detection results with SNR of 5 dB and 0 dB are shown in Figs. 3, 4 and 5, it can be seen that when the SNR is 5 dB, the detection method based on the DWT-MFCC cepstrum distance missed speech signals between 3 s and 3.5 s; when the SNR is 0 dB, the two comparison algorithms were not able to detect the behind speech segments while the improved

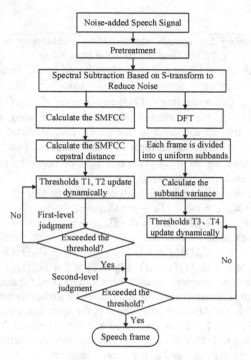

Fig. 2. Improved algorithm endpoint detection flowchart.

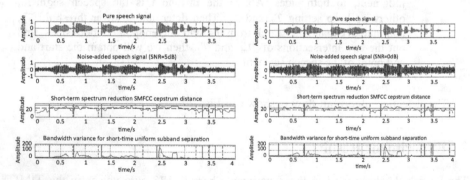

Fig. 3. The endpoint detection results of improved algorithm based on ST in SNR = 5 dB and SNR = 0 dB.

algorithm in this paper can still detect the position of each segment of speech. The experiment results can clearly show that the proposed algorithm has higher robustness for speech endpoint detection.

In order to further verify the stability and effectiveness of the proposed algorithm, the correct rate results are used to evaluate the detection results under different noise

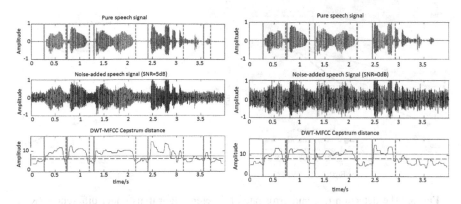

Fig. 4. The endpoint detection results based on DWT-MFCC cepstrum distance in SNR = 5 dB and SNR = 0 dB.

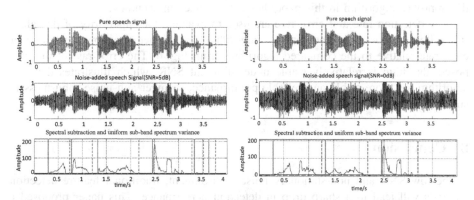

Fig. 5. The endpoint detection results based on spectral subtraction and uniform sub-band spectrum variance in SNR = 5 dB and SNR = 0 dB.

Table 1. The correct rate of different algorithms in different noises (SNR = 5 dB).

Noise	Proposed algorithm based on ST	DWT-MFCC cepstrum distance	Spectral subtraction + uniform sub-band spectrum variance	Proposed algorithm based on ST in pure speech
white	92.7%	84.4%	90.5%	96.2%
pink	91.6%	82.8%	90.6%	99.1%
volvo	91.3%	80.4%	90.3%	97.6%
babble	90.4%	81.3%	89.9%	96.4%
factory	90.2%	79.7%	89.5%	96.0%

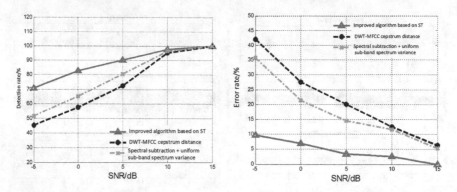

Fig. 6. The detection rate and error rate of different algorithms under different SNR

environments when the SNR is 5 dB. As shown in Table 1, it can be clearly seen that the improved algorithm in this paper has better detection accuracy.

The detection rate and error rate are used to evaluate the superiority of this algorithm. It is easy to see that the improved algorithm has a higher detection rate and lower error rate relative to the compared algorithms from Fig. 6. The error rate of the proposed algorithm is relatively stable under different SNR, which illustrates that this algorithm has more stable and reliable performance, stronger anti-noise robustness in speech endpoint detection.

8 Conclusion

In the low SNR and non-stationary noise environment, traditional feature detection methods will lead to a sharp drop in detection performance. This paper proposed a feature-improved speech endpoint detection algorithm based on s-transform. This method combines s-transform with MFCC and spectral subtraction to reduct noise. The experimental results show that this algorithm has a high accuracy and has advantages in the detection rate and error rate compared to the other two algorithms in Literature [4, 13]. It can effectively suppress noise and improve the quality of speech.

References

1. Stockwel, R.G., Mansinha, L., Lowe, R.P.: Localization of the complex spectrum: the S-transform. J. IEEE Trans. Signal Procesing. **44**(4), 998–1001 (1996)
2. Huang, L., Yang, C.: A novel approach to robust speech endpoint detection in car environments. In: IEEE International Conference on, vol. 3, pp. 1751–1754. IEEE (2000)
3. Nakagawa, S., Wang, L.: Speaker identification and verification by combining MFCC and phase information. In: IEEE International Conference on Acoustics, vol. 20, no. 4, pp. 4529–4532 (2009)
4. Yin, R., Cheng, J.: Improved feature extraction algorithm based on DWT-MFCC. J. Modern Electron. Technol. **40**(9), 18–21 (2017)

5. Zhang, Z., Yao, E., Shi, Y.: Audio endpoints detection algorithm based on wavelet analysis and MFCC. J. Electron. Meas. Technol. **39**(7), 62–66 (2016)
6. Zeng, S., Jingxiang, L.: Speech endpoint detection method based on fusion of MFCC distance and logarithmic energy parameter. J. Audio Eng. **40**(9), 51–55 (2016)
7. Cao, D., Gao, X., Gao, L.: An improved endpoint detection algorithm based on MFCC Cosine Value. J. Wirel. Pers. Commun. **95**, 2073–2090 (2017)
8. Wang, H., Yu, Z.: SMFCC: a novel feature extraction method for speech signal. J. Comput. Appl. **36**(6), 1735–1740 (2016)
9. Goh, Z., Tan, T.-C., Tan, B.T.G.: Postprocesing method for suppressing musical noise generated by spectral subtraction. IEEE Trans. Speech Audio Process. **6**(3), 28–292 (1998)
10. Paliwa, K., Wojcicki, K., Schwerin, B.: Single-channel speech enhancement using spectral subtraction in the short-time modulationdomain. J. Speech Commun. **52**(5), 450–475 (2010)
11. Wang, Z.-F.: Speech endpoint detection method research based on double threshold-frequency band variance. Electron. Des. Eng. **24**(19), 86–88 (2016)
12. Sun, Y., Wu, Y., Li, P.: Research on speech endpoint detection based on the improved dual-threshold. J. Chang. Univ. Sci. Technol. (Nat. Sci. Ed.) **39**(1), 92–95 (2016)
13. Wang, W., Hu, G., Yang, L., et al.: Research of endpoint detection based on spectral subtraction and uniform sub-band spectrum variance. Audio Eng. **40**(5), 40–43 (2016)

A Localization Evaluation System
for Autonomous Vehicle

Yuan Yin, Wanmi Chen[(✉)], Yang Wang, and Hongzhou Jin

School of Mechatronic Engineering and Automation, Shanghai University,
Shanghai 200072, China
{Alexx_Yin, wanmic, wy7ang}@163.com

Abstract. The autonomous vehicle is a kind of intelligent robot. At present, there are many algorithms for autonomous vehicle localization, but few methods for localization evaluation. To solve this problem, a grid hypothesis model using the existing prior information of the surrounding environment and posterior information of current laser real-time collection of autonomous vehicle is proposed, Kullback–Leibler divergence and Fourier transform are methods to evaluate the current location results. The above two methods can give relatively accurate evaluation results and corresponding evaluation method can be selected according to the actual speed and accuracy requirements.

Keywords: Autonomous vehicle · Localization evaluation
Grid hypothesis model · Kullback–Leibler divergence · Fourier transform

1 Introduction

The autonomous vehicle is an intelligent robot system that is driven by wheels or crawlers and has the ability to autonomously move on the ground under road or non-road conditions. An autonomous vehicle has been extensively studied in plenty of field in recent years. Localization, as one of the core of autonomous vehicle research, is the focus of many scientific research institutions and scholars. The accuracy and robustness of the localization is an important core indicator to measure the intelligence of the autonomous vehicle, and it is also one of the bottlenecks for the practical application of autonomous vehicle technology. Many researchers have developed different algorithms and models to solve this problem.

In [1], a self-localization algorithm consisting of a 2D laser range finder and the particle filter is proposed. The particle filter estimates the state of the vehicle by approximating the probability distribution of the system using a set of particles [2]. Each particle represents a possible state of the vehicle. While the literature [3] proposes a modified Markov localization algorithm for terrain-based navigation control of a light autonomous vehicle. Markov localization is a probabilistic algorithm. Instead of maintaining a single hypothesis as to which cell the vehicles might be, Markov localization maintains a probability distribution over the space of all such hypotheses [3]. Similarly, Kalman filter and its improved algorithm are also widely used in the positioning of autonomous vehicles [4–7].

© Springer Nature Singapore Pte Ltd. 2018
K. Li et al. (Eds.): ICSEE 2018/IMIOT 2018, CCIS 924, pp. 236–245, 2018.
https://doi.org/10.1007/978-981-13-2384-3_22

However, due to the uncertainty of the mobile robot itself, it will inevitably affect the accuracy of localization. Scholars have also conducted research on this issue. As the researches did in [8], using entropy and mutual information metrics to estimate quantitative uncertainty estimates and the effectiveness of information theory concepts within a probabilistic framework. In [9], it suggests a position estimation algorithm based upon an adaptive fading Kalman filter to overcome the inaccurate results due to limited linear approximation, which the adaptive fading factor enables the estimator to change the error covariance according to the real situation. And the literature [10] associates the new observations to existing estimates in terms of the Kullback-Leibler divergence to evaluate the proposed method to augment standard dynamic object trackers which solve the problem that other traffic participants are often occluded from sensor measurements by buildings or large vehicles in autonomous driving scenarios. But at present, there are few methods to evaluate the results of the localization of autonomous vehicles.

To solve this problem, we construct a localization evaluation system based on Gaussian distribution model that is independent of its own localization system and is related to the actual environmental information. The Kullback–Leibler divergence and Fourier transform methods are used to process the localization data to complete the evaluation of the localization effect.

2 Localization and Evaluation Model

2.1 Localization Model

Localization model is a three-dimensional Gaussian distribution model(X-Y-Z). The probability density function of a multidimensional Gaussian distribution is as follows:

$$p(x) = \det(2\pi\Sigma)^{-\frac{1}{2}} \exp\{-\frac{1}{2}(x - \mu)^T \Sigma^{-1}(x - \mu)\}. \tag{1}$$

In the formula, μ is the mean vector and Σ is a semi-positive definite symmetric matrix, which is the covariance matrix (in this model, the covariance matrix is a 3×3 semi-positive definite symmetric matrix). Gaussian model has a wide range of applications in robot localization, like in [11]. Gaussian techniques all share the basic idea that beliefs are represented by multivariate Gaussian distributions. The commitment to represent the posterior by a Gaussian has important ramifications. Most importantly, Gaussians are unimodal; they possess a single maximum. Such a posterior is characteristic of many tracking problems in robotics, in which the posterior is focused around the true state with a small margin of uncertainty [2].

In order to describe the pose of the unmanned vehicle more clearly, we introduce Euler angles (roll, pitch, yaw) to construct a model of pose6D (x, y, z, roll, pitch, yaw). Yaw represents the angle of rotation about the Y axis, Pitch the angle of rotation about the X axis, and Roll represents the angle of rotation about the Z axis, as shown in Fig. 1. Any rotation angle can be obtained by rotating these three times in order.

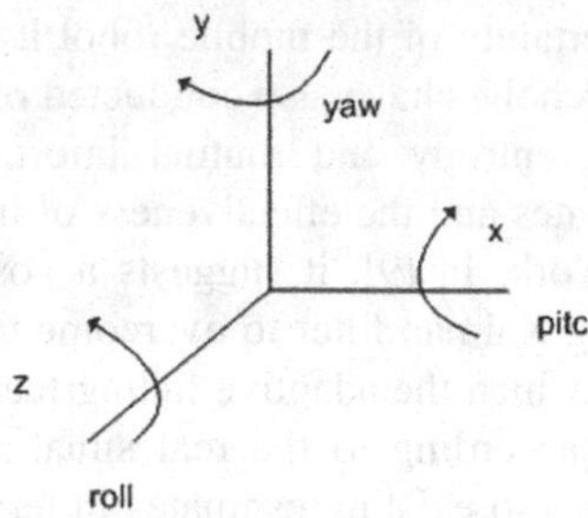

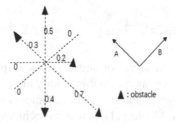

Fig. 1. Euler angle

2.2 Evaluation Model

Grid Hypothesis Model. Agrid hypothesis model using the existing prior information of the surrounding environment and posteriori information of current laser real-time collection of autonomous vehicle is constructed and it is the basis and focus of this localization evaluation system. The prior information is the set of existing high-definition maps and the array of data collected by the laser sensor in the area with a certain accuracy. The posterior information is the array of data of the current autonomous vehicle collected by the laser sensor in real time. Comparing the posteriori information with the priori information on the collected data of the corresponding position of the autonomous vehicle, the matching degree of the two can be obtained. We use the matching degree to evaluate the localization results of the autonomous vehicle. Figure 2 illustrates how to get the priori data array and posterior data array.

Fig. 2. Data collection schematic diagram

As shown in Fig. 2, if the data are collected in the A and B directions, the resulting data array is A = [0.3, 0.5, 0, 0.2, 0.7, 0.4, 0, 0], B = [0, 0.2, 0.7, 0.4, 0, 0, 0.3, 0.5]. The priori data array and an array of posterior data can be obtained by collecting data by laser. Then we construct a hypothesis grid to describe the model.

The output from the localization algorithm as a center to construct a localization frame composed of $m \times n$ grids. Each grid acquires data in l directions by laser and a total of $m \times n \times l$ sets of data are obtained. Figure 3 is a top view of the grid localization frame.

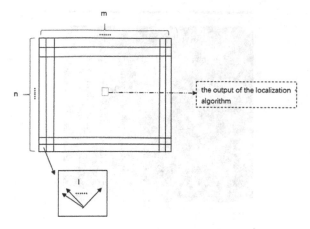

Fig. 3. Grid positioning frame top view

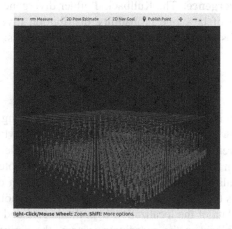

Fig. 4. A part of grid hypothesis (Color figure online)

Comparing the above $m \times n \times l$ sets of data with the corresponding current real-time laser acquisition data to obtain the matching degree, in order to better describe the matching degree in each grid, we simulated a visualized image of the matching degree. For the convenience to display, one of the l directions in each grid is taken, the red arrow shown in Figs. 4 and 5, and the height(ordinate) of the red arrow is the matching value of prior data and posterior data.

Finally, on the basis of constructing a real-time grid hypothesis evaluation model, Kullback–Leibler divergence and Fourier Transform methods are used to evaluate the current localization results.

Fig. 5. Grid hypothesis after scaling (Color figure online)

Kullback-Leibler Divergence. The Kullback–Leibler divergence (also called relative entropy) is a measure of how one probability distribution diverges from a second, expected probability distribution [12]. The definition formula is:

$$D_{KL}(P\|Q) = \sum_i P(i) \ln \frac{P(i)}{Q(i)}. \tag{2}$$

the value of $D_{KL}(P\|Q)$ indicates the information loss when using Q to approximate P, if it is close to 0, the two distributions have similar behavior, while a value close to 1 means two very different distributions. In the evaluation model, P denotes the data distribution collected in the localization hypothesis grid, Q denotes the theoretical data distribution of the localization hypothesis grid in the collection data set of the region and $D_{KL}(P\|Q)$ denotes the relative entropy of the two distributions. By calculating the distance between the data of the localization hypothesis grid and the priori data of the localization hypothesis grid in the coordinate system, the confidence is obtained by combining the $D_{KL}(P\|Q)$ parameter, thereby completing the localization evaluation.

Fourier Transform. Fourier Transform is an algorithm that samples a signal over a period of time (or space) and divides it into its frequency components. Fourier analysis converts a signal from its original time domain to a representation in the frequency domain and vice versa. The following are the formulas for the discrete Fourier forward and inverse transforms:

$$X(k) = \sum_{n=0}^{N-1} x(n) e^{-\frac{i2\pi kn}{N}}$$

$$= \sum_{n=0}^{N-1} x(n) \left[\cos \frac{2\pi kn}{N} - i \sin \frac{2\pi kn}{N}\right], k = 0, 1, \ldots, N-1. \tag{3}$$

$$x(n) = \frac{1}{N} \sum_{k=0}^{N-1} X(k) e^{\frac{i2\pi kn}{N}}$$

$$= \frac{1}{N} \sum_{k=0}^{N-1} X(k) [\cos \frac{2\pi kn}{N} + i \sin \frac{2\pi kn}{N}], n = 0, 1, \ldots, N-1. \tag{4}$$

where the latter expression follows from the former one by Euler's formula:

$$e^{ix} = \cos x + i \sin x. \tag{5}$$

In this model, evaluation with Fourier Transform method in three steps:

Step 1: Get error. First, we find the maximum data in grid hypothesis, then record the serial number and subtract the central serial number.

Step 2: Fourier Transform. Through the previous step we get the error sequence in time domain and then use the Fourier Transform to get the error result in frequency domain.

Step 3: Analyze the results. Low-frequency signal indicates false result to complete the evaluation of the localization result.

3 Experiments

3.1 Evaluation Steps

Step 1: Using the pose6D localization model introduced to Euler angles to locate the autonomous vehicle. A high-definition map and a collection of arrays of data collected by the laser sensor in that area are ready.

Step 2: After several experiments on the localization of the autonomous vehicle, the accuracy of the optimal localization frame is:

X dimension: 63; Y dimension: 63; theta dimension: 32; theta resolution: 0.00436; 0.16 meters per pixel.

The data in its localization frame are collected by laser sensor.

Step 3: Comparing the data obtained in the previous step with the priori data set corresponding to the first step to obtain the heat map.

In this heat map, red is darkest than other colors, from red to background blue is from dark to light. The darker the color, the closer the two sets of data are. The smaller offset in the first heat map in Fig. 6 indicates that the localization is more accurate, the offset in the second heat map is centered, and the third is larger, indicating poor localization results.

Step 4: Using Kullback–Leibler divergence and Fourier transform respectively for localization evaluation. We define $data\_from\_grid\_hypothesis[i]$ as $dfgh[i]$ and $data\_from\_grid\_pose[i]$ as $dfp[i]$. According to (2), we can obtain the relative entropy:

Fig. 6. Heat map (Color figure online)

$$KL_{param} = 100 \times \left| dfgh[i] \times \ln\frac{dfgh[i]}{dfp[i]} \right|. \tag{6}$$

Then obtain confidence for localization evaluation with the KL parameter.

According to the definition (3) and (4), one-dimension complex discrete Fourier Transform is performed on the difference discrete value over time, and the real part of the output value is judged. If it is greater than zero, the localization result is True, otherwise it is False. And calculate confidence for evaluation.

3.2   The Experimental Results

The Kullback–Leibler divergence and Fourier transform methods are used to evaluate the localization results of the autonomous vehicle, and calculating the confidence obtained by the two methods to judge whether the localization is correct or not, 1 for correct localization and 0 for localization failure. Figures 7 and 8 shown the evaluation confidence and localization results obtained by using the Fourier transform method in two time periods, Figs. 9 and 10 shown the evaluation confidence and localization results obtained by using the Kullback–Leibler divergence method.

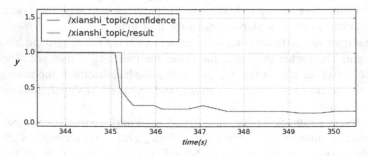

Fig. 7. Evaluation confidence and localization results by using the Fourier transform

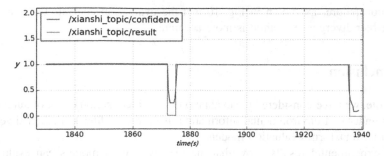

Fig. 8. Evaluation confidence and localization results by using the Fourier transform

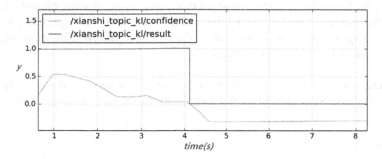

Fig. 9. Evaluation confidence and localization results by using the Kullback–Leibler divergence

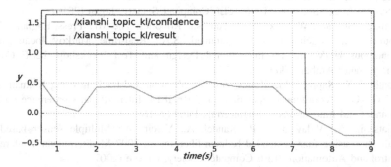

Fig. 10. Evaluation confidence and localization results by using the Kullback–Leibler divergence

In Figs. 7, 8, 9 and 10, the y axis represents the value of evaluation confidence and localization result that change with time. In Fig. 7, when the localization fails, the confidence changes obviously and the localization failure can be immediately judged based on the result, while in Fig. 9, the confidence changes slowly and the evaluation speed is slower. In Fig. 8, when some small localization errors occur (such as the impact of pedestrians on the road, changes in some buildings, etc.), result is judged as localization failure, as shown in Fig. 10 that the evaluation analysis using the Kullback–Leibler divergence method is more accurate.

4 Conclusion

In this note, we have considered the evaluation of the localization effect of autonomous vehicles under real environmental information using the Kullback–Leibler divergence and Fourier transform evaluation models.

The experimental results show that the two evaluation models can evaluate the localization effect. The Fourier transform evaluation model evaluates the localization of the autonomous vehicle faster than the Kullback–Leibler divergence evaluation model. However, the Kullback–Leibler divergence evaluation model is more effective than the Fourier transform evaluation model in dealing with some unexpected conditions encountered by autonomous vehicles under the real environmental information, and it is more accurate in localization evaluation.

Acknowledgments. This work is supported by Shanghai University, and we would like to appreciate the Prof. Wanmi Chen and M.E Yang Wang for the support of our paper.

References

1. Kurashiki, K., Fukao, T., Ishiyama, K., Kamiya, T., Murakami, N.: Orchard traveling UGV using particle filter based localization and inverse optimal control. In: The 3rd Symposium on System Integration, pp. 31–36. IEEE Computer Society, Japan (2010)
2. Thrun, S., Burgard, W., Fox, D.: Probabilistic Robotics. The MIT Press, England (2006)
3. Shoukry, Y., Abdelfatah, W.F., Hammad, S.A.: Real-time Markov localization for autonomous UGV. In: 4th International Design and Test Workshop. IEEE Computer Society, Saudi Arabia (2009)
4. Tripathi, S.K., Sapre, R.M.: Robust target localization and tracking using Kalman filtering for UGV-UAV coordinated operation. In: 2016 IEEE International Conference on Recent Advances and Innovations in Engineering, India (2016)
5. Tsalatsanis, A., Valavanis, K.P., Kandel, A., Yalcin, A.: Multiple sensor based UGV localization using fuzzy extended Kalman filtering. In: 2007 Mediterranean Conference on Control and Automation. IEEE Computer Society, Greece (2007)
6. Kwon, J.-W., Park, M.-S., Kim, T.-U., Chwa, D.-K., Hong, S.-K.: Localization of outdoor wheeled mobile robots using indirect Kalman filter based sensor fusion. J. Inst. Control. Rob. Syst. **14**, 800–808 (2008)
7. Nguyen, N., Tyagi, D., Shin, V.I.: An observation model based on polyline map for autonomous vehicle localization. In: Proceedings of the IEEE International Conference on Industrial Technology, India, pp. 2427–2431 (2006)
8. Messina, E., Madhavan, R.: Intelligent unmanned ground vehicle navigation via information evaluation. Adv. Rob. **20**, 1375–1400 (2006)
9. Sung, W.J., Choi, S.O., You, K.H.: TDoA based UGV localization using adaptive Kalman filter algorithm. In: 2008 2nd International Conference on Future Generation Communication and Networking Symposia, China, vol. 4, pp. 99–103. IEEE Computer Society (2008)

10. Galceran, E., Olson, E., Eustice, R.M.: Augmented vehicle tracking under occlusions for decision-making in autonomous driving. In: IEEE/RSJ International Conference on Intelligent Robots and Systems, Germany, pp. 3559–3565 (2015)
11. Pfaff, P., Plagemann, C., Burgard, W.: Gaussian mixture models for probabilistic localization. In: IEEE International Conference on Robotics and Automation, USA, pp. 467–472 (2008)
12. Wikipedia. https://en.wikipedia.org/wiki/Kullback%E2%80%93Leibler_divergence#cite_note-1

Cooperative Slip Detection Using a Dual-Arm Baxter Robot

Shane Trimble[✉], Wasif Naeem, and Seán McLoone

School of Electronics, Electrical Engineering and Computer Science,
Queen's University Belfast, Belfast, UK
strimble08@qub.ac.uk

Abstract. When dealing with robotic manipulation tasks, slip detection and control is vital to overcome payload uncertainties and to compensate for external disturbances. Many modern smart manipulators are shipped with integrated joint torque sensing capabilities providing a potential means of detecting slip and hence generating a feedback signal for slip control, without the need for additional external sensors. This paper investigates preliminary results on slip detection with an aim to extend the existing work on single manipulator to a dual arm cooperative manipulator system. The slip signal is obtained through filtering of onboard joint torque measurements when different materials are held in a friction grip between the two cooperating robotic end-effectors of a Baxter robot.

Frequency domain analysis of data from preliminary experiments shows a substantial frequency component in the vicinity of 12 Hz when slip is taking place. Consequently, a 9–15 Hz band-pass Chebyshev filtered torque signal is proposed as a real-time slip detection signal and its performance evaluated in experiments using a selection of materials with differing mass, coefficient of friction and thickness.

Analysis of the resulting filter output and threshold signal for each material revealed that the proposed approach was effective at detecting slip for some materials (laminated card, MDF, PVC and Perspex) but not for others (sheet steel, cardboard and polypropylene). This is attributed to the variation in consistency in slip behaviour of different material/weight combinations.

1 Introduction

The manipulation of objects by robots is typically accompanied by events such as slippage between a robot's fingers or, in the case of two non-dexterous end-effectors, robotic arms. Humans are able to identify such events using a combination of superficial and deep mechanoreceptors [1], but for robots, with more elementary mass, stiffness and friction sensing, such events can be hard to distinguish [2].

In industry many items manipulated by robots are too wide or heavy to be practically held in the grasp of a single enclosed end-effector due to size or payload limitations. In certain scenarios manipulators may work together in

© Springer Nature Singapore Pte Ltd. 2018
K. Li et al. (Eds.): ICSEE 2018/IMIOT 2018, CCIS 924, pp. 246–258, 2018.
https://doi.org/10.1007/978-981-13-2384-3_23

pairs, where an object may be held in a friction only grasp between the end-effectors, without additional support employed [3].

In the field of robotic slip detection and control, much work has been done on single dexterous end-effectors. While several methods exist to detect slip, such as the ones using accelerometers [4,5] and optical sensors [6,7] the main method of detecting slip is via pressure signal analysis of piezoresistive force sensing resistors (FSR) mounted on contact points [8]. These sensors encounter a change in resistivity which is directly proportional to the change in pressure. A typical time domain FSR sensor signal with slip occurring can be seen in Fig. 1. Such a sensor is incorporated into a control loop to detect slippage based on empirical mode decomposition in [2]. This approach relies on the analysis of vibrations generated during slippage, however challenges are faced in discriminating between noise and the small signals generated by slippage because of low signal-to-noise ratio, necessitating the use of time domain filtering on any feedback signals. In [9], a novel flexible, thin and lightweight FSR was developed in order to detect slip. The authors encountered issues differentiating between slip and changes in normal force, and so in [10], they investigated a method for identifying object slip by analysing the frequency components of the output measurements from the sensor. End-effector mounted strain gauge signals were analysed after Fast Fourier Transformation in [11]. Seven band-pass filters with different frequency bands were designed based on these signals and a threshold for each defined. Once slip is detected, the parameters of a sliding mode slip prevention controller are updated so that the grip force is increased in discrete, predetermined amounts to prevent the object slipping further.

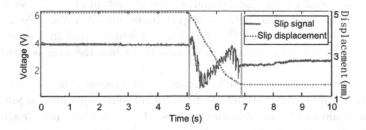

Fig. 1. A typical FSR time domain signal response with obvious high frequency components while slip is occurring, from 5 to 7 s [2].

Similarly, in [12], FSR sensor slip signals were transformed using FFT. This data was then used to train a standard artificial neural network for incipient slip detection, which successfully detected slippage of five different objects, of varying materials.

The optimal sensing layout for a single-end effector with two load cells measuring normal and tangential force used in conjunction with an optical sensor is investigated in [13]. Slip is induced through the modulation of grasp force applied to an object. The paper concludes that it is preferable to monitor normal force, tangential force and vertical slippage (optically) simultaneously. With feedback coming from this sensor combination no uncontrolled slip was observed.

Cooperating manipulators is currently an active area of study. In [6], interaction effect characterization during manipulation of a common object on such a system is explored. Kinematic constraints for the system are taken into account when modelling the overall system dynamics. The fundamental properties of the system during a manipulation task are derived and an experiment is conducted with two cooperating anthropomorphic robotic arms, which support the findings.

Coupled dynamics are presented in [14] for two cooperating mobile robotic arms manipulating a moving object with additional factors of external disturbances and other uncertainties accounted for. Centralized robust adaptive controls are introduced to guarantee set motion and force trajectories of an object. Closed-loop stability and the boundedness of tracking errors of the system are validated using Lyapunov stability synthesis.

A model for a cooperative continuum robot (CCR) concept is presented in [15]. These robots working in tandem allow for a large variety of new applications due to their flexibility, such as maintenance, search and rescue operations and medical interventions.

When selecting an appropriate controller feedback signal, it is desirable to utilize existing built-in sensors for both simplicity and economical reasons, as opposed to adding additional external circuitry.

Modern smart collaborative robots have spring loaded joints with torque sensing capabilities [16]. While these robots have many benefits which make them more suitable to a human workspace, such a system presents a number of challenges. Firstly, actuators can store unwanted energy in the elastic element which can potentially be dangerous and, secondly, system uncertainties and nonlinearities are present. The authors of [17] make use of a Variable Boundary Layer Sliding Mode Controller (VBSMC) to account for this on a single Baxter manipulator, showing an increase in compliance when the arm is moved by a human.

For object manipulation, a multi-purpose blank end-effector allows for a multitude of tasks to be done without the need for retooling for different jobs. While every task would not be suitable for this type of end-effector, most pushing, lifting and grasping jobs could be performed by robots with such devices attached. Two of these acting together allows for a wide range of objects to be manipulated, through the application of a normal force acting orthogonally to an object and the use of friction to overcome gravitational and motion acceleration forces.

Collaborating and general purpose robotics, two of the major focuses of *Industry* 4.0, are set to become more prevalent in the future [18]. It is therefore important to optimally design these systems for general purpose use on the shop floor.

The addition of slip control functionality increases the universal nature of a cooperating robot system, and so a natural extension to the field is slip detection and control using a pair of collaborating arms. In this paper, a preliminary study has been conducted to investigate the feasibility of using the built-in torque sensing capability of a Baxter dual arm robot, to be used ultimately as a feedback signal for control of slip between two collaborating manipulators. This has been analysed with a range of materials with differing weights for comparison.

The remainder of the paper is organised as follows. Section 2 presents a description of the robot and the related software and hardware including the end-effector, filter design and overall system architecture. Whilst the methodology of slip detection is discussed in Sect. 3 with Sect. 4 providing details of the experiments. Results are presented in Sect. 5 whereas Sect. 6 highlights ensuing discussions. Finally, Sect. 7 draws the concluding remarks and future work.

Table 1. ROS topics used in experiment

Rostopic	Built-in	Experiment usage	Pub freq [Hz]
.. /gravity_compensation_torques/actual_effort	Yes	$S0$ & $W0$ torque values	95
.. /suppress_collision_avoidance	Yes	Deactivate	10
.. /filter_output	No	Filter $W0$ orque	200

2   System Description

This section discusses the robotic platform employed in this study including the custom end-effectors and the Robot Operating System (ROS). The filter design and test objects used in the experiments are also described.

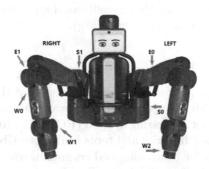

Fig. 2. Baxter robot with dual 7 degree-of-freedom manipulators [19].

2.1   The Baxter Robot

Baxter is a collaborative robot with two 7 degree-of-freedom manipulators designed to work on production lines side by side with human workers. The robot is safe to use around humans as each of it's 14 spring-loaded manipulator joints, as seen in Fig. 2, have built-in torque sensing capability providing feedback in case of a collision. Baxter also has a ring of ultrasonic sensors encircling the head module, allowing proximity detection of people or moving objects.

Fig. 3. 3D printed end-effector fitted to Baxter. Note the three rubber contact points for increased gripping.

Experimentation has revealed that the end-effector pose position accuracy deviates by a mean value of $+/-15\,\text{mm}$ [20]. The robot thus continues to correct for this error by constantly modifying the joint torque values. This makes it challenging to extract the desired frequency signal thus necessitating time domain filtering, as discussed in Sect. 2.4.

2.2 End-Effectors

For this experiment two customised 3D-printed end-effectors are attached to both manipulators, as shown in Fig. 3. Three rubber bumpers are added to each end-effector to increase contact quality and grip. The joint torque and gravity compensation values of the robot are recalibrated after attachment, to compensate for the slight increase in mass (circa $90\,\text{g}$).

2.3 System Architecture

In order to promote the platform, a research version of the robot was released in early 2013 along with an open-source Software Developement Kit (SDK), integrated with the Robot Operating System (ROS) [21]. ROS is an open-source, meta-operating system of libraries and tools built onto Ubuntu, which provides a networked framework for controlling and communicating with robots through publishing/subscribing to/from *Rostopics*. The Rostopics employed in this study are summarized in Table 1.

The ROS network and robot block diagram is shown in Fig. 4. This peer-to-peer network consists of one master and one client machine. The Rosmaster PC is an Ubuntu machine with ROS installed. On this machine three custom nodes are running. The torque control node is a custom script used to change the torque values of the *Rostopic .../gravity_compensation_torques/actual_effort*. It is commanded with an external hand-held controller, connected over USB. The collision avoidance suppression node publishes a simple message to the collision avoidance node to deactivate the subsystem. This normally-on safety feature is constantly reset, so the custom node needs to publish at a minimum of $10\,\text{Hz}$.

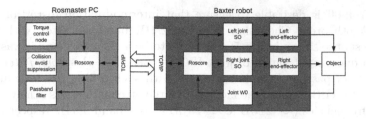

Fig. 4. System block diagram.

The Baxter robot communicates with the ROSmaster PC using TCP-IP protocol over ethernet, with a low latency of <1 ms. The robots $S0$ torque joint topics are passed torque values using *ROSmessages* sent from the torque control node in the ROSmaster PC. This applies normal force, F, through the end-effectors onto the test object. F can then be decremented by the user to entice slip.

2.4   Chebyshev Filter

Preliminary testing revealed a vast amount of undesirable signals and noise when attempting to detect slip, due to end-effector motion and constant error correction. The torque value of the joint $W0$ is measured in Nm at a sampling rate of 95 Hz, similar to the 100 Hz sampling rate used in [22], but below the 400 Hz used in [5,23].

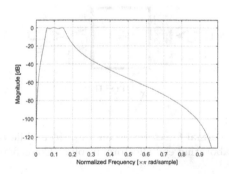

Fig. 5. Frequency response of 9 to 15 Hz passband filter applied to the torque value of joint $W0$.

Due to the real-time operation of the system, a low order infinite impulse response (IIR) filter was preferable to minimise excessive computation and ensure that the *rosnode* containing the filter would operate at the correct frequency of 200 Hz. This value was chosen as it is high enough to prevent aliasing ($>2Fs$), yet sufficiently low that the node scan-cycle does not have any latency issues.

A steep roll-off is desirable to ensure that intermodulation distortion is minimised. A 6th order Chebyshev 9 to 15 Hz IIR bandpass filter, with the frequency response shown in Fig. 5, was found to be satisfactory and it was applied to the torque output signal of joint $W0$, published as $Rostopic/filter\_output$. The effects of passband ripple associated with such a filter are insignificant in this case (≈ -1 dB), due to the fact that a large attenuation was achieved for the rejected frequencies (≈ -21 dB & ≈ -28 dB at passband ± 5 Hz respectively).

2.5   Experimental Objects

In order to conduct experiments with varying coefficients of friction, several everyday materials with different masses were selected. Among these, four materials which yielded consistent slip detection results were further tested with additional weights attached to examine the effect of an increased tangential force with a constant coefficient of friction on the magnitude of the frequency response.

3   Slip Detection Methodology

As mentioned earlier, in order to design a slip control system for a dual arm system, it is necessary to find an appropriate feedback signal for control purposes. Determination of normal force, F, the force applied to the object by the end-effectors during manipulation, is necessary to enable optimisation of the force in order to prevent slip.

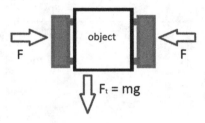

Fig. 6. Tangential and normal forces acting on an object while being manipulated by two non-dexterous collaborating end-effectors, in blue (Color figure online)

It can be established from Fig. 6 that if one or both manipulators are equipped with force feedback, F can be adjusted to a safe minimum in order to hold the object securely without any additional support. By applying minimal F the object can be held safely without the risk of crushing [13]. This can be calculated when the tangential force acting on the object, F_t, and the interface static coefficient of friction, μ_s, are known, as in Eq. 1:

$$F = \frac{F_t}{\mu_s} \tag{1}$$

where μ_s is dependant on the frictional properties of the two materials, their interaction and environmental factors [24,25]. In a non-laboratory environment, it is usually impractical to have the mass, and rare to have the coefficient of friction information available for different objects being manipulated.

In the case of this experimental platform, discussed in Sect. 2, the shoulder joint $S0$ (see Fig. 2) acts as a fulcrum applying torque, T in Newton-meters. F can be calculated from the torque at the joint, T_{S0}, and the perpendicular distance from the axis of rotation to the point of contact, d, in meters, as:

$$F = \frac{T_{S0}}{d} \tag{2}$$

The tangential force, F_t, pulling down on the object is given by:

$$F_t = m(g + a) \tag{3}$$

Z-plane acceleration of grippers, a, must be taken into account when the robot is in motion, along with g, acceleration due to gravity.

In order to apply the minimum grasping force to hold an object where μ_s and m are unknown, F cannot be calculated. When F_t is greater than F, the object will begin to move, therefore, the point at which minimum F is applied can be assumed as the point of impending slippage [13]. T_{S0}, torque at shoulder joint $S0$, and m is recorded for each test. Combining Eqs. 1, 2 and 3 gives the relationship:

$$\frac{T_{S0}}{m} = \frac{d(g + a)}{\mu_s} \tag{4}$$

Therefore for an object of the same μ_s and d acting on the same system but different m, it can be said that the ratio of threshold torque to mass remains the same, that is:

$$\frac{T_{S01}}{m_1} = \frac{T_{S02}}{m_2} \tag{5}$$

4   Experimental Methodology

The two end-effectors were commanded to identical Cartesian coordinates in the X and Z planes in order to keep them at the same height and distance from the robot. Both were also set to the same roll and yaw, with opposing pitch in order to get the flat surface of the end-effectors to face each other to allow for a grasping action as left and right F were increased.

Each object was held manually between the end-effectors and T_{S0} incremented, decreasing the difference in Y until a firm grasp was achieved, in the manner of Fig. 6. Torque was monitored to ensure a constant steady-state value before slipping is induced.

The torque level on the right $S0$ joint was decremented manually using an external hand-held controller until slipping was observed. The real-time torque value of left joint $W0$ was input into the filter discussed in Sect. 2.4 and the output recorded, along with all left arm joint torque values. Slip quality was monitored by the observer, watching for any sudden drops or unwanted paroxysmal movement, signifying a material that normal force is difficult to modulate for. The observer description of the contact properties of the intersection between the end-effectors and the object is recorded.

The experiment was repeated five times for each of the eight material/mass combinations where slip could be successfully detected. The average slip threshold torque values of left joint $S0$ and the filter output were recorded for each repetition, and the ratio of these values to mass calculated to validate Eq. 5.

5 Results

Quantitative analysis of four of the materials where slip was successfully recorded is provided in Table 2, which lists the type and description of materials used, their masses, average threshold forces at which slip occurs, average peak values of vibrations in joint $W0$ during slip and ratios of threshold and vibration forces to mass for each material. Figure 7 depicts torque (Nm) against time (samples) for time windows, in which slip occurs, of the eight experiments where the top rows (i) and (ii) correspond to the standard material whilst rows (iii) and (iv) correspond to the same material but with additional mass. The plots reveal the difference in slip threshold force at joint $S0$ and magnitude of vibrations observed at joint $W0$ as mass is increased and are typical of the materials where a consistent good quality slip signal was observed. It can be seen that when the slip threshold measured at $S0$ is crossed as in rows (i) and (iii) of Fig. 7, a spike

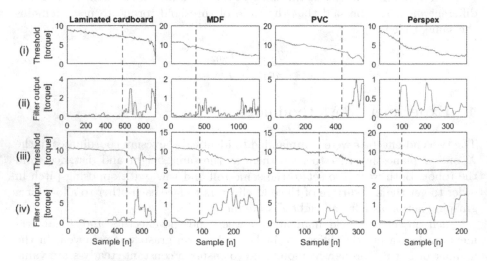

Fig. 7. Rows (i) and (ii) show the $S0$ force and absolute filter output respectively for time windows, in which slip occurs, of the lighter mass experiments; rows (iii) and (iv) for the heavier. The dashed lines mark the point of impending slip.

in the absolute filtered signal value $W0$ is observed (see corresponding rows (ii) and (iv)). The magnitude of the spike varies depending on a combination of mass and surface friction properties.

Table 2. Experimental torque/mass analysis

Material	Object description	Mass [kg]	T threshold [Nm]	T threshold/mass [Nm/kg]	Peak [Nm]	Peak/mass [Nm/kg]
Laminated card	glossy, sticky	0.8270	8.3024	10.0392	3.2904	3.9787
		1.3500	12.4563	9.2269	5.6785	4.2063
MDF	high friction	0.9900	5.4730	5.5283	0.9243	0.9336
		1.5150	9.7596	6.4420	2.6854	1.7725
PVC	glossy, sticky	1.1330	5.5640	4.9109	4.4427	3.9212
		1.6650	8.4640	5.0835	5.5422	3.3286
perspex	glossy, sticky	0.7440	6.8950	9.2675	0.8750	1.1761
		1.2730	10.9540	8.6049	1.0732	0.8430

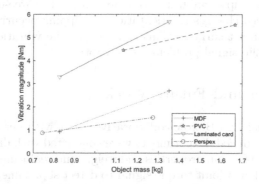

Fig. 8. Average frequency magnitude compared to the mass for four different objects.

The average magnitude of vibration against object's mass for the four materials is depicted in Fig. 8, showing that as mass increases, the frequency component of the force in the 9–15 Hz range during slip at $W0$ increases.

Additional materials including sheets of steel, cardboard, polypropylene and a hard card box were also tested but proved to be challenging with regard to slip. These are excluded from Table 2 as due to their slip behaviour it was not possible to acquire a satisfactory slip signal with such measurements. These issues are further discussed in the following section.

6 Discussion

As can be expected, for objects with the same coefficient of friction where slip could be modulated consistently, the magnitude of vibration is directly proportional to the mass due to additional tangential force. There is also a relationship between the threshold holding torque at joint $S0$ and this tangential force, as seen in Table 2. This was true in general for the experiments either with a glossy, but sticky material such as plastics or laminated card, and materials with a high friction surface, such as MDF. The ratios of both normal force to mass and vibration magnitude to mass are approximately adhered to, as per Eq. 5.

As mentioned earlier, it was not possible to detect slip for all the materials tested due to the intermittent or sudden nature of the slip observed. 'Slip-stick' is a complex known problem due to dynamic instabilities [4]. Materials with this characteristic are not best suited to a noisy moving robotic platform, and in the case of this study they made joint $S0$ force control difficult to modulate.

The strip of cardboard exhibited behaviour in this manner due to it being an easily compressible material with a non-uniform thickness. The polypropylene material exhibited similar behaviour, because, although smooth, it was very sticky and required a large mass in order to cause slip. This created undesirable torsion forces acting on the end-effectors which disrupted the contact shape between the material and the robot. The steel sheet, with it's relatively high mass and very slippery surface slid out of the grasp suddenly on all five occasions, preventing a distinct slip signal from being observed. The three-dimensional hard card box experienced changes in orientation as slipping occurred, thus shifting the angle of the contact surfaces. This caused sporadic vibrations forces acting on $W0$, making a slip signal problematic to capture.

7   Conclusions and Future Work

In this paper a dual-arm Baxter collaborative robot with custom friction grip end-effectors is introduced. Experiments were conducted with different materials with varying surface friction properties and weight and real-time time-domain filtering implemented on a joint torque signal to detect slip. Time domain analysis of the filtered and threshold signals revealed that the approach was effective at detecting slip for the laminated card, MDF, PVC and Perspex, as these materials slipped in a smooth manner. The steel, cardboard and polypropylene exhibited 'slip-stick' behaviour, making it difficult to capture a slip signal. It would be valuable to further investigate data in Fig. 7, by increasing data points with additional materials and weights. In future work, improved signal conditioning will be performed to enhance the slip detection signal. It would also be useful to investigate the filter time delay, as the filtered torque signal is to be used as a feedback signal for a fully automated closed-loop slip controller on the dual manipulator system.

References

1. Gerling, G.J., Rivest, I.I., Lesniak, D.R., Scanlon, J.R., Wan, L.: Validating a population model of tactile mechanotransduction of slowly adapting type I afferents at levels of skin mechanics, single-unit response and psychophysics. IEEE Trans. Haptics **7**, 216–228 (2014)
2. Deng, H., Zhong, G., Li, X., Nie, W.: Slippage and deformation preventive control of bionic prosthetic hands. IEEE/ASME Trans. Mechatron. **22**, 888–897 (2017)
3. Xian, Z., Lertkultanon, P., Pham, Q.C.: Closed-chain manipulation of large objects by multi-arm robotic systems. IEEE Rob. Autom. Lett. **2**, 1832–1839 (2017)
4. Won, H.-I., Chung, J.: Numerical analysis for the stick-slip vibration of a transversely moving beam in contact with a frictional wall. J. Sound Vibr. **419**, 42–62 (2018)
5. Khurshid, R.P., Fitter, N.T., Fedalei, E.A., Kuchenbecker, K.J.: Effects of grip-force, contact, and acceleration feedback on a teleoperated pick-and-place task. IEEE Trans. Haptics **10**, 40–53 (2017)
6. Erhart, S., Hirche, S.: Model and analysis of the interaction dynamics in cooperative manipulation tasks. IEEE Trans. Rob. **32**, 672–683 (2016)
7. Saen, M., Ito, K., Osada, K.: Action-intention-based grasp control with fine finger-force adjustment using combined optical-mechanical tactile sensor. IEEE Sens. J. **14**, 4026–4033 (2014)
8. Aqilah, A., Jaffar, A., Bahari, S., Low, C.Y., Koch, T.: Resistivity characteristics of single miniature tactile sensing element based on pressure sensitive conductive rubber sheet. In: 2012 IEEE 8th International Colloquium on Signal Processing and its Applications, pp. 223–227, March 2012
9. Teshigawara, S., Ishikawa, M., Shimojo, M.: Development of high speed and high sensitivity slip sensor. In: 2008 IEEE/RSJ International Conference on Intelligent Robots and Systems, pp. 47–52, September 2008
10. Teshigawara, S., Tadakuma, K., Ming, A., Ishikawa, M., Shimojo, M.: High sensitivity initial slip sensor for dexterous grasp. In: 2010 IEEE International Conference on Robotics and Automation, pp. 4867–4872, May 2010
11. Engeberg, E.D., Meek, S.G.: Adaptive sliding mode control for prosthetic hands to simultaneously prevent slip and minimize deformation of grasped objects. IEEE/ASME Trans. Mechatron. **18**, 376–385 (2013)
12. Schoepfer, M., Schuermann, C., Pardowitz, M., Ritter, H.: Using a Piezo-resistive tactile sensor for detection of incipient slippage. In: ISR 2010 (41st International Symposium on Robotics) and ROBOTIK 2010 (6th German Conference on Robotics), pp. 1–7, June 2010
13. Dzitac, P., Mazid, A.M., Ibrahim, M.Y., Appuhamillage, G.K., Choudhury, T.A.: Optimal sensing requirement for slippage prevention in robotic grasping. In: 2015 IEEE International Conference on Industrial Technology (ICIT), pp. 373–378, March 2015
14. Li, Z., Tao, P.Y., Ge, S.S., Adams, M., Wijesoma, W.S.: Robust adaptive control of cooperating mobile manipulators with relative motion. IEEE Trans. Syst. Man. Cybern. Part B (Cybern.) **39**, 103–116 (2009)
15. Lotfavar, A., Hasanzadeh, S., Janabi-Sharifi, F.: Cooperative continuum robots: concept, modeling, and workspace analysis. IEEE Rob. Autom. Lett. **3**, 426–433 (2018)
16. Arshad, A., Badshah, S., Soori, P.K.: Design and fabrication of smart robots. In: 2016 5th International Conference on Electronic Devices, Systems and Applications (ICEDSA), pp. 1–4, December 2016

17. Makrini, I.E., Rodriguez-Guerrero, C., Lefeber, D., Vanderborght, B.: The variable boundary layer sliding mode control: a safe and performant control for compliant joint manipulators. IEEE Rob. Autom. Lett. **2**, 187–192 (2017)
18. Chen, B., Wan, J., Shu, L., Li, P., Mukherjee, M., Yin, B.: Smart factory of industry 4.0: key technologies, application case, and challenges. IEEE Access **6**, 6505–6519 (2018)
19. ReThink Robotics: Baxter hardware specifications, May 2014. Accessed 14 Jan 2018
20. Cremer, S., Mastromoro, L., Popa, D.O.: On the performance of the baxter research robot. In: 2016 IEEE International Symposium on Assembly and Manufacturing (ISAM), pp. 106–111, August 2016
21. Rethink robotics opens up baxter robot for researchers (2018). Accessed 5 Feb 2018
22. Stachowsky, M., Hummel, T., Moussa, M., Abdullah, H.A.: A slip detection and correction strategy for precision robot grasping. IEEE/ASME Trans. Mechatron. **21**, 2214–2226 (2016)
23. Damian, D.D., Newton, T.H., Pfeifer, R., Okamura, A.M.: Artificial tactile sensing of position and slip speed by exploiting geometrical features. IEEE/ASME Trans. Mechatron. **20**, 263–274 (2015)
24. Tuononen, A.J.: Onset of frictional sliding of rubber–glass contact under dry and lubricated conditions. Sci. Rep. **6**(1) (2016)
25. Xu, F., Yoshimura, K.-I., Mizuta, H.: Experimental study on friction properties of rubber material: influence of surface roughness on sliding friction. Procedia Eng. **68**, 19–23 (2013)

Intelligent Control and Automation

Study on Swimming Curve Fitting of Biomimetic Carangiform Robotic Fish

Baodong Lou[1], Yu Cong[2], Minghe Mao[3(✉)], Ping Wang[2], and Jiangtao Liu[1]

[1] School of Mechanical and Electrical Engineering, Hohai University, Nanjing 210098, China

[2] School of Energy and Electrical, Hohai University, Nanjing 210098, China

[3] School of Computer and Information, Hohai University, Nanjing 210098, China
mmh_1988@126.com

Abstract. At present, the biomimetic carangiform robotic fish with infinite flexible structure has not been presented. In order to facilitate the robotic fish swimming mode control, based on a finite flexible structure a number of rigid joints are used instead. In order to overcome the existing curve fitting method which endpoint of each joint falls on the swimming curve, causing the deviation between the fitting curve and the real swimming curve is larger. In this paper, a minimum error criterion is proposed to fit the swimming curve for a three-joint biomimetic carangiform robotic fish. Experimental results show that the proposed method which causes the endpoints of robotic fish moving joints not falling on the fitted swimming curve can obtain more accurate swimming motion according to the real fish than that uses the conventional endpoints-on-fitted-curve method. Moreover and thus, using the proposed method the swimming velocity of the robotic fish is improved rapidly.

Keywords: Biomimetic carangiform robotic fish · Curve fitting
Motion equation · Minimum error

1 Introduction

After a long period of natural continuous choice, fabulous evolution of the fishes makes their swimming ability meet the needs of survival. According to the different swimming duration time the fish movement can be divided into two patterns: cruise and maneuvering. The cruise refers to the long-term steady-state swimming over a long period of time, while the maneuvering refers to generating a great acceleration or a large steering torque in a short period of time. Also, the propulsion patterns can be divided into two categories depending on the different parts of fish body that can generate thrust: Body and/or Caudal Fin propulsion (BCF) and Media and/or Paired Fin propulsion (MPF). The carangidae fish studied in this paper uses the BCF propulsion pattern, which relies on the swing of the 1/3 parts of the body and the caudal fins, to generate thrust. Based on the prototype of carangidea fish the study is implemented on both structural appearance and athletic stance of swimming in this paper. The

© Springer Nature Singapore Pte Ltd. 2018
K. Li et al. (Eds.): ICSEE 2018/IMIOT 2018, CCIS 924, pp. 261–271, 2018.
https://doi.org/10.1007/978-981-13-2384-3_24

propulsive efficiency of fish is more than 80%. Therefore, in order to generate high speed with high propulsive efficiency the motion control for the biomimetic robotic fish should be well studied.

The kinematics theory of robotic fish has been studied since 1920s. In 1960, Lighthill introduced the "slender body theory" in aerodynamics into the hydrodynamic analysis of fish swim. Using carangidae fish as the research object, he initially established the carangidae fish kinematic model. Experimental studies on fish dynamics mainly focused on kinematic parameters and various forms of fish movement. In 1933, Gary recorded the movement of fish by camera, and the theory of undulatory propulsion from the motion of the cross section. Domenici and Blake studied the C-shape start of the angel fish, suggesting that the size of the fish is independent of the duration of the escape process but linearly related to the turning radius. In 1999, Spierts gave the C-sharp and S-sharp turning curves of crucian carp, and studied the kinematics difference between the two starting methods respectively [11]. In 2001, Rosenberger observed the morphological parameters and swimming patterns of the myliobatis-shaped fish, and compared the effects of pectoral fin motion parameters on the swimming speed and propulsion performance. At present, there are two main control algorithms for robotic fish motion control: Central Pattern Generator (CPG) and curve fitting. CPG is a control algorithm using the neural network, which is based on the motion mechanism of the animal, and it is used as the bottom controller to generate the swimming posture of the robotic fish. Since CPG has a high degree of non-linear characteristic, which leads to big obstacles for its theoretical research and practical application. Moreover, the basic movement of the CPG is composed of a series of rhythmic movements, which can respond quickly for the robotic fish cruise movement, but it is difficult to achieve its maneuvering. The curve fitting is to fit the trajectory of the fish through each joint of the robotic fish, which is suitable for all kinds of motion forms, meanwhile the design process is simple and convenient. In the traditional curve fitting, the end points fall on the curve in the fitting process, which lead to larger fitting error. In this paper, the minimum error criterion is proposed for curve fitting as a metric.

In this paper, we use the curve fitting method to control the three-joint biomimetic carangiform robotic fish Based on the metric of minimum error criterion. Therefore, the end point of the joint does not fall on the fitted curve as the traditional methods. Experimental results show that the minimum error curve fitting method can make the robotic fish movement more smoothly and improve the velocity of biomimetic robotic fish movement compared with the traditional curve fitting method.

2   The Kinematic Equations of Biomimetic Robotic Fish

According to Lighthill's theory of slender body [8], the fish wave is a traveling wave group with a gradually increasing wave amplitude. It can be approximated by a polynomial and a sinusoidal curve:

$$F_B(x, t) = (c_1 x + c_2 x^2) \sin(\omega t + kx) \tag{1}$$

Where $F_B(x, t)$ is the lateral position of the fish;

c_1 is the primary coefficient of the fish wave envelope;

c_2 is the quadratic term coefficient of the fish wave envelope;

k is the number of fish waves ($k = 2\pi/\lambda$, λ is the wavelength of the fish body);

ω is the frequency of fish wave ($\omega = 2\pi f = 2\pi/T$).

Through the biological studies we can see that the swing amplitude of the tail motion joint is 0.075–0.1 times of the body length, and fish wave wavelength is usually $\lambda \geq 1L_B$, so the fish wave number is $k = 2\pi/\lambda \leq 2\pi/L_B$ [16]. Therefore, in the absence of special instructions, the parameters used in this paper are assumed as $c_1 = 0.05$, $c_2 = 0.03$, $k = 8$, $\omega = -2\pi/9$. The values here are negative because the origin point of the model is set the connection point of the head and tail movement joints, and then the fish head direction is negative. The body wave motion equations of the biomimetic robotic fish using $F_B(x, t)$ can be drawn by MATLAB shown in Fig. 1. Each curve in Fig. 1 corresponds to the movement posture of the robotic fish at a given moment, and the fluctuation starting point of the tail movement joint is 0 point.

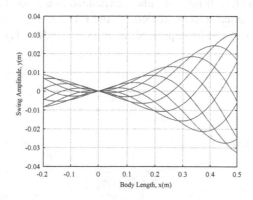

Fig. 1. Body wave curve cluster of biomimetic robotic fish

3 Kinematic Curve Fitting of Three-Joint Robotic Fish

Due to technical limitations, robotic fish can not be infinitely flexible at present, but instead of flexible curves it can be approximated by finite rigid joints. Because of the limitation of the biomimetic robotic fish joint length, it is difficult to use the analytical method to fit the equation of the multi-joint biomimetic robotic fish's body wave motion. Therefore, the numerical approximation method is used. The method firstly divides the body wave motion equation of the biomimetic robotic fish into N movements with time varying as $F_B(x, i)(i = 0. \ldots . N)$, and the gestures of each moment are fitted using three rigid joints as (l_1, l_2, l_3). In this way, the fish postures at all times can be replaced by approximated rigid joints of robotic fish. Figure 2 shows the robotic fish motion at a certain moment during cruise, while Fig. 3 shows the body wave motion curve corresponding to this posture.

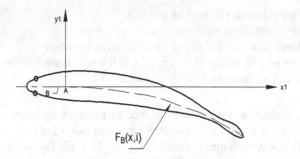

Fig. 2. Schematic diagram of biomimetic robotic fish at a certain time

In Fig. 3, $\theta_{i,j}(i = 0 \ldots M - 1, j = 1 \ldots 3)$ is the slip angle of each joint relative to the horizontal line, $\phi_{i,j}(i = 0 \ldots M - 1, j = 1 \ldots 3)$ is rotation angle which the individual joint of the biomimetic robotic fish need to be rotated, that is, the deflection angle of the back joint relative to the front joint. For example, "$\phi_{i,2}$" means the angle at which the second joint is required to be rotated relative to the first joint at the time of the movement posture $F_B(x, i)$. If this formula is expanded to a K-joint biomimetic robotic fish, the result of numerical approximation for the rotation angle using the body wave motion equation $F_B(x, t)$ can be expressed as $\phi_{i,j}(i = 0 \ldots M - 1, j = 1 \ldots K)$.

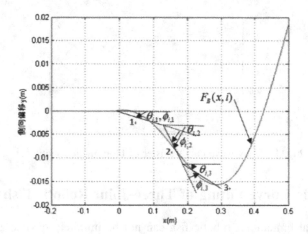

Fig. 3. The motion curve of biomimetic robotic fish

In references [18, 19], a method of curve fitting is proposed. In the case of known joint length, the starting point of the first joint coincides with the starting point of the wave, and then the circle is rounded with the length of the joint. The intersection with the curve is the coordinate of the other end point of the joint. The starting point of the second joint is the end point of the first joint, and the end point coordinate of the second joint is obtained by using the above mentioned method. Similarly, the coordinate of the third joint is obtained, then the fitted curves of the three-joint robotic fish motion are obtained.

In the process of fitting, the end of each joint falls on the theoretical fish wave curve, which causes large fitting errors, and the fluctuation curve of biomimetic robotic fish is not smooth enough to generate accurate biomimetic robotic fish swimming motion.

In this paper, the minimum error fitting method is proposed to fit the body wave motion curve of biomimetic robotic fish. Assuming that the biomimetic robotic fish has k joints with the length of each joint is $l_j (j = 1 \ldots k)$; the starting coordinate of each joint is (x_b, y_b), the end point coordinate is (x_e, y_e), which means that the starting coordinate of the j joint is the end coordinate of the $j-1$ th joint; finally, each joint can be represented by a linear equation $y = g(x)$. Then, the fitting error equation can be written as:

$$e(x) = \left| \int_{x_b}^{x_e} [g(x) - F_B(x)]dx \right|. \tag{2}$$

Although the fitting error includes amplitude error and direction error, only the amplitude error is considered in this paper, since the direction error is minimized to a certain small value at the same time when the amplitude error is minimized. Formula (6) represents only one joint fitting error, and it can be expanded to k th joint error equation as:

$$e_{i,j}(x) = \left| \int_{x_{b_{i,j}}}^{x_{e_{i,j}}} [g_{i,j}(x) - F_B(x, i)]dx \right|, \tag{3}$$

where $i = 0 \ldots M - 1, j = 1 \ldots k$,

$$g_{i,j}(x) = k_{i,j}x + b_{i,j} \tag{4}$$

where $k_{i,j} = \frac{y_{e_{i,j}} - y_{b_{i,j}}}{x_{e_{i,j}} - x_{b_{i,j}}}$ $b_{i,j} = y_{b_{i,j}} - k_{i,j}x_{b_{i,j}}$.

From the above analysis, we can see that the coordinates of each joint are related, so the starting coordinates of each biomimetic robotic fish joint can be described by the following equation:

$$\begin{cases} x_{b_{i,j}} = 0 & j = 0 \\ y_{b_{i,j}} = 0 & j = 0 \\ x_{b_{i,j}} = x_{e_{i,j-1}} & j = 2 \ldots k. \\ y_{b_{i,j}} = y_{e_{i,j-1}} & j = 2 \ldots k \end{cases} \tag{5}$$

The initial coordinate of the first joint is (0, 0), which is the connection point between the biomimetic robotic fish head and the tail movement joints. The connection point is the starting point of the fish wave motion. And since the length of each joint of the biomimetic robotic fish is given, the following equation can be obtained:

$$(x_{e_{i,j}} - x_{b_{i,j}})^2 + (y_{e_{i,j}} - y_{b_{i,j}}) = l_j^2 \tag{6}$$

Therefore, the problem of curve fitting is transformed into the problem of finding the joint end point coordinates in order to minimize the error equation $e_{i,j}(x)$ when the motion attitude equation $F_B(x, i)$ with the starting point coordinate and length of the joint are known at a certain moment. So that the following formula can be established:

$$\frac{de_{i,j}(x)}{dx} = 0 \tag{7}$$

It is obviously impossible to solve Eq. (11) by simultaneous Eqs. (7), (8), (9) and (10), because the constraint condition (9) and (10) themselves are interdependent and not completely independent of each other. Therefore, we assume that a length proportional correlation coefficient $R \in [0, 1]$ the ratio between the joint length between the starting point and the intersection of the rigid joint and the body wave curve and the total length of the joint. Then, for an arbitrary value of R, the intersection of the joint j and the motion curve $(x_{c_{i,j}}, y_{c_{i,j}})$ can be expressed by the following equation:

$$\begin{cases} (x - x_{b_{i,j}})^2 + (y - y_{b_{i,j}})^2 = (Rl_j)^2 \\ y = F_B(x, i), \end{cases} \tag{8}$$

where: $i = 0 \ldots M - 1, j = 1 \ldots k$

$(x_{c_{i,j}}, y_{c_{i,j}})$ can be obtained according to the above formula. Therefore, the linear equation $g_{i,j}(x)$ of the joint j can be easily obtained when knowing the coordinate of starting point and the intersection coordinate. $R_p = \frac{p}{n}, p = 0 \ldots n$ is introduced to calculate the minimum fitting error:

$$e_{i,jmin} = \min_{p=0\ldots n} (e_{i,j}(x)|R_p) \tag{9}$$

The fitting curve is obtained using the above equations, and then the rotation angle equation of each joint of the biomimetic robotic fish can be obtained by fitting the curve. The rotation angle equation is given as:

$$\begin{cases} \phi_{i,j} = \theta_{i,j} & j = 1 \\ \phi_{i,j} = \theta_{i,j} - \theta_{i,j-1} & j = 2 \ldots k \end{cases} \tag{10}$$

In order to control the motion of a robotic fish, the rotation angle $\phi_{i,j}$ at each moment is integrated into a time varying equation $\phi_j(t)$. Since the joint rotation of the robotic fish is a periodic motion that changes over time, the shape of the motion curve of each joint is similar to a sine function. It can be expressed by Fourier series as:

$$\phi_j(t) = \sum_{n=1}^{\infty} a_{n,j} \sin(n\omega t + \varphi_{n,j}), j = 1 \ldots k. \tag{11}$$

In order to limit the number of parameters to facilitate online optimization during engineering debugging, the results only retain the first term, and the joint angle control equations of the robotic fish can be obtained by discarding the higher order components, one has:

$$\phi_j(t) = a_j \sin(\omega t + \varphi_j), j = 1 \ldots k \tag{12}$$

The fitting curves of the traditional fish joint are plotted by using the angle control equation, as shown in Fig. 4. While the minimum error method for the robotic fish joint curves are shown in Fig. 5. One can see that there are no significant differences on the shape of the joint fitting curve using traditional fitting method and the proposed minimum error method. However, the initial phase angle and amplitude of each joint movement are different. And the difference between these two parameters will directly affect both the swimming posture and swimming speed of the robotic fish.

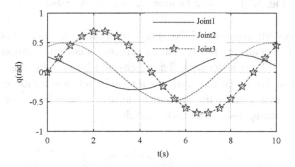

Fig. 4. Traditional fitting curve

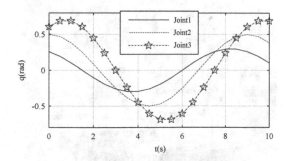

Fig. 5. Minimum error fitting curve

4 Experiment and Analysis

In order to verify the effect of the initial phase angle and amplitude of each joint on the swimming posture and swimming speed of the biomimetic robotic fish, a three-joint biomimetic carangiform robotic fish prototype is developed, as shown in Fig. 6, and the following experiment was carried out in the experimental system shown in Fig. 7.

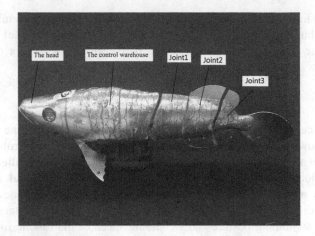

Fig. 6. Three-joint biomimetic carangiform robotic fish

The whole system consists of five parts: a three-joint biomimetic carangiform robotic fish, a PC client, an IDS industrial camera, a communication module and a 60 cm × 12 cm × 20 cm water tank. The three-joint biomimetic carangiform robotic fish is composed of five parts: the head, the internal control warehouse, the movement joint 1, the movement joint 2, the movement joint 3. The robotic fish communicates with the PC client using a 433 MHz RF module.

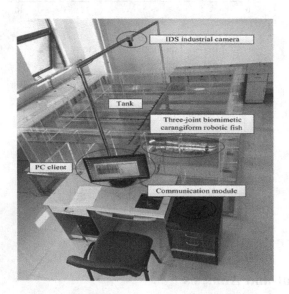

Fig. 7. Experimental environment and equipment

The fitting curves shown in Figs. 4 and 5 are realized on the three-joint biomimetic carangiform robotic fish prototype. Figure 8 is a set of continuous experimental pictures using the traditional fitting curve method for experimentation. While Fig. 9 is a set of continuous experimental pictures using the proposed minimum error fitting curve method for experimentation. Compared with the two sets of pictures, one can see that using the minimum error fitting curve to control the robotic fish swimming trajectory has a higher similarity with the swimming trajectory of real fish, and the curve is more smoothly in the process of movement. Comparing the two sets of pictures with the corresponding theoretical curve, one can find that the swimming curve of the robotic fish with the minimum error fitting curve is closer to the theoretical curve and has better linearity. Moreover, comparing the duration time taken by robotic fish after swimming the same distance, it can obviously be found that the duration time of the robotic fish using the minimum error fitting curve method is less than that of using the traditional method. The average velocity is improved by 7%, and the swimming posture is getting more stable.

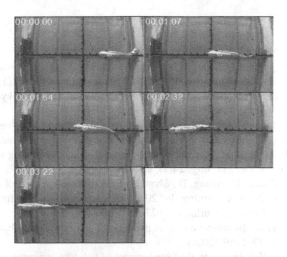

Fig. 8. Traditional curve fitting experiment

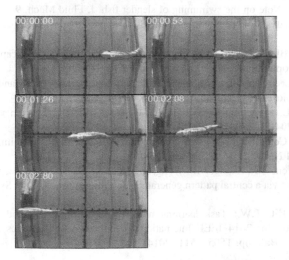

Fig. 9. Minimum error curve fitting experiment

5   Conclusion

In this paper, the curve fitting method of biomimetic carangiform robotic fish has been studied, and the experimental results have been validated. The following conclusions can be drawn as: A minimum error curve fitting method has been proposed for the three-joint biomimetic carangiform robotic fish. The method does not require the end point of the joint falling on the swimming curve. Experimental results have proved that the proposed method can make the fish swimming curve closer to that of the real fish. The fitted motion curve has been applied to a robotic fish prototype, which has proved that the proposed method can make the robotic fish swim more smoothly and improve the swimming speed rapidly.

References

1. Yu, J., Ding, R., Yang, Q., Tan, M., Wang, W., Zhang, J.: On a bioinspired amphibious robot capable of multimodal motion. IEEE/ASME Trans. Mechatron. **17**(5), 847–856 (2012)
2. Lu, X.Y., Yin, X.Z.: Propulsive performance of a fish-like travelling wavy wall. Acta Mech. **175**(1), 197–215 (2005)
3. Hong, C.: Kinematic mechanism research on the swimming and maneuvering of robot fish. Ph.D. dissertation, University of Science and Technology of China, China (2006)
4. Sfakiotakis, M., Lane, D.M., Davies, J.B.C.: Review of fish swimming modes for aquatic locomotion. IEEE J. Oceanic Eng. **24**(2), 237–252 (1999)
5. Hu, T., Lin, L., Zhang, D., Wang, D., Shen, L.: Effective motion control of the biomimetic undulating fin via iterative learning. In: 2009 IEEE International Conference on Robotics and Biomimetics (ROBIO), Guilin, pp. 627–632 (2009)
6. Low, K.H., Willy, A.: Biomimetic motion planning of an undulating robotic fish fin. J. Vib. Control **12**(12), 1337–1359 (2006)
7. Liu, J., Dukes, I., Knight, R., et al.: Development of fish-like swimming behaviours for an autonomous robotic fish. Univ. Bath **15**(1), 6–9 (2004)
8. Lighthill, M.J.: Note on the swimming of slender fish. J. Fluid Mech. **9**(2), 305–317 (1960)
9. Taylor, G.: Analysis of the Swimming of Microscopic Organisms. Proc. Roy. Soc. Math. Phys. Eng. Sci. **209**(209), 447–461 (1951)
10. Domenici, P., Blake, R.W.: The kinematics and performance of the escape response in the anglefish (Pterophyllum eimekei). J. Exp. Biol. **156**, 187–205 (1991)
11. Spierts, I.L., Leeuwen, J.L.: Kinematics and muscle dynamics of C- and S-starts of carp (Cyprinus carpio L.). J. Exp. Biol. **202**(Pt 4), 393 (1999)
12. Rosenberger, L.J.: Pectoral fin locomotion in batoid fishes: undulation versus oscillation. J. Exp. Biol. **204**(2), 379–394 (2001)
13. Ijspeert, A.J.: Central pattern generators for locomotion control in animals and robots: a review. Neural Netw. **21**(4), 642–653 (2008)
14. Chen, W.H., Ren, G.J., Zhang, J.B., Wang, J.H.: Smooth transition between different gaits of a hexapod robot via a central pattern generators algorithm. J. Intell. Rob. Syst. **67**(3–4), 255–270 (2012)
15. Chuan, L.K., Kit, T.W.: Task learning utilizing curve fitting method for kinect based humanoid robot. In: 2014 IEEE International Conference on Robotics and Biomimetics (ROBIO 2014), Bali, pp. 1505–1511 (2014)

16. Liu, Y.-X.: The entity design and dynamic research on the two-joint robot fish. Master dissertation, Harbin Institute of Technology, China (2007)
17. Liu, J., Hu, H.: Biological inspiration: from carangiform fish to multi-joint robotic fish. J. Bionic Eng. 7(1), 35–48 (2010)
18. Liu, J., Hu, H.: Mimicry of sharp turning behaviours in a robotic fish. In: 2005 IEEE International Conference on Robotics and Automation, pp. 3318–3323. IEEE (2005)

H_∞ Filter Designing for Wireless Networked Control Systems with Energy Constraints

Lisheng Wei[1]([✉]), Yunqiang Ma[2], and Sheng Xu[3]

[1] Anhui Polytechnic University, Wuhu 241000, An-Hui, China
lshwei_ll@163.com
[2] Anhui Technical College of Mechanical and Electrical Engineering,
Wuhu 241002, An-Hui, China
[3] Nantong Vocational University, Nantong 226007, Jiang-Su, China

Abstract. The issue of H_∞ filter designing for a class of Wireless Networked Control System (WNCS) with communication constraints was discussed in this paper. Firstly, the energy consumption of wireless sensor nodes in the data acquisition stage was reduced by using time-varying sampling strategy. And the wireless sensor nodes' energy consumption was reduced based on reducing-frequency in the data sending stage. Then the mathematical model of WNCS was described as the Asynchronous Dynamic System (ADS). By using Linear Matrix Inequality (LMI) technique, the sufficient condition of the WNCS to be stability was obtained. Finally, the numerical example was given to show the effectiveness of the proposed filter.

Keywords: Energy constraints · WNCS · Filtering · Time-varying sampling

1 Introduction

Over the past twenty years, WNCS has been widely expended in various kinds of applications including remote operations, aircraft, marine monitoring, intelligent transportation, and manufacturing plants [1]. These processes are often linked to pass the data collected through the sending of a real-time wireless network medium. WNCS has numerous advantages to energy saving optimization and actual industrial control system [2]. Nevertheless, a great many new problems and difficulties are created for the wireless network when it is applied to industrial control system. As the wireless network is an unstable shared channel, it will make stability analysis difficult and decrease the system control performance [3–5]. And the limited energy of wireless sensor nodes will reduce the lifetime of the WNCS. Consequently, it is of enormous scientific significance value to do research on the problem of filtering technique and controller design for WNCS with the energy constraints [3].

Two of the central issues are delay and packet-dropout, which has been extensively investigated in the last decade. A lot of researchers have tried to solve the control performance with delay and packet-dropout [4, 5]. Several good results have been available in the existing literatures. For instance, Zhen et al. [6] researched the problem of modeling and stabilization for WNCS with both time-varying delay and packet-dropout, which are modeled as an asynchronous dynamic system with three subsystems.

© Springer Nature Singapore Pte Ltd. 2018
K. Li et al. (Eds.): ICSEE 2018/IMIOT 2018, CCIS 924, pp. 272–280, 2018.
https://doi.org/10.1007/978-981-13-2384-3_25

And the sufficient condition for the system was obtained. Peng et al. [7] investigated the problem that the energy efficiency could be much improved while preserving the desired H_∞ performance. And the self-triggered sampling scheme was proposed. Dong et al. [8] designed the robust filter for a class of discrete-time WNCS with communication constraints and packet dropouts by using switched system theory. In conclusion, the majority of the above researches center on the issues of the delay and packet losses. The filtering technology is adopted in the external noise disturbance. On the foundation of the research achievements above, we are aimed at investigating the problem of filter designing and stabilization analysis for a class of WNCS with energy constraints.

The rest of paper is organized as follows. In Sect. 2, we propose a method to build a new modeling of WNCS with energy constraints. In Sect. 3, the sufficient conditions of the H_∞ filtering are given. In addition, and the gain used in the H_∞ filtering can be derived by LMI technology. Then the effectiveness of the proposed method is proved by the simulation results in Sect. 4. At last, the conclusions are given in Sect. 5.

2 Problem Formulations

The block diagram of a class of WNCS with filter is shown in Fig. 1. We can know that wireless sensor nodes contains a fixed topology previously, and transmits data from plant to filter nodes by reducing-frequency transmission.

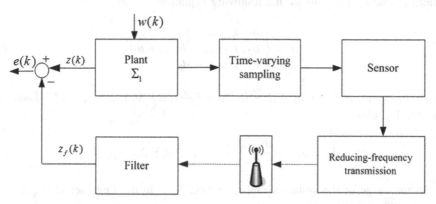

Fig. 1. The Block diagram of WNCS

Because the energy in WNCS is limited, the energy saving strategy is shown in Fig. 1 to prolong the service life of wireless sensor. The time-varying sampling is used to reduce the consumption of data acquisition of wireless sensor nodes, and then the reducing-frequency transmission is used to save the energy consumption of data transmission phase. The plant Σ_1 can be described as follows:

$$\begin{cases} \dot{x}(t) = \bar{A}x(t) + \bar{B}_1 w(t) \\ y(t) = \bar{C}x(t) + \bar{B}_2 w(t) \\ z(t) = \bar{\Gamma}_0 x(t) \end{cases} \tag{1}$$

where A, B_1, B_2, C and Γ_0 are constant matrices with appropriate dimensions. $x(k)=[x_1, x_2, \cdots, x_m]^T \in \mathbb{R}^m$ is the system state vector. $y(k) = [y_1, y_2, \cdots, y_n]^T \in \mathbb{R}^n$ is the output vector. $z(k) = [z_1, z_2, \cdots, z_p]^T \in \mathbb{R}^p$ is the estimated matrix of system and $w(k) \in l_2[0, \infty)$ is the disturbance noise with limited energy.

2.1 Energy Saving Strategy Based on Time-Varying Sampling

Without loss of generality and for convenience of discussion, the following assumptions are given for system (1) [8].

(1) Time driven is used in sensor nodes;
(2) The network induced delay is less than one sampling period;
(3) t_k represents the system sampling time, and $k = 0, 1, 2 \cdots \cdots$. h_k represents the system sampling period at the kth time. Then we have $h_k = t_{k+1} - t_k \in [d_1, d_2]$. d_1 is the allowable minimum sampling period of WNCS when the energy is sufficient. d_2 is the maximum allowable sampling period of WNCS when the energy is limited.

Using active variable sampling period strategy is applied to analyze time-varying sampling process of the system. The sampling period $[d_1, d_2]$ is divided into c equal interval, where c is positive integer. If the current sampling time is t_k, then the next sampling time t_{k+1} is satisfied the following Equation.

$$t_{k+1} = \begin{cases} b_1, & k = t_k + b_1 \\ b_2, & k \in (t_k + b_1, t_k + b_2] \\ d_2, & k > t_k + d_2 \end{cases} \tag{2}$$

where $b_1 = d_1 + a(\frac{d_2-d_1}{c})$, $b_2 = d_1 + (a+1)(\frac{d_2-d_1}{c})$, $a = 0, 1, 2, \cdots, c-1$. Then we have the Eq. (3).

$$h_k = d_1 + e(\frac{d_2 - d_1}{c}) \qquad e = 0, 1, 2, \cdots, c. \tag{3}$$

So the range of the system sampling period h_k is in the finite set $\Omega = \{d_1, \cdots, d_1 + e(\frac{d_2-d_1}{c}), \cdots, d_2\}$.

The plant Σ_1 can be described as follows:

$$\begin{cases} x(k+1) = Ax(k) + B_1 w(k) \\ y(k) = Cx(k) + B_2 w(k) \\ z(k) = \Gamma_0 x(k) \end{cases} \tag{4}$$

where $A = e^{\bar{A}h_k}$, $B_1 = \int_0^{h_k} e^{\bar{A}S} ds \bar{B}_1$.

Setting $\Delta h = h_k - d_1$ and $F_k = \int_0^{\Delta h} e^{\bar{A}S} ds = \bar{A}^{-1}(e^{\bar{A}\Delta h} - I)$, then we have $e^{\bar{A}\Delta h} = \bar{A} F_k + I$.

$$A = e^{\bar{A}(d_1 + \Delta h)} = e^{\bar{A}d_1} * e^{\bar{A}\Delta h} = e^{\bar{A}d_1}(\bar{A}F_k + I) = e^{\bar{A}d_1} + e^{\bar{A}d_1}\bar{A}F_k = \tilde{A} + M_1 F_k N_1 \quad (5)$$

where $\tilde{A} = e^{\bar{A}d_1}$, $M_1 = e^{\bar{A}d_1}\bar{A}$, $N_1 = I$.

Similarly, we have

$$
\begin{aligned}
B_1 &= \int_0^{d_1} e^{\bar{A}S} ds \bar{B}_1 + \int_{d_1}^{h_k} e^{\bar{A}S} ds \bar{B}_1 \\
&= \int_0^{d_1} e^{\bar{A}S} ds \bar{B}_1 + \int_0^{h_k - d_1} e^{\bar{A}(S + d_1)} ds \bar{B}_1 \\
&= \int_0^{d_1} e^{\bar{A}S} ds \bar{B}_1 + e^{\bar{A}d_1} \int_0^{\Delta h} e^{\bar{A}S} ds \bar{B}_1 \\
&= \tilde{B} + M_2 F_k N_2
\end{aligned}
\quad (6)
$$

where $\tilde{B} = \int_0^{d_1} e^{\bar{A}S} ds \bar{B}_1$, $M_2 = e^{\bar{A}d_1}$, $N_2 = \bar{B}_1$, $F_k = \int_0^{\Delta h} e^{\bar{A}S} ds$.

According to the above analysis, the discrete model of system (4) can be described as:

$$
\begin{cases}
x(k+1) = (\tilde{A} + M_1 F_k N_1)x(k) + (\tilde{B} + M_2 F_k N_2)w(k) \\
y(k) = Cx(k) + B_2 w(k) \\
z(k) = \Gamma_0 x(k)
\end{cases}
\quad (7)
$$

where $\tilde{A} = e^{\bar{A}d_1}$, $M_1 = e^{\bar{A}d_1}\bar{A}$, $N_1 = I$, $\tilde{B} = \int_0^{d_1} e^{\bar{A}S} ds \bar{B}_1$, $M_2 = e^{\bar{A}d_1}$, $N_2 = \bar{B}_1$, $F_k = \int_0^{\Delta h} e^{\bar{A}S} ds$

For the system (7), $\sigma_{\max}(\bar{A})$ is represent the largest singular value of system parameters. Then $F_k^T F_k \leq \lambda^2 I$, $\lambda > 0$ and satisfied the following Equation.

$$\lambda = \frac{e^{\sigma_{\max}(\bar{A}) * (d_2 - d_1)} - e^{\sigma_{\max}(\bar{A}) * (0)}}{\sigma_{\max}(\bar{A})} \quad (8)$$

2.2 Energy Saving Strategy Based on Reducing-Frequency Transmission

Considering the energy limitation of WNCS, the reducing-Frequency Transmission strategy can be used in this paper. The energy consumption of sensor nodes can be saved by reducing the amount of transmission data, that is, only updated data is allowed to be sent to filter nodes at the sampling time, and the remaining unupdated data are keeping the last sampling data. To simplify the description system, the function $\vartheta(k) \in N, N \triangleq \{1, 2, \cdots, n\}$ is introduced to represent the state of sending data from sensor nodes to the filter nodes. If $\vartheta(k) = d$, that is the dth sensor node can send the updated data to filter node, then the data of filter node is $\bar{y}_d(k) = y_d(k)$, the data of other filter node keep the last sampling data $\bar{y}_d(k) = \bar{y}_d(k-1)$. Setting the matrix form $\Xi_{\vartheta(k)} \in \{\Xi_1, \Xi_2, \cdots, \Xi_n\}$ representing the variable function $\vartheta(k)$, then we have

$\Xi_{\vartheta(k)} = diag[\delta(d-1), \delta(d-2) \cdots \delta(d-n)]$, δ is the Kronecker delta function. The data input of the filter for WNCS with energy constraints can be described as:

$$\begin{aligned} \bar{y}_d(k) &= \vartheta(k)y_d(k) + (1 - \vartheta(k))\bar{y}_d(k-1) \\ \bar{y}(k) &= \Xi_{\vartheta(k)}y(k) + (I - \Xi_{\vartheta(k)})\bar{y}(k-1) \end{aligned} \tag{9}$$

Considering the following filter,

$$\begin{cases} x_f(k+1) = A_f x_f(k) + B_f \bar{y}(k) \\ \quad\quad z_f(k) = C_f x_f(k) \end{cases} \tag{10}$$

where A_f, B_f and C_f are constant matrices of filter with appropriate dimensions. $x_f(k) = [x_{1f}, x_{2f}, \cdots, x_{mf}]^T \in \mathbb{R}^m$, $y(k) = [y_1, y_2, \cdots, y_n]^T \in \mathbb{R}^n$ and $z_f(k) = [z_{1f}, z_{2f}, \cdots, z_{pf}]^T \in \mathbb{R}^p$ are state vector, input vector and output vector respectively.

Combining the Eqs. (7), (9) and (10), the closed loop model of the filter error can be expressed by:

$$\begin{cases} X(k+1) = \Phi X(k) + Bw(k) \\ \quad\quad e(k) = \Gamma X(k) \end{cases} \tag{11}$$

where $X(k) = \begin{bmatrix} x^T(k) & x_f^T(k) & \bar{y}^T(k-1) \end{bmatrix}^T$ is the state augmented vector. $e(k) = z(k) - z_f(k)$ is the error vector. And

$$\Phi = \begin{bmatrix} \tilde{A} + M_1 F_k N_1 & 0 & 0 \\ B_f \Xi_{\vartheta(k)} C & A_f & B_f(I - \Xi_{\vartheta(k)}) \\ \Xi_{\vartheta(k)} C & 0 & I - \Xi_{\vartheta(k)} \end{bmatrix}, B = \begin{bmatrix} \tilde{B} + M_2 F_k N_2 \\ B_f \Xi_{\vartheta(k)} B_2 \\ \Xi_{\vartheta(k)} B_2 \end{bmatrix}$$

$$\Gamma = [\Gamma_0 \quad -C_f \quad 0], \tilde{A} = e^{\tilde{A}d_1}, M_1 = e^{\tilde{A}d_1}\tilde{A}, N_1 = I$$

$$\tilde{B} = \int_0^{d_1} e^{\tilde{A}S} ds \bar{B}_1, M_2 = e^{\tilde{A}d_1}, N_2 = \bar{B}_1, F_k = \int_0^{\Delta h} e^{\tilde{A}S} ds$$

Considering the scheduling matrix $\Xi_{\vartheta(k)}$ is a random matrix with time varying, the closed loop filtering error system can be described as a discrete system with n mode. In order to design the H_∞ filter for the discrete control system (7), which is shown in Eq. (10), we should get the following two conditions [7].

(1) When $w(k) = 0$, the closed loop model of the filter error (11) is stochastic stability, if and only if

$$lim \sum_0^\infty x(k)^T x(k) < \infty \tag{12}$$

(2) At the condition of zero initial state, the filtering error system (11) is used to suppress the disturbance level $\gamma > 0$, then the H_∞ performance γ can be described as:

$$\|e(k)\|_2^2 \leq \gamma^2 \|w(k)\|_2^2 \tag{13}$$

where $\|e(k)\|_2^2 = \sum_{k=0}^{\infty} e(k)^T e(k)$, $\|w(k)\|_2^2 = \sum_{k=0}^{\infty} w(k)^T w(k)$.

3 Main Results

Our work is aiming at designing the filter for WNCS so as to solve the problems of energy constraints. And prior to giving a detailed introduction of the main results, the sufficient convergence condition for WNCS is given.

Theorem 1: Considering the system (11), given positive constant $\gamma > 0$. Then the augmented system is asymptotical stable if there exist symmetric constant matrix $P_j > 0$, $P_i > 0$ and

$$\begin{bmatrix} -P_i & * & * & * \\ 0 & -\gamma^2 I & * & * \\ \Phi & B & -P_j^{-1} & * \\ \Gamma & 0 & 0 & -I \end{bmatrix} < 0 \tag{14}$$

where $*$ denotes the symmetric terms and

$$\Phi = \begin{bmatrix} \tilde{A} + M_1 F_k N_1 & 0 & 0 \\ B_f \Xi_\varphi C & A_f & B_f (I - \Xi_\varphi) \\ \Xi_\varphi C & 0 & I - \Xi_\varphi \end{bmatrix}, B = \begin{bmatrix} \tilde{B} + M_2 F_k N_2 \\ B_f \Xi_\varphi B_2 \\ \Xi_\varphi B_2 \end{bmatrix}, \Gamma = [\Gamma_0 \quad -C_f \quad 0]$$

Theorem 2: Considering the system (7), given a positive scalar $\gamma > 0$ and $\varepsilon > 0$, if there exist $P_i > 0$ and $P_j > 0 (i, j \in [1, \cdots, N])$, J_{11}, J_{12}, J_{13}, J_{22}, J_{31}, J_{32}, J_{33}, V and W with proper dimensions such that the LMI (15) holds.

$$\begin{bmatrix} \tilde{\Pi} & * & * \\ \tilde{M} & -\lambda^{-1}\varepsilon^{-1}I & * \\ \tilde{N}^T & 0 & -\lambda^{-1}\varepsilon I \end{bmatrix} < 0 \tag{15}$$

Hence the system (11) is asymptotically stable as well as having the H_∞ performance index.
where

$$\tilde{\Pi}_1 = \begin{bmatrix} \Pi_1 & * & * & * \\ 0 & -\gamma^2 I & * & * \\ \Pi_2 & \Pi_3 & \Pi_4 & * \\ \Pi_5 & 0 & 0 & -I \end{bmatrix}, \Pi_1 = -P_i$$

$$\Pi_2 = \begin{bmatrix} J_{11}^T \tilde{A} + V \Xi_{\vartheta(k)} C + J_{31}^T \ \Xi_{\vartheta(k)} C & U & V(I - \Xi_{\vartheta(k)}) + J_{31}^T(I - \Xi_{\vartheta(k)}) \\ J_{12}^T \tilde{A} + V \Xi_{\vartheta(k)} C + J_{32}^T \ \Xi_{\vartheta(k)} C & U & V(I - \Xi_{\vartheta(k)}) + J_{32}^T(I - \Xi_{\vartheta(k)}) \\ J_{13}^T \tilde{A} + J_{33}^T \ \Xi_{\vartheta(k)} C & 0 & J_{33}^T(I - \Xi_{\vartheta(k)}) \end{bmatrix}$$

$$\Pi_3 = \begin{bmatrix} J_{11}^T \tilde{B} + V \Xi_{\vartheta(k)} B_2 + J_{31}^T \ \Xi_{\vartheta(k)} B_2 \\ J_{12}^T \tilde{B} + V \Xi_{\vartheta(k)} B_2 + J_{32}^T \ \Xi_{\vartheta(k)} B_2 \\ J_{13}^T \tilde{B} + J_{33}^T \ \Xi_{\vartheta(k)} B_2 \end{bmatrix}$$

$$\Pi_4 = P_j - J - J^T, \ \Pi_5 = [\Gamma_0 \ \ -W \ \ 0]$$

$$\Pi_6 = \begin{bmatrix} J_{11}^T M_1 & 0 & 0 \\ 0 & 0 & 0 \\ 0 & 0 & 0 \end{bmatrix}, \ \Pi_7 = \begin{bmatrix} J_{11}^T M_2 & 0 & 0 \\ 0 & 0 & 0 \\ 0 & 0 & 0 \end{bmatrix}$$

$$\tilde{M} = \begin{bmatrix} 0 & 0 & 0 & 0 \\ 0 & 0 & 0 & 0 \\ \Pi_6 & \Pi_7 & 0 & 0 \\ 0 & 0 & 0 & 0 \end{bmatrix}, \ \tilde{N} = \begin{bmatrix} \hat{N}_1 & 0 & 0 & 0 \\ 0 & \hat{N}_2 & 0 & 0 \\ 0 & 0 & 0 & 0 \\ 0 & 0 & 0 & 0 \end{bmatrix}$$

$$\hat{N}_1 = \begin{bmatrix} N_1 & 0 & 0 \\ 0 & 0 & 0 \\ 0 & 0 & 0 \end{bmatrix}, \ \hat{N}_2 = \begin{bmatrix} N_2 \\ 0 \\ 0 \end{bmatrix}, \ J = \begin{bmatrix} J_{11} & J_{12} & J_{13} \\ J_{22} & J_{22} & 0 \\ J_{31} & J_{32} & J_{33} \end{bmatrix}$$

And the parameters matrix of filter are $A_f = J_{22}^{-T} U$, $B_f = J_{22}^{-T} V$ and $C_f = W$.

Remark: The optimal performance γ^* can be obtained by solving the convex optimization problem as follows:

$$min \ \mu \ subject \ to \ (15) \ with \ \mu = \gamma^2$$

$$J_{11} \sim J_{33}, \ P_i, \ P_j, \ U, \ V, \ W$$

So the optimal performance is $\gamma^* = \sqrt{\mu_{min}}$.

4 Numerical Simulations

In this segment, an illustrative instance, taking the following discrete-time control systems into account, is showed to testify the validity of the raised theorems.

$$\dot{x}(t) = \begin{bmatrix} -12 & 7 \\ 9 & -10 \end{bmatrix} x(t) + \begin{bmatrix} -13 \\ 8 \end{bmatrix} w(t)$$

$$y(t) = \begin{bmatrix} 0.6 & 0.2 \\ -0.3 & 0.4 \end{bmatrix} x(t) + \begin{bmatrix} 0.8 \\ -0.3 \end{bmatrix} w(t)$$

$$z(t) = [0.5 \ \ 0.5] x(t)$$

Assuming the minimum allowed sampling period of the system $d_1 = 0.1s$ when WNCS energy is sufficient, and the maximum allowed sampling period of the system $d_2 = 0.2s$ when WNCS energy is limited. The sampling period $h_1 = 0.1s$, $h_2 = 0.15s$ and $h_3 = 0.2s$. So the sampling period is randomly switched over in a finite set $\Omega = \{0.1, 0.15, 0.2\}$. Setting $\vartheta_d(k) = \{1, 2, 1, 2, \cdots\}$, $\Xi_1 = diag[1\ 0]$ and $\Xi_2 = diag[0\ 1]$, then by using Eq. (8), we have $\lambda = 0.3014$. When choosing the noise $w(k) = 2e^{-0.3k}\sin(0.5\pi k)$ and using theorem 2 and Matlab LMI Toolbox, we obtain the optimal suppression level $\gamma^* = 0.6427$. At the same time, the feasible solution of a set of H_∞ filter parameters under the optimal suppression level state is obtained as follows.

$$A_f = \begin{bmatrix} -0.1586 & -0.0983 \\ 0.2366 & 0.1466 \end{bmatrix}, B_f = \begin{bmatrix} -1.6748 & 0.5342 \\ 1.1469 & -0.3615 \end{bmatrix}$$

$$C_f = [-0.6331 \quad -0.6664]$$

Assuming that the initial values $x_f(0) = [0\ 0\ ]^T$ and $x(0) = [0.5 - 0.5]^T$, the state tracking curves of system and filter can be shown in Figs. 2 and 3 respectively.

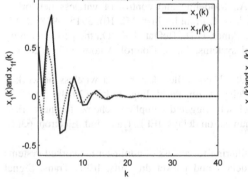

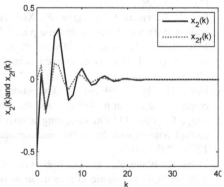

Fig. 2. State trajectory of $x_1(k)$ and $x_{1f}(k)$ **Fig. 3.** State trajectory of $x_2(k)$ and $x_{2f}(k)$

In Figs. 2 and 3, $x_1(k)$ and $x_2(k)$ are the state of plant, and $x_{1f}(k)$ and $x_{2f}(k)$ are the state of filter. It can be observed that $x_{if}(k)$ can track $x_i(k)$ effectively in 20 time steps.

5 Conclusions

In this paper, the filtering problem for WNCS with energy constraints was considered. By using time-varying sampling strategy, the energy consumption of wireless sensor nodes in the data acquisition stage was reduced. And the mathematical model of

WNCS could be described as an asynchronous dynamic system. The sufficient conditions of H_∞ filter were derived. Then by the simulation, the effectiveness of the proposed method was proved.

Acknowledgments. This work was supported by natural science research programme of colleges and universities of an-hui province under grant KJ2016A062, natural science foundation of an-hui province under grant 1608085MF146, foundation for talented young people of an-hui polytechnic university under grant 2016BJRC008, visiting study Foundation for outstanding young talent of an-hui educational committee under grant gxfxZD2016108, and the applied basic research plan of nan-tong under grant GY12017015.

References

1. Ge, X., Yang, F., Han, Q.-L.: Distributed networked control systems: A brief overview. Inf. Sci. **380**, 117–131 (2017)
2. Zhang, X., Han, Q.: Event-triggered H∞ control for a class of nonlinear networked control systems using novel integral. Int. J. Robust Nonlinear Control **27**(4), 679–700 (2017)
3. Sadi, Y., SC, E.: Joint optimization of wireless network energy consumption and control system performance in wireless networked control systems. IEEE Trans. Wirel. Commun. **16**(4), 2235–2248 (2017)
4. Bai, J., Renquan, L., Hongye, S., Xue, A.: Modeling and control of wireless networked control system with both delay and packet loss. J. Franklin Inst. **352**(10), 3915–3928 (2015)
5. Makled, E.A., Halawa, H.H., Daoud, R.M., Amer, H.H., Refaat, T.K.: On the perform ability of hierarchical wireless networked control systems. Intell. Control Autom. **6**(2), 126–133 (2015)
6. Hong, Z., Gao, J., Wang, N.: Output-feedback controller design of a wireless networked control system with packet loss and time delay. Math. Probl. Eng. **1**, 1–7 (2014)
7. Peng, C., Han, Q.: On designing a novel self-triggered sampling scheme for networked control systems with data losses and communication delays. IEEE Trans. Ind. Electron. **63**(2), 1239–1248 (2016)
8. Dong, H., Wang, Z., Gao, H.: Robust H_∞ filtering for a class of nonlinear networked systems with multiple stochastic communication delays and packet dropouts. IEEE Trans. Signal Process. **58**(4), 1957–1966 (2010)

Distance Overestimation Error Correction Method (DOEC) of Time of Flight Camera Based on Pinhole Model

Le Wang, Minrui Fei, Hakuan Wang[✉], Zexue Ji, and Aolei Yang

Shanghai Key Laboratory of Power Station Automation Technology,
School of Mechatronic Engineering and Automation, Shanghai University,
Shanghai 200072, China
{wangle,mrfei,HKWang,Zexueji,aolei}@shu.edu.cn

Abstract. Depth cameras with Time of Flight (ToF) technology are widely used in machine vision and various measurement tasks. However, due to hardware conditions and imaging characteristics, multiple errors limit the further application of the ToF camera. This paper classified errors into errors caused by non-imaging principle and error caused by imaging principle. In order to simplify the experimental procedure and improve the efficiency of errors correction, a simple and feasible method is used to correct errors caused by non-imaging principle, and an evaluation function is proposed to determine the optimal reference distance, so as to select appropriate integration time and global offsets. To tackle the radial distance error, Distance Overestimation Error Correction method (DOEC) based on the principle of pinhole imaging is proposed to further improve the accuracy of depth data. Finally, error correction methods proposed in this paper are verified by experiments, and the segmentation of different depth ranges is successfully achieved by using the modified data, prove the effectiveness of the proposed methods.

Keywords: Time of flight · Error correction · Pinhole imaging
Plan segmentation · Data accuracy

1 Introduction

With the rapid development of machine vision system, different types of cameras play significant roles in industrial intelligence more and more. Because of compact structure and being less sensitive to illumination, time-of-flight (ToF) camera is widely applied into many fields, such as mobile robot avoidance and navigation [1], object detection and recognition [2, 3], 3D reconstruction and gesture recognition [4, 5].

Time-of-flight camera is a kind of active sensors, it emits near infrared (NIR) and receive reflected light [6], and calculate the distance from the optical center of the camera to an target object surface. There are some noise and errors exist in TOF camera [7, 8], which cause negative impact on the accuracy of distance measurement [9]. Thus it is essential to correct the data error of ToF camera at the initial procedure. There are several source of errors in ToF camera, generally the error can be classified as systematic errors and non-systematic errors [10]. Systematic errors can be predicted and

© Springer Nature Singapore Pte Ltd. 2018
K. Li et al. (Eds.): ICSEE 2018/IMIOT 2018, CCIS 924, pp. 281–290, 2018.
https://doi.org/10.1007/978-981-13-2384-3_26

corrected by different calibration methods, but the non-systematic errors are complexed and unpredicted and generally removed by filtering.

Several phenomena from the idealistic model of ToF camera are analyzed, but the temperature, multi-path reflections and ambient light effects are still hard to solve [11]. An error model is utilized to estimate ground and wall planes, acquisition geometry and noise characteristic are analyzed in this error model [12]. A 2.5D pattern board with holes is used to capture both color and ToF depth images for feature detection. The transformation of the ToF camera is reset. In order to get accurate bias after ray correction, k-means clustering and B-spline functions are utilized [1].

In ToF camera, the radial distance is acquired between the optical center to an target object surface, which is longer than the actual distance. To remove the radial distance error, this paper divides the various errors in the TOF camera into errors caused by the non-imaging principle and error caused by the imaging principle. When compensating errors caused by the non-imaging principle, data error caused by temperature changes and integration time are analyzed and corrected, multipath errors and other noises are compensated by taking offsets, and an evaluation function is proposed to determine the optimal reference distance. To tackle the radial error caused by imaging principle, Distance Overestimation Error Correction method (DOEC) based on the principle of pinhole imaging is proposed. By analyzing the positional relationship between the center pixel and other pixels in depth image, the angle relationship between the two is obtained, and the radial distance is convert to vertical distance. Thus the right distance of ToF camera is obtained.

The remainder of this paper is organized as follows. Section 2 is errors caused by non-imaging principle in ToF camnera. Section 3 corrects the radial error caused by the imaging principle. Section 4 states the experimental results.

2   Errors Caused by Non-imaging Principle in ToF Camnera

TOF cameras are able to obtain distance information by utilizing the time of flight measurement of photons. Photons are emitted by modulated infrared light. The modulated infrared light determines the phase shift φ between reference signal and reflected light. where c is the speed of light, f is the modulation frequency. The distance value d is formulated as:

$$d = \frac{1}{2} \times c \times \frac{\varphi}{2\pi f} \tag{1}$$

The temperature of the chip changes with the operating time, which will cause drift of depth data, especially when the temperature of the chip changes significantly when the ToF camera is just started. In order to reduce the deviation caused by temperature changes, warm-up time of the chip is required before the measurement of ToF camera. Observed from the experimental results of EPC660 chip, it takes about 15–20 min to warm up before the depth image is acquired, and the obtained depth data is relatively more stable and accurate.

Integration Time (IT) is the time span when ToF camera computes multiple phase of photons and obtain the distance. Thus the Integration Time is important to the accuracy of ToF camera data. In this paper, when the integration time is 1500 μs, the effect of integration time on the depth data is studied by taking pictures of flat walls at different distances. As shown in Fig. 1(a), (b), (c), (d) is depth images acquired at different distance. Different colors represent different distances and black represents invalid points. It can be seen that when the integration time is fixed, the larger the measurement distance is, the more invalid points are, and the more pixels that appear jitter at the edge of the image, the accuracy of the measurement decreases. Therefore, it is necessary to select an appropriate integration time.

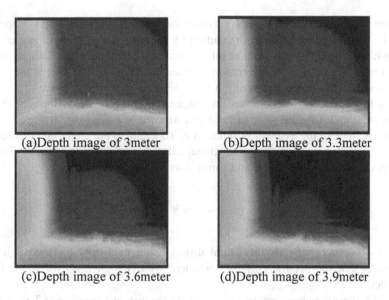

(a)Depth image of 3meter   (b)Depth image of 3.3meter

(c)Depth image of 3.6meter   (d)Depth image of 3.9meter

Fig. 1. Depth image of different distance with integration time is 1500 μs (Color figure online)

Multipath errors and other noises can be eliminated through precise modeling, but the implementation process is more complex. Some nonlinear errors will change with distance, which are difficult to solve. In order to simplify the errors correction procedure, this paper sets offsets to correct such errors.

Through the above analysis of the source of error, this paper corrects the error of ToF camera under the range of 0–4 m. Since the nonlinear errors are related to the distance, 1 m, 2 m, 3 m, and 4 m are utilized as the distance baseline for the experiment. The experiment steps of errors correction caused by non-principle are shown as follows, where 1 m is sets as the distance baseline firstly.

Step1: Warm up before starting. To reduce errors due to temperature changes, image acquisition should start after 20 min so that the ToF camera has enough time to warm up, meanwhile the data fluctuation range is small.

Step2: Adjust the integration time. The integration time was adjusted enable the amplitude at 1 m distance baseline reach about 1000LSB regarded as suitable amplitude. Integration time did not change during the subsequent experiment.

Step3: Set the global offset. Since the data accuracy of the pixel at the optical center is less affected by various errors than other pixels in the depth image, the trueness of the data is higher. Therefore, the measured depth data at the optical center denoted as $basemea_i$ is used to compute the global offset at the distance baseline of 1 m. i is the representation of different distance baseline from 1 m to 4 m. The value of global $offset_i$ can be formula as follow:

$$offset_i = distancebaseline_i - basemea_i \quad i = 1, 2, 3, 4 \tag{2}$$

Where the $distancebaseline_1$ is 1 m. After the value of global $offset_1$ is acquired, it can be used to compensate errors caused by multiple path and other noises.

Step4: Measure the depth data at other distances. To analyze the data accuracy at different distance after the integration time and global offset were set at the distance baseline of 1 m, the camera position was adjust at the actual distance of 2 m, 3 m, and 4 m respectively, denoted as act_i. Measured distance data of optical center at different actual distance were marked and denoted as mea_i.

Step5: Calculate the evaluation function v. To evaluate the effect on data accuracy by changing integration time and global offset set at different distance baseline, evaluation function v is used and formula as follow:

$$v = \sum_{i=1}^{4} (act_i - mea_i)^2 \quad i = 1, 2, 3, 4 \tag{3}$$

If the difference between the actual distance and measured distance is smaller, indicates that the accuracy of the measured data is higher, so the value of v is smaller.

Step6: Repeat the above process by changing the distance baseline to 2 m, 3 m, and 4 m respectively.

Experiment results are shown in Table 1. When the distance baseline is 2 m, the value of evaluation function v is the smallest than that of other distance baseline. It indicates that the distance data obtained are more reliable, and errors caused by the non- imaging principle have been improved to some extent. Thus the integration time and global offset set at the distance baseline of 2 m are chosen as the better experiment parameters in the 0–4 m operating range of ToF camera. Depth data acquired at distance baseline of 2 m are also saved as data sample, which are used to correct the errors caused by imaging principle in the next section.

Table 1. Experiment results and value of v

Actual distance	mea_i at 100 cm	mea_i at 200 cm	mea_i at 300 cm	mea_i at 400 cm	v
100 cm	100	98.7	97.1	94.7	62.82
200 cm	203.5	200	198.1	196.3	**16.61**
300 cm	305.4	301.4	300	298.2	19.31
400 cm	407.1	403.6	402.7	400	45.02

3   Error Caused by Imaging Principle

After correcting errors caused by the non-imaging principle, a more accurate depth image is obtained. In this section, we analyze the error caused by the imaging principle and propose a Distance Overestimation Error Correction method (DOEC) based on the pinhole imaging principle.

3.1   Distance Overestimation Error

The distance overestimation error means that the distance measured by ToF camera is longer than the actual distance. In actual measure process, as shown in Fig. 2, there are three test points A, B, C on the same object plane need to be measured, just imaging that there are three test points A, B, C on a smooth wall, test point B is the intersection of the line started from optic center O_C and the object plane. The straight line distance of test point A, test point B, test point C between optic center O_C denoted as r_A, r_B, r_C, and the vertical distance between object plane and camera plane is denoted as d. it is clear to see that d is equal to r_B, r_A and r_C are longer than the true distance r_B, this phenomena is called distance overestimation error. The overestimated distance r_A and r_C can be corrected by the following formula:

$$d = r_B = r_A \times \sin\theta_A = r_C \times \sin\theta_C \tag{4}$$

Where θ_A is the angle between the straight line r_A to camera plane, θ_C is the angle between the straight line r_C to camera plane. This kind of distance overestimation will have a great impact on reconstruction of the 3D image.

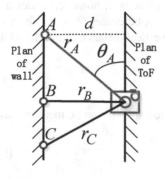

Fig. 2. Distance overestimation error

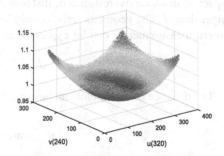

Fig. 3. Distance data at 1 m of wall

Experiment has been done in front of smooth wall, the vertical distance between the wall to the camera optical center O_c is 1 m. Figure 3 is the scatter diagram of the wall after using the depth data collected from the experiment. It can be seen that the farther the test point is away from the optic center O_c, the more obvious the overestimation of the depth in the 3D image is, that means the depth value of points near the optical center are closer to 1 m and the depth value near edge points are greater, even though they are in same plane. So it is necessary to compensate such error in accurate measurement.

3.2   Distance Overestimation Error Correction Method (DOEC)

Aim to remove the distance overestimation error, this paper proposed Distance Overestimation Error Correction method (DOEC) by exploiting the principle of pinhole imaging, a model is built to correct such error, which is shown in Fig. 4. Where imaging plane, camera plane and object plane are shown in Fig. 4. O_b is the center point of imaging plane, O_c is the optic center of camera plane, and O_a is the center point of object plane. p is an arbitrary point on object plane, p' is the corresponding point of p on imaging plane. f is the focal length, d is the vertical distance from the object plane to the depth camera plane, r is the actual distance measured by the depth camera. θ is the angle between the laser light and the line started from optic center O_c.

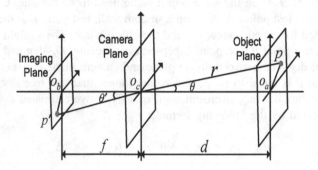

Fig. 4. Imaging model of ToF

According to the principle of linear propagation of light, it is easy to know that $\theta = \theta'$. The actual distance of camera plane and object plane is d, however, under the impact of distance overestimated, distance of point p to optic center O_c is r, which is longer than d. The geometric relationship between the vertical distance d and the TOF camera measurement r can be expressed as (5):

$$d = r \times \cos \theta \tag{5}$$

The distance of each point can be corrected if θ is knowable. θ' can be measured as:

$$\theta' = \arctan(\frac{O_b p'}{f}) \tag{6}$$

where $O_b p'$ is the image distance between p and image plane center O_b. The depth map exists as a two-dimensional pixel matrix in the depth camera. Since there is a conversion relationship between successive imaging plane and discrete image pixel coordinate system, $O_b p'$ actually represents the true distance of pixel point in the discrete image pixel coordinate system, and the position of p' in the continuous imaging plane coordinate system is known as (x, y). The coordinate transformation between the continuous imaging plane and the discrete image pixel coordinate is shown in Fig. 5.

where $u - v$ represents the discrete pixel coordinate system, $x - y$ represents the continuous image coordinate system, and from a continuous imaging plane to a discrete image pixel coordinate system, $p'(x, y)$ will be transformed into $(u_{p'}, v_{p'})$, which is shown in (7):

$$u_{p'} = \frac{x}{dx} + u_0 \qquad v_{p'} = \frac{y}{dy} + v_0 \tag{7}$$

where dx represents the true physical width of one pixel in the x-axis direction, and dy represents the same in the y-axis direction. These two widths are intrinsic parameters of the imaging chip and can be found by consulting the chip manual. If the chip is stable, dx and dy will not change. (u_0, v_0) is the center point of the image plane, which is the projection point of the camera aperture center on the image plane and can be obtained by calibration. So $O_b p'$ can be calculated by (8).

$$o_b p' = \sqrt{(u_{p'} - u_0)^2 + (v_{p'} - v_0)^2} \tag{8}$$

Then the final depth vertical distance can be computed as

$$
\begin{aligned}
d &= r \times \cos(\arctan(\frac{\sqrt{(u_{p'} - u_0)^2 + (v_{p'} - v_0)^2}}{f})) \\
z &= r \times \cos(\arctan(\frac{\sqrt{(x/dx)^2 + (y/dy)^2}}{f}))
\end{aligned}
\tag{9}
$$

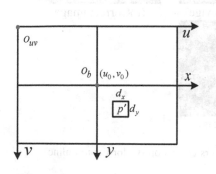

Fig. 5. Coordinate transformation

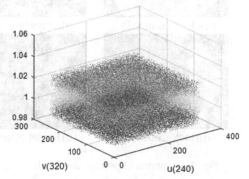

Fig. 6. Experiment result of DOEC

Through the above steps, the distance overestimated has been corrected, final result of the correction are shown in Fig. 6. It can be seen that depth data of points far from the optical center point are corrected, and the measured data fluctuate around 1 m about ±2 cm of 1 m. Thus the effectiveness of the DOEC has been proved.

4   Experiment Results

By correcting errors caused by the non-imaging principle and the error caused by imaging principle, the accuracy of the depth data is greatly improved, and the depth data in the same plane can be kept within a small fluctuation range. To prove the effectiveness of the above method, objects on the desktop and the desktop are taken as the experimental objects. By analyzing the scope of the depth data, the plane where the desktop is located and the plane where the objects are located are divided.

Figure 7(b) is a grayscale image, as shown in Fig. 7(a) is a depth map after non-imaging principle error correction, it can be seen that the overall image data after the error correction caused by the non-imaging principle is relatively stable, but due to the impact of errors caused by imaging principle, radiating radially from the center of the depth image, the color gradually darkens from yellow to blue. This phenomenon indicates that the depth data is different at different locations although they are in the same plane. The accuracy of the depth data is not high, the fluctuation range is large, and it is difficult to distinguish between the target object and the background. Therefore, in order to further improve the accuracy of the depth data, it is necessary to correct the depth overestimation error caused by the imaging principle.

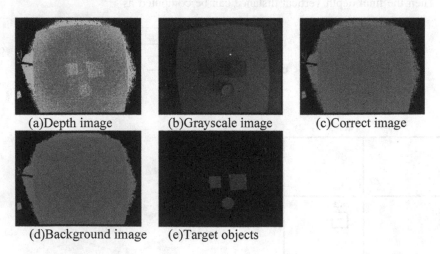

(a)Depth image   (b)Grayscale image   (c)Correct image

(d)Background image   (e)Target objects

Fig. 7. Experiment process and results of errors correction (Color figure online)

After correcting errors caused by non-imaging principle and error caused by imaging principle, the corrected depth image is finally obtained as shown in Fig. 7(c)–(e). In order to facilitate the analysis and processing of the image, this paper maps the

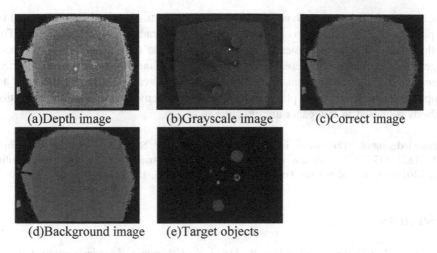

(a)Depth image   (b)Grayscale image   (c)Correct image

(d)Background image   (e)Target objects

Fig. 8. Experiment process and results of errors correction

data after the overestimation error correction to the range of 0–255, so that the corrected depth image is represented by a grayscale image, as shown in Fig. 7(c). Different depth data corresponds to different gray values in the range of 0–255. The greater the depth distance is, the greater the gray value is. It can be seen from the Fig. 7(c) that the gray value on the same plane after the error correction is relatively uniform, indicating that the fluctuation range of the depth data on the same plane is small, so the background and the target object can be separated according to the depth distance range of different planes. Figure 7(d) is a divided background, and Fig. 7(e) is a divided target object. Because the distance from the center of the camera to the desktop is greater than the distance from the surface of the article, the gray value corresponding to the desktop after correction is greater than the corresponding gray value of the surface of the target object.

After change the number and shape of target objects, final results are shown in Fig. 8. The background planes and the target objects are well separated, proved that the two error correction methods are valid.

5   Conlusion

Due to the imaging characteristics and various factors in the external environment, there are many kinds of errors exist in the depth data of ToF camera. Starting from the imaging principle, this paper classifed errors into two categories: errors caused by the non-imaging principle and errors caused by imaging principle. To improve errors correction efficiency of errors caused by non-imaging principle, temperature changes, amplitude intensities and integration time are analyzed and corrected in this paper, multipath errors and other noises are compensated by taking offsets, an evaluation function is proposed to determine the optimal reference distance, so as to select appropriate integration time and global offsets. In the correction of errors caused by imaging principle, Distance Overestimation Error Correction method (DOEC) based on the pinhole imaging principle is proposed to remove the radial distance error of the ToF depth camera, which contributes to limit the data on the same plane within a certain range. Finally, objects of different heights in different planes were taken as experiment objects, and plans are segment by depth data range. Even the shape of the item are complicated, the background plan can be split, which demonstrates that the correction methods proposed in this paper are effective.

Acknowledgement. This work is supported by National Science Foundation of China (61473182, 61773253), Science and Technology Commission of Shanghai Municipality (15JC1401900), Natural Science Foundation of Shanghai (No. 18ZR1415100).

References

1. Pertile, M., Chiodini, S., Giubilato, R., Debei, S.: Calibration of extrinsic parameters of a hybrid vision system for navigation comprising a very low resolution time-of-flight camera. In: IEEE International Workshop on Metrology for Aerospace, pp. 391–396 (2017)
2. Lin, J., Liu, Y., Suo, J., Dai, Q.: Frequency-domain transient imaging. IEEE Trans. Pattern Anal. Mach. Intell. **39**, 937–950 (2016)
3. Adam, A., Dann, C., Yair, O., Mazor, S., Nowozin, S.: Bayesian time-of-flight for realtime shape, illumination and albedo. IEEE Trans. Pattern Anal. Mach. Intell. **39**, 851–864 (2017)
4. Anwer, A., Ali, S.S.A., Khan, A., Mériaudeau, F.: Underwater 3D scene reconstruction using Kinect v2 based on physical models for refraction and time of flight correction. IEEE Access **5**, 1–11 (2017)
5. Shim, H., Lee, S.: Recovering translucent objects using a single time-of-flight depth camera. IEEE Trans. Circuits Syst. Video Technol. **26**, 841–854 (2016)
6. Francis, S.L.X., Anavatti, S.G., Garratt, M., Shim, H.: A ToF-camera as a 3D vision sensor for autonomous mobile robotics. Int. J. Adv. Robot. Syst. **12**, 1 (2015)
7. Illadequinteiro, J., Brea, V.M., López, P., Cabello, D., Doménechasensi, G.: Distance measurement error in time-of-flight sensors due to shot noise. Sensors **15**, 24–42 (2015)
8. Fürsattel, P., et al.: A comparative error analysis of current time-of-flight sensors. IEEE Trans. Comput. Imaging **2**, 27–41 (2016)
9. Belhedi, A., Bartoli, A., Bourgeois, S., Gay-Bellile, V.: Noise modelling in time-of-flight sensors with application to depth noise removal and uncertainty estimation in three-dimensional measurement. Comput. Vis. IET **9**, 967–977 (2015)
10. Ghorpade, V.K., Checchin, P., Trassoudaine, L.: Line-of-sight-based ToF camera's range image filtering for precise 3D scene reconstruction. In: European Conference on Mobile Robots, pp. 1–6 (2015)
11. Hertzberg, C., Frese, U.: Detailed modeling and calibration of a time-of-flight camera. In: International Conference on Informatics in Control, Automation and Robotics, pp. 568–579 (2015)
12. Konno, Y., et al.: Accurate plane estimation based on the error model of time-of-flight camera. In: Second IEEE International Conference on Robotic Computing, pp. 304–307 (2018)

Discrete Event-Triggered H_∞ State-Feedback Control for Networked Control Systems

Weili Shen[1], Jingqi Fu[1(✉)], Weihua Bao[2], and Zhengming Gao[2]

[1] Department of Automation, College of Mechatronics Engineering
and Automation, Shanghai University, No. 149, Yanchang Road,
200072 Shanghai, China
jqfu@staff.shu.edu.cn
[2] Shanghai Automation Instrumentation Co., Ltd., Shanghai, China

Abstract. This paper is concerned with H_∞ controller design problem for event-triggered networked control systems with bounded time-varying transmission delay and packet losses. The state-feedback controller proposed in this paper deals with event-triggered model and guarantees a required disturbance attenuation level γ subject to external bounded disturbances. Firstly, an improved event-triggered communication scheme is proposed. Secondly, an event-based system is transformed into a delay system. Thirdly, the asymptotical stability criterion in the sense of mean-square for the delay-dependent H_∞ control, and the collaborative approach of the state-feedback control gain and the event-triggered scheme parameters are derived by using LMIs technique and Lyapunov stability theory which lead to less conservatism. Finally, two examples are provided to illustrate the effectiveness of the proposed event-triggering transmission scheme and the co-design method.

Keywords: H_∞ controller · Event-triggered communication scheme
Lyapunov-Krasovskii functional · Time-delay · NCSs

1 Introduction

The cross-infiltration and development of Sensors, microelectronics and communication technologies contribute to the research and accelerate the application of the network control systems (NCSs). The components of NCSs are modularized and share the communication networks, which brings a series of advantages, such as low installation and maintenance costs, high information integration, flexible scalability, and the capacity of meeting the requirements of some special occasions [1–3]. Up to now, the NCSs have a wide range of applications in various fields [2]. However, its limited energy resources are the bottleneck restricting its forward development.

In order to solve the above problem, the event-triggered mechanism(ETM) comes into being. Event-triggered techniques for control design guarantee the signals which are really needed to be sent or the control actions which are really necessary to be executed by using a judgement function [3, 4]. Typically, the function contains the state or output information of the systems, when the information satisfies a certain condition, the task is executed. Thus, the amount of the sent state signals is relatively less

© Springer Nature Singapore Pte Ltd. 2018
K. Li et al. (Eds.): ICSEE 2018/IMIOT 2018, CCIS 924, pp. 291–301, 2018.
https://doi.org/10.1007/978-981-13-2384-3_27

compared with time-triggered method. With the reduction of transmission data, the problems of limited bandwidth, packet loss and network delay in NCSs will be alleviated and the lifespan of the battery of the nodes will also increase.

However, compared with the theory of time sampling, the theoretical research on ETM is relatively lacking, and the main reason caused that is the theoretical analysis on the latter is much more complex. Even for a simple system, the complexity and challenge for analysis and design is apparently. Time delay system method is one of the main modeling and analysis methods of event triggered control system [1, 5–8]. The linear system is modeled as a system model with internal delay, which facilitates the consideration of network constraints such as induced delays and designing controllers. In [1], theorems are proposed to preserve the desired control performance of the event-triggered linear system and evaluate the upper bound of the event-triggered condition; and to avoid the sensor nodes keeping radio on to wait for reception of the sampled data, a novel self-triggered sampling scheme is developed based on event-triggered theorems. In [5], a sufficient condition is derived to co-design both the desired dynamic output feedback controls and the event-triggering parameters considering not all state of the system is measurable. In [9], a more general forms of the event-triggered paradigm than [5] refers is used for both state-feedback and static output-feedback control; the maximum verifying period is obtained by solving a generalized eigenvalue problem. For the linear system with constant delay, a state feedback controller based on event triggered mechanism is designed, which can offer the optimal control performance while reducing the control task executions and the data transmissions [6]. In [7], an improved event-triggered mechanism is proposed which can obtain low transmission rate during the whole operation time by using both the state and state-independent information. In [8], for the case that the statistical information on the external noises is not precisely known, an event-triggered method to ensure the exponential stability as well as prescribed H_∞ performance for the filtering error system are derived. However, there are a few studies on event-triggered control considering time delay and packet loss simultaneously, which is the motivator of the study in this paper.

Referring to the above literature, the time-delay system modeling method is applied in this paper to the stability analysis and controller design of event-triggered systems. Considering that most research is a continuous trigger mechanism depending on hardware, a discrete event-triggered communication mechanism with variable weight, which can be implemented by software and guarantee the minimum lower limit of the release period in principle, is proposed in this paper. Take the effect of both time delay and packet losses into account, the NCS is remodeled. The results show that the joint design method of the event-triggered method and the state feedback controller proposed in this paper can achieve longer average control period, i.e. reduce more resources in NCSs.

Notation: R^n and $\mathbb{N}$ denote the n-dimensional Euclidean space and natural number, respectively. The notation $X > 0 (X \geq 0)$ stands for a real symmetric positive definite (positive semidefinite). X^T denotes the transpose of matrix X. $Diag\{\}$ denotes the block-diagonal matrix. "*" is used as the ellipsis for terms induced by symmetry. $Sym\{X\}$ represents $X + X^T$.

2 Problem Statement

2.1 System Description

Consider the following continuous-time linear system governed by

$$\begin{cases} \dot{x}(t) = Ax(t) + B\hat{u}(t) + B_\omega \omega(t) \\ z(t) = Cx(t) \end{cases} \tag{1}$$

where $\hat{u}(t) \in R^m$ is the control input vector, $\omega(t) \in L_2[0, \infty)$ is the disturbance, and $z(t) \in R^p$ is the control output; A, B, C, D and B_ω are constant matrices with appropriate dimensions; the initial condition of the system (1) is given by $x(t_0) = x_0$.

The structure of NCSs with network latency and ETM is constructed in Fig. 1.

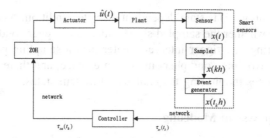

Fig. 1. The structure of the NCSs based on event-triggered scheme

The sensor collects the information of a plant; In this paper, it is used to monitor changes in the state $x(t)$. The sampler detects the continuous signal acquired by the sensor in a fixed period h, and obtains discrete signals $x(kh)$. The sampling time is set as $S_s = \{0, h, 2h, \ldots\}(k \in \mathbb{N})$. Whether the sampled data is transmitted to the controller depends on the event-triggered condition predefined by event generator.

The control signal is transmitted in a single packet. First do not consider the packet loss, the successful transmitted instant sequence of the event generator can be described as $S_g = \{0, b_1h, b_2h, \ldots\}$ $(b_k \in \mathbb{N})$. With the rapid development of electronic technology and chips, and the wide use of high-speed digital processors, the computational delay is negligible compared with transmission delays in the NCSs [2]. The network induced delay can be expressed and $\tau_k = \tau_{sc}(t_k) + \tau_{ca}(t_k)$ and $\tau_k \in [\tau_m, \tau_M]$, where $\tau_{sc}(t_k)$, $\tau_{ca}(t_k)$ are the transmission delay between sampler to controller and controller to actuator respectively; $\tau_m = \min\{\tau_k\}$, $\tau_M = \max\{\tau_k\}$. The input of the actuator is generated by the ZOH, and the holding time is $t \in [t_k, t_{k+1})(t_k = b_kh + \tau_k)$.

2.2 An Event-Triggered Mechanism

In order to reduce the data transmission in the NCSs, the following event-triggered algorithm is designed for the event generator in Fig. 1:

$$[x(b_kh+jh) - x(b_kh)]^T W[x(b_kh+jh) - x(b_kh)] > \delta \Xi^T W \Xi \qquad (2)$$

where $\Xi = (1 - \sigma)x(b_kh) + \sigma x(b_kh + jh);x(b_kh + jh)$ represents the value of the plant state at the current sampling instant, and $x(b_kh)$ represents the value of the latest trigger instant of the plant state; W is a symmetric positive definite matrix, known as the event-triggered matrix; $\delta \geq 0$ is a given scalar parameter named threshold; $0 \leq \sigma \leq 1$ is a given scalar parameter as well. Once $x(b_kh + jh)$ satisfies (2), it will be sent immediately and the control law will be updated accordingly; otherwise, it will be completely discarded. In terms of the above ETM, the controlled system can achieve low average transmission rate while ensuring a satisfactory system performance by adjusting the parameters δ, σ, W. By changing the magnitude of the parameter σ, the weight of the current sampled data and the latest release data can be adjusted. A larger threshold can bring a smaller transmission data rate under the premise of a stable control system.

The trigger condition (2) is state-dependent discrete condition. As described, it only needs to determine whether the sampled signals meet the trigger condition at sampling instants, thus ensuring the trigger interval greater than a sampling period, i.e. strictly positive, by which avoiding zone phenomenon in essence, and there is no need to the extra hardware devices monitoring the changes of system status.

2.3   Closed Loop System Modeling

Assume that the all state of the system can be measured, a static linear state feedback controller $u(t) = Kx(b_kh)$ $(t \in [t_k, t_{k+1}))$ is designed for the system. And the ZOH retention time $\Omega = [t_k, t_{k+1})$ can be divided into subintervals according to the time delay analysis method in reference [7]:

$$\Omega = \bigcup_{i_k=0}^{d} \Omega_{i_k} \qquad (3)$$

where $d = b_{k+1} - b_k - 1$,

$$\Omega_{i_k} = \begin{cases} [b_kh + i_kh + \tau_k, b_kh + (i_k + 1)h + \tau_k), & i_k = 1, 2, \ldots, d-1 \\ [b_kh + dh + \tau_k, b_{k+1}h + \tau_{k+1}), & i_k = d \end{cases}$$

Defining a time delay function:

$$\eta(t) = \begin{cases} t - b_kh, & t \in [b_kh + \tau_k, b_kh + h + \tau_k) \\ t - (b_kh + h), & t \in [b_kh + h + \tau_k, b_kh + 2h + \tau_k) \\ \quad \vdots \\ t - (b_kh + dh), & t \in [b_kh + dh + \tau_k, b_{k+1}h + \tau_{k+1}) \end{cases} \qquad (4)$$

Obviously $\eta(t)$ is a piecewise linear function and bounded, that is $\eta_1 \leq \eta(t) \leq \eta_2$, where $\eta_1 = \tau_m$, $\eta_2 = s\tau_M + h$; and the derivative in the subinterval is 1.

Define an error function $e(t)$:

$$e(t) = \begin{cases} x(b_k h) - x(b_k h), & t \in \Omega_0 \\ x(b_k h + h) - x(b_k h), & t \in \Omega_1 \\ \quad\vdots \\ x(b_k h + dh) - x(b_k h), & t \in \Omega_d \end{cases} \tag{5}$$

Thereby control input can be represented as $u(t) = K[x(t - \eta(t)) - e(t)]$ $(t \in [t_k, t_{k+1}))$. Take the packet losses into account next. Assume that the random packet losses under the network condition of this paper is described with a stochastic variable $\beta(t)$ which follows the Bernoulli distribution:

$$\begin{cases} P(\beta(t) = 1) = E\{\beta(t)\} = \bar{\beta} \\ P(\beta(t) = 0) = 1 - \bar{\beta} \end{cases} \tag{6}$$

where $0 < \bar{\beta} < 1$. data not be lost when $\beta(t) = 1$. Then the final input signal translates into: $\hat{u}(t) = \beta(t) K x(b_k h)$, and the spatial model of the system is as follows:

$$\begin{cases} \dot{x}(t) = Ax(t) + B\hat{u}(t) + B_\omega \omega(t) \\ z(t) = Cx(t) \\ \hat{u}(t) = \beta(t) K x(b_k h), t \in [t_k, t_{k+1}) \end{cases} \tag{7}$$

In combination with the above analysis, a closed loop system model based on event triggered mechanism is obtained:

$$\begin{cases} \dot{x}(t) = \psi_1(t) + (\beta(t) - \bar{\beta})\psi_2(t) \\ z(t) = Cx(t) \end{cases} \tag{8}$$

In which, the initial function of the system is $x(t) = \varphi(t)$, $t \in [\eta_2, 0]$. Where $\psi_1(t) = Ax(t) + \bar{\beta}BK[x(t - \eta(t)) - e(t)] + B_\omega \omega(t)$, $\psi_2(t) = BK[x(t - \eta(t)) - e(t)]$.

3 H_∞ Control Stability Analysis

In this section, for a given disturbance attenuation level γ, we will obtain a sufficient condition on the design of the state feedback controller such that the system described by (8) with the event generator (2) meets the following two requirements.

(1) The closed-loop system described by (8) with $\omega(t) = 0$ is asymptotically stable;
(2) Under zero initial condition, the controlled output $z(t)$ satisfies $\|z(t)\|_2 \leq \gamma \|\omega(t)\|_2$ for any nonzero $\omega(t) \in L_2[0, \infty)$.

Theorem 1: For the given positive parameters $\eta_1, \eta_2, \gamma, \sigma, \delta, \bar{\beta}$ and the feedback gain K, under the event-triggered communication scheme (2), the closed-loop system (8) is asymptotically stable with an H_∞ performance constraint index γ for the disturbance

attention, if there exist matrices $P = P^T > 0, W > 0, Z_i = Z_i^T > 0, Q_i = Q_i^T > 0,$
$R_i = R_i^T > 0 (i = 1, 2)$, and matrix S with appropriate dimensions such that

$$\begin{bmatrix} Z_2 & * \\ S & Z_2 \end{bmatrix} > 0 \tag{9}$$

$$\begin{bmatrix} \Phi_{11} & * \\ \Phi_{21} & \Phi_{22} \end{bmatrix} < 0 \tag{10}$$

where

$$\Phi_{11} = sym\{\Gamma_1^T P e_1\} + \begin{bmatrix} e_1 \\ e_2 \end{bmatrix}^T Q_1 \begin{bmatrix} e_1 \\ e_2 \end{bmatrix} - \begin{bmatrix} e_2 \\ e_3 \end{bmatrix}^T Q_1 \begin{bmatrix} e_2 \\ e_3 \end{bmatrix} + \begin{bmatrix} e_1 \\ e_2 \end{bmatrix}^T Q_2 \begin{bmatrix} e_1 \\ e_2 \end{bmatrix} - \begin{bmatrix} e_3 \\ e_4 \end{bmatrix}^T Q_1 \begin{bmatrix} e_3 \\ e_4 \end{bmatrix} + \begin{bmatrix} e_1 \\ e_6 \end{bmatrix}^T R_1 \begin{bmatrix} e_1 \\ e_6 \end{bmatrix}$$

$$- \begin{bmatrix} e_6 \\ e_7 \end{bmatrix}^T R_1 \begin{bmatrix} e_6 \\ e_7 \end{bmatrix} + \begin{bmatrix} e_1 \\ e_6 \end{bmatrix}^T R_2 \begin{bmatrix} e_1 \\ e_6 \end{bmatrix} - \begin{bmatrix} e_7 \\ e_8 \end{bmatrix}^T R_2 \begin{bmatrix} e_7 \\ e_8 \end{bmatrix} - (e_1^T - e_2^T) Z_1 (e_1 - e_2) - \gamma^2 e_{10}^T e_{10} - (e_4^T - e_5^T) Z_2 (e_4 - e_5)$$

$$- (e_5^T - e_8^T) Z_2 (e_5 - e_8) + (e_5^T - e_8^T) S (e_4 - e_5) + (e_4^T - e_5^T) S (e_5 - e_8) - e_9^T W e_9$$

$$+ \delta [(\sigma - 1) e_9^T + e_5^T] W [(\sigma - 1) e_9 + e_5]$$

$$\Phi_{21}^T = col\{\frac{\eta_1}{3} \Gamma_1, \eta_{21} \Gamma_1, \Gamma_2, \frac{\eta_1}{3} \Gamma_3, \eta_{21} \Gamma_3\}, \quad \Phi_{22}$$

$$= diag\{-Z_1^{-1}, -Z_2^{-1}, I, -\hat{\beta}^{-1} Z_1^{-1}, -\hat{\beta}^{-1} Z_2^{-1}\}$$

Proof: Construct a Lyapunov-Karsovskii functional as following

$$V(t) = V_1(t) + V_2(t) + V_3(t) \tag{11}$$

where $V_1(t) = x^T(t) P x(t)$

$$V_2(t) = \int_{t-\frac{\eta_1}{3}}^{t} \omega_1^T(s) Q_1 \omega_1(s) ds + \int_{t-\frac{2\eta_1}{3}}^{t} \omega_1^T(s) Q_2 \omega_1(s) ds$$

$$+ \int_{t-\frac{\eta_2}{3}}^{t} \omega_2^T(s) R_1 \omega_2(s) ds + \int_{t-\frac{2\eta_2}{3}}^{t} \omega_2^T(s) R_2 \omega_2(s) ds$$

$$V_3(t) = \frac{\eta_1}{3} \int_{-\frac{\eta_1}{3}}^{0} \int_{t+\theta}^{t} \dot{x}^T(s) Z_1 \dot{x}(s) ds d\theta + \eta_{21} \int_{-\eta_2}^{-\eta_1} \int_{t+\theta}^{t} \dot{x}^T(s) Z_2 \dot{x}(s) ds d\theta, \ \eta_{21}$$

$$= \eta_2 - \eta_1$$

Taking the derivation of $V(t)$ for $t \in [b_k h + \tau_k, b_{k+1} h + \tau_{k+1})$ along the trajectory of the system, obtain:

$$E\{\dot{V}_1(t)\} = E\{2x^T(t) P \dot{x}(t)\} = 2x^T(t) P \psi_1(t) \tag{12}$$

$$E\{\dot{V}_2(t)\} = \omega_1^T(t)Q_1\omega_1(t) - \omega_1^T(t - \frac{\eta_1}{3})Q_1\omega_1(t - \frac{\eta_1}{3}) + \omega_1^T(t)Q_2\omega_1(t)$$

$$- \omega_1^T(t - \frac{2\eta_1}{3})Q_1\omega_1(t - \frac{2\eta_1}{3}) + \omega_2^T(t)R_1\omega_2(t) - \omega_2^T(t - \frac{\eta_2}{3})R_1\omega_2(t - \frac{\eta_2}{3}) \quad (13)$$

$$+ \omega_2^T(t)R_2\omega_2(t) - \omega_2^T(t - \frac{2\eta_2}{3})R_2\omega_2(t - \frac{2\eta_2}{3})$$

$$E\{\dot{V}_3(t)\} = \frac{\eta_1^2}{9}[\psi_1^T(t)Z_1\psi_1(t) + \hat{\beta}\psi_2^T(t)Z_1\psi_2(t)] - \frac{\eta_1}{3}\int_{t-\frac{\eta_1}{3}}^{t} \dot{x}^T(s)Z_1\dot{x}(s)ds$$

$$+ \eta_{21}^2[\psi_1^T(t)Z_2\psi_1(t) + \hat{\beta}\psi_2^T(t)Z_2\psi_2(t)] - \eta_{21}\int_{t-\eta_2}^{t-\eta_1} \dot{x}^T(s)Z_2\dot{x}(s)ds \quad (14)$$

where $\omega_1(t) = [x^T(t) \; x^T(t - \frac{\eta_1}{3})]^T$, $\omega_2(t) = [x^T(t) \; x^T(t - \frac{\eta_2}{3})]^T$, $\hat{\beta} = \bar{\beta}(1 - \bar{\beta})$.

The formula (14) contains two integral terms. In order to reduce conservatism, we use Jensen's inequality [7] and reciprocally convex method to scale the two integral terms respectively:

$$-\frac{\eta_1}{3}\int_{t-\frac{\eta_1}{3}}^{t} \dot{x}^T(s)Z_1\dot{x}(s)ds \leq -\left[x(t) - x(t - \frac{\eta_1}{3})\right]^T Z_1\left[x(t) - x(t - \frac{\eta_1}{3})\right] \quad (15)$$

$$-\eta_{21}\int_{t-\eta_2}^{t-\eta_1} \dot{x}^T(s)Z_2\dot{x}(s)ds \leq -[x(t - \eta_1) - x(t - \eta(t))]^T Z_2[x(t - \eta_1) - x(t - \eta(t))]$$
$$-[x(t - \eta(t)) - x(t - \eta_2)]^T Z_2[x(t - \eta(t)) - x(t - \eta_2)]$$
$$+ sym\{[x(t - \eta(t)) - x(t - \eta_2)]^T S[x(t - \eta_1) - x(t - \eta(t))]\} \quad (16)$$

For $\dot{V}(t)$, plus and minus the corresponding items, obtains:

$$E\{\dot{V}(t)\} = E\{\dot{V}(t)\} - e^T(t)We(t) + e^T(t)We(t) - z^T(t)z(t)$$
$$+ z^T(t)z(t) - \gamma^2\omega^T(t)\omega(t) + \gamma^2\omega^T(t)\omega(t) \quad (17)$$

Within the trigger interval, the following formula is satisfied:

$$e^T(t)We(t) \leq \delta\vartheta^T(t)W\vartheta^T(t) \quad (18)$$

where $\vartheta(t) = (1 - \sigma)[x(t - \eta(t)) - e(t)] + \sigma x(t - \eta(t))$.

Combine (15), (16), (17) and (18), obtain:

$$E\{\dot{V}(t)\} \leq \chi^T(t)\Theta\chi(t) - z^T(t)z(t) + \gamma^2\omega^T(t)\omega(t) \quad (19)$$

where $\chi(t) = \{x(t), x(t - \frac{\eta_1}{3}), x(t - \eta_1), x(t - \eta(t))x(t - \frac{\eta_2}{3}), x(t - \frac{2\eta_2}{3}), x(t - \eta_2),$
$e(t), \omega(t)\}$, $\Theta = \Phi_{11} + \frac{\eta_1^2}{9}\Gamma_1^T Z_1\Gamma_1 + \eta_{21}^2\Gamma_1^T Z_2\Gamma_1 + \Gamma_2^T\Gamma_2 + \frac{\eta_1^2}{9}\hat{\beta}\Gamma_3^T Z_1\Gamma_3 + \eta_{21}^2\hat{\beta}\ \Gamma_3^T Z_2$
$\Gamma_3, \Gamma_1 = Ae_1 + \bar{\beta}BKe_5 - \bar{\beta}BBKe_9 + B_\omega e_{10}, \Gamma_2 = Ce_1, \Gamma_3 = BKe_5 - BKe_9, e_i(i = 1, 2,$
..., 10) is a block coordinate matrix, for example $e_2 = [0\,I\,0\,0\,0\,0\,0\,0\,0\,0]$.

By applied the Schur complements, obtains:

$$\begin{bmatrix} \Phi_{11} & * \\ \Phi_{12}^T & \Phi_{22} \end{bmatrix} < 0 \Rightarrow \Theta < 0 \tag{20}$$

Stated thus, the system (18) satisfying Theorem 1 with $\omega \equiv 0$ is asymptotically stable and meets the H_∞ performance index γ. This completes the proof.

On the basis of Theorem 1, the design method of controller K is given by Theorem 2.

Theorem 2: For the given positive parameters η_1, η_2, γ, σ, δ and $\bar{\beta}$, under the event-triggered communication scheme (2), the closed-loop system (8) is asymptotically stable with an H_∞ performance index γ for the disturbance attention, and the feedback gain $K = YX^{-1}$, if there exist matrices $X = X^T > 0$, $\tilde{W} = \tilde{W}^T > 0$, $\tilde{Z}_i = \tilde{Z}_i^T > 0$, $\tilde{Q}_i = \tilde{Q}_i^T > 0, \tilde{R}_i = \tilde{R}_i^T > 0 (i = 1, 2)$, and matrix S with appropriate dimensions such that

$$\begin{bmatrix} \tilde{Z}_2 & * \\ \tilde{S} & \tilde{Z}_2 \end{bmatrix} > 0 \tag{21}$$

$$\begin{bmatrix} \Phi_{11} & * \\ \Phi_{21} & \Phi_{22} \end{bmatrix} < 0 \tag{22}$$

Where

$$\tilde{\Phi}_{11} = sym\{e_1^T \tilde{\Gamma}_1\} + \begin{bmatrix} e_1 \\ e_2 \end{bmatrix}^T \tilde{Q}_1 \begin{bmatrix} e_1 \\ e_2 \end{bmatrix} - \begin{bmatrix} e_2 \\ e_3 \end{bmatrix}^T \tilde{Q}_1 \begin{bmatrix} e_2 \\ e_3 \end{bmatrix} + \begin{bmatrix} e_1 \\ e_2 \end{bmatrix}^T \tilde{Q}_2 \begin{bmatrix} e_1 \\ e_2 \end{bmatrix} - \begin{bmatrix} e_3 \\ e_4 \end{bmatrix}^T \tilde{Q}_1 \begin{bmatrix} e_3 \\ e_4 \end{bmatrix}$$

$$+ \begin{bmatrix} e_1 \\ e_6 \end{bmatrix}^T \tilde{R}_1 \begin{bmatrix} e_1 \\ e_6 \end{bmatrix} - \begin{bmatrix} e_6 \\ e_7 \end{bmatrix}^T \tilde{R}_1 \begin{bmatrix} e_6 \\ e_7 \end{bmatrix} + \begin{bmatrix} e_1 \\ e_6 \end{bmatrix}^T \tilde{R}_2 \begin{bmatrix} e_1 \\ e_6 \end{bmatrix} - \begin{bmatrix} e_7 \\ e_8 \end{bmatrix}^T \tilde{R}_2 \begin{bmatrix} e_7 \\ e_8 \end{bmatrix} - (e_1^T - e_2^T)\tilde{Z}_1(e_1 - e_2)$$

$$- e_9^T \tilde{W} e_9 - \gamma^2 e_{10}^T e_{10} - (e_4^T - e_5^T)\tilde{Z}_2(e_4 - e_5) - (e_5^T - e_8^T)\tilde{Z}_2(e_5 - e_8) + (e_5^T - e_8^T)\tilde{S}(e_4 - e_5)$$

$$+ (e_4^T - e_5^T)\tilde{S}(e_5 - e_8) + \delta[(\sigma - 1)e_9^T + e_5^T]\tilde{W}[(\sigma - 1)e_9 + e_5]$$

$$\tilde{\Phi}_{21} = col\{\frac{\eta_1}{3}\tilde{\Gamma}_1, \eta_{21}\tilde{\Gamma}_1, \tilde{\Gamma}_2, \frac{\eta_1}{3}\tilde{\Gamma}_3, \eta_{21}\tilde{\Gamma}_3\}$$

$$\tilde{\Phi}_{22} = diag\left\{-X\tilde{Z}_1^{-1}X, -X\tilde{Z}_2^{-1}X, I, -\hat{\beta}^{-1}X\tilde{Z}_1^{-1}X, -\hat{\beta}^{-1}X\tilde{Z}_2^{-1}X\right\}$$

$$\tilde{\Gamma}_1 = AXe_1 + \bar{\beta}BYe_5 - \bar{\beta}BYe_9 + B_\omega e_{10}, \tilde{\Gamma}_2 = CXe_1, \Gamma_3 = BYe_5 - BYe_9.$$

Proof: Define matrices $\xi = diag\{X, X, X, X, X, X, X, X, X, I, I, I, I, I\}$, $\varsigma = diag\{X, X\}$, $X = P^{-1}$, $\tilde{W} = XWX$, $\tilde{Z}_i = XZ_iX$, $\tilde{Q}_i = XQ_iX$, $\tilde{R}_i = XR_iX(i = 1, 2)$. The congruent transformation is then performed for the condition (9) and (10) in Theorem 1.

$$\begin{bmatrix} \tilde{Z}_2 & * \\ \tilde{S} & \tilde{Z}_2 \end{bmatrix} = \varsigma^T \begin{bmatrix} Z_2 & * \\ S & Z_2 \end{bmatrix} \varsigma > 0 \tag{23}$$

$$\begin{bmatrix} \tilde{\Phi}_{11} & * \\ \tilde{\Phi}_{21} & \tilde{\Phi}_{22} \end{bmatrix} = \xi^T \begin{bmatrix} \Phi_{11} & * \\ \Phi_{21} & \Phi_{22} \end{bmatrix} \xi < 0 \tag{24}$$

This completes the proof.

CCL algorithm is adopted to solve the non-linear terms $-X\tilde{Z}_1^{-1}X$, $-X\tilde{Z}_2^{-1}X$ in inequality (22), details of which can be found in reference [10].

4 Illustrative Examples

Assume that the systems described in Fig. 1 is the satellite control system [5]. The state equation of the satellite system is described as follows:

$$\begin{cases} \dot{x}(t) = \begin{bmatrix} 0 & 1 & 0 & 0 \\ -\frac{k}{J_2} & -\frac{d}{J_2} & \frac{k}{J_2} & \frac{d}{J_2} \\ 0 & 0 & 0 & 1 \\ -\frac{k}{J_1} & -\frac{d}{J_1} & \frac{k}{J_1} & \frac{d}{J_1} \end{bmatrix} x(t) + \begin{bmatrix} 0 \\ 0 \\ 0 \\ \frac{1}{J_1} \end{bmatrix} u(t) + \begin{bmatrix} 1 \\ 1 \\ 1 \\ 1 \end{bmatrix} \omega(t) \\ z(t) = [1 \ \ 0 \ \ 0 \ \ 0]x(t) \end{cases} \tag{25}$$

where $J_1 = J_2 = 1$, $k = 0.09$ and $d = 0.0219$. Our task is to design an H_∞ state feedback controller for the satellite control system so that the system is stable with H_∞ performance norm bound γ when existing the disturbance of external noise The parameters are set as $\tau_m = 20$ms, $\tau_M = 60$ms, $h = 100$ms, $\delta = 0.1$, $\sigma = 0.5$, $\gamma = 10$. For $t \in [10 \text{ s}, 20 \text{ s}]$, imposing a perturbation $w(t) = e^{-2t}$ on the system. Using Theorem 2 to solve the state feedback parameter K and the event-triggered matrix W.

Under this condition, setting $\beta = 0.05$ yields:

$$K = [-0.0273 - 0.8072 - 0.3140 - 0.7013]$$

$$W = \begin{bmatrix} 1.3671 & -0.6341 & -0.6846 & -0.0483 \\ -0.6341 & 1.3326 & -0.6341 & -0.0643 \\ -0.6846 & -0.6341 & 1.3668 & -0.0481 \\ -0.0483 & -0.0643 & -0.0481 & 0.1607 \end{bmatrix}$$

In Fig. 2, the abscissa and the ordinate show the release instants for the signal and the time interval between two transmission instants. From the diagram, we can see that under the event-triggered communication mechanism, the control cycle of the system is not fixed, and the maximum execution cycle is 1.6 s, which is larger than the sensor sampling period h. For $t \in (0, 60 \text{ s})$, the number of data obtained from the sampler is 600. If the traditional periodic trigger control strategy is adopted, 600 packets have to be transmitted, although some of which is unnecessary. However, the simulation results show that the amount of transmitted data is 78 with proposed ETM, that is, the average data transmission rate is 13.00%. Compared with the time-triggered mechanism, it saves 87.00% of the bandwidth resources. The frequency of task execution is reduced in the NCS with ETM, but the control effect is not affected when some control data lost (Fig. 3).

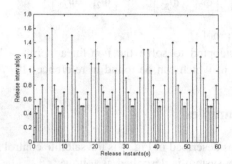

Fig. 2. The release instants and release interval

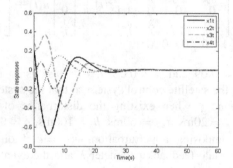

Fig. 3. The event-triggered state responses

5 Conclusion

To save the NCSs with limited resources and increase its life-span, in this paper, we have studied a kind of discrete event-triggered scheme for continuous-time system when existing time-varying delay and packet loss constrains. The data is transmitted in the form of a single packet in the network, and the loss of packets is described by a stochastic variable that satisfies the Bernoulli distribution. For the resulting delay system, a Lyapunov-Karsovskii functional with the delay information has been constructed. A new stabilization criterion in the sense of mean-square expressed in the form of matrix inequalities with H_∞ norm bounds and H_∞ control design has been developed. As shown by simulation results, the proposed method can significantly reduce data transmission while normal operation of the system, despite delay and packet loss.

Acknowledgments. This work was financially supported by the Science and Technology Commission of Shanghai Municipality of China under Grant (No. 17511107002).

References

1. Peng, C., Han, Q.L.: On designing a novel self-triggered sampling scheme for networked control systems with data losses and communication delays. IEEE Trans. Ind. Electron. **63** (2), 1239–1248 (2016)
2. Zhang, L., Gao, H., Kaynak, O.: Network-induced constraints in networked control systems —a survey. IEEE Trans. Ind. Inform. **9**(1), 403–416 (2013)
3. Liu, Q., Wang, Z., He, X., Zhou, D.H.: A survey of event-based strategies on control and estimation. Syst. Sci. Control. Eng. **2**(1), 90–97 (2014)
4. Trimpe, S., Campi, M.C.: On the choice of the event trigger in event-based estimation. In: 2015 International Conference on Event-based Control, Communication, and Signal Processing (EBCCSP), pp. 1–8, 17–19 June 2015
5. Zhang, X.M., Han, Q.L.: Event-triggered dynamic output feedback control for networked control systems. IET Control Theory Appl. **8**(4), 226–234 (2014)
6. Wu, W., Reimann, S., Görges, D., Liu, S.: Suboptimal event-triggered control for time-delayed linear systems. IEEE Trans. Autom. Control **60**(5), 1386–1391 (2015). https://doi.org/10.1109/TAC.2014.2347214
7. Li, F., Fu, J., Du, D.: An improved event-triggered communication mechanism and$L\infty$control co-design for network control systems. Inf. Sci. **370–371**, 743–762 (2016)
8. Hu, S., Yue, D.: Event-based H_∞ filtering for networked system with communication delay. Signal Process. **92**(9), 2029–2039 (2012)
9. Chen, X., Hao, F.: Periodic event-triggered state-feedback and output-feedback control for linear systems. Int. J. Control Autom. Syst. **13**(4), 779–787 (2015)
10. Peng, C., Han, Q.L.: A novel event-triggered transmission scheme and L2 control co-design for sampled-data control systems. IEEE Trans. Autom. Control **58**(10), 2620–2626 (2013)

Brief Technical Analysis of Facial Expression Recognition

Lei Xu, Aolei Yang$^{(\boxtimes)}$, Minrui Fei, and Wenju Zhou

Shanghai Key Laboratory of Power Station Automation Technology,
School of Mechatronic Engineering and Automation, Shanghai University,
Shanghai 200072, China
{XuLeiaa,aolei}@shu.edu.cn, mrfei@staff.shu.edu.cn,
zhouwenju2004@126.com

Abstract. Facial expression recognition (FER) is the current hot research topic, and it is widely used in the fields of pattern recognition, computer vision and artificial intelligence. As it is an important part of intelligent human-computer interaction technology, the FER has received widespread attention in recent years, and researchers in different fields have proposed many approaches for it. This paper reviews recent developments on FER approaches and the key technologies involved in the FER system: face detection and preprocessing, facial expression feature extraction and facial expression classification, which are analyzed and summarized in detail. Finally, the state-of-the-art of the FER is summarized, and its future development direction is pointed out.

Keywords: Computer vision · Artificial intelligence · Facial expression
Feature extraction · Classification

1 Introduction

As an aspect of emotion recognition, the FER plays a very important role in interpersonal communication. Facial expression is an important way to express emotion and information exchange. According to research conducted by the social psychologist Albert Mehrabian, in the daily human communication, emotional information transmitted through facial expressions is as high as 55% of the total amount of information [1], while information transmitted through voice and language accounts for 38% and 7% of the total amount of emotional information. The FER is the foundation of emotional understanding, and it has injected new blood for artificial intelligence.

In 1971, Ekman and Friesen made groundbreaking work [2]. They defined six basic types of facial expression for human expression recognition: happiness, sadness, surprise, fear, anger, disgust. In 1978, Ekman and Friesen et al. developed the famous Facial Action Coding System (FACS) to detect subtle changes in facial expressions [3]. In 1991, MASE and Kenji proposed a new theory that uses the optical flow method to recognize facial expressions. Since then, researchers have used computer technology to extract and classify facial expression features that have attracted widespread attention.

FER system includes three major technical steps: face detection and preprocessing, facial expression feature extraction and facial expression classification. As shown in

© Springer Nature Singapore Pte Ltd. 2018
K. Li et al. (Eds.): ICSEE 2018/IMIOT 2018, CCIS 924, pp. 302–310, 2018.
https://doi.org/10.1007/978-981-13-2384-3_28

Fig. 1, FER system is established to first detect and preprocess the face, which includes image rotation correction, face location, and scale normalization of the expression image, etc. The feature information that can represent the essence of the input expression is extracted from the static images or the dynamic image sequences. In order to avoid excessive dimensions, features such as dimension reduction and feature decomposition are required in the process of extracting feature data. Finally, the relationship between features is analyzed and the input facial expressions are classified into corresponding categories. At present, the FER plays an important role in interactive game platforms, safe driving, intelligent recommendation, distance education, criminal investigation and security, auxiliary medical and other fields, and it has tremendous space for development and application.

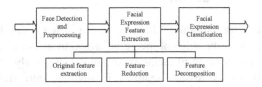

Fig. 1. Facial expression recognition system framework

According to the relevant literatures on the FER studies in recent years, this paper analyzes face detection and preprocessing, facial expression feature extraction, expression classification technology. It reviews the research results of facial expression recognition, and then looks forward to its development trend.

2 Face Detection and Preprocessing

The most importance for FER is to be able to completely extract feature information of the entire face on an original image. Before feature extraction, it is necessary to preprocess the original image. Image preprocessing is mainly divided into two aspects: removing the unwanted background of the facial expression image and image normalization.

The development of face detection technology provides an effective way to remove the complex background of the original image in the FER system. Viola and Jones used cascaded classifiers on Haar-like features to detect face [4]. However, sometimes it is failed to detect contours or partially occluded faces by this method. Due to the different image acquisition methods, the size and format of the generated images are different. The original images need to be normalized to make the full use of the images. The image normalization includes three parts: face normalization, plane face rotation correction and depth face rotation correction. The problem of large difference in gradation due to uneven illumination can also be solved by gray-scale normalization after the geometric normalization is achieved. After a series of steps, the normalization of the original picture is finally completed. For example, as shown in Fig. 2, facial images in the Japanese Female Facial Expression (JAFFE) database are detected and preprocessed, and they are classified into seven basic expressions.

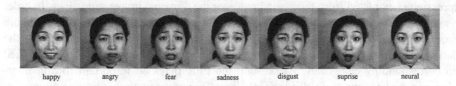

happy   angry   fear   sadness   disgust   suprise   neural

Fig. 2. Sample images of one subject with seven expressions on JAFFE database

3   Facial Feature Extraction

Feature extraction plays an important role in the entire FER system. Under the premise of ensuring the integrity of the original image information of the images, the approach for extracting useful information of facial expressions can greatly improve the rate of FER. The extraction of expression features is divided into static image feature extraction and dynamic sequence image feature extraction according to the different nature of the image. However, most feature extraction processes have excessive dimensions or the high volume of data, and it is necessary to perform dimension reduction, feature decomposition and etc. At present, various feature extraction algorithms have been continuously proposed and improved.

3.1   Extraction of Facial Expression Features in Static Images

Static images are unchanged still pictures, and they are prepared for follow-up processing after a series of preprocessing. Usually, it is divided into two major categories including geometric feature extraction and appearance feature extraction.

The method of extracting geometric features is a macroscopic method that generally represents the structural changes of human faces. According to geometric relationship between the feature points, the main task of this method is to extract the feature points of human face and facial expression features. The three representative geometric feature extraction methods include Active Shape Model (ASM), Active Appearance Models (AAM) and Scale Invariant Feature Transform (SIFT). ASM uses a local texture model to find the best position of the feature point in the facial expression image, and adjusts the parameters of the statistical model. The model gradually approaches the outline of the facial expression and achieves the accurate position of the target. It can extract facial features rapidly and have high accuracy [5]. Antonakos et al. built AAMs and experimental results prove that it has a good recognition effect for unseen faces such as poses and occlusion. SIFT is a kind of local descriptor, and it has scale invariance and can detect key points in the image. Li et al. [6] proposed the new method based on SIFT, and it improved the performance of feature extraction in multispectral graphics.

The appearance feature extraction method is a microscopic method. The appearance feature is based on the feature of using the pixel properties of the entire face image, which reflects the information of the bottom face of the face image, and particularly shows the information of the local minute change. The appearance feature extraction methods mainly include Local Binary Pattern (LBP) and Gabor Filter. LBP is used to compare the local features of an image. It can extract and measure the texture information of the local neighborhood in a grayscale image, and can effectively suppress the influence of illumination. Chao et al. [7] proposed the expression-specific LBP with symmetric extension features, and it can better extract important face points of the human face. Gabor Filter is a classic method for facial expression feature extraction. A set of filters are used to filter the image. The result can reflect the relationship between local pixels. The Gabor filter can detect texture changes of the multi-scale and multi-directional, and it is less affected by light changes. A novel approach for FER is proposed, and the facial feature is extracted from image by applying Gabor wavelet filter on an image and computing local transitional pattern (LTP) code from the transformed image. Extensive experiments illustrate that it is effective and efficient for the FER.

3.2 Extraction of Facial Expression Features in Dynamic Image Sequences

The process of continuous facial expression movement is reflected in the dynamic sequence images. The expression features of the dynamic image sequences are manifested by the deformation of the human face and the muscle movement in each area of the face. Currently, feature extraction methods based on dynamic image sequences mainly include optical flow, feature point tracking method, model tracking method and the elastic map matching.

The optical flow is often used to extract the expression features of the dynamic image sequence. It has the advantages of highlighting the face deformation and reflecting the movement tendency of the face image sequences. In facial expression recognition, the dynamic descriptor itself is more suitable than the static descriptor because different parts of the facial expression change with time. The proposed method based on optical flow by Fan et al. has a better recognition rate than using separate descriptors in the FER.

The feature points are selected in regions where the gray level changes are relatively large, such as corners of the eyes, corners of the mouth, etc. Displacement or deformation information of facial features is easily obtained by tracking these points. Ghimire et al. [8] proposed facial system can achieve good result of the FER. Unlike the tracking of feature points, the goal based on model tracking is the entire face. The model here can be 2D or 3D, but more complex calculations are required in most models. Dewan et al. [9] proposed a novel method based on model tracking, and it can gradually learn the trajectory model of human face and improve the performance of the system.

The basic principle of the elastic map matching method is that select feature points on the input facial expression image to construct an elastic map with a certain topological structure. Then the feature vectors on each node and structure are extracted and a similarity function is constructed to compare the degree of similarity between the feature vector and the topology. If the similarity is the greatest, the match could be completed. Zafeiriou and Pitas [10] propose a new technique based on the elastic map matching improves the performance of the selection of the most discriminant facial landmarks for the FER.

3.3 Feature Reduction Method

After the facial expression image is extracted from the original features, some features often have very large spatial dimensions, such as appearance features. These features need to be represented by converting from high-dimensional features to low-dimensional subspaces through some mapping and transformation. The dimension of the feature is significantly reduced, and the effectiveness of these features is improved. Feature reduction methods can be further divided into two categories including linear and nonlinear methods.

Linear dimensionality reduction methods commonly used in the FER include principal component analysis (PCA), linear discriminant analysis (LDA), etc. The PCA can effectively extract the local features that make a great contribution to the FER, eliminate redundancy and reduce the dimension, but the distinction between different types of data in this method is not considered. The LDA based on the Fisher criterion is a more successful feature extraction algorithm. It selects the proper projection direction by maximizing the dispersion of the data between classes and minimizing the intra-class dispersion of data, mainly to find the direction with the greatest resolution. In [11], stepwise linear discriminant analysis which is based on the LDA is proposed, and it selects the localized features with the partial F-test value from the expression frames. It is a significant improvement for the FER.

There are two representative manifold learning methods for nonlinear dimensionality reduction including local linear embedding and isometric mapping (Isomap). Local linear embedding (LLE) which focus on preserving the local structures can also reduce the dimension of data, and it can also make the data better retain the original geometric relationship in the local sense after dimension reduction. A new kernel-based supervised manifold learning algorithm based on LLE is proposed for the FER [12], and it has the effectiveness and promising performance. Isomap is based on the Multidimensional Scale Transform (MDS). The goal is to maintain the intrinsic geometric properties of the data points by keeping the geodesic distance between the two points constant. Isomap based on expression weighted distance is proposed [13]. In order to take the advantage of knowledge of expression classes, Isomap assigns weighed values according to different sample distance, and it performs very well on the JAFFE database.

3.4 Feature Decomposition Method

Face images contain a wealth of information, and the information used varies for different identification requirements. For example, what is needed in face detection is common information in face images, and what is needed in face recognition is face difference information. In the FER, it is necessary to use the information of the differences between various expression features, and perhaps information that is favorable for one identification requirement interferes with another. Therefore, a solution is to separate the different face factors, so that the various types of recognition can be performed in different subspaces to avoid interference from other factors. A dictionary-based approach for the FER by decomposing expressions is proposed by Taheri et al. [14]. They achieve expression decomposition and recognition by computing the facial expression sparse code matrix.

4   Facial Expression Classification

The expression classification method and the expression feature extraction method are closely related. It refers to defining a set of categories and designing a corresponding classification mechanism to recognize expressions and classify them into corresponding categories. At present, the main expression classification methods include Hidden Markov Model (HMM), K-Nearest Neighbor (KNN), Support Vector Machines (SVM), AdaBoost, Artificial Neural Network (ANN), and so on.

4.1   Hidden Markov Modeling (HMM)

The HMM contains hidden unknown parameters, and it is a Markov process based on the Markov chain. One of them is the Markov chain, and it is a random process that describes the transfer of states; another one describes the statistical correspondence between observations and states. The whole process of the HMM algorithm is that the observed values are generated with the transition of the state, and we are concerned with judging the hidden state through the existing observations. It uses a long series of observation sequences to extrapolate possible state sequences that lead to this result. The random signal information can be effectively described in the statistical model by the HMM. Wu et al. [15] proposed a novel method based on the HMM for the FER. It can locate apex frames of sequences with multiple peaks and label the sequences effectively.

4.2   K-Nearest Neighbor (KNN)

The KNN algorithm is a mature classification method and it is also one of the machine learning algorithms. The principle of this method is that if the majority of the k most similar samples (the nearest neighbors in the feature space) in a sample belong to the same class. The main idea of KNN is to determine its own category based on the similar neighbor categories. The premise of the algorithm is that it needs to have a set of training data that has been marked. First, it calculates the distance between the test object and all objects in the training set. Then, it finds the nearest K objects in the distance calculated in the previous step as the neighbors of the test object. Finally, it finds out the most frequently occurring objects among the K objects, and its category is the category to which the test object belongs. Bahari et al. [16] apply the KNN to classify the features into the emotional states, and it has better classification accuracy.

4.3 Support Vector Machine (SVM)

The SVM is a classifier with strong generalization ability. It has many advantages in solving identification problems such as nonlinearity, small sample sets and high-dimensional patterns. The basic model of SVM is to find the best separating hyperplane in the feature space so that the interval between positive and negative samples is the largest in the training set. SVM is a supervised learning algorithm used to solve the two-category problem. SVM can also be used to solve nonlinear problems after the introduction of the kernel method. The SVM not only increases the computational complexity, but also avoids the curse of dimensionality compared with the linear model [17]. It proves that the polynomial kernel function has good real-time performance in FER, while radial basis kernel function has better generalization and learning ability.

4.4 AdaBoost

AdaBoost is an iterative algorithm, and its basic principle of Adaboost algorithm is to combine several weak classifiers (weak classifiers generally use a single-level decision tree) to make it a strong classifier. It adopts an iterative idea that only one weak classifier is trained per iteration and the weak classifier trained will participate in the use of the next iteration. The AdaBoost algorithm which is proposed by Freund and Schapire, is first practical boosting algorithm, and it is one of the most widely used and studied [18]. Owusu et al. proposed a new method which is based on the AdaBoost, and it can enhance accuracy and speed with the expression dataset reduced [19].

4.5 Artificial Neural Networks (ANN)

The ANN massively parallel computing system composed of a large number of connected neurons, and learns complex nonlinear input-output relations through a training process. Its principle can be summarized as follows: for nonlinear separable samples, the input space is first converted to a high-dimensional space by nonlinear transformation, and then the optimal linear interface is obtained in the high-dimensional space, and this nonlinear transformation is achieve by defining a proper kernel function. Different architectures and models of ANN are used for the FER in the recent years, such as Convolutional Neural Network (CNN), Polynomial Neural Network (PNN), Recurrent Neural Networks (RNN), Retinal Connected Neural Network (RCNN), etc. For example, Lopes et al. [20] combined the CNN and the specific image pre-processing steps to recognize the facial expressions, and the CNNs achieved better accuracy with big data.

5 Conclusion

The FER is a cross-disciplinary research topic and has become a very popular research topic in the fields of psychology, medicine, computer vision, pattern recognition, etc. It has important application value in the field of intelligent human-computer interaction. This paper describes the key technologies involved in facial expression recognition:

face detection and preprocessing, expression feature extraction and expression classification. The paper categorizes the research results on facial expression recognition technology at home and abroad, and introduces the problems existing in some technologies and the latest technologies related to facial expression recognition.

Although many achievements have been made in the study, many problems still need to be solved. For example, expression classification is too restrictive and human expressions are not only six basic expressions, but there are also many complex and superimposed expressions. Face expressions in dynamic images and facial expressions in 3D real life are easily affected by illumination, occlusion, etc. The robustness of the FER is poor, and the effectiveness of the recognition algorithm still needs improvement. Therefore, many expression recognition algorithms have not yet been applied to specific projects or products, and it is still a challenging topic. With the arrival of the era of big data, the demand for real-time facial expressions has increased dramatically. The application of the FER technology has a broader scope of development and utilization value. In the future, facial expressions can be assisted by integrating sound, heat, and environmental factors. Expression recognition system adds depth information based on 2D to support 3D face analysis. Taking time changes into consideration helps to improve expression recognition rates by analyzing the correlation between consecutive adjacent frames.

Acknowledgements. This work is supported by Natural Science Foundation of Shanghai (No. 18ZR1415100), National Science Foundation of China (61473182, 61773253), Science and Technology Commission of Shanghai Municipality (15JC1401900) and Key research and development project of Yantai (2017ZH061).

References

1. Mehrabian, A.: Communication without words. Psychol. Today **2**, 53–55 (1968)
2. Ekman, P., Friesen, W.V.: Constants across cultures in the face and emotion. J. Pers. Soc. Psychol. **17**, 124–129 (1971)
3. Ekman, P.: Facial Action Coding System. A Technique for the Measurement of Facial Action (1978)
4. Hu, P.: Application research on face detection technology based on OpenCV in mobile augmented reality. Int. J. Sign. Process. Image Process. Pattern Recogn. **8**, 249–256 (2015)
5. Shbib, R., Zhou, S.: Facial expression analysis using active shape model. Int. J. Sign. Process. Image Process. Pattern Recogn. **8**, 9–22 (2016)
6. Li, Y., Liu, W., Li, X., Huang, Q., Li, X.: GA-SIFT: a new scale invariant feature transform for multispectral image using geometric algebra. Inf. Sci. **281**, 559–572 (2014)
7. Chao, W.L., Ding, J.J., Liu, J.Z.: Facial expression recognition based on improved local binary pattern and class-regularized locality preserving projection. Signal Process. **117**, 1–10 (2015)
8. Ghimire, D.: Recognition of facial expressions based on tracking and selection of discriminative geometric features. Int. J. Multimed. Ubiquitous Eng. **10**, 35–44 (2015)
9. Dewan, M.A.A., Granger, E., Marcialis, G.L., Sabourin, R., Roli, F.: Adaptive appearance model tracking for still-to-video face recognition. Pattern Recogn. **49**, 129–151 (2016)

10. Zafeiriou, S., Pitas, I.: Discriminant graph structures for facial expression recognition. IEEE Trans. Multimed. **10**, 1528–1540 (2008)
11. Siddiqi, M.H., Ali, R., Khan, A.M., Park, Y.T., Lee, S.: Human facial expression recognition using stepwise linear discriminant analysis and hidden conditional random fields. IEEE Trans. Image Process. **24**, 1386–1398 (2015)
12. Zhao, X.: Facial expression recognition using local binary patterns and discriminant kernel locally linear embedding. EURASIP J. Adv. Signal Process. **2012**, 20 (2012)
13. Wang, S., Yang, H., Li, H.: Facial expression recognition based on incremental isomap with expression weighted distance. J. Comput. **8**, 2051–2058 (2013)
14. Taheri, S., Qiu, Q., Chellappa, R.: Structure-preserving sparse decomposition for facial expression analysis. IEEE Trans. Image Process. **23**, 3590–3603 (2014)
15. Wu, C., Wang, S., Ji, Q.: Multi-instance hidden Markov model for facial expression recognition. In: IEEE International Conference and Workshops on Automatic Face and Gesture Recognition, pp. 1–6 (2015)
16. Bahari, F., Janghorbani, A.: EEG-based emotion recognition using recurrence plot analysis and K nearest neighbor classifier. In: Biomedical Engineering, pp. 228–233 (2013)
17. Wang, F., He, K., Liu, Y., Li, L., Hu, X.: Research on the selection of kernel function in SVM based facial expression recognition. In: Industrial Electronics and Applications, pp. 1404–1408 (2013)
18. Schapire, R.E.: Explaining AdaBoost. Springer, Heidelberg (2013)
19. Owusu, E., Zhan, Y., Mao, Q.R.: A neural-AdaBoost based facial expression recognition system. Expert Syst. Appl. **41**, 3383–3390 (2014)
20. Lopes, A.T., Aguiar, E.D., Souza, A.F.D., Oliveira-Santos, T.: Facial expression recognition with convolutional neural networks: coping with few data and the training sample order. Pattern Recogn. **61**, 610–628 (2017)

Application of Intelligent Virtual Reference Feedback Tuning to Temperature Control in a Heat Exchanger

Yalan Wen[1], Ling Wang[1(✉)], Weiqing Peng[1],
Muhammad Ilyas Menhas[1,2], and Lin Qian[1,3]

[1] Shanghai Key Laboratory of Power Station Automation Technology,
School of Mechatronics Engineering and Automation, Shanghai University,
Shanghai 200072, China
{phoenixwen,wangling,candidates}@shu.edu.cn,
ilyasminhas75@yahoo.com, ql_spcti@163.com
[2] Department of Electrical Engineering,
Mirpur University of Science and Technology, Mirpur A.K., Pakistan
[3] Shanghai Power Construction Testing Institute, Shanghai 200031, China

Abstract. Heat exchangers are frequently incorporated in industrial processes. Temperature control in heat exchangers is very important for the safety and economic benefits of the industrial system. However, it is still challenging to control the temperature of heat exchangers because of the complicated thermal dynamic phenomena. In this paper, an improved data-driven control method, i.e. intelligent virtual reference feedback tuning based on multi-population cooperative human learning optimization (IVFRT-MCHLO), is developed to design the optimal controller for a water heat exchanger. The controller is designed based on IVRFT method and a novel multi-population cooperative human learning optimization (MCHLO) algorithm is proposed to find out the optimal controller. The experimental results demonstrate that the proposed IVFRT-MCHLO has better control performance as the multi-population cooperation strategy of MCHLO improves the global search ability greatly.

Keywords: Heat exchanger · Temperature control
Human learning optimization · Intelligent virtual reference feedback tuning
Data-driven

1 Introduction

Heat exchangers are extensively utilized in many industrial fields, including power generation systems [1], chemical processes [2] and district heating systems [3]. Efficient temperature control can improve the dynamic performance and enhance stability of the system involving the heat exchanger significantly [4]. However, it is a major challenge to control the fluid temperature being heated at a specific and stable reference value because heat exchangers are extremely complex devices involving a large number of thermal dynamic phenomena, for which the prediction of their operation from first principles seems to be impossible [5]. Therefore, researchers proposed

© Springer Nature Singapore Pte Ltd. 2018
K. Li et al. (Eds.): ICSEE 2018/IMIOT 2018, CCIS 924, pp. 311–320, 2018.
https://doi.org/10.1007/978-981-13-2384-3_29

various advanced approaches to design and improve temperature controllers for heat exchangers over past few decades. However, most of those methods [4, 6, 7] are designed based on mathematical models, which means that plenty of effort has to be spent on system modelling. Furthermore, it is difficult to construct a perfect model and some complex nonlinear systems are even unlikely to be modelled.

Virtual reference feedback tuning (VRFT) is a data-driven control (DDC) approach. As a hotspot, VRFT approaches have been improved substantially and applied to a wide range of control systems [8–10]. However, the optimal controller cannot be designed successfully because the performance indices are not included in its objective function in the standard VRFT method. Therefore, Wang et al. [11] developed an intelligent VRFT (IVRFT), in which a potential performance metric, i.e., the reference model parameter, was included in the controller design to achieve the optimal control performance. Compared with VRFT approaches, the controller design problem in the IVRFT is transformed from a parameter identification problem into an optimization problem. Traditional derivative-based methods including the least square method, which is adopted in VRFT approaches, cannot be used to solve such an optimization problem.

Obviously, the optimization method has a significant impact on the controller design based on IVRFT method [11]. Human learning optimization (HLO) is an simple yet efficient optimization tool, which mimics the human learning process [12]. In previous works, HLO has obtained the best-so-far results on two well-studied sets of multi-dimensional knapsack problems, i.e. 5.100 and 10.100 [13], which shows its advantages. In this paper, a multi-population cooperative human learning optimization (MCHLO) is proposed as an optimization tool to design the optimal controller for a water heat exchanger based on IVRFT.

The reminder of this paper is organized as follows. Section 2 introduces the IVRFT briefly. MCHLO is described in Sect. 3. Section 4 presents the optimal controller design based on IVRFT and MCHLO (IVRFT-MCHLO) in details. Then IVRFT-MCHLO is utilized to control the temperature in a water heat exchanger and compared with the other control approaches in Sect. 5. Finally, we draw the conclusions in Sect. 6.

2 Intelligent Virtual Reference Feedback Tuning

The VRFT approach [14] aims to solve a model-reference problem in discrete time. The objective function adopted in the VRFT method does not include any performance index, and thus it is almost impossible to design the optimal controller through the original VRFT method. However, for practical engineering applications, the dynamic performance is of great importance because it significantly influences the efficiency of systems and the benefit of enterprises. Considering that the reference model determines the closed-loop control performance of a controller tuned by the VRFT method, Wang et al. [11] presented a novel intelligent VRFT approach in which the reference model and the controller are both optimized. Consequently, the controller with the best performance can be found in the framework of IVRFT.

Consider a first-order reference model as Eq. (1), where A is a parameter related to the speed of response and d refers to the delay time.

$$M(z^{-1}) = \frac{(1-A)z^{-1}}{1-Az^{-1}} z^{-d} \tag{1}$$

Apparently, the reference model with a relatively small A will have a better dynamic performance. The controller design based on such a reference model is bound to result in better control performance. Encouraged by that fact, a novel objective function is proposed in IVRFT as Eq. (2)

$$J_{IVRFT} = J_{VRFT} + k \times A \tag{2}$$

where J_{VRFT} denotes the objective function of the standard VRFT approach, and k denotes the weight of A which should be small enough to make sure that J_{VRFT} dominates this objective function.

3   Multi-population Cooperative Human Learning Optimization

Social entities such as organizational units are often drawn by boundaries of knowledge [15]. Individuals shape their own organizations and are also impacted by them. Levels of cooperation have great impacts on knowledge sharing among organizational units [16]. It is natural that proper knowledge sharing can speed up the knowledge conversion process. Inspired by this fact, a multi-population cooperative strategy is introduced into HLO, and a novel multi-population cooperative human learning optimization is proposed, where the whole population is divided into a master subpopulation and S slave subpopulations as Fig. 1. The master population involves S individuals and the remaining individuals are shared by the slave subpopulations equally.

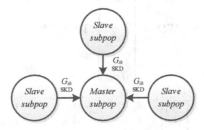

Fig. 1. Schematic of MCHLO strategy

In MCHLO, the cooperation between the master subpopulation and each slave subpopulation works together. The master subpopulation and slave subpopulation are evolved in parallel, which can take full advantage of the emerging solutions saved in the master subpopulation. Besides, the proposed multi-population cooperative strategy can increase the population diversity. Therefore, the global search ability is further improved by the enhanced exploration and exploitation.

In MCHLO, an individual is encoded as a binary string like Eq. (3), in which each bit stands for a basic component of knowledge.

$$x_i = [x_{i1} \quad x_{i2} \quad \cdots \quad x_{ij} \quad \cdots \quad x_{iM}], \, x_{ij} \in \{0,1\}, 1 \leq i \leq N, 1 \leq j \leq M \quad (3)$$

where x_i is ith individual, N refers to the number of individuals in a population, and M denotes the length of solutions. Each bit is stochastically initialized with 0 or 1.

3.1   Learning Operators

Random Learning Operator (RLO). Human learning processes are always accompanied by randomness. When learning new things, people usually attempt to solve problems by using random methods for lack of prior knowledge [17]. The individual has random learning behaviors to explore new knowledge during the search process, which are defined in MCHLO as Eq. (4).

$$x_{ij} = R(0,1) = \begin{cases} 0, \, 0 \leq r_1 \leq 0.5 \\ 1, \, else \end{cases} \quad (4)$$

where r_1 is a stochastic number between 0 and 1.

Individual Learning Operator (ILO). External stimuli can motivate people to build skills and knowledge through individual reflection [18]. For each subpopulation, individual best solutions are saved in the individual knowledge database (IKD) like Eqs. (5)–(6)

$$IKD = \begin{bmatrix} ikd_1 \\ ikd_2 \\ \vdots \\ ikd_i \\ \vdots \\ ikd_N \end{bmatrix}, 1 \leq i \leq N \quad (5)$$

$$ikd_i = \begin{bmatrix} ikd_{i1} \\ ikd_{i2} \\ \vdots \\ ikd_{ip} \\ \vdots \\ ikd_{iL} \end{bmatrix} = \begin{bmatrix} ik_{i11} & ik_{i12} & \cdots & ik_{i1j} & \cdots & ik_{i1M} \\ ik_{i21} & ik_{i22} & \cdots & ik_{i2j} & \cdots & ik_{i2M} \\ \vdots & \vdots & & \vdots & & \vdots \\ ik_{ip1} & ik_{ip2} & \cdots & ik_{ipj} & \cdots & ik_{ipM} \\ \vdots & \vdots & & \vdots & & \vdots \\ ik_{iL1} & ik_{iL2} & \cdots & ik_{iLj} & \cdots & ik_{iLM} \end{bmatrix}, 1 \leq p \leq L \quad (6)$$

where ikd_i is the IKD of individual i, L indicates the number of solutions stored in the IKD, and ikd_{ip} is known as pth best solution for individual i. For the slave subpopulation, when MCHLO performs the individual learning operator (ILO), it generates new solutions according to the knowledge in the IKD as Eq. (7)

$$x_{ij} = ik_{ipj} \tag{7}$$

For the master subpopulation, the IKD$_{master}$ directly inherits G_{ib}, i.e., the iteration-best solution generated by the slave subpopulation.

$$ikd_{master,i} = \begin{bmatrix} ik_{i1} & ik_{i2} & \cdots & ik_{ij} & \cdots & ik_{iM} \end{bmatrix}, 1 \leq i \leq S, 1 \leq j \leq M \tag{8}$$

where $ikd_{master,\,i}$ is the IKD of the ith individual in the master subpopulation. When an individual in the master subpopulation yields the new candidate, it generates new solutions from the knowledge stored in the IKD$_{master}$ as Eq. (9).

$$x_{ij} = ik_{ij} \tag{9}$$

Social Learning Operator (SLO). As human beings are social animals, human learning cannot be separated from interaction among each other. To accelerate the learning processes, it is natural for an individual to learn from his/her own organization. For the slave population in MCHLO, the social knowledge database (SKD) is utilized to reserve the knowledge of the subpopulation as Eq. (10)

$$SKD = \begin{bmatrix} skd_1 \\ skd_2 \\ \vdots \\ skd_q \\ \vdots \\ skd_H \end{bmatrix} = \begin{bmatrix} sk_{11} & sk_{12} & \cdots & sk_{1j} & \cdots & sk_{1M} \\ sk_{21} & sk_{22} & \cdots & sk_{2j} & \cdots & sk_{2M} \\ \vdots & \vdots & & \vdots & & \vdots \\ sk_{q1} & sk_{q2} & \cdots & sk_{qj} & \cdots & sk_{qM} \\ \vdots & \vdots & & \vdots & & \vdots \\ sk_{H1} & sk_{H2} & \cdots & sk_{Hj} & \cdots & sk_{HM} \end{bmatrix}, 1 \leq q \leq H \tag{10}$$

where skd_q is the qth solution, and H denotes the size of the SKD. For an individual in the slave subpopulation, the social learning operator (SLO) is performed as Eq. (11)

$$x_{ij} = sk_{qj} \tag{11}$$

For the master subpopulation, only the best-so-far solution is stored in the SKD$_{master}$ as Eq. (12). Each individual in the master subpopulation executes SLO as Eq. (13)

$$SKD_{master,j} = \begin{bmatrix} sk_1 & sk_2 & \cdots & sk_j & \cdots & sk_M \end{bmatrix}, 1 \leq j \leq M \tag{12}$$

$$x_j = sk_j \tag{13}$$

In summary, an individual in MCHLO employs the RLO, ILO and SLO in the search process to generate new candidates, which can be formulated as Eq. (14)

$$x_{ij} = \begin{cases} RLO, & if\ 0 \le r \le pr \\ ILO, & if\ pr < r \le pi \\ SLO, & if\ pi < r \le 1 \end{cases} \tag{14}$$

where pr, $(pi - pr)$ and $(1 - pi)$ represent the probability of executing RLO, ILO and SLO, respectively. Note that ILO and SLO for the master subpopulation are different from those for each slave subpopulation, which has been described before.

3.2 Update of IKDs and SKD

IKDs and SKDs are updated so as to simulate people evaluating their performance and updating the experience in the learning process. The sizes of IKDs and SKDs were both equal to 1 as recommended in [17].

For the slave subpopulation, the solution in IKDs is substituted by a new candidate if the new one has a better fitness value. SKD is updated in the same way. For an individual in the slave subpopulation, its IKD will be re-initialized if its optimal solution is not updated in the consecutive rl iterations to avoid premature. For the master subpopulation, as mentioned above, IKD$_{master}$ is updated through copying the iteration-best solution G_{ib} generated by each slave subpopulation. SKD$_{master}$ is updated when the new best solution is found by any subpopulation.

4 Controller Design Based on IVRFT-MCHLO

Consider a typical PID controller as Eq. (15)

$$u(k) = u(k-1) + K_p[e(k) - e(k-1)] + K_i e(k) \\ + K_d[e(k) - 2e(k-1) + e(k-2)] \tag{15}$$

where $u(k)$ represents the manipulated variable at the kth sampling instant, $e(k)$ refers to the error between the process output and its set-point at the kth sampling instant, and K_p, K_i and K_d are parameters of a PID controller. The corresponding controller transfer function can be formulized as Eq. (16), and its parametric form is as Eq. (17)

$$C(z^{-1}; \theta) = K_p + \frac{K_i}{1 - z^{-1}} + K_d(1 - z^{-1}) \tag{16}$$

$$C(z^{-1}; \theta) = \beta^T(z)\theta \tag{17}$$

where

$$\beta^T(z) = \left[1 \frac{1}{1-z^{-1}} 1 - z^{-1} \right] \tag{18}$$

$$\theta = [K_p \quad K_i \quad K_d]^T \tag{19}$$

From Eqs. (1) and (16), $u^{vir}(t)$ can be deduced as Eqs. (20)–(21)

$$u^{vir}(z^{-1}) = \left[K_p + \frac{K_i}{1-z^{-1}} + K_d(1-z^{-1}) \right] \times \left[\frac{1-z^{-1}}{(1-A)z^{-1}} z^{-d} \right] y \tag{20}$$

$$u^{vir}(z^{-1}) = \varphi^T(t)\theta = [\varphi_p(t) \quad \varphi_i(t) \quad \varphi_d(t)] \begin{bmatrix} K_p \\ K_i \\ K_d \end{bmatrix} \tag{21}$$

where $\varphi_p(t)$, $\varphi_i(t)$, $\varphi_d(t)$ denote the ratio of K_p, K_i and K_d respectively.

In IVRFT-MCHLO, MCHLO is used to search for the best K_p, K_i, K_d and A by following Eq. (2), in order to tune the controller with superior performance. The implementation of IVRFT-MCHLO can be summarized as follows:

Step 1: initialize the algorithm parameters included in MCHLO;
Step 2: set the length of each decision variable; in this paper, each decision variable is coded by 30 bits;
Step 3: initialize the master subpopulation and each slave subpopulation randomly;
Step 4: initialize the IKDs and SKD of each slave subpopulation, as well as the IKDs$_{master}$ and SKD$_{master}$;
Step 5: generate new solutions by performing learning operators as Eq. (14);
Step 6: evaluate the fitness of each individual according to Eq. (2);
Step 7: update the IKDs and SKD of each slave subpopulation, as well as the IKDs$_{master}$ and SKD$_{master}$ according to the updating rules of MCHLO;
Step 8: output the optimal solution in SKD$_{master}$ if the termination criterion is met; otherwise go back to step 5.

5 Temperature Control in a Water Heat Exchanger

As Fig. 2 shows, the valve V that manipulates the input water is utilized to control the temperature T of output water in a water heat exchanger. The input water is from a storage tank, whose temperature can be kept at a certain point by an independent controller. The behavior of this process can be modeled as Eq. (22) [19]. Note that IVRFT-MCHLO and VRFT are model-free approaches, and the model is only utilized to collect the I/O data and validate the controller designed by IVRFT-MCHLO.

$$\frac{T(s)}{V(s)} = P(s) = \frac{0.12}{1+6s} e^{-3s} \tag{22}$$

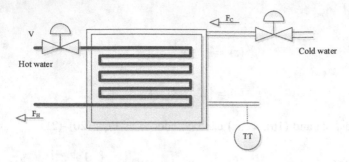

Fig. 2. Schematic diagram of the water heat exchanger

IVRFT-MCHLO was implemented to control the water temperature in the heat exchanger, as well as IVRFT [11] and the other model-based control approaches, i.e. the Z-N method [20] and model-based optimal PID controller design with harmony search (MPID) [21]. The parameter settings for MCHLO are obtained by trial and error, that is, $pr = 5/M$, $S = 2$, $rl = 100$, $pi = 0.85 + 2/M$. For the MPID approach, its objective function is formulated as Eq. (23)

$$F = w_1 \times \text{IAE} + w_2 \times t_{up} + w_3 \times \text{OS} \tag{23}$$

where IAE, t_{up}, and OS refer to the integral of absolute error, rise time and overshoot, respectively. w_1, w_2 and w_3 are the corresponding weight coefficients which are the recommended values in [21]. Note that the ideal model as well as the model with 0.5% error is taken as a competitor in this paper. The control performance of the above-mentioned approaches is depicted in Fig. 3, and the corresponding results are listed in Table 1. Non-overshoot control is achieved by all approaches except the Z-N method. It is undoubted that the results obtained by the IVRFT approaches are inferior to the MPID method with the perfect model. However, it should be emphasized that the results obtained by IVRFT-MCHLO are very close to that of MPID and significantly better than that of MPID with 0.5% model error. IVRFT-MCHLO outperforms IVRFT on each performance index except OS, which reflects that the optimization algorithm is important to the control performance in the framework of IVRFT.

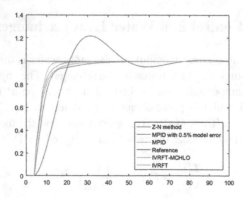

Fig. 3. Step response curves of all the control methods

Table 1. Results of MCHLO-IVRFT and other control approaches on the temperature control

Methods	$T_{up}(s)$	OS(%)	IAE	Fitness
Z-N	12	21.88	17.5284	1123.5000
MPID with 0.5% model error	9	0	8.6685	17.6685
MPID	6	0	6.4707	12.4707
IVRFT-MCHLO	7	0	6.8822	13.8822
IVRFT	8	0	7.6210	15.6210

6   Conclusions

Heat exchangers widely exist in industrial processes. However, its temperature control is still challenging in engineering applications. Therefore, we proposed an improved intelligent virtual reference feedback tuning based on a novel multi-population cooperative human learning optimization algorithm (IVFRT-MCHLO), which can design the optimal temperature controller of heat exchangers only based on the collected data of the system efficiently. With the enhanced exploration and exploitation abilities, MCHLO can be combined with the IVRFT to find out the optimal controller. Experimental results display that IVRFT-MCHLO can be utilized to design the temperature controller for a water controller successfully and achieve the desirable control performance.

Acknowledgments. This work is supported by National Natural Science Foundation of China (Grant No. 61633016 & 61703262), Key Project of Science and Technology Commission of Shanghai Municipality under Grant No. 16010500300 and 15220710400, Shanghai Sailing Program under Grant No. 16YF1403700, and Natural Science Foundation of Shanghai (No. 18ZR1415100).

References

1. May, P., Ehrlich, H.-C., Steinke, T.: ZIB structure prediction pipeline: composing a complex biological workflow through web services. In: Nagel, W.E., Walter, W.V., Lehner, W. (eds.) Euro-Par 2006. LNCS, vol. 4128, pp. 1148–1158. Springer, Heidelberg (2006). https://doi.org/10.1007/11823285_121
2. Anxionnaz, Z., Cabassud, M., Gourdon, C., Tochon, P.: Heat exchanger/reactors (HEX reactors): concepts, technologies: state-of-the-art. Chem. Eng. Process.: Process. Intensif. **47**, 2029–2050 (2008)
3. Tol, Hİ., Svendsen, S.: A comparative study on substation types and network layouts in connection with low-energy district heating systems. Energy Convers. Manag. **64**, 551–561 (2012)
4. Wang, Y., You, S., Zheng, W., Zhang, H., Zheng, X., Miao, Q.: State space model and robust control of plate heat exchanger for dynamic performance improvement. Appl. Therm. Eng. **128**, 1588–1604 (2018)
5. Díaz, G., Sen, M., Yang, K., McClain, R.L.: Dynamic prediction and control of heat exchangers using artificial neural networks. Int. J. Heat Mass Transf. **44**, 1671–1679 (2001)

6. Vasičkaninová, A., Bakošová, M., Čirka, Ľ., Kalúz, M., Oravec, J.: Robust controller design for a laboratory heat exchanger. Appl. Therm. Eng. **128**, 1297–1309 (2018)
7. Wang, S., Yu, X., Liang, C., Zhang, Y.: Enhanced condensation heat transfer in air-conditioner heat exchanger using superhydrophobic foils. Appl. Therm. Eng. **137**, 758–766 (2018)
8. Formentin, S., De Filippi, P., Corno, M., Tanelli, M., Savaresi, S.M.: Data-driven design of braking control systems. IEEE Trans. Control Syst. Technol. **21**, 186–193 (2013)
9. Formentin, S., Karimi, A.: Enhancing statistical performance of data-driven controller tuning via L2-regularization. Automatica **50**, 1514–1520 (2014)
10. Yan, P., Liu, D., Wang, D., Ma, H.: Data-driven controller design for general MIMO nonlinear systems via virtual reference feedback tuning and neural networks. Neurocomputing **171**, 815–825 (2016)
11. Wang, L., Ni, H., Yang, R., Pardalos, P.M., Jia, L., Fei, M.: Intelligent virtual reference feedback tuning and its application to heat treatment electric furnace control. Eng. Appl. Artif. Intell. **46**, 1–9 (2015)
12. Sörensen, K., Sevaux, M., Glover, F.: A history of metaheuristics. In: Martí, R., Panos, P., Resende, M. (eds.) Handbook of Heuristics, pp. 1–18. Springer, Cham (2018). https://doi.org/10.1007/978-3-319-07153-4_4-1
13. Wang, L., Yang, R., Ni, H., Ye, W., Fei, M., Pardalos, P.M.: A human learning optimization algorithm and its application to multi-dimensional knapsack problems. Appl. Soft Comput. **34**, 736–743 (2015)
14. Campi, M.C., Lecchini, A., Savaresi, S.M.: Virtual reference feedback tuning: a direct method for the design of feedback controllers. Automatica **38**, 1337–1346 (2002)
15. von Krogh, G.: Individualist and collectivist perspectives on knowledge in organizations: implications for information systems research. J. Strat. Inf. Syst. **18**, 119–129 (2009)
16. Hansen, M.T.: The search-transfer problem: the role of weak ties in sharing knowledge across organization subunits. Adm. Sci. Q. **44**, 82–111 (1999)
17. Wang, L., Ni, H., Yang, R., Fei, M., Ye, W.: A simple human learning optimization algorithm. In: Fei, M., Peng, C., Su, Z., Song, Y., Han, Q. (eds.) LSMS/ICSEE 2014. CCIS, vol. 462, pp. 56–65. Springer, Heidelberg (2014). https://doi.org/10.1007/978-3-662-45261-5_7
18. Wang, L., Ni, H., Yang, R., Pardalos, P.M., Du, X., Fei, M.: An adaptive simplified human learning optimization algorithm. Inf. Sci. **320**, 126–139 (2015)
19. Normey-Rico, J.E., Camacho, E.F.: Unified approach for robust dead-time compensator design. J. Process Control **19**, 38–47 (2009)
20. Åström, K.J., Hägglund, T.: Revisiting the Ziegler-Nichols step response method for PID control. J. Process Control **14**, 635–650 (2004)
21. Wang, L., Yang, R., Pardalos, P.M., Qian, L., Fei, M.: An adaptive fuzzy controller based on harmony search and its application to power plant control. Int. J. Electr. Power Energy Syst. **53**, 272–278 (2013)

Design and Realization of 108MN Multi-function Testing System

Shutao Zheng$^{(\boxtimes)}$, Yu Yang, Zhiyong Qu, and Junwei Han

Harbin Institute of Technilogy, Harbin Heilong Provience, China
{zhengst77, hjw}@hit.edu.cn, yangyu@fyty2010.cm,
quzhiyong@fyty2010.com

Abstract. With the rapid development of China economics, large buildings are beginning to appear. In order to ensure safety of the large buildings, 108MN Multi-Function Testing System (MFTS) built by HIT with 6-DOF and large loading force was proposed by China State Construction Engineering Corporation (CSCEC), which can research and evaluate the seismic performance of structures such as long columns building, cross shape joints, shear walls and 8 floors full scale building. This paper shows you the base function, system main structure parameter and performance characteristics of MFTS, detailed design process was given, inverse kinematics model based Hydraulic servosystem and compound control model of force and displacement were built to analysis the performance, simulation analysis results show that the MFTS can meet design requirements and the proposed controller has good abilities. The related experiments will be tested after MFTS is built.

Keywords: Seismic · Inverse kinematics model · Hydraulic servosystem
Mixed controller

1 Introduction

As everyone knows, earthquake has extensive damage for building structure etc. which lead to loss of many people's lives and impact on the local economy (e.g. 1994 Northridge earthquake which occurred on January 17 with 60 deaths and property damage between \$13 billion and \$50 billion; 1995 Hyogo-ken Nambu earthquake which occurred on January 17 with over 5000 deaths and property damage \$150 billion [1]; 2008 wenchuan earthquake which occurred on May 12 with 69225 deaths and property damage RMB 8451 hundreds of millions [2]). In order to reduce the destroy associated with large earthquakes, the seismic performance of building structures should be evaluated. Because of the simulation models are often inconformity to capture complex response, and the seismic characteristics is difficult to be precise evaluated when multi-dimensional and continuously varying are acting on large and complex building structure during earthquakes [3, 4], many large scale structural seismic tables have been built and used for performance evaluation. The University of Minnesota's Multi-Axial Subassemblage Testing (MAST) [5] System provides a powerful tool for investigating effects of earthquakes with 6-DOF control system and high speed data acquisition system, the Multi-Axial Testing System (MATS) in the

© Springer Nature Singapore Pte Ltd. 2018
K. Li et al. (Eds.): ICSEE 2018/IMIOT 2018, CCIS 924, pp. 321–329, 2018.
https://doi.org/10.1007/978-981-13-2384-3_30

NCREE [6], E-Defense [7] which is the largest 3-D shaking table in the world, the Multi-Axial Full-Scale Sub-Structured Testing and Simulation Facility (MUST-SIM) is a state-of-the-art physical and analytical simulation facility [8], SRMD [9] consists of prestressed concrete reaction frame and a moving platen with four hydrostatic low friction hydraulic has the ability to test dampers and isolator bearings. Above those loading facilities have the capacity of multiaxis, multifunctional and full-scale tests which greatly fulfil the experiment demand for buildings.

China is the country with frequent earthquakes, large high-rise buildings and complex structural bridges are becoming more and more with the rapid economic development, 108MN Multi-Function Testing System (MFTS) with high speed and large-scale loading force was proposed and developed jointed by CSCEC (China State Construction Engineering Corporation) and HIT (Harbin Institute of Technology), which can provide real-time, full-scale, 6-DOF dynamic and static performance testing for bearings and all kinds of structural components including shear walls, long columns, and complex cross shape joints. MFTS is full scale and multi scope powerful experiment tool in earthquake engineering research field when it is finished.

First the paper gives the main construct and characteristics of MFTS,then shows the detailed design and analysis process,the inverse kinematics model based hydraulic servosystem of MFTS is derived for understanding the characteristics of the system, a mixed controller with loading force in out loop and displacement in inner loop is designed to resolve the control problem of MFTS, simulation and experiment shows the MFTS has good control performance.

2   MFTS Description

Figure 1 shows the main components of the MFTS, 6DOF loading system is the core of MFTS. The MFTS is placed in a 25 m × 25 m × 9 m (length * width * depth) base pit. In order to ensure the system performance requirement, Hydraulic Power Unit (HPU) is provided with 1750 L/min at 21 MPa for system supply and 350 L/min at 14 MPa for pre-stage supply for servo valve and 700 L/min at 21 MPa for system supply or at 31 MPa for accumulator charging. The accumulator is composed of 15,480 L accumulator volume and 19,440 L gas volume pressurized up to 31 MPa. The oil tank is 68 m^3 for oil storage. The 6DOF loading system is made up of 18 actuators, and a loading platform which can simultaneously impose different vertical loading force and double direction horizontal displacement. Isolation system with 52 vibration isolators is placed between reinforced concrete base and concrete base to prevent the impact on the surrounding facilities when the MFTS is working. Four lift cylinders can drive the movable platform move to adjust the distance between 6-DOF loading system and movable platform for adapting to different parts.

The performance parameter of the MFTS are summarized in Table 1. MFTS can satisfy four kinds of specimens including long column, shear wall, complex cross shape joints, and rubber bearings. Testing objectives range from slow-speed unidirectional testing for basic performance characterization to high-speed, 3-D dynamic testing for energy-based analysis. The clearance for specimen installation is up to 9.1 m × 6.6 m in plane and up to 10 m in height between movable platform and 6-DOF loading

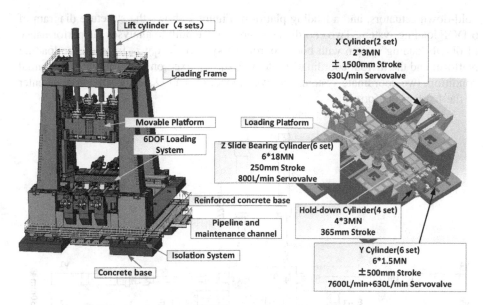

Fig. 1. MFTS overall structure and 6-DOF loading system

system. In order to solve the problem of 108MN large loading force in Z direction, Static pressure support actuators with very low friction are adopted which are fixed together with the loading platform.

Table 1. Perfomance parameter of MFTS

Degree of freedom	x	y	z
Loading force	6MN(tension)	±6MN (dynamic)	108MN
	10MN (compression)	±9MN	(Compression)
Velocity (mm/s)	±53	±1571	±22
Displacement (mm)	±1500	±500	250
Relative platform rot.	±2° (φ)	±2° (θ)	±10° (ψ)
Capacity of specimen	9.1 m (length) × 6.6 m (width) × 10 m (height)		

3   System Modeling

According to the above description, MFTS is a complex loading system. System modeling should be derived to analyze the system characteristics. This section shows the system model and mixed controller adopt displacement and force.

3.1   Inverse Kinematics

6DOF loading system of the MFTS is composed of Y-direction hydraulics cylinder with 6, X-direction hydraulic cylinder with 2, Z-direction hydraulic cylinder with 6, 4 hold-down actuators, and a loading platform. Figure 2 shows the structure diagram of 6-DOF loading system. Two coordinate systems were built to analyses the performance of 6DOF loading system with body coordinate system O_p-$x_p y_p z_p$ fixed on the loading platform and the inertial coordinate system O_b-$x_b y_b z_b$ fixed on the ground. In the initial condition, two coordinate systems are overlapped, O_b and O_p at the top surface center of the loading platform.

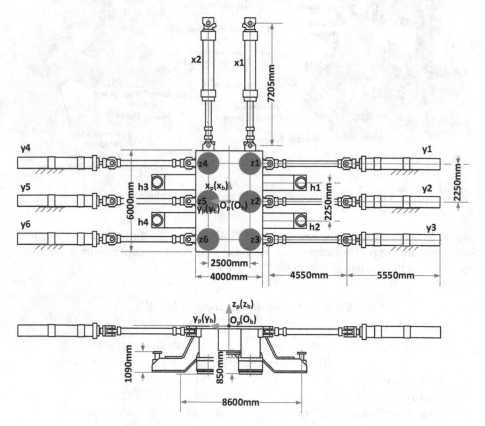

Fig. 2. Schematic diagram of 6DOF loading system

Figure 3 shows you the three kinds of articulated joints in the system: x direction (a) is SPS (P-prismatic joint, S-spherical joint, E-epitaxy), y direction (b) is PSS, and the z direction ((c) is EPS which including z1 ∼ z6 and h1 ∼ h4).

The inverse kinematics model of x direction is as following:

$$l_i = \left\| R(q_o)a_i - b_i + q_p \right\| = \left\| g_i - b_i \right\| \ (i = 1, 2) \tag{1}$$

where a_i, and g_i are the (3×1) vectors of upper joint point A_i in two coordinate system respectively, b_i is the (3×1) vector of the lower joint point B_i in O_b-$x_b y_b z_b$. R_i is a rotation matrix of transformation from O_p-$x_p y_p z_p$ to O_b-$x_b y_b z_b$. $q_p = [x \ \ y \ \ z]^T$ is the

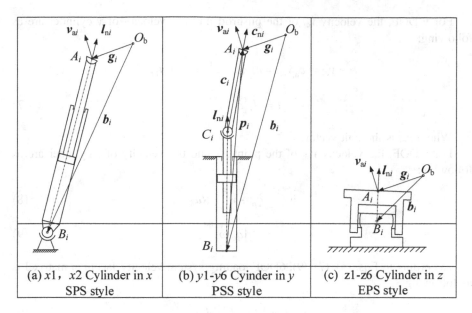

(a) $x1$, $x2$ Cylinder in x SPS style	(b) $y1$-$y6$ Cyinder in y PSS style	(c) $z1$-$z6$ Cylinder in z EPS style

Fig. 3. Structure diagram of three types kinematic chains

position vector, $q_o = [\varphi \quad \theta \quad \psi]^{\mathrm{T}}$ the orientation vector, $\| \ \|$ is the Euclidean norm operator, l_i is the ith actuator length.

For Y direction, the jth actuator length vector l_j is as following:

$$p_j = p_j - c_j = g_j - b_j - c_j \ (j = 1, 2, 3, 4, 5, 6) \tag{2}$$

For Z direction, the kth actuator length vector l_k is as following:

$$l_k = z_{ak} - z_{bk}/z_{nk} \ (k = 1, 2, 3, 4, 5, 6) \tag{3}$$

According to the Eqs. (1), (2), and (3), 6DOF loading system's inverse kinematic can be obtained.

3.2 6DOF Loading System Jacobian Matrix

6DOF loading system Jacobian matrix shows the relationship between the loading platform and the actuator lengths.

For x DOF, the velocity v_{ai} of upper joint point A_i and the velocity of x cylinder are as following:

$$v_{ai} = \dot{q}_p + w \times Ra_i \tag{4}$$

$$\dot{l} = J_x [\dot{q}_p \omega]^T \tag{5}$$

For y DOF, the velocity v_{cj} of the pushrod and the velocity of y cylinder are as following:

$$v_{ci} = c_{nj}^T v_{aj} = c_{nj}^T \dot{q}_p + c_{nj}^T (w \times Ra_j) \tag{6}$$

$$\dot{l} = J_y [\dot{q}_p \ \omega]^T \tag{7}$$

Where c_{ni} is the unit vector.

For z DOF, the velocity v_{nk} of the point A_k and the velocity of z cylinder are as following:

$$v_{nk} = \dot{q}_p + w \times Ra_k \tag{8}$$

$$\dot{l} = J_z [\dot{q}_p \ \omega]^T \tag{9}$$

According to Eqs. (5), (7), (9), 6DOF loading system velocity Jacobian matrix J is as following:

$$J = [J_x \ J_y \ J_z] \tag{10}$$

3.3   Controller Design

Controller of MFTS is mainly used to control the displacement and pose of the loading platform accurately, according to the system requirement Z direction is force control in outer loop and position control in inner loop and other five direction is position control. Figure 4 shows you the structure of controller, in order to speed up the simulation and

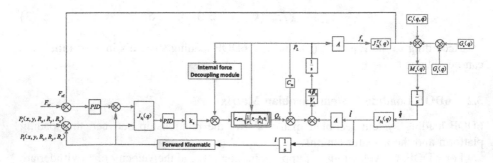

Fig. 4. Structure diagram of MFTS controller

check the control effect, Matlab/Simulink was used to develop the control system model and XPC-target real time kernel are adopted to run control model, the sample time is 1 ms.

4 Simulation Experiments

According to the requirement, seven cycle of Y direction is designed to performed to validate the performance of the proposed controller, Fig. 5 shows the neoprene pad test of MFTS. Four hold-down cylinders can provide 12MN downward force to prevent the loading platform tip-over. Only z DOF is force mode and other five DOFs are position mode. Because of the max velocity need the large flow and large power, only 7 cycles $(A = 0.2$ m, $f = 0.5$ Hz) in y direction were designed to guarantee test and the start and the end are half cycle and six whole cycle. Figure 6 shows that the curve has a good position dynamic tracking ability as (a), z direction force keeps changing(c) between 57.5MN and 62.5MN because of the displacement fluctuation.

Fig. 5. Neoprene pad test of MFTS

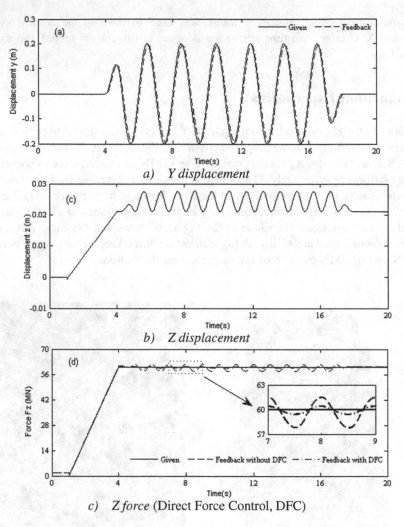

a) *Y displacement*

b) *Z displacement*

c) *Z force* (Direct Force Control, DFC)

Fig. 6. Test curve of Neoprene pad based MFTS

5   Conclusion

In order to satisfy the requirement of China's economic development, MFTS was proposed to build. The system structure and performance characteristics of MFTS were given which is a 6DOF static and dynamic real-time testing facility. In order to better analysis the system characteristics, the 18 cylinders inverse kinematics model and Jacobian matrix are built. Mix controller structure was given and simulation model was built. Finally, an experiment of neoprene pad to check whether the mixed controller can be used. The results demonstrate that MFTS can use the proposed controller to gain good effect.

References

1. Elnashai, A.S., Di Sarno, L.: Fundamentals of Earthquake Engineering, pp. 18–19. Wiley Press, Chicheste (2008)
2. http://www.baike.com/wiki/wenchuanearthquake
3. Gao, C., Zheng, S., Cong, D., Han, J., Yang, Z., Sun, J.: Modeling and control of the CSCEC multi-function testing system. J. Earthq. Eng. **22**, 1–14 (2016)
4. Nakata, N., Spencer, B.F.: Multi-dimensional hybrid simulation using a six-actuator self-reaction loading system. In: The 14th World Conference on Earthquake Engineering, China (2008)
5. http://nees.umn.edu
6. Chen, J.C., Lin, T.H., Chen, P.C., Lin, K.C., Tsai, K.C.: Advanced seismic testing using the multi-axial testing system (MATS) in NCREE. In: Proceedings of the 3rd International Conference on Advances in Experimental Structural Engineering, San Francisco (2009)
7. Xianchang, L.: E-defense and research tests. J. Earthq. Eng. Eng. Vib. **28**(4), 111–116 (2008)
8. http://www.structures.ucsd.edu/
9. Shortreed, J.S., Benzoni, G.: Characterization and testing of the caltrans seismic response modification device test system. Philos. Trans. Roy. Soc. Math. Phys. Eng. Sci. **359**(1786), 1829–1850 (2001)

Research on Vibration Suppression for Boom Luffing of Telescopic Boom Aerial Work Platform

Ru-Min Teng[✉], Xin Wang[✉], Ji-Zhao Wang[✉],
and Ji-Fei Liang[✉]

Mechanical and Engineering Department, Dalian University of Technology,
Dalian 116024, Liaoning, People's Republic of China
tengrumin@163.com, 1063140310@qq.com,
1296151011@qq.com, 3234875883@qq.com

Abstract. With the increase in the length of the boom for aerial work vehicles, the boom vibrates in rapid motion. Therefore, how to suppress the boom vibration and achieve good stability and safety is significant. Based on the research of telescopic boom aerial vehicles, the mathematical models of the link hydraulic system of telescopic boom aerial vehicles are established. According to the state equation of the boom system, the feedback gain vector is designed based on the linear quadratic optimal control theory, the feedback value is fed back to the signal input end of the solenoid valve to construct the closed loop control system which restrains the boom vibration, and the simulation of the closed loop control system is made to analyze the vibration suppression effect of the boom. Through the control of luffing motion, a vibration control method of telescopic boom aerial vehicle is put forward, which has a good reference function for similar products.

Keywords: Aerial work platform · Hydraulic system · Vibration suppression
Feedback

1 Introduction

Aerial work platforms are widely used in building, manufacturing and maintenance. The vibration will be generated on the platform when the boom luffing motion occurs. Especially while the boom works with full boom extension, the vibration is obvious. So it is necessary to study the vibration suppression for improving the quality of the aerial work platform.

Now the researches mainly aimed at the study of the state equation, dynamic analysis and vibration suppression. For example, the mathematical model of the folding aerial platforms was established by Jing through the Lagrange equations [1]; Tan proposed a rapid method of acquiring modal parameters for the high platform fire engine [2]; Sawodny of the University of Stuttgart, Germany designed a kind of motion planner for the boom elevation angle of the fire ladder car [3], and got the state space equation of the boom system [4–6]. Based on study of vibration suppression, this paper adds the electro-hydraulic proportional control model and a new control system is built.

© Springer Nature Singapore Pte Ltd. 2018
K. Li et al. (Eds.): ICSEE 2018/IMIOT 2018, CCIS 924, pp. 330–341, 2018.
https://doi.org/10.1007/978-981-13-2384-3_31

2 Modeling Electro-Hydraulic Proportional Control System

An electro-hydraulic proportional control system is applied to determinate the displacement of the hydraulic cylinders, and the specific working theory of the system is shown in Fig. 1.

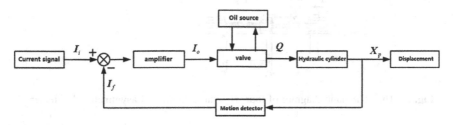

Fig. 1. The schematic diagram of electro-hydraulic proportional position control system of hydraulic system

1. Transfer function of the proportional amplifier

$$G_1(s) = \frac{I_0(s)}{I_i(s)} = K_a \tag{1}$$

where, K_a - Proportional amplification factor.

2. Transfer function of electro-hydraulic proportional valve

The transfer function of the proportional valve output flow Q to the input current I is [8]:

$$G_{sv} = \frac{Q(s)}{I(s)} = \frac{K_{sv}}{\frac{s^2}{w_{sv}^2} + \frac{2\zeta_{sv}}{w_{sv}}s + 1} \tag{2}$$

where, K_{sv} - Proportional valve gain, $m^3/s \cdot A$; $m^3/s \cdot A$
   w_{sv} - The natural frequency of the proportional valve, rad/s;
   ζ_{sv} - Proportional valve damping ratio.

3. The transfer function of the hydraulic cylinder

Modeling the transfer function based on symmetrical valve control theory [8–11]. Figure 2 is a schematic diagram of the asymmetric hydraulic cylinder based on the four-way valve. Table 1 shows the parameters of the cylinder.

In the symmetrical valve asymmetric cylinder system, the effective area acting on the hydraulic cylinder is inconsistent when the hydraulic cylinder is extended and retracted. As a result, the open loop gain of the transfer function is not equal when the hydraulic cylinder stays extended and retracted. Therefore, different situations need to be considered separately [8].

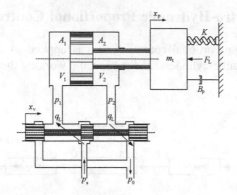

Fig. 2. The schematic diagram of four-way valve-controlled asymmetrical cylinder

Table 1. The parameters of luffing cylinder

	Name	Symbol	Value	Unit
Variable luff hydraulic cylinder	Hydraulic cylinder inner diameter	D	200	mm
	Piston rod diameter	d	140	mm
	Cylinder stroke	L	1902	mm
	Rodless cavity area	A_1	31415.93	mm^2
	Rod cavity area	A_2	16024.65	mm^2
	Effective area ratio of two cavities	n	0.51	
	Fluid equivalent elastic modulus	β_e	1.4×10^9	Pa
	Drive equivalent load	m	11551.02	kg
	Hydraulic damping ratio	ζ_n	0.3	
	Natural frequency	w_h	37.09	rad/s

4. The transfer function of the displacement sensor

$$K_s = \frac{I_{max}}{L_{max}} \tag{3}$$

among, I_{max} - Maximum output current value of the sensor output, A;
   L_{max} - Maximum length of the sensor measurement, m.

5. Luffing hydraulic control system mathematical model

Through the solution of the transfer function, the final system block diagram is shown in Fig. 3.

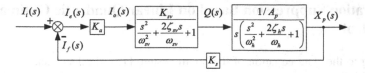

Fig. 3. The block diagram of valve-controlled cylinder electro-hydraulic proportional position control system

3   The Geometric Relationship Between the Expansion of the Hydraulic Cylinder and the Luffing Angle

The luffing angle is achieved by controlling the displacement of the luffing hydraulic cylinder, so the geometric relationship of the expansion and luffing angle of the hydraulic cylinder can be derived. The structure dimension diagram of the telescopic boom aerial platform is shown in Fig. 4.

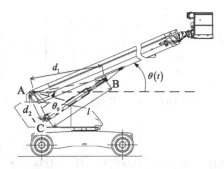

Fig. 4. The dimension of telescopic boom aerial platform

d_1 - the distance between A and B. The A indicates the hinges between the boom and the turntable, B indicates the hinge point between the boom and the variable luff hydraulic cylinder;

d_2 - the distance between A and C. C indicates the hinge point between the turntable and the variable luff hydraulic cylinder;

l - luffing hydraulic cylinder length;

θ_0 - When the boom is in horizontal position, the angle between AB and AC;

$\theta(t)$ - luffing angle.

According to the triangular relationship:

$$\cos(\theta + \theta_0) = \frac{d_1^2 + d_2^2 - l_2}{2d_1 d_2} \tag{4}$$

4 Vibration Suppression Based on Linear Quadratic Optimal Control

According to the state equation of the boom system [12], the feedback gain vector is designed by linear quadratic optimal control theory, and the feedback signal is input into the electro-hydraulic proportional valve and the closed loop control system is constructed to suppress the vibration of the boom. The control system is simulated in the Simulink and the effect of vibration suppression is analyzed.

4.1 Design Based on Linear Quadratic Controller

In Wang master's thesis [13], the state equation of the boom is:

$$\dot{x} = Ax + Bu$$
$$y = Cx + Du$$

among,

$$A = \begin{bmatrix} 0 & 1 & 0 & 0 \\ -17.99 & -0.424 & 0 & 0 \\ 0 & 0 & 0 & 1 \\ 0 & 0 & -538.9 & -0.232 \end{bmatrix}, B = \begin{bmatrix} 0 \\ 10355 \\ 0 \\ 65822 \end{bmatrix}$$

$$C = [0.00191 \quad 0 \quad -0.00095 \quad 0], D = 0$$

Output deviation is

$$e(t) = y(t) = Cx(t) + Du(t) = [0.00191 \quad 0 \quad -0.00095 \quad 0]x(t) - u(t) \quad (5)$$

Because output $y(t)$ and input $u(t)$ are one-dimensional functions, the weight function Q and R can be represented by the constant Q and R. The optimal objective function (6) is

$$J = \frac{1}{2}\int_0^\infty \left\{ x^T(t)(C^T qC)x(t) + u^T(t)(D^T qD + r)u(t) + 2x^T(t)(C^T qD)u(t) \right\} dt \quad (6)$$

further,

$$J = \frac{1}{2}\int_0^\infty \left[x^T(t)Q_1 x(t) + u^T(t)R_1 u(t) + 2x^T(t)N_1 u(t) \right] dt \quad (7)$$

among, $Q_1 = C^T qC, R_1 = D^T qD + r, N = C^T qD$

For q = 0.05, r = 1 and C, D is known, the feedback gain vector is obtained through MATLAB optimal control toolbox:

$$[-0.5318 \quad 0.6443 \quad 0.5337 \quad 0.0578] \times 10^{-4}$$

4.2 Vibration Response Analysis Based on Linear Quadratic Optimal Control

Figure 5 is a simulation model based on the linear quadratic optimal control. After the state equation coefficient matrix C and D are adjusted, the state variable of the boom is obtained on the basis of the boom output angular displacement and the speed of the boom tip. According to the previous feedback gain vector obtained, the feedback value of the LQR optimal control is calculated and fed back to the signal input end of the solenoid valve, and the flow of the solenoid valve is adjusted to control the motion of the hydraulic cylinder, then, the vibration suppression of the boom is achieved. Meanwhile, the linear acceleration response of boom tip can be obtained by deriving.

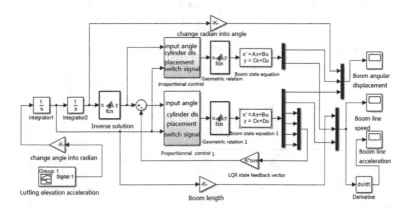

Fig. 5. The simulation model based on linear quadratic suboptimal control

4.2.1 Design of Luffing Angle

The boom luffing motion is designed that the boom luffing angle rises from 0° to 32° at the first stage and stays with a interval. At the second stage, the angle changes to 47°, then the boom luffing angle declines to 32°, then to 16°. The acceleration changed curve of the boom luffing angle is shown in Fig. 6, and the specific data is shown in Table 2.

4.2.2 Response Analysis of the Boom Angular Displacement

Figure 7 is the angular displacement response curve of the boom. At the beginning, it is not easy to observe because of the superposition of the vibration and the luffing. Therefore, in order to facilitate the expression, this paper uses the method of analyzing

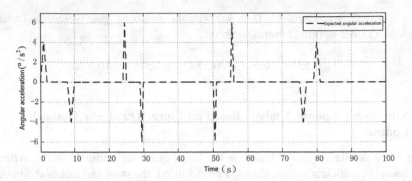

Fig. 6. The curve of acceleration variation of boom luffing angel

Table 2. Acceleration variation of the boom angle

Operation stage	Time (s)	Change time of boom acceleration (s)	Maximum acceleration (°/s²)	Boom working time at uniform speed (s)
First rise	0–10	2	±4	6
Second rise	24–30	1	±6	4
First decline	50–56	1	±6	4
Second decline	75–81	2	±4	22

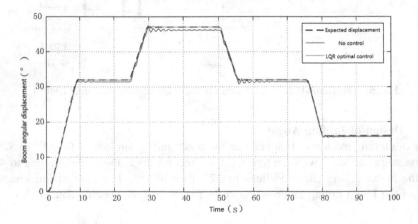

Fig. 7. The response of angel displacement of boom tip

the residual vibration, and extracts the boom tip angular displacement curve in the four stages. Figures 8 and 9 are respectively the boom angular displacement response curve in rising stage and decline stage.

Figure 8, The specific change of expected angular displacement, angular displacement under uncontrolled condition and the angular displacement under LQR control are shown in Tables 3 and 4.

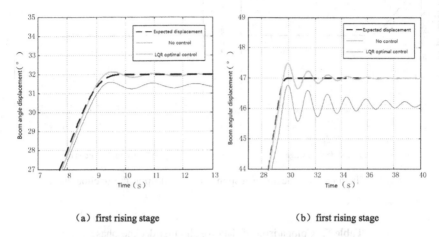

(a) first rising stage　　　　　　　　　(b) first rising stage

Fig. 8. The angel displacement response of boom tip at the rising stage

Table 3. Comparison of data for the first ascending phase

Control method	Peak (°)	Phases (°)	The difference between peaks and troughs (°)	Steady state value (°)
Desired angular displacement	–	–	–	32
uncontrolled	31.59	31.25	0.34	31.41
LQR optimal control	32.14	31.97	0.17	31.97

Table 4. Data comparison for the second ascending phase

Control method	Peak (°)	Phases (°)	The difference between peaks and troughs (°)	Steady state value (°)
Desired angular displacement	–	–	–	47
uncontrolled	46.78	45.58	1.2	46.21
LQR optimal control	47.5	46.65	0.85	47

Figure 9, The specific change of expected angular displacement, angular displacement under uncontrolled condition and the angular displacement under LQR control are shown in Tables 5 and 6.

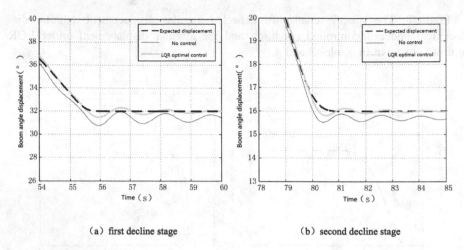

(a) first decline stage   (b) second decline stage

Fig. 9. The angel displacement response of boom tip at the decline stage

Table 5. Comparison of data for the first decline phase

Control method	Peak (°)	Phases (°)	The difference between peaks and troughs (°)	Steady state value (°)
Desired angular displacement	–	–	–	32
uncontrolled	31.96	30.76	1.2	31.41
LQR optimal control	32.32	31.47	0.85	31.97

Table 6. Comparison of data for the second decline phase

Control method	Peak (°)	Phases (°)	The difference between peaks and troughs (°)	Steady state value (°)
Desired angular displacement	–	–	–	16
uncontrolled	15.87	15.53	0.34	15.7
LQR optimal control	16.12	15.81	0.31	15.99

Through the response analysis of the angular displacement of the boom tip, it can be found that the vibration of the boom is suppressed by the LQR optimal control. As time increases, the suppression effect is more and more obvious. In addition, although the angle displacement of the boom tip has some overshoot, the steady-state value is basically same with the expected value, which eliminates the steady-state deviation. And through data analysis, it can be found that the angular displacement response of the boom tip is basically consistent when the LQR optimal control system stays at the rising and decline stages.

4.2.3 The Response Analysis of the Boom Tip Line Speed

The boom line speed analysis process is consistent with the analysis process of the boom angle displacement, and no specific data analysis is performed here. Figure 10 shows the boom tip line speed response curve.

Figure 11 is the response curve of the boom line speed in the rising phase. Through observation, it is known that the system based on LQR optimal control has more and more obvious advantage, and the speed of the tip line speed tends to be stable after fifth cycles.

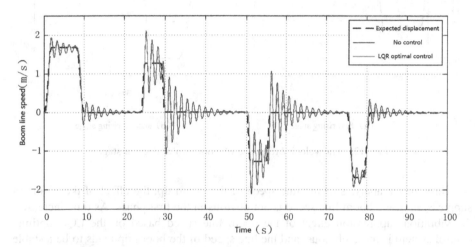

Fig. 10. The velocity response of boom tip

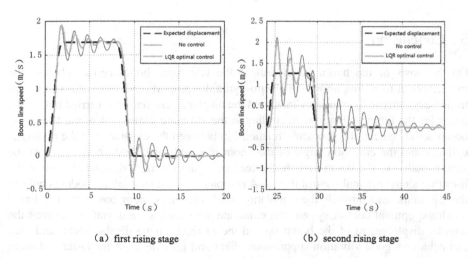

(a) first rising stage   (b) second rising stage

Fig. 11. The velocity response of boom tip at rising stage

Figure 12 is the response curve of the tip line speed at the decline stage. Under the same variable luffing angle, the effect of LQR optimal control is almost consistent with the rising stage, namely, the vibration luffing and vibration attenuation time are basically consistent.

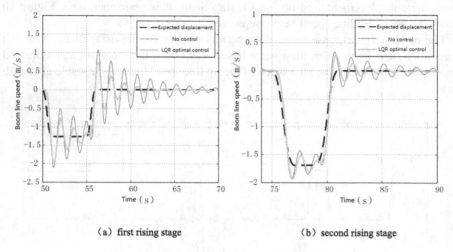

(a) first rising stage   (b) second rising stage

Fig. 12. The velocity response of boom tip at decline stage

Through the analysis of the line speed of the boom tip, the effect of the vibration suppression of the boom line speed is not obvious in the first phase. As time increases, the vibration suppression effect of the boom line speed based on the LQR optimal control system is more obvious, and the line speed of the boom tip tends to be a stable value of 0 after about four to five cycles. Compared with the uncontrolled system, the system has a good effect on suppressing the vibration of the boom.

5 Conclusion

On the basis of the hydraulic system of the telescopic boom aerial vehicles, the mathematical modeling about the electro-hydraulic proportional valve, the valve controlled asymmetric hydraulic cylinder and the displacement sensor is carried out in this paper for the luffing vibration; According to the structure dimension of the telescopic boom aerial vehicle, the geometric relationship between the expansion of the hydraulic cylinder and the elevation angle of the boom is established. And on the basis of the state equation of the boom system, the feedback gain vector is designed by using the linear quadratic optimal control theory. A complete system simulation model is built in the Simulink and through the simulation analysis, the system based on the linear quadratic optimal control system can eliminate the steady-state deviation between the angular displacement of the boom tip and the expected angle displacement, and then can achieve a good vibration suppression effect and provide ideas for faster and more stable motion of the aerial platform vehicle.

References

1. Jing, Y.L., Xiong, J.Q., Wang, F.L.: Application of input shaper in anti-swing control of folding aerial work vehicles. Noise Vibr. Syst. (4), 38–42 (2011). (in Chinese)
2. Tan, J.H.: Dynamic analysis and vibration control of fire truck boom based on platform. Xiangtan University, Xiangtan (2014). (in Chinese)
3. Sawodny, O., Aschemann, H., Bulach, A., Hofer, E.P.: Online generation of trajectories considering kinematic constraints. In: Proceedings of 7th IEEE International Conference on Methods & Models in Automation & Robotics, Miedzydroje, Poland, pp. 7133–7188 (2001)
4. Sawodny, O., Lambeck, S., Hildebrandt, A.: Trajectory generation for the trajectory tracking control of a fire rescue turntable ladder. In: Proceedings of the Third International Workshop on Robot Motion and Control, RoMoCo 2002, pp. 411–416 (2002)
5. Zuyev, A., Sawodny, O.: Observer design for a flexible manipulator model with a payload. In: Proceedings of 45th IEEE International Conference on Decision and Control, pp. 4490–4495 (2006)
6. Kharitonov, A., Zimmert, N., Sawodny, O.: Active oscillation damping of the fire-rescue turntable ladder. In: Proceedings of the IEEE Conference on Control Applications, pp. 391–396 (2007)
7. Yang, Z.R., Hua, K.Q., Xu, Y.: Electro-Hydraulic Ratio and Servo Control. Metallurgical Industry Press, Beijing (2009). (in Chinese)
8. Wu, Z.S.: Hydraulic Control System. Higher Education Press, Beijing (2008). (in Chinese)
9. Zhao, C.L.: Adaptive controller and its application in valve-controlled asymmetric cylinder speed system. Harbin Institute of Technology, Heilongjiang (2006). (in Chinese)
10. Zhang, Y.: Discrete adaptive controller in valve-controlled asymmetric cylinder electro-hydraulic servo system. Harbin Institute of Technology, Heilongjiang (2008). (in Chinese)
11. Zhang, L.C.: Adaptive controller and its application in valve-controlled asymmetric cylinder force system. Harbin Institute of Technology, Heilongjiang (2006). (in Chinese)
12. Gao, L.C.: Research on vibration suppression of vertical arm system of aerial work vehicle. Dalian University of Technology, Liaoning (2015). (in Chinese)
13. Wang, J.Z.: Study on amplitude suppression of arm boom for telescopic boom aerial work truck. Dalian University of Technology, Dalian (2016). (in Chinese)

Intrusion Detection in SCADA System: A Survey

Pu Zeng and Peng Zhou[✉]

School of Mechatronic Engineering and Automation, Shanghai University,
Shanghai 200072, China
{plovehui, pzhou}@shu.edu.cn

Abstract. Nowadays, the industrial systems are more and more interconnected with the outside world. However, the interconnection of Supervisory Control and Data Acquisition (SCADA) systems with the outside world using Internet-based standards introduce numerous vulnerabilities to these systems. Although awareness is constantly rising, the SCADA systems are still exposed to serious threats. In this paper, a review of Intrusion Detection and report results is conducted in the surveyed works. In the end, we also discuss the potential research directions on this topic.

Keywords: Intrusion Detection · SCADA system · Survey · Machine learning

1 Introduction

The importance of Supervisory Control and Data Acquisition (SCADA) systems has increased in the past years [1]. And there are more and more cyber incidents in recent years, which have caused serious damage to the critical infrastructures with very important economic losses, especially after the Stuxnet incident in 2010 [2]. The malware which was targeting the PLCs connected to a nuclear centrifuge, and its ultimate goal was to sabotage the nuclear plant. Besides, a city water utility was hacked (2011) [3], fully demonstrated the great threat of attacks to industrial control systems.

Intrusion Detection technology is becoming a major research direction for solving the problem of attacks to SCADA systems which detect attacks by analyzing network characteristics (such as network traffic, packet loss rate, etc.) after occurring of attacks. During the last years, many papers about the Intrusion Detection in SCADA system were reported [9–29]. Therefore, we will make a survey about them in this paper.

This paper is organized as follows: background on SCADA systems is reviewed in Sect. 2. Taxonomy of detection approach is overviewed in Sect. 3. Intrusion Detection methodologies are discussed in Sect. 4. This paper is ended with the final conclusion in Sect. 6.

2 Background

In this section, we propose some necessary introduction of SCADA systems to support the argumentation in next sections.

© Springer Nature Singapore Pte Ltd. 2018
K. Li et al. (Eds.): ICSEE 2018/IMIOT 2018, CCIS 924, pp. 342–351, 2018.
https://doi.org/10.1007/978-981-13-2384-3_32

2.1 Supervisory Control and Data Acquisition

Supervisory control: SCADA systems are highly distuributed, so that they can be used to control critical infrastructure, which often distributes over thousands of square kilometers. Though SCADA system, managers can monitor and control field sites over long-distance communication networks.

Data acquisition: SCADA systems collect data from one or more distant facilities. Then they display the data to the operators graphically or textually and transfer it to a central computer facility so that to record it and log it in the system databases.

Data acquisition allows the operators not only monitor but also control the system in real time, and to send control instructions to those facilities [1]. Therefore, the system makes supervisory control possible. Common SCADA systems include SCADA electric power grids, SCADA gas pipelines, SCADA water networks and SCADA storage tanks. In this paper, we mainly survey papers which make research in electric power systems.

2.2 Components of SCADA System

There are four main components of SCADA systems [39]:

- The Human Machine Interface (HMI) is not only a hardware but also a software which can display process status information, reports, and other information to systems.
- The Master Terminal Unit (MTU), which can also be called SCADA Server, give all commands to other different components of SCADA system. The MTU gathers data, stores some information about system and pass other to associated components.
- The Remote Terminal Units (RTUs) or remote telemetry units, can converts sensor signals to digital data. So it can support SCADA remote stations as a data acquisition and control unit designed. The RTUs gather information from different devices and keep it in the memory. When MTU needs it, RTUs code and transmit the information back to the MTU.
- The Programmable Logic Controllers (PLCs) are small industrial computers which are connected to the physical process sensors and convert sensor signals to digital data. Because PLCs are more economical, flexible and versatile than RTUs, they are sometimes implemented as field devices instead of RTUs.

2.3 Security of SCADA System

Threats by insiders include employees who introduce malware into control systems which are extremely dangerous. Knowledgeable insiders could control systems without connected networks [5]. And other kinds of security threats would also cause serious damage to critical infrastructure, especially threats by nation-states which could get many resources for attacking the SCADA system by highly capable organizations [6] (Fig. 1).

Before we make research of intrusion detection, we should make investigation of SCADA vulnerabilities, which can help us understand about how they are exploited for attacks. The SCADA systems can be divided into four major types [7]: security policy,

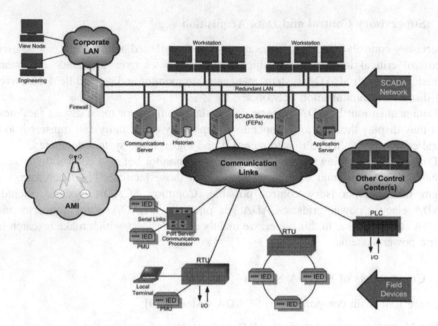

Fig. 1. The SCADA system [1]

communication protocol, architectural and software and hardware vulnerabilities. Nowadays, SCADA system have become more and more complicated not only in software but also in hardware. The model of attacks is shown in Fig. 2.

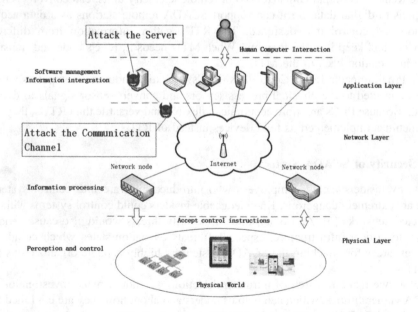

Fig. 2. Attacks in SCADA system [4]

3 Taxonomy of Detection Method

In this section, we introduce taxonomy of detection approach, which can be roughly divided into three categories: data-based method, model-based method and information security method [3].

3.1 Data-Based Method

The data-based method uses pattern recognition techniques and machine learning to analyze data which we acquires from SCADA system. It do not require models of systems and attacks for the detection. The training dataset is observed, such as command signals, sensor measurements and control signals. The benefit of data-based is we can study classification without using the machine learning model directly. There are two main categories of machine learning which is divided into supervised and unsupervised. Classification and regression represent the supervised learning, while clustering represents the unsupervised learning.

3.2 Model-Based Method

The model-based method which develops the SCADA systems models under both proper functioning and different attack scenarios. The comparison between system outputs and observations model makes a decision about whether system is under attack. The system could be considered to be suffer from attacking, when data are not consistent with the normal. This method often requires professional prior knowledge which is based to build a model for attacks detection. And then, we can check the consistency of the observed data with the output of this attack pattern, if the model we build are available.

3.3 Information Security Method

Information security method focuses broadly on three main categories [8]. Firstly, data confidentiality, which is generally performed by access control methods or authentication methods. Secondly, the integrity of data is related to the trustworthiness of data. And the integrity of data is implemented by prevention mechanisms and detection mechanisms. Thirdly, the availability of data is when you need the information or resources you can get them from system. The Dos attacks is a classic example of the data which is unavailability. By using the characteristic of information security, we can improve the security of SCADA systems against attacks

4 Intrusion Detection Methodologies

In this section, we survey existing Intrusion Detection methodologies recent years. Proposals are divided according to the taxonomy described in Sect. 3.

Lahza et al. [9] propose a method which use knowledge of domain to construct new features which include three SCADA-protocol-specific steps. The result of this method have a better performance than those described in previous research used with several other classifiers.

Lin et al. [10] propose a semantic analysis framework. The framework combines Intrusion Detection System (IDS) with a power flow analysis that can estimate the execution results of control commands.

Wan et al. [11] propose a method which use One Class Support Vector Machine (OC-SVM) as the first layer to detect misbehaviors. For the process data behavior, they use Reconstruction Error based on Kernel Principal Component Analysis (RE-KPCA) method to detect data exceptions. This approach has a better performance in classification accuracy than those methods mentioned in the paper.

Shitharth et al. [12] propose an Intrusion Weighted Particle-based Cuckoo Search Optimization (IWP-CSO) method which combines Hierarchical Neuron Architecture based Neural Network (HNA-NN) techniques is proposed in this paper. The IWP-CSO method is used to select the best feature when the input data is clustered. And then, the HNA-NN is used to classify the intrusions in SCADA system.

Sadhasivan et al. [13] propose an approach which uses the Linear Weighted Cuckoo Search Optimization (LWCSO) algorithm to get the best features. A Probabilistic Kernel Model (PKM) is used to update the weight function to form a cluster that represents the best features.

Kleinmann et al. [14] use algorithms which first build a Discrete-Time Markov Chain (DTMC). Then, the symbols are split into sets. And they use the Deterministic Finite Automata (DFA) in the work to build a graph model.

Giuseppe et al. [15] introduce models that are developed with the Control Theory perspective. This research highlights the role of determining the reaction that the monitoring system may experience when it undergoes different types of cyberattacks.

Yang et al. [16] propose detection method based on expert knowledge. The advantage of this method is that it does not take into account the actual operating environment because it has clear advantages over existing more general proposals.

Cruz et al. [17] use an IT-OCSVM method which perform intrusion detection with high accuracy and low overhead in a time step. The algorithm introduced at most a 96.3% detection accuracy and a 2.5% false alarm rate in the experiments.

Bermudez et al. [18] propose a system named FieldHunter. The system which extracts fields and infers their types automatically. And it can detect realistic zero-day attacks on SCADA networks, as result of the valuable information about network protocol specification it provides.

Almalawi et al. [19] propose a method which uses a data-driven clustering method and the DBSCAN is selected as the base clustering algorithms. And the method can identify whether the given system is normal or critical.

Zhou et al. [20] propose a method which use the hidden Markov model. The method is designed to distinguish between attacks and failures and overcome the shortcomings of anomaly detection. The research limits the false alarm rate to less than 1.61%. Besides, the designed system has little influence on the performance of control system.

Erez et al. [21] propose a new domain-aware intrusion detection system. The system can detect unusual changes in SCADA control register values within Modbus/TCP protocols, which use Incremental classification and Single-window classification. The experimental result shows that the system have a 93% classification accuracy. Besides, it has a 0.86% false alarm rate.

Nader et al. [22] propose a work which can detect anomaly. The anomaly will happen after malicious have already passed the IDS. This paper uses machine learning method for anomaly detection by using one-class classification method including SVDD and KPCA.

Yang et al. [23] propose a system which provide a considerate method to solve intrusion detection, by analyzing multiple attributes. And the system uses whitelists and behavior-based concept, so as to make SCADA systems more safety.

Goldenberg et al. [24] propose a method which use the DFA algorithm by an HMI-PLC channel. The DFA-based intrusion detection system delve into Modbus/TCP packets and generate a very detailed model.

Carcano et al. [25] present a method which is based on the critical state analysis and state proximity concepts. Because the detection is based on the system evolution analysis, and not on the analysis of the attack evolution, the IDS can detect also "zero-day attacks".

Yoo et al. [26] propose a method which extracts the main fields from the GOOSE/MMS packets using 3-phase preprocessing. And then they removed outliers by an EM algorithm. Besides, it uses the OCSVM algorithm to learn and detection normal behavior.

Hink et al. [27] propose a power system classification framwork by using machine learning method. With the JRipper + AdaBoost approach, they could dependably classify SCADA system with low false positive rates.

Pan et al. [28] propose a method which uses a Bayesian network graph and gets data logs from the perspective of relay in the SCADA system. The resulting IDS was used to classify data get from the perspective of each relay station.

Pan et al. [29] propose another approach which uses the common paths mining-based method. The common paths is complex specifications which could describe patterns of system behavior connected with SCADA systems. The IDS which is mentioned in this paper correctly classifies 90.4% of tested instances. And the average detection accuracy of this IDS for zero-day attack is 73.43%.

5 Discussion

In this section, we make a discussion about intrusion detection methodologies provided in Sect. 4. We compare recent papers and make Tables 1 and 2 as follows:

Table 1 shows the trend of writing papers about Intrusion Detection in SCADA systems.

As Table 1 shows, the Data-based approach is more used than the other two approaches because of the rapid development of machine learning techniques. And we can see that there are more and more researchers which focus on the security of SCADA systems in recent years.

Table 2 shows the surveyed works of Intrusion Detection in SCADA systems by listing the following metrics: protocol, datasets or testbed, and main detection technique. As Table 2 lists, the systems which use the protocol of Modbus are studied most

Table 1. Papers about Intrusion Detection in SCADA systems

Years	Data-based method	Model-based method	Information security method
2015–2018	[9, 11–13, 17, 19–21, 29]	[10, 14–16, 18]	
2011–2014	[22, 26, 27]	[24, 28]	[23, 25]

Table 2. Comparison of the surveyed works

Author	Ref.	Protocol	Datasets or testbed	Main detect. technique
Lahza et al.	[9]	MMS/GOOSE	Power system	SVM/DT/NN
Lin et al.	[10]	DNP3	Power system	Semantic analysis framework
Wan et al.	[11]	Modbus/TCP	TEP system	OCSVM and RE-KPCA
Shitharth et al.	[12]	No mentioned	ADFA IDS datasets	IWP-CSO and HNA-NN
Sadhasivan et al.	[13]	Modbus	MSU SCADA datasets	LWCSO and PKM
Kleinmann et al.	[14]	S7-0x72	S7-0x72 datasets	DTMC and DFA
Giuseppe et al.	[15]	Modbus/TCP	Water distribution system	Control Theory
Yang et al.	[16]	GOOSE/SMV	Power system	multi-layered IDS
Cruz et al.	[17]	TCP/IP	Power system	IT-OCSVM
Bermudez et al.	[18]	Binary protocols	Power system	FieldHunter
Almalawi et al.	[19]	Modbus/TCP	Water treatment system	DBSCAN
Zhou et al.	[20]	Powerlink/CAN	TEP system	HMM
Erez et al.	[21]	Modbus/TCP	Power system	Incremental classification and Single-window classification
Nader et al.	[22]	No mentioned	Gas Pipeline Testbed and water treatment	SVDD and KPCA
Yang et al.	[23]	IEC 60870-5	Photovoltaic system	Access-Control Whitelists
Goldenberg et al.	[24]	Modbus/TCP	Power system	DFA
Carcano et al.	[25]	Modbus	Boiling Water Reactor	The critical state validation
Yoo H et al.	[26]	MMS/GOOSE	Power system	EM and OCSVM
Hink et al.	[27]	Modbus	MSU SCADA datasets	JRipper + AdaBoost
Pan et al.	[28]	Modbus	MSU SCADA datasets	Bayesian network
Pan et al.	[29]	Modbus	MSU SCADA datasets	Common path algorithm

frequently in the papers we survey. And then, the power systems are the main field that investigators study in, which causes frequent using of Modbus protocol. Mississippi State University SCADA Security Laboratory integrates control systems within numerous critical infrastructure industries to create a testbed and datasets (MSU SCADA datasets) [30]. These datasets are very widely used in various related studies.

6 Conclusion

We present a survey paper comprising three main contributions: (i) a review of current proposals of Intrusion Detection in SCADA system, (ii) a taxonomy to classify existing intrusion detection methodologies and (iii) a comparison of the surveyed works by which we can see the research trends.

Intrusion Detection in SCADA system is still a developing field. With the development of machine learning algorithms [31], researchers achieve a higher detection accuracy. In the future research, we can combine the machine learning methodologies with other approach (such as trust management systems [32, 33], adversarial learning [34, 35] and game theory [36–38]) to get better practical results.

Acknowledgments. This work was partially supported by the National Natural Science Foundation of China (Nos. 61502293, 61775058 and 61633016), the Shanghai Young Eastern Scholar Program (No. QD2016030), the Young Teachers' Training Program for Shanghai College & University, the Science and Technology Commission of Shanghai Municipality (Nos. 18ZR141 5000 and 17511107002) and the Shanghai Key Laboratory of Power Station Automation Technology.

References

1. Nader, P.: One-class classification for cyber intrusion detection in industrial systems. IEEE Trans. Ind. Inf. **10**(4), 2308–2317 (2015)
2. Chen, T.M., Abu-Nimeh, S.: Lessons from Stuxnet. Computer **44**(4), 91–93 (2011)
3. Do, V.L., Fillatre, L., Nikiforov, I., et al.: Feature article: security of SCADA systems against cyber-physical attacks. IEEE Aerosp. Electron. Syst. Mag. **32**(5), 28–45 (2017)
4. Dong, Y., Zhou, P.: Jamming attacks against control systems: a survey. In: Yue, D., Peng, C., Du, D., Zhang, T., Zheng, M., Han, Q. (eds.) LSMS/ICSEE -2017. CCIS, vol. 762, pp. 566–574. Springer, Singapore (2017). https://doi.org/10.1007/978-981-10-6373-2_57
5. Cardenas, A., Amin, S., Sinopoli, B., et al.: Challenges for securing cyber physical systems. In: First Workshop on Cyber-physical Systems Security, vol. 2010, pp. 363–369 (2010)
6. Kushner, D.: The Real Story of Stuxnet. IEEE Spectr. **50**(3), 48–53 (2013)
7. Fovino, I.N., Coletta, A., Masera, M.: Taxonomy of security solutions for the SCADA sector. Joint Research Centre of the European Commission (2010)
8. Bishop M.: Introduction to computer security. In: Euromicro International Conference on Parallel, Distributed, and Network-Based Processing, pp. 170–174. IEEE (2004)
9. Lahza, H., Radke, K., Foo, E.: Applying domain-specific knowledge to construct features for detecting distributed denial-of-service attacks on the GOOSE and MMS protocols. Int. J. Crit. Infrastruct. Prot. **20**, 48–67 (2017)

10. Lin, H., Slagell, A., Kalbarczyk, Z.T., et al.: Runtime semantic security analysis to detect and mitigate control-related attacks in power grids. IEEE Trans. Smart Grid 9(1), 163–178 (2017)

11. Wan, M., Shang, W., Zeng, P.: Double behavior characteristics for one-class classification anomaly detection in networked control systems. IEEE Trans. Inf. Forensics Secur. 12(12), 3011–3023 (2017)

12. Shitharth, S., Winston, D.P.: An enhanced optimization based algorithm for intrusion detection in SCADA network. J. Comput. Secur. 70, 16–26 (2017)

13. Sadhasivan, D.K., Balasubramanian, K.: A novel LWCSO-PKM-based feature optimization and classification of attack types in SCADA network. Arab. J. Sci. Eng. 42(8), 3435–3449 (2017)

14. Kleinmann, A., Wool, A.: Automatic construction of statechart-based anomaly detection models for multi-threaded industrial control systems. ACM Trans. Intell. Syst. Technol. 8(4), 55 (2016)

15. Giuseppe, B., Miciolino, E.E., Pascucci, F.: Monitoring system reaction in cyber-physical testbed under cyber-attacks. Comput. Electr. Eng. 59, 86–98 (2017)

16. Yang, Y., Xu, H.Q., Gao, L., et al.: Multidimensional intrusion detection system for IEC 61850-based SCADA networks. IEEE Trans. Power Deliv. 32(2), 1068–1078 (2017)

17. Cruz, T., Rosa, L., Proença, J., et al.: A cybersecurity detection framework for supervisory control and data acquisition systems. IEEE Trans. Ind. Inf. 12(6), 2236–2246 (2017)

18. Bermudez, I., Iliofotou, M., et al.: Towards automatic protocol field inference. Comput. Commun. 84(C), 40–51 (2016)

19. Almalawi, A., Fahad, A., Tari, Z., et al.: An efficient data-driven clustering technique to detect attacks in SCADA systems. IEEE Trans. Inf. Forensics Secur. 11(5), 893–906 (2016)

20. Zhou, C., Huang, S., Xiong, N., et al.: Design and analysis of multimodel-based anomaly intrusion detection systems in industrial process automation. IEEE Trans. Syst. Man Cybern. Syst. 45(10), 1345–1360 (2015)

21. Erez, N., Wool, A.: Control variable classification, modeling and anomaly detection in Modbus/TCP SCADA systems. Int. J. Crit. Infrastruct. Prot. 10, 59–70 (2015)

22. Nader, P., Honeine, P., Beauseroy, P.: Ip-norms in one-class classification for intrusion detection in SCADA systems. IEEE Trans. Ind. Inf. 10(4), 2308–2317 (2014)

23. Yang, Y., Mclaughlin, K., Sezer, S., et al.: Multiattribute SCADA-specific intrusion detection system for power networks. IEEE Trans. Power Deliv. 29(3), 1092–1102 (2014)

24. Goldenberg, N., Wool, A.: Accurate modeling of Modbus/TCP for intrusion detection in SCADA systems. Int. J. Crit. Infrastruct. Prot. 6(2), 63–75 (2013)

25. Carcano, A., Coletta, A., Guglielmi, M., et al.: A multidimensional critical state analysis for detecting intrusions in SCADA systems. IEEE Trans. Ind. Inf. 7(2), 179–186 (2011)

26. Yoo, H., Shon, T.: Novel approach for detecting network anomalies for substation automation based on IEC 61850. Multimed. Tools Appl. 74(1), 303–318 (2015)

27. Hink, R.C.B., Beaver, J.M., Buckner, M.A., et al.: Machine learning for power system disturbance and cyber-attack discrimination. In: International Symposium on Resilient Control Systems, pp. 1–8. IEEE (2014)

28. Pan, S., Morris, T., Adhikari, U.: A specification-based intrusion detection framework for cyber-physical environment in electric power system. Int. J. Netw. Secur. 17(2), 174–188 (2015)

29. Pan, S., Morris, T., Adhikari, U.: Developing a hybrid intrusion detection system using data mining for power systems. IEEE Trans. Smart Grid 6(6), 3104–3113 (2015)

30. Morris, T., Srivastava, A., Reaves, B., et al.: A control system testbed to validate critical infrastructure protection concepts. Int. J. Crit. Infrastruct. Prot. 4(2), 88–103 (2011)

31. Mitchell, T.M., Carbonell, J.G., Michalski, R.S.: Machine Learning. McGraw-Hill, New York (2003)
32. Zhou, P., Chang, R., Gu, X., et al.: Magic train: design of measurement methods against bandwidth inflation attacks. IEEE Trans. Dependable Secure Comput. **PP**(99), 1 (2018)
33. Zhou, P., Jiang, S., Irissappane, A., et al.: Toward energy-efficient trust system through watchdog optimization for WSNs. IEEE Trans. Inf. Forensics Secur. **10**(3), 613–625 (2015)
34. Lowd, D., Meek, C.: Adversarial learning. In: Eleventh ACM SIGKDD International Conference on Knowledge Discovery in Data Mining, pp. 641–647. ACM (2005)
35. Dalvi, N., Domingos, P., Sanghai, S., et al.: Adversarial classification. In: Tenth ACM SIGKDD International Conference on Knowledge Discovery and Data Mining, pp. 99–108. ACM (2004)
36. Li, Y., Shi, L., Cheng, P., et al.: Jamming attacks on remote state estimation in cyber-physical systems: a game-theoretic approach. IEEE Trans. Autom. Control **60**, 2831–2836 (2015)
37. Yuan, Y., Yuan, H., Guo, L., et al.: Resilient control of networked control system under DoS attacks: a unified game approach. IEEE Trans. Ind. Inf. **12**(5), 1786–1794 (2016)
38. Huang, J.Y., Liao, I.E., Chung, Y.F., et al.: Shielding wireless sensor network using markovian intrusion detection system with attack pattern mining. Inf. Sci. **231**, 32–44 (2013)
39. Stouffer, K., Falco, J., Kent, K.: Guide to supervisory control and data acquisition (SCADA) and industrial control systems security, Spin (2006)

Intelligent Servo Feedback Control
for Hydrostatic Journal Bearing

Waheed Ur Rehman[1] [iD], Jiang Guiyun[1(✉)], Nadeem Iqbal[1],
Luo Yuanxin[1], Wang Yongqin[1], Shafiq Ur Rehman[2], Shamsa Bibi[2],
Farrukh Saleem[1], Irfan Azhar[3], and Muhammad Shoaib[1]

[1] The State Key Laboratory of Mechanical Transmission, Chongqing University,
Chongqing 400030, China
{wrehman87,L1600316,yxluo,Wyq,L1700258,
L1700263}@cqu.edu.cn, Gyjiang_1@163.com
[2] Chemistry Department, University of Agriculture Faisalabad,
Faisalabad, Pakistan
{Shafiq.urrehman,Shamsa.shafiq}@uaf.edu.pk
[3] Koc University, Istanbul, Turkey
mazhar13@ku.edu.tr

Abstract. The purpose of current research work is to improve dynamics characteristics of hydrostatic journal bearing which is integral part of high speed and heavy load machinery nowadays. Current work presents hydrostatic journal bearing with servo control. Mathematical model is derived for hydrostatic journal bearing and two control strategies were presented. Result shows that hydrostatic journal bearing with self-tuning PID control has better results than PID control. The performance of active hydrostatic journal bearing under two different control strategies were checked with respect to different conditions of speed, viscosity, load, pressure, bearing clearance. The numerical result shows that proposed hydrostatic journal because of active lubrication has better performance including stability and controllability, high stiffness, faster response, strong resistance under Self tuning PID control. Furthermore, proposed hydrostatic journal bearing with servo control has no eccentricity under new equilibrium position after being applied load which is big advantage on conventional hydrostatic journal that always face some amount of eccentricity under external load due to absent of servo feedback. All simulations were performed in Matlab/Simulink. The numerical result shows that proposed active hydrostatic journal due to active lubrication has good performance including stability and controllability, high stiffness, faster response, strong resistance in Matlab/Simulink which shows effectiveness of proposed system.

Keywords: Self tuning PID · PID · Tribology · Fluid mechanics
Hydrostatic journal bearing · Fluid film lubrication theory · Servo valve etc.

© Springer Nature Singapore Pte Ltd. 2018
K. Li et al. (Eds.): ICSEE 2018/IMIOT 2018, CCIS 924, pp. 352–364, 2018.
https://doi.org/10.1007/978-981-13-2384-3_33

1 Introduction

Rotary equipment's for precision applications have been long utilized hydrostatic journal bearing due to their many useful features. These journal bearing offer greater position accuracy, enhanced stability, and low friction. For the reasons mentioned earlier, numerous researchers have conducted studies on hydrostatic journal bearings. Matthew et al. [1] studied the dynamic performance using linear and non-linear numerical methods for complaint cylindrical journal bearings. Kim et al. [2] derived equations of perturbation and general Reynold equation. He accomplished this by analyzing the behavior of journal bearings and studying effects of different recess shapes on it. Thomsen and Klit [3] further focused their studies on analyzing the effects of compliant layers over the behavior of hydrodynamic journal bearings. De Pellegrin et al. [4] derived isothermal and iso-viscous models for hydrostatic journal bearing by keeping in view the behavioral characteristics of tilt pad type hydrostatic journal bearing. Phalle et al. [5] studied the effect of wear on performance of a hybrid journal bearing system which employ membrane type of compensation. Above mentioned research findings demonstrated to play a vibrant role in successful improvement of the performance under normal operational environmental conditions in traditionally used journal bearings.

Considering the operational conditions, these conditions severely restrict behavior of journal bearings and also play an important part too. So numerous studies have been conducted in this field by great number of researchers to enhance the dynamic characteristics of these bearing, the rigidness of fluid film and rigid rotor's stability. Bouaziz et al. [6] studied the dynamic behavior of the misaligned rotor. Sharma et al. [7] examined the wear-tear phenomena on a hybrid conical journal bearing with four pockets. The research findings of this study proposed that with augmented radial position accuracy and stationarity of traditional journal bearings, we can directly influence the behavior of mechanical equipment under harsh operational conditions. It is also tried to control oil film thickness in [8, 9] and some control strategies were presented.

After this above conclusion, it is probable to increase the performance of a journal bearing using an active control technology. Using several types of actuators like piezoelectric, magnetic & hydraulic to control the vibrations in rotor (Nicoletti and Santos [10]. The Morosi and Santos [11] have effectively validated that it is likely to apply active lubrication to the gas journal. The Santos and Watanabe [12] further explored the applications of the active lubrication in journal bearings, in order to get enhanced damping coefficients and to have a reduced cross-coupling stiffness. With that it considerably augmented the threshold for the stability of the journal bearing. Santos suggested an active control for the control of vibration in a flexible rotor, using an output feedback controller and computed gains of the controllers. Kim and Lee [13] focused on improvement of dynamic pressure by examining the properties of a sealed squeeze film type damper. And the results of their study showed that active control technology is effective in dampers. Ho et al. [14] worked and analysed the effects of thrust magnetic bearings on the stability and bifurcation of the flexible rotor with active magnetic bearing system. Nicoletti and Santos [15] focused on the analysis of the frequency response tilt type active hydrostatic bearing. Estupinan and Santos [16] effectively studied multi-body systems which were inter-connected through thin films of fluid and derived the mathematical modeling and showed that it can be easily controlled by using several types of actuators. Haugaard and Santos [17] and Nicoletti and Santos [15] studied the dynamic performance in theory and focused on active lubrication of tilting-pad journal bearings. These research studies were concentrated on customary analysis of stiffness in bearings and the damping in the frequency domain. Most of the precision rotary equipment have been extensively and more commonly employing these hydrostatic journal bearings, which led to the requirement of having a bearing with improved performance and reliability. Santos and Watanabe [12] worked on the extension of the stability-threshold of the hydrostatic journal bearing and studied the viability of reduced vibrations in theory. With most of the researchers discovering these areas, none of them have previously worked or studied on controlling the journal position accuracy and precision of a hydrostatic journal bearing under external load conditions and not much existing literature addresses this topic.

In our pursuit to realize our objectives, first we made mathematical model for hydrostatic journal bearing using servo control and then two different control strategies are presented. Self-tuning PID control and PID control. A numerical comparison has been done in Result and discussion part which show effectives of proposed system.

2   Problem Formulation for Coupled System

The Structure of hydrostatic journal bearing is shown in Fig. 1, it consists of servo valve, filter, regulator and some electronics components. Hydrostatic journal bearing has advantage over hydrodynamic bearing that is surface of journal remain separated from bearing under different speeds and loads. So that is why, hydrostatic journal bearing has less wear and less friction as compared to hydrodynamic bearing under low speed or under starting condition of rotary machinery. The performance of hydrostatic journal bearing depends upon gap between journal and surface. Throttlers have big influence on efficiency of hydrostatic journal bearing. Fixed throttlers have problem as they are limited in term of stiffness and load carrying capacity. This paper present active throttling device called servo valve to control clearance gap between inner and outer periphery of hydrostatic journal bearing.

3   Modelling for Hydrostatic Journal Bearing System

Servo valve is key component of proposed system. It controls the flow towards bearing. Flow through servo valve is describe by second order differential equation in [18]. The coefficients such as gain, frequency and damping are obtained from manufacturers [19, 20].

Let suppose non linearities are ignored for derivation of a mathematical model of Electro hydraulic servo valve (EHSV). The EHSV current i_s is related to spool displacement x_v by first order transfer function [21, 22].

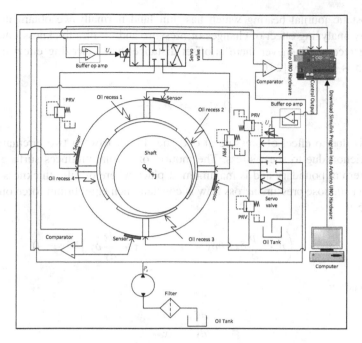

Fig. 1. Hydrostatic journal bearing attached with feedback servo control

$$\tau_v \dot{x}_{vi} = K_i i_i - x_{vi} \qquad i \in x, y \tag{1}$$

Flow for hydrostatic bearing along recess aligned in vertical and horizontal direction is given by [23];

$$
\begin{cases}
Q_2 = C_d w x_{vx} \sqrt{\dfrac{2}{\rho}(P_s - P_0 - P_x)} \\[4mm]
Q_4 = C_d w x_{vx} \sqrt{\dfrac{2}{\rho}(P_s - P_0 + P_x)}
\end{cases}
\tag{2}
$$

Similarly for Y direction, is given by;

$$
\begin{cases}
Q_1 = C_d w x_{vy} \sqrt{\dfrac{2}{\rho}(P_s - P_0 - P_y)} \\[4mm]
Q_3 = C_d w x_{vy} \sqrt{\dfrac{2}{\rho}(P_s - P_0 + P_y)}
\end{cases}
\tag{3}
$$

Hydrostatic journal bearing which has thin land normally we obtain its transfer function by analyzing effect of changes of pressure and oil film thickness into and out of bearing recess. Whenever there is offset distance then squeezing effect come into play which is given by [23],

$$Q_{squeeze} = A_e \frac{dh_i}{dt}$$ (4)

Flow is due to effect of pressure at one end. Fluid between two circular surfaces faces restriction due to shear stress. The motion of journal produces surface velocity which is zero at boundary and is maximum at place where oil film thickness center is present. Let suppose pressure across flow is constant then equilibrium force on element of width b is

$$pb\delta y - \left(p + \frac{dp}{dx}\delta x\right)b\delta y - \tau b\delta x + \left(\tau + \frac{d\tau}{dy}\delta y\right)b\delta x = 0$$

This leads to

$$\frac{d\tau}{dy} = \frac{dp}{dx}$$ (5)

Substituting $\tau = \eta(du/dy)$ into Eq. (5).

$$\eta\frac{d^2u}{dy^2} = \frac{dp}{dx}$$ (6)

Applying boundary conditions and integrating such as $u = 0$ & u = U when $y = 0$ & $y = h$, respectively, to get velocity distribution that is;

$$u = \frac{Uy}{h} - \frac{1}{2\eta}\frac{dp}{dx}\left(yh - y^2\right)$$ (7)

Flow rate is often integral of velocity that is given by;

$$Q_{PU} = \frac{1}{2}Uhb - \frac{bh^3}{12\eta}\frac{dp}{dx}$$ (8)

Let suppose there is a recess or pocket of width b and length l, then pressure gradient in an Eq. (8) will take the form of P_L/l

$$Q_{PU} = \frac{1}{2}Uhb - \frac{bh^3}{12\eta}\frac{P_{Li}}{l}$$ (9)

Equation (9) is very useful; it is employed to flow that is due to surface velocity and pressure. Pressure is obtained from external source of energy while surface velocity is produced because of relative motion between two surfaces such as journal and bearing surface.

Compressibility has good influence on bearing stiffness and damping. It depends upon bulk modulus which is relationship between change in volume and change in pressure, is described by relationship;

$$dV = \frac{V_e}{\beta_e} dP_{Li} \tag{10}$$

Rearranging Eq. (10) while taking changes with respect to time

$$\frac{dV}{dt} = \frac{V_e}{\beta_e} \frac{dP_{Li}}{dt} \tag{11}$$

Time rate of change of volume is called is flow for hydrostatic bearing termed as compressible flow, so Eq. (11) takes form that is given by;

$$Q_{Compressibility} = \frac{V_e}{\beta_e} \frac{dP_{Li}}{dt} \tag{12}$$

One can get overall flow in hydrostatic bearing by employing equation of continuity [24, 25]. Where flow from servo valve is employed in term of squeezing flow, pressure velocity flow and compressibility flow. Motion dynamics of hydrostatic bearing can be described by considering factors such as; arrangement of masses, fluid film stiffness and structure linkages. The equation of motion for hydrostatic bearing in term of masses, stiffness and coefficients, is given by;

$$F_{film} = m\ddot{h}_i + B_d\dot{h}_i + F_{Li} \tag{13}$$

4 Design Strategy

In this paper two design strategies are proposed for HJBSC, one is PID control and second is Intelligent Control.

4.1 PID Design Strategy

PID control is best controller which is used in a lot of engineering aplications due to their ease of operations and good performance characteristics. PID consists of Proportional (reduces rise time, make system fatser), Derivative (smooth signal over time) and Integral (reduce staedy state error part of signal). PID controller takes error signal and produces corresonding controller signal for plant. Error signal is genereted with differential amplifier which takes output feedback signal and reference bearing clearance for comparison. The PID controller drives servo valve by generating appropriate signal. A simulink program is written in the form of algorithim to find efficient and optimal parameters. A fittness function is used to find precise and accurate values of controller parameters. This fitness function finds sum of errors between refrence and current value and it is given by;

$$F(e_i) = sum(abs(e_i - e_0))$$ (14)

4.2 Proposed Design Staretgy

In order to improve further effeciency of active hydrostatic journal bearing, a self tuning PID control method is introduced in this part.

Self tuning PID controller is best option to compensate error caused by external laoding and inaccuracies. Conventional PID controller are used in a lot of industrial process and automatic control system due to their ability of simpilcity and ease of operation. Fuzzy control is a good method for systems such as complex systems, time-delay linear systems and higher-order nonlinear systems that have no accurate and precise mathematical models. Keeping in view the problems to get an accurate mathematical model of the proposed system and to achieve good load rejection performance and good stiffness. A self tuning PID controller is designed in this paper. The structure of self tuning PID controller or Intelligent controller is shown in Fig. 2. It is just like a parallel structure where fuzzy logic is used for tuning the parameters of a PID controller. In Fig. 2, e_p is the error between reference bearing clearance and output bearing clearance while D_{p1} and D_{p2} are gain that covert signal into such a form which is suitable for fuzzy logic controller, while controller parameters are D_1, D_2, C_1, C_2, G_1, G_2 and tuning parameters are K_p' and K_i', K_d'. The fuzzy logic controller is a parallel structure where fuzzy logic is used to tune the parameter of PID controller. The "rule base" keeps the knowledge in the form of rules and each rule present a certain state called member function. The triangular member function is used which has general formula as:

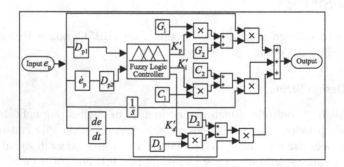

Fig. 2. Structure of self-tuning PID controller

$$\mu_r = \begin{cases} 0 & x \le a_r \\ (x - a_r)/(b_r - a_r) & a_r < x < b_r \\ (c_r - x)/(c_r - b_r) & b_r < x < c_r \\ 0 & c_r \le x \end{cases} \qquad (15)$$

Where $r \in \{$NB, NS, ZE, PS, PB, S, MS, M, MB, B$\}$.

Let suppose the range of parameters K_p, K_d and K_i of the PID controller are bounded. A suitable range of each parameter is found by the simulation of the convention PID controller. The range of each parameter for the fuzzy logic controller is $K_p \in [K_{pmin}, K_{pmax}]$, $K_d \in [K_{dmin}, K_{dmax}]$ and $K_i \in [K_{imin}, K_{imax}]$. They can be calibrated by using an adjustment mechanism;

$$K_z = (K_{zmax} - K_{zmin})K_z' + K_{zmin} \qquad (16)$$

Where subscript z presents the type of the tuning parameter. It may be derivative, proportional or integral.

5   Simulation Results and Discussion

In order to check effectiveness of proposed strategy experiments have been done in matlab/Simulink by using parameters which are given in Table 1. Simulations are performed under different dynamics conditions which are explained in next part.

5.1   Influence of Initial Oil Pressure

Whenever we use rotational machinery then high speed and high load is always demand in operationg conditions. Such applications where high speed and high load is common operationg conditions, demand hydrostatic jornal bearing. The pressure of oil is one of the most important component that has influence on the working of active hydrostatic journal bearing. So its effects must be analyzed. A number of experiments have been done in matlab/simulink and it is observed that the performance of self-tuning PId controller is better than coventional PID controller under same initial oil pressure as shown in Fig. 3.

5.2   Influence of External Load

The shaft cannot get its equilibrium position after being applied load. There are some reasons behind this phenomena such as; throttling effect, bearing component's mass and stiffness as well as inertia of hydrostatic bearing.

There are two important factors such eccentricity and response time to get new equilibrium position. These factors are very important for performance of active hydrostatic journal bearing. Active hydrostatic journal has servo valve which adjust flow in real time so that hydrostatic journal bearing can get zero eccentricity under equilibrium conditions. In order to improve performance of active hydrostatic journal bearing, two strategies are proposed one is conventional PID control and second is self-

Table 1. Simulation parameters

Parameter	Symbol	Values
Recess	$h_0(m)$	2.5×10^{-5}
	$l(m)$	0.08
	$l_1(m)$	0.01
	$b(m)$	0.08
	$b_1(m)$	0.01
	$m(kg)$	23
Shaft (Spindle)	$d(m)$	0.06
	$N(rpm)$	1500
Oil	$B_e(Pa)$	7×10^8
	$\rho(Kg/m^3)$	900
	$B_d(Ns/m)$	5×10^5
	$\eta(Pas)$	0.025
Bearing	$L(m)$	0.06
	$L_1(m)$	0.012
	$D(m)$	0.025
	$B_1(m)$	$\pi D/16$
	$C(m)$	2.5×10^{-5}
	$A_e(m^2)$	1.88×10^{-2}
	$V_e(m^3)$	2.8×10^{-4}
	$F(N)$	1200
	$D(m)$	0.06006
Servo valve	$K_i(m/A)$	3.04×10^{-5}
	$K_q(m^2/s)$	2.7
	$K_c(m^3 s^{-1} Pa)$	1.75×10^{-11}
	$\tau_v(s)$	0.001

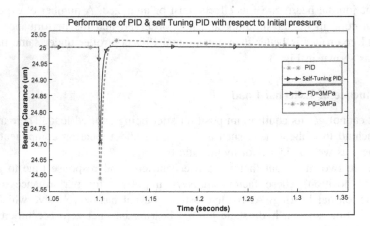

Fig. 3. Influence of initial oil pressure on performance of bearing

tuning PID control. The external load of 800 N and 1600 N is applied at a time 1.1 s as shown in Fig. 4. Result shows that under same external load, the stiffness and load rejection performance of self-tuning PID control based active hydrostatic journal is better than PID control based active hydrostatic journal bearing. This thing provides the system good rotation and stationary characteristics as well provides rotor or shaft more stability.

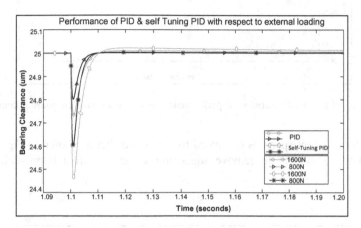

Fig. 4. Influence of external load on performance of active hydrostatic journal bearing

5.3 Influence of Oil Viscosity

During working, there is some separation between journal and surface and this separation kept constant by a pressurized oil film. This separation help hydrostatic journal bearing to exhibit good stiffness and better rejection performance as well as low friction and good damping characteristics. Investigation reveals that temperature has important effect on viscosity of oil. Operations of high speed and high load produce a lot heat which has effect to change viscosity of oil. So oil under temperature condition will affect the efficiency of hydrostatic journal bearing. This problem has been removed in active hydrostatic journal bearing; temperature does not affect much more due to servo feedback. Furthermore, Self-tuning PID control is less sensitive to temperature changes as compared to conventional PID. It has also better stiffness under same viscosity conditions as compared to conventional PID as shown in Fig. 5.

5.4 Influence of Spindle Speed

Whenever there is eccentricity then offset distance come to play which produce squeezing effect and squeezing effect produce film oscillation. Conventional hydrostatic journal bearing produces eccentricity even once system settled down and gets new equilibrium position while hydrostatic journal bearing with proposed strategy has no eccentricity under equilibrium position and also Self tuning PID controller has better

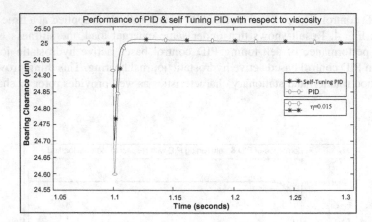

Fig. 5. Influence of viscosity on performance of active hydrostatic journal bearing

results under different speed as compared to PID controller as shown in Fig. 6. Servo valve is key component to remove squeezing effect in active hydrostatic journal bearing.

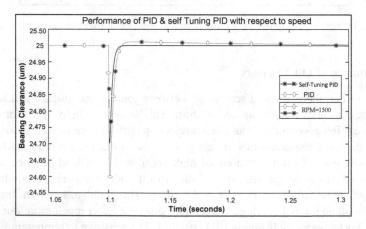

Fig. 6. Influence of external load on performance of active hydrostatic journal bearing

6 Conclusions

The current work presents an accurate and precise mathematical model that consists of active hydrostatic journal bearing and servo feedback control. The proposed mathematical model is checked under two different strategies. Experiments are carried out in Matlab/Simulink. The problem of traditional hydrostatic journal bearing is eccentricity under different loads which is removed by proposed active hydrostatic journal bearing. Furthermore, Proposed active hydrostatic journal bearing is checked under two different strategies such PID controller and intelligent Controller. Results show that active hydrostatic journal bearing with intelligent Controller has better stiffness, load rejection, rotor stability, less vibration and no wear under different dynamic conditions of rotating velocity, temperature, initial oil pressure and varying load. Proposed active hydrostatic journal bearing monitors bearing clearance in real time and adjust oil film thickness in such a way so that eccentricity is zero under new equilibrium after being applied load. Current work involves simulation work while future work will be to validate proposed system on test bench.

Acknowledgement. This work is supported by the National Natural Science Foundation of China (Grant No. 51075409).

References

1. Cha, M., Kuznetsov, E., Glavatskih, S.: A comparative linear and nonlinear dynamic analysis of compliant cylindrical journal bearings. Mech. Mach. Theory **64**, 80–92 (2013)
2. Kim, H., Jang, G., Ha, H.: A generalized Reynolds equation and its perturbation equations for fluid dynamic bearings with curved surfaces. Tribol. Int. **50**, 6–15 (2012)
3. Thomsen, K., Klit, P.: A study on compliant layers and its influence on dynamic response of a hydrodynamic journal bearing. Tribol. Int. **44**, 1872–1877 (2011)
4. De Pellegrin, D.V., Hargreaves, D.J.: An isoviscous, isothermal model investigating the influence of hydrostatic recesses on a spring-supported tilting pad thrust bearing. Tribol. Int. **51**, 25–35 (2012)
5. Phalle, V.M., Sharma, S.C., Jain, S.: Influence of wear on the performance of a 2-lobe multirecess hybrid journal bearing system compensated with membrane restrictor. Tribol. Int. **44**, 380–395 (2011)
6. Bouaziz, S., Hili, M.A., Mataar, M., Fakhfakh, T., Haddar, M.: Dynamic behaviour of hydrodynamic journal bearings in presence of rotor spatial angular misalignment. Mech. Mach. Theory **44**, 1548–1559 (2009)
7. Sharma, S.C., Phalle, V.M., Jain, S.: Influence of wear on the performance of a multirecess conical hybrid journal bearing compensated with orifice restrictor. Tribol. Int. **44**, 1754–1764 (2011)
8. Rehman, W.U., Yuanxin, L., Guiyun, J., Yongqin, W., Rehman, S.U., Bibi, S., et al.: Control of oil film thickness for hydrostatic journal bearing using PID disturbance rejection controller. In: 2017 IEEE 3rd Information Technology and Mechatronics Engineering Conference (ITOEC), pp. 543–547 (2017)
9. Rehman, W.U., Yuanxin, L., Guiyun, J., Yongqin, W., Yun, X., Iqbal, M.N., et al.: Control of an oil film thickness in a hydrostatic journal bearing under different dynamic conditions. In: 2017 29th Chinese Control And Decision Conference (CCDC), pp. 5072–5076 (2017)
10. Nicoletti, R., Santos, I.F.: Control system design for flexible rotors supported by actively lubricated bearings. J. Vib. Control **14**, 347–374 (2008)
11. Morosi, S., Santos, I.F.: Active lubrication applied to radial gas journal bearings. Part 1: modeling. Tribol. Int. **44**, 1949–1958 (2011)
12. Santos, I.F., Watanabe, F.Y.: Compensation of cross-coupling stiffness and increase of direct damping in multirecess journal bearings using active hybrid lubrication: part I—theory. J. Tribol. **126**, 146–155 (2004)

13. Kim, K.-J., Lee, C.-W.: Dynamic characteristics of sealed squeeze film damper with a central feeding groove. J. Tribol. **127**, 103–111 (2005)
14. Ho, Y., Liu, H., Yu, L.: Effect of thrust magnetic bearing on stability and bifurcation of a flexible rotor active magnetic bearing system. Trans. Am. Soc. Mech. Eng. J. Vib. Acoust. **125**, 307–316 (2003)
15. Nicoletti, R., Santos, I.F.: Frequency response analysis of an actively lubricated rotor/tilting-pad bearing system. In: ASME Turbo Expo 2004: Power for Land, Sea, and Air, pp. 735–744 (2004)
16. Estupinan, E.A., Santos, I.F.: Linking rigid multibody systems via controllable thin fluid films. Tribol. Int. **42**, 1478–1486 (2009)
17. Haugaard, A.M., Santos, I.F.: Multi-orifice active tilting-pad journal bearings—harnessing of synergetic coupling effects. Tribol. Int. **43**, 1374–1391 (2010)
18. Merritt, H.E.: Hydraulic Control Systems. Wiley, Hoboken (1967)
19. Edelmann, H.: Schnelle Proportionalventile und ihre Anwendug, Sonderdruck aus Ölhydraulic und Pneumatik. Schnelle Proportionalventile und ihre Anwendug, Sonderdruck aus Ölhydraulic und Pneumatik **30**, 1 (1986)
20. Neal, T.: Performance estimation for electrohydraulic control systems. Moog Tech. Bull. **126** (1974)
21. Rehman, W.U., Wang, S., Wang, X., Shi, C., Zhang, C., Tomovic, M.: Adaptive control for motion synchronization of HA/EHA system by using modified MIT rule. In: 2016 IEEE 11th Conference on Industrial Electronics and Applications (ICIEA), pp. 2196–2201 (2016)
22. Rehman, W.U., Wang, S., Wang, X., Fan, L., Shah, K.A.: Motion synchronization in a dual redundant HA/EHA system by using a hybrid integrated intelligent control design. Chin. J. Aeronaut. **29**, 789–798 (2016)
23. Rehman, W.U., Jiang, G., Luo, Y., Wang, Y., Khan, W., Rehman, S.U., et al.: Control of active lubrication for hydrostatic journal bearing by monitoring bearing clearance. Adv. Mech. Eng. **10**, 1687814018768142 (2018)
24. Rehman, W.U., Wang, X., Wang, S., Azhar, I.: Motion synchronization of HA/EHA system for a large civil aircraft by using adaptive control. In: 2016 IEEE Chinese Guidance, Navigation and Control Conference (CGNCC), pp. 1486–1491 (2016)
25. Rehman, W.U., Nawaz, H., Wang, S., Wang, X., Luo, Y., Yun, X., et al.: Trajectory based motion synchronization in a dissimilar redundant actuation system for a large civil aircraft. In: 2017 29th Chinese Control And Decision Conference (CCDC), pp. 5010–5015 (2017)

Iterative Feedback Tuning
for Two-Degree-of-Freedom System

Hui Pan[1]([⊠]), Yanjin Zhang[1] [iD], and Ling Wang[2]

[1] College of Automation Engineering, Shanghai University of Electric Power,
Shanghai 200090, China
panhui001@163.com
[2] Shanghai Key Laboratory of Power Station Automation Technology,
Shanghai University, Shanghai 200072, China

Abstract. This paper is concerned with Iterative Feedback Tuning (IFT) for Two-degree-of- freedom (2-DOF) system. The IFT is a data-driven method for tuning controller parameters, which uses the closed-loop system input-output data directly, and without establishing a mathematical model for the controlled system. The design of control system is a multi-objective problem, so a 2-DOF control system naturally has advantages over a one-degree-of- freedom (1-DOF) control system. When tuning 2-DOF system controllers, two-step method is firstly concerned. While in this paper, the application of IFT method in a 2-DOF control system is studied, which can make controllers' parameters tuned at the same time, and the IFT method is more accurate and efficient in tracking performance and robustness. The feasibility and effectiveness of the method are verified by numerical simulation and comparison.

Keywords: IFT · 2-DOF · Data-driven · PID · Parameter tuning

1 Introduction

In this paper, the problem of tuning Two-degree-of-freedom (2-DOF) system controllers is concerned, when no mathematical description of the plant dynamical behavior is available. The degree of freedom of the control system can be defined as the number of independently adjustable closed-loop transfer functions [1, 2]. When designing a control system for a multi-objective optimization problem, 2-DOF control has more advantages than one-degree-of-freedom (1-DOF), for example, system tracking performance and robustness. This fact was already stated by the article [3]. In [4, 5], various 2-DOF PID controllers were proposed for industrial use and detailed analyses were made, also the further study were made about optimal tuning [6–9]. The main methods are Two-step Tuning Method (TSTM) [3], Frequency-domain Method (FDM) [9], Virtual Reference Feedback Tuning (VRFT) [10], and so on.

It has been more than twenty years since the Iterative Feedback Tuning (IFT) was put forward by Hjalmarsson [11]. As one of the methods that belongs to data-driven control (DDC) [12], IFT has attracted many scholars' attention since its emergence. After years of development, IFT has gradually become a well-established design methodology [13, 14], and which has been applied into many control systems that

© Springer Nature Singapore Pte Ltd. 2018
K. Li et al. (Eds.): ICSEE 2018/IMIOT 2018, CCIS 924, pp. 365–379, 2018.
https://doi.org/10.1007/978-981-13-2384-3_34

input-output data is available. Similar to other DDC methods [15–19], IFT does not need to establish the mathematical model of the controlled system, and only uses the input-output data of the closed-loop experiments of the system to tuning the controller parameters directly. IFT theory was originally proposed for single-loop control systems, and with the development, it has been studied and extended to many advanced control systems, such as multi-input-multi-output systems [20], internal model control [21], cascade control [22] and so on. IFT method has been extended to various industrial applications [23–26].

In this paper, the IFT method is studied to tuning the parameters of the PID controllers in the 2-DOF control system. In IFT method, at each iteration, the experimental input-output data of the system are utilized to tuning the parameters of the 2-DOF PID controllers' parameters directly. The feasibility and effectiveness of the method are proved by the numerical simulation and comparison of the typical 2-DOF control system.

The paper is organized as follows. Section 2 illustrates the basic theory of 2-DOF system and IFT method. In Sect. 3, the IFT theory is extend to the 2-DOF system, which contains the derivation of correlation variables. Section 4 gives two numerical examples of the given method, and Sect. 5 is the summary of this paper and some future work.

2 Preliminaries

2.1 2-DOF Control System

A general form of the 2-DOF control system is shown in Fig. 1, where the controller consists of two conventional controllers: $C(s)$ and $C_f(s)$. $C(s)$ is called the serial (or main) controller and $C_f(s)$ is called the feed-forward controller. The transfer function $P_d(s)$ from the disturbance d to controlled variable y is assumed different from the transfer function $P(s)$ from the manipulated variable u to y. Variable r is the set value of the system, and $H(s)$ is a detector. The closed-loop transfer functions from r to y and d to y are respectively given by:

$$G_r(s) = \frac{P(s)\big(C(s) + C_f(s)\big)}{1 + P(s)C(s)H(s)} \tag{1}$$

$$G_d(s) = \frac{P_d(s)}{1 + P(s)C(s)H(s)} \tag{2}$$

To simplify the problem, the following two assumptions that are appropriate for many practical design problems with some exceptions, are introduced for the control system shown in Fig. 1.

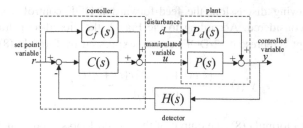

Fig. 1. Two-degree-of-freedom (2-DOF) control system.

Assumption 1: The detector has sufficient accuracy and speed for the given control purpose, i.e.,

$$H(s) = 1 \tag{3}$$

Assumption 2: The main disturbance enters at manipulating point, i.e.,

$$P_d(s) = P(s) \tag{4}$$

As a result, the control system shown in Fig. 1 can be simplified to the feed-forward type of 2-DOF control system shown in Fig. 2 under assumptions 1 and 2 [3].

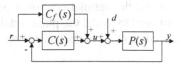

Fig. 2. Feed-forward type of 2-DOF PID control system.

The controller of the Fig. 2 system consists of $C(s)$ and $C_f(s)$, where the $C(s)$ is a conventional PID controller and $C_f(s)$ is a feed-forward compensation PID controller.

$$C(s) = K_p\left(1 + \frac{1}{T_i s} + T_d D(s)\right) \tag{5}$$

$$C_f(s) = -K_p(\alpha + \beta T_d D(s)) \tag{6}$$

Where the K_p is the proportional gain, T_i is the integral time and T_d is the differential time. α and β are 2-DOF parameters, and the above five parameters can be adjusted. $D(s)$ can be expressed by formula (7), where $\tau = T_d/\delta$, and δ is a differential gain which is a fixed value and does not affect the optimization of other parameters, but the characteristics of the actual controlled object need to be considered.

$$D(s) = \frac{s}{1 + \tau s} \tag{7}$$

In the following discussion, the feed-forward 2-DOF control system shown in Fig. 2 will be considered. According to the Fig. 2, the closed-loop transfer function $y^2(t)$ (superscript 2 represents 2-DOF) can be expressed by formula (8).

$$y^2(t) = \frac{(C(s) + C_f(s))r(t) + d(t)}{1 + P(s)C(s)} P(s) \tag{8}$$

According to formula (8), the output of the closed-loop system can be divided into two parts: one is the output caused by the set value $r(t)$, which is recorded as $y^{2r}(t)$; and the other is the output caused by the disturbance $d(t)$, which is recorded as $y^{2d}(t)$.

$$y^{2r}(t) = \frac{C(s) + C_f(s)}{1 + P(s)C(s)} P(s)r(t) \tag{9}$$

$$y^{2d}(t) = \frac{1}{1 + P(s)C(s)} P(s)d(t) \tag{10}$$

2.2   Iterative Feedback Tuning Theory

IFT is one of the DDC methods, which puts forward a performance criterion function (for example, LQG type) for the control system. Based on the input-output data of the closed-loop control system, to find the optimal controller parameters that is based on gradient iteration. IFT does not need to model the plant and directly tunes the controller parameters, which makes the controller parameters tuning more direct and accurate [14].

As is shown in Fig. 3, the conventional 1-DOF closed-loop control system, the output of the Closed-loop system $y^1(t)$ (superscript 1 represents 1-DOF) can be expressed by formula (11) and (12).

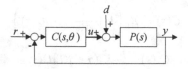

Fig. 3. Conventional closed-loop PID control system.

Where $r(t)$ is the system set value input; $d(t)$ is the disturbance; $P(s)$ is the unknown plant; $u(t)$ is the control signal. The controller structure of $C(s, \theta)$ has been selected beforehand, the controller parameter vector θ is adjustable, and the parameter vector θ is differentiable. $\theta = [\theta_1 \cdots \theta_n]$, n is the number of the parameters. In practice, the controller $C(s, \theta)$ is usually chosen as the conventional PID controller, then $n = 3$.

$$y^1(t) = (u(t) + d(t))P(s) \tag{11}$$

$$u(t) = C(s, \theta)(r(t) - y^1(t)) \tag{12}$$

Where $r(t)$ is the system set value input; $d(t)$ is the disturbance; $P(s)$ is the unknown plant; $u(t)$ is the control signal. The controller structure of $C(s, \theta)$ has been selected beforehand, the controller parameter vector θ is adjustable, and the parameter vector θ is differentiable. $\theta = [\theta_1 \cdots \theta_n]$, n is the number of the parameters. In practice, the controller $C(s, \theta)$ is usually chosen as the conventional PID controller, then $n = 3$.

The expected closed-loop response of the system from set value input $r(t)$ to output $y_d^1(t)$, which is expressed by formula (13). $T_d^1(s)$ is the expected closed-loop system transfer function.

$$y_d^1(t) = T_d^1(s)r(t) \tag{13}$$

The tracking error between the actual output $y^1(t)$ and the expected output $y_d^1(t)$ is $\tilde{y}^1(t)$.

$$
\begin{aligned}
\tilde{y}^1(t) &= y^1(t) - y_d^1(t) \\
&= \frac{P(s)C(s, \theta)}{1 + P(s)C(s, \theta)} r(t) - T_d^1(s)r(t) + \frac{P(s)}{1 + P(s)C(s, \theta)} d(t)
\end{aligned}
\tag{14}
$$

The design goal of the controller $C(s, \theta)$ is to minimize the tracking error $\tilde{y}^1(t)$ between the $y^1(t)$ and the $y_d^1(t)$, so that the system performance criterion function $J(\theta)$ can be chosen as quadratic criterion.

$$J(\theta) = \frac{1}{2N} \sum_{k=1}^{N} \left[(y^1(k, \theta) - y_d^1(k))^2 \right] \tag{15}$$

$$\theta^* = \arg \min_{\theta} J(\theta) \tag{16}$$

When the sampling data length N is fixed, the value of $J(\theta)$ is only related to the controller parameters vector θ. The goal of the IFT method is to find the θ^* when the performance function $J(\theta)$ gets the minimum value, and define it as the optimal controller parameter. To find the optimal θ^* can be regarded as the problem of finding the minimum value of the quadratic function $J(\theta)$.

To obtain the minimum of $J(\theta)$, a solution for θ to the Eq. (17) is found:

$$\frac{\partial J(\theta)}{\partial \theta} = \frac{1}{N} \sum_{k=1}^{N} \left[(y^1(k, \theta) - y_d^1(k)) \frac{\partial y^1(k, \theta)}{\partial \theta} \right] = 0 \tag{17}$$

If the gradient $\partial J(\theta)/\partial \theta$ could be computed, then the solution of (17) would be obtained iteratively by the following Algorithms:

$$\theta_{i+1} = \theta_i - \gamma_i R_i^{-1} \frac{\partial J(\theta_i)}{\partial \theta} \tag{18}$$

Here, R_i is some appropriate positive definite matrix at iteration i, typically a Gauss-Newton approximation of the Hessian of $J(\theta)$, while γ_i is a positive real scalar that determines the step size. The sequence γ_i, must obey some constraints for the algorithm to converge to a local minimum of the performance criterion function $J(\theta)$.

As stated, this problem is intractable since it involves expectations that are unknown. However, such problem can be solved by using a stochastic approximation algorithm of the form (18). The gradient $\partial J(\theta)/\partial \theta$ evaluated at the current controller can be replaced by an unbiased estimate. In order to solve this problem, one thus needs to generate the following quantities:

(i) the signals $\tilde{y}^1(t)$ and $r(t)$;
(ii) the gradients $\partial \tilde{y}^1(t, \theta)/\partial \theta$ and $\partial y^1(t, \theta)/\partial \theta$.

Because the $P(s)$ is unknown, the input-output data of the system are required which are obtained by closed-loop system experiments.

3   Iterative Feedback Tuning for 2-DOF Controllers

The IFT for 1-DOF system and the typical structure of 2-DOF are given in previous section. In this section, the IFT is extended for the 2-DOF case shown in Fig. 2.

3.1   Derivation of Correlation Variables

For the 2-DOF control system shown in Fig. 2, the system output is expressed by formula (8). To facilitate the following derivation, rewrite the conventional controller $C(s)$ to $C(\theta_c)$, and rewrite the feed-forward controller $C_f(s)$ to $C_f(\theta_f)$. Notice that, $C(\theta_c)$ and $C_f(\theta_f)$ respectively relate to the adjustable PID controller of parameters θ_c and θ_f. Now that:

$$\theta_c = \begin{bmatrix} \theta_{c1} \\ \theta_{c2} \\ \theta_{c3} \end{bmatrix} = \begin{bmatrix} K_p \\ \frac{K_p}{T_i} \\ K_p T_d \end{bmatrix}, \quad \theta_f = \begin{bmatrix} \theta_{f1} \\ \theta_{f2} \end{bmatrix} = \begin{bmatrix} \alpha\theta_{c1} \\ \beta\theta_{c3} \end{bmatrix} \tag{19}$$

Where $\theta = [\theta_c \quad \theta_f]^T$. The error $\tilde{y}^2(t)$ between actual output and expected output of the Fig. 3 system can be expressed by formula (20).

$$\begin{aligned} \tilde{y}^2(t) &= y^2(t) - y_d^2(t) \\ &= \frac{(C(\theta) + C_f(\theta_f))r(t) + d(t)}{1 + P(s)C(\theta)}P(s) - T_d^2(s)r(t) \end{aligned} \tag{20}$$

Similar to 1-DOF system, a performance criterion function of quadratic form like formula (15) is selected.

$$J(\theta) = \frac{1}{2N} \sum_{k=1}^{N} \left[\left(y^2(k, \theta) - y_d^2(k) \right)^2 \right] \tag{21}$$

The gradient $\partial J(\theta)/\partial \theta$ can be obtained from the derivation of θ on both sides of the Eq. (21).

$$\frac{\partial J(\theta)}{\partial \theta} = \frac{1}{N} \sum_{k=1}^{N} \left[\tilde{y}^2(k, \theta) \frac{\partial \tilde{y}^2(k, \theta)}{\partial \theta} \right] \tag{22}$$

In order to achieve iterative optimization of controller parameters vector θ, calculation can be carried out according to formula (17). However, when using formula (17), it is necessary to figure out the gradient $\partial J(\theta)/\partial \theta$ by using formula (22), but in fact, the value of $\partial \tilde{y}^2(t, \theta)/\partial \theta$ must be obtained, which greatly increases the difficulty of the solution process. For this purpose, it is necessary to use the input-output data of the system to solve $\partial \tilde{y}^2(t, \theta)/\partial \theta$ by stochastic approximation, and it means that to replace $\partial \tilde{y}^2(t, \theta)/\partial \theta$ after the calculation and processing of the sampling data currently. As a result, the error signals $\tilde{y}^2(t, \theta_i)$ of the system must be obtained, which is used for the gradient $\partial \tilde{y}^2(t, \theta)/\partial \theta$. When the controller parameters of the system is θ_i, the gradient of the error signal $\partial \tilde{y}^2(t, \theta)/\partial \theta$ can be obtained by the following formula.

$$\frac{\partial \tilde{y}^2(t, \theta_i)}{\partial \theta} = \frac{\partial \left(y^2(t, \theta_i) - y_d^2(t) \right)}{\partial \theta} = \frac{\partial y^2(t, \theta_i)}{\partial \theta} \tag{23}$$

Obviously, by calculating the gradient $\partial y^2(t, \theta_i)/\partial \theta$ to estimate $\partial \tilde{y}^2(t, \theta)/\partial \theta$. For the following calculation, the controller parameters θ_c and θ_f are differentiated respectively.

$$\begin{aligned}
\frac{\partial y^2(t, \theta_i)}{\partial \theta_c} &= \frac{\partial y^{2r}(t, \theta_i)}{\partial \theta_c} + \frac{\partial y^{2d}(t, \theta_i)}{\partial \theta_c} \\
&= \frac{\partial C(\theta_c)}{\partial \theta_c} \frac{P(s)}{1 + C(\theta_c)P(s)} \left(r(t) - y^{2r}(t, \theta_i) \right) \\
&\quad - \frac{\partial C(\theta_c)}{\partial \theta_c} \frac{P(s)}{1 + P(s)C(s)} y^{2d}(t, \theta_i)
\end{aligned} \tag{24}$$

$$\begin{aligned}
\frac{\partial y^2(t, \theta_i)}{\partial \theta_f} &= \frac{\partial y^{2r}(t, \theta_i)}{\partial \theta_f} + \frac{\partial y^{2d}(t, \theta_i)}{\partial \theta_f} \\
&= \frac{\partial C(\theta_f)}{\partial \theta_f} \frac{P(s)}{1 + C(\theta_c)P(s)} r(t)
\end{aligned} \tag{25}$$

Notice that the model of the $P(s)$ is unknown and there is no need to model it. $\partial y^2(t, \theta_i)/\partial \theta_c$ and $\partial y^2(t, \theta_i)/\partial \theta_f$ are obtained by using the input-output data from three experiments in IFT method.

3.2   Closed - Loop System Experiment

Through the derivation of Sect. 3.1, the key to the iterative optimization of controller parameter vector θ is to get the values of $\partial y^2(t,\theta_i)/\partial \theta_c$ and $\partial y^2(t,\theta_i)/\partial \theta_f$, which can be used for the estimation of $\partial \bar{y}^2(t,\theta_i)/\partial \theta$ and $\partial J(\theta_i)/\partial \theta$. To this end, three closed-loop system tests are required to obtain relevant data.

(i) the first is called basic experiment. With $r_1 = r(t)$ as the input of the set value of the system, the system output $y_1^2(t,\theta_i)$ (subscript 1 represents the first experiment) with a data length of N is obtained.

$$y_1^2(t,\theta_i) = \frac{C(s) + C_f(s)}{1 + P(s)C(s)} r(t)P(s) + \frac{1}{1 + P(s)C(s)} d(t)P(s) \qquad (26)$$

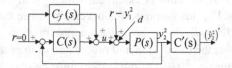

Fig. 4. Schematic diagram of the second experiment.

(ii) the second experiment is described in Fig. 4, set $r_2 = 0$ and $r(t) - y_1^2(t,\theta_i)$ as the input of the set value of the system. The output $y_2^2(t,\theta_i)$ with data length N should be collected. The gradient $\partial \bar{y}^2(t,\theta_i)/\partial \theta_f$ can be calculated by formula (28).

$$y_2^2(t,\theta_i) = \frac{P(s)}{1 + P(s)C(\theta_c)} \left[(r(t) - y_1^2(t,\theta_i)) + d(t) \right] \qquad (27)$$

$$\begin{aligned}
\frac{\partial \bar{y}_2^2(t,\theta_i)}{\partial \theta_c} &= \frac{\partial C(\theta_c)}{\partial \theta_c} y_2^2(t,\theta_i) \\
&= \frac{\partial C(\theta_c)}{\partial \theta_c} \frac{P(s)}{1 + P(s)C(\theta_c)} \left[(r(t) - y_1^2(t,\theta_i)) + d(t) \right] \qquad (28) \\
&= \frac{\partial y^2(t,\theta_i)}{\partial \theta_c} + w(t,\theta_i)
\end{aligned}$$

Where

$$w(t,\theta_i) = \frac{\partial C(\theta_c)}{\partial \theta_c} \frac{P(s)}{1 + P(s)C(\theta_c)} \left(d(t) + y_1^{2d}(t,\theta_i) \right) \qquad (29)$$

(iii) the third experiment is described in Fig. 5, to set $r_3 = 0$ and $r(t)$ as the input of the set value of the system. Similarly, to get the output $y_3^2(t,\theta_i)$ with data length N. The gradient $\partial \bar{y}^2(t,\theta_i)/\partial \theta_f$ can be calculated by formula (30).

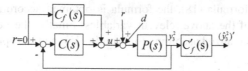

Fig. 5. Schematic diagram of the third experiment.

$$y_3^2(t, \theta_i) = \frac{P(s)}{1 + P(s)C(\theta_c)} (r(t) + d(t)) \tag{30}$$

$$
\begin{aligned}
\frac{\partial \tilde{y}_3^2(t, \theta_i)}{\partial \theta_f} &= \frac{\partial C(\theta_f)}{\partial \theta_f} y_3^2(t, \theta_i) \\
&= \frac{\partial C(\theta_f)}{\partial \theta_f} \frac{P(s)}{1 + P(s)C(\theta_c)} (r(t) + d(t)) \\
&= \frac{\partial y^2(t, \theta_i)}{\partial \theta_f} + v(t, \theta_i)
\end{aligned}
\tag{31}
$$

Where

$$v(t, \theta_i) = \frac{\partial C(\theta_f)}{\partial \theta_f} \frac{P(s)}{1 + P(s)C(\theta_c)} d(t) \tag{32}$$

Through three experiment, the related input-output data are obtained, and can be calculate for $\partial \tilde{y}^2(t, \theta_i)/\partial \theta_c$ and $\partial \tilde{y}^2(t, \theta_i)/\partial \theta_f$.

When there is no noise or mean value of noise in the system is zero, or in another word, the mean values of Eqs. (30) and (33) are zero, $\partial y^2(t, \theta_i)/\partial \theta_c$ and $\partial y^2(t, \theta_i)/\partial \theta_f$ are unbiased estimates of $\partial \tilde{y}^2(t, \theta_i)/\partial \theta_c$ and $\partial \tilde{y}^2(t, \theta_i)/\partial \theta_f$ [14].

Based on the above analysis, the gradient $\partial J(\theta_i)/\partial \theta$ can be rewritten as follows:

$$
\begin{cases}
\dfrac{\partial J(\theta_i)}{\partial \theta_c} = \dfrac{1}{N} \displaystyle\sum_{k=1}^{N} \left[(y^2(k, \theta_i) - y_d^2(k)) \dfrac{\partial \tilde{y}^2(k, \theta_i)}{\partial \theta_c} \right] \\[4mm]
\dfrac{\partial J(\theta_i)}{\partial \theta_f} = \dfrac{1}{N} \displaystyle\sum_{k=1}^{N} \left[(y^2(k, \theta_i) - y_d^2(k)) \dfrac{\partial \tilde{y}^2(k, \theta_i)}{\partial \theta_f} \right]
\end{cases}
\tag{33}
$$

The positive definite matrix R_i can be obtained by using the Hessian estimation of $J(\theta_i)$.

$$
\begin{cases}
R_{ci} = \dfrac{1}{N} \displaystyle\sum_{k=1}^{N} \left[\left(\dfrac{\partial \tilde{y}^2(t, \theta_i)}{\partial \theta_c} \right)^T \left(\dfrac{\partial \tilde{y}^2(t, \theta_i)}{\partial \theta_c} \right) \right] \\[4mm]
R_{fi} = \dfrac{1}{N} \displaystyle\sum_{k=1}^{N} \left[\left(\dfrac{\partial \tilde{y}^2(t, \theta_i)}{\partial \theta_f} \right)^T \left(\dfrac{\partial \tilde{y}^2(t, \theta_i)}{\partial \theta_f} \right) \right]
\end{cases}
\tag{34}
$$

On the basis of formula (18), the formula is obtained according to the derivation and transformation of the above relevant variables. Finally, the iteration of controller parameter vector θ is realized according to formula (35), and the optimal value is finally achieved.

$$\begin{cases} \theta_{ci+1} = \theta_{ci} - \gamma_{ci}R_{ci}^{-1}\dfrac{\partial J(\theta_i)}{\partial \theta_c} \\ \theta_{fi+1} = \theta_{ci} - \gamma_{fi}R_{fi}^{-1}\dfrac{\partial J(\theta_i)}{\partial \theta_f} \end{cases} \tag{35}$$

4 Numerical Example

Based on the above theoretical derivation, this section extends the application of IFT in 2-DOF system by numerical simulation, to compare the feasibility and effectiveness of this method. In the following discussion, two numerical examples are chosen for the simulation, which come from reference [3].

4.1 Numerical Example 1

For a typical plant model with first-order inertia plus hysteresis, when $L/T = 0.2$ and $T = 1$. Selection of the expected Closed-Loop transfer function of the system is $T_d^2(s) = 1$, and the structure of PID controllers are shown in formula (37).

The sampling time of the system is $T_s = 0.01\,s$, $\tau = 0.001\,s$, runtime is 10 s. According to the reference data in the literature, the initial controller parameters are as follows: $\theta_{c1} = 5$, $\theta_{c2} = 10$, $\theta_{c3} = 0.25$, $\theta_{f1} = 3.5$, $\theta_{f1} = 0.45$. Iterative data is shown in Fig. 6.

$$P_1(s) = \frac{1}{1+Ts}e^{-Ls} \tag{36}$$

$$\theta_c = \begin{bmatrix} 1 & \frac{1}{s} & \frac{s}{1+\tau s} \end{bmatrix}\begin{bmatrix} \theta_{c1} \\ \theta_{c2} \\ \theta_{c3} \end{bmatrix}, \quad \theta_f = -\begin{bmatrix} 1 & \frac{s}{1+\tau s} \end{bmatrix}\begin{bmatrix} \theta_{f1} \\ \theta_{f2} \end{bmatrix} \tag{37}$$

From the data in Fig. 6, it can be seen that the value of the performance criterion function $J(\theta)$ obtained from the previous iterations decreases at a relatively large rate, and the range of parameter changes is relatively large. But with the iteration i increases, the $J(\theta)$ decreases slowly and tends to be stable.

The above initial parameters and optimization parameters are brought into the simulation experiment respectively, and the optimized controller parameters in the literature are taken as reference. To set up $r(t) = 1$, with the starting time is 0 s and the running time is 3.5 s. The simulation figure is shown in a diagram in Fig. 7. In the following figures, Ini represents the initial parameters of the controller, IFT represents the optimal parameters, and Ref represents the parameters in the reference [3].

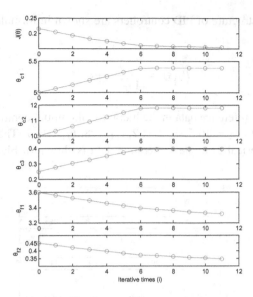

Fig. 6. Parameters iterative graph of numerical example 1.

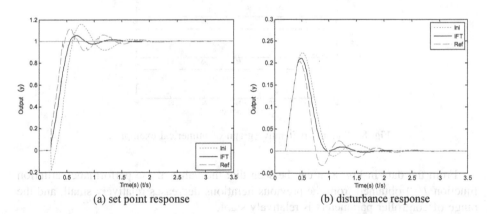

(a) set point response   (b) disturbance response

Fig. 7. Comparison of set point response and disturbance response in numerical examples 1.

Setting up $r(t) = 0$, and adding the disturbance $d(t) = 1$ to the system. The start time is 0 s, the simulation figure is shown in b diagram in Fig. 7. It can be seen from Fig. 7 that the comprehensive control effect of the IFT parameters is better than that of the initial parameters and the reference parameters.

4.2   Numerical Example 2

For a typical plant model with second-order inertia plus hysteresis, when $L/T = 0.2$ and $T = 1$. Selection of the expected Closed-Loop transfer function of the system is

$T_d^2(s) = 1$, and the structure of PID controllers are shown in formula (38) in numerical example 1.

$$P_2(s) = \frac{1}{(1 + Ts)^2} e^{-Ls} \tag{38}$$

According to the reference data in the literature, the initial controller parameters are as follows: $\theta_{c1} = 10$, $\theta_{c2} = 10.5$, $\theta_{c3} = 2.2$, $\theta_{f1} = 8$, $\theta_{f1} = 1.7$. The running condition is the same as numerical example 1. Iterative data is shown in Fig. 8.

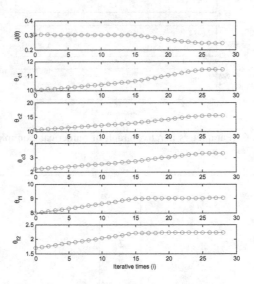

Fig. 8. Parameters iterative graph of numerical example 2.

From the data in Fig. 8, it can be seen that the value of the performance criterion function $J(\theta)$ obtained from the previous iterations decreases relatively small, and the range of controller parameters is relatively stable.

The initial parameters and optimization parameters are brought into the simulation experiment respectively, and the optimized controller parameters in the literature are taken as reference. Setting up $r(t) = 1$ with the starting time is 0 s, and the running time is 7 s. The simulation result is shown in a graph in Fig. 9.

Setting up $r(t) = 0$, and adding the disturbance $d(t) = 1$ to the system. The simulation result is shown in b graph in Fig. 9.

According to Fig. 9, to conclude that the comprehensive control effect of the IFT parameters is better than that of the initial parameters and the reference parameters, though the anti-disturbance is not as good as reference parameters.

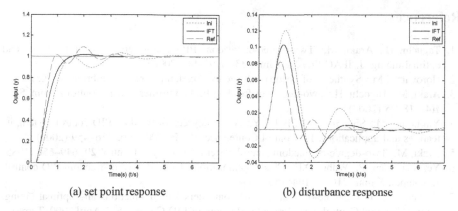

(a) set point response   (b) disturbance response

Fig. 9. Comparison of set point response and disturbance response in numerical examples 2.

5 Summary

In this paper, we extend the IFT method to tuning the parameters of the PID controllers in the 2-DOF structure control system, and the typical feed-forward 2-DOF control is considered as the research object. Compared with the conventional TSTM, the 2-DOF PID controllers can be tuned by using the input-output data of the closed-loop control system without establishing a mathematical model, also two PID controllers' parameters can be tuned at the same time, which makes the controller parameter tuning more direct and accurate. The simulation results show that the tracking performance of the system is better than that of the TSTM, and the anti-interference performance of the system is slightly worse than that of the TSTM. However, the IFT method has less oscillation and faster stability. It is feasible and effective to tune the parameters of 2-DOF PID controllers by integrating the control effect of the whole system.

The following two points should be noted when applying the IFT method in tuning the 2-DOF parameters:

(i) It is necessary to select an appropriate reference model, otherwise, the local optimum is easy to appear in the IFT iteration, and the control effect of the obtained parameters is not satisfactory.

(ii) It is necessary to select the appropriate initial value of the controller parameters, so that the whole control system can be in a stable state, and all the controller parameters can reach the optimum or near the optimum synchronously, which requires some experience in the controlled system.

Currently, the IFT is still under study.

Acknowledgments. This work is supported by Shanghai Key Laboratory of Power Station Automation Technology (No.13DZ2273800).

References

1. Taguchi, H., Araki, M.: Two-degree-of-freedom PID controllers — their functions and optimal tuning. J. IFAC Proc. Volumes **33**(4), 91–96 (2000)
2. Horowitz, I.M.: Synthesis of Feedback Systems. Academic Press, Cambridge (1963)
3. Araki, M., Taguchi, H.: Two-degree-of-freedom PID controller. Int. J. Control Autom. Syst. **1**(4), 18–25 (2003)
4. Yukitomo, M., Shigemasa, T., Baba, Y.: A two degrees of freedom PID control system, its features and applications. In: Control Conference, IEEE, 2004, pp. 456–459 (2004)
5. Araki, M.: Two-degree-of-freedom control system – I. J. Syst. Control **29**, 649–656 (1985)
6. Ye, S.U., Han, P., Wang, D.F.: Chaos optimization of two degree-of-freedom PID control. J. Comput. Simul. **21**(11), 164–166 (2004)
7. Taguchi, H.: Two-degree-of-freedom PID controllers - their functions and optimal tuning. In: IFAC Digital Control: Past, Present and Future of PID Control, 5–7 April 2000, Terrassa, Spain (2000)
8. Taguchi, H., Kokawa, M., Araki, M.: Optimal tuning of two-degree-of-freedom PD controllers. In: Proceedings of the 4th Asian Control Conference, 25–27 September 2002, Singapore (2002)
9. Taguchi, H., Doi, M., Araki, M.: Optimal parameters of two-degrees-of-freedom PID control systems. J. Trans. Soc. Instrum. Control Eng. **23**(9), 889–895 (2009)
10. Lecchini, A., Campi, M.C., Savaresi, S.M.: Virtual reference feedback tuning for two degree of freedom controllers. Int. J. Adapt. Control Signal Process. **16**(5), 355–371 (2002)
11. Hjalmarsson, H., Gunnarsson, S., Gevers, M.: A convergent iterative restricted complexity control design scheme. In: 1994 Proceedings of the IEEE Conference on Decision and Control, pp. 1735–1740 (1994)
12. Xu, J.X., Hou, Z.S.: Notes on data-driven system approaches. J. Acta Autom. Sinica **35**(6), 668–675 (2009)
13. Hjalmarsson, H., Gevers, M., Gunnarsson, S.: Iterative feedback tuning: theory and applications. J. IEEE Control Syst. **18**(4), 26–41 (1998)
14. Hjalmarsson, H.: Iterative feedback tuning—an overview. J Int. J. Adapt. Control Signal Process. **16**(5), 373–395 (2002)
15. Arimoto, S., Kawamura, S., Miyazaki, F.: Bettering operation of dynamic systems by learning: a new control theory for servomechanism or mechatronics systems. In: 2007 IEEE Conference on Decision and Control, pp. 1064–1069 (1984)
16. Han, Z.G., Hou, Z.S.: Robust model-free learning adaptive control for nonlinear systems. Control Decis. (2), 137–142 (1995)
17. Spall, J.C.: Multivariate stochastic approximation using a simultaneous perturbation gradient approximation. IEEE Trans. Autom. Control **37**(3), 332–341 (1992)
18. Campi, M.C., Lecchini, A., Savaresi, S.M.: Brief virtual reference feedback tuning: a direct method for the design of feedback controllers. Automatica **38**(8), 1337–1346 (2002)
19. Safonov, M.G., Tsao, T.C.: The unfalsified control concept: a direct path from experiment to controller. In: Francis, B.A., Tannenbaum, A.R. (eds.) Feedback Control, Nonlinear Systems, and Complexity. LNCIS, vol. 202, pp. 196–214. Springer, Heidelberg (1995). https://doi.org/10.1007/BFb0027678
20. Nakamoto, M.: Parameter tuning of multiple PID controllers by using iterative feedback tuning. In: 2004 SICE 2003 Conference, IEEE, pp. 183–186. IEEE (2003)
21. Bruyne, F.D.: Iterative feedback tuning for internal model controllers. Control Eng. Pract. **11**(9), 1043–1048 (2003)

22. Tesch, D., Eckhard, D., Bazanella, A. S.: Iterative feedback tuning for cascade systems. In: 2017 Control Conference, pp. 495–500. IEEE (2017)
23. Ren, Q., Xu, J., Li, X.: A motion control approach for a robotic fish with iterative feedback tuning. In: 2015 IEEE International Conference on Industrial Technology, pp. 40–45. IEEE (2015)
24. Navalkar, S.T., Wingerden, J.W.V.: Iterative feedback tuning of an LPV Feedforward controller for wind turbine load alleviation. IFAC PapersOnLine **48**(26), 207–212 (2015)
25. Rădac, M.B., Precup, R.E., Petriu, E.M.: Stable iterative feedback tuning method for servo systems. In: 2011 IEEE International Symposium on Industrial Electronics, pp. 1943–1948. IEEE (2011)
26. Precup, R., Mosincat, I., Radac, M.: Experiments in iterative feedback tuning for level control of three-tank system. In: 2010 IEEE Mediterranean Electrotechnical Conference, Melecon 2010, pp. 564–569. IEEE (2010)

IoT Systems

Data Monitoring for Interconnecting Microgrids Based on IOT

Weihua Deng[(⊠)] and Shufen Wang

Shanghai University of Electric Power, Shanghai 200090, China
dwh197859@126.com

Abstract. The real time monitoring is very important for the interconnecting microgrids. The power production status is not only grasped by watching the real time data, but also some optimization approach can be employed to improve operation mode thus dispatching power reasonably. But now a full range of monitoring of interconnecting microgrids is not implemented yet. In the present age of big data, the computing capability and storage space have been developing fast. These advanced techniques enable the large-scale data monitoring system. The big data from monitoring can be analyzed and applied into the optimization of production process. Motivated by this, a real-time data monitoring system simulation platform is developed. Specially, ThingSpeak platform is validated in our work.

Keywords: Microgrid · IOT · Thingspeak · Monitoring

1 Introduction

The Microgrid (MG) is considered to be the most promising intelligent power management system that can be operated in parallel or on an island. The power generated by a single microgrid is limited and can only provide a maximum load capacity of approximately 10 MVA. However, several MGs can be interconnected to provide more power to meet greater load requirements. It also has more redundancy and ensures better power supply reliability [1]. Multiple interconnected microgrids are often referred to as Multi Microgrid (MMG) [2]. The MMG system connects multiple individual microgrids and other distributed generation to a medium voltage distribution network. Currently, each MG is usually based on the local control strategy and does not coordinate with other microgrids according to local requirements and goals [3, 4]. However, it is expected that future subtransmission and distribution systems will consist of several interconnected microgrids and form a complex grid [5].

In an interconnected microgrid, each microgrid will be connected to the next microgrid by High Voltage DC (HVDC) transmission based on Voltage-Sourced Converter (VSC). With the rapid development of fully-controlled power electronic devices and power electronics, high-voltage direct current (HVDC) systems based on voltage source converters (VSC-HVDC) and pulse width modulation technologies have been extensively studied and applied [6]. The VSC-HVDC system provides an economical and reliable solution for large-capacity long-distance power transmission.

© Springer Nature Singapore Pte Ltd. 2018
K. Li et al. (Eds.): ICSEE 2018/IMIOT 2018, CCIS 924, pp. 383–389, 2018.
https://doi.org/10.1007/978-981-13-2384-3_35

Recently, the development process of the VSC-HVDC system shows that they are a better alternative to the traditional thyristor-based HVDC system [7].

A large range of modeling and control of the VSC-based HVDC system have been published in the last few years [8]. From these studies, it becomes clear that the control and the system impedance can have the impact on the stability of the system. Usually, we need to pre-assess their impact on the system stability before connecting to the main grid [9, 10]. Interconnecting together multiple microgrids can lead to undesirable dynamic behaviors, that is why we must monitor some of the important parameters.

It is, therefore, necessary to data monitoring based on IOT. In particular, this paper investigates interconnecting together multiple microgrids, thus provide a method for monitoring data. The remote monitoring center can read the data stored in ThingSpeak from any microgrid at any time. The main objective in this paper is to use thingspeak on the microgrid data monitoring, and the remote monitoring center can access microgrid data at any time for data analysis.

2   System Model

A single microgrid system operated in islanded mode and data monitoring center can monitor data by the communications network. In other words, each microgrid can transmit data in real time, and for the data monitoring center can always get any time required data from any microgrid. Figure 1 shows the comprehensive architecture of IOT framework with ThingSpeak cloud service for microgrid data monitoring. Where P1, P2, P3 respectively are active power of each microgrid, Q1, Q2, Q3 respectively are reactive power of each microgrid, and Udc is DC voltage of VSC-HVDC link.

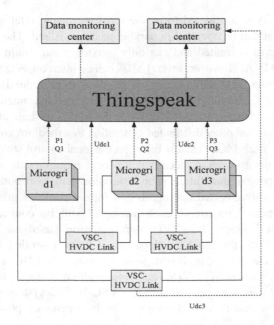

Fig. 1. architecture of IOT framework with ThingSpeak cloud service

2.1 VSC-Based HVDC System Model

The two-terminal VSC-based HVDC system under this study is depicted in Fig. 2. The HVDC system consists of the converter transformers, ac filters, two VSC HVDC converters named VSC1 and VSC2, and the dc cable. Both the VSC1 and VSC2 are assumed to be identical in structure. The electrical circuit of a VSC-HVDC converter for analytical modeling is shown in Fig. 3.

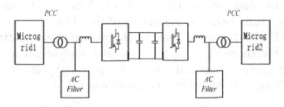

Fig. 2. VSC-based HVDC system

Overview of the control system of a VSC converter and interface to the main circuit shows an overview diagram of the VSC control system and its interface with the main circuit.

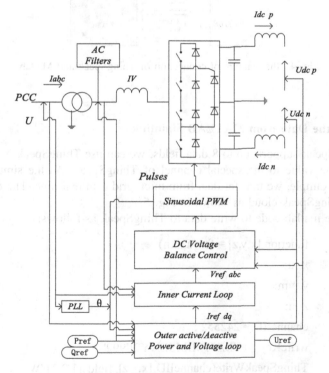

Fig. 3. VSC-HVDC converter

The converter 1 and converter 2 controller designs are identical. The two controllers are independent with no communication between them. Each converter has two degrees of freedom. In our case, these are used to control: P and Q in station 1 (rectifier); Udc and Q in station 2 (inverter).

2.2 IOT with ThingSpeak

ThingSpeak is an IOT analytics platform service that allows you to aggregate, visualize, and analyze live data streams in the cloud [11]. You can send data to ThingSpeak from your devices, create instant visualizations of live data.

With MATLAB analytics inside ThingSpeak, you can write and execute MATLAB code to perform preprocessing, visualizations, and analyses. You can collect and analyze data from internet connected sensors using ThingSpeak. Matlab Simulink is connected with ThingSpeak by the channel as shown Fig. 4.

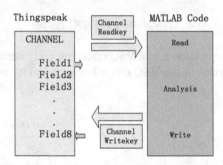

Fig. 4. the diagram of connection of ThingSpeak and Matlab

3 Results

3.1 Write the Data from MATLAB Simulink

Since ThingSpeak supports up to 8 data fields, we can use ThingSpeak. write to send more than one value to the special channel of ThingSpeak. As the simulation progresses, for example, we transfer data from microgrid 1 in real-time. The data will be passed in ThingSpeak cloud as shown in Fig. 5.

There are matlab code to write data to ThingSpeak as follows:

```
function [x,y,z] = fcn(u,m,n)
x=u;
y = m;
z=n;
channelID = 242552 ;
writeKey   = 'BZ57MIMSENY2F992'
ThingSpeakWrite(channelID,[x,y,z],'field',[1,2,3],'W
riteKey', writeKey);
pause(15);
```

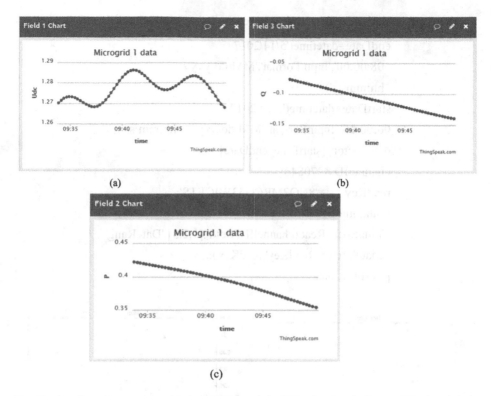

(a)   (b)

(c)

Fig. 5. the data from microgrid 1 is displayed in ThingSpeak platform with simulation. (a) microgrid 1 Udc, (b) microgrid 1 P, (c) microgrid 1 Q

3.2 Read the Data Stored in ThingSpeak

We will use another computer as a remote monitoring center. The monitoring center can be build in any place where it is needed. Our remote monitoring center can read the data stored in ThingSpeak from any microgrid at any time. We can always read the data stored in ThingSpeak, next we will verify its feasibility.

Before we have transfer the VSC-based HVDC simulation data to ThingSpeak, now we read the data from 2017/5/17 08:00:00 to 2017/5/17 10:00:00. Firstly, we begin by specifying a start date and an end date using a datetime object. And we use ThingSpeak. read to read the stored in ThingSpeak. We then append the data and time from each field into two vectors, called data and time. Next we plot the data and time as shown in Fig. 6. (a) microgrid 1 Udc, (b) microgrid 1 P, (c) microgrid 1 Q.

There are matlab code to read data stored in ThingSpeak channel as follows:

```
endDate=datetime('5/14/2017
  08:00:00','InputFormat','MM/dd/yyyy
  hh:mm:ss');
startDate=datetime('5/12/2017
06:00:00','InputFormat','MM/dd/yyyy   hh:mm:ss');
.dateVector=[startDate, endDate];
channelID =270840;
readKey    ='8NQ2MRCG53WICFTS';
[data,time]=
ThingSpeakRead(channelID,'field',[1,2,3],'DateRang
e',dateVector,'ReadKey',readKey);
plot(time, data)
```

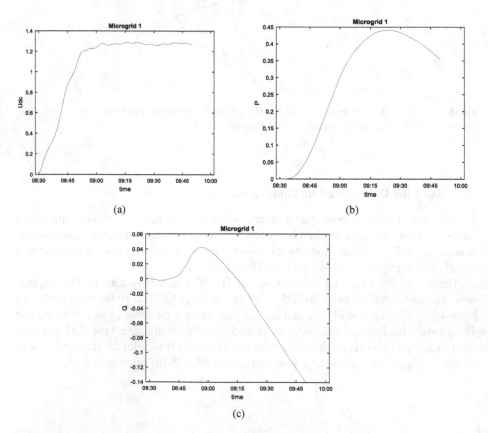

(a)   (b)

(c)

Fig. 6. read the data from ThingSpeak platform (a) microgrid 1 Udc, (b) microgrid 1 P, (c) microgrid 1 Q

4 Conclusions

Data monitoring based on internet of thing for interconnecting together multiple microgrids in this paper. It is shown that even systems that are far apart can share information and monitor data through ThingSpeak. This paper can be applied to multiple microgrids, and we can remotely monitor the dynamic interaction between microgrids thereby controlling the flow of energy. And then an intelligent power management system is proposed to facilitate power trading among microgrids and improved reliability.

References

1. Chowdhury, S., Chowdhury, S.P., Crossley, P.: Microgrids and Active Distribution Networks, Renewable Energy Series, vol. 6. Institution of Engineering and Technology, Stevenage (2009)
2. Gil, N.J., Lopes, J.A.P.: Hierarchical frequency control scheme for islanded multi-microgrids operation. In: IEEE Lausanne Power Tech Lausanne, pp. 473–478 (2007)
3. Lopes, J.A.P., Hatziargyriou, N., Mutale, J., Djapic, P., Jenkins, N.: Integrating distributed generation into electric power systems: A review of drivers, challenges and opportunities. Lecct. Rower Syst. Rest. **77**(9), 1189–1203 (2007)
4. Buayai, K., Ongsakul, W., Mithulananthan, N.: Multi-objective micro-grid planning by NSGA-II in primary distribution system. Eur. Trans. Elect. Power **22**(2), 170–187 (2012)
5. Koyanagi, K., et al.: Electricity cluster-oriented network: a gridindependent and autonomous aggregation of micro-grids. In: Proceedings of the International Symposium: Modern Electric Power System, Wroclaw, Poland, pp. 1–6, September 2010
6. Aditya, S.K., Das, D.: Load-frequency control of an interconnected hydro-thermal power system with new area control error considering battery energy storage facility. Int. J. Energy Res. **24**, 525–538 (2000)
7. Usama, M.U., Kelle, D., Baldwin, T.: Utilizing spinning reserves as energy storage for renewable energy integration. In: Power Systems Conference, pp. 1–5 (2014)
8. Ktiraei, F., Iravani, R., Hatziargyriou, N., Dimeas, A.: Microgrids Management: Controls and Operation Aspects of Microgrids. IEEE Power and Energy Magazine (2008)
9. Beerten, J., Cole, S., Belmans, R.: Modeling of multi-terminal VSC HVDC systems with distributed DC voltage control. IEEE Trans. Power Syst. **29**(1), 34–42 (2014)
10. Lu, W., Ooi, B.-T.: Optimal acquisition and aggregation of offshore wind power by multiterminal voltage-source HVDC. IEEE Trans Power Deliv. **18**, 201–206 (2003)
11. Maureira, G.A.M., Oldenhof, D., Teernstra, L.: ThingSpeak—an API and Web Service for the Internet of Things. World Wide Web, 7 November 2015

A Hybrid Routing Control Mechanism for Dual-Mode Communication of Streetlight Information Acquisition System

Min Xiang$^{(\boxtimes)}$, Xudong Zhao$^{(\boxtimes)}$, and Yongmin Sun$^{(\boxtimes)}$

Key Laboratory of Industrial Internet of Things & Networked Control,
Chongqing University of Posts and Telecommunications,
Chongqing 400065, China
xiangmin@cqupt.edu.cn, 272690907@qq.com,
2729193509@qq.com

Abstract. In order to improve network stability and data acquisition success rate of streetlight information acquisition network, a hybrid routing control mechanism is proposed. Combining the distribution and access mode of streetlight node, and signal attenuation differences between wireless and power line carrier, a dual-tree network is constructed. Firstly, wireless and carrier next hop nodes are respectively calculated in dual-tree network by post-order traversal algorithm. Secondly, next hop node of forwarding packet is selected from wireless and carrier next hop node by the index of transformation rate of signal. The test results show that hybrid routing control mechanism can improve network stability and data acquisition success rate of streetlight information acquisition network.

Keywords: Dual-mode communication · Hybrid routing control
Dual-tree network · Streetlight information acquisition system

1 Introduction

With the development of Internet of Things (IOT) technology, it is a trend that streetlight control system gradually turns to be intelligent [1]. Now, Power Line Communication (PLC) and wireless technology are widely applied in streetlight information acquisition network [2, 3], but it is hard to improve network stability and data acquisition success rate only using PLC or wireless technology in streetlight information acquisition network. Now, dual-mode communication technology is used in smart streetlight, and how to build a reasonable dual-mode network and be efficient to select routing has become a hot issue.

Min Xiang, born in 1974, Ph.D., Professor. His research interests include Smart Grid, wireless sensor network and industrial internet of things.

Xudong Zhao, born in 1993, M.S., His research interests include Smart Grid and industrial internet of things.

Yongmin Sun, born in 1988, M.S., His research interests include Smart Grid and industrial internet of things.

© Springer Nature Singapore Pte Ltd. 2018
K. Li et al. (Eds.): ICSEE 2018/IMIOT 2018, CCIS 924, pp. 390–399, 2018.
https://doi.org/10.1007/978-981-13-2384-3_36

In recent years, there has been relevant research on the application of dual-mode communication technology in streetlight information acquisition network. In [4], a comparison between PLC and wireless used in streetlight control system is proposed, and the advantages and disadvantages about them are introduced. In [5], a design of remote control system based on PLC in the internet of things is proposed. The node can get the RSSI decision channel by obtaining the power carrier and the radio receiving signal intensity. In [6], a method of channel selection and routing strategy is proposed based on the ladder algorithm. The node makes the decision channel through the field strength and the pre divided channel priority.

In order to improve network stability and data acquisition success rate of streetlight information acquisition network, a hybrid routing control mechanism is proposed. Firstly, a dual-tree network is constructed. Secondly, routing of streetlight node forwarding packets is calculated by post-order traversal algorithm and index of transformation rate of signal (TROS).

2 Dual-Mode Communication Architecture

In the streetlight information acquisition network, communication network includes long-distance communication network and local dual-mode communication network. The long-distance communication network is constructed for communicating between the master station and the concentrator node. Local communication network is constructed for communicating between the concentrator node and the streetlight node [7]. The dual-mode communication modules are used in the device of concentrator and the streetlight. The dual-mode communication architecture of streetlight information acquisition system is shown in Fig. 1.

Concentrator node consists of concentrator and dual-mode communication module, which builds and manages streetlight information acquisition network. Streetlight node which consists of master streetlight and dual-mode communication module is responsible for measuring streetlight data.

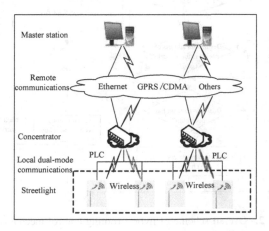

Fig. 1. Dual-mode communication architecture of streetlight information acquisition system

3 Hybrid Routing Control Mechanism

3.1 Overall Scheme Design

Dual-tree network is proposed by combining the distribution of streetlight equipment, access mode of streetlight equipment and signal attenuation differences between wireless and PLC. In the streetlight information acquisition system, the distribution of streetlight nodes have the following characteristics: streetlight nodes are in a parallel strip distribution. Streetlight nodes are mostly tree-like access to streetlight information acquisition network, and the network topology of streetlight nodes is designed to be dual-tree network. There is signal attenuation differences between wireless and PLC. Wireless signals are mainly affected by buildings, distances and weather. After streetlight nodes are deployed, buildings and distances of two nodes are stable, but weather would affect larger areas and lots of nodes. Carrier signals are mainly affected by distances and power line load. After streetlight node is deployed, the distances of two streetlight nodes is stable, but power line load only affects small area and a little nodes. Relay is an effective method to improve the reliability of carrier network. Nodes build wireless and carrier routing metric by hop and RSSI. Wireless routing metric tends to RSSI, and carrier routing metric tends to hop count.

When streetlight node forwards packet, the post-order traversal algorithm is adopted to calculate the wireless and carrier next hop node in dual-tree network. Wireless and carrier next hop node of streetlight node forwarding packet is calculated by post-traversing wireless and carrier routing forwarding tree. $TROS_w$ is transformation rate of signal between current node and wireless next hop node. $TROS_p$ is transformation rate of signal between current node and carrier next hop node. The overall scheme of hybrid routing control mechanism is shown in Fig. 2.

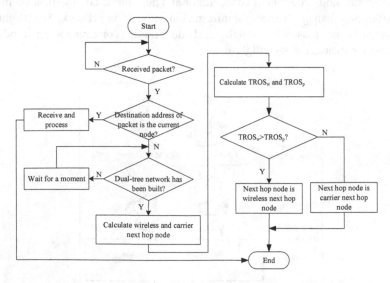

Fig. 2. Overall scheme of hybrid routing control mechanism

3.2 Dual-Tree Network Construction

Streetlight node combines the distribution of streetlight equipment, access mode of streetlight equipment and signal attenuation differences between wireless and PLC, and dual-tree network is constructed. Four network control message frames is defined, and the dual-tree network construction process is divided into three stages.

(1) Network control message frame. In order to build a dual-tree network, four network control message frames are defined. Four network control message frames consists of network beacon frame, route request frame, route reply frame and routing update frame. Streetlight node broadcasts route request frame to get network beacon frame, unicasts route reply frame to parent node to update current node route, and unicasts routing update frame to update child node route to concentrator node. The format of network beacon frame is shown in Fig. 3. The Source Address is 48-bit MAC address. The MAC payload includes one-byte HOP count, one-byte control domain C and one-byte child node number N. High four bit of control domain C identifies the network type, and network beacon frame consists of wireless and carrier network beacon frame.

0 7		55 63	71	79 80 87
32H	Source Address	C	HOP	N	16H
MHR		MAC payload		MFR

Fig. 3. Format of Network beacon frame

(2) Network initialization stage. When streetlight node and concentrator node are powered on, firstly the network will initialized. The dual-mode communication modules of concentrator and streetlight node are initialized on software and hardware. For example, IPv6 protocol stack, software state machine and hardware I/O. The IPv6 address of concentrator node is set by information from the master station. After its IPv6 address is configured, the wireless routing forwarding tree and carrier routing forwarding tree is built by concentrate node, and the wireless and carrier network beacon frame is broadcasted.

(3) Network discovery stage. Streetlight node needs to wait for a while and judge whether network beacon frame is received. If streetlight node hasn't received network beacon frame since node began to wait, it will broadcasts a route request frame to its neighboring neighbor nodes and requests a network beacon frame. If the network beacon frame is received, streetlight node will analyze network beacon frame to obtain hop count, the content of control domain C, and source address. Streetlight node calculates RSSI in data link layer. At the same time, the streetlight receive IPv6 network prefix by neighbor discovery protocol (NDP).

(4) Access control stage. The streetlight node firstly evaluates communication performance of the network to be accessed. The streetlight node sets wireless and carrier routing metric by hop count and RSSI. When streetlight node evaluates the communication performance of wireless network, node focuses on RSSI rather

hop count. When streetlight node evaluates the communication performance of carrier network, streetlight node focuses on hop count rather RSSI. Streetlight node evaluates communication performance of wireless and carrier network by Eq. 1. The β is weight coefficient, $0.5 < \beta < 1$, normally $\beta = 0.6$, the C_m is the permitted biggest number of child node. The L_m is the permitted biggest number of child node. Streetlight node joins the network which has the highest communication performance, and itself hop count is set as a value which is equal to parent hop count plus one. The hop parent is the hop count of parent streetlight node. Then, streetlight node unicasts routing reply frame to parent node, and broadcasts wireless and carrier network beacon frame.

$$\sigma = \begin{cases} \beta \frac{rssi}{10 \lg w} + (1 - \beta)(1 - \frac{hop}{C_m}), & wireless \\ \beta(1 - \frac{hop}{C_m}) + (1 - \beta)\frac{rssi}{10 \lg w}, & plc \end{cases} \tag{1}$$

When streetlight node firstly joins the network, its parent node assigns a two-byte short address A_c to current streetlight node by Eq. 2 and Eq. 3 [8, 9]. The A_p is two-byte short address of parent node, and the n is the number of child node of parent node. In Eq. 3. The d is the hop count of current node. After having set two-byte short address, the streetlight node can obtain the PANID and obtain 64-bit IPv6 network prefix of parent streetlight node.

$$A_C = A_P + 1 + Cskip(d)(n - 1), \quad (1 \leq n \leq C_m). \tag{2}$$

$$Cskip(d) = \begin{cases} 1 + C_m(L_m - d - 1), & C_m = 1 \\ \frac{1 - C_m^{L_m - d}}{1 - C_m}, & C_m > 1 \end{cases}. \tag{3}$$

A dual-tree network is built by one concentrator and seven streetlight nodes, which is shown in Fig. 4. The concentrator node is the root node of this dual-tree network, and each streetlight node has one wireless and carrier parent node. When streetlight node C joins dual-tree network, streetlight node C doesn't choose concentrator node as wireless parent node because there is a barrier between concentrator node and streetlight node C, but streetlight node C still choose concentrator node as carrier parent node because barrier can't affect carrier signal. In dual-tree network, some streetlight nodes have the same wireless and carrier parent nodes while some streetlight nodes have different wireless and carrier parent nodes. When concentrator node and seven streetlight nodes all use wireless channel to communicate, dual-tree network can be regarded as wireless routing forwarding tree, and the wireless next hop count of the streetlight node C is two.

3.3   Hybrid Routing Control

When packet is received by streetlight node, if destination address of packet is the current node, node will receive and handle this packet. If not, node will forward this packet. Firstly wireless and carrier next hop node is calculated. Secondly, TROS is

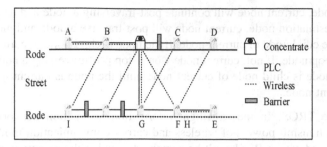

Fig. 4. Dual-tree network

calculated between current node and wireless and carrier next hop node. Finally, next hop node is calculated by TROS and wireless and carrier next hop.

(1) Calculate wireless and carrier next hop node. Wireless next hop node of forwarding packet is calculated by post-traversing wireless routing forwarding tree, and carrier next hop node of forwarding packet is calculated by post-traversing carrier routing forwarding tree. The process of streetlight node post-traversing routing forwarding tree is shown in Fig. 5.

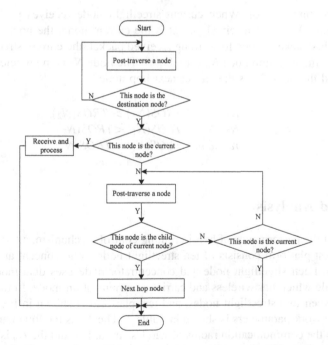

Fig. 5. Process of streetlight node post-traversing routing forwarding tree

In Fig. 5, when current node post-traverses a node in the routing forwarding tree, it will judge whether the node is destination node of packet. If this node isn't the destination node, current node will continue post-traversing a node and judging. If this node is the destination node, current node will post-traverse a node and judge whether the node is the child node of current node. If the node is child node of current node, the node is next hop node. If not, current node won't stop post-traversing a node and judge whether the node is child node of current node until the node is current node or child node of current node.

(2) Calculate TROS. In the streetlight information acquisition network, there are different transmit powers of wireless and carrier communication modules, so the wireless and carrier RSSI can't be compared to judge the communication quality of wireless and carrier channels, and the index of TROS is defined. The current streetlight node calculates TROS by Eq. 4. The *rssi* is the received signal strength of the channel by which current streetlight node communicates with node N, *and* the *w* is the transmit power value in milliwatts. The current streetlight node should calculate wireless and carrier transformation rate of signal.

$$TROS(N) = \frac{10\lg w - rssi}{10\lg w} \times 100\%. \tag{4}$$

(3) Hybrid routing control. When current streetlight node receives packet and the destination address of received packet is the current node, the node receive and process this packet. When forwarding received packet, the current streetlight node calculates the next hop node N_{next} by Eq. 5. The node N_1 is the wireless next hop node, and the node N_2 is the carrier next hop node.

$$N_{next} = \begin{cases} N_1, & TROS(N_1) > TROS(N_2) \\ N_2, & TROS(N_1) < TROS(N_2) \\ random, & TROS(N_1) = TROS(N_2) \end{cases} . \tag{5}$$

4 Test and Analysis

In order to test the performance of hybrid routing control mechanism, a test platform is set up. This test platform consists of ten streetlight nodes, one concentrator node and master station. Each streetlight node and concentrator node uses dual-mode communication module which has wireless and carrier communication mode. In the test, there are walls between two streetlight nodes, and test platform is shown in Fig. 6.

Related network parameters is shown in Table 1. The N_w is the total barriers in test area, the R_w is the communication radius of wireless modules, and the L_m is the biggest permissible number of child nodes.

(1) Parent node update times. In order to verify the ability of improving network stability by hybrid routing control mechanism (HRCM), HRCM is compared with carrier communication scheme proposed in [10] and the wireless communication

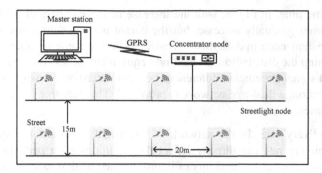

Fig. 6. Test platform

Table 1. Network parameters

Parameter	Value	Definition
N_w	10	Total barrier number
R_w	80 m	Communication radius of wireless
R_p	310 m	Communication radius of PLC
C_m	5	The biggest hop
L_m	6	The biggest number of child node
β	0.6	Scale factor

scheme proposed in [11]. The devices shown in test platform are adopted to build network of streetlight information acquisition by three communication schemes, and concentrator node calculates the parent node update times. The parent node update times under different time is shown in Fig. 7. The parent node update times under different numbers of wall is shown in Fig. 8.

In Fig. 7, the parent node update times in the daytime is more than it at night, but the parent node update times of HRCM is less than the parent node update times of

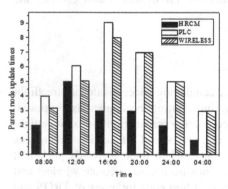

Fig. 7. The parent node update times under different time

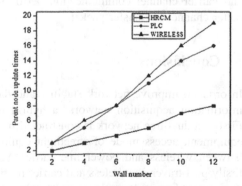

Fig. 8. The parent node update times under different numbers of wall

PLC in the same time. In Fig. 8, with the increase of the numbers of wall, the parent node update times gradually increase, but the parent node update times of HRCM is less than the parent node update times of wireless in the same number of streetlight nodes. Combining the distribution of streetlight equipment, access method of streetlight equipment and signal attenuation differences between micro power wireless and power line communication, a dual-tree network is proposed. The dual-tree has the less parent node update times.

(2) Packet delivery rate. In the network of streetlight information acquisition, the packet delivery rate can directly reflect the communication performance of network. In order to verify the ability of improving acquisition success rate streetlight information, HRCM is compared with PLC and wireless by the index of packet delivery rate. The devices shown in test platform are adopted to build network of streetlight information acquisition by three communication schemes, and concentrator node calculates packet delivery rate. The packet delivery rate under different time and wall number is shown in Table 2.

Table 2. Packet delivery rate under different time and nodes

T	N	N_w	Size	HRCM	PLC	WIRELESS
08:00	10	0	1000	100%	99.3%	100%
12:00	10	2	1000	100%	98.2%	100%
16:00	10	4	1000	99.8%	98.3%	99.7%
20:00	10	6	1000	99.6%	98.5%	99.5%
24:00	10	8	1000	99.9%	99.3%	98.9%
04:00	10	10	1000	100%	99.8%	98.1%

In Table 2, with the increasing number of streetlight nodes, the packet delivery rate of wireless is gradually reduced, and the packet delivery rate of PLC in the day time is less than at night. The packet delivery rate of HRCM is the highest in three communication schemes. In the network built by HRCM, streetlight node evaluates wireless and carrier channel communication performance by TROS index, and chooses the better channel to transfer packet.

5   Conclusions

In order to improve network stability and data acquisition success rate of streetlight information acquisition network, a hybrid routing control mechanism is proposed. Firstly, a dual-tree network is constructed by combining the distribution of streetlight equipment, access mode of streetlight equipment, and signal attenuation differences between wireless and power line carrier. Secondly, when node forwards packet, it firstly post-traverses wireless and carrier routing forward tree to calculate wireless and carrier next hop node; node secondly calculates next hop node by index of TROS and wireless and carrier next hop node. The test results show that hybrid routing control mechanism can improve network stability and data acquisition success rate of street-light information acquisition network.

Acknowledgments. This work is supported by Key R&D program of common key technology innovation for key industries in Chongqing (cstc2017zdcy-zdyfX0032).

References

1. Bai, C.-L., Ma, J.: Intelligent street lamp monitoring system based on internet of things. J. Appl. Electron. Tech. **40**(3), 82–85 (2014)
2. Yan, Z.-L., Gao, S.-J., Huang, X.-Y.: Application of wireless sensor network based on IPv6-based low-power wireless personal area network in smart street lights. J. China Electric Power **23**, 78–79 (2016)
3. Gao, Y.-H., Liang, X.-Y.: Design of intelligent streetlight control system based on Zigbee. J. Modern Electron. Technol. **19**, 29–32 (2013)
4. Zhu, M.: Comparison of Zigbee and power line carrier in street lamp single lamp control system. J. China New Commun. **17**(19), 39–40 (2015)
5. Li, Z.-Z., Du, Y., Fan, X.-Z.: Research and design of dual mode heterogeneous communication based on ladder algorithm. J. Electro Tech. Appl. **17**, 118–121 (2015)
6. Kong, Y.-H., Li, J.-C., Chen, Z.-X.: Design and Realization of an Adaptive Dual-mode Communication Module Based on RSSI. J. Sci. Technol. Eng. **16**(23), 203–207 (2016)
7. Zhu, Y.-N., Liu, J., Xu, Q.: Application of dual-mode communication in bidirectional interaction of smart meters. J. Appl. Electron. Tech. (z1), 210–213 (2015)
8. Qi, Z.-Y., Li, Z.-F.: Microgrid monitoring network based on Zigbee communication. J. Comput. Eng. **43**(4), 79–83 (2017)
9. Zhou, S.-Y., Gao, J.-Z., Zou, S.-H.: Energy-efficient data storage with non-uniform nodes distributed wireless sensor networks. J. Chongqing Univ.: Nat. Sci. Edn. **40**(9), 57–66 (2017)
10. Xiang, M., He, J.-X., Du, Y.-H.: An IPv6 based-tree routing control mechanism for low-voltage power line communication. J. Power Syst. Technol. **40**(06), 1874–1880 (2016)
11. Huang, Z.-C., Yuan, F., Li, Y.: Implementation of IPv6 over low power wireless personal area network based on wireless sensor network in smart lighting. J. Comput. Appl. **34**(10), 3029–3033 (2014)

An RF Energy Harvesting Approach for Secure Wireless Communication in IoT

Cheng Yin[1]([✉]), Emiliano Garcia-Palacios[1], and Hien M. Nguyen[2]

[1] Queen's University Belfast, Belfast, UK
cyin01@qub.ac.uk, e.garcia@ee.qub.ac.uk
[2] Duy Tan University, Da Nang, Vietnam
nguyenminhhien2501@gmail.com

Abstract. Mobile terminals and base stations are being deployed globally resulting in an increase in carbon emissions. Energy harvesting is attracting considerable attention and an environment- friendly communication system is desirable. In this paper, we demonstrate such a system. A power beacon provides energy for a transmitting source and for a relay using time switching radio frequency energy harvesting technique. We demonstrate that when an eavesdropper tries to wiretap the signals transmitted from the source and the relay the system remains secure. The closed-form expression for secrecy outage probability is derived. Our results show how the performance varies with the SNR of the power beacon and the distance from the relay and the source to the power beacon. In addition, we show that the duration of energy harvesting process in relation to the time used for transmitting information has a significant impact on the system security.

1 Introduction

In early Internet of Things (IoT) applications batteries are being used in plenty of sensor devices and embedded equipment but their lifespan is limited and they need replacement and maintenance. Most batteries end up in landfills and this has a bad impact on the environment. To reduce the use of batteries, energy harvesting (EH) techniques are gaining increasing interest. Devices and equipment can derive energy by themselves using energy harvesting technology from environmental resources and prolong their lifetime. Ideally sensors could derive enough energy to become battery-less! When performing a harvesting process, energy is gathered from the external environment, i.e., solar, wind, vibration, electromagnetic, thermoelectric phenomena. In this way, sufficient energy could be harvested to drive a wireless sensor network (WSN) for an IoT application. To compare the amount of harvested energy from these resources, we show some figures from [4,5] in Table 1. Although solar, vibration, thermal have more power density, they are not always available, moreover, the cost of energy such as solar is still high.

Compared with other sources in Table 1, due to the increase in mobile terminals and base stations, electromagnetic energy is available anywhere (both

© Springer Nature Singapore Pte Ltd. 2018
K. Li et al. (Eds.): ICSEE 2018/IMIOT 2018, CCIS 924, pp. 400–407, 2018.
https://doi.org/10.1007/978-981-13-2384-3_37

Table 1. an overview of different energy sources and harvested energy [4,5]

Source	Harvested power
Vibration	
Human	$4\,\mu\text{w}/\text{cm}^2$
Industrial	$100\,\mu\text{w}/\text{cm}^2$
Thermal	
Human	$30\,\mu\text{w}/\text{cm}^2$
Industrial	$1-10\,\text{mw}/\text{cm}^2$
Solar	
Indoor	$10\,\mu\text{w}/\text{cm}^2$
Outdoor	$10\,\text{mw}/\text{cm}^2$
Radio Frequency (RF)	
Cell phone	$0.1\,\mu\text{w}/\text{cm}^2$
Wi-Fi	$1\,\text{mw}/\text{cm}^2$
GSM	$0.1\,\mu\text{w}/\text{cm}^2$

indoor and outdoor) and anytime. In addition, it can be retrieved boundlessly from multiple power sources in various scenarios, e.g., TV, radio stations, satellite stations, cell phones masts, Wi-Fi, etc. In order to capture electromagnetic energy, some authors have already designed a system to realize it [4]. The key modules are the antenna and rectifier circuit which can transfer RF signals or alternating current (AC) to direct current (DC) [4]. The process of harvesting energy from RF signals is clean and does not produce any pollution to the environment. Several schemes have been proposed for RF energy harvesting because simultaneously harvesting power and transmitting information is not practical due to the limitation of hardware [2]. There are two main protocols to tackle this problem, i.e. time switching (TS) protocol and power splitting (PS) protocol. In TS protocol, during a given period, time is dived into two parts for energy harvesting and information transmitting. If PS protocol is used instead, some power is used for energy harvesting and the rest is used for signal transmitting. In [8] a TS protocol was considered in a cognitive radio context and the impact of the position of the primary user (far or near) upon secondary transmitters was studied.

In IoT and WSN where communication technologies are limited in transmission range from source to destination the use of relays is desirable. Relays help to extend the range of sensor nodes thus helping to interconnect nodes in the sensor network or helping a given sensor to reach a distant destination. Existing research has shown that relaying networks can enhance the system performance [7]. At the radio layer there are two relay alternatives, amplify-and-forward (AF) and decode-and-forward (DF). Compared with AF, a relay network operating with DF relays has better performance because the interference is lower [6].

However, DF relays require more power to operate due to its complexity. Relay nodes can only be equipped with finite energy to work for a functioning time [1]. Replacing and charging batteries is not desirable. This motivate us to consider exploiting RF energy harvesting for relays too. We could envisage a sensor network where sensors and relays are now battery-less.

In future sensor applications, security is also a crucial problem that we cannot ignore. Because of the broadcast nature of wireless channel, information is vulnerable to eavesdropping [6]. Traditional way to secure wireless information is to deploy cryptographic techniques at higher layers despite consuming huge power for encrypting, decrypting data and burdening the protocol stack which is to be avoided in energy constrained sensor networks. At the lower layer, physical layer security (PLS) has gained popularity in recent years to secure wireless communication.

In this research, we propose a mathematical approach and system model to obtain the system performance, i.e. secrecy outage probability (SOP). In the system, an information source (e.g. a sensor) transmits desired signals to a destination (e.g. a base station or sink) with the help of a relay node. In the future we envisage IoT scenarios where the sensors and relay nodes are battery-less. To enable such a system, a power beacon is assumed to provide energy for the information source and the relay node. Then the information source and the relay forward the signals with the harvested energy. To assess security, an eavesdropper is also considered in the system, and it can wiretap signals from the source and the relay. In our model, an outage occurs when either the system is not reliable or not secure, hence we assess the secrecy outage probability as a performance parameter. Our contributions are summarized as:

- We propose a system model including an information source, a relay, a destination, an eavesdropper and a power beacon. The information source and relay node harvest energy from the power beacon using TS protocol.
- The impacts of the location and the signal-to-noise ratio (SNR) of power beacon on the system performance are investigated.
- The fraction of time dedicated for energy harvesting in a TS frame α versus the time dedicated for information transmission to the relay and destination has a direct impact on performance. This is investigated to find the optimum value of alpha.
- Closed-form expression for SOP is derived. In addition, Monte Carlo method is used to evaluate simulation results.

2   System Model

We consider a network with a power beacon B, an information source S, a DF relay R, a destination D and an eavesdropper E, as shown in Fig. 1. All the nodes are equipped with one antenna and all the channels are independent and identically distributed. The additive white Gaussian noise (AWGN) at R_k and D has zero mean and variance N_0. Assuming all the channels are Rayleigh fading and the channel power gains follow exponential distribution with parameter λ_{AB}, where $A \in \{B, S, R\}$ and $B \in \{S, R, D, E\}$.

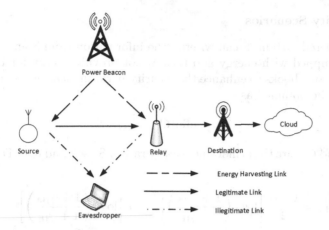

Fig. 1. An RF energy harvesting system model for secure IoT

2.1 Energy Harvesting Scheme

In the considered system, B provides energy for S and R using TS protocol based energy harvesting technique, as shown in Fig. 2, because of its high throughput. α is the EH time fraction $(0 < \alpha < 1)$ that has been chosen as a design parameter. In a transmission block time T, it takes S and R a period of αT to harvest energy from B and then both S and R use $\frac{(1-\alpha)T}{2}$ to transmit information to R and D.

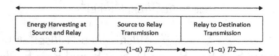

Fig. 2. TS Protocol

Hence, the energy harvested at S and R are

$$E_{\mathsf{S}} = \eta \mathcal{P}_{\mathsf{B}} \alpha T |h_{\mathsf{BS}}|^2, \tag{1}$$

$$E_{\mathsf{R}} = \eta \mathcal{P}_{\mathsf{B}} \alpha T |h_{\mathsf{BR}}|^2, \tag{2}$$

where η is the efficiency coefficient of the energy conversion ratio between the power delivered to the load and the harvested power at the antenna $(0 < \eta < 1)$ [4]. $\mathcal{P}_{\mathsf{B}}$ is the transmit power of power beacon. $|h_{\mathsf{BS}}|^2$ is the channel power gains of B $\rightarrow$ S and $|h_{\mathsf{BR}}|^2$ is the channel power gains of B $\rightarrow$ R. The transmit power at S and R can be derived as below,

$$\mathcal{P}_{\mathsf{S}} = \frac{2\eta \mathcal{P}_{\mathsf{B}} |h_{\mathsf{BS}}|^2 \alpha}{(1-\alpha)}, \tag{3}$$

$$\mathcal{P}_{\mathsf{R}} = \frac{2\eta \mathcal{P}_{\mathsf{B}} |h_{\mathsf{BR}}|^2 \alpha}{(1-\alpha)}. \tag{4}$$

2.2 Security Scenarios

In the considered system, E can wiretap the information from S and R. Assume that E is equipped with energy and B does not provide energy for E. S and R use different code books to enhance the security performance. Hence, the secrecy capacity can be obtained as

$$C_s = \min(C_{1s}, C_{2s}), \tag{5}$$

where C_{1s} and C_{2s} are the achievable secrecy rate of S $\rightarrow$ R and R $\rightarrow$ D, expressed as follows:

$$C_{1s} = \frac{1-\alpha}{2} \left[\log_2\left(\frac{1+\gamma_{1M}}{1+\gamma_{1E}}\right)\right]^+ = \epsilon \left[\log_2\left(\frac{1+\gamma_{1M}}{1+\gamma_{1E}}\right)\right]^+, \tag{6}$$

$$C_{2s} = \frac{1-\alpha}{2} \left[\log_2\left(\frac{1+\gamma_{2M}}{1+\gamma_{2E}}\right)\right]^+ = \epsilon \left[\log_2\left(\frac{1+\gamma_{2M}}{1+\gamma_{2E}}\right)\right]^+, \tag{7}$$

where $\epsilon = \frac{1-\alpha}{2}$ clarify the fact that in a block time T, both S $\rightarrow$ R and R $\rightarrow$ D use $(1-\alpha)T/2$ to transmit information, γ_{1M} is the SNR at R, γ_{2M} is the SNR at D, γ_{1E} and γ_{2E} are the SNRs of the links S $\rightarrow$ E and R $\rightarrow$ E,

$$\gamma_{1M} = \xi\gamma_M|h_{BS}|^2|h_{SR}|^2, \tag{8}$$

$$\gamma_{2M} = \gamma_M\xi|h_{BR}|^2|h_{RD}|^2, \tag{9}$$

$$\gamma_{1E} = \gamma_E\xi|h_{BS}|^2|h_{SE}|^2, \tag{10}$$

$$\gamma_{2E} = \gamma_E\xi|h_{BR_k}|^2|h_{RE}|^2, \tag{11}$$

where $\gamma_M = \frac{P_B}{N_0}$, $\gamma_E = \frac{P_B}{N_E}$, $\xi = \frac{2\eta\alpha}{(1-\alpha)}$. $|h_{SR}|^2, |h_{RD}|^2, |h_{SE}|^2$ and $|h_{RE}|^2$ are the channel power gains of S $\rightarrow$ R$_{k^*}$, R$_{k^*}$ $\rightarrow$ D, S $\rightarrow$ E, and R $\rightarrow$ E. N_E is the variance of the AWGN at E.

The secrecy capacity of the proposed system is given as,

$$C_s = \epsilon\left[\log_2 \min\left(\frac{1+\gamma_M\xi|h_{BS}|^2|h_{SR}|^2}{1+\gamma_E\xi|h_{BS}|^2|h_{SE}|^2},\right.\right.$$

$$\left.\left.\frac{1+\gamma_M\xi|h_{BR}|^2|h_{RD}|^2}{1+\gamma_E\xi|h_{BR}|^2|h_{RE}|^2}\right)\right]^+. \tag{12}$$

3 Secrecy Outage Probability

In this section, SOP is derived to obtain the secrecy performance of the considered system. The concept of SOP is that the probability of secrecy capacity is below a certain rate [3],

$$P_{out} = \mathbb{P}\left\{C_S < R_{th}\right\}, \tag{13}$$

where C_s is the secrecy capacity of the system, and R_{th} is the secrecy target rate ($R_{th} > 0$). An outage occurs when either the system is not reliable or not secure.

From (12), we have

$$\mathbb{P}\left\{C_s < R_{th}\right\} = \mathbb{P}\left\{\gamma_{\mathsf{PRS}} < \beta\right\}$$
$$= F_{\gamma_{\mathsf{PRS}}}\left(\beta\right), \tag{14}$$

where

$$\gamma_{\mathsf{PRS}} = \min\left(\frac{1 + \gamma_{\mathsf{M}}\xi|h_{\mathsf{BS}}|^2|h_{\mathsf{SR}}|^2}{1 + \gamma_{\mathsf{E}}\xi|h_{\mathsf{BS}}|^2|h_{\mathsf{SE}}|^2},\right.$$
$$\left.\frac{1 + \gamma_{\mathsf{M}}\xi|h_{\mathsf{BR}}|^2|h_{\mathsf{RD}}|^2}{1 + \gamma_{\mathsf{E}}\xi|h_{\mathsf{BR}}|^2|h_{\mathsf{RE}}|^2}\right). \tag{15}$$

$F_{\gamma_{\mathsf{PRS}}}\left(\beta\right)$ is the CDF of γ_{PRS}, and $\beta = 2^{\frac{R_{th}}{\epsilon}}$.

From (14) we have the following lemma.

Lemma 1. *The SOP of the considered system is formulated as follows:*

$$F_{\gamma_{\mathsf{PRS}}}\left(\beta\right) = 1 - \frac{4\gamma_{\mathsf{M}}(\beta - 1)\lambda_{\mathsf{SE}}\lambda_{\mathsf{RE}}\sqrt{\lambda_{\mathsf{BS}}\lambda_{\mathsf{BR}}\ \lambda_{\mathsf{SR}}\lambda_{\mathsf{RD}}}}{\xi(\gamma_{\mathsf{E}}\lambda_{\mathsf{SR}}\beta + \gamma_{\mathsf{M}}\lambda_{\mathsf{SE}})(\gamma_{\mathsf{E}}\lambda_{\mathsf{RD}}\beta + \gamma_{\mathsf{M}}\lambda_{\mathsf{RE}})}$$
$$\times \mathbf{K}_1\left(2\sqrt{\frac{\lambda_{\mathsf{RD}}\lambda_{\mathsf{BR}}(\beta - 1)}{\gamma_{\mathsf{M}}\xi}}\right)\mathbf{K}_1\left(2\sqrt{\frac{\lambda_{\mathsf{SR}}\ \lambda_{\mathsf{BS}}(\beta - 1)}{\gamma_{\mathsf{M}}\xi}}\right), \tag{16}$$

where $\mathbf{K}_1(\cdot)$ is the modified Bessel function of the second kind.

4 Numerical Results

In this section, the simulation results using Monte Carlo approach are evaluated to prove the accuracy of above performance analysis. The 'Sim' curves are the simulation results and 'Ana' curves are analytical results. In the figures, we can observe that both the simulation curves and analytical curves match very well.

Moreover, the parameters are fixed as: $\gamma_{\mathsf{E}} = 20$dB, $R_{th} = 0.2$ bits/s/Hz and $\eta = 0.5$. It is assumed that the position of the nodes are located in Cartesian coordinate system as $\mathsf{S} = (0,0), \mathsf{R} = (2,0), \mathsf{D} = (3,0)$ and $\mathsf{E} = (1,-4)$ respectively. The location of B is not fixed because the impact of the location of B is investigated later. Hence, the distance between two nodes can be described as $d_{AB} = \sqrt{(x_A - x_B)^2 + (y_A - y_B)^2}$ where $A, B = \{\mathsf{S}, \mathsf{B}, \mathsf{D}, \mathsf{R}, \mathsf{E}\}$. A and B have the co-ordinates (x_A, y_A) and (x_B, y_B). It is assumed that average SNR of each link is dependent on the path loss as $1/\lambda_X = 1/d_X^{pl}$, where pl is the path loss exponent. In this section, $pl = 4$ is assumed.

In Fig. 3, the impacts of γ_{M} and the position of B are investigated. We can observe that with the increase of γ_{M}, the system has a better performance due to the decrease of SOP. The position of B varies from $(1, 0), (1, 1)$ to $(1, 2)$

which means it moves vertically, further from S and R. We can observe from the figure that the distance between B to R and S increases, the system has a worse performance because the SOP increases. This demonstrates the fact that as the distance between B to R and S increases, R and S harvest less energy for transmission, thus decreasing the system performance.

In Fig. 4, SOP is plotted as function of α. We assume that $\gamma_E = 20$ dB and B $= (1, 0)$. It can be observed that SOP is extremely high when α is too small or too large. This is because when α is small, S and R can not harvest enough energy. In addition, when α is large, the transmit period will be short, so the secrecy capacity is low. Therefore, we should design α carefully in order to achieve a secure wireless system. In our examples, $\alpha = 0.6$ is nearly an optimum point.

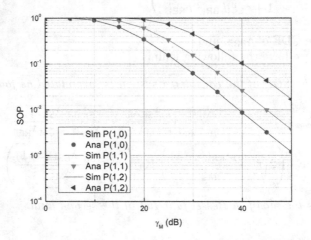

Fig. 3. SOP with different position of B

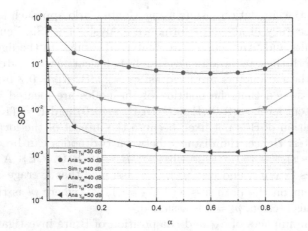

Fig. 4. SOP is plotted as a function of α with different γ_M

5   Conclusion

In this paper, an EH system with a DF relay and a power beacon is proposed. The information source and the relay can harvest energy from the power beacon and then forward the signal to the destination. The eavesdropper can wiretap the signals transmitted from the source and the relay. Time switching protocol based EH is used. The closed-form expression for SOP is derived. The results have shown that γ_M and the distance between the power beacon and the source and the relay can affect the performance of the considered EH system significantly. When the power beacon locates closer to the source and the relay as well as γ_M is high, the system performs significantly better. Moreover, the time dedicated to harvesting energy in a TS frame α can affect the secrecy performance of the considered system significantly. Hence, α should be designed carefully. We show the optimum value in our examples. In summary, we have demonstrated that it is possible to harvest enough energy from RF sources to transmit information, to extend the range via a relay and more significantly for the system to be resilient to an eavesdropper attack.

Acknowledgement. This work was supported by a Research Environment Links grant, ID 339568416, under the Newton Programme Vietnam partnership. The grant is funded by the UK Department of Business, Energy and Industrial Strategy (BEIS) and delivered by the British Council. For further information, please visit www.newtonfund. ac.uk.

References

1. Akhtar, F., Rehmani, M.H.: Energy replenishment using renewable and traditional energy resources for sustainable wireless sensor networks: a review. Renew. Sustain. Energy Rev. **45**, 769–784 (2015)
2. Benedict, F.P., Maji, P., Roy, S.D., Kundu, S.: Secrecy analysis of a cognitive radio network with an energy harvesting AF relay. In: 2017 International Conference on Wireless Communications, Signal Processing and Networking (WiSPNET), pp. 1358–1363. IEEE (2017)
3. Bloch, M., Barros, J., Rodrigues, M.R., McLaughlin, S.W.: Wireless information-theoretic security. IEEE Trans. Inf. Theory **54**(6), 2515–2534 (2008)
4. Tran, L.G., Cha, H.K., Park, W.T.: RF power harvesting: a review on designing methodologies and applications. Micro Nano Syst. Lett. **5**(1), 14 (2017)
5. Vullers, R., van Schaijk, R., Doms, I., Van Hoof, C., Mertens, R.: Micropower energy harvesting. Solid-State Electron. **53**(7), 684–693 (2009)
6. Yin, C., Nguyen, H.T., Kundu, C., Kaleem, Z., Garcia-Palacios, E., Duong, T.Q.: Secure energy harvesting relay networks with unreliable backhaul connections. IEEE Access **6**, 12074–12084 (2018)
7. Yin, C., Nguyen, N.P., Garcia-Palacios, E., Tran, X.N., Le-Tien, T.: Secure energy harvesting communications with relay selection over nakagami-m fading channels. Mob. Netw. Appl. 1–8 (2017)
8. Zhang, J., Nguyen, N.P., Zhang, J., Garcia-Palacios, E., Le, N.P.: Impact of primary networks on the performance of energy harvesting cognitive radio networks. IET Commun. **10**(18), 2559–2566 (2016)

Low-Cost, Extensible and Open Source Home Automation Framework

Che Cameron[1(✉)] and Kang Li[2]

[1] Queens University Belfast, University Road, Belfast BT7 1NN, UK
ccameron07@qub.ac.uk
[2] University of Leeds, Leeds LS2 9JT, UK

Abstract. The implementation of an IoT application usually depends on a framework, platform or ecosystem - of which there are many choices available, both closed- and open-source, each presenting their own vision. By reviewing a range of different options with respect to features, price and customisability it is shown that each provider tends to limit the available opportunities in their platform, either intentionally or unintentionally. Therefore an open-source framework with NodeRED at its core is developed and presented which imposes minimal constraints upon the user/developer, encourages novices to learn and safeguards the privacy of its users.

This approach is verified by building a demonstration system which is retrofitted to an old property and successfully provides heating system control and finger print entry. The use of heterogeneous nodes and the integration of 2 radio technologies serve to underscore the technological agnosticism and flexibility of this framework.

Keywords: Home automation · IoT · Open-Source · Low cost
NodeRED · MQTT

1 Introduction

The field of IoT has been the topic of much discussion and development over the past few years, and has arguably suffered from its own hype. The stunning array of low-cost sensors, actuators and controllers presents a panoply of possible applications - and in so doing, runs the risk of an over-abundance of choice. This is reflected in the lack of harmonisation or standardisation throughout the field [1].

However, some standard tools and techniques have started to emerge which are helping to increase interoperability between ecosystems and devices [10] - an important aspect of the interconnected world which is striven for. In this fluid and constantly developing landscape, a strong strategy for platform development focuses upon wide compatibility, technological agnosticism and quick reconfigurability [6].

Useful technology can be defined by the impact it has upon our lives, and the home environment presents a prime opportunity for this impact. Some schools of

K. Li et al. (Eds.): ICSEE 2018/IMIOT 2018, CCIS 924, pp. 408–418, 2018.
https://doi.org/10.1007/978-981-13-2384-3_38

architecture consider the home as a *machine for living* and in this vein, the most important functions of that machine could be considered as suitable targets for IoT technologies.

The temperature of a dwelling is one of the most important aspects of comfort (and even safety, in extreme conditions) and usually consumes the largest proportion of the total energy expended in the home - both in empirical terms and in cost. Central heating control is a natural starting point for many home IoT systems, which often build out their functionality from this foundation [4]. Proactive energy management of a home plays a large role in setting household running costs and influences environmental impact - and is greatly assisted and optimised through the use of smart interconnected systems.

A selection of available IoT platforms will be overviewed (with a focus on Open-Source) in Sect. 2, then this paper will introduce the framework in Sect. 3, including the details of the software packages, then go on to describe the demonstration system in Sect. 4, with information about the implementation in hardware and software. Section 5 offers some observations and thoughts on the results of using this framework in a practical setting, and the work is briefly concluded in Sect. 6.

2   IoT Platforms

The framework that will be presented here is more akin to an architecture than any individual products and so it is most fruitful to consider the major Home IoT ecosystems in use today rather than attempt to review the wide range of individual products available.

Amazon Alexa, Google Home and Apple Homekit, nest products and Samsung Smartthings make up a large segment of the market and give a fair representation of the shape of closed-source Home IoT technologies. They are characterised by expensive components, centralised servers for management and beautiful, highly developed interfaces that require minimal effort from the end-user to set up.

Initially, each company tried their best to create a closed ecosystem with a monopoly on compatible products, however consumer pressure is forcing them to gradually open their platforms to more devices [5]. The support that each offers is still far from universal, ultimately restrictive in what can be accomplished and largely pre-defines how the user interacts with their system.

Open source solutions are available for IoT and there are many, and ever-changing choices (as is custom in this arena). These solutions vary from presenting a complete management suite down to aggregation of control panels for disparate devices/systems. Some closed-source projects also aim to integrate disparate IoT ecosystems and generally monetise this effort by offering enhanced features for a price.

The general advantages of an open-source approach are transparency of operation (helping to safeguard security and privacy), the ability to customise the elements as desired and a reduction in cost. In a less tangible fashion, the community surrounding an open-source project is often passionate about what they are building and using, which is commonly reflected in the level of help that is available from developers and peers.

Many of these platforms provide built-in support for a wide range of end devices and hubs, along with a community that continues to develop plug-ins. Without a specific application in mind, it is counter-productive to attempt to definitively rank the different projects - Table 1 shows a comparison of the important characteristics and features of a variety of systems.

Table 1. Comparison of IoT platforms

PLATFORM	SET UP & CONFIGURATION	AUTOMATION / FEATURES	DEVICE INTEGRATION	PRICE
Calaos [Open Source]	GUI Configuration of plugins	Scripted Rules Engine, LUA Scripting	Wago PLC, multimedia, additional devices as developed	FREE
Domoticz [Open Source]	GUI Configuration of plugins, Auto-Detection of Devices	Simple Event Scripting, Notifications, Master/Slave Devices,	Wide Range of Plug-Ins	FREE
Home Assistant [Open Source]	YAML, Add-On Store, Text Config Files	Scripted Rules Engine (States Based), AppDaemon (Python),	1000+ Devices	FREE
openHAB [Open Source]	JVM Environment, Text Config Files, Limited GUI Config	Bindings API (text based), Experimental Rules Engine	Wide Range of Plug-Ins	FREE
OpenRemote [Closed Source]	Web Based UI Designer, Text Config Files, Scripting	Scripted Rules Engine (Drools)	Wide Range of Plug-Ins (variable quality and completeness)	Private: FREE, Commercial: $150
ThingsBoard [Open Source]	GUI Device Manager, Text Config Files	Rules Engine, Asset Tracking, Cluster Servers	MQTT, CoAP and HTTP with provision for legacy systems (eg. Modbus)	Basic:FREE, Advanced: $1999/year
iRule [Closed Source]	Web Based UI Builder	Device Commands only	Plug-Ins for Major EcoSystems, IR remote, NO custom plugin development	Basic: $49.99, Advanced: $99.99

The implementation of rules engines, scripting and programming languages is often proprietary (or at least non-standard). This means that basic, pre-defined or anticipated tasks are relatively easy, but a steep learning curve often presents itself upon any attempt to customise functionality outside of the designated development path. Therefore any large project is likely to generate significant amounts of code and effort that cannot be reused elsewhere [9].

Each platform tends to have a particular philosophy or paradigm to champion, however therein lies a problem - the presupposition of applications, tasks and functionality. The framework described in Sect. 3 addresses this issue by connecting generalised tools with an open and flexible approach.

3   Home IoT Framework

3.1   Overview

This framework is composed of a networked hub, sensor/actor nodes and a web interface suitable for computer or mobile use.

The hub is responsible for node management, data handling (aggregation, storage and processing) and it integrates a web interface which may be optionally forwarded to the WAN for remote access. Programming and implementation is achieved primarily through the flow-based Node-RED software on the hub, and inter-component communication is via the MQTT protocol making use of JSON encoding for data structures.

Physical nodes may be composed of any technologies that the user desires, the only requirement being that some form of MQTT is supported for integration with NodeRED. Most modern homes incorporate a wireless network already, which this system can connect to - alternatively a separate air-gapped network or different radio technology can be used if desired. The intent is to demonstrate a low-cost, hardware agnostic approach to Home IoT which trades some ease of installation for large cost savings, fast development of applications and huge customisability.

An important note should be made with respect to privacy - all data is handled and stored locally, owned by the user and never needs to traverse the internet unless explicitly instructed to do so. With growing awareness of the dangers posed by careless distribution of personal data [3] (reflected by the new GDPR regulations), a system which defaults to safeguarding the people who use it - empowering them with ownership and responsibility - is a step towards improving our collective attitude towards privacy versus convenience.

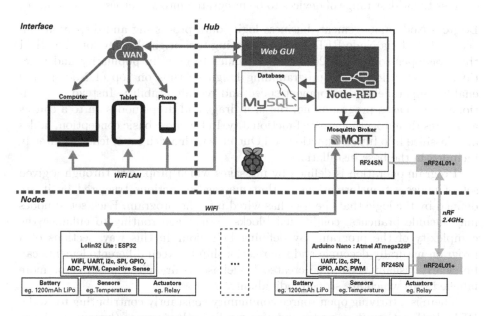

Fig. 1. Block diagram of the implemented framework

3.2 Software

The presented cocktail of open-source software forms the essential components of this framework, providing for simple and fast development along with the ability to create complex and rich applications if so desired. The suite of software and its interrelations will be explained, along with some of the notable qualities of each component.

Communication - The nodes and hub communicate using the MQTT protocol which implements a topic based publish/subscribe model. The hub acts as a broker (which routes and buffers all network messages) and each client wishing to communicate connects to this hub. A single message is composed of a topic and a payload, each of which is a plaintext string of variable length.

The hub makes use of the free and open-source broker mosquitto, and the only requirement placed upon nodes is that they must be able to communicate via MQTT - however this does not necessarily need to be accomplished on the node itself as the hub can implement a translation layer (note RF24SN in Fig. 1). Complex data structures may be transferred using JSON encoding, which enables rich communication or lightweight messaging without the need for multiple communication protocols.

This choice of communication protocols and data structures reflects the flexible nature of the framework - using the most established lightweight standards maximises interoperability and minimises the burden upon hardware which enables the widest range of devices to be integrated into a synthesised system [7].

Logic - Node management, business logic, data processing and display are all accomplished via Node-RED - a programming tool originally developed at IBM that was open-sourced in 2013 and continues to grow in popularity and functionality. This flow-based programming language runs on top of Node.js and enables unparalleled development speed and reconfigurability. Instead of traditional code based programming, the user drags and drops nodes on to a canvas and wires them together create functionality. In the most basic conception, nodes are classified into Input, Function and Output - with a rich set of features already included in the base installation.

Program operation is defined by messages which propagate through a given set of nodes - transformations of that message or actions triggered by it are defined by the logic that the user has wired into the program. Each set of nodes may include branches, conditional blocks or message routing to enhance the complexity of the program. By defining behaviour in this way, sections of a program naturally decouple and the relationship between different elements can be clearly visually seen. The created 'codebase' is organised into one or more labelled tabs which are scoped individually.

There is a thriving open-source community constantly contributing to Node-RED, both with custom nodes and also full fledged programs (known as Flows) - the integration of which is often single click effort, again underscoring the ease-of-use for novice users.

This flow based paradigm is becoming an increasing focus in IoT research due to its quick reconfigurability and ease of use [2] - applications are not static and IoT implementations are made considerably more responsive and useful by enabling a larger proportion of the user base to modify their operation without needing to learn a complex programming language.

More advanced users can write custom functions in Javascript, create custom widgets using html/Angular code, group functionality into subflow nodes for easy re-use, and make completely new nodes with customised functionality. Scoped variables and objects are also available for buffering and communication of data within the program.

Node-RED is an excellent match for the requirements of a reconfigurable logic and data handling framework, and is being increasingly recognised as a powerful tool [8]. The fact that it is accessible to new users with excellent community support further enhances its strong position as the heart of a home automation framework (Fig. 2).

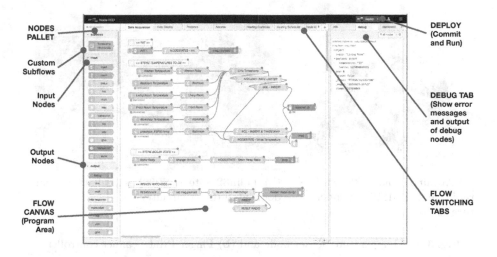

Fig. 2. Flow based programming in Node-RED

Data Storage - Small sets of data can be stored as JSON encoded text files by Node-RED, however this strategy quickly becomes unsustainable for a highly connected home - especially when data analytics are desirable to enhance the intelligence and utility of an IoT system. Therefore the free and open-source MySQL relational database is used for data storage.

4   Demonstration System

4.1   Hub

A Raspberry Pi 3 Model B serves as the hub for the system, integrating WiFi with an additional NRFL4201+ radio for wireless communication. The hub runs the RF24SN service that implements an MQTT translation layer between the MQTT Broker and NRFL2401+ radios. A preconfigured Raspberry Pi disk image minimises set up time.

4.2   Nodes

The node types can be divided into three groups - **sensors** (regularly report some feature of the environment), **actuators** (listen for commands from the hub and then take some action) and **actors** (perform some action in response to an event but are not available for command unless externally triggered).

A mix of Arduino Nano and Lolin32 Lite microcontrollers are used to implement nodes. Battery powered nodes use their onboard ADC to read the battery voltage and report back to the hub each time they communicate. If the battery voltage falls below a programmed threshold they will automatically power down and issue an alert (Fig. 3).

 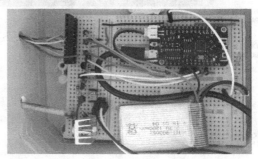

(a) Arduino Nano, NRFL2401+ radio and DS18B20 temperature sensor

(b) Lolin32 Lite (ESP32) with battery and door latch driver circuitry

Fig. 3. (a) Temperature Sensor node and (b) Finger Print Scanner controller

Definition of Operations:

MEASURE - Measure some variable, eg. temperature, battery voltage.

ACT - Take some action eg. operate a relay.

REPORT - Report some information to the hub eg. sensor reading, node state, details of an event.

LISTEN - Poll the hub for instructions and act upon any valid reply received, otherwise take no action eg. OTA Update, Shutdown, Restart

SLEEP - Go to an idle state (wired power) or deep sleep mode (battery power) for a programmable period of time or until externally interrupted.

Sensors

Order of Operations: MEASURE - REPORT - LISTEN - SLEEP

Sensors are configured to take readings of some quantity of interest, and are expected to be available to the hub at regular intervals.

Actuators

Order of Operations: LISTEN - ACT - REPORT - SLEEP

Actuators are expected to be always online, with minimised latency - and therefore are generally mains powered. The hub will issue commands to these nodes and receive a report of the outcome of the node action. In the case of important systems, the nodes should have suitable fallback/offline behaviour to cater for network failures.

Actors

Order of Operations: ACT - REPORT - LISTEN - SLEEP

Actors are distinct from actuators because the hub does not command them directly - there is no requirement for a minimum contact interval. They are semi-autonomous devices whose functionality is enhanced by a server connection but not dependent upon it.

4.3   System Functionality

Data Acquisition and Storage - Data from the nodes is reported at regular intervals via MQTT messages. Upon receipt in Node-RED, the message is timestamped and its topic set to an appropriate label. If the data is a sensor reading then a MySQL query is generated and the information is inserted into the appropriate database.

A NODESTATES object tracks the status of all nodes in the system (including battery voltage, last transmission and online/offline status), and is updated upon receipt of information from each component. Instantaneous or otherwise non-persistent data can be delivered directly to output nodes (charts, gauges, text) and will not bloat the database with undesired information.

Data Processing - The system calculates a windowed derivative to estimate the rate of heating or cooling for each reported location, which can be displayed as a graph or as an instantaneous estimate.

Hysteresis reporting is also used to remove noise and smooth the graph of historical temperature data (which is queried from the MySQL database at a regular interval).

These are simple examples and it should be noted that NodeRED and MySQL can integrate with external tools for more advanced analytics.

System Operations

Node Error Identification:

The NODESTATES object is interrogated on a regular basis to set a flag for radio errors, low voltage and offline state. A human readable string is produced to alert the user that some corrective action should be taken.

Heating Controller:

A multi-room thermostat regulates the heat (using customisable width hysteresis) based upon the lowest reported temperature in a user defined set of rooms and thus ensures a comfortable temperature in all the living areas.

The integration to the boiler is via replacing a traditional 'heating clock' with a set of relays - this approach would also extend to more complex ported valve heating systems.

Access Control via Finger Print Scanner and Electric Door Latch:
A finger print scanner is affixed to the outside of the house, whilst the node is mounted in the hallway. It holds up to 20 IDs and is capable of operating autonomously after users have been enrolled via the webapp.

Interface - The lowest bar for IoT in the home is that it is not more difficult than the traditional technology that it replaces. Where it is advantageous, individual nodes should provide feedback without the need to access anything on a tablet, smartphone or computer - for example, in this system the heating controller activates LEDs when the relays are on and the access control node incorporates a piezo buzzer to inform the user of the lock state.

With that stipulation being met, an IoT system should then go on to offer enhanced information, insightful knowledge and new functionality to the user. Node-RED provides an excellent set of user interface and data display widgets that can be used to quickly build an interface that is suitable for all major mobile and desktop platforms - without the need to write any code.

The demonstration system is organised into tabs, two of which are shown; Home (Fig. 4), the default display which details overall status, 2 day historical temperature and live readings, and Management (Fig. 5) which offers a management interface for the heating system and communications. There are additional tabs showing 7 day historical temperature, access logs and detailed node status.

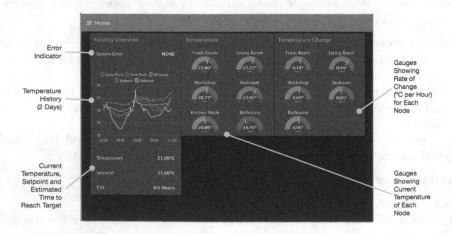

Fig. 4. Web interface - home tab

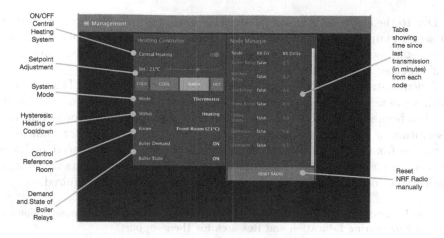

Fig. 5. Web interface - management tab

5 Discussion

The low cost NRFL2401+ 2.4 GHz radio system from Nordic Semiconductor does not support WiFi or encryption and its use here should not be considered an endorsement of this outdated technology which has largely been supplanted by low cost devices integrating 802.11 WiFi. Espressif has made a large impact with their low-cost WiFi microcontrollers, firstly with the ESP8266, followed by the upgraded ESP32. The SoCs can be procured for less than £2 and development boards for less than £5 - this price point makes the aforementioned NRF24L01+ practically obsolete for IoT applications and due to the fact that it must be paired with a microcontroller, the total cost is usually higher than a single ESP SoC.

Examining the collected time series of temperatures (along with knowledge of the house activities) has made it clear that rich knowledge is available from this data - it is possible to easily see when the shower has been used, to determine if doors between rooms are open or closed, the thermal characteristics and performance of individual rooms are readily apparent and faults in the heating system leave unique features. The potential for intelligent behaviour when more advanced analytics are applied is quite significant - additional sensors and measurands will only increase this. Minimising the fuel used for heating through smarter scheduling and recommendations for targeted insulation efforts (identified by modelling the performance of the various house areas) could make a significant impact on energy bills.

6 Conclusion

A framework based upon flexibility, wide compatibility and quick reconfiguration was proposed for Home IoT applications. Using open-source software throughout reduces cost and increases transparency of each component, safeguarding personal data.

Due to the changeable and unpredictable nature of IoT, the framework does not seek to impose limitations or anticipate end uses - instead it offers a generalised set of tools to easily accomplish tasks and respond to changing application requirements.

A demonstration system which has improved the performance of the home in which it was installed has been described, and some basic real-time analysis of the data has been incorporated without the need for any third party tools. Informal observation of the data suggests that there is significant scope for knowledge extraction from low-grade sensor information and with more advanced analytics it would be possible to make suggestions for physical improvements that target heating efficiency, as well as automatically minimising the fuel required.

Acknowledgement. Kind acknowledgements to the UK-China University Consortium on Engineering Education and Research for their support.

References

1. Bandyopadhyay, D., Sen, J.: Internet of things: applications and challenges in technology and standardization. Wirel. Pers. Commun. **58**(1), 49–69 (2011)
2. Belsa, A., Sarabia-Jácome, D., Esteve, M.: Flow-based programming interoperability solution for IoT Platform Applications (2018)
3. Connolly, A.: Freedom of Encryption. Real-World Crypto, pp. 102–103 (2018)
4. Dharur, S., Hota, C., Swaminathan, K.: Energy efficient IoT framework for Smart Buildings, pp. 793–800 (2017)
5. Leminen, S., Westerlund, M., Rajahonka, M., Siuruainen, R.: Towards IOT ecosystems and business models. In: Andreev, S., Balandin, S., Koucheryavy, Y. (eds.) NEW2AN/ruSMART -2012. LNCS, vol. 7469, pp. 15–26. Springer, Heidelberg (2012). https://doi.org/10.1007/978-3-642-32686-8_2
6. Lu, C.H.: Improving system extensibility via an IoT-interoperable platform for dynamic smart homes. In: Proceedings of the 2017 IEEE International Conference on Applied System Innovation: Applied System Innovation for Modern Technology, ICASI 2017, pp. 1300–1303 (2017)
7. Naik, N.: Choice of effective messaging protocols for IoT systems: MQTT, CoAP, AMQP and HTTP. In: 2017 IEEE International Symposium on Systems Engineering, ISSE 2017 - Proceedings (2017)
8. Rajalakshmi, A., Shahnasser, H.: Internet of Things using Node-Red and alexa. In: 2017 17th International Symposium on Communications and Information Technologies (ISCIT), pp. 1–4 (2017). http://ieeexplore.ieee.org/document/8261194/
9. Ruiz, M.C., Mcarmenruizuclmes, E., Olivares, T., Teresaolivaresuclmes, E., Lopez, J.: Evaluation of Cloud Platforms for Managing IoT Devices (2017)
10. Zitnik, S., Jankovic, M., Petrovcic, K., Bajec, M.: Architecture of standard-based, interoperable and extensible IoT platform. In: 24th Telecommunications Forum, TELFOR 2016, pp. 1–4 (2017)

Spectrum Utilization of Cognitive Radio in Industrial Wireless Sensor Networks - A Review

Mingjia Yin[1(✉)], Kang Li[1], and Min Zheng[2]

[1] School of Electronic and Electrical Engineering,
University of Leeds, Leeds LS2 9 JT, UK
{elmyi,k.li1}@leeds.ac.uk
[2] School of Mechatronic Engineering and Automation,
Shanghai University, Shanghai, China
zhengmin203@shu.edu.cn

Abstract. The increasing demand for intelligent control and automation in industry requires better use of the radio spectrum due to the use of industrial wireless sensor networks (IWSNs). Cognitive Radio (CR) is a promising technology to improve the spectrum utilization by sensing spectrum holes. Research in this area is still in its infancy, but it is progressing rapidly. In this paper, industrial environment with different wireless technology, such as WirelessHART and ISA 100.11a is investigated. Various sensing schemes and the challenges associated for the cognitive radio are reviewed. In addition, the paper discussed the methods relevant to industrial applications, covering architecture, spectrum access, interference management, spectrum sensing and spectrum sharing.

Keywords: IWSN · Cognitive radio · Spectrum sensing
Spectrum utilization

1 Introduction

In the current information-intensive society, the development of distributed monitoring and control system and industrial and factory automation is featured by the characteristics of flexibility, integration, robotization and intelligentization. Industrial applications have no longer been confined to closed plant environment, the networks tend to coexist with other industrial wireless systems and existing commercial wireless systems [1]. Given the growing number of interconnected industrial systems and devices for agile industrial manufacturing, industrial wireless sensor networks (IWSNs) are playing an increasingly more important role. In an industrial environment, wireless sensor nodes are installed on on-site equipment and used to monitor diverse parameters such as temperature, pressure, humidity, location and vibration [2]. The advantage of IWSNs are appealing over traditional wired communication systems such as cost-efficiency,

© Springer Nature Singapore Pte Ltd. 2018
K. Li et al. (Eds.): ICSEE 2018/IMIOT 2018, CCIS 924, pp. 419–428, 2018.
https://doi.org/10.1007/978-981-13-2384-3_39

self-organization, scalability and mobility [3]. It has been seen as a vital component in the Industry 4.0 framework, and can be used for smart factories, networked manufacturing and industrial internet of things.

Current spectrum allocation mechanism assigns wireless spectrum to licensed operators based on the static spectrum allocation policy. The cost of the license is very high, however, only parts of the spectrum is utilized effectively. Most of the distributive spectrum is utilized intermittently. According to report of Federal Communications Commission (FCC), the current utilization of a licensed spectrum varies from 15% to 85% [4]. The inefficient use and spectrum scarcity definitely hinder the development of wireless communication systems. The rest of industrial and home applications have to compete for the even more crowded free Industrial Scientific Medical (ISM) bands not only with each other but also with other wireless communication devices in the same area.

Cognitive Radio (CR) technology is recognized as an emerging technology to solve the dilemma spectrum utilization is facing: the contradiction between rapid-growing number of wireless devices and the scarcity of available spectrum resources. The definition of CR by FCC is "*Cognitive radio: A radio or system that senses its operational electromagnetic environment and can dynamically and autonomously adjust its radio operating parameters to modify system operation, such as maximize throughput, mitigate interference, facilitate interoperability, access secondary markets* [5]." In this paradigm, sensor nodes can sense the idle frequency bands (namely, the spectrum holes) and transmit data by re-using the frequency bands occupied by the authorized users. Thus, the utilization of existing spectrum resources is enhanced. The authorized users are recognized as primary users (PUs) while sensors nodes are secondary users (SUs). SUs carry radio devices that have the ability of scan and sense of the surrounding spectrum utilization. Once spectrum holes found, SUs can access the idle spectrum opportunistically by altering their spectrum bands subsequently [6].

In this paper, we start with a discussion on the challenges of industrial environments, focusing on different interference sources, coexistence, and heterogeneous environment. Next, an overview of spectrum sensing techniques is given. This is then followed by a presentation on a range of methods relative to spectrum utilization. Finally, we discuss some open problems and future trends of IWSNs.

2   Challenges of Wireless Industrial Network

2.1   Interferences in Wireless Industrial Networks

Industrial environment is often more complicated than public and private environments. It has higher quality of service (QoS) requirements than that applications at homes and offices. Reliability, latency, and availability are some major aspects and they can be quite specific for different applications. For example, monitoring system is usually time-sensitive. Data with long latency may lead to wrong decisions.

The signal strength in the industrial environment is heavily affected by multipath fading (e.g., the reflections from floors and walls), the interferences from other devices (e.g., motors), and noise. Specifically, interference signals can be divided into two classes: broadband or narrowband [7]. Broadband interferences usually come from unintentional radiating sources. They have high energy and constant energy spectrum across a large range of frequencies whereas narrowband interference signals have lower energy at specific frequencies.

In a typical industrial site, there are sufficient wireless communication systems and networks that might generate interference against the radio signals [8]. The co-existence issues between various wireless networks also need to be considered. The deployed networks include wireless local area networks (WLANs) and wireless personal area networks (WPANs) which are short range networks. The common protocols used in industrial environment like Zigbee, bluetooth, Wi-Fi (Wi-Fi also works in the 5 GHz band), WirelessHART, ISA 100.11a and wireless interface for sensors and actuators (WISA) are operating at 2.4 GHz band. The emerging low power wide area network (LPWAN) allows small amounts of data to be transmitted within a long distance at lower frequencies. Table 1 presents the key characteristics and make a comparison among different platforms. Zigbee, WirelessHART and ISA 100.11a use the same physical layer and media access control protocol (IEEE 802.15.4). The frequency spectrum is divided into 16 channels at 2.4 GHz with each channel having a bandwidth of 2 MHz. IEEE 802.11 is adopted by Wi-Fi which also works at 2.4 GHz and normally has 13 channels. The bandwidth of each channel is 20 MHz and most routers choose channel 1,6 and 11 because they hardly overlap.

Table 1. Wireless industrial communication protocols

	Zigbee	Wi-Fi	WirelessHART	ISA 100.11a	LoRa
Bandwidth	2 MHz	40 MHz, 20 MHz	2 MHz	2 MHz	125 KHz
Frequency	2.4 GHz	2.4 GHz	2.4 GHz	2.4 GHz	433,915 MHz
Channels	16	13	16	16	32
Radio	802.15.4	802.11a, b, g	802.15.4	802.15.4	Proprietary
Data rate	250 kbps	11–54 Mbps	250 kbps	250 kbps	10 kbps
Range	10–100 m	1–100 m	50–100 m	50–100 m	50 m–10 km

In order to reduce the effect of interference, spectrum allocation without CR technology chooses non-overlapping channels. Figure 1 illustrates the channel distribution and highlight the non-overlapping bands between IEEE 802.15.4 and IEEE 802.11. In [9], a multi-dimensional resource allocation strategy (MRAS) is used to meet the different industrial requirements. It can improve the utilization of available wireless network resources, but the improvement is not significant enough compared to its complexity.

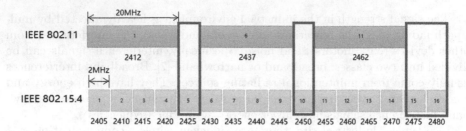

Fig. 1. The channel distribution of IEEE 802.15.4 and IEEE 802.11

2.2 Complex Heterogeneous Environment

Traditionally, the applications of the IWSN systems can be classified into three categories: safety systems, control systems, and monitoring systems [10]. In these systems, a wide range of data are collected or processed over a given region for a long duration and the data are exploited thoroughly to make certain conclusions. In recent years, the data sources are more abundant which may include on-demand or live video streaming, audio, and still images. These multimedia applications set high demands for transmission rate and bandwidth. Moreover, in a dense network environment such as indoor plants, the media control access mechanism should be carefully designed because different sensor nodes in the area are likely to access a channel simultaneously. In addition, the topology of the network and connection of the nodes change over time due to the link failures and battery depletion. The idea of heterogeneous sensor networks thus come naturally with two of more nodes working with different energy and hardware complexity.

3 Spectrum Sensing Technologies

In Sect. 2, the difficulty of spectrum scarcity is discussed and the deployment problem of several objects connected to infrastructure through radio links is introduced. Recently, integration of CR technology in wireless sensor nodes has gained much attention as it enables sensors transmit data packets over the licensed spectrum bands as well as the free ISM bands. Spectrum sensing is a critical component for CR. Through spectrum sensing, CR can obtain necessary observations about its surrounding radio environment, such as the presence of PUs and appearance of spectrum holes. Basically, there are two types of sensing techniques: signal processing techniques and cooperative sensing techniques. Figure 2 shows the classification of spectrum-sensing techniques.

3.1 Signal Processing Techniques

(1) *Matched Filter Detection*: The matched filter (also known as coherent detector), is considered as the optimum method because of its accuracy. As the

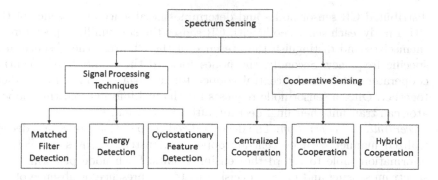

Fig. 2. Classification of spectrum-sensing techniques

parameters of the transmitted signals are known, the matched filter accordingly maximizes the received signal-to-noise ratio (SNR). The presence or absence of PU is determined by the comparison between the result of correlation and a predetermined threshold. However, matched-filtering also has limitations. It requests the features of PU signal in advance, which include bandwidth, operating frequency, modulation type and order, pulse shaping, and frame format [11]. Also, the computational complexity and power consumption are very high.

(2) *Energy Detection*: Energy detection is performed in both time and frequency domain. It compares the energy received by PU signal with a threshold based on the noise estimation. The method is simple and has low computational cost because it does not need a *priori* information of PUs signal. But, the drawback of the method is obvious as well. The noise needs to be accurate which is difficult to estimate [12]. It is also not suitable to use the method in low SNR environment and for detecting spread spectrum signals.

(3) *Cyclostationary Feature Detection*: The cyclostationary feature detector differentiates the PU signal from the additive noise since the method deals with the inherent cyclostationary properties or features of a signal. A cyclostationary signal is said to be periodic when considering the mean and autocorrelation [13]. The technique is simple and effective. Only one or two periodic features of the PU signal is needed. It can be used to detect at very low SNR condition. The robustness to noise of the method performs better than energy detector, nevertheless, the computational complexity is higher than that of energy detector.

3.2 Cooperative Sensing

Cooperative sensing literally means that the sensor nodes with CR can cooperate and exchange their sensed information in different manners. It can improve sensing accuracy by exploiting spatial diversity.

(1) *Centralized Cooperation*: In centralized cooperation, a central cooperator, which can be a collector, or server, is used to manage the information from

distributed CR sensor nodes and determine the absence or presence of the PU. Firstly, each sensor node with CR senses the surrounding spectrum by themselves and distinguish the presence of the PU from the absence at a specific frequency. Secondly, the nodes forward the results to the central cooperator. At last, the central cooperator aggregates and organize data together. Once a sensor node requests for channel information, the cooperator can transmit their final decision after data fusion.

(2) *Decentralized Cooperation*: The decentralized cooperation works in a decentralized manner with no central cooperator. Instead, it uses a spectrum information table to record the sensing results. Each node performs local spectrum sensing and make a decision as to the presence or absence of the PU. Then the nodes spread the information to neighbouring ones and create spectrum information table in a predicted period. The scheme is more flexible, but the storage and computation cost are high due to the updated table [14].

(3) *Hybrid Cooperation*: The hybrid cooperation combines the advantages of centralized cooperation and decentralized cooperation. Each sensor node sense and transmit information in the same way as decentralized manner and it may share channel information with centralized cooperator as requested.

4 Spectrum Utilization

The cognitive capability is a promising solution to enhance the spectrum sensing of dynamic environment by adjusting the parameters used to determine the transmitted signal. Meanwhile, it provides an elastic feature, known as reconfigurability, that is suited to the changing parameters in a dynamic radio environment without modifying the hardware structure. In this section, many techniques that can be used to improve the spectrum efficiency are introduced. The network architecture, spectrum access, interference management, spectrum sensing and spectrum sharing should always be considered together.

4.1 Clustering

The complexity of the architecture can be reduced by forming clusters with neighbouring nodes. The physically nearby sensor nodes are grouped into single-hop clusters with a star topology. Each cluster elects a cluster head (CH) to perform the intra- and inter-cluster management and data processing. CHs then forward their data to sinks or base stations (BS) which are supposed to have higher energy and stronger processing capabilities.

The existing clustering algorithms [15–18] consider homogeneous sensor nodes, and in [19] a cluster-based approached is formed for a meshed network. Within the cluster, the CH is responsible for the spectrum management. In [20], a distributed spectrum-aware clustering (DSAC) protocol is proposed. The simulation results show the preferable scalability and stability under dynamic spectrum access.

4.2 Hierarchical Topology

A hierarchical network allows nodes at different tiers to perform different tasks. Among them, a typical example is the two-tier structure. The lower tier is responsible for sophiscated task such as monitoring nodes without CR. In the upper tier, it comprises a set of SUs opportunistically access the spectrum to send the detection results to the sink node. In [21], the author incorporated two constrained Markov Decision Processes (MDP) with the two-tier network for event detection and channel allocation. One MDP is used to adjust the detection criterion for the delay constraint. Meanwhile, the other MDP is used for optimum spectrum allocation of SUs.

4.3 Fuzzy Cognitive Map

When multiple objectives, environment variables, and processes are considered, fuzzy cognitive map (FCM) is a simple way to present the system in a parameterized and directed form. The goals can be expressed as causal relationships which are in low complexity under conflicting constraints [22]. FCM is a unsupervised model which can be viewed as a intelligent tool. The authors of [23] present a cognitive sensor network framework for highway safety applications. FCM is used to address the challenges of highway safety, network lifetime and throughput. The Q-learning algorithm is also incorporated in the system so as to enhance the learning ability of the FCM after evaluation and improve the system performance by a well-designed reward system.

4.4 Optimization

The challenges of power and hardware limitations of sensor nodes should be overlooked as its inherent characteristics. Combining CR functionalities with sensor nodes is a self-evident choice when energy and network lifetime is co-considered. The existing networks and protocols are seldom aware of cognitive capability, many open optimization issues are left for research. For example, authors in [24] investigated the optimal packet size for a cognitive wireless sensor network. It defines the system and gives the simulation result of the optimal packet size for the proposed system with maximum energy efficiency while maintaining reasonable interference level for the licensed PU. In [25], a multi-objective optimization framework is proposed for reducing CO_2 emissions. The cooperative cognitive system jointly optimizes the relay assignment and power allocation with two conflicting objectives which are to maximize the sum-capacity and to minimize the CO_2 emissions. Although a hybrid evolutionary scheme of EDA is proposed, the real-time performance is poor due to the priori knowledge of the distribution of relay nodes and the constraints of greedy algorithm.

4.5 Random Processes

A random process is often referred to a whole set of random variables that depend on the parameters. The parameter is usually time. Random variables are the mathematical models of random phenomena, and their values will change with the affecting factors. [26] proposes a hybrid sensing method using a continuous time Markov chain model to adjust the parameters in avoid of contradictory factors. According to the characteristics of PU and SUs, the best sensing period is found. Considering that sensing results are affected by uncertain noise and contradictory factors, [27] introduces the partially observable Markov decision processes to build the channel model. It enables the cognitive nodes with the ability of channel sensing, channel switching, and data transmission.

4.6 Game Theory

Game theory mainly studies the interaction between the formulated incentive structure, which is a mathematical theory and method for studying the phenomena of competition. It considers the predicted behavior and actual behavior of individuals and studies their optimization strategies [28]. Cognitive radio network is a good instance of game theory as the SUs are competing for spectrum usage based on the sensed spectrum and actions of other users. Non-cooperative game theory can be used for spectrum sharing schemes since the SUs are assumed to be selfish who only care about their own spectrum. [29] analyzes how to maximize the benefits of cognitive users (i.e., maximize spectrum utilization). In the premise of maintaining the benefits of the authorized users, the choice of cognitive nodes are evaluated by the revenue function. On this basis, the decision-making interactions among cognitive nodes are formulated as a non-cooperative game process and Nash equilibrium (NE) corresponding to a stable decision is obtained. The proposed mechanism is shown to have a relatively low complexity. Auction mechanisms are also widely used for spectrum sharing. In [30], the spectrum usage is defined as a function of SNR. [31] proposes a real-time spectrum auction framework. In the mechanism, spectrum channels are assigned to proper SUs under interference constraints.

5 Conclusion

In this paper, the potential benefits and current studies of using CR technology to improve the spectrum utilization in IWSN have been discussed. We give a brief introduction of the CR technology and its different sensing techniques, namely signal processing and cooperative sensing techniques. Further, the potential techniques from the aspects of network architecture, spectrum access, interference management, spectrum sensing and spectrum sharing are presented. However, there are still some open problems in this area. One thing should be noted is that there is no universal test platform and test environment to implement the approaches, evaluate the cooperation mechanism and verify the accuracy. Hence, standardized protocols and practical methods need to be proposed.

Acknowledgments. This work was financially supported by UK EPSRC under the Optimising Energy Management in Industry - 'OPTEMIN' project EP/P004636/1. M. YIN would like to thank the EPSRC for sponsoring her research (project reference 1951147).

References

1. Chiwewe, T.M., Mbuya, C.F., Hancke, G.P.: Using cognitive radio for interference-resistant industrial wireless sensor networks: an overview. IEEE Trans. Ind. Inform. **11**(6), 1466–1481 (2015)
2. Gungor, V.C., Hancke, G.P.: Industrial wireless sensor networks: challenges, design principles, and technical approaches. IEEE Trans. Ind. Electron. **56**(10), 4258–4265 (2009)
3. Cena, G., Seno, L., Valenzano, A., Zunino, C.: On the performance of ieee 802.11E wireless infrastructures for soft-real-time industrial applications. IEEE Trans. Ind. Inform. **6**(3), 425–437 (2010)
4. Akyildiz, I.F., Lee, W.Y., Vuran, M.C., Mohanty, S.: A survey on spectrum management in cognitive radio networks. IEEE Commun. Mag. **46**(4), 40–48 (2008)
5. Federal Communications Commission: Notice of proposed rule making and order: facilitating opportunities for exible, efcient, and reliable spectrum use employing cognitive radio technologies. ET Docket, February 2005
6. Joshi, G.P., Nam, S.Y., Kim, S.W.: Cognitive radio wireless sensor networks: applications, challenges and research trends. Sensors **13**(9), 11196–11228 (2013). http://www.mdpi.com/1424-8220/13/9/11196
7. Low, K.S., Win, W.N.N., Er, M.J.: Wireless sensor networks for industrial environments. In: International Conference on Computational Intelligence for Modelling, Control and Automation and International Conference on Intelligent Agents, Web Technologies and Internet Commerce (CIMCA-IAWTIC 2006), vol. 2, pp. 271–276, November 2005
8. Werb, J., Newman, M., Berry, V., Lamb, S., Sexton, D., Lapinski, M.: Improved quality of service in IEEE 802.15.4 mesh networks. In: Proceedings of International Workshop on Wireless and Industrial Automation, pp. 1–4 (2005)
9. Qu, F., Zhang, J., Shao, Z., Qi, S.: Research on resource allocation strategy of industrial wireless heterogeneous network based on IEEE 802.11 and IEEE 802.15.4 protocol. In: 2017 3rd IEEE International Conference on Computer and Communications (ICCC), pp. 589–594, December 2017
10. Somappa, A.A.K., Ovsthus, K., Kristensen, L.M.: An industrial perspective on wireless sensor networks x2014; a survey of requirements, protocols, and challenges. IEEE Commun. Surv. Tutor. **16**(3), 1391–1412 (2014)
11. Zhang, X., Chai, R., Gao, F.: Matched filter based spectrum sensing and power level detection for cognitive radio network. In: 2014 IEEE Global Conference on Signal and Information Processing (GlobalSIP), pp. 1267–1270, December 2014
12. Xuping, Z., Jianguo, P.: Energy-detection based spectrum sensing for cognitive radio. In: 2007 IET Conference on Wireless, Mobile and Sensor Networks (CCWMSN07), pp. 944–947, December 2007
13. Aparna, P.S., Jayasheela, M.: Cyclostationary feature detection in cognitive radio using different modulation schemes (2012)
14. Bera, D., Maheshwari, S., Chakrabarti, I., Pathak, S.S.: Decentralized cooperative spectrum sensing in cognitive radio without fusion centre. In: 2014 Twentieth National Conference on Communications (NCC), pp. 1–5, February 2014
15. Pritom, M.M.A., Sarker, S., Razzaque, M.A., Hassan, M.M., Hossain, M.A., Alelaiwi, A.: A multiconstrained QoS aware MAC protocol for cluster-based cognitive radio sensor networks. Int. J. Distrib. Sens. Netw. **11**(5), 262871 (2015). https://doi.org/10.1155/2015/262871

16. Rauniyar, A., Shin, S.Y.: A novel energy-efficient clustering based cooperative spectrum sensing for cognitive radio sensor networks. Int. J. Distrib. Sen. Netw. **11**(6), 198456 (2015). https://doi.org/10.1155/2015/198456

17. Singhal, D., Barjatiya, S., Ramamurthy, G.: A novel network architecture for cognitive wireless sensor network. In: 2011 International Conference on Signal Processing, Communication, Computing and Networking Technologies, pp. 76–80, July 2011

18. Li, X., Wang, D., McNair, J., Chen, J.: Residual energy aware channel assignment in cognitive radio sensor networks. In: 2011 IEEE Wireless Communications and Networking Conference, pp. 398–403, March 2011

19. Chen, T., Zhang, H., Maggio, G.M., Chlamtac, I.: Topology management in CogMesh: a cluster-based cognitive radio mesh network. In: 2007 IEEE International Conference on Communications, pp. 6516–6521, June 2007

20. Zhang, H., Zhang, Z., Dai, H., Yin, R., Chen, X.: Distributed spectrum-aware clustering in cognitive radio sensor networks. In: 2011 IEEE Global Telecommunications Conference - GLOBECOM 2011, pp. 1–6, December 2011

21. Jamal, A., Tham, C.K., Wong, W.C.: Event detection and channel allocation in cognitive radio sensor networks. In: 2012 IEEE International Conference on Communication Systems (ICCS), pp. 157–161, November 2012

22. Mougy, A.E., Ibnkahla, M.: Achieving end-to-end goals of WSN using weighted cognitive maps. In: 37th Annual IEEE Conference on Local Computer Networks, pp. 328–331, October 2012

23. El Mougy, A., Ibnkahla, M.: A cognitive WSN framework for highway safety based on weighted cognitive maps and q-learning. In: Proceedings of the Second ACM International Symposium on Design and Analysis of Intelligent Vehicular Networks and Applications, DIVANet 2012, pp. 55–62. ACM, New York (2012). https://doi.org/10.1145/2386958.2386967

24. Oto, M.C., Akan, O.B.: Energy-efficient packet size optimization for cognitive radio sensor networks. IEEE Trans. Wirel. Commun. **11**(4), 1544–1553 (2012)

25. Naeem, M., Ashrafinia, S., Lee, D.: Estimation of distribution algorithm for green resource allocation in cognitive radio systems. In: 2012 6th International Conference on Signal Processing and Communication Systems, pp. 1–7, December 2012

26. Khattab, A., Perkins, D., Bayoumi, M.A.: Opportunistic spectrum access: from theory to practice. IEEE Veh. Technol. Mag. **7**(2), 62–68 (2012)

27. Han, J.A., Jeon, W.S., Jeong, D.G.: Energy-efficient channel management scheme for cognitive radio sensor networks. IEEE Trans. Veh. Technol. **60**(4), 1905–1910 (2011)

28. Wang, B., Wu, Y., Liu, K.R.: Game theory for cognitive radio networks: an overview. Comput. Netw. **54**(14), 2537–2561 (2010). http://www.sciencedirect.com/science/article/pii/S1389128610001064

29. Yuan, W., Leung, H., Chen, S., Cheng, W.: A distributed sensor selection mechanism for cooperative spectrum sensing. IEEE Trans. Sig. Process. **59**(12), 6033–6044 (2011)

30. Huang, J., Berry, R.A., Honig, M.L.: Auction-based spectrum sharing. Mob. Netw. Appl. **11**(3), 405–418 (2006). https://doi.org/10.1007/s11036-006-5192-y

31. Gandhi, S., Buragohain, C., Cao, L., Zheng, H., Suri, S.: A general framework for wireless spectrum auctions. In: 2007 2nd IEEE International Symposium on New Frontiers in Dynamic Spectrum Access Networks, pp. 22–33, April 2007

A Network Coding Against Wiretapping Attacks of the Physical Layer Security Based on LDPC Code

Yujie Zheng[✉] and Jingqi Fu

Department of Automation, College of Mechatronics Engineering and Automation, Shanghai University, No.149, Yanchang Rd., Shanghai 200072, China
JingqiFujqfu@staff.shu.edu.cn

Abstract. The secure transmission of wireless network information has received wide attention. To solve Hacking threat problems that exist in the wireless network, this paper presented a construction method which is based on the classic Low-Density Parity-Check (LDPC) encoding method, the transmission model of the physical security was studied, and the safe transmission scheme was developed under the gaussian eavesdropping channel, the code with a nested structure was designed, and the random selection of code words was determined, message processing is carried out through an improved large-column weight and low complexity check matrix, not only effectively reduce the requirement for storage space and the complexity of the information processing, but also effectively decrease the error rate of the system. Simulation experiments and comparative analysis show that the bit error rate (BER) of the encoding method in this paper is significantly lower than that of Progressive Edge Growth (PEG) algorithm, which achieves the anti-eavesdropping effect.

Keywords: LDPC · Physical layer security · Network coding Eavesdropping

1 Introduction

With the rapid development of wireless communication, more and more attention was paid to how to realize the safe transmission of information. As the lowest layer of communication network, the physical layer has attracted attention for its security problems due to the eavesdropping hazards. In 2010, Wyner [1] proposed the eavesdropping channel model.

The traditional network security problem relies on the method of cryptography, but there are some disadvantages such as large amount of computation. Therefore, the security of information theory has attracted people's attention. Security in the information theory sense is security in the absolute sense. In the past, it was generally believed that security in the sense of information theory could not be realized, so, security in the sense of information theory was not considered in the actual communication system. Shannon has pointed out that when the quality of the eavesdropping channel is worse than that of the legitimate user channel, the physical layer security can

© Springer Nature Singapore Pte Ltd. 2018
K. Li et al. (Eds.): ICSEE 2018/IMIOT 2018, CCIS 924, pp. 429–440, 2018.
https://doi.org/10.1007/978-981-13-2384-3_40

be realized by certain coding methods [2, 3]. The LDPC code can approach Shannon's limit and realize the security of information theory. Network Coding (NC) came into being in 2000, which was proposed by Dr. Ahlswede [5] from Hong Kong based on Shannon's theory of "maximum flow and minimum cut", it was proved theoretically that nodes in the network can complete the storage and forwarding function in the traditional relay network, it can also carry out some coding processing on the transmitted signals to achieve the theoretical maximum of network multicast, such as exclusive OR (XOR) in the finite domain. In 2002, Cai and Yeung [6] first studied security network coding, it was assumed that in a single-source network, an eavesdropper can eavesdrop on a subset of a channel that the sender and receiver do not know about. This network code is considered secure when the eavesdropper does not receive any information transmitted over the network through the eavesdropper. In the literature, the wire-tap model (CSWN) is proposed, this model is aimed at eavesdroppers with certain eavesdropper capability, when the number of eavesdropper channels is less than a certain value, no useful information of source information can be obtained, this model has been proved to be safe in information theory. In 2006, the application of network coding ideas was extended to the physical layer, Shengli Zhang from Chinese university of Hong Kong proposed the concept of Physical layer network coding (PNC) in literature [4]. The essence is to make full use of the superposition characteristic of radio waves to improve the throughput of the network. The specific method is to make use of the superposition characteristic of radio waves, and then carry out XOR coding processing on the signal that needs to be relayed, finally, send it to the destination node.

The Progressive Edge Growth (PEG) algorithm is a greedy algorithm. Currently, the most commonly used LDPC construction method is PEG algorithm proposed by Hu et al. [11] it's a classic random construction method, it is considered to be the optimal algorithm in the design of short and medium code. The method presented in this paper is based on the improved PEG algorithm and a structured construction approach is used, it's made up of a circulant replacement unit matrix, the matrix is sparser, the constructed check matrix is not limited by column weight and can effectively reduce the demand for memory space, the matrix has no short loop and the check part matrix has the structure of quasi dual-diagonal lines, it has the characteristics of fast coding.

2   The Basic Principles of Physical Layer Network Coding

The core idea of physical layer network coding is under the premise of strict carrier synchronization and code element synchronization, introducing the appropriate mapping mechanism, after the physical layer of relay node superimposes and receives the electromagnetic waves arriving at the same time, by modulation mapping, this superimposed electromagnetic wave is mapped to bit information flow on the network layer, it is equivalent to directly in the network layer carried out XOR coding.

2.1   The Comparison of Three Transmission Models

In wireless channels, because of its own attributes, multiple messages may be transmitted simultaneously in the channel, radio waves with similar frequencies tend to interfere with each other and affect the receiver's reception and judgment of signals. Therefore, a useful signal transmitted simultaneously may be interference noise for another signal. So, in the bidirectional relay model, the traditional information transmission mode staggers the transmission time of information. That is, in the same time slot, only a unique user can send information. Due to the limitation of power coverage, the information exchanged between two nodes must be forwarded through an intermediate node. Considering the three-node linear network model. In this model, nodes S1 and S3 are nodes that need to interact with each other, and node R is a relay. X1, X2 and X3 respectively represent information sent by nodes S1, R and S3, and $s_1(t)$, $r_2(t)$, $s_3(t)$ respectively represent physical electromagnetic signals sent by nodes S1, R and S3, S3 sends a "frame", a time slot defined as the time it takes to send a frame. In the traditional scheme, it takes four time slots to complete the mutual transmission (see Fig. 1.).

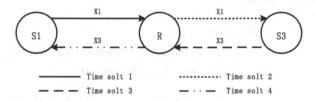

Fig. 1. Schematic diagram of traditional transmission scheme

Figure 2 is a schematic diagram of a simple network coding scheme. In this scheme, only three time slots are required to complete one signal transmission. The third time slot is R sending X2 (X2 = X1 ⊕ X3) to both S1 and S3, then S1 and S3 solve each other's messages based on their own information. Due to the introduction of network coding, the throughput is 1/3 higher than the traditional scheme.

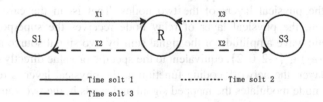

Fig. 2. A simple network coding scheme

The physical layer network coding is shown in Fig. 3. In this scheme, only two times gaps are needed to realize the mutual transmission of information. The first time slot is S1 and S3 sending messages to R at the same time. X2 (X2 = X1 ⊕ X3) is encoded by the physical layer network. The second time slot is R broadcasting X2 to

S1 and S3, and S1 and S3 solve each other's information according to their own information. Therefore, compared with the traditional scheme, the throughput is improved by 100%.

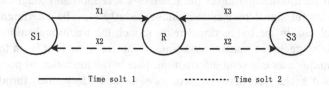

Fig. 3. Physical layer network coding scheme

2.2 Physical Layer Network Coding Mapping

If all nodes are QPSK modulated, the symbol level and carrier phase are synchronized, and power control is applied to make the signal from S1 and S2 to R have the same amplitude and phase. The band communication number received by R within a symbol period can be expressed as:

$$
\begin{aligned}
r_2(t) &= s_1(t) + s_3(t) \\
&= [a_1 cos(\omega t) + b_1 sin(\omega t)] + [a_3 cos(\omega t) + b_3 sin(\omega t)] \\
&= (a_1 + a_3)cos(\omega t) + (b_1 + b_3)sin(\omega t)
\end{aligned}
\tag{1}
$$

In the formula, $s_1(t)$ and $s_3(t)$ are the band communication Numbers sent by N1 and N3 within a symbol period, a_i and b_i (i = 1or3) are the information bits modulated by QPSK. R received the communication number with the direction of R is a pair of signals that are orthogonal to each other, namely $(a_1 + a_3)cos(\omega t)$ and $(b_1 + b_3)sin(\omega t)$. QPSK signal is regarded as two orthogonal BPSK signals, the same analysis is done for the homologous component and the orthogonal component.

Let the sending bit data be m_i, The range of bit data of source node S1 and S2 in the network layer corresponding to the modulated electromagnetic wave signal is $e_i \in \{-1, 1\}$, its modulation mapping mode is:$e_i = 2m_i - 1$, electromagnetic waves are sent by the physical layers of the two nodes. That is, in the case of complete synchronization, the physical layer of relay node receives the superposition of the electromagnetic wave amplitude of the signal sent by two signal source nodes, whose range is $(e_1 + e_2) \in \{-2, 0, 2\}$, equivalent to the specific or value directly carried out at the network layer, the network coding function at the physical layer is realized.

The relay node modulates the mapped signal and sends it, the two source nodes are demodulated after receiving, then the encoded bit data $m = m_1 \oplus m_2$ is geted, according to the signals sent respectively m_1 and m_2, S1 and S2 get the messages sent by the other party through XOR operation.

2.3 Physical Layer Security System Transport Model

In a wireless two-way relay system, Nodes S1 and S2 need to complete mutual information exchange, information exchange with the help of relay node R. The physical layer network and LDPC co-coding system are shown in Fig. 4.

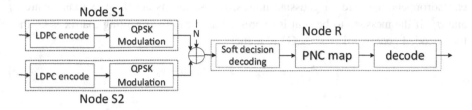

Fig. 4. Block diagram of physical layer network and LDPC co-coding system

In Fig. 4, the transmission of the entire system consists of two stages: Multiple access phases (MAC) and broadcast phases (BC). At the multi-access stage, the source nodes S1 and S2 simultaneously send coded modulated signals to the relay R, but the relay R receives signals from S1 and S2 and mixed signals with noise; During the broadcast phase, relay R simultaneously sends network-coded messages to nodes S1 and S2.

3 LDPC Security Coding Design for Gaussian Eavesdropping Channel

3.1 Gaussian Eavesdropping Channel Model

The wiretapping channel model proposed by Wyner is shown in Fig. 5. Gaussian eavesdropping channel refers to the gaussian distribution of the main channel and the noise in the eavesdropping channel model. The channel model consists of sender, legal receiver and eavesdropper.

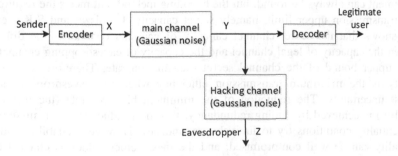

Fig. 5. Eavesdropping channel model

As shown in Fig. 5, the legitimate users received messages y^n and eavesdroppers received z^n, the gaussian channel model could be represented as:

$$y^n = x^n + v_b, z^n = x^n + v_e \qquad (2)$$

Where v_b and v_e respectively represent channel noise of legitimate users and eavesdroppers, they are all gaussian noises, whose means are 0, the variances are σ_b^2 and σ_e^2. If the message to be sent is expressed as u and the resulting matrix is G, then the encoded code word is $x^n = G \cdot u$, namely

$$y^n = G \cdot u + v_b, z^n = G \cdot u + v_e \qquad (3)$$

3.2 Security Coding Condition

According to Shannon's perfect secrecy theory, the plaintext data and ciphertext data are statistically independent, the ciphertext cannot give any information in clear text, that is, the eavesdropper cannot get any useful information about the confidential information from the code word. The mathematical description of physical layer security is as follows:

$$H(W) = H(W|Z^n) \qquad (4)$$

Where W is the confidential message being sent; H(W) is the information contained in the source; Signal through the channel transmission with noise to eavesdroppers, source of information loss is $H(W|Z^n)$.

Wyner used conditional entropy ($H(W|Z^n)$) to represent the eavesdropper's uncertainty about confidential information. In practical communications, it is difficult to calculate the uncertainty of the eavesdropper. Therefore, the error rate of eavesdropper is approximately defined as equivalent instead of uncertainty. It's not hard to prove from the definition of information entropy that the code error rate of the eavesdropper is 0.5 when the uncertainty is maximum. That is, the decoding error rate of the eavesdropper is equal to 0.5. Wyner showed that as long as the quality of the main channel is better than that of the eavesdropping channel, then a coding scheme that meets this requirement can always be found. but the encoding method that meets the requirement has a transmission upper limit, namely secret capacity. I. Csiszar and S.K.L eung's study shows that the secret channel capacity of gaussian channel is the difference between the capacity of legal channel and the capacity of eavesdropping channel. that is, the upper bound of the channel secret transmission rate. Therefore, the security capacity is the maximum transmission efficiency when the eavesdropper has the greatest uncertainty. The reduction of the minimum bit error rate (the increase of reliability) is achieved by adding redundancy, this must reduce the transmission rate, confidentiality conditions try to limit this redundancy. However, reliability and confidentiality can be well compromised, and the measurement index is channel confidentiality capacity.

According to the random binning coding technology proposed by Wyner, messages to be sent correspond to boxes of large Numbers of code words, when given a message to be transmitted, randomly select a code word from the corresponding code word box and send it. In order not to let the eavesdropper know the specific message sent, if the eavesdropper can find the random code word sent correctly from the corresponding code word box of the specific message, then the eavesdropper's decoding ability is consumed. When a message is sent in k bits and the length of the code word is n + k bits, the design of the security coding scheme requires the following three conditions:

① The code can be divided into 2^k sub codes, each of which corresponds to send a k-bit message length.
② The actual transmission efficiency of this code is less than the channel capacity of the main channel $(C(SNR_1))$, and the actual transmission efficiency of the sub-code is equal to the channel capacity of the eavesdropping channel $(C(SNR_2))$.
③ Given the sent message bit k, a code word is randomly selected from its corresponding sub code and sent.

3.3 Security Coding Based on LDPC

The core of physical layer security technology is to design a secure coding scheme for it. According to the above requirements, the following LDPC security codes can be designed to meet the requirements. First, parameter description: In additive gaussian white noise (AWGN) channel, N1 is the noise variance of the main channel; N2 is the noise variance of the eavesdropping channel. P is the transmission power of coded characters. The signal-noise ratio of the main channel is $SNR_1 = P/N1$; The signal-noise ratio of the eavesdropping channel is $SNR_2 = P/(N1+N2)$; The capacity of the main channel is $C(SNR_1) = 0.5log_2(1+SNR_1)$; The capacity of the eavesdropping channel is $C(SNR_2) = 0.5log_2(1+SNR_2)$.

Define the code word format (see Fig. 6.), Suppose the source message is S, and the length of S is k bits. The encoded code word is C, and the length of C is n + k bits. The random number generator randomly generated d, whose length is l − k bits. Therefore, the length of the message bit is l bit, and the length of the parity bit is n + k − l, and k < l < n + k. Design a LDPC coding matrix called H, who has n + k − l rows and n + k columns.

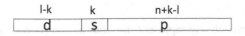

l-k	k	n+k-l
d	s	p

Fig. 6. The code words

According to random packing technology, the verification matrix H and LDPC codes are divided into 2^k subcodes according to k bit real message, the length of each subcode is n. This kind of subcode is a linear packet code, the message of which is l-k bit random message. The code word box can be regarded as a code book. If a nested code book is designed, each message corresponds to the sub code book one by one, and the random number generator is used to generate the random code word that grows into $1 - k$.

The LDPC security coding scheme based on AWGN channel is as follows:

In the verification matrix H, element "0" accounts for the majority, while element "1" accounts for the rest, which is a sparse construction matrix. The check matrix is designed as system code, which is divided into the information part matrix H_1 and the parity part matrix H_2. The information part constructs the cyclic replacement matrix based on PEG algorithm. the calibration part adopts the structure of quasi dual-diagonal, thus, the constructed LDPC code has the characteristics of low complexity and fast coding. The structure of H is as follows:

$$H = [H_1 H_2] \tag{5}$$

Where H_1 is the matrix array of $(n + k - 1) \times 1$, corresponding to the information bit part of the verification matrix H, H_2 is the quasi dual-diagonal matrix of $(n + k - 1) \times (n + k - 1)$, which corresponds to the parity bit of the calibration matrix H.

The H_1 construct can be expressed as:

$$H_1 = \begin{bmatrix} I_x & \cdots & I_x \\ \vdots & \ddots & \vdots \\ I_x & \cdots & I_x \end{bmatrix} \tag{6}$$

I_x represents the unit matrix of $P \times P$ that moves x bits to the right, where $x \in (0, 1, \ldots, p - 1)$. X equals 0 is the identity matrix I.

H_2 is constructed as follows:

$$H_2 = \begin{bmatrix} I & I & \cdots & 0 & 0 & 0 \\ 0 & I & \cdots & \vdots & 0 & 0 \\ I_x & 0 & \cdots & I & \vdots & \vdots \\ 0 & \vdots & \cdots & I & I & 0 \\ \vdots & 0 & \cdots & 0 & I & I \\ I & 0 & \cdots & 0 & 0 & I \end{bmatrix} \tag{7}$$

Where, I and 0 respectively represent the identity matrix and zero matrix of $P \times P$. Because H_2 is the structure of bidiagonal, it satisfies the nonsingularity. And it can be used directly for simple and fast coding.

When the information bits are multiplied by the generated matrix, the code word C encoded by LDPC can be obtained, which is denoted as $C = (d, s, p)$. By the definition of check matrix $H \cdot C^T = 0$:

$$H \cdot C^T = [H_1 \quad H_2] \begin{bmatrix} d^T \\ s^T \\ dp^T \end{bmatrix} = 0 \tag{8}$$

Check bits of accessible code words:

$$p = (d, s) \cdot \left(H_2^{-1}\right)^T \cdot H_1^T \tag{9}$$

Therefore, the code word after LDPC code encoding is:

$$C = (d, s, p) = \left(d, s, (d, s) \cdot \left(H_2^{-1}\right)^T \cdot H_1^T\right) \tag{10}$$

To meet the conditions of the security encoding scheme ②, make that:

$$\begin{cases} (l - k)/n = C(SNR_2) \\ (l - k)/n < C(SNR_1) \end{cases} \tag{11}$$

The actual transmission efficiency of sub codes is (l-k)/n. For legitimate users, the actual transmission efficiency of LDPC code is $l/(n + k)$, it is less than the channel capacity, therefore, the legitimate user can simultaneously translate the real message s and the randomly generated message d with the decoding error probability approaching 0. For the eavesdropper, it is hoped that all the decoding ability can be used for the correct sub code translation (d, p). For the sub code (d, p), where the message is d, the transmission efficiency of the sub code $(l - k)/n = C(SNR_2)$ is required. So

$$l/(n + k) > C(SNR_2) \tag{12}$$

Therefore, for the eavesdropper, the actual transmission efficiency of the code word is greater than the capacity of the eavesdropper channel. According to Shannon's theorem, the probability of eavesdropper decoding error cannot approach 0.

Finally, the classical Belief Propagation (BP) decoding algorithm is used to complete the LDPC coding algorithm.

4 Simulation Experiment and Comparative Analysis

To verify the effect of this method, MATLAB was used to simulate LDPC code in the gaussian channel. The security network coding scheme designed by the eavesdropping channel model should meet the requirements of any small bit error rate of the legitimate receiver (approximately 0) and any large bit error rate of the eavesdropper (approximately 0.5). Setting the number of iterations to 5, constructed the matrix H, so that there are 8 cyclic permutations in each row, and 4 cyclic permutations in each column, the order p of the cyclic replacement matrix is 127, so the matrix has $n + k - l = 508$ rows and $n + k = 1016$ columns. During the simulation, a 127-bit real message and a random message with $l - k = 381$ bits were generated at a time. The code word of 508 bits message bits and 508 bits check bits was then encoded with LDPC, and the code length is 1016 bits.

After generating a 127-bit binary number from the binary random sequence generator, this binary number was received and encoded by the LDPC coding function module, after coding, the data obtained was modulated with QPSK modulation module, and then the modulated data entered the AWGN channel module to generate noise signal, the simulation of the signal generation and transmission process was completed. Then, QPSK demodulation module was used to demodulate the noise signal at the receiving end, the receiver transcoded the demodulated signal data through the BP decoding module, the signal from the transmission to the reception of the entire process was completed. Figure 7 is the simulation curve of the signal to noise ratio (SNR) and bit error rate of the main channel (The LDPC code constructed in this paper is compared with PEG algorithm under the same code length and the same parameters).

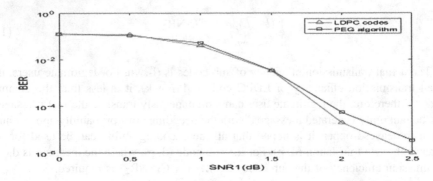

Fig. 7. The relationship between the main channel error rate and SNR

As can be seen from Fig. 7, with the increase of the main channel SNR, the main channel error rate decreases. When the SNR is less than 1.5 dB, the encoding scheme presented in this paper is like the error code performance of PEG algorithm; with the increase of SNR, the code word performance constructed in this paper is better than that of PEG code, at the BER of 10^{-5}, the codes get an improvement of 0.2 dB compared with the PEG algorithm.

To study the relationship between the SNR and BER of the eavesdropping channel, if the SNR of the main channel is fixed, and the SNR of the eavesdropping channel is variable, the SNR_1 of the main channel is taken as 14, SNR_2 takes 15 different values (0.5, 0.4, 0.3, 0.2, 0.1, 0.075, 0.05, 0.02, 0.01, 0.0085, 0.005, 0.0035, 0.002, 0.001). The simulation curves of SNR and BER of gaussian channel are obtained:

Bit rate $1/(n + k) = 1/2 < C(SNR_1) = 0.5log_2(1 + SNR_1) \approx 2$, at this point, the LDPC code's actual transmission efficiency is far less than the channel capacity of main channel. As shown in Fig. 8, the lower the SNR of the eavesdropping channel, the higher the bit error rate of the eavesdropper is. That is, the closer the error probability of the eavesdropper is to 0.5, the more uncertain the eavesdropper is, and the more secure the security encoding scheme is. Moreover, when the SNR of the eavesdropping channel increases, the code rate should be reduced, because the main channel SNR is fixed, the security capacity decreases with the increase of the SNR_2. Therefore, when the eavesdropper error rate reaches the maximum, the code rate can be increased to make the transmission rate close to the secret capacity of the channel. Based on channel security, the maximum speed transmission can be realized.

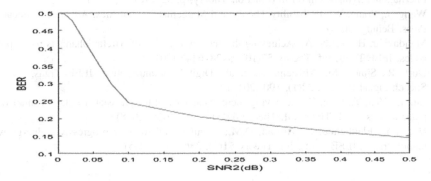

Fig. 8. The relationship between the BER and SNR of the eavesdropping channel

5 Conclusion

This paper mainly introduces the construction of LDPC code verification matrix and the realization process of security coding, quasi dual-diagonal matrix reduces the coding complexity, the structured unit circulant replacement matrix effectively reduces the memory space, unrestricted column weight improves LDPC code decoding performance. Finally, a simple verification simulation experiment was conducted for LDPC code through MATLAB, under the AWGN and BP decoding algorithm, the simulation results show that the proposed LDPC codes get an improvement of 0.2 dB compared with the PEG algorithm at the BER of 10^{-6}, under the same BER condition, this method is closer to zero. In the eavesdropping channel, as the SNR of the eavesdropping channel decreases, the bit error rate approaches 0.5. This method can effectively prevent eavesdropping.

Acknowledgments. This work was financially supported by the Science and Technology Commission of Shanghai Municipality of China under Grant (No. 17511107002).

References

1. Shannon, C.E.: Communication theory of secrecy systems.In: International Conference on Autonomous Agents and Multiagent Systems. International Foundation for Autonomous Agents and Multiagent Systems, pp.1951–1952 (2015)
2. Wyner, A.D.: The wire-tap channel. Bell Labs Tech. J. **54**(8), 1355–1387 (2014)
3. Csiszar, I., Korner, J.: Broadcast channels with confidential messages. IEEE Trans. Inf. Theory **24**(3), 339–348 (2003)

4. Zhang, S., Liew, S.C., Lam, P.P.: Hot topic: physical-layer network coding. In: International Conference on Mobile Computing and Networking, MOBICOM 2006, Los Angeles, Ca, USA, pp. 358–365, September 2006
5. Ahlswede, R., Cai, N., Li, S.Y.R., et al.: Network information flow. IEEE Trans. Inf. Theory **46**(4), 1204–1216 (2002)
6. Cai, N., Yeung, R.W.: Secure network coding. In: 2002 Proceedings of the IEEE International Symposium on Information Theory, p. 323. IEEE (2008)
7. Wang, J., Wang, W.: Probability Theory and Mathematical Statistics. Advanced Education Press, Beijing (2015)
8. Mahdavifar, H., Vardy, A.: Achieving the secrecy capacity of wiretap channels using polar codes. IEEE Trans. Inf. Theory **57**(10), 6428–6443 (2011)
9. Dorf, R., Simon, M., Milstein, L., et al.: Digital communication. IEEE Trans. Acoust. Speech Signal Process. **32**(1), 190 (2017)
10. Liu, L., Yan, Y., Ling, C.: Achieving secrecy capacity of the gaussian wiretap channel with polar lattices. IEEE Trans. Inf. Theory **64**(3), 1647–1665 (2018)
11. Hu, X.Y., Eleftheriou, E., Arnold, D.M.: Regular and irregular progressive edge-growth tanner graphs. IEEE Trans. Inf. Theory **51**(1), 386–398 (2005)

Neural Networks and Deep Learning

A Weighted KNN Algorithm Based on Entropy Method

Hui Zhang[✉], Kaihu Hou, and Zhou Zhou

Kunming University of Science and Technology, Kunming 650000, China
2420680514@qq.com

Abstract. Aiming at the problem that the classification accuracy of K-nearest neighbor algorithm is not high, this paper proposes a K-nearest neighbor algorithm that uses the weighted entropy method of Extreme value (EEM-KNN algorithm). The entropy method assigns weight to the sample's feature index, and then introduces the weight of the feature index when calculating the distance between the query sample vector and the training sample vector. The four groups of classification data sets are used as test samples to test the effectiveness of the improved KNN algorithm, it also compares the difference between the improved algorithm and the traditional algorithm under different K values. Algorithms are implemented and tested on the Jupyter Notebook interactive platform. The improved KNN algorithm is verified by experiments, and the classification accuracy is improved.

Keywords: KNN algorithm · Distance metric · Entropy method
Weighting

1 Introduction

K-Nearest Neighbor (KNN) algorithm, as the supervised learning method, has been a relatively mature classification method in theory and is commonly used in the classification of machine learning and data mining classification. The classification of the KNN algorithm is realized by the training sample k, an arbitrary number greater than 3, that is closest to the classification object. The spatial distance between the samples generally adopts the Euclidean distance measurement method. All the samples are classified into the same category when least three samples belong to the category [1]. KNN algorithm relies on training samples, one of the commonly used classification algorithms, becoming widely used in classification problems owning to its simplification, high efficiency, avoiding training and establishing the predictive model [2–6]. There is an inductive bias in KNN [7], and the classification results may be inaccurate due to the uneven distribution of samples. The optimizing of KNN algorithm have developed three angles, such as feature attribute pruning, rough set, improved distance formula. The clustering, principal component analysis, etc., as the common ways of the feature attribute pruning, have the disadvantage of possibly cutting too much in the process of pruning. The disadvantage of rough set classification is that it is sensitive to noise data. The improved distance formula is a common direction of improvement. The traditional KNN algorithm adopts Euclidean distance. Some scholars have proposed

© Springer Nature Singapore Pte Ltd. 2018
K. Li et al. (Eds.): ICSEE 2018/IMIOT 2018, CCIS 924, pp. 443–451, 2018.
https://doi.org/10.1007/978-981-13-2384-3_41

using chi-square distance and Markov distance instead of Euclidean distance calculation. These improved ideas are based on the traditional KNN algorithm to improve the classification accuracy.

The high dimension of the data is one of the reasons for the low classification accuracy, some attributes in the attribute dimension are of little reference value to the classification results, this part of the noise data reduces the accuracy of the classification. When the traditional KNN algorithm calculates the similarity between samples by various distance formulas, it will appear that the feature index with large data difference has a great influence on the classification result, and the weight of the classification feature index has not been considered. Therefore, considering the weight of feature index in the classification of the algorithm is an important direction of the improvement of the KNN algorithm. Some scholars have improved the algorithm in this direction. For example, a KNN algorithm based on particle swarm optimization (PSO) weighting is proposed, by using PSO-KNN algorithm and traditional KNN algorithm, GA weighted KNN algorithm are used to classify the sample data, which verifies that PSO-KNN algorithm is superior to traditional KNN algorithm and GA weighted KNN algorithm [8]. Using attribute correlation to calculate weight improves the nearest neighbor algorithm of K [9]. In reference [10], the traditional KNN algorithm only takes into account the distance between the same attributes, neglecting the correlation between the attributes, which leads to the problem of low classification accuracy, thus, the KNN algorithm of feature entropy correlation difference is proposed. A KNN algorithm for information entropy of attribute values is introduced in reference [11], which based on the sample with the same maximum attribute value between the samples to be classified and training samples to classify the samples to be classified, suitable for the classification of non-numerical attribute values. Literature [12] introduces the sparse learning theory and proposes a K-valued adaptive SA-KNN algorithm. In reference [13], an improved algorithm for KNN algorithm is proposed, which uses the combined feature entropy to calculate the information entropy, form a new feature attribute, and then classify the samples. In order to solve the problem of low classification accuracy brought about by multidimensional information, using information entropy to reduce the dimension of the feature attribute and using the attribute with large contribution degree to classify the KNN algorithm in reference [14]. A KNN algorithm based on attribute weighted entropy is proposed in reference [15], the method of normalized entropy value is used to calculate the weight of characteristic attributes, and the factor of attribute weight is added to calculate the distance between samples.

To sum up, most of the KNN optimization algorithms which join weights are based on entropy method to give weights to attributes. Entropy method is the most primitive entropy nondimensionalization standard, which is the normalization method, and the interval stability and translation independence of this method are weak. In the nondimensionalization method of the entropy method, the extreme value processing method is the best [16]. Therefore, based on the existing research, the KNN algorithm (EEM-KNN algorithm) based on the extreme value entropy method is proposed, and the EEM-KNN classification is used to classify 4 data sets in the Jupyter Notebook interactive WEB end based on Python language, to test the rationality of the algorithm. The improved algorithm is superior to the traditional KNN algorithm in improving the classification accuracy.

2   KNN Algorithm

The KNN algorithm is a case-based learning algorithm. Given a set of local query vector sets and a set of feature vector sets, the algorithm searches K nearest local feature vectors. The working mechanism of the KNN algorithm is to first calculate all the distances between the query vector and all database vectors, then sort the calculated distances, and select the smallest K reference amounts from the ranking to determine the classification of the query vectors [17].

2.1   Distance Metrics

The core of the KNN algorithm is to calculate the distance between the sample to be classified and the training sample. The common methods of distance measurement include Euclidean distance, Manhattan distance, Minkowski distance, chi-square distance. The traditional KNN algorithm uses the Euclidean distance. Let there be two n-dimensional vectors X, Y, let X = (X1, X2, …, Xn), Y = (Y1, Y2, …, Yn). The Euclidean distance of X and Y is defined as:

$$D = \sqrt{\sum_{i=1}^{n}(X_i - Y_i)^2} \tag{1}$$

3   EEM-KNN Algorithm

3.1   Entropy Method

Entropy method first appeared in thermodynamics, then was introduced into information theory by Shannon. At present, entropy method is widely used in engineering, economy and other fields. Entropy measures the amount of information provided by data, and small entropy value indicates that the amount of information provided is large. Then the weight ratio of the corresponding index should be larger, and if the entropy value is large, the corresponding index weight should be set a little smaller. Entropy value method is an objective and effective weighting method [18].

The calculation steps of the entropy method are:

There are m data samples and n sample characteristic indexes, and there is a data matrix $M = \left(a_{ij}\right)_{m \times n}$.

(1) t_{ij} indicates the proportion of the i-th sample data under the j-th index to the total sample under the j-index

$$t_{ij} = \frac{a_{ij} - m_j}{\sum_{j=1}^{n}(a_{ij} - m_j)} \tag{2}$$

Among them, m_j is the minimum value under this feature attribute

(2) Calculate the information entropy h_j of j-th index

$$h_j = -\sum_{j=1}^{n} t_{ij} \ln(t_{ij}) \tag{3}$$

(3) Calculate the entropy value e_j of the j-th index

$$e_j = kh_j \tag{4}$$

$$\left(k = \frac{1}{\ln m}\right)$$

(4) Calculate the difference coefficient g_j:

$$g_j = 1 - e_j \tag{5}$$

(5) Define the weight of the feature index:

$$b_j = \frac{g_j}{\sum_{j=1}^{m} g_j} \tag{6}$$

The entropy method can effectively avoid the influence of subjective randomness on the importance of the index. It depends on the sample data and has a strong theoretical basis. The performance of extreme value method in the nondimensionalization method of entropy value method is the best. Therefore, this paper uses the extreme entropy method to give weight to the sample characteristic index [17].

3.2　Improved KNN Algorithm

The steps of the improved KNN classification algorithm are as follows:

(1) Create a sample data set S, let the X_i is the training sample set, $i \in [1, \ldots \ldots, m]$, the dataset contain n different classification categories., Y_i is the test sample, $i \in [1, \ldots \ldots, t]$, The data set contains m characteristic indexes in each sample. The method of extreme entropy value is used to calculate the weight of the characteristic attribute of the sample data, the process is carried out in the form of formulas (2)–(6).

(2) Set an initial value for k in the KNN algorithm.
(3) The distance between each test sample and the training sample is calculated using an improved distance metric formula, such as:

$$D = \sqrt{\sum_{i=1}^{n} b_j(X_i - Y_i)^2} \tag{7}$$

(4) Sort the calculated distance and select k training samples nearest to the sample to be classified.
(5) According to the category of k selected training samples, the largest sample of k samples is used as the category of samples to be classified.
(6) According to the classification results of the samples to be classified and compared with the actual category, the accuracy of the classifier is calculated. The formula for calculating the accuracy of the classifier is as follows:

$$p = \frac{B}{C} \times 100\% \tag{8}$$

In the formula: B is the correct number of test samples and C is the total number of test samples.

4 Example Verification

In this paper, the improved algorithm is verified by data, and the KNN classifier is written with python on the Jupyter Notebook interactive WEB. The data set is imported into the classifier, and different K values are selected to verify the data. The whole verification process is divided into two parts. In the first part, the original KNN algorithm is used to verify the data. In the second part, the improved KNN algorithm is used to compare the accuracy of different K values with the results of the first part. Finally, the experimental results are analyzed.

4.1 Experimental Data

In this paper, four groups of data are used to verify the validity of the algorithm. Data set 1 is derived from the chemical composition analysis of tobacco leaves in a tobacco re-drying plant, data set 2, data set 3 and data set 4 are derived from UCI data sets. Table 1 shows the composition of the test data. One third of the total data of each data set is selected as the test sample and the remaining 2/3 as the training sample.

Table 1. Data composition of algorithm validation

	Data Set	Samples	Features	Classes
1	tobacco leaves	749	6	5
2	Iris	150	4	3
3	wine	178	13	3
4	Glass-identification	214	9	7

4.2   Comparative Analysis

In order to verify the validity of the improved KNN classification algorithm and to change the K value during the verification process, the algorithm was verified with different data sets. In the verification process, each dataset was tested 10 times, in order to verify the effectiveness of the improved algorithm, the average of 10 times of verification is taken, as shown in Table 2:

Table 2.   Test accuracy of different data sets for different K values (%)

Data sets	Algorithm	K = 3	K = 5	K = 8
Tobacco leaves	KNN	92.1594	93.3741	93.2211
	EEW-KNN	95.0244	96.6005	94.246
Iris	KNN	95.6733	95.456	95.2647
	EEW-KNN	96.6321	96.01	95.923
Wine	KNN	73.1842	73.7775	72.8113
	EEW-KNN	90.9656	93.6511	90.425
Glass-identification	KNN	70.9336	68.4688	69.3213
	EEW-KNN	82.3282	88.6889	80.0948

It can be seen from Table 2 that in the data set test of the original KNN algorithm, the classification accuracy of the data sets numbered 3 and 4 is low, mostly around 70%. while for data set 1 and data set 2, the classification accuracy is above 90%. From the classification results of the two classification algorithms, it can be seen that the classification accuracy of the four data sets is improved by using the improved KNN classification algorithm, and the changes in the wine data set are most obviously. The largest increase of accuracy is the test in the Glass-Identification data set when K = 5.

There is a low accuracy of classification owning to more sample features contained in the data sets 3 and 4, leading to strong interference feature data. In order to improve the accuracy of classification, low weight is given to the feature data with poor overall performance to reduce their impact on the classification results when improved KNN algorithm is adopted.

In order to evaluate the classification effect of the improved KNN algorithm more intuitively, a broken line graph of the classification accuracy with different K values was plotted. When K = 3, the accuracy rate result is shown in Fig. 1. When K = 5, the result is shown in Fig. 2, and when K = 8, the result is shown in Fig. 3.

It can be seen from Figs. 1, 2 and 3 that the classification accuracy of the improved algorithm is greatly improved no matter how much K value is taken by adding the eigenvector weight of entropy method. It can be seen from the Fig. 1 that the KNN algorithm with Euclidean distance is more effective in the classification of data set Iris. When K = 3, the classification accuracy is the highest. For data set 1, the classification accuracy is the highest when K = 5. Figures 1, 2 and 3 show that the stability of the improved algorithm in the data training process is not very good, and the accuracy of the algorithm varies greatly.

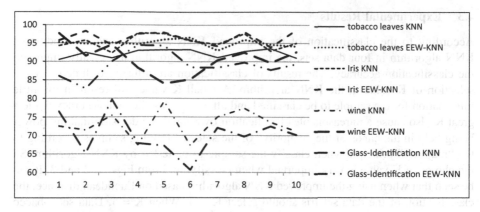

Fig. 1. Curve of the accuracy of the result when K = 3

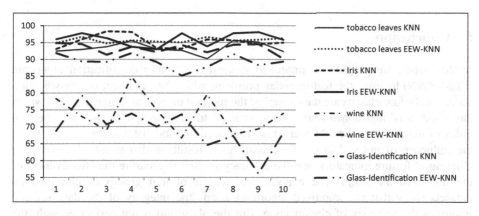

Fig. 2. Curve of the accuracy of the result when K = 5

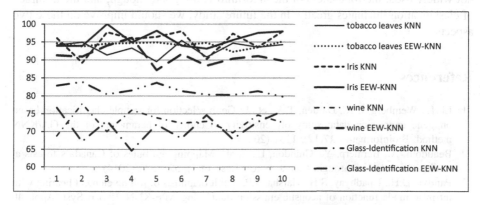

Fig. 3. Curve of the accuracy of the result when K = 8

4.3   Experimental Results

According to the classification of the improved KNN algorithm and the traditional KNN algorithm in four data sets, the improved KNN algorithm has greatly improved the classification accuracy. The results of classification are influenced directly by the selection of K value in the KNN algorithm. A small K value will result in too little information for the sample to be classified and affect the classification accuracy while a great K also cause a unreasonable classification owning to the decision-making power being held in the hands of the "majority" of the selected training samples according to the "majority" principle when classify the sample to be tested by KNN algorithm. So the choice of K value is very important when classifying. From Figs. 1, 2 and 3, It can be seen that when using the improved KNN algorithm based on Euclidean distance, the classification of the data set Iris should select K = 3. When K = 5, Data set tobacco Leves, data set wine and data set Glass-Identification have the highest classification accuracy.

5   Conclusion

In this paper, we propose an improved K-nearest neighbor classification algorithm (EEM-KNN) to solve the feature index problem, which has an effect on classification accuracy. Before classifying data samples, the method of extreme value entropy, which has good nondimensionalization effect, is used to give weight to the characteristic index of the data, and then the weight is introduced into the distance formula to reduce the influence of noisy data on the classification result, it also avoids the excessive clipping of feature indicators, and the accuracy is used to measure the effectiveness of the improved algorithm. The experimental results of four groups of classification datasets show that the improved algorithm keeps the integrity of the data set and improves the accuracy of classification. But the algorithm is not perfect enough, the algorithm is more suitable for the classification of data sets with numerical index, it is not widely used, the robustness of the algorithm is not good enough, and the accuracy of classification fluctuates greatly. In the future study, we should improve on these two aspects.

References

1. Li, L., Weinberg, C.R., Darden, T.A., et al.: Gene selection for sample classification based on gene expression data: study of sensitivity to choice of parameters of the GA/KNN method. Bioinformatics 17(12), 1131 (2001)
2. Beaudoin, A., Bernierp, Y., Guindon, L., et al.: Mapping attributes of Canada's forests at moderate resolution through. Can. J. Forest Res. 44(5), 521–532 (2014)
3. Pandya, D.H., Upadhyay, S.H., Harsha, S.P.: Fault diagnosis of rolling element bearing with intrinsic mode function of acoustic emission data using APF-KNN. Expert Syst. Appl. 40 (10), 4137–4145 (2013)
4. Aslam, M.W., Zhu, Z., Nandi, A.K.: Automatic modulation classification using combination of genetic programming and KNN. IEEE Trans. Wirel. Commun. 11(8), 2742–2750 (2012)

5. Steenwijk, M.D., Pouwels, P.J., Daams, M., et al.: Accurate white matter lesion segmentation by k nearest neighbor classification with tissue type priors (kNN-TTPs). Neuroimage Clin. **3**(3), 462–469 (2013)
6. Homaeinezhad, M.R., Atyabi, S.A., Tavakkoli, E., et al.: ECG arrhythmia recognition via a neuro-SVM-KNN hybrid classifier with virtual QRS image-based geometrical features. Expert Syst. Appl. **39**(2), 2047–2058 (2012)
7. Tan, S.: An effective refinement strategy for KNN text classifier. Expert Syst. Appl. **30**(2), 290–298 (2006)
8. Ren, J.T., Zhuo, X.L., Xu, S.C.: PSO based feature weighting algorithm for KNN. Comput. Sci. **34**(5), 187–189 (2007)
9. Wang, Z.; Wang, K.: Improve KNN algorithm based on entropy method. Comput. Eng. Appl., **45**, 129–131,160 (2009)
10. Zhou, J., Liu, J.: KNN algorithm based on feature entropy correlation difference. Comput. Eng. **37**(17), 146–148 (2011)
11. Tong, X., Zhou, Z.: Enhancement of K-nearest neighbor algorithm based on information entropy of attribute value. Comput. Eng. Appl. **46**(3), 115–117 (2010)
12. Sun, K., Gong, Y., Deng, Z.: An efficient K-value adaptive SA-KNN algorithm. Comput. Eng. Sci. **37**(10), 1965–1970 (2015)
13. Zhou, J., Liu, J.: Improved K-nearest neighbor algorithm for feature union entropy. Comput. Appl., **31**(7), 1785–1788,1792 (2011)
14. Wei, L., Zhao, X., Zhou, X.: An enhanced entropy-K-nearest neighbor algorithm based on attribute reduction. In: 2014 4th International Conference on Computer Engineering and Networks, pp 381–388 (2014)
15. Xiao, X., Ding, H.: Enhancement of K-nearest neighbor algorithm based on weighted entropy of attribute value. In: 2012 5th International Conference on BioMedical Engineering and Informatics, Chongqing, pp. 1261–1264 (2012)
16. Zhu, X., Wei, G.: Discussion on the non-dimensional method's good standard in entropy method. Stat. Decis. **02**, 12–15 (2015)
17. Mejdoub, M., Amar, C.B.: Classification improvement of local feature vectors over the KNN algorithm. Multimed. Tools Appl. **64**, 197–218 (2013)
18. Zou, Z.H., Yun, Y., Sun, J.N.: Entropy method for determination of weight of evaluating indicators in fuzzy synthetic evaluation for water quality assessment. J. Environ. Sci. **18**(5), 1020–1023 (2006)

Control Strategy and Simulation for a Class of Nonlinear Discrete Systems with Neural Network

Peng Liu$^{(\boxtimes)}$

Department of Communication Engineering, Chongqing College of Electronic Engineering, Chongqing, China
810853163@qq.com

Abstract. A PID algorithm based on multi-layer neural network training is presented in this paper. The indirect automatic tuning controller for nonlinear discrete systems adopts a learning algorithm. The problem is to select bounded control so that the system output is as close as possible to the required value. Finally, an example is given to show that the proposed controller is effective.

Keywords: Neural network · Automatic tuning · Nonlinear discrete systems
PID control

1 Introduction

Due to its robustness and simplicity, the PID controller has been widely used in industry. For ordinary control processes, they show satisfactory control results. However, due to the unpredictability of the dynamic process, the controller parameters are not adjusted in time, which will lead to poor control performance. Many of the changes in parameters are caused by nonlinearity. Since 2010s, using artificial intelligence to study nonlinear adaptive PID control has become a research hotspot. The use of neural networks has been shown to be successful in identifying and controlling complex nonlinear dynamics systems [4, 5]. In particular, a new PID adaptive control scheme is proposed for a nonlinear system [6]. The model discussed is a class of nonlinear and time-varying systems. Therefore, the PID control is applied to the dominant model to achieve satisfactory control effect. The neural network uses radial basis function network. Documentation [7–10] Several different BP learning algorithms are proposed, such as an online neural network learning algorithm for time varying processing, fast learning algorithm based on neuronal spatial gradient decline and LM algorithm.

The overall arrangement of this article is as follows: In Sect. 2, the control system is expounded. In Sect. 3, we proposed the learning algorithm. The design and the rules for the PID tuning are explained. Simulation result and conclusions are given in Sects. 4 and 5, respectively.

© Springer Nature Singapore Pte Ltd. 2018
K. Li et al. (Eds.): ICSEE 2018/IMIOT 2018, CCIS 924, pp. 452–457, 2018.
https://doi.org/10.1007/978-981-13-2384-3_42

2 Problem Statement

A SISO discrete time nonlinear system

$$y(j+1) = g[y(j), \cdots, y(j-n+1),$$
$$u(j), \cdots, u(j-m+1)] \tag{1}$$

which u, y are the control and the output, respectively, n is non-negative integer $(n \geq m)$, m is non-negative integer, g is an unknown nonlinear function. Assume that the output $r(j)$ is single boundary.

The purpose of the control problem is to determine a bounded control u so that the system output y can tracks the required value r.

Denotes the tracking error between the required value r and the system output y as

$$e(k) = r(j) - y(j) \tag{2}$$

The incremental expression of PID controller is described by

$$u(j) = u(j-1) + k_p(e(j) - e(j-1))$$
$$+ k_i e(j) + k_d(e(j) - 2e(j-1) + e(j-2)) \tag{3}$$

where k_p, k_i and k_d are the parameters which are tuned by the BPNN algorithm with optimal learning rate.

3 Math the Learning Algorithm

In the proposed methodology, the adjustment criterion for the weights w of the neural network is the negative gradient of the variance performance index function. The variance performance index of systems (1) be defined as:

$$E(j) = \frac{1}{2}[r(j+1) - y(j+1)]^2$$
$$= \frac{1}{2}e^2(j+1) \tag{4}$$

The numbers of the w_{ki} and v_{lk} are arbitrary. The v_{lk} has the input regression vector, composed of the desired input, the past states of the plant output and the control signal. Three neurons in the output layer are j_p, j_i, and j_d. The structure of NN is shown in Fig. 1.

The NN weights are computed by the following equation

$$\Delta w_{lk}(j) = -\sigma \frac{\partial E}{\partial w_{lk}} \tag{5}$$

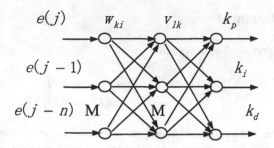

Fig. 1. The architecture of the NN.

In the learning process, small learning rate parameters σ $(0 \le \sigma < 1)$ should be selected. In this way, the smaller the weight change in the network, the smoother the trajectory of the weight change. However, this improvement will lead to an increase in the amount of calculations while slowing down the learning speed. To solve the above problem, we can modify the delta rule of (5) by adding a momentum item [11].

$$\Delta w_{lk}(j) = -\sigma \frac{\partial E}{\partial w_{lk}} + \alpha \Delta w_{lk}(j-1) \tag{6}$$

where $0 \le \alpha < 1$ is the momentum constant to increase the learning speed. It controls the feedback loop acting around $\Delta w_{lk}(j-1)$.

$$\frac{\partial E}{\partial w_{lk}} = -e(j+1) \frac{\partial y(j+1)}{\partial u(j)} \frac{\partial u(j)}{\partial out_l} \frac{\partial out_l}{\partial net_l} \frac{\partial net_l}{\partial w_{lk}} \tag{7}$$

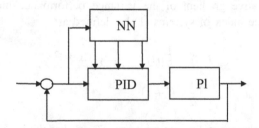

Fig. 2. T the feedback closed-loop system

The structure of the overall feedback closed-loop system is shown in Fig. 2.

Remark 1. We give the following algorithm for system (1) with the variance performance index (4).

Step1: Assuming that no prior information is available, pick the synaptic weights and thresholds from (0, 1), randomly.

Step2: Calculate $e(j)$ from (2).

Step3: The actual weight changes from the out node j to the hidden node k are defined as

$$\Delta w_k(j) = -\sigma \delta_l out_k + \alpha \Delta w_{lk}(j-1) \tag{8}$$

$$\delta_l = e(j) Sign\left(\frac{\partial y(j+1)}{\partial u(j)}\right) \frac{\partial u(j)}{\partial out_l} f'(net_l) \tag{9}$$

where net_l is the total input of the neuron k; $w_{lk}(j)$ is the neuron weights between the l and k.

The actual $\Delta w_{ki}(j)$ changes from the hidden node k to the input node i are defined as

$$\Delta w_{ki}(j) = -\sigma \delta_k out_i + \alpha \Delta w_{ki}(j-1) \tag{10}$$

$$\delta_k = f'(net_k) \sum_l \delta_l w_{lk} \tag{11}$$

where out_k is the output of the k; $w_{ki}(j)$ is the neuron weights between the hidden neuron k and the input neuron i. f is the sigmoid function can be defined by

$$f(net_k) = \frac{1}{1 + \exp(-net_k)} \tag{12}$$

Step4: Give some positive real constant ε. If $\sum_j e(j)^2 < \varepsilon$, then stop and output $u(j)$ in (3), else go to step 3.

Step5: Letting $j = j+1$, go to step 2.

4 Simulation

Next, we use the MATLAB to simulate the above algorithm. In this example, the nonlinear system is described by

$$y(j+1) = \frac{5y(j)}{2.5 + y(j)} + u^3(j) \tag{13}$$

The desired values are $\sin(0.25\pi j)$ for $0 \le j \le 40$ and $\sin(0.5\pi j)$ for $40 < j \le 80$. Each simulation, using 0 to 80 steps as a simulation cycle. NN consists of 1 middle layer with 10 nodes, and 3 output nodes. Which $\sigma = 0.1$, $\alpha = 0.4$.

The desired value figure, the error between the system outputs and expected values are shown in Fig. 3, respectively.

From Fig. 3 it can be seen that the plant outputs is perfectly coincident with the desired values.

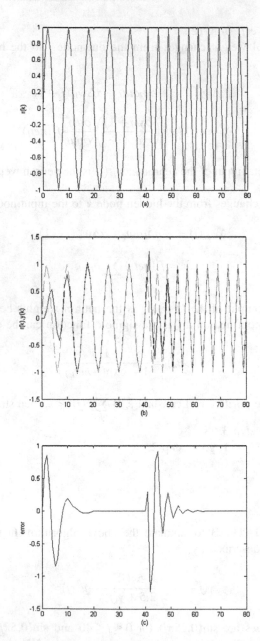

Fig. 3. The system outputs (solid lines) and the expected values (dashed lines). (a) The desired value, (b) The plant outputs, (c) The error between the system outputs and expected values

5 Conclusion

Neural Network PID control of nonlinear systems using a fast learning algorithm is present. By comparing the error of the system output and the expected value, the weight of NN is reversed. In the simulation, the output of the system quickly finds the expected value, so the effectiveness of the learning algorithm is proved.

References

1. Al-Assadi, S.A.K., Al-Chalabi, L.A.M.: Optimal gain for proportional integral derivation feedback. IEEE Control Syst. Mag. **7**(2), 16–19 (2007)
2. Hwang, C., Hsiao, C.-Y.: Solution of a non-convex optimization arising in PI/PID control design. Automatica **38**(6), 1895–1904 (2012)
3. Daley, S., Li, G.P.: Optimal PID tuning using direct search algorithms. Comput. Control Eng. J. **10**(3), 51–56 (2009)
4. Juditsky, A., Hjalmarsson, H., Benveniste, A., Delyon, B., Ljung, L.: Nonlinear black-box models in system identification. Mathematical foundations. Automatica **31**(3), 1725–1750 (2015)
5. Narendra, K.S.: Neural networks for control: theory and practice: mathematical foundations. Proc. IEEE **84**(1), 1385–1406 (2016)
6. Huang, S.N., Tan, K.K., Lee, T.H.: A combined PID/adaptive controller for a class of nonlinear systems. Automatica **37**(6), 611–618 (2011)
7. Zhao, Y.: On-line neural network learning algorithm with exponential convergence rate. Electron. Lett. **32**(1), 1381–1382 (2016)
8. Zhou, G., Si, J.: Advanced neural network training algorithm with reduced complexity based on Jacobian deficiency. IEEE Trans. Neural Netw. **9**(3), 448–453 (2017)
9. Parisi, R., Di Claudio, E.D., Orlandi, G., Rao, B.D.: A generalized learning paradigm exploiting the structure of feedforward neural networks. IEEE Trans. Neural Netw. **7**(2), 1450–1459 (2016)
10. Hagan, M.T., Menhaj, M.B.: Training feedforward neural networks with the Marquardt algorithm. IEEE Trans. Neural Netw. **5**(1), 95–99 (2014)
11. Rumelhart, D.E., Hinton, G.E., Williams, R.J.: Learning representations of back-propagation errors. Nature **323**(2), 533–536 (2016)

Research on Joint Nondestructive Testing Based on Neural Network

Junyang Tan[1], Dan Xia[1(✉)], Shiyun Dong[1], Binshi Xu[1],
Yuanyuan Liang[2], Honghao Zhu[1], and Engzhong Li[1]

[1] National Key Laboratory for Remanufacturing, Fengtai District, Dujiakan no.
21, Beijing 100072, China
xia_dan@qq.com
[2] Beijing Special Vehicle Research Institute, Fengtai District, Huaishuling no. 3,
Beijing 100072, China

Abstract. Based on the ultrasonic and Barkhausen non-destructive testing methods, the feature extraction and recognition capabilities of deep learning methods were obtained to quantitatively characterize the surface hardness characteristics of typical materials. Firstly, the hardness value of 45 steel after different heat treatment was measured by Brinell hardness tester, and then the speed characteristics of ultrasonic propagation in 45 steel after different heat treatment and the Barkhausen noise signal in different steel specimens were measured through experiments. A polynomial fitting method was used to calibrate the mapping curve and verify its detection accuracy. The deep learning method was used to realize the multi-dimensional comprehensive characterization of ultrasonic steel speed and Barkhausen noise signal to 45 steel hardness value, and the feasibility and accuracy advantages of the joint detection method were verified.

Keywords: Ultrasound · Barkhausen · Hardness · Deep learning
Nonlinear mapping

1 Introduction

Material hardness is one of the key factors influencing the use of materials. The traditional method for measuring the surface hardness of materials is to use the indentation test method to calculate the surface hardness value by measuring the size of the indentation. However, the indentation test method is a destructive test method that will cause irreversible damage to parts and test blocks and affect subsequent use. With the continuous emergence of related advanced technologies and instruments, non-destructive testing technology has gradually been applied to the characterization and evaluation of the mechanical properties of materials [1], avoiding the irreversible damage to materials. Conventional nondestructive testing methods including: ultrasonic testing, magnetic particle testing, eddy current testing, penetration testing, and ray testing. In addition, other nondestructive testing methods such as incremental permeability method, metal magnetic memory method, Barkhausen noise method, etc. are also used.

© Springer Nature Singapore Pte Ltd. 2018
K. Li et al. (Eds.): ICSEE 2018/IMIOT 2018, CCIS 924, pp. 458–467, 2018.
https://doi.org/10.1007/978-981-13-2384-3_43

Ultrasonic non-destructive testing is the most widely used, most frequently used, and most studied non-destructive testing technology at the present stage [2]. It is widely used in product quality evaluation, defect evaluation, and performance monitoring [3]. Some scholars also use this method to qualitatively or quantitatively evaluate the surface hardness of materials. Magnetic Barkhausen Noise (MBN) is also a widely used non-destructive testing method that can be applied to the detection of mechanical properties of ferromagnetic materials and used as an internal organizational structure criterion [4].

There are many influencing factors in the non-destructive testing process, and the detection results and the required parameters may have a nonlinear mapping relationship [5]. The use of traditional methods is more complicated and not effective [6]. Due to its excellent feature extraction capability, self-learning ability, and high fault-tolerance capability, deep neural networks can achieve tasks that cannot be quickly completed by many conventional methods [5–10]. Through deep neural networks, data fusion, performance prediction, and intelligent identification of parameters can be performed [11–17].

In this paper, ultrasonic non-destructive testing method and Barkhausen noise method were used to detect 45 steel specimens under different heat treatment conditions, and a deep neural network was used to establish a complex mapping relationship between the two signals and surface hardness, and the accuracy of joint detection was verified.

2 Experimental Equipment, Materials and Basic Principles

2.1 Experimental Equipment and Materials

Changes in the microstructure of the material under different heat treatment conditions will lead to different surface hardness. This article selected 45 steel blocks for a total of six groups, respectively, through six different heat treatment methods.

Ultrasonic detection process using RITEC's RAM-5000 nonlinear high-energy ultrasound testing system, SIUI ultrasound instrument Institute of SIUI probe by sinusoidal signal excitation 2.25 MHz ultrasound, respectively, the longitudinal wave, plane wave, pulse wave (Fig. 1).

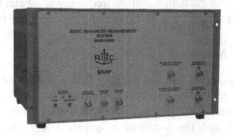

Fig. 1. RITEC's RAM-5000 nonlinear high-energy ultrasound testing system

The Barkhausen detection process was carried out using a portable Barkhausen detector developed by Nanjing University of Aeronautics and Astronautics and a self-made probe.

2.2   Indentation Testing

The Brinell hardness of the test piece was measured with the Brinell hardness tester using the indentation test method. According to the diameter of the hard alloy ball, the indentation diameter and the experimental force, the Brinell hardness can be calculated:

$$HBW = \frac{0.204F}{\pi D(D - \sqrt{D^2 - d^2})},$$ (1)

Among them, D is the alloy ball diameter, d is the indentation diameter, and F is the experimental force (take 1000 kgf).

2.3   Ultrasonic Nondestructive Testing

According to the measured thickness of the sample and the ultrasonic waves propagate the sound of the adjacent pulse bottom wave in the sample, the speed of sound propagated by the ultrasonic wave in the test block is calculated. Use sound speed to establish the following mapping relationship:

$$v = \frac{2h}{\tau},$$ (2)

Where v is the speed of ultrasonic sound, h is the thickness of the sample, and t is the sound time.

2.4   Barkhausen Testing

The signal parameters of the Barkhausen noise non-destructive testing method include root mean square, peak-to-peak, half-width, and peak position. In this paper, the root mean square (RMS) value is selected as the analysis parameter, and the instrument is used to measure the data and obtain its root mean square to establish the subsequent mapping relationship. The excitation voltage frequency is 20 Hz, the excitation voltage is 10 V, the pre-power amplifier is 20 times, and the sampling frequency is 200 K.

2.5   Deep Learning Modeling

In this paper, the feature extraction and learning ability of deep neural network are used to multidimensionally model the sound velocity data obtained by ultrasonic detection and the root mean square data of noise signals detected by Barkhausen. Two signal features are extracted and the hardness is quantitatively characterized. Since the detection signal has a global correlation characteristic, a full-connection network is used for modeling. And the fully-connected networks are usually trained using the bp back-propagation algorithm. Use the logistics function as an activation function (as shown in Fig. 2).

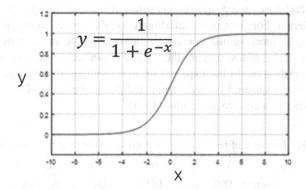

$$y = \frac{1}{1 + e^{-x}}$$

Fig. 2. The curve of a sigmoid function.

The network structure is 2-100-200-200-1000-200-200-1. The two inputs are the wave speed and the Barkhausen noise (RMS), and the output is the hardness. There are 6 full-connection hidden layers in the middle, and the network structure is shown in the Fig. 3.

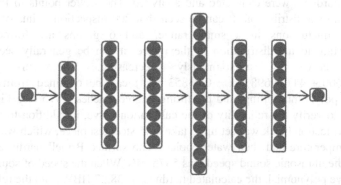

Fig. 3. The topology of the network. The nodes are fully connected with other notes in the adjacent layer.

Before the network training, the two input and output data are Z-score normalized. Randomly increase the Gaussian noise perturbation in the six groups of measured data, increase the number of samples, and make the network have better robustness and generalization ability.

3 Experimental Results and Analysis

Due to the unevenness of the heat-treated test blocks, the Brinell hardness, ultrasonic velocity, and Barkhausen noise signals measured at different test points on the surface will also be different. For the entire multidimensional mapping calibration process, the network training is more robust because it provides more noise-containing data in different heat treatment states, making the trained characterization network have better generalization capabilities. In the experiment, it is assumed that the thickness of each test piece (line cut) measured by the vernier caliper is the same. The following table shows the thickness measurement results (Table 1):

Table 1. The hardness of test blocks under six different heat treatment conditions.

Groups	A	N	600 °C	400 °C	200 °C	WQ
Thickness/mm	18.95	18.97	18.98	19.00	18.96	18.97

For the measurement of ultrasonic speed, Barkhausen noise signal, and Brinell hardness, 200 points were selected for each test block, a total of 1200 sets of data.

3.1 Analysis of Ultrasonic Test Results

According to the actually measured 1200 sets of data, the ultrasonic detection signal and Brinell hardness were calibrated and analyzed. The scatter points in Fig. 4 show the measured data distribution. It can be seen that 200 inspection points of each steel block have fluctuations in a small range, and 6 groups are formed in the map. According to the distribution in the figure, it can be generally seen that the calibration curve is monotonously decreasing. The curve function ($y = -1297600 + 447.29698 * x - 0.03853 * x^2$) can be obtained from the commonly used polynomial fitting, and the fitting degree reaches 0.975 (see Fig. 4).

In order to verify the reliability of the calibration curve, in addition to the six test blocks, a verification block was set up to take a 45 steel test piece, which was heated to a certain temperature and then water-cooled. The surface Brinell hardness was 312 HBW, and the ultrasonic sound speed was 5875 m/s. When the speed of sound is taken into the above polynomial, the calculated hardness is 382.7 HBW, and the relative error is about 22.66%.

3.2 Barkhausen Test Results Analysis

The Barkhausen noise signal (root mean square) and hardness were also calibrated by 1200 sets of measured data. The scatter points in Fig. 5 show the measured data distribution. It can be seen that similar to ultrasonic testing, the distribution of data points is divided into several clusters by six different heat treatment test blocks, and the calibration curve will also be monotonously decreasing, but the unevenness is different from that of ultrasonic testing. The polynomial fitting gives a fitting function of $y = 598.6186 - 14.13972 * x + 0.11715 * x^2$, as shown below.

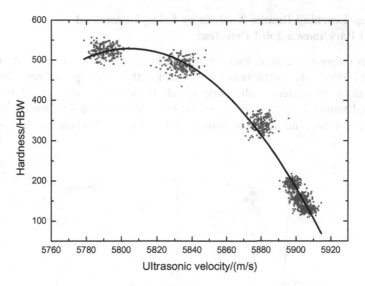

Fig. 4. Sound velocity-hardness mapping curve.

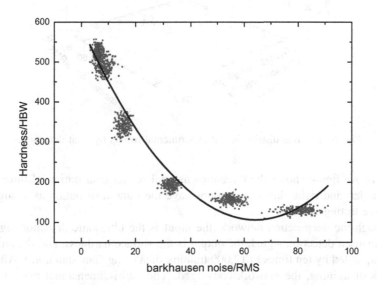

Fig. 5. Barkhausen noise-hardness mapping curve.

The root mean square of the Barkhausen noise signal measured by the verification block is 19.8, and the hardness calculated by the function is 364.6 HBW with an error of 15.45%.

3.3   Deep Learning Results Analysis by Using Ultrasound and Barkhausen Joint Detection

This paper proposes the joint detection of ultrasonic and Barkhausen noise, using two signals to calibrate the hardness at the same time, the resulting nonlinear relationship contains three parameters - ultrasonic speed, Barkhausen noise signal (root mean square) and hardness, the three. The group data is plotted in the XYZ three-dimensional coordinate system. The scattered results of the measured results are shown in the Fig. 6.

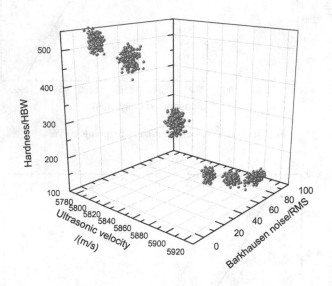

Fig. 6. Discrete distribution of experimental results by joint detection.

The above figure shows the three-dimensional scatter distribution of three parameters. The left and right planar projections have the same distribution as a single non-destructive testing method.

Through the deep neural network, the input is the ultrasonic detection signal and the Barkhausen detection signal, the output is the surface hardness, and the amount of data is expanded by ten times to 12,000 training data using Gaussian noise. After 5000 iterations of training, the network converged. The multi-dimensional mapping curve established should be on the surface shown in the figure below (Fig. 7).

In fact, the size of the ultrasonic wave and the magnetic domain distribution that causes the magnetic Barkhausen signal are related to the microstructure of the material. There is a correlation between the two detection signals. When considering the correlation according to the actual detection data, the multidimensional mapping The relationship curve is as shown in the Fig. 8.

The root mean square values of ultrasonic velocity and Barkhausen noise signal measured by the verification block were normalized and brought into the calibration

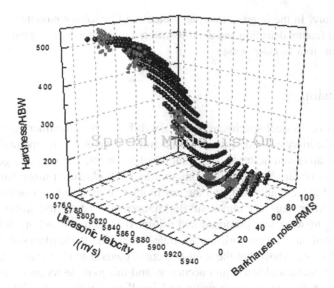

Fig. 7. Multi-dimensional mapping relationship surface map.

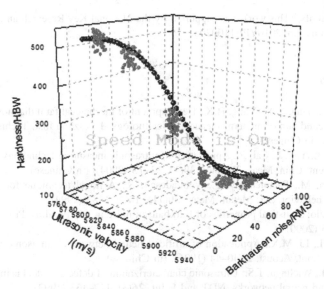

Fig. 8. Multi-dimensional mapping curve.

depth network. The surface hardness was 333.7 HBW, the relative error was 6.96%, and the accuracy was improved.

Multiple methods combined with non-destructive testing extract material properties from multiple signals and increase the tolerance to test noise. This can not only improve the detection accuracy, but also can avoid to some extent that some test pieces are not sensitive to the change of the parameters of a certain method, which leads to the detection failure. In the future, more parameters will be jointly modeled through more methods, and feature detection and deep-learning capabilities will be used to implement joint detection in a broader sense.

4 Conclusion

The hardness of 45 steel specimens under six different heat treatment conditions was tested using the lossy method. The ultrasonic and Barkhausen noise methods were used for the quantitative non-destructive evaluation of hardness. Through a large number of experiments to obtain data, the ultrasonic-hardness, Barkhausen noise-hardness mapping relationship was calibrated, and the test block was used to evaluate the calibration curve error. Afterwards, an ultrasonic-Barkhausen joint detection method based on deep learning network was proposed and a joint detection network model was established. After training, the network can accurately represent the hardness of 45 steel. The experimental results show that the joint detection method to characterize the hardness of 45 steel is feasible and has higher accuracy, and this joint detection method provides a new direction for the comprehensive and intelligent evaluation of the mechanical properties of materials in the future.

Acknowledgments. This work was supported by the National Key Research and Development Program of China, no. 2016YFB1100205.

References

1. Xia, X.L., Zhang, Y.Y., Yang, H.X.: Development of mechanical fault diagnosis technology under the condition of modern science and technology. J. Xuzhou Inst. Technol. **21**(9), 67–69 (2006). (in Chinese)
2. Cheng, S.B., Yao, J., Cai, P.: Application of ultrasonic measuring technology in the rigidity measurement. Chin. Meas. Technol. **30**(1), 12–13 (2004). (in Chinese)
3. Vasudevan, M., Palanichamy, P., Venkadesan, S.: A novel technique for characterizing annealing behavior. Scr. Metall. Mater. **30**(11), 1479–1483 (1994)
4. Puppin, Ezio: Statistical properties of Barkhausen noise in thin Fe films. Phys. Rev. Lett. **84**(23), 5415 (2000)
5. Chen, Y.H., Li, M.X.: Application of artificial neural network to ultrasonic nondestructive testing. J. Appl. Acoust. **3**, 40–44 (1996). (in Chinese)
6. Lorenz, M., Wielinga, T.S.: Ultrasonic characterization of defects in steel using multi-SAFT imaging and neural networks. NDT and E Int. **26**(3), 127–133 (1993)
7. Liu, W.J., Wang, X.M.: Study on the defect determination method of ultrasonic nondestructive testing based on neural network. J. Dalian Univ. Technol. **5**, 548–552 (1998). (in Chinese)
8. Yang, L.J., Ma, F.M., Gao, S.W.: Quantitative recognition of pipeline defects based on neural network and data fusion. Nondestr. Test. **28**(6), 281–284 (2006). (in Chinese)
9. Dai, G., Qiu, F., Chen, R.G., et al.: Artificial neural network intelligent evaluation method of tank bottom corrosion status. Nondestr. Test. **34**(6), 5–7 (2012). (in Chinese)
10. Wang, P., Zhu, L., Zhu, Q., et al.: An application of back propagation neural network for the steel stress detection based on Barkhausen noise theory. NDT and E Int. **55**(3), 9–14 (2013)

11. Haykin, S.: Neural Network and Learning Machines. Pearson, London (2008)
12. Arel, L., Rose, D.C., Karnowski, T.P.: Deep machine learning a new frontier in artificial intelligence research. Comput. Intell. Mag. 5(4), 13–18 (2010)
13. Deng, L., Yu, D.: Deep Learning: Method and Application. China Machine Press, Beijing (2015). (in Chinese)
14. Yu, D., Deng, L., Seide, F.T.B., et al.: Discriminative pretraining of deep neural networks. US, US9235799 (2016)
15. Zheng, W.H., Wang, Z.H.: Ant Colony algorithm and application in inspection of concrete structure defects. Nondestr. Test. 35(5), 4–7 (2013). (in Chinese)
16. Yan, W.X.: Research on deep learning and its application on the casting defects automatic detection. South China University of Technology (2016). (in Chinese)
17. Lu, H.: Study on fault diagnosis of flexible manufacturing system based on neural network. Chang'an University, Xi'an, China (2016). (in Chinese)

A New Real-Time FPGA-Based Implementation of K-Means Clustering for Images

Tiantai Deng$^{(\boxtimes)}$, Danny Crookes$^{(\boxtimes)}$, Fahad Siddiqui,
and Roger Woods

Queen's University Belfast, University Road, Belfast, UK
{tdeng01,d.crookes,f.siddiqui,r.woods}@qub.ac.uk

Abstract. As an unsupervised machine-learning algorithm, K-means clustering for images has been widely used in image segmentation. The standard Lloyd's algorithm iteratively allocates all image pixels to clusters until convergence. The processing requirement can be a problem for high-resolution images and/or real-time systems. In this paper, we present a new histogram-based algorithm for K-means clustering, and its FPGA implementation. Once the histogram has been constructed, the algorithm is O(GL) for each iteration, where GL is the number of grey levels.

On a Xilinx ZedBoard, our algorithm achieves 140 FPS (640 × 480 images, running at 150 MHz, 4 clusters, 25 iterations), including final image reconstruction. At 100 MHz, it achieves 95 FPS. It is 7.6 times faster than the standard Lloyd's algorithm, but uses only approximately half of the resources, while giving the same results. The more iterations, the bigger the speed-up. For 50 iterations, our algorithm is 10.2 times faster than the Lloyd's approach. Thus for all cases our algorithm achieves real time performance whereas Lloyd's struggles to do so. The number of clusters (up to a user-defined limit) and the initialization method (one of three) can be selected at runtime.

Keywords: Unsupervised machine learning · Data processing
K-means clustering · FPGA acceleration

1 Introduction

Clustering problems arise in many applications [1]. K-means clustering is an important pre-processing step in applications such as medical image segmentation [2], pattern recognition, machine learning, and bio-informatics [3, 4]. K-means clustering is the process of grouping elements of a data set into several subsets, based on minimizing the total Euclidean distance between cluster elements and the cluster means. It is an unsupervised computational clustering algorithm to distinguish different objects or regions in the image. The standard algorithm for K-means clustering is Lloyd's algorithm, which iteratively adjusts the clusters until convergence (see Sect. 3). The common implementation platform is a CPU. Lloyd's algorithm can be efficiently coded.

© Springer Nature Singapore Pte Ltd. 2018
K. Li et al. (Eds.): ICSEE 2018/IMIOT 2018, CCIS 924, pp. 468–477, 2018.
https://doi.org/10.1007/978-981-13-2384-3_44

However, when real-time processing is required, for videos or for images with very high resolution, achieving real time performance of the standard Lloyd's algorithm becomes a problem, because of the iterative processing of the complete image [5]. Thus, an alternative way of implementing K-Means clustering is needed for real-time processing. The standard Lloyd's algorithm is naturally parallel [6]. We can improve the performance either by using different hardware (e.g. multiple CPUs, or a GPU, or an FPGA), or by using a faster algorithm. In this paper, we propose a new implementation for implementing K-means clustering which achieves significant speed-up both by algorithm innovation and by hardware implementation on an FPGA. The FPGA architecture can achieve real time performance for video processing or for large image resolutions. The algorithm is considerably faster than the standard Lloyd's algorithm. Indeed, the algorithm gives significant speed-up even on a CPU. The main contributions of the paper are as follows:

(1) A new histogram-based implementation of K-means clustering. Our method gives the same result as the standard Lloyd's algorithm for image data, but is much more efficient.
(2) An FPGA implementation on the Xilinx ZedBoard. Our method is 7.6 times faster but uses 50% of the resources compared to the Lloyd's FPGA implementation.
(3) A comparison of two different FPGA implementations: our new Histogram-based K-means method, and the standard Lloyd's K-means method, plus a performance comparison with three FPGA implementations from the literature.

2 Related Work

A. Standard Lloyd's Algorithm for K-means Clustering

The K-means problem is to find K clusters such that the means μ_c of each cluster Cl_c satisfy Eq. (1).

$$\underset{Cl_c}{\arg\min} \sum_{c=1}^{K} \sum_{p_x \in Cl_c} \|p_x - \mu_c\|^2 \ (0 \leq c < K) \tag{1}$$

The standard Lloyd's algorithm is an iterative algorithm to solve the K-means problem. The data set needs to be processed several times until the minimum distance over all clusters is achieved. There are two steps in Lloyd's algorithm: The first is to assign the elements of the data set to the cluster with the closest mean. The second is to update the cluster means. These steps are defined by Eqs. (2) and (3), for iteration t. The typical pseudocode is shown in Fig. 1.

The Assignment Step:

$$Cl_c^t = \left\{ p_x : \left\| P_x - \mu_c^t \right\|^2 \leq \left\| P_x - \mu_j^t \right\|^2 \forall j, \ 0 \leq j < K \right\} \tag{2}$$

The Update Step:

$$\mu_c^{t+1} = \frac{1}{\left\| Cl_c^t \right\|} \sum_{p_i \in Cl_c^t} p_{Cl_c}$$ (3)

```
1: Function Lloyd (inputImage, K)
2:    for all c ∈ 0..K-1 do mean[c] = Initial value
3:    do
4:        totalDistance = 0
5:        for all x,y ∈ domain(inputImage) do
6:            p = inputImage[x,y]
7:            find c ∈ 0..K-1 such that abs(p-mean[c]) is minimum
8:            totalDistance += (p-mean[c])²
9:            sum[c] += p
10:           size[c] += 1
11:       for all c ∈ 0..K-1 do
12:           if (size[c] ≠ 0) mean[c] = sum[c] / size[c]
13:   while (totalDistance has not converged)
14:   return result, means
15: end
        Pseudocode for Standard Lloyd's
```

```
1: Function HistoKmeans (inputImage, K)
2:    Calculate histogram H of the inputImage
3:    B[0] = 0;  B[K] = 256
4:    for all c ∈ 1..K-1 do B[c] = Initial value
5:    do
6:        for all c ∈ 0..K-1 do
7:            totalTop = 0 ;  totalBottom = 0
8:            for i ∈ B[c]..B[c+1]-1  do
9:                totalTop += H[i] × i ;  totalBottom += H[i]
10:               if (totalBottom ≠ 0)  mean[c] = totalTop / totalBottom
11:       for all c ∈ 1..K-1 do
12:           B[c] = ( mean[c-1] + mean[c] ) / 2
13:   while (termination condition not met)
14:   return B, mean
15: end
        Pseudocode for Histogram-based
```

Fig. 1. Pseudocode for the standard Lloyd's algorithm

Since the algorithm needs to access the data set to calculate the means and distances at each iteration, it is necessary to keep a copy of the original data set in memory throughout the FPGA implementation.

B. FPGA Implementation of K-means Clustering

A number of researchers have already studied the FPGA implementation of K-means clustering. In [7], Lavenier feeds the image into the distance calculation units, and indexes every pixel in another array. Due to limited resources on the FPGA, the image is stored in off-chip memory, and must then be streamed multiple times. This entails extra communication overheads between the FPGA and off-chip memory. Estlick et al. implemented K-Means in hardware using software/hardware co-design. The distance calculation is computed in hardware and the rest of the algorithm is completed on a CPU to avoid using a huge amount of hardware resources [8]. And in [4], Yuk-Ming and Choi etc. use three FPGAs which work together to deal with the large amount of data because of the limited resources on each FPGA. In [9], Benkrid implemented a highly parameterized parallel system, and his implementation is not dedicated to image clustering but shows the potential of using FPGAs to accelerate the clustering process. Takashi, Tsutomu et al. implemented K-means on a Xilinx FPGA, using KD-Tree, but they are limited by the resources on the FPGA, and they have to store the image in an off-chip SRAM. They report a performance of 30FPS on an RGB 24-bit image [10, 11]. In [11], the approach replaces the Euclidean distance into the multiply-less Manhattan distance and reduces the word length to save resources. The approaches above focus on achieving greater efficiency by adjusting the word-length, simplifying the distance calculation or using a heterogeneous platform.

Others try to reduce the amount of data. In [1], a filter algorithm is applied first before K-means to reduce the amount of data. Tsutomu reduces the scanning data size by doing partial K-means, whereby the algorithm is applied on 1/8, 1/4, and 1/2 sampled data. This simplifies the K-means algorithm to get better performance but also introduces inaccuracy into the result [12].

Another way to speed up Lloyd's algorithm is to reduce the number of iterations. The performance of Lloyd's is very dependent on the starting point. In [13], Khan and Ahmad used a small amount of data to execute K-means to get a better estimate of the initial mean for each cluster. Pena, Lozano, and Larranaga compared four classical initialization methods for the K-means algorithm: Random, Forgy, MacQueen, and Kaufman. The author found that the Random and Kaufman initialization make the algorithm more effective and independent of the initial value which means it is more robust and effective [14].

The Soft-processor approach is another way of using FPGAs. This retains the high level programming approach, and hides much of the complexity of hardware from developers. In [15], a multi-processor architecture is proposed for K-means based on a network on chip, and using a shared memory to support communication between processors.

To summarize the above approaches, there are three existing ways to speed up the process of K-means clustering using an FPGA. One is to focus on the system architecture, parallelizing the system and finding more effective ways to allocate memory, such as in [7, 9, 10]. The second way is to reduce the amount of data, such as in [1, 12]. The third way is to reduce the number of iterations by finding better initial means for each cluster, as in [13, 14].

We now present our novel approach to implementing K-means clustering, and then present its implementation on a single chip of FPGA including camera and display control.

3 Histogram-Based K-Means Clustering

We first note that the K-means problem for image processing is more constrained than K-means for other kinds of data. The range of the input data is discrete, e.g. for an 8-bit grayscale image, the grey levels are from 0 to 255.

Secondly, the clustering of pixels does not need to take the location of pixels into account. Therefore, we can represent the input image by the image histogram (for the purposes of clustering). The image histogram (which does not change throughout the iterative clustering process) is effectively a compressed version of the image. For any grey level value g, all pixels with that value can be clustered at the same time, with a single calculation.

Thirdly, we can represent each cluster c merely as a sub-range of the histogram, from column B_c to column $B_{(c+1)-1}$ inclusive, where B_i is the lower bound of cluster i.

Fourthly, given the means of each cluster μ_c, the new bounds, which define the new clusters, will be simply half way between the respective means. Figure 2 shows a typical histogram and the representation of four clusters.

For an $N_x \times N_y$ image, and doing L iterations, the complexity of the standard Lloyd's algorithm is $N_x \times N_y \times L$. The complexity of our new histogram-based algorithm will be $N_x \times N_y + 256 \times L$ (assuming 256 grey levels), where the $N_x \times N_y$ component is for calculating the histogram. For example, for a 512×512 image with L = 20, the standard method will require around 5.2M steps, whereas our histogram-based method will require around 0.267M steps – an improvement, in theory, of the

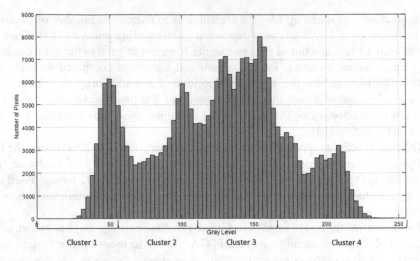

Fig. 2. An image histogram and representation of four clusters

order of 20x. In practice, there will be the additional overhead of image input and perhaps reconstruction of the output image and the number of iterations will be image-dependent. These factors will typically have the effect of reducing the apparent speed-up.

For an 8-bit image, the histogram is a one-dimensional vector with 256 elements, where each element in the histogram represents the number of pixels having that grey level. After generating the histogram, bounds are needed to divide the histogram into different clusters. Each cluster is defined by a pair of bounds, which define the part of the histogram corresponding to the cluster. If we have K clusters, there will be K + 1 bounds, where $B_0 = 0$, and $B_K = 256$. Cluster c ($0 \leq c < K$) is the part of the histogram from column B_c to $B_{(c+1)-1}$ inclusive. The inner bounds ($0 < c < K$) can be initialized in different ways (see later). Then, the means for the current clusters are calculated as defined by Eq. (4).

$$\mu_c = \frac{\left(\sum_{i=B_C}^{B_{C+1}-1} H_i \times i \right)}{\left(\sum_{i=B_C}^{B_{C+1}-1} H_i \right)} \quad (0 < C < K) \tag{4}$$

Once the updated means are calculated, the next iteration first assigns the clusters by merely updating the bounds. To assign a pixel to the correct new cluster, we have to see which mean it is closest to. Consider a pixel with value g (say, 150) in an image with a histogram such as in Fig. 2, and the means are [0.0, 27.5, 90.5, 165.0, 220.0, 256.0]. Column g will be part of the cluster whose mean is closest to g. We can achieve this simply by moving the bounds so that each bound is half way between the two respective means. The updating of the clusters is defined by Eq. (5).

$$B_C = \frac{(\mu_{C-1} + \mu_C)}{2} \, (0 \le C < K) \tag{5}$$

The iteration can then be completed by updating the means using Eq. (4).

We use integers to hold the bounds, so that they correspond to actual pixel grey levels. In our FPGA implementation, we use simple fixed point to represent the means.

Termination of the iterative algorithm could be brought about under several conditions. The total distance can be readily calculated as in the standard Lloyd's algorithm. However, in our preferred approach, the termination condition is that none of the bounds are changed by the updating (Eq. (5)). This has the advantage that the total (squared) distance does not need to be calculated. A third option is to set a fixed number of iterations (say, 50), which can be sufficient for many applications in practice. This number may be application–specific, and can be set at runtime.

There are several ways to initialize the K-means algorithm such as Random, or MacQueen and Kaufman, as mentioned in [14]. Actually, in our histogram method, we initialize the cluster bounds rather than the means. We provide two particular ways to do this. The first is simply to divide the grey level range into K equal parts. The second way is to divide all the pixels into K equally sized clusters. The latter can be achieved by using the cumulative histogram and setting the bounds to the columns which have the appropriate height.

Dividing the histogram range into K equal parts takes the least resources in a hardware implementation. However, in an image with an unevenly distributed histogram, some clusters may be empty (for instance, if the image is overexposed or too dark). The danger condition of calculating the mean of a zero-element cluster can be overcome with a suitable condition; however, if we have two adjacent zero-element clusters, the bounds would not move and those clusters would not grow. Thus, the safest way to initialize the clusters is to set each cluster initially to have the same number of pixels (approximately), using the cumulative histogram. We can build the cumulative histogram from the histogram during initialization. A refinement which is easy to implement is for the user to supply an initial, application-specific estimate of the relative sizes of each cluster as a parameter.

4 System Implementation

We implemented the histogram-based K-means Clustering algorithm on a Xilinx FPGA, using Vivado HLS on a ZedBoard and running at either 150 MHz or 100 MHz. And the architecture is shown in the Fig. 3 below.

The architecture of the FPGA implementation is simple. The system is made up of two parts, the I/O part and the processing part. The whole system is controlled by the AXI-Lite bus. The camera repeatedly captures a frame and stores it in the frame buffer. Then the data is streamed to the input FIFO and fed into the K-means hardware. After the image is processed, the bounds and means are sent to the image reconstruction hardware and the output frame buffer. We use a physical VGA interface for display. The architecture is shown in Fig. 3. The K-means hardware and the image reconstruction hardware are programmed in HLS. The input and output images are

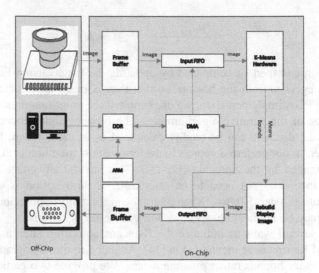

Fig. 3. System architecture

transferred using the AXI-Stream interface. The means and bounds of each cluster are held in a BRAM.

Our architecture is parameterized to provide some flexibility for the user. Our K-means hardware can support any number of clusters up to a defined maximum (in our case, 10 clusters). Within this limit, the actual number of clusters can be selected, and changed during the run time by setting the control registers in the control bus. Extending the maximum number requires re-synthesis the hardware and pay more hardware resources.

The method for setting the initial value of the bounds, as mentioned above, can be selected at runtime via a control register as well.

For comparison purposes, we run both the Lloyd's and our K-means at both 100 MHz and 150 MHz. The ARM output 100/150 MHz clock is divided into 50 MHz and 25 MHz. 50 MHz is used in the camera and display, and 25 MHz is used in the data transfer through the FIFOs and frame buffers. The FIFOs are used to help synchronise data across the clock domain between the frame buffer and our K-means hardware.

Both Lloyd's and our histogram-based algorithm can run at 150 MHz. However, the hardware resources for both these higher speed implementations are noticeably higher than for the 100 MHz version. In the next section, we discuss the performance and resources in detail.

5   Results and Comparison

We compare the performance of two designs: the standard Lloyd's algorithm and our new histogram-based algorithm. For the hardware versions, we consider several factors: hardware usage, the clock cycles required to process an image (4 clusters), and the actual number of frames per second (FPS). The utilization of the different designs is shown in Table 1. It can be seen that the histogram-based algorithm takes about half the LUT (Look up table) and FF (Flip-Flop) resources.

Table 1. Comparison of performance (including reconstruction of output image)

100 MHz	LUTs	FFs	DSPs	BRAMs
Histogram	1194	749	1	40.5
Lloyd's	2641	1535	3	38.5
150 MHz	LUTs	FFs	DSPs	BRAMs
Histogram	1807	2770	4	40.5
Lloyd's	3793	4350	3	38.5

Since even at 100 MHz our histogram-based architecture is able to achieve real time performance, the clustering itself does not demand using the fastest clock speed; and since the 100 MHz version uses rather less hardware resources, its use would therefore normally be preferred (Table 2).

Table 2. Comparison with other literatures

100 MHz, L = 25	FPS	Iterations
Histogram (HW)	95	25
Lloyd's (HW)	12.5	25
[13]	30	–
[14]	38.6	–
[12]	45.8	–

We also compare the performance of our algorithm to the implementations in [13–15]. The work in [14] takes a 24-bit RGB image of size 640 × 480 and has a performance of 30 FPS; the pixels in RGB channel are clustered in parallel. And the work in [13, 15] is using 640 × 480 grayscale image. [15] uses the Manhattan distance to replace Euclidean distance, and [13] reduces the data set by sampling the image to get better performance. Those two approaches are based on the standard Lloyd's algorithm but cannot guarantee full accuracy, and have less performance than our new implementation. The superiority of our new method can be seen.

Hence, the new histogram-based algorithm is the best choice when multi-clusters is needed. It has more advantages over the existing algorithms, it takes fewer resources, better performance than full K-means, and it is easy to adapt the stream implementation.

6 Conclusion and Future Work

This paper has presented a new K-means clustering algorithm, based on iteratively processing the image histogram rather than the image. The main contributions are as follows:

1. A new histogram-based K-means clustering algorithm, which transforms the 2-D image into a 1-D histogram. The histogram retains all the details which are needed to perform K-means clustering. The method is equivalent to Lloyd's, and gives the same results.
2. An FPGA implementation of the new histogram-based K-means clustering algorithm. On an FPGA, the histogram-based takes approximately half the resources compared to Lloyd's, and a speed-up of approximately 7.6. Even at 100 MHz and with 50 iterations, we achieve 82 FPS for 640×480 images.

Future work will look at providing greater flexibility in the FPGA architecture, including a wider range of cluster initialization strategies, and some possible further optimizations. Using the histogram-based algorithm to cluster RGB color image will be challengeable, we are going to find a way to optimize the algorithm and make it suitable for RGB color image.

Acknowledgement. This work was supported by the Chinese Scholarship Council.

References

1. Kanungo, T., Mount, D.M., Netanyahu, N.S., et al.: An efficient K-means clustering algorithm: Analysis and implementation. IEEE Trans. Pattern Anal. Mach. Intell. **24**(7), 881–892 (2002)
2. Ng, H.P., Ong, S.H., Foong, K.W.C., et al.: Medical image segmentation using K-means clustering and improved watershed algorithm. In: Proceedings of 2006 IEEE Southwest Symposium on Image Analysis and Interpretation, pp. 61–65. IEEE (2006)
3. Duda, R.O., Hart, P.E., Stork, D.G.: Pattern Classification and Scene Analysis, 2nd edn. Wiley Interscience, Hoboken (1995)
4. Choi, Y.M., So, H.K.H.: Map-reduce processing of K-means algorithm with FPGA-accelerated computer cluster. In: Proceedings of the 2014 IEEE 25th International Conference on Application-Specific Systems, Architectures and Processors, ASAP, pp. 9–16. IEEE (2014)
5. Neshatpour, K., Koohi, A., Farahmand, F., et al.: Big biomedical image processing hardware acceleration: a case study for K-means and image filtering. In: 2016 IEEE International Symposium on Circuits and Systems, ISCAS, pp. 1134–1137. IEEE (2016)
6. Farivar, R., Rebolledo, D., Chan, E., et al.: A parallel implementation of K-means clustering on GPUs. In: PDPTA 2008, vol. 13, no. 2, pp. 212–312 (2008)
7. Lavenier, D.: FPGA implementation of the K-means clustering algorithm for hyperspectral images. In: Proceedings of Los Alamos National Laboratory LAUR (2000)
8. Estlick, M., Leeser, M., Theiler, J., et al.: Algorithmic transformations in the implementation of K-means clustering on reconfigurable hardware. In: Proceedings of the 2001 ACM/SIGDA Ninth International Symposium on Field Programmable Gate Arrays, pp. 103–110. ACM (2001)

9. Hussain, H.M., Benkrid, K., Erdogan, A.T., et al.: Highly parameterized K-means clustering on FPGAs: comparative results with GPPs and GPUs. In: Proceedings of 2011 International Conference on Reconfigurable Computing and FPGAs, ReConFig, pp. 475–480. IEEE (2011)
10. Saegusa, T., Maruyama, T., Yamaguchi, Y.: How fast is an FPGA in image processing? In: Proceedings of International Conference on Field Programmable Logic and Applications, FPL 2008, pp. 77–82. IEEE (2008)
11. Saegusa, T., Maruyama, T.: An FPGA implementation of K-means clustering for color images based on Kd-tree. In: Proceedings of International Conference on Field Programmable Logic and Applications, FPL 2006, pp. 1–6. IEEE (2006)
12. Maruyama, T.: Real-time K-means clustering for color images on reconfigurable hardware. In: Proceedings of 18th International Conference on Pattern Recognition, ICPR 2006, vol. 2, pp. 816–819. IEEE (2006)
13. Khan, S.S., Ahmad, A.: Cluster center initialization algorithm for K-means clustering. Pattern Recogn. Lett. 25(11), 1293–1302 (2004)
14. Pena, J.M., Lozano, J.A., Larranaga, P.: An empirical comparison of four initialization methods for the K-means algorithm. Pattern Recogn. Lett. 20(10), 1027–1040 (1999)
15. Khawaja, S.G., Akram, M.U., Khan, S.A., et al.: A novel multiprocessor architecture for K-means clustering algorithm based on network-on-chip. In: Proceedings of 2016 19th International Multi-topic Conference, INMIC, pp. 1–5. IEEE (2016)

Neural Network Identification of an Axial Zero-Bias Magnetic Bearing

Qing Liu[1], Li Wang[1(✉)], and Yulong Ding[1,2(✉)]

[1] School of Energy and Environmental Engineering, University of Science and Technology Beijing, Beijing 100083, China
liwang@me.ustb.edu.cn, Y.Ding@bham.ac.uk
[2] Birmingham Center for Energy Storage, School of Chemical Engineering, University of Birmingham, Birmingham B15 2TT, UK

Abstract. System identification for magnetic bearings can be used for various purposes, such as aggressive control design, on-line monitoring and early diagnosis of upcoming faults in rotating machinery, etc. Especially for the zero-bias active magnetic bearing (AMB) system, which omits the bias current/flux to reduce power loss and rotor heating, whereas brings out the problem of highly nonlinearity. Here, we applied the NARX neural network to the identification of an axial zero-bias magnetic bearing system. The I/O data are acquired through a stabilized magnetic bearing test rig, which are more accurate than data that generated by simulation. Two kinds of training methods are compared in different working conditions. The results show a good ability of generalization, which prove the feasibility of the NN identification.

Keywords: Zero-bias · Magnetic bearing · Neutral networks
System identification

1 Introduction

Active magnetic bearings (AMBs) generate controlled electromagnetic forces to levitate the rotor to balancing positions (Fig. 1), thus there is no mechanical contact or abrasion to the magnetic bearings. Therefore, AMB provides many unique and practical merits compared with traditional bearings, such as free of lubrication, no contamination, higher rotating speed and higher precision. Consequently, AMBs have been widely utilized in various fields, including high-speed electrical spindle, flywheel energy storage systems, turbine engines and vacuum pumps. In addition, the apparent noncontact and frictionless characteristics make the AMB irreplaceable at harsh working conditions such as in extreme temperature or vacuum environment. Further, both the bearing stiffness and damping are controllable which make the AMB adjustable in case of sudden imbalance or vibration.

Due to the intrinsic nonlinear characteristics of magnetic forces, a constant current or flux is supplied to each electromagnet (EM), which is referred as the bias current/flux, to improve the linearity of the force-current relationships around the operating point and allow for a higher slew rate of force. Meanwhile, a variable current/flux which is calculated by the controller is superimposed on the bias

© Springer Nature Singapore Pte Ltd. 2018
K. Li et al. (Eds.): ICSEE 2018/IMIOT 2018, CCIS 924, pp. 478–488, 2018.
https://doi.org/10.1007/978-981-13-2384-3_45

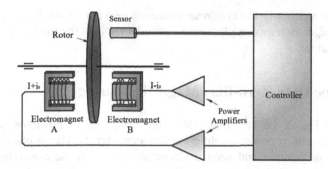

Fig. 1. Schematic of one-DOF active magnetic bearings

current/flux, referring as the control current/flux. Although a bias current/flux linearizes the relationship between the force and the control current, it also results in rotor heating and power loss [1] (the copper loss in the windings, eddy-current loss and hysteresis loss). In certain situations, large bias current/flux is designed to improve bearing stiffness and load capacity, yet causes huge copper losses and cuts down the running time of the AMB system [2].

Based on this, there are several viable drive modes to reduce power loss of the AMBs. For one, the bias currents/fluxes are lowered and the control current is merely superimposed on one side of the pair of coils. Consequently, the energy consumption can be reduced efficiently. Nevertheless, this operating mode is merely appropriate for low bearing stiffness and low vibration applications due to poor slew rate and controllability of the force. For the other, there is no bias current/flux and only the control current/flux is exerted on one side of the pair of coils, which is also called the zero-bias AMB. In spite of the least rotor heating of all kinds, high nonlinearity of the electromagnetic force degrades the control characteristic greatly.

According to the highly nonlinearity of the zero-bias magnetic bearings, precise modelling is of essence for several reasons. First is that it enables prediction of the system dynamics under different working situations. Then, identification for AMB systems could be used for on-line monitoring and early diagnosis of upcoming faults in rotating machinery [3]. Next, a concise model of the zero-bias AMB plant is required for the controller design [4]. Otherwise the controllers have to be robust with respect to the plant uncertainty [5].

Generally, the dynamic model of the AMB is established on the basis of theoretical knowledge, which mainly relies on the identification of the model parameters. For example, the linearized magnetic force around the equilibrium position is $f = k_i i + k_x x$, where k_i and k_x are the current-force coefficient and the displacement-force coefficient, which are related to coil turns, geometry, nominal air gap and the bias current. Moreover, the dynamics of the flexible rotor is calculated by FE model. Nonetheless, this kind of methods are not accurate enough for controller design. Besides, many parts are not covered, including sensors, power amplifiers, eddy current and hysteresis effects.

Apart from that, the linearized model based on Taylor expansion around the equilibrium position is no longer suitable for the zero-bias AMBs. Accordingly, effective ways to identify the nonlinear system of zero-bias AMB is of significance to controller design. Here, we apply neural networks (NN) to the modelling of zero-bias magnetic bearings.

2 The One-DOF Zero-Bias Magnetic Bearing

As shown in Fig. 2, the zero-bias AMBs are comprised of the rotor, displacement sensors, the controller, power amplifiers and electromagnets. The displacement sensors detect the rotor position and send the position signals to the controller. After AD conversion and data filtering, the controller calculates the control value and outputs it as PWM wave. The power amplifiers connect the controller with the electromagnets, which act as an electronic switch and meanwhile drive the EM.

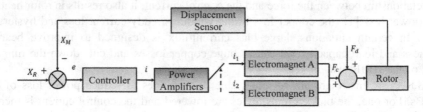

Fig. 2. Block diagram of zero-bias AMBs

Compared with conventional AMBs, there is no constant bias current and only one electromagnet being electrified at any moment. In an attractive type bearing configuration of electromagnets demonstrated in Fig. 1, when the rotor is deviating from the balanced position due to a disturbance, the coil current of the EM that the rotor is approaching reduces to zero, while the other EM on the opposite is switched on to produce attractive magnetic force to drag the rotor back to the equilibrium position and stabilized. The motion equation for the one-DOF zero-bias AMB system is derived as

$$m\ddot{x} = f_1 - f_2. \tag{1}$$

where m is the rotor mass and f_1, f_2 are the nonlinear control force of each EM, which can be denoted as

$$f_1 = \frac{ki_1^2}{(x_0 + x)^2} \quad f_2 = \frac{ki_2^2}{(x_0 - x)^2}. \tag{2}$$

where k is a constant $(= \mu_0 N^2 S/4)$, i_1, i_2 are the EM's currents, x_0 is the nominal air gap and x is the rotor displacement. The total force to the rotor f is

$$f = \begin{matrix} -f_1 & (x > 0, i_2 = 0) \\ f_2 & (x < 0, i_1 = 0) \end{matrix}. \tag{3}$$

As demonstrated, the relationship between the magnetic force and the control current is nonlinear. Meanwhile, only one control input is effective at any moment which is depended on the rotor position [6, 7].

3 Architecture and Algorithm of the NARX Network

System identification is a process of estimating parameters of a system model, which also allows fast and accurate modelling of magnetic bearings [5]. Identification for AMB systems could be used for on-line monitoring and early diagnosis of upcoming faults in rotating machinery [3]. Artificial intelligence theory such as neural networks and fuzzy logic, have also been used in identification and control of AMBs [8]. Compared with classical system identification methods, such as prediction error (PE) method, the output error (OE) method, the instrumental variable (IV) method [9], NN has an ability of approaching any continuous nonlinear mapping, therefore the NN is generally applied to system identification and control.

NN comprises of many simple processing elements operating in parallel whose function is determined by network structure, connection strength, and the processing preformed at computing elements or nodes [10]. Common approaches such as BP, RBP or SVM are static neural networks, which add TDL (Tapped Delay Line) in front of the input to realize dynamic characteristics. Nonetheless, the TDL is not an internal component of the neural networks, therefore increases the training complexity. Besides, the order of the TDL is generally 2 order, which reduces the model accuracy. Hence, dynamic neural networks are preferred. Here NARX network is presented since the TDL unit is the interior structure of the NN and can be adjusted dynamically, therefore reduce the training complexity. Besides, compared with another dynamic neural networks, i.e. NAR, which only uses past values of network output, NARX is more accurate. The NARX model can be expressed as [11]

$$y(t) = f(u(t-1), \ldots, u(t-n_u), y(t-1), \ldots, y(t-n_y)). \tag{4}$$

where $u(t)$ and $y(t)$ denote the I/O of the network at time t, n_u and n_y represent the input and output order, and function f is a nonlinear function. When function f can be approximated by a multilayer perception, the resulting system is called a NARX network. As shown in Fig. 3, the NARX network mainly consists of the input layer, the hidden layer, the output layer, and the TDL. The output of the hidden layer i at time k can be described as

$$p_i(k) = f_{sig}\left(\sum_{r=1}^{n_u} w_{ir}(k)u(k-r) + \sum_{l=1}^{n_y} w_{il}(k)y(k-l) + b_i\right). \tag{5}$$

where f_{sig} is the Sigmoid function of the hidden layer, n_u is the length of time delay of the external input, and n_y is the length of time delay of the output feedback. $w_{ir}(k)$ is the weight value between the input $u(t-r)$ and the hidden unit i at time k; $w_{il}(k)$ is the weight value between the output feedback $y(t-l)$ and the hidden unit i at time k; b_i is

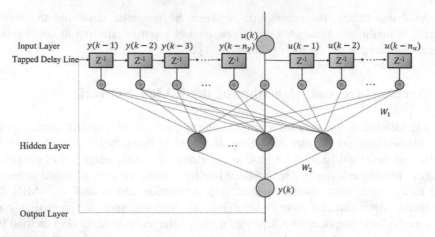

Fig. 3. The structure of NARX neural network model

the threshold value of the unit i. Hence, the output $y_j(k)$ of the output layer j can be expressed as

$$y_i(k) = \sum_{i=1}^{N} w_{ji}(k)d_i + T_j. \tag{6}$$

where $w_{ji}(k)$ is the weight value between the hidden unit i and the output layer j; T_j is the threshold value of the output layer j; N is the number of the hidden units. Therefore, the expression of NARX network can be expressed by combining Eqs. (5) and (6).

The NN configurations are demonstrated in Fig. 4. There are two kinds of configurations. One is called parallel architecture and the other is series-parallel architecture. For the former structure, the output of the NARX network is fed back to the input of the feedforward neural network as part of the standard NARX architecture. For the latter one, the true output is used instead of feeding back the estimated output, which possesses two advantages. Firstly, the input to the feedforward network is more accurate. Secondly, the resulting network has a purely feedforward architecture, and static backpropagation can be used for training.

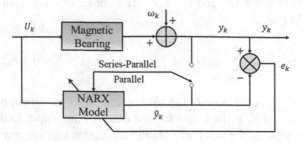

Fig. 4. Two kinds of architectures of NARX model

As shown in Fig. 4, the aim of the NN training algorithm is to minimize the error between the sample output and the corresponding NN model output estimation. The training algorithm applies some parameter-searching strategy, such as the Levenberg-Marquardt (LM) and back-propagation (BP) training function with momentum weight/bias learning function, to adjust the parameters of all neurons in the NN. These parameters mainly contain two groups, i.e. bias and weight.

The performance criteria for the network model can be classified into two types: mean square error (MSE) and error range, which can be described as follows

$$MSE = \frac{1}{N} \sum_{i=1}^{N} \left(y(i) - \hat{y}(i)\right)^2. \tag{7}$$

$$\Delta \delta = [\min(y(i) - \hat{y}(i)), \max(y(i) - \hat{y}(i))]. \tag{8}$$

where $y(i)$ is the output of the zero-bias AMB system, and $\hat{y}(i)$ is the prediction of the model output. N is the number of the samples. The smaller the MSE and $\Delta \delta$ are, the more accurate the network model is.

As for the training algorithms for the NN, there are many choices. Here we compare two kinds of algorithms, i.e. the LM and Scaled Conjugate Gradient (SCG). The LM interpolates between the Gauss–Newton algorithm (GN) and the method of gradient descent. For well-behaved functions and reasonable starting parameters, the LM tends to be a bit slower than the GN. Nevertheless, the LM is more robust than the GN, which means that in many cases it finds a solution even if it starts very far off the final minimum. In addition, a supervised learning algorithm (SCG) with super linear convergence rate is applied, which is based upon Conjugate Gradient Methods. SCG uses second order information from the neural network yet demands only O(N) memory usage (N is the number of weights in the network) [12].

4 Simulation Results

In this section, system identification was applied to a one-DOF zero-bias magnetic bearing test rig based on different working conditions. Moreover, different training algorithms are compared.

The AMB plant is open loop unstable, thus to fulfil system identification, it must be stabilized [13]. An embedded control system was implemented with a micro-controller (Fig. 5). The test rig is comprised of two EMs, a rotor, a displacement sensor, a controller and two power amplifiers. The EMs are two small attracted-disk type with EI shaped cores. The rotor is an iron disc with wall thickness 2.5 mm and diameter 60 mm. The displacement sensor is eddy current type with an output range of 0–10v, 1%FS. The controller is based on K60 microprocessors (Freescale 32-bit), and the control algorithm is designed in IAR development environment. In addition, two switching power amplifiers which mainly constitute of MOSFET (IRF540N) are applied to actuate the EMs.

Fig. 5. The test rig of the one-DOF zero-bias AMB

Two group of data were acquired, the first was under the steady state with 2000 timesteps and a sampling time of 1 ms (Fig. 6). The second group covered an external disturbance and the relaxation process, which contained 6000 timesteps with a sampling time of 1 ms (Fig. 10). The number of hidden neurons is ten, and both the input order and output order of the NARX model are two.

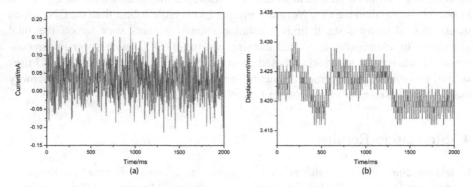

Fig. 6. Snapshot of: (a) input data sequences; (b) output data sequences (steady state)

The simulation results of the steady state were displayed in Figs. 7 and 8. The total time of training, validation, and test for LM is 1 s, whereas that of the SCG is more than 2 s. Specifically, Fig. 7. is about the MSE, which represents the average squared difference between actual output and the targets [14]. Lower values are better, and zero means no error. Figure 8 is about the error histogram. Obviously, the majority of the error concentrated on zero, however, the error distribution was more dispersed using LM. Moreover, the overall regression (R) values for LM is 0.97065, while that of SCG is 0.9552. The regression measures the correlation between the output and target. An R value of 1 means a close relationship, 0 a random relationship. Overall, LM has a far faster convergence speed and smaller regression value, whereas the epoch iteration is more. Besides, both algorithms are sensitive to initial parameters.

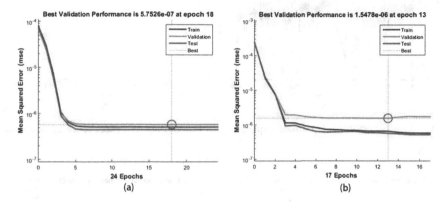

Fig. 7. Mean squared error and epochs number of the steady state: (a) LM; (b) SCG

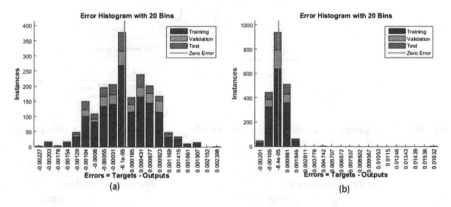

Fig. 8. Error histogram with 20 bins (steady state): (a) LM; (b) SCG

As for the second group, the simulation results of the steady state are demonstrated in Figs. 9, 10, 11 and 12. The total time of training, validation, and test for LM is around 10 s, whereas that of the SCG is more than 20 s. The LM algorithm has smaller MSE and regression value compared with SCG. Overall, both algorithm can approach the nonlinear system very well. Although the LM requires large calculation, it prevails in convergence speed and regression.

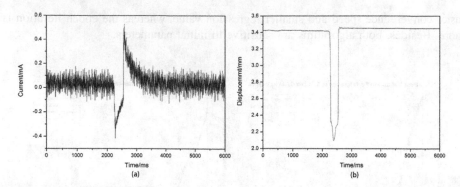

Fig. 9. A snapshot of: (a) input data sequences; (b) output data sequences (under disturbance)

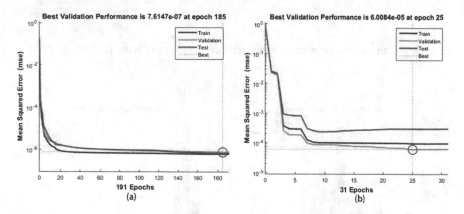

Fig. 10. Mean squared error and epochs number of: (a) LM; (b) SCG (under disturbance)

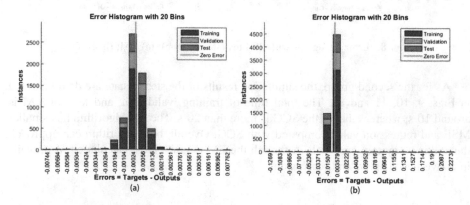

Fig. 11. Error histogram with 20 bins (under disturbance): (a) LM; (b) SCG

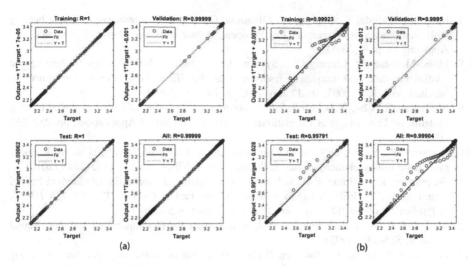

Fig. 12. The regression values of the training, validation, test process (under disturbance): (a) LM; (b) SCG

5 Conclusion

Zero-bias magnetic bearing is a highly-nonlinear system and the design of the controller needs to include the nonlinear characteristics. Based on the fact that the NN can approach any nonlinear mapping, here we present the system identification of the zero-bias AMB with a NARXNET. Two kinds of training algorithms are compared in different operation conditions. The results show the feasibility and effectiveness of NN identification.

References

1. Kato, Y., Yoshida, T., Ohniwa, K.: Self-sensing active magnetic bearings with zero-bias current control. Electr. Eeg. Jpn. **165**, 69–76 (2008)
2. Rong, H., Zhou, K.: Nonlinear zero-bias current control for active magnetic bearing in power magnetically levitated spindle based on adaptive backstepping sliding mode approach. Proc. Inst. Mech. Eng. Part C: J. Mech. Eng. Sci. **231**, 3753–3765 (2017)
3. Gahler, C., Mohler, M., Herzog, R.: Multivariable identification of active magnetic bearing systems. JSME Int. J. Ser. C Mech. Syst. Mach. Elem. Manuf. **40**, 584–592 (1997)
4. Cho, Y.M., Srinavasan, S., Oh, J.-H., Kim, H.S.: Modelling and system identification of active magnetic bearing systems. Math. Comput. Model Dyn. **13**, 125–142 (2007)
5. Gähler, C., Herzog, R.: Identification of magnetic bearing systems. Math. Model. Syst. **1**, 29–45 (1995)
6. Sivrioglu, S., Saigo, M., Nonami, K.: Adaptive backstepping control design for a flywheel zero-bias AMB system. In: Proceedings of 2003 IEEE Conference on Control Applications, CCA 2003, pp. 1106–1111. IEEE (2003). B 7

7. Kato, Y., Yoshida, T., Ohniwa, K., Miyashita, O.: A self-sensing active magnetic bearing with zero-bias-current control. In: European Conference on Power Electronics and Applications, p. 9 (2005)
8. Mohd-Mokhtar, R., Liuping, W.: System identification of MIMO magnetic bearing via continuous time and frequency response data. In: IEEE International Conference on Mechatronics, ICM 2005, 10–12 July 2005, p. 191–196 (2005)
9. Srinivasan, S., Cho, Y.M.: Modeling and system identification of active magnetic bearing systems. In: Proceedings of International Conference on Control Applications, pp. 252–260 (1995)
10. Jayaswal, P., Verma, S.N., et al.: Development of EBP-artificial neural network expert system for rolling element bearing fault diagnosis. J. Vib. Cont. **17**, 1131–1148 (2010)
11. Siegelmann, H.T., Horne, B.G., Giles, C.L.: Computational capabilities of recurrent NARX neural networks. IEEE Trans. Syst. Man Cybern. Part B Cybern. **27**, 208–215 (1997). A Publication of the IEEE Systems Man & Cybernetics Society
12. Møller, M.F.: A scaled conjugate gradient algorithm for fast supervised learning. Neural Netw. **6**, 525–533 (1993)
13. Gibson, N.S., Heeju, C., Buckner, G.D.: H∞ control of active magnetic bearings using artificial neural network identification of uncertainty. In: 2003 IEEE International Conference on Systems, Man and Cybernetics, vol.1442, pp. 1449–1456 (2003)
14. Hamamreh, J., Dama, Y.: Self-organizing schedulers in LTE system for optimized pixel throughput using neural network (2013)

Precision Measurement and Instrumentation

A Novel Bench of Quarter Vehicle Semi-active Suspension

Xiaomin Dong[1,2(✉)], Wenfeng Li[1,2], Chengwang Pan[1,2], and Jun Xi[1,2]

[1] State Key Laboratory of Mechanical Transmission, Chongqing University, Chongqing, China
xmdong@cqu.edu.cn
[2] School of Mechanical Engineering, Chongqing University, Chongqing, People's Republic of China

Abstract. According to the requirements of automotive performance evaluation standards, a typical quarter vehicle suspension model was established, and the correlation between the suspension model transfer function and the vehicle performance evaluation criteria was analyzed. Because the current lack of a standard bench of car suspension, this paper has established a universal and efficient standard bench of quarter car semi-active suspension. The bench is composed of the hardware system part, the sensing scheme and software system part. The bench can not only be used as a passive suspension development platform, but also can be used as a semi-active suspension control test platform. With the technology of Rapid Control Prototype (RCP), a variety of control schemes for verifying the semi-active suspension can be compared to find a suitable control algorithm, which is very significant for improving ride comfort and safety of vehicle suspension. In addition, the bench is equipped with a force sensor on the piston rod of the damper to monitor the real-time output force value of the damper, and to achieve real-time tracking and correction of the control output in the semi-active suspension control test.

Keywords: Quarter vehicle suspension model
Bench of quarter car suspension · RCP · Real-time tracking

1 Introduction

Suspension system is one of the most important assembly of modern automobiles. It is the mechanism of elastic connection between the frame and the wheels. The main task of suspension system is to transfer all forces and moments between the wheel and the body. At the same time, it will buffer the impact load transmitted from the road to the body, which causes the passenger's discomfort. Suspension system has a significant impact on the performance of a car such as ride stability, driving stability, ride comfort, etc. [1]. Therefore, the suspension system has always been one of the most important issues for car designers and researchers [2]. For the traditional design of automotive passive suspension, the task of the matching between the stiffness coefficient and damping coefficient requires much time and effort. An effective vehicle suspension

© Springer Nature Singapore Pte Ltd. 2018
K. Li et al. (Eds.): ICSEE 2018/IMIOT 2018, CCIS 924, pp. 491–501, 2018.
https://doi.org/10.1007/978-981-13-2384-3_46

bench is promising but difficult to achieve. Some researchers investigated the development of vehicle suspension test rig, e.g., Liu et al. [3] constructed a performance testing system that can measure the absorption efficiency, vibration frequency, phase difference and corresponding vibration wave form of suspension. It provides a basis for comprehensive evaluation and fault diagnosis of suspension performance. Based on the existing automobile suspension test platform, Chen et al. [4] designed a high precision force sensor and the adjustment module of the output signal of the speed sensor, which improved the accuracy and real time of the test system. By simplifying the actual vehicle, Geng et al. [5] established the physical model of the two degree of freedom Mcpherson suspension system. On this basis, the research and construction of the performance test bench for the Mcpherson suspension system were designed and constructed. Omar et al. [6] designed a universal suspension test rig for electrohydraulic active and passive automotive suspension system, and demonstrated the effectiveness of the platform through simulation and experimentation.

However, these suspension test rig has less adaptive ability. There is a difficulty in tuning damping coefficient. They are not suitable to study the semi-active suspension and control algorithms. Consequently, the contribution of this study is to develop a bench for study vehicle suspension. According to the vehicle suspension performance evaluation criteria, a two-degree-of-freedom vehicle suspension physical model was developed. This bench can not only be used for passive suspension training to match the test of passive vehicle suspension stiffness and damping, but also for semi-active suspension testing. By adopting rapid control prototype (RCP) technology, the comparison of different control algorithms on the impact of suspension performance can be realized, the cost and time of the control algorithm test can be saved. The effectiveness of the quarter car suspension bench system was verified through experiments.

The organization of this study is as following. Test standard for vehicle suspension performance is addressed in the Sect. 2. In Sect. 3, the theoretic analysis for the bench test system of a quarter car suspension is analyzed. The design of the bench test system of a quarter car suspension is proposed in the Sect. 4. The prototype test and discussion are investigated in the Sect. 5. Section 6 concludes this study.

2 Study on Evaluation Standard of Automobile Suspension

Vehicle suspension evaluation methods can be roughly divided into subjective sensory evaluation and objective physical quantity evaluation methods. Since subjective evaluation methods vary from person to person, the discrete type is very large, and it is unfavorable to explain the performance of the automotive suspension. With the development of measurement technology and signal processing technology, the objective physical quantity evaluation method has been widely used.

2.1 International Standard Evaluation Method of Vehicle Drive Stability and Riding Comfort

The drive stability of the car is closely related to the ride comfort. The total weighted acceleration root mean square (RMS) value is generally used to evaluate the car ride stability in the international standard.

For the evaluation method of ride comfort, vibration dose values (EVDV) are generally used in the international standard to evaluate human response to vibration.

When the crest factor is less than 12, the frequency-weighted acceleration RMS value is used to evaluate the person's response to vibration and to calculate the estimated vibration dose value (EVDV).

$$EVDV = 1.4 \cdot \left[\frac{1}{T} \int_0^T a_w^2(t) dt \right]^{\frac{1}{2}} \cdot T^{\frac{1}{4}} \quad \text{m/s}^{-1.75} \tag{1}$$

where a_w is the equivalent vibration value for the entire exposure time (m/s^2); T is the vibration analysis time (s).

When the crest factor is greater than 12, the method of average quadripartite value can better estimate the severity of the high crest factor vibration, and vibration dose value (VDV) can be obtained.

$$VDV = \left[\int_0^T a_w^4(t) dt \right]^{\frac{1}{2}} \quad \text{m/s}^{-1.75} \tag{2}$$

If the vibration exposure consists of two or more vibrations of different intensity, the total exposure EVDV (or VDV) is.

$$EVDV = \left[\sum EVDV_i^4 \right]^{\frac{1}{4}} \tag{3}$$

$$VDV = \left[\sum VDV_i^4 \right]^{\frac{1}{4}} \tag{4}$$

For the same vibration with a crest factor less than 12, EVDV is basically the same as VDV. If the difference between the two values is less than 25%, the RMS method can be used [7].

2.2 Other Commonly Used Vehicle Suspension Evaluation Methods

Many scholars have concluded a lot of suspension evaluation methods through experiments and experiences. At present, the most common method to objectively evaluate the suspension performance is based on the RMS value of the sprung mass acceleration, the root mean square value of the suspension dynamic deflection, and the RMS value of the dynamic tire load [8].

The RMS value of sprung mass acceleration indicates the ride stability and ride comfort of the car. The RMS of suspension dynamic deflection reflects the deformation of the suspension. The RMS value of the dynamic load of the tire directly affects the grounding of the vehicle. The excessive dynamic load of the tire will seriously affect the safety of the grounding of the vehicle, which will degrade the steering stability.

Based on the above evaluation indicators, it can be seen that the ride stability and comfort of the vehicle are affected by the sprung mass acceleration and suspension dynamic deflection. Stability of vehicle operation is affected by tire dynamic load. According to different vehicle suspension requirements, different vehicle suspension parameters are selected to obtain the required suspension performance.

3   Theoretic Analysis for Bench Test System

The working principle of the vehicle suspension system. The unevenness of the road surface is transmitted to four dampers of suspension systems through the wheels, and then transmitted to the vehicle body through the suspension system. The vehicle system in motion is a multi-degree-of-freedom vibration system. Research on the car suspension is based on the dynamic model of the suspension. The vehicle model can accurately predict the impact of the suspension parameters on its performance, thus it can reflect the performance of real suspension system. However, the establishment of an accurate model is a complex process. The establishment of a complete vehicle model requires more relevant parameters, and the accuracy of the parameters will inevitably affect the accuracy of the model.

The quarter-vehicle suspension model is the most basic model for the research of the suspension system. Although it cannot be used for the attitude control of the vehicle, it is sufficient to reflect the relevant indicators that reflect the performance of the suspension: the sprung mass acceleration and the sprung mass displacement, suspension dynamic deflection and tire dynamic load. In addition, the quarter vehicle suspension model involves fewer parameters, which facilitates in-depth study on the suspension system. Therefore, the test object of the vehicle suspension characteristic test system in this paper is the quarter vehicle suspension model [9, 10].

3.1   Establishment of Physical Model of a Quarter Vehicle Suspension

The simplified model of an automotive passive suspension model and magneto-rheology (MR) suspension model are shown in Figs. 1 and 2.

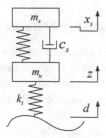
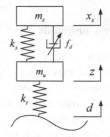

Fig. 1. 1/4 car passive suspension model   **Fig. 2.** 1/4 car semi-active suspension model

In the figure: m_s, x_s are body masses and displacements, respectively. m_u, z are tire mass and displacement, respectively. k_s is the stiffness of the suspension. k_t is the tire stiffness. c_s is the viscous damping coefficient of the suspension. d is random road input. f_d is the damping force of a MR damper.

3.2 Establishment of Two-Degree-of-Freedom Mathematical Model for the Quarter-Vehicle Suspension

The quarter vehicle suspension mathematic model with two-degree-of-freedom is usually represented by the Newtonian mechanics method. The dynamic equation of the passive suspension is.

$$m_s\ddot{x}_s + c_s(\dot{x}_s - \dot{z}) + k_s(x_s - z) = 0 \tag{5}$$

$$m_s\ddot{z} - c_s(\dot{x}_s - \dot{z}) - k_s(x_s - z) + k_t(z - d) = 0 \tag{6}$$

Where $\ddot{x}_s$, $\dot{x}_s$ are the sprung mass accelerations and speeds, respectively. $\ddot{z}$, $\dot{z}$ are unsprung mass accelerations and speeds, respectively.

For a MR semi-active suspension, the corresponding passive damper can be replaced with a magneto-rheological damper, and its kinetic equation is.

$$m_s\ddot{x}_s + k_s(x_s - z) + f_d = 0 \tag{7}$$

$$m_u\ddot{z} - k_s(x_s - z) + k_t(z - d) - f_d = 0 \tag{8}$$

Here, only the passive suspension is taken as an example for illustration.

Performing Laplace transformation on Eqs. 1 and 2. The transfer function of the sprung mass acceleration with respect to the road surface input.

$$H_A = \frac{\ddot{X}_s(s)}{D(s)} = \frac{k_t(C_s s + k_s)s^2}{\Delta s} \tag{9}$$

in which,

$$\Delta s = m_u m_s s^4 + (m_s C_s + m_u C_s)s^3 + (m_s k_s + m_s k_t + m_u k_s)s^2 + k_t C_s s + k_s k_t$$

The transfer function of the sprung mass displacement with respect to the road surface input:

$$H_{DI} = \frac{X_s(s)}{D(s)} = \frac{k_t(C_s s + k_s)}{\Delta s} \tag{10}$$

The transfer function of the suspension deflection relative to the road surface input,

$$H_{DE} = \frac{X_s(s) - Z(s)}{D(s)} = \frac{k_t m_s s^2}{\Delta s} \tag{11}$$

The transfer function of the tire dynamic load with respect to the road surface input,

$$H_F = \frac{k_t(Z(s) - D(s))}{D(s)} = \frac{k_t Z(s)}{D(s)} - k_t = \frac{k_t^2(m_s s^2 + C_s s + k_s)}{\Delta s} - k_t \tag{12}$$

As described in Sect. 2, the sprung mass acceleration is often used as an important index for evaluating the ride comfort in the evaluation of the automobile performance. The suspension deflection seriously affects the ride stability and riding comfort. The tire dynamic load affects the stability of the car's operation. In the process of vehicle suspension test, due to the small rolling of the tire, it is difficult to test the dynamic load of the tire. Therefore, in the process of vehicle suspension test, the dynamic load of vehicle suspension is indirectly obtained by testing the tire dynamic deflection and un-sprung mass acceleration.

4 Quarter Vehicle Semi-active Suspension Bench System Design

The quarter car semi-active suspension bench system is mainly designed to simulate the vibration characteristics of the quarter vehicle suspension system. Its overall structure is shown in the Fig. 3.

The quarter vehicle semi-active suspension bench system consists of two parts, the hardware system part and the sensing and software system part. The hardware system part completes all physical movements of the vehicle suspension system. The sensing scheme and software system part complete signal acquisition, feedback and control of hardware.

The quarter vehicle semi-active suspension bench system working principle is as follows, the electric servo vibration excitation system sends excitation signals for simulating the road surface excitation to the vibration table, and the vibration table produces corresponding vertical vibration, the vibration is transmitted to the inner frame by the tire assembly and the damper assembly. The inner frame is vibrated by the roller to move relative to the guide rail of the outer frame, thus the vertical vibration of

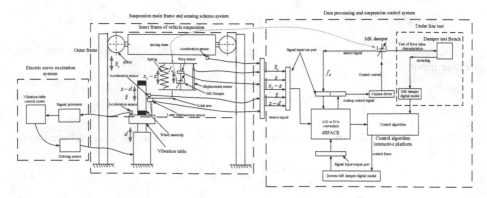

Fig. 3. The quarter vehicle semi-active suspension bench system block diagram

the inner frame is achieved. Through the sensors at the specified position of the inner frame, the status information of different parts of the suspension is transmitted to dSPACE. The signal is converted by dSPACE and transmitted to the control algorithm interaction platform. The control algorithm interactive platform outputs the control signal to the damper after the signal is calculated and processed. The control signal is applied through the current driver to the coil of the semi-active MR damper, thus the suspension damping is changed and the suspension control is achieved.

4.1 Hardware System Part

The hardware system part of the quarter car semi-active suspension bench system is mainly composed of two parts, the vibration control cabinet and the vibration platform part, the suspension main frame part. The vibration control cabinet and the vibration table part are used to provide excitation input for the semi-active suspension platform of the quarter vehicle. The suspension main frame part is used to simulate 1/4 semi-active suspension and related motion.

4.1.1 The Vibration Control Cabinet and the Vibration Table Part

The vibration control cabinet includes servo amplification system and vibration table system, etc. The servo amplifier system is designed to drive a vibration table, including a power amplifier, a power amplifier cabinet, a system control box, etc. By modulating the signal, conducting electrical control, measuring and controlling the output voltage and output current of the power amplifier, the excitation function of the vibration table can be completed.

The vibration table system is mainly composed of an excitation part, a moving coil and its supporting and guiding, a vibration isolation mechanism and a bearing. In the moving coil and its support and guide, an air spring is used for support.

4.1.2 Suspension Main Frame Part

The suspension main frame is mainly composed of an inner frame of a simulated vehicle suspension and a fixed vertical guide rail outer frame for restraining the inner frame of the vehicle suspension. The inner frame includes the wheel assembly, damper assembly, connecting arms, the frame that simulates the sprung mass of the suspension, the fork arms that connect the wheels to the frame and the pulley of the inner frame for sliding freely in the vertical direction. The outer frame part consists of a fixed pillar and a guide rail mounted on the pillar surface and matched with the inner frame roller. The specific structure is shown in Fig. 3.

The main points of the technical design are as follows.

To ensure that the un-sprung mass is closer to the real vehicle, the system adopts a real-tire assembly.

In order to pledge the normal operation of the damper assembly part, a real car damper assembly is adopted in the passive suspension; when the MR semi-active damper assembly is configured, the travel of the MR damper is designed to satisfy suspension requirements, outer contours and passive dampers are matched, and spring of damper assemblies are used to ensure suspension stiffness matching.

The pulley guide is used between the internal and external frames. The pulley is evenly arranged along the vertical direction of the guide rail, a certain pre-pressure is exerted between the pulley and the guide rail to eliminate the shake due to the movement of the inner frame.

With the aim of guaranteeing that the sprung mass is close to the real vehicle, the counterweights are evenly and symmetrically arranged on the top platform of the inner frame according to requirements. The counterweight and the top platform of the inner frame are fixed by set screws to prevent vibration.

4.2   Sensing Scheme and Software System Part

4.2.1   Sensing Scheme System

According to the requirements of vehicle suspension performance evaluation in the Sect. 3.2 and the requirements of ensuring the completeness of vehicle suspension performance parameters, the sensing scheme of the platform is worked out.

The installation of the sensor and the testing parameters of the sensor are detailed in Fig. 3.

4.2.2   Software System

The software part is composed of two parts. One is the excitation control center for controlling the excitation platform, and the other is the data processing and suspension control system.

The vibration platform control center consists of human-computer interaction interface and signal receiver. The input of different excitation signals can be achieved, and the final excitation value can be corrected by adjusting the excitation input value in real time according to the feedback of the acceleration signal.

Data processing and suspension control system is mainly established in this paper for the MR semi-active suspension, including dSPACE system, offline MR damper modeling and interactive platform for control algorithm. As shown in Fig. 3.

The dSPACE system is used for analog-to-digital conversion of the sensor signal, digital-to-analog conversion of the control signal, and also for establishment of interface with control algorithm program software, interaction between dSPACE and control software.

With the dSPACE system, RCP technology can be achieved, the comparison of different control algorithm tests for semi-active suspension can be accomplished. By replacing the control algorithm module with the required control algorithm, and the control experiment of the relevant control algorithm can be carried out based on the rapid control prototype technology.

The offline MR damper modeling is a preparatory work. For details, please refer to [11] Sect. 3.1.3. Through the treatment of the damper mathematical model, the inverse model of the damper is obtained, and the control algorithm is used to control the output characteristics of the damper.

The control algorithm interaction platform is used to operation the control algorithm program. Download the required control algorithm into the software and establish the interaction between the control program and dSPACE through the interface program between the software and dSPACE. Through the force sensor installed between the damper piston rod and the frame bottom plate of the vehicle suspension, the output force value of the damper can be monitored in real time, the real-time correction of the control signal can be realized.

5   Prototype Test and Discussion

According to the function and structure of the semi-active suspension characteristic test platform system of the vehicle as description in the third section, the prototype of the test platform system is designed and constructed as shown in Fig. 4.

1-MR suspension system; 2-Vibration table; 3-dSPACE; 4-DC power supply;

5-Control algorithm interactive platform; 6, 9-Acceleration sensor; 7-Displacement sensor;

8-MR damper assembly; 10-Laser displacement sensor.

Fig. 4. Auto semi-active suspension characteristic test platform system prototype schematic

By the vehicle semi-active suspension characteristics test platform system, various suspension vibration tests can be carried out. In this paper, the simulation of the sinusoidal spectrum excitation input is taken as an example to test the system, the suspension characteristics of the MR semi-active suspension at different currents are experimentally investigated.

The input excitation which is a displacement excitation of the vibrating table is as $A = 5 \cdot \sin(2 \cdot \pi \cdot 8 \cdot t)$. The results of the test are shown in Fig. 5. The test results show that the test platform system can simultaneously test multiple parameters of suspension system, such as suspension spring load acceleration, un-sprung load acceleration, suspension dynamic deflection, tire displacement and damper force value. From the test results, we can clearly know the characteristics of the MR semi-active suspension with different currents. We can combine and calculate the above test results to evaluate the suspension performance according to the evaluation index of the second section. This test proves the integrity and effectiveness of the test platform system.

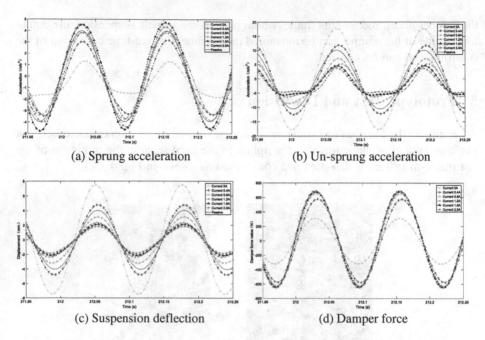

(a) Sprung acceleration

(b) Un-sprung acceleration

(c) Suspension deflection

(d) Damper force

Fig. 5. Characteristics of semi-active suspension under different current

6   Conclusion

In this paper, a universal and efficient standard bench of quarter car semi-active suspension is proposed, designed and configured, and the effectiveness of the bench is verified through experiments. Four main conclusions can be drawn as followings.

(1) During the design process of the quarter car semi-active suspension bench, it is ensured that the bench is close to the real vehicle model, and that the testing result of the test platform is relatively high relative to the spoilage of the real vehicle model.

(2) The bench can be equipped with a passive suspension training platform to match the stiffness coefficient and the damping coefficient of passive suspension.

(3) The bench based on dSPACE system can realize RCP technology and multiple real-time tests of control algorithms, thus avoiding the time and cost loss caused by designing and manufacturing the control algorithm hardware.

(4) By arranging the force sensor on the MR damper, real-time tracking and correction of the control force value can be realized, and the real-time performance of the control effect can be detected.

Acknowledgment. The authors disclosed receipt of the following financial support for the research, authorship, and/or publication of this article: This work was financially supported by the National Natural Science Foundation of People's Republic of China (Project NO. 51675063), this research is also supported by graduate research and innovation foundation of Chongqing, China (Grant No. CYB17023). These supports are gratefully acknowledged.

References

1. Dong, X., Zhang, Z., Yu, J., Tuo, F.: Partial fault sliding mode fault-tolerant control for magneto-rheological semi-active suspension actuators considering temperature effect. In: 13th National Rheology Conference Proceedings, pp. 36–38, Xi'an (2016)
2. Dong, X., Yu, M., Liao, C., Chen, W., Huang, S.: Research on adaptive fuzzy logic control for automobile magneto-rheological semi-active suspension. J. China J. Highw. Transp. **19**(2), 111–115 (2006)
3. Liu, Y., et al.: Study on testing method and testing system of vehicle suspension performance. J. Highw. Transp. Res. Dev. **23**(9), 126–130 (2006)
4. Chen, G., et al.: Research and design of the suspension performance test system for automobiles. J. Chang. Univ. Sci. Technol. (Nat. Sci. Ed.) **32**(3), 388–391 (2009)
5. Geng, X., Xu, W., Li, B., Wang, Z., Chen, Q.: The design of McPherson suspension system performance test platform. J. Mach. Des. Manuf. (11), 163–165 (2012)
6. Omar, M., et al.: A universal suspension test rig for electrohydraulic active and passive automotive suspension system. J. Alex. Eng. J. **56**(4), 1–11 (2012)
7. ISO 2631-1: Mechanical vibration and shock-Evaluation of human exposure to whole-body vibration-part 1: General requirements. S, pp. 3–10 (2003)
8. Miao, Y.: Study on control system of automobile magneto-rheological semi-active suspension, pp. 46–51. Chongqing University, Chongqing (2003)
9. Tuo, F.: Research on fault-tolerant control of MR semi-active suspension with partial fault in actuator considering temperature effect, pp. 32–34. Chongqing University, Chongqing (2015)
10. Zhao, M., Liu, X., Pan, G.: Study on magneto-rheological damper model and semi-active suspension control. J. Vib. Eng. **17**, 1051–1053 (2004)
11. Dong, X.: Human simulated intelligent control of automobile magneto-rheological semi-active suspension, pp. 44–49. Chongqing University, Chongqing (2006)

Research on Nondestructive Testing
for the Depth of Hardening Zone

Ping Chen, Tao Xiang$^{(\boxtimes)}$, Song Guo, Jie Fang, and Xin Xu

School of Mechanical Engineering, Chongqing University, Chongqing 400030,
People's Republic of China
781905415@qq.com

Abstract. In view of the problem of depth of hardening zone measurement for quenching work-piece, this paper analyzes the advantages of new nondestructive testing methods compared with traditional destructive testing methods. The nondestructive testing method, principle and achievable precision index of depth of hardening zone based on eddy current, ultrasonic and magnetic effects are reviewed. Combining the deficiencies in the research status of nondestructive testing technique, the development trend of nondestructive testing technology for depth of hardening zone is prospected.

Keywords: Quenching work-piece · Depth of hardening zone
Nondestructive testing · Development trend

1 Introduction

Quenching is an important heat treatment process for the performance enhancement of metal parts, and then the mechanical properties and physical properties of the parts can be greatly improved with proper tempering process. Therefore, it is widely used in the heat treatment process, such as the rotary support track, the gear rack surface, the machine tool guide, the important shaft parts and so on [1]. The combination of suitable hardening depth and suitable inner ductility can make these parts perform the best comprehensive property. Therefore, accurate measurement of hardening depth is of great significance in industrial production.

The traditional measurement of quenching depth usually uses the metallographic method (from the quenching surface to the martensitic zone's half of the depth), the microhardness method (the hardness of semi-martensitic zone as the standard) or the macro fracture method [2]. But these methods all need to damage the parts to varying degrees. This not only affects the property of parts but also greatly increases the cost of inspection, which this do not meet the development needs of Industry 4.0, either. In particular, as for the large or high-precision quenched parts, the above method can't be effectively detected, which urgently requires an efficient nondestructive testing technique to measure quenching depth of the work-piece. Therefore, the researchers tried to detect the quenching depth through different detection principles and methods. These testing methods include nondestructive testing methods of based on eddy current, ultrasonic and magnetic effects [3]. Finally, this paper will discuss the principle, research status and development trend of the quenching depth's nondestructive testing method.

© Springer Nature Singapore Pte Ltd. 2018
K. Li et al. (Eds.): ICSEE 2018/IMIOT 2018, CCIS 924, pp. 502–511, 2018.
https://doi.org/10.1007/978-981-13-2384-3_47

2 Eddy Current Testing Technology

The basic principle of eddy current nondestructive testing: the exciting coil will generate an alternating magnetic field around the coil after energizing the exciting coil. The eddy current shown in Fig. 1(a) will be generated, when the work-piece is placed in the alternating magnetic field. However, the eddy currents will in turn generate a magnetic field in the opposite direction compared with the excitation magnetic field so that the original magnetic field in the coil is reduced, thus causing the change of the coil impedance. Since the distribution of the eddy current depends on excitation conditions. Therefore, when some exciting parameters are kept constant, the change of exciting coil impedance or the voltage in another dedicated detecting coil can be measured so that the researcher calculate the parameter that the test can need.

The eddy current in the measured work-piece is unevenly distributed because the frequency of the exciting current, the conductivity and the magnetic permeability of the tested work-piece can influence the eddy current generated in the work-piece. The eddy

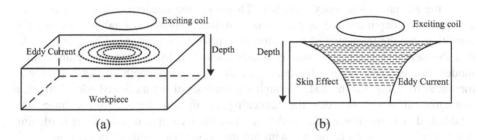

Fig. 1. Principle of eddy current generation

current density is the largest and the densest on the work-piece surface, and the eddy current density gradually decreases with the increase of depth. The attenuation amplitude shows an exponential decay function with the increase of depth and also shows the skin effect of eddy current, as shown in Fig. 1(b) [4].

The distance that the eddy current penetrates into the work-piece is called the depth of penetration. Usually the depth that the eddy current density is attenuated to 1/e (37%) of work-piece surface's eddy current density is defined as the standard penetration depth, also called the skin depth. Its calculation formula is as follows [4]:

$$\delta = \frac{1}{\sqrt{\pi f \mu \sigma}} . \tag{1}$$

In the formula, δ is the standard penetration depth (skin depth), σ is the conductivity, μ is the magnetic permeability, and f is the frequency of the exciting current.

According to the calculation formula, it can be known that the skin depth is inversely proportional to the 1/2 order power of the current frequency for a given quenched work-piece. Therefore, the reasonable detecting frequency can be selected by the calculation formula so that the skin depth includes the entire quenched layer and the detection made can be more accurate and faster.

The measurement of hardening depth by using eddy current is essentially based on establishing mathematical model between the hardening depth and the induced voltage of detecting coil, so as to achieve the goal of measuring the hardening depth. For example, the calculation formula of induction voltage for cylindrical quenching parts is as follows [5]:

$$V_m = (2\pi f)N_s \frac{\pi d^2}{4} \mu_r \mu_{eff} H_0 \times 10^{-8}. \tag{2}$$

Where V_m is the induced voltage of detecting coil, N_s is the number of coil turn, f is the frequency of the exciting current, μ_r is the relative magnetic permeability, μ_{eff} is the effective magnetic permeability, and H_0 is the magnetic field strength.

It can be known from the above formula that the induced voltage increases with the increase of excitation frequency, but the excitation frequency can also affects the effective permeability. So the induced voltage will show a non-linear increasing trend when the excitation frequency increases. Therefore, the mathematical model between the hardening depth and the detecting coil's induced voltage is established under the condition that the frequency of excitation current remains unchanged by this formula, and the depth of hardening zone is finally measured by solving the mathematical model. For example, in the literature [6], the hardening depth of 40Cr steel was measured by using this method. Through the analysis of the measured eddy current, a mathematical model between the hardening depth and the induced voltage was established. The maximum relative deviation of the measured results of the hardening depth was less than 6% compared with the metallographic method on average.

3   Ultrasonic Testing Technology

Ultrasonic nondestructive testing is a new nondestructive testing method with many advantages, which is widely used in detection of defects, cracks and thicknesses. The attenuation measurement and backscatter measurement are the two main technical means of ultrasonic nondestructive testing [7–12], and ultrasonic backscatter measurement is just used for nondestructive testing of hardening depth based on ultrasonic [1]. Beecham and Fay were the earliest scholars who used ultrasonic scattering technique to evaluate grain size of metal material [13–15], then Du and Lonsdale used ultrasonic backscattering technique to measure the quenching depth of railroad wheels on the basis of Beecham's and Fay's studies and good results have been achieved [16]. Specifically, the grain size of quenching work-piece is from the small grain size of the hardening layer in transition to the large grain size of substrate material. So the microstructure size of the work-piece surface's quenched layer is small, the energy loss of ultrasonic wave is less and the ultrasonic reflection is very little when the ultrasonic wave enters the work-piece surface through different methods. But it will encounter with relatively bulky pearlite and ferrite when the ultrasonic wave penetrates into the boundary between the hardened layer and the substrate material layer, so there will form backscattered echo. Therefore, the depth of hardening zone can be calculated by measuring the time when the ultrasonic wave is emitted to the receiving echo.

At present, the most widely used method in the field of ultrasonic nondestructive testing is the piezoelectric ultrasonic nondestructive testing technology. Figure 2 shows the detection principle. After the ultrasonic wave enters into work-piece by the couplant, the backscattering phenomenon will occur when ultrasonic wave passes through the interface. Therefore, the time that the ultrasonic wave transmits from the work-piece surface to the interface can be measured by the detection of backscatter signals, and then the depth of hardening zone is calculated by the path formula.

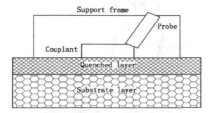

Fig. 2. Principle of the piezoelectric ultrasonic non-destructive testing

According to the theory of acoustic scattering, the size of microstructure and the frequency of ultrasonic wave both have a great influence on the detection. Therefore, it is necessary to determine the frequency range that can generate backscattered echo according to the Eq. (3) before testing [1]. It can not only improve the efficiency of experimental detection, but also make the detection more accurate.

$$d \approx \lambda = \frac{v}{f}.$$ (3)

Where d is the microstructure sizes, λ is the wavelength, v is the wave velocity, f is the ultrasonic frequency.

For example, in the literature [17], the hardening depth of specimen was detected by the piezoelectric ultrasonic nondestructive testing method, and the final measurement error was about 1 mm.

4 Magnetic Effect Testing Technology

4.1 Magnetic Coercivity Testing Technology

The magnetic hysteresis loop is a curve describing the magnetization phenomenon and reverse magnetization phenomenon of the ferromagnetic material under the external magnetic field. That is to say, it describes that the magnetic induction intensity B changes with the external magnetic field intensity H, which reflects the basic magnetic properties of the material and is one of the fundamental bases of the material for the use. The magnetic hysteresis loop of magnetic material is shown in Fig. 3, showing three important parameters: B_r (remanent magnetic induction intensity), B_m (saturated magnetic intensity), H_c (magnetic coercive force). On the magnetic hysteresis loop, B_r, B_m and H_c are all the characteristic parameters which can reflect the properties of the material [20–23]. What's more, the magnetic coercive force is related to the grain size and the carbon content in the material. Therefore, the hardening depth of the quenched work-piece can be characterized by the magnetic coercive [18, 19].

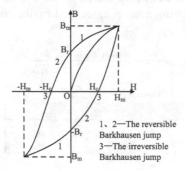

Fig. 3. The magnetic hysteresis loop

In order to obtain the value of the magnetic coercive force to characterize the depth of hardening zone, the magnetic hysteresis loop is measured by the RC indirect measurement method shown in Fig. 4. According to the following formula [18]:

$$B = \frac{CR_2}{SN_2} U_B.$$

(4)

The magnetic induction intensity in the tested piece can be calculated by measuring the output voltage U_B at the two ends of the integration capacitor C. Where B is the magnetic induction intensity, C is the integration capacitor, R_2 is the Integral resistance, S is the effective magnetic flux area of detecting coil and N_2 is the turn number of detecting coil.

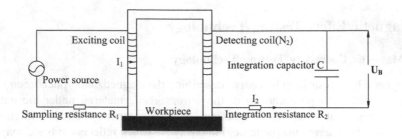

Fig. 4. The principle of nondestructive testing based on magnetic coercive force

After measuring the magnetic induction intensity B under different the external magnetic field intensity, the magnetic hysteresis loop can be obtained and the value of magnetic coercive force can be similarly obtained. Since the magnetic coercive force is closely related to the carbon content and the grain size (the grain size increases gradually from the work-piece surface to the interface) of material, the depth of hardening zone can be obtained by establishing the mathematical model between the magnetic coercive force and the hardening depth and then solving the model. For example, the carburizing and quenching hardening layer depth is measured by magnetic coercive force in the literature [18], and the relationship between the magnetic coercive force and the quenching depth was established.

4.2 Barkhausen Effect Testing Technology

The magnetic domain is many tiny regions formed by the spontaneous magnetization of ferromagnetic materials. In these regions, the orientation of the atomic magnetic moment are the same, but the magnetic moments of the magnetic domain between different magnetic domains are inconsistent. Thus, there is a transition region where the atomic magnetic moments change from one direction to another direction among the different magnetic domains is called the domain wall. In the magnetization process of ferromagnetic materials, the Barkhausen jump is induced by the discontinuous movement of the domain wall [24]. It is found that the magnetization is a stepwise irreversible jump process in the steepest region of the magnetic hysteresis loop when the ferromagnetic material is magnetized, as shown in Fig. 3. This discontinuous jumping phenomenon is called the Barkhausen effect, and the discontinuous jumping signal can be received in the detecting coil on the material surface, called Barkhausen Noise [28–30]. In the movement process of the domain wall, the magnetization of an external magnetic field is the motive force of the domain wall moving, besides the change of microstructure inside the material and the residual stress are the resistance of the domain wall moving. Since the Barkhausen Noise is induced by the discontinuous movement of the domain wall, the Barkhausen Noise signal carries information on the microstructure and residual stress inside the material. Therefore, the Barkhausen Noise signal can be used to detect the depth of hardened layer [25–27].

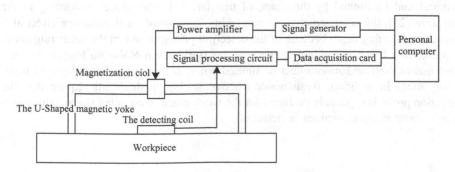

Fig. 5. Principle of non-destructive testing based on Barkhausen effect

The method shown in Fig. 5 is used to measure the Barkhausen Noise. After establishing the mathematical model between the strength of noise signal and the depth of hardening zone, and solving the mathematical model can finally achieve the goal of measuring the depth of hardening zone. For example, the Barkhausen effect was used to detect the depth of hardening zone in the literature [25]. The fitting straight line equation of the strength of noise signal and the depth of hardening zone was $MP = 14.688H^{-0.6828}$, and the relative error of the fitting straight line equation was measured to be within 4% at last.

5   Research Status and Deficiency

The detecting methods of hardening depth that are referred to above are all non-destructive testing method. These methods can directly detect the work-piece and the operation is simple and quick. What's more, it can achieve the goal of large-scale detection for the quenched work-piece and eliminate the disadvantage that the traditional method needs to damage the specimen and needs to do sampling detection.

So these methods have a wide application prospect.

Although nondestructive testing of the hardening depth has many advantages, there are still many limitations. For example, the eddy current nondestructive testing technology can only detect work-piece with the shallow depth of hardening zone because of the skin effect. If the tested work-piece has the large depth of hardening zone, the measurement result will be inaccurate due to the skin effect. What's more, the eddy current nondestructive testing technology can only be used for conductive materials. With regard to ultrasonic nondestructive testing technology, the excitation frequency of ultrasonic wave has great influence on the detection. If the inappropriate excitation frequency is selected, the scattered echo signal may be extremely weak and difficult to recognize. So the reasonable excitation frequency must be selected in the experiment. In addition, the couplant must be also used between the piezoelectric ultrasonic probe and the work-piece to measure. Then, the type of couplant, its thickness, and other factors must also be taken into account. This makes the detection more complicated. Since the nondestructive testing technology based on magnetic coercive force is limited to the detection principle, it can only detect the work-piece made of ferromagnetic material and be limited by the shape of the detected work-piece. According to the literature [25], the nondestructive testing technology based on Barkhausen effect also limits the detecting depth because of the detection principle. When the hardening depth is more than 4 mm, the signal strength of the Barkhausen Noise no longer changes. This makes the Barkhausen effect be limited when detecting the large depth of hardening zone. In addition, these nondestructive testing methods all require that the detection probe is separately designed for the work-piece of complex shape, which also brings about many difficulties in detection.

6 The Development Tendency and Prospects

In view of the above deficiency, the development of nondestructive test methods for the depth of hardening zone can be considered according to the following points. For the quenched work-piece with shallow depth of hardening zone, the eddy current nondestructive testing and the Barkhausen Noise nondestructive testing can be used, and the optimization research is carried out for two kinds of nondestructive testing technology on this basis. For the optimization research, it can be considered from the following two aspects:

(1) For traditional eddy current nondestructive testing technology, the detection of depth is limited due to the skin effect. So pulsed eddy current testing technology can be considered to take place of traditional eddy current testing technology. The pulse eddy current nondestructive testing technology is a new detection method developed on the basis of traditional eddy current nondestructive testing technology. It uses pulsed current signal as excitation signal. Compared with single-frequency excitation signal, the frequency spectrum of pulsed excitation signal has a wider range. The secondary induced electric field is easier to identify and detect. The final induced voltage signal carries more abundant and diverse information, which can increase its detection depth.

(2) For the nondestructive testing of hardening depth based on Barkhausen effect, a mathematical model between the hardening depth and grain size can be considered to establish. Because the Barkhausen Noise signal carries grain size information, this can make the depth of hardening zone that is measured further increase by the grain size information carried in the noise signal.

For the quenched work-piece with deep hardened layer, ultrasonic nondestructive testing technology and nondestructive testing technology based on magnetic coercivity can be considered to use, and the optimization research was carried out for two kinds of nondestructive testing technology on this basis. The optimization research can be considered from the following two aspects:

(1) For the piezoelectric ultrasonic testing technology, it is difficult to control the thickness of couplant. Therefore, the electromagnetic ultrasonic transducer can be used to replace the piezoelectric ultrasonic transducer. Electromagnetic ultrasonic transducer is a new type ultrasonic receiving and transmitting device. It relies on the electromagnetic effect to transmit and receive ultrasonic. What's more, it doesn't need the couplant in the detection process and contact with the work-piece. So it can avoid the problems and disadvantages because of using the couplant.

(2) For the nondestructive testing technology based on magnetic coercive force, the detection process is limited to the detection probe. When the shape of work-piece is complicated, different structure size's probes need to be designed for different work-pieces each time the detection is performed. Therefore, it can consider the miniaturized and flexible design of the probe, which can make the probe adapt to most of the different shapes of work-piece. If the problem of probe can be solved, the nondestructive testing technology based on magnetic coercive force can be applied more widely.

The above four detection methods all measure the depth of hardening zone by establishing a mathematical model of the special signal parameters and the depth of hardening zone. But they all ignore the relationship between grain size and the depth of hardening zone. Therefore, the next research can focus on the relationship between the grain size and the depth of the hardened layer. That is, the mathematical model between the hardening depth and grain size is established by the grain size information carried in the detected signal. Finally, solving the mathematical model achieves the goal of measuring the depth of hardening zone.

When the nondestructive testing technology is used to measure the depth of hardening zone of quenched work-piece, it can greatly improve the production efficiency of actual quenched work-piece and greatly reduce the cost of metallographic detection because of its nondestructive, convenient, rapid, efficient and low-cost characteristics. Therefore, there is extremely important economic value and industrial value to carry out further research, exploration and optimization on the nondestructive testing method for the depth of hardening zone.

References

1. Shi, J.C.: Nondestructive testing technology of hardened layer of 45 steel based on ultrasonic wave. Anhui University of Technology (2016)
2. Guan, Y.Q.: The ultrasonic measurement of the depth of hardening zone. J. Constr. Mach. **6**, 106–107 (2015)
3. Xu, G.Q., Zhong, X.L., Zhan, S.F.: Ultrasonic testing technology for quenching depth of cummins crankshaft. **28**(4), 196–197 (2016)
4. Cheng, X.M.: Research on carburized layer characteristics and eddy current testing system of carburized materials. Wuhan University of Technology (2003)
5. Li, J.W.: Nondestructive Testing Manual. China Machine Press, Beijing (2012)
6. Wang, C.Y., Chen, T.Q., Song, L., et al.: Eddy current nondestructive testing of the hardening depth of 40Cr steel. J. Nondestruct Test. **31**(6), 8–13 (2007)
7. He, X.P., Tian, Y.P., Zhang, H.P.: Ultrasonic nondestructive evaluation on the grain size of metal materials. J. Tech. Acoust. **6**, 445–451 (2013)
8. Lobkis, O.I., Rokhlin, S.I.: Characterization of polycrystals with elongated duplex microstructure by inversion of ultrasonic backscattering data. J. Appl. Phys. Lett. **96**(16), 161905 (2010)
9. Weaver, R.L.: Diffusivity of ultrasound in polycrystals. J. Mech. Phys. Solids **38**, 55–86 (1990)
10. Papadakis, E.P.: Ultrasonic attenuation caused by scattering in polycrystalline media. In: Mason, W. (ed.) Physical Acoustics, vol. IV, no. Part B, pp. 269–328. Academic Press, New York (1968)
11. Merkulov, L.G.: Investigation of ultrasonic scattering in metals. Sov. J. Tech. Phys. **26**, 59–69 (1956)
12. Hirsekorn, S.: The scattering of ultrasonic waves by polycrystals. J. Acoust. Soc. Am. **72**, 1021–1031 (1982)
13. Beecham, D.: Ultrasonic scatter in metals its properties and its application to grain size determination. J. Ultrason. **4**(2), 67–76 (1966)
14. Fay, B.: Theoretical considerations of ultrasound backscatter. J. Acta Acust. United Acust. **28**(19), 354–357 (1973)

15. Fay, B., Brendel, K., Ludwig, G.: Studies of inhomogeneous substances by ultrasonic back-scattering. J. Ultrasound Med. Biol. **2**(3), 195–198 (1976)
16. Du, H., Lonsdale, C., Oliver, J., et al.: Evaluation of railroad wheel steel with lamellar duplex microstructures using diffuse ultrasonic backscatter. J. Nondestruct. Eval. **32**(4), 331–340 (2013)
17. Zhao, Z.K., Kong, C.H., Bao, W.B.: The principle and application of ultrasonic backscatter hardening layer depth detector. In: 8th National Electromechanical Technology Annual Meeting and Machinery Industry Energy Saving and Emission Reduction Process Technology Seminar, pp. 95–101, Hangzhou (2014)
18. Li, D.P.: Research on detection technology of carburized and hardened depth of the magnetic coercivity. Nanchang Hangkong University (2015)
19. Luo, X., Wu, W., Li, D.P., et al.: Detection of 20CrMnTi steel carburizing hardening depth by magnetic coercive force. J. Nondestruct. Test. **38**(7), 47–50 (2016)
20. Sun, J.M.: Study on measurement technology of stress measurement system on coercive force measuring for ferromagnetic materials. Shenyang University of Technology (2016)
21. Lv, Z.: Ferromagnetic material stress testing technology research based on the coercivity. Shenyang University of Technology (2016)
22. Zhou, Y.: Based on coercivity of ferromagnetic materials stress detecting technology. Shenyang University of Technology (2015)
23. Zhang, L.: Coercive force of ferromagnetic materials testing technology research. Shenyang University of Technology (2014)
24. Wang, W.T.: Research on the key technology of nondestructive testing based on Barkhausen effect. Zhengzhou University (2017)
25. Liu, Y.B., Shi, H.J., Meng, F.Q., et al.: The research for Barkhausen noise to test the hardened depth. J. Coal Mine Mach. **10**, 24–25 (2001)
26. Liu, Y.B., Yang, Z.Y., Shi, X.J., et al.: Nondestructive determination of hardening depth in an induction hardened bearings by Barkhausen noise. In: 1th International Mechanical Engineering Conference, p. 547. Machinery Industry Press, Shanghai (2000)
27. Du, F.M., Xu, X.C., Xu, Y.H., et. al.: Nondestructive testing of hardening depth with Barkhausen effect. In: 8th National Acoustic Emissions Academic Symposium, pp. 62–65, Shanghai (1999)
28. Yuan, H.J., Fu, J., Li, H.M., et al.: Application status of nondestructive testing technology based on Barkhausen effect. J. Acta Metrol. Sin. **37**(01), 75–78 (2016)
29. Pan, L., Zhang, S.J., Wan, G., et al.: The detection of ferromagnetic material hardness based on Barkhausen effect. J. Nondestruct. Test. **38**(12), 28–31 (2016)
30. Zhang, Y.: Study on nondestructive testing of high strength steel plate based on Barkhausen effect. Huazhong University of Science and Technology (2015)

Distributed Fusion Estimation Based on Robust Kalman Filtering for 3D Spatial Positioning System

Li Liu[1]([⊠]), Wenju Zhou[1]([⊠]), Aolei Yang[2], Jun Yue[1], and Xiaofeng Zhang[1]

[1] School of Information Science and Electrical Engineering, Ludong University,
Yantai 264025, China
liulildu@163.com, zhouwenju2004@126.com
[2] Shanghai Key Laboratory of Power Station Automation Technology,
School of Mechatronic Engineering and Automation,
Shanghai University, Shanghai 200072, China

Abstract. Because of the requirements of growing measurement scale, the issue of the networked high-precision positioning has been developed rapidly, and this paper designs a 3D spatial positioning system. With the aid of the spatial positioning principle, the 3D spatial positioning system is used to enlarge communication constraint and increase signal coordination processing. A information fusion estimation method is presented for the distributed networked systems with data transmission delays. The proposed distributed fusion estimation scheme employs the transformation of measurement and the weighted fusion of innovation sequence. To reduce the communication burden and computational cost with transmission delays, a re-optimal weighted fusion estimator is designed. Moreover, the proposed method reduces the information redundancy and maintains the higher measurement accuracy. An illustrative example obtained from the 3D spatial positioning system is given to validate the effectiveness of the proposed method.

1 Introduction

In recent decades, to solve the problem of high-precision measurement and positioning, the space measurement and positioning systems with relevant measurement methods have been developed rapidly. With the increasing of the network scale, the scope of the measurement and positioning systems has been growing much larger; meanwhile, the coverage mode has been growing much more flexible. Therefore, the application of distributed network structure can able to increase

L. Liu—This work was supported by Natural Science Foundation of China (61772253, 61633016, 61473182, 61472172), Key Research and Development Project of Yantai (2017ZH061), Key Project of Science and Technology Commission of Shanghai Municipality (15411953502), Key Technical of Key Industries of Shandong (2016CYJS03A02-1), and Key Research and Development Project of Shandong (2016ZDJS06A05).

K. Li et al. (Eds.): ICSEE 2018/IMIOT 2018, CCIS 924, pp. 512–521, 2018.
https://doi.org/10.1007/978-981-13-2384-3_48

the reliability of information, and improve the precision of collaborative calculation. Moreover, the distributed network structure reduces the burden of communication [1]. Large-scale networked systems have been successfully applied in some important research fields, such as network physical systems (cyber-physical systems, CPSs), Smart grid, and intelligent transportation.

The distributed estimation strategy [2–4] is applied to target tracking and positioning, fault diagnosis and so on. The objective is that state estimation accuracy after fusion is higher than that of each local estimation. Research on filtering is the basis of the information perception and fusion, according to different performance indicators, the relevant distributed filtering has aroused more and more attention, including distributed particle filtering [5], distributed H_∞ filtering [6], distributed Kalman Filtering [2,3,7,8] and so on. Furthermore, distributed Kalman filtering is used to realize the coordination and fusion of error estimation, which is an important scheme to solve the state estimation for large-scale systems [2].

Due to the restriction of communication facilities and scale for networked systems, the measurement information is inevitably affected by the unpredictable interference. Note that the fundamental Kalman filtering method can not satisfy the performance requirement, such that the robust Kalman filtering method is designed considering various noise sequences. For example, the uncertainty of system parameters can be described by state-dependent noise [9,10]. Costa et. al. [11] investigated robust pattern independent filtering for discrete-time Markov jump systems with state-correlated noises. Considering the correlation for noise, the distributed Kalman filtering fusion method [7,12] was presented with cross correlation between measurement noise and process noise. In addition, for a class of noisy sequences with uncertain variance, the method of the least upper bound in [13–15] for all admissible uncertainties was proposed. In order to reduce the influence of transmission delays for the measured value, the measurement transformation [15] was proposed, which used the Kalman filter of recombination the innovation sequence to deal with multiple delays system. Therefore, it is transformed into the correlative system with no time delay, and the computational complexity is reduced.

According to the above analysis, based on the principle of spatial positioning of linear CCD, the information measured by 3D photoelectric sensor is considered to be influenced by the uncertain factors, such as transmission delays and cross correlation noise. In order to improve the robustness of the estimator, the innovation sequence of weighted fusion is used to optimize the interference of cross correlation noise during the information exchange. Developing the reorganized measurement sequence and the innovation sequence, the Kalman filtering is transformed into Kalman prediction to reduce the computational complexity. The proposed weighted fusion method of filtering error covariance is used to coordinate and exchange the measurement information between two subsystems. Therefore, the distributed fusion estimation is based on the optimal information fusion criterion. It is worth noting that the re-optimization of the local estimate is able to get higher estimation precision than the local one.

The remainder of the paper is organized as follows. The space positioning system model is established in Sect. 2. Section 3 presents the distributed fusion method using weighted innovation sequence method. Simulation results and analysis are presented in Sect. 4 and the concluding remarks are given in Sect. 5.

2   Space Positioning System Model

Based on the principle of spatial positioning, the photoelectric sensor is designed in this section. Furthermore, considering the uncertainty of the distributed systems, the system model is established from the system state and measure information, which is obtained by the sensor with noise correlation and transmission delays.

2.1   Principle of Spatial Positioning

Firstly, the Metris Krypton Measurement approach based on the three-coordinate positioning measurement is introduced, which is obtained by using the optical tracker and the special light emission device (LED).

The 3D photoelectric sensor, as shown in Fig. 1(a), is composed of three linear CCD, which is embedded three fixed-focus cylindrical optical mirrors. The three linear CCD has a "Y" shape distribution on the same plane.

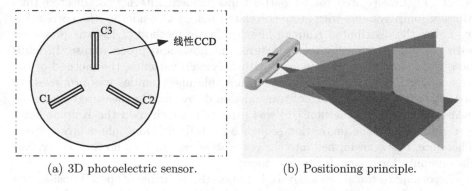

(a) 3D photoelectric sensor.   (b) Positioning principle.

Fig. 1. 3D photoelectric sensor and its principle.

The system principle of 3D photoelectric sensor positioning is shown in Fig. 1(b). The measured target is composed of the special LED. And then, each cylindrical optical mirror through the light only project to its corresponding plane under the CCD. A point light source of space is projected into each CCD plane by a cylindrical optical mirror, which is a straight line light intersecting with the CCD, and can perceive its position information on the CCD. If the target is in the measurement range of the 3D photoelectric sensor, the target will form three planes with three CCD lenses. Therefore, processor computes the intersection point of three planes, that is, the coordinates of the light source for the space points (X, Y, Z).

2.2   System Model Establishment

The information measured by 3D photoelectric sensor is disturbed by the uncertain factors in the process of network communication. Based on the experimental analysis, the distributed uncertainty system for sensor networks can be described as following:

$$x_{k+1} = (A_k + \Delta A_k)\, x_k + B_k w_k, \quad k = 1, 2, \cdots \tag{1}$$

$$z_k^i = H_k^i x_{k-\tau_k} + \varpi_k^i, \quad i = 1, \cdots, n, \tag{2}$$

in which, $x_k \in \mathbb{R}^r$ is the estimated state, $z_k^i \in \mathbb{R}^{m_i}$ represents the measured value of the i-th sensor, and $\tau_k > 0$ denotes the transmission delay. $A_k \in \mathbb{R}^{r \times r}$ expresses the state transition matrix, $B_k \in \mathbb{R}^r$ is a time-varying vector with known dimensions, and $H_k^i \in \mathbb{R}^{m_i \times r}$ is the measurement matrix. Meanwhile, the state-dependent matrix $\Delta A_k = C_k \xi_k$ is used for expressing the uncertainty within the system [7], where $C_k \in \mathbb{R}^{r \times r}$ is the state transition matrix, and the state-dependent noise $\xi_k \in \mathbb{R}$ is independent of zero mean white noise. $w_k \in \mathbb{R}$ represents the process noise with variance Q_k, and $\varpi_k^i \in \mathbb{R}^{m_i}$ represents the measurement noise of the i-th sensor with variance R_k^i. Furthermore, the initial state x_0 is not correlated with other noise signals with the mean μ_0, and covariance are set as P_0.

Considering the effect of transmission delay, the noise from the previous sampling time is more important than the current measurement value. Therefore, it is assumed that the process noise and measurement noise for the subsystems and different sensors are one-step related. Accordingly, the relation has the following statistical properties:

$$E\left(w_k\right) = 0, \quad E\left(\varpi_k^i\right) = 0,$$
$$E\left(\begin{pmatrix} w_k \\ \varpi_k^i \end{pmatrix} \begin{pmatrix} w_l^T & \left(\varpi_l^i\right)^T \end{pmatrix}\right)$$
$$= \begin{pmatrix} Q_k \delta_{k-l} + Q_{k,l}\delta_{k-l+1} & S_k^i \delta_{k-l} + S_{k,l}^i \delta_{k-l+1} \\ 0 & R_k^i \delta_{k-l} + R_{k,l}^i \delta_{k-l+1} \end{pmatrix} \tag{3}$$

where δ_{k-l} is the Kronecker function, satisfying $Q_k = Q_k^{\,T}$ and $R_k^i = \left(R_k^i\right)^T$.

3   Distributed Fusion Estimation

Based on the Kalman filtering, a distributed weighted fusion estimation method is proposed for weighted fusion of the innovation sequence and error covariance matrix.

3.1   Filter Parameters

At the time instant of k, the i-th subsystem employs the minimized one-step prediction error covariance, to probe the appropriate filter parameters. For the local one-step prediction $\hat{x}_{k+1|k}^i$, the covariance $P_{k+1|k}^i$ from the prediction error is computed by the following equation:

$$P_{k+1|k}^i = E\left(\tilde{x}_{k+1|k}^i\left(\tilde{x}_{k+1|k}^i\right)^T\right)$$

$$= \Phi_k^i P_{k|k-1}^i\left(\Phi_k^i\right)^T + B_k Q_k B_k^T + K_k^i R_k^i\left(K_k^i\right)^T + C_k X_k C_k^T$$
$$+ \Phi_k^i W_k^i B_k^T + B_k\left(W_k^i\right)^T\left(\Phi_k^i\right)^T - B_k S_{k,k+1}^i\left(K_k^i\right)^T \tag{4}$$
$$- K_k^i\left(V_k^i\right)^T\left(\Phi_k^i\right)^T - \Phi_k^i V_k^i\left(K_k^i\right)^T - K_k^i\left(S_{k,k+1}^i\right)^T B_k^T$$

in which, $P_{k|k-1}^i$ denotes the one-step prediction error covariance at the time instant of $k-1$.

Since the local estimate $\hat{x}_{k+1|k}^i$ satisfies as following:

$$\hat{x}_{k+1|k}^i = \Phi_k^i \hat{x}_{k|k-1}^i + K_k^i y_k^i \tag{5}$$

the expectation X_k is solved according to the state x_k. It is defined as:

$$X_{k+1} = A_k X_k A_k^T + C_k X_k C_k^T + B_k Q_k B_k^T$$
$$+ A_k B_{k-1} Q_{k-1,k} B_k^T + B_k Q_{k,k-1} B_{k-1}^T A_k^T \tag{6}$$

and the initial value is set to $X_0 \triangleq \mu_0 \mu_0^T + P_0$ [7].

Then, W_k^i and V_k^i are obtained by the following means, respectively.

$$W_k^i = E\left(\tilde{x}_{k|k-1}^i w_k^T\right) = B_{k-1} Q_{k-1,k} - K_{k-1}^i\left(S_k^i\right)^T \tag{7}$$

$$V_k^i = E\left(\tilde{x}_{k|k-1}^i\left(v_k^i\right)^T\right) = B_{k-1} S_{k-1,k+1}^i - K_{k-1}^i R_{k-1,k}^i \tag{8}$$

Thus, the optimal filter gain matrix K_k^i is evolved, i.e.

$$K_k^i = \Xi_k^i\left(H_k^i P_{k|k-1}^i\left(H_k^i\right)^T + R_k^i + \tilde{\Xi}_k^i\right)^{-1} \tag{9}$$

where $\Xi_k^i = A_k P_{k|k-1}^i\left(H_k^i\right)^T + B_k\left(W_k^i\right)^T\left(H_k^i\right)^T + A_k V_k^i + B_k S_{k,k+1}^i$ and $\tilde{\Xi}_k^i = H_k^i V_k^i + \left(V_k^i\right)^T\left(H_k^i\right)^T$.

Substituting Eqs. (9) into (4), error covariance matrix $P_{k+1|k}^i$ is rewritten as

$$P_{k+1|k}^i = A_k P_{k|k-1}^i A_k^T + \Gamma_k^i - K_k^i\left(\Xi_k^i\right)^T \tag{10}$$

Note that $\Gamma_k^i = B_k Q_k B_k^T + C_k X_k C_k^T + A_k W_k^i B_k^T + B_k\left(W_k^i\right)^T A_k^T$. Based on the above analysis, the matrix Σ_k can be calculated as following:

$$\Sigma_k^{i,j} = H_k^i P_{k|k-1}^{i,j}\left(H_k^j\right)^T + H_k^i V_k^{i,j} + \left(H_k^j V_k^{j,i}\right)^T + R_k^{i,j} \tag{11}$$

here $\Sigma_k^{i,j}$ is an $nm \times nm$-dimensional matrix.

3.2   Estimation Error Cross-Covariance

The weighted fusion strategy based on the Kalman one-step prediction $\hat{x}^i_{k+1|k}$ and filter gain K^i_k, the predicted error covariance between the i-th and j-th subsystems, at the time instant k can be obtained as following:

$$\hat{x}^i_{k+1|k} = A_k\hat{x}^i_{k|k-1} + K^i_k\tilde{Y}_k \tag{12}$$

$$K^i_k = \Xi^i_k \left(H^i_k P^i_{k|k-1}\left(H^i_k\right)^T + R^i_k + \tilde{\Xi}^i_k \right)^{-1} \tag{13}$$

$$\begin{aligned}
P^{i,j}_{k+1|k} &= A_k P^{i,j}_{k|k-1} A^T_k + B_k Q_k B^T_k + C_k X_k C^T_k + K^i_k P_k \left(K^j_k\right)^T \\
&+ A_k W^i_k B^T_k + B_k \left(W^j_k\right)^T A^T_k - A_k M^i_k \left(K^j_k\right)^T \\
&- B_k L^T_k \left(K^j_k\right)^T - K^i_k \left(M^j_k\right)^T A^T_k - K^i_k L_k B^T_k
\end{aligned} \tag{14}$$

where,

$$\begin{aligned}
P_k &= E\left(\tilde{Y}_k \tilde{Y}^T_k\right) \\
W^i_k &= B_{k-1} Q_{k-1,k} - K^i_{k-1}\left(S^i_k\right)^T \\
X_{k+1} &= A_k X_k A^T_k + C_k X_k C^T_k + B_k Q_k B^T_k \\
&\quad + A_k B_{k-1} Q_{k-1,k} B^T_k + B_k Q_{k,k-1} B^T_{k-1} A^T_k \\
M^i_k &= \sum_{q=1}^n \left(P^{i,q}_{k|k-1}(H^q_k)^T + V^{i,q}_k \right) \theta^q_k \\
L_k &= \sum_{q=1}^n (\theta^q_k)^T \left(H^q_k W^q_k + \left(S^q_{k-1,k}\right)^T \right)
\end{aligned} \tag{15}$$

Next, the weighted fusion strategy is used for fusing the cross-correlated covariance, which is defined as

$$J = \left(Ix_k - \hat{x}_{k|k-1}\right)^T \Sigma^{-1}_{k|k-1} \left(Ix_k - \hat{x}_{k|k-1}\right) \tag{16}$$

Since the optimal Kalman filter uses the weighted fusion method of linear minimum variance [12], the corresponding optimal information fusion estimates covariance $P_{k|k-1}$ satisfies $P_{k|k-1} \leq P^i_{k|k-1}$, $i = 1, 2, \cdots, n$.

4   Experimental Results and Analysis

In order to verify the robustness of the proposed weighted fusion estimation, a 3D photoelectric sensor positioning measurement platform is designed. The experimental results of this paper is supported by the relation of the algorithm and platform, the research of the distributed fusion estimation algorithm is the

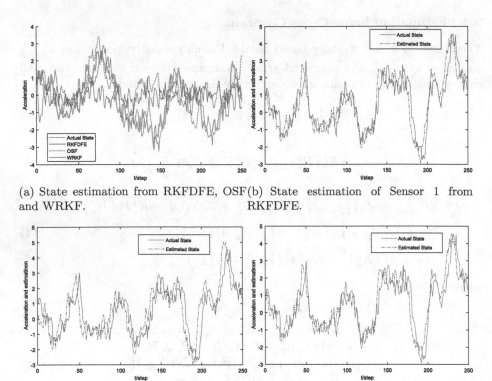

(a) State estimation from RKFDFE, OSF(b) State estimation of Sensor 1 from and WRKF.   RKFDFE.

(c) State estimation of Sensor 2 from(d) State estimation of Sensor 3 from RKFDFE.   RKFDFE.

Fig. 2. Comparison of state estimation for acceleration.

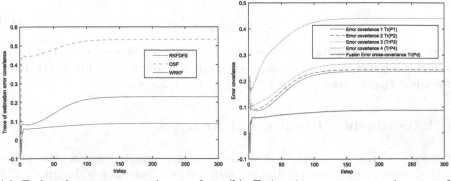

(a) Estimation error covariances from (b) Estimation error covariances of OSF, WRKF and RKFDFE.   RKFDFE from each sensor and fusion center.

Fig. 3. Comparison of filtering error covariance.

support of the 3D photoelectric sensor positioning system. The mathematical description of the target tracking system used in the experiment is:

$$x_{k+1} = \left(\begin{pmatrix} 0.96 & T & T^2/2 \\ 0 & 0.96 & T \\ 0 & 0 & 0.96 \end{pmatrix} + \begin{pmatrix} 0.01 & 0 & 0 \\ 0 & 0.01 & 0 \\ 0 & 0 & 0.01 \end{pmatrix} \xi_k \right) x_k + \begin{pmatrix} T^2/2 \\ T \\ 1 \end{pmatrix} w_k$$
$$k = 1, 2, \cdots$$

(17)

$$z_k^i = H_k^i x_{k-\tau_k} + \varpi_k^i, \quad i = 1, 2, 3, 4 \tag{18}$$

$$w_k = \eta_k + \eta_{k-1} \tag{19}$$

$$\varpi_k^i = \beta_i w_{k-1} + \beta_i \eta_k, \quad i = 1, 2, 3, 4 \tag{20}$$

The sample period is $T = 0.1s$. The state $x_k = \begin{pmatrix} s_k & \dot{s}_k & \ddot{s}_k \end{pmatrix}^T$ represents the position, velocity, and acceleration of the target at the instant of kT. $\xi_k \in \mathbb{R}$ represents a state-dependent noise with a zero mean value of and variance $\sigma_\xi^2 = 1$. $\eta_k \in \mathbb{R}$ is independent on the variance for white noise $\sigma_\eta^2 = 0.09$. z_k^i represents the time delay value measured by the i-th sensor. In which, $H_1 = \begin{bmatrix} 1 & 0.6 & 0.8 \end{bmatrix}$, $H_2 = \begin{bmatrix} 0.8 & 1 & 0.5 \end{bmatrix}$, $H_3 = \begin{bmatrix} 0.8 & 0.3 & 1 \end{bmatrix}$ and $H_4 = \begin{bmatrix} 0.6 & 0.5 & 1 \end{bmatrix}$. Variable β_i is used to determine the intensity of the noise correlation, and set $\beta_1 = 1$, $\beta_2 = 0.8$, $\beta_3 = 2$ and $\beta_4 = 5$.

The initial value is $\hat{x}_{0|0}^{z_0} = \mu_0 = E(x_0) = \begin{pmatrix} 1 & 1 & 1 \end{pmatrix}^T$ and $P_{0|0}^{z_0} = 0.01 I_3$. Compare the proposed distributed fusion estimation (RKFDFE) with the weighted robust Kalman filtering (WRKF) [7] and the optimal sequential fusion (OSF) method [12]. In the mathematical analysis of signal and system, the noise sequence adopts the white noise processing method.

In order to demonstrate the estimation results clearly, the state of the acceleration and its estimation are shown in Fig. 2. In contrast to these three methods, Fig. 2(a) shows the best performance of RKFDFE in state estimation with cross-correlation noise and transmission delays. Figures 2(b)–(d) show the state estimate of the acceleration computed by each sensor. Because the cross-correlation for noise, the filtering estimation for target tracking is more dependent on the RKFDFE method, when the cross-correlated strength is small.

Figure 3 compares and analyzes the corresponding estimation error covariance results. Figure 3(a) illustrates the trace of estimated error covariance by the above three methods, and verifies that the trace of the estimated error covariance matrix obtained by RKFDFE is less than the other two methods. Figure 3(b) using the RKFDFE method, the trace (i.e. $Tr(Pi)$, $i = 1, \cdots, 4$) of the error covariance matrix between each filter and the trace (i.e. $Tr(Pd)$) of the fused matrix is compared. Furthermore, the weighted fusion method is able to improve the robustness for the state estimation and get the optimal steady value, and then obtain a higher measurement accuracy.

5   Conclusion

Based on the principle of spatial positioning of linear CCD, the 3D photoelectric sensor has been designed. The spatial target information has been measured, and the trajectory has been tracked and estimated. This paper has studied the state estimation problem of distributed uncertain systems with cross correlation noise and transmission delays. To deal with the stochastic transmissions and reduce the network communication burden, the reorganized weighted fusion estimation and innovation sequence method has been proposed. It has realized the information interaction between any two neighboring subsystems due to the communication constraints. Finally, numerical experiments have shown that the proposed distributed fusion estimation algorithm has a better dynamic tracking effect for state estimation, to improve the spatial positioning accuracy.

References

1. Ge, X., Han, Q.-L.: Distributed event-triggered H_∞ filtering over sensor networks with communication delays. Inf. Sci. **291**, 128–142 (2015)
2. Li, D., Kar, S., Moura, J.M., Poor, H.V., Cui, S.: Distributed Kalman filtering over massive data sets: analysis through large deviations of random Riccati equations. IEEE Trans. Inf. Theory **61**(3), 1351–1372 (2015)
3. Song, E., Xu, J., Zhu, Y.: Optimal distributed Kalman filtering fusion with singular covariances of filtering errors and measurement noises. IEEE Trans. Autom. Control **59**(5), 1271–1282 (2014)
4. Hu, J., Wang, Z., Chen, D., Alsaadi, F.E.: Estimation, filtering and fusion for networked systems with network-induced phenomena: New progress and prospects. Inf. Fus. **31**, 65–75 (2016)
5. Zhong, X., Mohammadi, A., Premkumar, A., Asif, A.: A distributed particle filtering approach for multiple acoustic source tracking using an acoustic vector sensor network. Sig. Process. **108**, 589–603 (2015)
6. Song, B., Wu, Z.-G., Park, J.H., Shi, G., Zhang, Y.: H_∞ filtering for stochastic systems driven by Poisson processes. Int. J. Control **88**(1), 2–10 (2015)
7. Feng, J., Wang, Z., Zeng, M.: Distributed weighted robust Kalman filter fusion for uncertain systems with autocorrelated and cross-correlated noises. Inf. Fus. **14**(1), 78–86 (2013)
8. Song, H., Yu, L., Zhang, W.-A.: Distributed consensus-based Kalman filtering in sensor networks with quantised communications and random sensor failures. IET Sig. Process. **8**(2), 107–118 (2014)
9. Zhang, W., Zhao, Y., Sheng, L.: Some remarks on stability of stochastic singular systems with state-dependent noise. Automatica **51**, 273–277 (2015)
10. Tian, T., Sun, S., Li, N.: Multi-sensor information fusion estimators for stochastic uncertain systems with correlated noises. Inf. Fus. **27**, 126–137 (2016)
11. Costa, O., Benites, G.: Robust mode-independent filtering for discrete-time Markov jump linear systems with multiplicative noises. Int. J. Control **86**(5), 779–793 (2013)
12. Yan, L., Li, X.R., Xia, Y., Fu, M.: Optimal sequential and distributed fusion for state estimation in cross-correlated noise. Automatica **49**(12), 3607–3612 (2013)
13. Qi, W., Zhang, P., Deng, Z.: Robust weighted fusion Kalman filters for multisensor time-varying systems with uncertain noise variances. Sig. Process. **99**, 185–200 (2014)
14. Zhang, P., Qi, W., Deng, Z.: Hierarchical fusion robust Kalman filter for clustering sensor network time-varying systems with uncertain noise variances. Int. J. Adapt. Control Sig. Process. **29**(1), 99–122 (2015)

15. Qi, W.-J., Zhang, P., Deng, Z.-L.: Robust sequential covariance intersection fusion Kalman filtering over multi-agent sensor networks with measurement delays and uncertain noise variances. Acta Automatica Sinica **40**(11), 2632–2642 (2014)
16. Rezaei, H., Esfanjani, R.M., Sedaaghi, M.H.: Improved robust finite-horizon Kalman filtering for uncertain networked time-varying systems. Inf. Sci. **293**, 263–274 (2015)

Image Processing

A Novel 3D Head Multi-feature Constraint Method for Human Localization Based on Multiple Depth Cameras

Feixiang Zhou[1], Haikuan Wang[1(✉)], Zhile Yang[2], and Dong Xie[1]

[1] School of Mechatronics Engineering and Automation, Shanghai University,
Shanghai 200444, China
HKWang@shu.edu.cn
[2] Shenzhen Institute of Advanced Technology, Chinese Academy of Sciences,
Shenzhen 518055, Guangdong, China

Abstract. Up to date, the majority of existing spatial localization methods is based on visual positioning methods and non-visual positioning methods. In the vision-based positioning method, the traditional 2D human detection method are vulnerable to tackle with environmental changes including illumination, complex background, object occlusion, shadow interference and other factors, due to which the algorithm is less robust and difficult to achieve accurate target positioning. In respects to 3D human positioning, binocular vision or multi-vision approaches have been widely used to acquire depth information. The complexity of the algorithm is high, and the detection range is limited. To deal with this, a spatial location method based on multiple depth cameras is proposed in this paper. Multiple 3D-TOF depth cameras are jointly used to directly obtain depth information. Histograms of Oriented Depth (HOD) features are then extracted and trained to find the human head and shoulder region. Moreover, Spatial Density of Head (SDH) and the Convexity and Square Similarity of Head (CSSH) features are combined to determine the human target. Finally, the positioning data of multiple cameras are determined by using Nearest Center Point (NCP) to obtain the final human body positioning information. Experimental results show that the proposed method can not only obtain higher recognition rate and positioning accuracy, but also enable a larger detection range, meeting the needs of large-scale spatial positioning.

Keywords: Multiple depth cameras · Human localization · SDH
CSSH · NCP

1 Introduction

With the unprecedented development of information technology and artificial intelligence, human detection and positioning has been widely used in video surveillance, virtual reality, human-computer interaction, planetary detection, behaviour understanding, and other areas, achieving public safety monitoring and management, accidents Precaution, detection and treatment, nursing care for young and old patients, and autonomous navigation.

© Springer Nature Singapore Pte Ltd. 2018
K. Li et al. (Eds.): ICSEE 2018/IMIOT 2018, CCIS 924, pp. 525–535, 2018.
https://doi.org/10.1007/978-981-13-2384-3_49

At present, various methods [1–3] have been proposed in addressing this research area, the majority of which are based on 2D images. Ma *et al.* [4] first obtained the motion vector by the optical flow method, and then applied it into a shape model for human detection and tracking. However, such methods are easily affected by the external environment. The depth image has many advantages over the 2D gray image and the color image. First, the depth image is robust to the changes in color and illumination. In addition, the depth image directly represents the target's 3D information. Therefore, researchers began to use depth information to study the detection and positioning of moving targets. The RDSF algorithm (Relational Depth Similarity Features) proposed by Ikemura *et al.* [5] makes full use of the difference in the frequency distribution of the depth values of different objects, and divides the depth map into blocks that do not overlap each other. Yu *et al.* [6] proposed SLTP (Simplified Local Ternary Patterns) to perform histogram statistics on the edge information of depth images. Wang *et al.* [7] proposed a depth feature extraction algorithm PDSS (Pyramid depth self-similarities) due to strong local self-similarity of depth information of the human body. Spinello *et al.* [8] proposed HOD depth feature extraction algorithm that mimics the HOG algorithm, and performs histogram statistics on the magnitude and direction of depth difference to extracts depth features. Shen *et al.* [9] improved the HOG features and proposed an HDD feature extraction algorithm. The algorithm extends the gradient direction from the original 180-degree statistical space to 360-degree, and makes statistics on the gradients in different directions more precise. When shooting vertically, the head area is closest to the camera, and the human body target can be detected and positioned by recognizing the head area. Xia *et al.* [10] proposed a model-based human detection system. The algorithm uses 2D head contour model and 3D head surface geometry model for human detection. The literature [11] relies on the relationship between the pixels at the edge of the head region to create a head template to realize the recognition of the head. Meanwhile, the author also proposed a human template matching algorithm [12] to further improve the accuracy of the head recognition. The algorithm has a strong recognition effect on multi-person environment and strong ability to eliminate human-like targets.

Aiming at the practical needs of large space, this paper proposes a 3D head multi-feature constraint method based on multiple depth cameras to detect and locate the human body. According to the multi-camera spatial structure, NCP is used to determine the positioning data of multiple cameras to obtain the final body positioning information.

The rest of the paper is organized as follows: Sect. 2 presents the human positioning method based on multiple depth cameras; Sect. 3 proposes the nearest center point method. The Sect. 4 analyses the experimental results, followed by that Sect. 5 concludes the paper.

2 Multi-feature Constraint Method for Human Localization

Figure 1 shows the flow chart of human positioning method based on multiple depth cameras. Using multiple cameras avoids the disadvantages of a single camera with a small coverage and improves the detection accuracy.

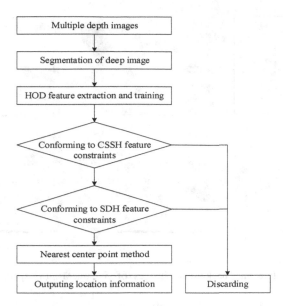

Fig. 1. Flow chart of human location method

2.1 Segmentation of Depth Image

In image processing, we normally have interest only in some particular areas of an image. It is assumed that the actual scene in this paper is fixed, and depth background difference is used to segment the human target. In this paper, the five depth images acquired by the five cameras in their respective positions are reserved as fixed background images. The spatial structure and background image are shown in Fig. 2.

Due to that the camera shoots downwards, the legs of the human body can be considered as invalid areas. This paper controls the quantified depth range at $[D_{near}, D_{far}]$. Firstly, Gaussian filtering is performed on the original depth data to filter out noise and suppress the drift of depth data. Then the original depth image is subtracted from the background image, and the foreground target is extracted according to the threshold T, as shown in Formula (1).

$$D_i(\text{x}, \text{y}) = |I_i(x, y) - B(x, y)|$$
$$T_i(\text{x}, \text{y}) = \begin{cases} 1, & D_i(x, y) \geq T \\ 0, & D_i(x, y) < T \end{cases} \tag{1}$$

where $B(x, y)$ is the background image, $I_i(x, y)$ is the i-th frame image, $T_i(x, y)$ is the binary image, and it is the effective target point.

Then the depth image of the corresponding area is extracted, as shown in Formula (2).

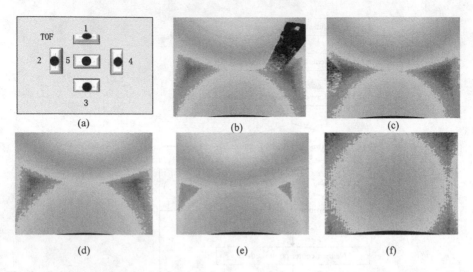

Fig. 2. Spatial structure and background images of 5 cameras. (a) spatial structure; (b–f) background images.

$$S_i(x,y) = \begin{cases} I_i(x,y), & D_i(x,y) \geq T \\ 0, & D_i(x,y) < T \end{cases} \tag{2}$$

where $S_i(x,y)$ is the effective human region, and $S_i(x,y) \subseteq [D_{near}, D_{far}]$.

2.2   Extraction and Training of HOD Feature

The traditional HOG feature is generally used to describe the local area of the image. It composes the target feature by calculating the gradient direction histogram on the local area. This article utilises the HOD feature to detect depth images, which is very similar to HOG. The only difference is that HOD calculates the depth difference in the depth image, and HOG calculates the gray value or RGB value of the pixel in the 2D image.

After obtaining the HOD feature vector, SVM classifier is used in this paper to train the features. In this paper, SVM is used to classify and recognize the HOD features of human head and shoulders in real space. The positive and negative samples are trained to obtain the decision function, and different feature vectors are distinguished.

2.3   3D Head Feature Constraints

According to Sect. 2.2, head and shoulder detection of human targets can be accomplished, but over-fitting or under-fitting is often caused by feature training, resulting in missing or false detection. Therefore, two human character constraints (SDH and CSSH) are proposed in this paper to further improve detection accuracy.

In the depth image, the entire human head area can be considered as a standard sphere, and the upper half of the human head is like a circular arc convexity, as shown in Fig. 3(a). The depth of the edge is greater than the depth of the middle. The convex surface can be considered to be composed of an infinite number of circular arc curves, and for a single circular arc curve, the slope of positive and negative changes only once during the process from one side to the other. According to this feature, a CSHA-based head feature discriminate method is proposed. The n points on the edge of the convexity $d_1, d_2, d_3 \ldots d_n$ are selected as shown in Fig. 3(b). Then the n points are not repeatedly linked to obtain $n/2$ circular arc curves, as shown in the colored curves in Fig. 3(b), and the number of points that conform to the law of slope change is counted. Finally the head convexity similarity S_{con} is calculated.

$$S_{con} = \frac{N}{n/2} \tag{3}$$

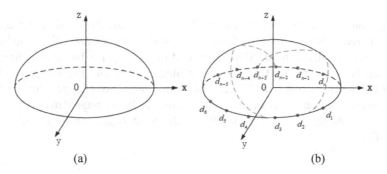

Fig. 3. Circular arc convexity of head area: (a) circular arc convexity; (b) circular arc curves.

In the 2D image, an approximate ellipse target head region will also be obtained, as shown in the red circle in Fig. 6. To simplify the calculation, the rectangular region of $M \times N$ is taken as the head *Harea*, as shown in the blue rectangle in Fig. 4. The pixels in the rectangular area $H_i(x, y)$ can be represented as

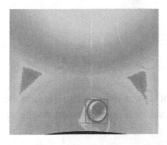

Fig. 4. Top area of head. (Color figure online)

$$H_i(x, y) = \begin{cases} 1, & D_i(x, y) \in Harea \\ 0, & D_i(x, y) \notin Harea \end{cases} \tag{4}$$

The square similarity of head is

$$S_{squ} = \frac{16 \times \sum\limits_{x=0}^{N-1} \sum\limits_{y=0}^{M-1} H_i(x, y)}{(C_{head})^2} \tag{5}$$

where C_{head} is the perimeter of a rectangular region. When the head is more like a standard circle, the rectangle resembles a square, and the value of S_{squ} is closer to 1.

Finally, CSSH is defined by combining these two features, as shown in Formula (6).

$$S_{cs} = k_1 * S_{con} + k_2 * S_{squ} \tag{6}$$

where k_1, k_2 are the weight coefficients, and $T_k \in [0, 1]$ is the threshold. When $S_{cs} \geq T_k$, the current area satisfies the CSSH feature. Otherwise, it does not satisfy the feature.

The spatial density of head (SDH) proposed in this paper is based on a fixed ratio relationship between the head region of the human body and the space area of the shoulder and head, as shown in Fig. 5. This feature does not change with height and weight. When a person walks in the scene, there will be no huge deformation on the shoulders and above. The spatial density of the head D_{head} can be calculated with Formula (7).

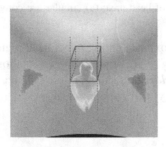

Fig. 5. Spatial distribution of head area.

$$D_{head} = \frac{V_{Head}}{V_{Rec}} \tag{7}$$

where V_{Rec} is the volume of space where the human head is located; V_{Head} is the volume of the head, which can be approximated as the sphere volume, and it can be calculated with Formula (8).

$$V_{Head} = \frac{4}{3}\pi \left(\sqrt{\frac{\sum\limits_{(x,y)\in hz} T_i(x,y)}{\pi}} \right)^3 \tag{8}$$

When $V_{Head} \geq V_k$ and $V_k \in [0, 1]$, the current region satisfies the SDH feature, and otherwise, it do not satisfy the feature.

The effects of over-fitting and under-fitting caused by training can be prevented by combining the above two features, and the detection accuracy of the human body can be improved.

3 Nearest Center Point Method

After determining the head area of the human body, the central point of the head region (l_x, l_y) is selected as the positioning point of the human body, as shown in formula (9).

$$
\begin{aligned}
l_x &= \frac{\sum\limits_{x=0}^{N-1}\sum\limits_{y=0}^{M-1} x \cdot H_i(x,y)}{\sum\limits_{x=0}^{N-1}\sum\limits_{y=0}^{M-1} H_i(x,y)} \\
l_y &= \frac{\sum\limits_{x=0}^{N-1}\sum\limits_{y=0}^{M-1} y \cdot H_i(x,y)}{\sum\limits_{x=0}^{N-1}\sum\limits_{y=0}^{M-1} H_i(x,y)}
\end{aligned}
\tag{9}
$$

Since multiple cameras may detect the head region at the same time, it is necessary to determine which camera data is valid. In this paper, the nearest center point method is proposed to select an effective location point. The pixel distance between the center point of the head and the center point of the image (u_0, v_0) is calculated, and the closest point is selected as the final human body target location point, as shown in formula (10). This can prevent the problem of incomplete depth data when the target deviates from the center of the image, thus ensuring the accuracy of positioning information.

$$D = \sqrt{(l_x - u_0)^2 + (l_y - v_0)^2} \tag{10}$$

Finally, according to the camera coordinate transformation, the actual spatial position of the center point of the head can be obtained, that is, the position coordinate of the human body.

4 Experimental Results and Analysis

In order to verify the stability of the system and the effectiveness of proposed algorithm, the positioning test of the human target was performed in the actual space. In this experiment, a total of 10 individuals were tested in sequence. Firstly, 5000 frames of depth images were collected for training, including head-up, head-down, head-turn, squat, and other movement states. Some of the positive and negative samples used in this paper are shown in Figs. 6 and 7 respectively, and all training samples are normalized to the same size (32×32). The algorithm is written in C++ and compiled and run in Visual Studio 2013. The test computer uses an Intel core i5-4570 processor clocked at 3.20 GHz. The five TOF depth cameras used in this paper have a resolution of 320×240, and they are fixed at a height of 3 m above the ground. The lens of the middle camera is parallel to the ground, and the remaining four cameras are oriented in the four directions towards the east, west, south and north respectively, and have a certain angle with the horizontal plane.

Fig. 6. Positive samples. (Color figure online)

SVM classifier combining the SDH and CSSH features is used to determine the human head region. The results are shown in Fig. 8, and the point on the head is the positioning point of this target.

In addition, the detection effect of human detection algorithm combining HOD with SVM is compared with the algorithm combining SDH and CSSH feature constrains, as shown in Table 1.

It can be seen from Table 1 that the 3D head feature constraint method proposed in this paper can effectively improve the detection precision of the human target, and the total running time of the algorithm is controlled within 100 ms, e.g. 10 frames of depth images can be processed per second.

In order to further verify the accuracy of location, the relationship between the outputs of the 3D coordinates of the center of the head and the location in the actual space is compared in this paper. Figure 9(a) shows the change in the height of a person with 1.70 m height, and he is positioned in real time when walking in the space. The results show that the height error is ±3 cm, while Fig. 9(b) shows the 2D track of human target is compared with the track of walking in real space. It can be found that the positioning is more accurate near the central point (0, 0), while in the place close to

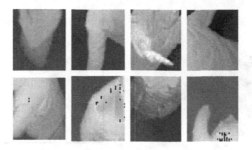

Fig. 7. Negative samples.

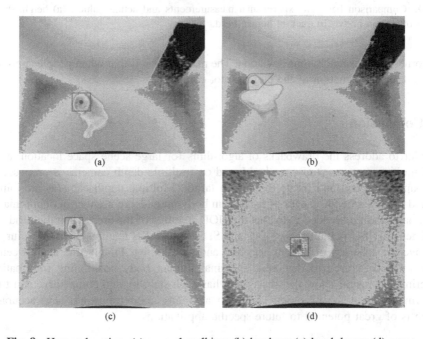

Fig. 8. Human location: (a) normal walking; (b) head-up; (c) head-down; (d) squat.

Table 1. Comparison of accuracy and real time of two algorithms for human detection

Algorithm	Training samples	Test samples	False positive rate	False negative rate	Detection rate	Running time
HOD + SVM	3000	270	4.67%	4.83%	95.33%	82 ms
HOD + SVM + SDH + CSSH	3000	350	2.87%	3.96%	97.13%	94 ms

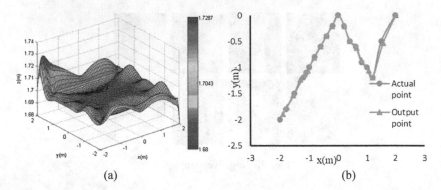

(a)   (b)

Fig. 9. Comparison between experimental measurements and actual values: (a) height distribution of human body; (b) track of human head.

the corner, there is an obvious deviation. The main reason is that when people approach the wall, the information of the target is not complete.

5 Conclusion

In order to address the drawbacks of algorithms for large scene space location, a 3D head multi-feature constraint method based on multiple depth cameras is proposed in this paper to detect and locate the human target. Multiple depth cameras are jointly applied to obtain depth images of the human body and a large number of depth images of human head are divided to extract the HOD features of the area. Then the head and shoulder classifier is trained by SVM, and SDH and CSSH features are used to further improve the accuracy of human detection and positioning. Finally, the nearest center point method is used to determine the final human body positioning information. Experimental results show that the system has high stability and competitive real-time performance, and the proposed algorithm also has good robustness and accuracy, which is of great potential to future specific applications.

References

1. Dalal, N., Triggs, B.: Histograms of oriented gradients for human detection. In: IEEE Computer Society Conference on Computer Vision & Pattern Recognition, pp. 886–893 (2005)
2. Dalal, N., Triggs, B., Schmid, C.: Human detection using oriented histograms of flow and appearance. In: Leonardis, A., Bischof, H., Pinz, A. (eds.) ECCV 2006. LNCS, vol. 3952, pp. 428–441. Springer, Heidelberg (2006). https://doi.org/10.1007/11744047_33
3. Schwartz, W.R., Kembhavi, A., Harwood, D., Davis, L.S.: Human detection using partial least squares analysis. In: IEEE International Conference on Computer Vision, pp. 24–31 (2010)

4. Ma, J., Ren, F.: Detect and track the dynamic deformation human body with the active shape model modified by motion mectors. In: IEEE International Conference on Cloud Computing and Intelligence Systems, pp. 587–591 (2011)
5. Ikemura, S., Fujiyoshi, H.: Real-time human detection using relational depth similarity features. In: Kimmel, R., Klette, R., Sugimoto, A. (eds.) ACCV 2010. LNCS, vol. 6495, pp. 25–38. Springer, Heidelberg (2011). https://doi.org/10.1007/978-3-642-19282-1_3
6. Yu, S., Wu, S., Wang, L.: SLTP: a fast descriptor for people detection in depth images. In: IEEE Ninth International Conference on Advanced Video and Signal-Based Surveillance, pp. 43–47 (2012)
7. Wang, N., Gong, X., Liu, J.: A new depth descriptor for pedestrian detection in RGB-D images, pp. 3688–3691 (2012)
8. Spinello, L., Arras, K.O.: People detection in RGB-D data. In: International Conference on Intelligent Robots & Systems, vol. 38, no. 2, pp. 3838–3843 (2011)
9. Shen, Y., Hao, Z., Wang, P., Ma, S., Liu, W.: A novel human detection approach based on depth map via kinect. In: IEEE Conference on Computer Vision and Pattern Recognition Workshops, pp. 535–541 (2013)
10. Xia, L., Chen, C. C., Aggarwal, J.K.: Human detection using depth information by kinect. In: Computer Vision and Pattern Recognition Workshops, pp. 15–22 (2011)
11. van Oosterhout, T., Bakkes, S., Kröse, B.: Head detection in stereo data for people counting and segmentation (2011)
12. van Oosterhout, T., Englebienne, G., Kröse, B.: RARE: people detection in crowded passages by range image reconstruction. Mach. Vis. Appl. 26(5), 561–573 (2015)

Head Ternary Pattern-Head Shoulder Density Features Pedestrian Detection Algorithm Based on Depth Image

Haikuan Wang, Haoxiang Sun$^{(\boxtimes)}$, Kangli Liu, and Minrui Fei

School of Mechatronics Engineering and Automation, Shanghai University,
99 Shangda Road, BaoShan District, Shanghai 200444, China
haden@shu.edu.cn

Abstract. The existing pedestrian detection algorithms are mostly based on 2D image processing, which are susceptible to complex background, the changes of light intensity, and many other factors. For these reasons, the robustness and accuracy of traditional algorithms are not ideal. Moreover, for other few algorithms that use 3D vision, the core process is to extract features by converting 3D images to grayscale images, which cannot make full use of depth information. To solve these problems, a pedestrian detection algorithm based on depth image is proposed in this paper. For depth image preprocessing, a 3D dilation and erosion algorithm based on probability density is proposed. Combined with the Head Ternary Pattern-Head Shoulder Density (HTP-HSD) features proposed in this paper, the implement of pedestrian detection can be ensured using SVM classifier to classify the features. Experimental results show that the HTP-HSD features meet the actual needs of pedestrian detection with higher recognition rate and recognition speed.

Keywords: Depth image · Pedestrian detection · 3D dilation and erosion
HTP-HSD

1 Introduction

With the enhancement of hardware and the richness of AI application scenarios, pedestrian detection plays an increasingly important role in image processing. Besides, pedestrian detection has made great contributions in many fields, such as traffic accident warning, intelligent service robots, etc. According to the cameras, pedestrian detection algorithms can be divided into (a) pedestrian detection algorithm based on color images and (b) pedestrian detection algorithm based on depth images.

In the pedestrian detection based on color images, the Histogram of Oriented Gradient (HOG) proposed by Dalal and Triggs [1] is currently the most widely used pedestrian feature descriptor. However, the HOG algorithm is based on gradient features, which leads to high dimensions and slow calculations. In order to solve this problem, Zhu et al. [1] allow the block size in the HOG to be variable to increase the speed of operation. Malysiak and Markard [2] used parallel technology to implement HOG on the GPU. The Local Binary Pattern (LBP) is a feature extraction method for texture classification, which is first proposed by Liu et al. [3]. Based on the characteristics of

© Springer Nature Singapore Pte Ltd. 2018
K. Li et al. (Eds.): ICSEE 2018/IMIOT 2018, CCIS 924, pp. 536–545, 2018.
https://doi.org/10.1007/978-981-13-2384-3_50

pedestrians, Mu et al. [4, 5] proposed two variants of LBP: Semantic-LBP (S-LBP) and Fourier LBP (F-LBP). Considering the basic features detected by the color images are susceptible to light, Cosmo et al. [6] used the relative stability of human body structure to propose a color self-similarity (CSS) feature, which can be combined with the HOG feature to greatly improve the detection performance.

In recent years, with the development of hardware technology, depth cameras can capture three-dimensional information of the shooting scene with a greater range and higher accuracy. In terms of the fact, depth cameras can meet the requirements of system stability on the industrial site, and therefore have more advantages in obstacle positioning and detection. Compared with the color image, the depth information only depends on the three-dimensional features of the object, which has nothing to do with the light intensity and contrast. All the above advantages let depth cameras bypass the problems faced by existing pedestrian detection algorithms. Xia et al. [7] proposed a template-matching method based on depth image for human detection, using Canny operator for edge extraction, and then calculating template matching of depth image to locate the human body. Spinello and Arras [8] attempted to use depth information instead of gray information for calculating traditional HOG feature, and proposed a Histogram of Oriented Depth (HOD). Zhang et al. [9] proposed the Water-fill algorithm which is based on the flow characteristics of water in reality. This algorithm obtains the local extremum of the head by imitating the flow direction of the water droplets and the stopping point of the water droplets and has a high recognition rate. The literature [10] relies on the relationship between the pixel points at the edge of the head region to create a head template and to achieve head recognition.

Based on the above research, this paper proposes an HTP-HSD features pedestrian detection algorithm based on depth vision collected by ToF cameras. After the pre-process of original images, the HTP-HSD combined features is used for pedestrian detection and localization.

The structure of this paper is organized as follows: this section is an introduction; specific scheme of pedestrian detection is introduced in Sect. 2; experiments for the algorithm and analyzes the results are conducted in Sect. 3; Sect. 4 is a summary.

2 Scheme of Pedestrian Detection

The depth-based pedestrian detection process is shown in Fig. 1.

2.1 Depth Image Preprocessing

Depth image preprocessing, which provide support for subsequent detection algorithms, is an important part of the entire machine vision inspection system, including spatial filtering, morphological processing and preliminary extraction of some primary features. However, when using the depth camera to capture the image of the application scene, the complex background environment will bring difficulties to the classification and recognition. First, the uncertainty of the ambient light source causes depth information anomalies. Second, the materials, finish, and flatness of different surfaces are different from each other, leading to the fluctuations or lack of depth information.

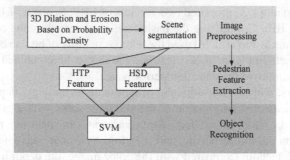

Fig. 1. The flow chart of pedestrian detection algorithm.

Based on these problems, spatial domain and morphological filtering in image pre-processing can weaken the fluctuation of depth information, fill in the missing depth information, and thus improve the quality of the image.

3D Dilation and Erosion Based on Probability Density

Traditional morphological processing mostly uses fixed templates to process images in binary images. Therefore, when dealing with depth images with complex scenes, the traditional morphological filtering has more limitations [11]. In this paper, a 3D dilation and erosion method based on probability density is proposed, which is used to fill missing depth information in depth images and remove isolated points and noises.

First, the depth histogram of the original image is counted, and then the depth interval between the obstacle and the pedestrian is located. Second, the original image is projected onto the corresponding depth interval D_R. The standard deviation of the normal distribution is σ_α and expected $D(i,j)$ defined as follows:

$$D(x,y) = \frac{\sum_{i,j} [P(i,j) \cdot D(i,j)]}{\sum_{i,j} P(i,j)} \tag{1}$$

And the probability density function $H(i,j,\sigma_\alpha)$ of the normal distribution is

$$H(i,j,\sigma_\alpha) = \exp(-\frac{|D_m - D(i,j)|^2}{2\sigma_\alpha^2}) \cdot k \tag{2}$$

$$k = \frac{1}{\sqrt{2\pi}\sigma_\alpha - 1} \tag{3}$$

Let the dilation factor α and the erosion factor β are defined as:

$$\alpha = \frac{\sum_{i,j} P(i,j) \cdot H(i,j,\sigma_\alpha)}{m \cdot n - 1} \tag{4}$$

$$\beta = 1 - \alpha \tag{5}$$

Thus, the symbolic function $P(x, y)$ be defined as

$$P(x,y) = \begin{cases} 1, & D(x,y) \in D_R \\ 0, & D(x,y) \notin D_R \end{cases} \tag{6}$$

Let T_P and T_F be thresholds of dilation and erosion respectively. When the dilation factor of the invalid point $\alpha > T_P$, the depth of the point will be filled according to the Eq. (1). And when the erosion factor of valid point $\beta > T_F$, this point will be removed. An adaptive threshold is obtained by learning the probability distribution of all pixels with the dilation factor and the erosion factor in the neighborhood of the center point. The application of this method can effectively suppress noise of the depth image after depth projection and can fill in the black hole to improve the effect of preprocessing. Increasing the number of iterations of 3D dilation and erosion can better fill in the black holes, remove noise, and enhance the effect of image preprocessing in the depth image.

The experiments show that, in Fig. 2, the human profile is more obvious traditional method. It is more conducive to the final identification and classification.

(a)   (b)   (c)

Fig. 2. Comparison of effects of different dilation and erosion methods. (a) the original image. (b) the image after 3D Dilation and Erosion Based on Probability Density processing. (c) the image after traditional template-based processing.

Scene Segmentation

The objects themselves have a certain spatial thickness, therefore the use of depth information for segmentation can effectively separate the complex foreground and background in the depth image. Because the interference around the object within a single scene after segmentation is relatively small, it is beneficial to improve the accuracy of obstacle location. The positioning of obstacles uses the following equations:

$$C_x = \frac{\sum_{i=1}^{X}\sum_{j=1}^{Y} i \cdot D(i,j)}{\sum_{i=1}^{X}\sum_{j=1}^{Y} D(i,j)} \tag{7}$$

$$C_y = \frac{\sum\limits_{i=1}^{X}\sum\limits_{j=1}^{Y} j \cdot D(i,j)}{\sum\limits_{i=1}^{X}\sum\limits_{j=1}^{Y} D(i,j)} \tag{8}$$

where $D(i,j)$ is the depth value of the point (i,j), X and Y respectively denotes the total number of pixels in the horizontal and vertical directions. The region of the obstacle can be completely located by using the region growing method.

The result of image segmentation using the depth information is shown in Fig. 3.

Fig. 3. The result of image segmentation. (a) the original depth image. (b) three images after segmentation.

2.2 HTP-HSD Pedestrian Features Extraction

As the preprocessing is described in Sect. 2.1, the scenario can be described more accurately and completely in depth image which prepares for the next step of pedestrian features extraction.

The traditional detection methods are mostly based on the pedestrian's outline features and shape features. [12] proposed a Head-Shoulder-Body Density (HSBD) based pedestrian detection method. The application of these features shows good robustness in dealing with images with complex environments. These features can discriminate pedestrians and other obstacles effectively and accurately.

In the application scenario, the HSBD feature may be falsely detected or missed because of the blockage of the body part. Analysis of the actual application sample shows that there is a relatively fixed ratio between the width of the head and the shoulder. In addition, the situation that the human head is shielded is very rare, therefore Head-Shoulder-Density (HSD) features can improve the accuracy of pedestrian detection. So, a model based on depth image is introduced and a Head Ternary Pattern-Head Shoulder Density (HTP-HSD) features in proposed. According to the depth interval to which the object belongs, the HSD can be calculated as:

$$HSD = \frac{\sum\limits_{(i,j)\in H} P(i,j)}{H} \tag{9}$$

where H is the selected region of head and $P(i,j)$ is the symbolic function:

$$P(i,j) = \begin{cases} 1, & D(i,j) \in D_R \\ 0, & D(i,j) \notin D_R \end{cases} \tag{10}$$

D_R denotes the depth interval where the object is located. The extraction result of HSD feature is shown in Fig. 4.

Fig. 4. The result of HSD feature extraction.

In the positioned region of head, HTP feature are extracted from its outline. Because the detected region and the number of pixels is small, the stability of the gradient features can be improved by using the Sobel operator to calculate the gradient of the depth around the center point. The extraction HTP feature is as shown in Fig. 5.

Fig. 5. HTP feature extraction diagram.

Let $\Delta x = d(x, y+1) - d(x, y-1)$ be the gradient of X axis and $\Delta y = d(x+1, y) - d(x-1, y)$ be the gradient of Y axis. HTP feature of center point is computed as:

$$HTP(x_c, y_c) = h(t_x, t_y) \tag{11}$$

where

$$t_x = \begin{cases} 1, & \Delta x > T_d \\ 0, & |\Delta x| \leq T_d \\ -1, & \Delta x \leq T_d \end{cases} \tag{12}$$

$$t_y = \begin{cases} 1, & \Delta y > T_d \\ 0, & |\Delta y| \le T_d \\ -1, & \Delta y \le T_d \end{cases} \tag{13}$$

in which $\Delta x_c = (2\Delta x + \Delta(x-1) + \Delta(x+1))/4$ is denoted as the horizontal gradient and $\Delta y_c = (2\Delta y + \Delta(y-1) + \Delta(y+1))/4$ is denoted as the vertical gradient of the center pixel calculated by Sobel operator and T_d denotes the threshold for adjusting the HTP feature.

Using the HTP-HSD feature can detect pedestrians accurately and effectively because this feature is less affected by the environment. It is suitable for implementing pedestrian detection in application scenarios with complex backgrounds. The ToF camera directly obtains the depth information of each pixel in the scene. The adoption of scale information avoids the disadvantage of the long time-consuming disadvantage of the traditional image detection that requires the construction of an image pyramid to obtain scale-invariant features.

2.3 Support Vector Machine

In order to distinguish between pedestrians and other obstacles, features of objects extracted from image should be classified and identified. Most classification algorithms are based on the theory of statistics. By training the positive and negative samples in advance, the criteria for classification are obtained. Then the new samples are identified according to the criteria.

Support Vector Machine (SVM) was first proposed by Cortes and Vapnik in the 1990s [13]. It is a supervised machine learning method that trains a large amount of sample data with tagged information. The support vector, which minimizes the error and maximizes the separation interval, is usually used for classification and regression analysis. This support vector is also known as the maximum interval classifier.

Assuming the number of data samples is n: $x_1 \sim x_n$, the classified hyperplane can be represented as:

$$w^T x + b = 0 \tag{14}$$

where x denotes the point on the classification hyperplane, and w denotes the vector perpendicular to the classification hyperplane, and b denotes the displacement which is used to improve the flexibility of classified hyperplane. In order to make all the training samples outside two parallel hyperplane spacing regions, it is necessary to ensure that all samples $x_1 \sim x_n$ satisfies:

$$\begin{aligned} w^T x_i + b &\ge 1, or \\ w^T x_i + b &\le -1 \end{aligned} \tag{15}$$

According to the content of Sects. 2.1 and 2.2, the HTP-HSD features are extracted from massive depth images collected by ToF cameras, which are preprocessed by 3D dilation and erosion based on probability density. HTP-HSD features are trained by the SVM classifier to achieve pedestrian detection and classification.

3   Experiments

In order to verify the effectiveness of the algorithm, 2400 depth images collected in the actual application scene are divided into three parts in this experiment, in which 1440 training samples are for SVM training, and 480 cross verified samples are for validating model validity, and the rest 480 test samples are for testing the generalization capability of the model. The results of some different positions about obstacles and humans are shown below (Fig. 6):

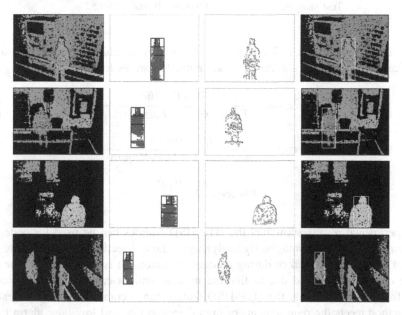

Fig. 6. The original image, segmented image, HTP-HSD features image and result of pedestrian detection in different situation. (a) pedestrian in front of an obstacle. (b) pedestrian between two obstacles. (c) pedestrian image is incomplete. (d) pedestrian standing sideway.

After training 1440 training samples, the parameters of the SVM were obtained. Then cross verified samples are used to verify that whether the model parameters are reasonable. The precision is 98.81% and there is no false alarm which indicates that the trained SVM model is effective. Test samples are used to test the generalization ability of the pedestrian detection method proposed in this paper. The false detection rate is 0.74% which shows that the HTP-HSD pedestrian detection algorithm has better generality and universal applicability. The result and analysis of experiments are shown in Tables. 1 and 2.

Table 1. The result of experiments.

	Positive samples	Negative samples	True positive	False positive	False negative	True negative
Cross validation samples	252	228	249	0	3	228
Test samples	208	272	208	2	0	270

Table 2. The analysis of experiments

	Precision	Recall	F Score
Cross validation samples	100.00%	98.81%	99.40%
Test samples	99.04%	100.00%	99.52%

Precision, Recall, and F Score are usually used in machine learning to evaluate classification models and algorithms. The definitions are as follows:

$$Precision = \frac{TruePositive}{TruePositive + FalsePositive} \tag{16}$$

$$Recall = \frac{TruePositive}{TruePositive + FalseNegative} \tag{17}$$

$$FScore = 2 \cdot \frac{P \cdot R}{P + R} \tag{18}$$

Experimental results show that the HTP-HSD features can be used for pedestrian detection based on depth images. By analyzing the false detection, images that are false alarmed or missed were taken during outdoor operations. It is inspected that the HTP feature cannot be matched due to that the intense sunlight caused abnormal fluctuations. In normal situations, the HTP-HSD feature can accurately classify pedestrian. This method meets the requirements of high detection rate and low false alarm rate in application scenarios.

The test platform is a personal computer with an i5-4570 CPU and the development environment is Windows. The software development platform is Microsoft Visual Studio 2013. The average time of each image is 35 ms, and 28 frames of depth images can be processed every second.

4 Conclusion

An HTP-HSD features pedestrian detection algorithm based on depth images is proposed in this paper. It avoids the disadvantages of traditional 2D pedestrian positioning. By filtering and preprocessing the original depth image using the 3D dilation and erosion based on probability density, the HTP-HSD features proposed in this paper are extracted. The pedestrian detection is implemented using criteria trained by SVM. Experiments show that this method can detect and identify pedestrian more accurately, and it meets the requirements of practical applications for real-time pedestrian detection.

References

1. Dalal, N., Triggs, B.: Histograms of oriented gradients for human detection. In: 2005 IEEE Computer Society Conference on Computer Vision and Pattern Recognition, pp. 886–893. IEEE, San Diego (2005)
2. Malysiak, D., Markard, M.: Increasing the efficiency of GPU-based HOG algorithms through tile-images. In: Nguyen, N.T., Trawiński, B., Fujita, H., Hong, T.P. (eds.) ACIIDS 2016. LNCS (LNAI), vol. 9621, pp. 708–720. Springer, Heidelberg (2016). https://doi.org/10.1007/978-3-662-49381-6_68
3. Liu, L., Fieguth, P., Wang, X., Pietikäinen, M., Hu, D.: Evaluation of LBP and deep texture descriptors with a new robustness benchmark. In: Leibe, B., Matas, J., Sebe, N., Welling, M. (eds.) ECCV 2016. LNCS, vol. 9907, pp. 69–86. Springer, Cham (2016). https://doi.org/10.1007/978-3-319-46487-9_5
4. Xu, F., Zhang, J., Wang, J.Z.: Microexpression identification and categorization using a facial dynamics map. IEEE Trans. Affect. Comput. **8**, 254–267 (2017)
5. Mu, Y., Yan, S., Liu, Y., Huang, T., Zhou, B.: Discriminative local binary patterns for human detection in personal album. In: 2008 IEEE Conference on Computer Vision and Pattern Recognition, pp. 1–8. IEEE, Anchorage (2008)
6. Cosmo, D.L., Salles, E.O.T., Ciarelli, P.M.: Pedestrian detection system based on HOG and a modified version of CSS. In: Seventh International Conference on Machine Vision (ICMV 2014), pp. 5–15. SPIE, Milan (2015)
7. Xia, L., Chen, C.C., Aggarwal, J.K.: Human detection using depth information by kinect. In: 2011 Conference on Computer Vision and Pattern Recognition, pp. 15–22. IEEE, Colorado Springs (2011)
8. Spinello, L., Arras, K.O.: People detection in RGB-D data. In: 2011 International Conference on Intelligent Robots and Systems, pp. 3838–3843. IEEE, San Francisco (2011)
9. Zhang, X., Yan, J., Feng, S., Lei, Z., Yi, D., Li, S.Z.: Water filling: unsupervised people counting via vertical kinect sensor. In: 2012 IEEE Ninth International Conference on Advanced Video and Signal-Based Surveillance, pp. 215–220. IEEE, Beijing (2012)
10. Hou, Y.-L., Pang, G.K.H.: Multi-cue-based crowd segmentation in stereo vision. In: Real, P., Diaz-Pernil, D., Molina-Abril, H., Berciano, A., Kropatsch, W. (eds.) CAIP 2011. LNCS, vol. 6854, pp. 93–101. Springer, Heidelberg (2011). https://doi.org/10.1007/978-3-642-23672-3_12
11. Hasan, S.M.A., Ko, K.: Depth edge detection by image-based smoothing and morphological operations. J. Comput. Des. Eng. **3**, 191–197 (2016)
12. Qi, X., Fei, M., Hu, H., Wang, H.: A novel 3D expansion and corrosion method for human detection based on depth information. In: Fei, M., Ma, S., Li, X., Sun, X., Jia, L., Su, Z. (eds.) LSMS/ICSEE -2017. CCIS, vol. 761, pp. 556–565. Springer, Singapore (2017). https://doi.org/10.1007/978-981-10-6370-1_55
13. Wang, X., Han, T.X., Yan, S.: An HOG-LBP human detector with partial occlusion handling. In: 2009 IEEE 12th International Conference on Computer Vision, pp. 32–39. IEEE, Kyoto (2009)

Maximally Stable Extremal Regions Improved Tracking Algorithm Based on Depth Image

Haikuan Wang, Dong Xie$^{(\boxtimes)}$, Haoxiang Sun, and Wenju Zhou

School of Mechatronics Engineering and Automation,
Shanghai University, 99 Shangda Road, BaoShan District,
Shanghai 200444, China
xiedong@shu.edu.cn

Abstract. In order to solve the problem that traditional Camshift algorithm can easily fail to track overlapping targets and multiple similar depth targets, a new improved maximally stable extremal regions (MSER) algorithm is presented in this paper. Firstly, the suspected target contour is extracted and similarity analysis is performed. Secondly, the improved MSER algorithm is used to confirm the target contour and update the similarity library. Finally, combined with the physical properties unique to the depth image and based on the Kalman filter, it is possible to predict the tracking target's moving position. The experimental results show that the real-time performance and recognition rate are improved, and robustness to the situation of target overlap and occlusion is better with the improved MSER algorithm.

Keywords: Depth image · MSER algorithm · Target tracking
Camshift algorithm

1 Introduction

Traditional digital image processing technology [1] has gradually matured, but it is greatly affected by light, and meanwhile stability is difficult to control at times, which greatly restricts its further development. The depth information of the target can be reflected directly and identified with the structural information due to that the depth image [2] is not affected by the light intensity nor the surface characteristics of the object, and binocular imaging can be replaced by depth images, because of which more and more applications are developed.

Nowadays, there are many classic methods, e.g. eigen pictures and eigen shapes [3], using the depth information for target tracking, among which the continuous adaptive mean shift (Camshift) [4] algorithm attracts much attention. The algorithm effectively solves human target deformation and achieves better results in the simple background environment. However, when there are multiple targets of similar depth in the image, simple layering alone cannot be multi-targeted.

The MSER algorithm [5] marks a series of discernible detection areas as suspicious target areas for the current frame image by processing the images, and determines the exact boundary of the detected area. However, when the pixel change is not obvious, the algorithm will not be able to extract valid information, resulting in tracking failure.

K. Li et al. (Eds.): ICSEE 2018/IMIOT 2018, CCIS 924, pp. 546–554, 2018.
https://doi.org/10.1007/978-981-13-2384-3_51

Kalman filter [6], which is low computational complex and better real time, is an algorithm calculating the linear minimum variance estimate of the state sequence of the dynamic system.

Based on the content above, a new MSER improved tracking algorithm based on depth image is proposed in this paper. Firstly, the depth image is extracted and the contour curve and local surface features [7] are extracted, and the similarity is analyzed. The contour will be considered invalid and ignored when the similarity is low and considered valid when the similarity is high. If the similarity stays in the middle, the improved MSER algorithm will be used to determine the target contour, and to extract the contour features of the confirmed target, and to update the similarity database, so as to improve the accuracy of the similarity analysis. The Kalman filter at last is used to predict the position of the target in the three-dimensional scene which keeps the target's motion consistent and coherent.

2 Features and Acquisition of Depth Image

The depth image is usually converted into a grayscale image [8] for intuitive display, but the meaning of the depth image and the ordinary grayscale image is obviously different. Every point of the depth image represents the distance between the point and the depth camera, which is a solid physical meaning that will be used to determine the position of the target in a three-dimensional scene.

There are many popular methods to acquire depth image such as stereo matching [9] method of a binocular camera, ToF method [10, 11] based on the principle of time-of-flight, depth measurement method based on the structure light [12] and the moiré fringe characteristics. These methods have their own strengths in different fields. In this paper, depth information is collected with time-of-flight method, which has high real-time performance more advantages compared to the other measurement methods, and is less influenced by the environment and less complex.

3 Specific Algorithm Flow

The overall framework of this algorithm is shown in Fig. 1.

3.1 Similarity Analysis

The outer contour of objects is acquired and then extracted into contour curves, on which the largest curvature point is set as a feature and projected on the original contour as marked point [13]. The contour, presented by the sequence of the marked points, is analyzed by similarity with the contours in the similarity library. The precision of the object is realized by ruling out the contours of low similarity.

A discrete set $p = \{p_1, p_2, p_3, \ldots p_n\}$ is collected from the contour. The relative positions between p_i and the rest points are reduced to the distribution counts of every sector on the model. Denote $k = \{1, 2, \ldots K\}$ as a number set in which $K = M * N$. The statistical distribution histograms is denoted by $h_i(k)$ which satisfies

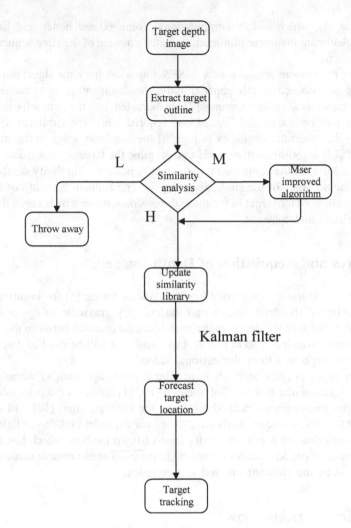

Fig. 1. Algorithm flow chart

$$h_i(k) = \#\{q \neq p_i : (q - p_i) \in bin(k)\} \tag{1}$$

Then calculate the cost matrix which satisfies

$$C_{i,j} = C(p_i, q_j) = 0.5 * \sum_{k=1}^{K} \frac{[h_i(k) - h_j(k)]^2}{h_i(k) + h_j(k)} \tag{2}$$

where $h_j(k)$ denotes the point q_i shape histogram of the target Q what satisfies

$$H(\pi) = \sum C(p_i, q_\pi(i)) \tag{3}$$

The larger the value of H is, the lower the similarity will be, and vice versa. Target Depth map and outline map are simply shown in Fig. 2.

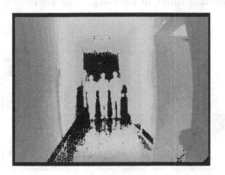

Fig. 2. Three target depth maps and contour maps

3.2 Improved MSER Algorithm

The MSER detection algorithm is based on the orderly arrangement of the pixel values in the image, and then sets the sorted pixel values into a component tree. The maximum stable extremum area of the merged area is determined by the determination criterion to clean up the invalid area.

Bucket sorting [14], also called Binsort sorting, can greatly reduce the complexity of conventional sorting methods. When the pixels are bucket sorted, they will be distributed at its position in the image where the extremum area can be found by merging pixels with similar properties via union-find method. The two sets must be examined if they are intersected before merging. As is shown in Fig. 3.

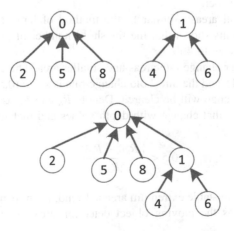

Fig. 3. Union-find sets

When using the recursive method to find the root node, the complexity of each algorithm is $o(n)$, which greatly increases the overall algorithm's consumption time. Therefore, a path compression method is used to reduce the complexity (see Fig. 4). When all the algorithms are completed, only the final connected component remains. The neighborhood quadtree method is used to extract the MSER in order to save the originally connected regions at different times in the image and improve the efficiency of the algorithm.

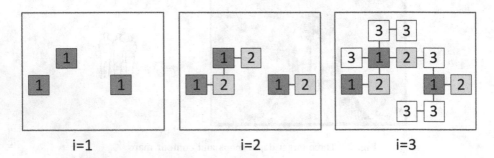

i=1   i=2   i=3

Fig. 4. Extremum area search

Before nodes are merged, function Make Set is used to complete the creation of the initial node, and the presence of neighboring nodes within the four-neighborhood of the pixel should be checked. The invalid region is deleted via the stability condition, and the maximum stable extremum region that meets the conditions is obtained.

When the areas are merged, all the extremum regions in the image are obtained, but not all of the regions are the maximum stable extremum region. For invalid areas, the specific removal rules are as follows:

(1) Removal of oversized areas: the threshold number of pixels occupied by the largest area is set to 3000 through experimental analysis of the tested images pixel numbers in this paper.

(2) Removal of small areas: Similar to the method of large areas, the analysis of experimental results shows that the threshold number of pixels occupied by the minimum area is set to 400.

(3) Removal of larger change rate areas and smaller area: The area change rate is set according to (3.4), and the threshold change rate is set to (0.5, 1). Extremum areas that exceed this range will be cleared. Denote R_a and R_b as the areas of adjacent areas respectively that change with depth values and that satisfy

$$0.5 < \frac{||R_a| - |R_b||}{|R_a|} < 1 \tag{4}$$

When the maximum stable extremum area is found, the remaining area in the depth image is considered as the moving object detection area. By performing the AND operation with the suspected target contour previously analyzed by similarity, the target contour to be tracked can be confirmed.

3.3 Predicting the Target Location

In the tracking process, the target may move in the vertical direction, so the depth value may also change. In order to solve this problem, according to the physical meaning of depth, the actual position of the target in the scene is displayed by establishing a spatial rectangular coordinate system. The noise matrices of the observation matrix and the state transition matrix are mutually independent Gaussian white noise matrices.

Denote (x_k, y_k) as the centroid of the horizontal plane, and (v_{x_k}, v_{y_k}) as its speed. Denote G as the top point of the target in the Z direction G, which moves at the speed of v_{z_k}, is at z_k. The interval between the two continuous frames is short and it can be considered as uniform motion. Denote Δt as the interval between two adjacent images as.

The target's motion state vector X_k satisfies

$$X_k = [x_k \ y_k \ z_k \ v_{x_k} \ v_{y_k} \ v_{z_k}]^T \tag{5}$$

The observation state vector Z_k satisfies:

$$Z_k = [x_k \ y_k \ z_k]^T \tag{6}$$

$$z_k = z_{k-1} + (\Delta t)v_{z_{k-1}} \tag{7}$$

$$v_{z_k} = v_{z_{k-1}} \tag{8}$$

Therefore, the system state transition matrix A satisfies:

$$A = \begin{pmatrix} 1 & 0 & 0 & \Delta t & 0 & 0 \\ 0 & 1 & 0 & 0 & \Delta t & 0 \\ 0 & 0 & 1 & 0 & 0 & \Delta t \\ 0 & 0 & 0 & 1 & 0 & 0 \\ 0 & 0 & 0 & 0 & 1 & 0 \\ 0 & 0 & 0 & 0 & 0 & 1 \end{pmatrix} \tag{9}$$

The observation matrix C is:

$$C = \begin{pmatrix} 1 & 0 & 0 & 0 & 0 & 0 \\ 0 & 1 & 0 & 0 & 0 & 0 \\ 0 & 0 & 1 & 0 & 0 & 0 \end{pmatrix} \tag{10}$$

So the Kalman filter can be used to predict the motion of the target in the Z axis. The highest point as a reference point is shown in Fig. 5.

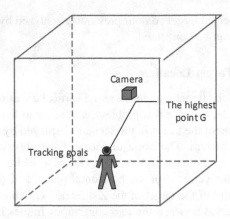

Fig. 5. Tracking target

4 Experimental Results and Analysis

Overlapping and occlusion experiments were carried out using the ToF camera in order to validate the accuracy of the improved MSER tracking algorithm. The ToF camera was placed on the top of the testing area to collect the images of the moving targets. Tracking effect images with two and three targets can be seen in Fig. 6.

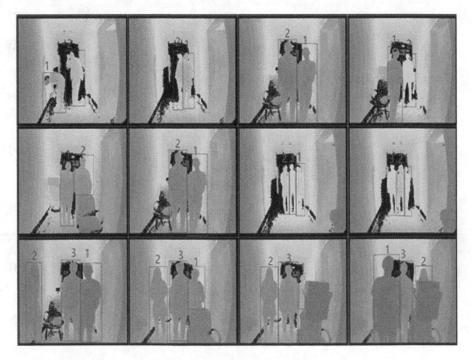

Fig. 6. Track multiple targets

The overlapped targets will be considered as one with traditional Camshift for that the targets to be tracked cannot be distinguished from the disturbance of similar characteristics and failed to be tracked when the target is sheltered (see Fig. 7). The traditional Camshift algorithm works well when the targets do not overlap. However, when the targets overlap, the target cannot be distinguished correctly, and the two targets are mistaken as one. These problems are solved with an improved MSER tracking algorithm in this paper where the targets can be precisely tracked when there are many targets or the targets are sheltered (Tables 1 and 2).

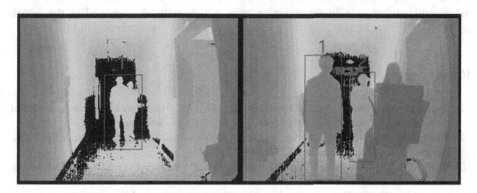

Fig. 7. Traditional camshift algorithm tracking error map

Table 1. Track statistics of experimental results with overlapping targets

Tracking the number of targets	Tracking algorithm	Test samples	Misuse rate (%)	Detection rate (%)
2	Camshift	500	2.6%	97.4%
	Improved MSER		1.5%	98.5%
3	Camshift	500	7.2%	92.8%
	Improved MSER		3.6%	96.4%

Table 2. Track statistics of experimental results of target occlusion

Tracking the number of targets	Tracking algorithm	Test samples	Misuse rate (%)	Detection rate (%)
2	Camshift	500	5.7%	94.3%
	Improved MSER		2.5%	97.5%
3	Camshit	500	11.2%	88.8%
	Improved MSER		5.6%	94.4%

5 Conclusion

In this paper, using the unique physical properties of depth images, an improved tracking algorithm for MSER is proposed, and Kalman filter is used to achieve accurate prediction and tracking of target locations. The target's contour is extracted and confirmed iteratively. The accuracy of the similarity analysis is improved with the similarity database update. However, this algorithm based on the contour curve and local area feature matching in the depth image has a large amount of computation and increases the complexity. At the same time, the effect is good in the stable area while many problems remain in the complex ones which will be improved in the future research.

References

1. Baqersad, M., Hamedi, A., Mohammadafzali, M., Ali, H.: Asphalt mixture segregation detection: digital image processing approach. Adv. Mater. Sci. Eng. (2017)
2. Shotton, J., et al.: Efficient human pose estimation from single depth images. IEEE Trans. Pattern Anal. Mach. Intell. **35**, 2821–2840 (2013)
3. Biskup, M., Procaccia, E.B.: Eigenvalue vs perimeter in a shape theorem for self-interacting random walks (2018)
4. Hou, H.N., Wu, T.: Pedestrian tracking algorithm based on camshift multi-feature adaptive fusion. Electron. Qual. **3**, 007 (2017)
5. Donoser, M., Bischof, H.: Efficient maximally stable extremal region (MSER) tracking. In: 2006 IEEE Computer Society Conference on Computer Vision and Pattern Recognition, pp. 553–560 (2006)
6. Nguyen, T., Mann, G.K.I., Vardy, A., Gosine, R.G.: Developing a cubature multi-state constraint Kalman filter for visual-inertial navigation system. In: Conference on Computer and Robot Vision, pp. 321–328 (2017)
7. Lo, T.W.R., Siebert, J.P.: Local feature extraction and matching on range images: 2.5D SIFT. Comput. Vis. Image Underst. **113**, 1235–1250 (2009)
8. Qiao, B., Jin, L., Yang, Y.: An adaptive algorithm for grey image edge detection based on grey correlation analysis. In: International Conference on Computational Intelligence and Security, pp. 470–474 (2017)
9. Sun, C.: A Fast Stereo Matching Method. Digital Image Computing Techniques and Applications, pp. 95–100 (1997)
10. Eichhardt, I., Jankó, Z., Chetverikov, D.: Novel methods for image-guided ToF depth upsampling. In: IEEE International Conference on Systems, Man, and Cybernetics (2017)
11. Bevilacqua, A., Stefano, L.D., Azzari, P.: People tracking using a time-of-flight depth sensor. In: IEEE International Conference on Video and Signal Based Surveillance, p. 89 (2006)
12. Sitnik, R.: New method of structure light measurement system calibration based on adaptive and effective evaluation of 3D-phase distribution. In: Proceedings of SPIE - The International Society for Optical Engineering, vol. 5856, pp. 109–117 (2005)
13. Salve, S.G., Jondhale, K.C.: Shape matching and object recognition using shape contexts. In: IEEE International Conference on Computer Science and Information Technology, pp. 483–507 (2010)
14. Astrachan, O.: Bubble sort: an archaeological algorithmic analysis. ACM (2003)

Dynamic Hand Gesture Recognition Based on the Three-Dimensional Spatial Trajectory Feature and Hidden Markov Model

Kangli Liu[1], Feixiang Zhou[1], Haikuan Wang[1(✉)], Minrui Fei[1,2], and Dajun Du[1]

[1] School of Mechatronics Engineering and Automation, Shanghai University, Shanghai, China
HKWang@shu.edu.cn
[2] Shanghai Key Laboratory of Power Station Automation Technology, Shanghai University, Shanghai 200444, China

Abstract. In the process of the traditional hand gesture recognition, complex backgrounds, illumination and hand gesture changes in space can seriously affect the accuracy of the dynamic hand gesture recognition. In this paper, an improved dynamic hand gesture recognition method based on Three-dimensional Time of Flight (3D-TOF) camera is proposed. Firstly, an adaptive segmentation algorithm is used for the hand gesture segmentation combining the frame difference method and the depth threshold. Then a dynamic hand gesture recognition algorithm based on the three-dimensional (3D) spatial trajectory feature and Hidden Markov Model (HMM) is proposed which takes full advantage of the depth data. And in order to improve the recognition rate of the dynamic hand gesture, the misidentified samples are trained again. Experimental results show that the algorithms proposed in this paper have a high recognition rate of the dynamic hand gestures and a good robustness to the different backgrounds and illumination.

Keywords: 3D-TOF · Dynamic hand gesture recognition
3D spatial trajectory feature · HMM

1 Introduction

With the progress of science and technology and the development of computer application technology, the traditional mouse, keyboard and other human-computer interaction means have been unable to meet the requirements of current users. Therefore, how to develop a natural, friendly and harmonious human-computer interaction which conforms to the human's behaviour becomes a hot issue in the present research. In recent years, hand gesture recognition has attracted much attention as one of the most natural and friendly human-computer interaction [1, 2]. And it has been widely applied to various fields such as virtual reality, unmanned vehicles and smart home, etc.

© Springer Nature Singapore Pte Ltd. 2018
K. Li et al. (Eds.): ICSEE 2018/IMIOT 2018, CCIS 924, pp. 555–564, 2018.
https://doi.org/10.1007/978-981-13-2384-3_52

In the traditional hand gesture recognition based on vision, the accuracy of recognition can be easily affected by the complex background and illumination, etc. With the constant progress of the depth sensing technology [3, 4], a hand gesture recognition method based on the depth vision is proposed using the depth information acquired from a depth camera, which successfully overcomes the problems existing in the traditional hand gesture recognition to some extent. At present, more and more scholars use the depth camera to accomplish the dynamic hand gesture recognition. Hsieh *et al.* [5] adopted Haar features and support vector machine (SVM) to recognize the dynamic hand gestures. Rahmani *et al.* [6] proposed a real-time dynamic hand gesture recognition method based on histogram of depth gradients (HDG) and RF. Yang *et al.* [7] proposed a method based on depth motion map (DMM). First, calculate the three views of the depth map of each frame, then normalize the hand regions in each view, after that divide each frame and accumulate to obtain the DMM, then extract the corresponding HOG features, and finally use the SVM to classify. Premaratne *et al.* [8] employed the changes of the direction angles of the hand gesture trajectory as the features, and then achieved the recognition based on HMM. In the above literatures, depth information is mostly applied to segment hand gesture regions, but not directly used to extract the three-dimensional (3D) features of the hand gesture. Scholars gradually introduced depth information into gesture description features, such as 3D HOG (Histogram of Oriented Gradient) features and 3D HOF (Histograms of Oriented Optical Flow) features based on 2D image features. Oreifej *et al.* [9] proposed a four-dimensional (4D) HOG feature by adding a one-dimensional time factor on the basis of the 3D HOG features. Geng *et al.* [10] proposed the hand shape features extracted from the depth images and the spherical coordinate (SPC) feature extracted from the 3D hand motion trajectories for sign language recognition. Yang *et al.* [11] presented a flexible 3D trajectory indexing method for complex 3D motion recognition. Trajectories are represented in the subprimitive level, the level between the point level and primitive level.

The dynamic hand gesture recognition method based on 3D-TOF camera [12, 13] studied in this paper takes full advantage of the depth information. In order to overcome the changes of the complex background and illumination, an adaptive hand gesture segmentation method is presented which combines the frame difference method with the depth threshold. Then based on the HMM, this paper proposed a dynamic hand gesture recognition algorithm based on the direction angle features of the 3D spatial trajectory. Experimental results show that the average recognition rate of dynamic hand gestures using the above algorithms reaches 94.5%, and the algorithms have a good robustness to the different backgrounds and illumination.

The structure of this paper is organized as follows: This section is an introduction. Section 2 describes the hand gesture segmentation under complex background and different illumination. Section 3 describes a dynamic gesture recognition method based on the 3D spatial trajectory feature and HMM. In Sect. 4, the experimental results are analysed. Finally, some important conclusions and future work are discussed.

2 Hand Gesture Segmentation Under Complex Background and Different Illumination

Hand gesture segmentation is the first and crucial step of the dynamic hand gesture recognition. It means detecting and segmenting the motion hand region of interest accurately from the complex background. The result of the hand gesture segmentation will directly affect the recognition rate of dynamic hand gestures.

In this paper, a TOF camera with a resolution of 320×240 is used to obtain depth images. Considering the actual situation, the hand gestures are closer to the camera than the background and the human body. Therefore, the method based on the depth threshold is usually applied for the hand gesture segmentation. In this paper, an adaptive hand gesture segmentation method with the combination of the frame difference method and the depth threshold is put forward. This method not only overcomes the influence of complex fore-background and different illumination, but also realizes the adaptive hand gesture segmentation. The specific steps are as follows:

Step 1: Detect the depth image of the motion region of the current frame.

$$D(x,y) = \begin{cases} I_t(x,y) & |I_t(x,y) - I_{t-1}(x,y)| > T_1 \\ 0 & |I_t(x,y) - I_{t-1}(x,y)| \leq T_1 \end{cases} \quad (1)$$

Where $I_t(x,y)$ is the depth image of the current frame, $I_{t-1}(x,y)$ is the depth image of the previous frame, $D(x,y)$ is the depth image of the motion region.

Step 2: Calculate the average depth d of the depth image of the motion region, and take the average d as the depth threshold T for the hand gesture segmentation, as shown in the formula (2):

$$T = d = \frac{1}{240 \times 320} \sum_{i=240} \sum_{j=320} D(x_i, y_j) \quad (2)$$

Step 3: According to the depth threshold T, the hand gesture segmentation is performed on the current frame, as shown in formula (3):

$$T(x,y) = \begin{cases} 255 & I_t(x,y) < T \pm \delta \\ 0 & otherwise \end{cases} \quad (3)$$

Where $T(x,y)$ is the binary image of the segmented hand gesture region, δ is the given error of the depth threshold.

The result of the hand gesture segmentation is shown in Fig. 1. Figure 1(a) shows the depth image from the TOF camera. Figure 1(b) shows the segmented hand region by the above method. It can be seen that the hand gesture region is completely segmented.

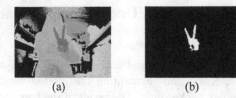

(a)   (b)

Fig. 1. (a) The original depth image (b) the binary image of the segmented hand gesture region

3   Dynamic Gesture Recognition Based on 3D Spatial Trajectory Feature and HMM

3.1   Hand Gesture Tracking

Unlike the static hand gesture recognition in which the changes of the shapes and geometric features of the hand are focused mostly, the dynamic hand gesture recognition is more concerned about the motion trajectory of the hand gesture. In this paper, the trajectory of the gravity center of the dynamic hand gesture represents the trajectory of the hand gesture. According to the features of the moment of the contours, the gravity center of the contour can be extracted, as shown in formula (4):

$$p = (x_0, y_0) = (\frac{m_{10}}{m_{00}}, \frac{m_{01}}{m_{00}}) \tag{4}$$

Where m_{10} and m_{01} are the first-order geometric moments of the contour image and m_{00} is the zero-order geometric moment of the contour image.

Then the trajectory points are extracted every three frames denoted as $P(x, y, z)$, where z represents the depth value of the point.

3.2   3D Spatial Trajectory Feature Extraction

The extraction of hand gesture features is a very critical procedure in the hand gesture recognition and can directly decide the accuracy of the recognition. In general, the extraction of the dynamic hand gesture features is transformed into the extraction of the dynamic hand gesture trajectory features. The common hand gesture trajectory features include position, direction angles, and movement rate. In this paper, the direction angle which contributes most to the recognition rate is selected as the hand gesture trajectory feature. And in order to take full advantage of the depth information provided by the TOF camera, the original the two-dimensional (2D) trajectory is replaced by a 3D trajectory to increase the motion features in the depth direction. Thus, the 3D trajectory features can not only reflect the plane hand gesture trajectory features but also the spatial trajectory features, which is very effective for improving the accuracy of the dynamic hand gesture recognition. Figure 2 shows the spatial trajectory and projections of a dynamic hand gesture.

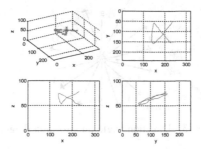

Fig. 2. 3D trajectory and projection of the gesture

Assuming that the hand gesture trajectory points obtained at $t-1$ and t are $P_{t-1}(x_{t-1}, y_{t-1}, z_{t-1})$ and $P_t(x_t, y_t, z_t)$ respectively. The direction angle of $\overline{P_{t-1}P_t}$ is defined as $[\theta_{xyt}, \theta_{yzt}, \theta_{xzt}]$, where θ_{xyt}, θ_{yzt}, and θ_{xzt} respectively are the orientation angles of the trajectory points P_{t-1} and P_t in the *XOY*, *YOZ*, and *XOZ* plane. The calculation method is shown in formula (5), (6) and (7):

$$\theta_{xyt} = \begin{cases} \arctan\left(\frac{y_t-y_{t-1}}{x_t-x_{t-1}}\right) + \pi & x_2 - x_1 < 0 \\ \arctan\left(\frac{y_t-y_{t-1}}{x_t-x_{t-1}}\right) + 2\pi & y_2 - y_1 < 0 \\ \arctan\left(\frac{y_t-y_{t-1}}{x_t-x_{t-1}}\right) & otherwise \end{cases} \tag{5}$$

Where θ_{xyt} is the direction angle in the *XOY* plane.

$$\theta_{yzt} = \begin{cases} \arctan\left(\frac{z_t-z_{t-1}}{y_t-y_{t-1}}\right) + \pi & y_2 - y_1 < 0 \\ \arctan\left(\frac{z_t-z_{t-1}}{y_t-y_{t-1}}\right) + 2\pi & z_2 - z_1 < 0 \\ \arctan\left(\frac{z_t-z_{t-1}}{y_t-y_{t-1}}\right) & otherwise \end{cases} \tag{6}$$

Where θ_{yzt} is the direction angle in the *YOZ* plane.

$$\theta_{xzt} = \begin{cases} \arctan\left(\frac{z_t-z_{t-1}}{x_t-x_{t-1}}\right) + \pi & x_2 - x_1 < 0 \\ \arctan\left(\frac{z_t-z_{t-1}}{x_t-x_{t-1}}\right) + 2\pi & z_2 - z_1 < 0 \\ \arctan\left(\frac{z_t-z_{t-1}}{x_t-x_{t-1}}\right) & otherwise \end{cases} \tag{7}$$

Where θ_{xzt} is the direction angle in the *XOZ* plane.

Then the extracted direction angle features are quantized into 12 levels using 12-direction chain codes. As shown in Fig. 3, the direction angle of each level is expressed as a corresponding number between 0 and 11. Finally, the discrete eigenvectors are obtained as the input to the HMM.

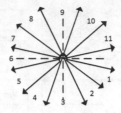

Fig. 3. Direction angle quantization diagram

3.3 Dynamic Hand Gesture Recognition Based on the 3D Trajectory Feature and HMM

The HMM describes a double stochastic process that randomly generates observation sequences from a hidden Markov model. Because HMM has a strong ability to model the atypical hand gestures and can describe the complex gestures and it has the advantage of predefining the gesture models [14]. Therefore, the HMM algorithm [15–17] has always been dominant in the dynamic hand gesture recognition. This paper selects the HMM algorithm based on the 3D trajectory features to implement the dynamic hand gesture recognition.

The complete set of parameters for an HMM can be represented as $\lambda = \{M, N, A, B, \pi\}$, where N is the number of hidden states of the HMM, M is the number of the observed values of the HMM, A is the state transition probability matrix, B is the observation probability matrix, and π is the initial probability vector. This paper adopts the simpler parameter representation of the HMM, that is, $\lambda = \{\pi, A, B\}$. Once the model parameters of the HMM are determined, the HMM is developed.

The dynamic hand gesture recognition based on the HMM is mainly divided into two stages, namely the training stage of the HMM and the recognition stage of the dynamic hand gestures. The basic steps are as follows:

Step 1: Use the left-right strip HMM topology and initialize the model parameter to $\lambda = \{\pi, A, B\}$.

Step 2: Using the Baum-Welch learning algorithm, estimate the new model parameters $\overline{\lambda} = (\overline{\pi}, \overline{A}, \overline{B})$ through continuous iterative operations based on the 3D gesture spatial trajectory feature vectors which is input as the observation sequence O.

Step 3: Use the fore-backward algorithm to calculate $P(O|\lambda)$ and $P(O|\overline{\lambda})$, that is, the probability of the observation sequence O under the model parameters λ and $\overline{\lambda}$, and then calculate $\left|\log P(O|\overline{\lambda}) - \log P(O|\lambda)\right|$. If $\left|\log P(O|\overline{\lambda}) - \log P(O|\lambda)\right| < \varepsilon$ (ε is a given convergence threshold value), then converges. The HMM trained at this time is closest to the observed value. So far, the training process is completed. Otherwise making $\lambda = \overline{\lambda}$, continue the step 2 until $P(O|\overline{\lambda})$ converges.

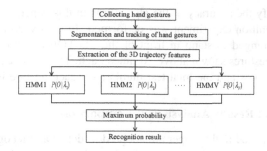

Fig. 4. Flow chart of dynamic hand gesture recognition

An HMM is trained for each given dynamic hand gestures, then the motion trajectory direction angle feature vector of a sample is taken as the input observation sequence of the HMM. Finally calculate $P(O|\lambda_i)$ ($0 \leq i \leq V$, where V is the number of the defined dynamic hand gestures). The hand gesture of the corresponding HMM with the highest probability is considered as the recognition result. The dynamic hand gesture recognition flow chart is as shown in Fig. 4.

Since all the samples are treated uniformly by using the Baum-Welch classic training algorithm, $P(O|\lambda_i)$ may eventually converge to the local optimal value resulting in the poor recognition of some samples. On the basis of this circumstance, some improvements have been made in this paper. The training process of the hand gesture samples is linked with the test results of the model, and the HMM is corrected by using the test results of the model. If some hand gesture samples are misrecognized as other gestures, then those samples will be input into the corresponding HMM again for a second training to correct the model parameters. Finally, after performing this operation several times, the optimal parameters of the HMM is determined.

4   Experimental Results and Analysis

Based on the principles of the practicality, simplicity and identifiability of the hand gestures and conforming to people's habits, this paper defines four basic dynamic hand gestures, as shown in Fig. 5, which are the trajectories of the four specific dynamic hand gestures respectively. The small solid black circle represents the starting position of the hand gesture, and the direction of the black solid arrow is the direction of the motion trajectory of the dynamic hand gesture, wherein the gesture 4 represents moving hand from far to close.

(a)   (b)   (c)   (d)

Fig. 5. The trajectories of the four specific dynamic hand gestures: (a) gesture1, (b) gesture2, (c) gesture3, (d) gesture4

In order to verify the accuracy of the algorithms in this paper, a real-time dynamic hand gesture recognition experiment was performed. In the experiment, a total of ten volunteers were arranged to stand in front of the 3D-TOF camera and repeated four kinds of dynamic gestures shown above 20 times each. Therefore, each volunteer need to complete 80 gestures and the total test number for each gesture is 200.

4.1   Experimental Results Analysis and Comparison

The algorithms proposed in this paper are adopted to detect and recognize the dynamic hand gestures in the real time. The experimental results show that the accuracy of these four specific dynamic hand gesture recognition is higher than 90%, and the average recognition accuracy is 94.5%.

When processing a relatively simple gesture, such as gesture 1, the recognition rate is highest up to 100%. When processing a gesture with complicated changes, such as the gesture 3, the accuracy of the recognition is reduced to some extent. But generally, the recognition effect satisfies the requirements. The specific recognition results are shown in Table 1.

Table 1. The accuracy of dynamic hand gesture recognition

Dynamic hand gesture	Test samples	Correct	Accuracy	Average accuracy
gesture1	200	200	100%	94.5%
gesture2	200	190	95%	
gesture3	200	180	90%	
gesture4	200	186	93%	

At the same time, the recognition accuracy of dynamic hand gesture based on the 3D trajectory features is evaluated by comparing with the 2D trajectory features used in the past. The comparison result is shown in Fig. 6.

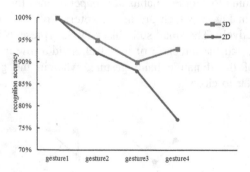

Fig. 6. Comparison of hand gesture recognition accuracy based on 3D trajectory features and 2D trajectory features.

The experimental results show that when recognizing gesture 2, gesture 3 and gesture 4, the recognition accuracy is certainly improved by extracting the 3D trajectory features proposed in this paper instead of the previous 2D trajectory features. This shows that the depth information does increase the recognition accuracy.

4.2   Robust Verification

In order to verify the robustness of the algorithms under different backgrounds and illumination, the defined dynamic hand gesture 2 was recognized in the four cases of natural light & simple background, natural light & complex background, dim light & simple background and dim light &complex background. And 50 experiments were performed in each case. The experimental results are shown in the following Table 2:

Table 2. Recognition accuracy under different backgrounds and lighting conditions

	Simple background	Complex background
Natural light	95.1%	94.3%
Dim light	94.2%	93.5%

From the table above, it can be seen that there is no dramatic change of the recognition rate of the dynamic hand gestures when the background and illumination change. Therefore, the proposed algorithms for the dynamic hand gesture recognition have a good robustness to the different backgrounds and illumination.

5   Conclusion

In this paper, the dynamic hand gesture recognition method based on 3D-TOF camera is principally investigated. In the preprocessing stage, an adaptive hand gesture segmentation method combining the frame difference method and depth threshold is adopted to successfully overcome the influence of complex background and different illumination. In the process of the dynamic hand gesture recognition, the 3D spatial trajectory feature vectors of the dynamic gestures are input into the HMM for training and recognition. In addition, the misidentified samples are trained for the second time to improve the training method of the HMM. The experimental results show that the dynamic gesture recognition algorithms based on 3D trajectory features and HMM are very effective for improving the accuracy of the hand gesture recognition and increasing the range of the hand gesture recognition, and have a good robustness to different backgrounds and illumination.

In the actual human-computer interaction, more abundant hand gesture changes are needed. At the same time, more 3D space trajectory features should be explored to improve the accuracy and generalizability of the algorithm presented in this paper.

References

1. Rautaray, S.S., Agrawal, A.: Vision based hand gesture recognition for human computer interaction: a survey. Artif. Intell. Rev. **43**, 1–54 (2015)
2. Song, Y., Demirdjian, D., Davis, R.: Continuous body and hand gesture recognition for natural human-computer interaction. ACM Trans. Interact. Intell. Syst. (TiiS)-Spec. Issue Affect. Interact. Nat. Environ. **2**, 1–28 (2012)
3. Liu, K., Chen, C., Jafari, R., Kehtarnavaz, N.: Fusion of inertial and depth sensor data for robust hand gesture recognition. IEEE Sens. J. **14**, 1898–1903 (2014)
4. Munaro, M., Basso, A., Fossati, A., Gool, L.V., Menegatti, E.: 3D reconstruction of freely moving persons for re-identification with a depth sensor. In: 2014 IEEE International Conference on Robotics and Automation (ICRA), pp. 4512–4519. IEEE, Hong Kong (2014)
5. Hsieh, C.-C., Liou, D.-H.: Novel Haar features for real-time hand gesture recognition using SVM. J. Real-Time Image Process. **10**, 357–370 (2015)
6. Rahmani, H., Mahmood, A., Huynh, D.Q., Mian, A.: Real time action recognition using histograms of depth gradients and random decision forests. In: IEEE Winter Conference on Applications of Computer Vision, pp. 626–633. IEEE, Steamboat Springs (2014)
7. Yang, X., Zhang, C., Tian, Y.: Recognizing actions using depth motion maps-based histograms of oriented gradients. In: Proceedings of the 20th ACM international conference on Multimedia, pp. 1057–1060. ACM, Nara (2012)
8. Premaratne, P., Yang, S., Vial, P., Ifthikar, Z.: Dynamic hand gesture recognition using centroid tracking. In: Huang, D.-S., Bevilacqua, V., Prashan, P. (eds.) ICIC 2015. LNCS, vol. 9225, pp. 623–629. Springer, Cham (2015). https://doi.org/10.1007/978-3-319-22180-9_62
9. Oreifej, O., Liu, Z.: HON4D: histogram of oriented 4D normals for activity recognition from depth sequences. In: 2013 IEEE Conference on Computer Vision and Pattern Recognition, pp. 716–723. IEEE, Portland (2013)
10. Lubo, G., Xin, M., Haibo, W., Jason, G., Li, Y.: Chinese sign language recognition with 3D hand motion trajectories and depth images. In: Proceeding of the 11th World Congress on Intelligent Control and Automation, pp. 1457–1461. IEEE Shenyang (2014)
11. Yang, J., Yuan, J., Li, Y.F.: Flexible trajectory indexing for 3D motion recognition. In: 2015 IEEE Winter Conference on Applications of Computer Vision, pp. 326–332. IEEE, Waikoloa (2015)
12. Corti, A., Giancola, S., Mainetti, G., Sala, R.: A metrological characterization of the kinect V2 time-of-flight camera. Robot. Auton. Syst. **75**, 584–594 (2016)
13. Li, L., Xiang, S., Yang, Y., Yu, L.: Multi-camera interference cancellation of time-of-flight (TOF) cameras. In: 2015 IEEE International Conference on Image Processing (ICIP), pp. 556–560. IEEE, Quebec City (2015)
14. Kumar, P., Gauba, H., Roy, P.P., Dogra, D.P.: Coupled HMM-based multi-sensor data fusion for sign language recognition. Pattern Recogn. Lett. **86**, 1–8 (2017)
15. Raheja, J.L., Minhas, M., Prashanth, D., Shah, T., Chaudhary, A.: Robust gesture recognition using Kinect: a comparison between DTW and HMM. Opt.-Int. J. Light. Electron Opt. **126**, 1098–1104 (2015)
16. Liu, K., Chen, C., Jafari, R., Kehtarnavaz, N.: Multi-HMM classification for hand gesture recognition using two differing modality sensors. In: 2014 IEEE Dallas Circuits and Systems Conference (DCAS), pp. 1–4. IEEE, Richardson (2014)
17. Zhang, X.H., Wang, J.J., Wang, X., Ma, X.L.: Improvement of dynamic hand gesture recognition based on HMM algorithm. In: 2016 International Conference on Information System and Artificial Intelligence (ISAI), pp. 401–406. IEEE, Hong Kong (2016)

Author Index